A HISTORY OF THE CHURCHES
IN THE UNITED STATES AND CANADA

A HISTORY OF THE
CHURCHES IN
THE UNITED STATES
AND CANADA

———

ROBERT T. HANDY

OXFORD UNIVERSITY PRESS
Oxford   New York   Toronto   Melbourne

Oxford University Press
Oxford   London   Glasgow
New York   Toronto   Melbourne   Wellington
Nairobi   Dar es Salaam   Cape Town
Kuala Lumpur   Singapore   Jakarta   Hong Kong   Tokyo
Delhi   Bombay   Calcutta   Madras   Karachi

First published by the Clarendon Press, Oxford, 1976

First issued as an Oxford University Press paperback, 1979

Library of Congress Cataloging in Publication Data

Handy, Robert T.
A history of the churches in the United States and Canada.

(Oxford history of the Christian Church)
Bibliography: p.
Includes index.
1. North America—Church history. I. Title.
II. Series.
BR510.H35 1978   277
ISBN 0-19-826910-2   77-015360
ISBN 0-19-502531-8 pbk.

Printed in the United States of America

TO

BARBARA MITCHELL HANDY

PREFACE

WHEN the Christian Church was first brought to North American shores by European travellers and settlers, it was already divided into the various branches that had developed during the course of western history. As six nations contended for colonial possessions in the New World, their established national churches founded congregations and missions there. Although five of those nations gave up claims to the territory that eventually became part of the United States or Canada, the churches they had founded remained.

Representatives of dissenting traditions also came to the western wilderness, seeking a place of refuge where they hoped to be free to follow their distinctive beliefs. The early immigrants were followed by millions of others, who introduced further diversities into the religious picture of the continent. Most of the newcomers came willingly, in search of freedom and prosperity, but those from Africa were brought primarily as slaves, many of whom in time became Christians. Some of the native Indians were also won to the faith, though never in the numbers that missionaries hoped. In due course, certain indigenous churches arose—North American additions to the complex patterns of modern Christianity.

For many reasons both the United States and Canada gave up established churches, and accepted patterns of religious freedom. As voluntary agencies, the churches have played important roles in both American and Canadian life, and the histories of these nations cannot be fully understood without attention to them.

The religious patterns of the two countries have shown both similarities and differences from the early days to the present. A number of the same denominational structures, types of piety, and general trends can be discerned. But from the start there were tensions on both sides of what finally became fixed as the boundary between the two lands, for the English colonies were predominantly Protestant while New France was conspicuously Catholic. Then when the British conquered New France in the course of the Seven Years' (French and Indian) War, the Protestant churches were strengthened. During the American Revolution, however, both Nova Scotia and Quebec refused to support the drive of the thirteen colonies to the south for independence, and in turn received as immigrants many Loyalists who reinforced the ties of the Canadian provinces with the British Empire. So despite many important similarities and continuing relationships, the religious life of the two nations developed in somewhat distinctive ways, especially during recurring periods of strain between them. For various reasons, including important geographic, economic, and climatic factors, the United States grew much faster than Canada, which was not consolidated as a nation until 1867, and which in population remains about one-tenth the size of its southern neighbour.

The historical study of the churches of the United States has been going on longer, and has engaged more scholars, than has been the case for Canada. For more than a century and a quarter a distinguished line of historians from Robert Baird to Winthrop S. Hudson and Sydney E. Ahlstrom have written over-all studies of religion in America. But only in the last few years, with the production of general books on Canadian church history by such scholars as H. H. Walsh, John S. Moir, and John Webster Grant has an inclusive treatment of the Christian churches of both lands become possible. The present book, which is the first to undertake such a study, examines the church histories of both nations together for the early colonial period. Then, as distinctive developments appear, separate chapters are devoted to following the course of church life in the two countries. In the years since World War I, however, the similarities in the situation of the churches in North America have enabled the two stories to be brought together, for the churches north and south have similar problems and opportunities as the long-familiar cultural patterns of western Christendom continue to be eroded.

It would be impossible to thank all those who have helped me to write this book, for I am indebted to many teachers, colleagues, and students, as well as to researchers and writers on whose works I have drawn. To those who have read all or parts of this study as it was in preparation I am especially grateful. Professors Robert W. Lynn, Glenn T. Miller, and Gerald P. Fogarty, S.J., have read the entire text, and saved me from various errors of fact and infelicities of style. Professors John Webster Grant and John S. Moir have read certain of the sections on Canada, and have helped this American to see some things through Canadian eyes. Professor Lawrence N. Jones has read much of the typescript, and has been especially helpful in commenting on the sections dealing with black religion. Among the many others who could be mentioned for help with various details, my thanks go to Dr. Robert H. Craig, Mrs. Gail Craig, and Mrs. Karen Osborne, and to those who typed the final draft, Mrs. Kay Mounger and Mrs. Ruth James. Even with all the assistance I have received, I know there will be certain slips and one-sided interpretations for which I alone must accept responsibility.

ROBERT T. HANDY

Union Theological Seminary
New York
Christmas 1974

CONTENTS

LIST OF MAPS

INTRODUCTION

THE Christian Church was brought to North American shores in various forms during an age of faith in which, with few exceptions, Christian churches and European states formed close alliances, mutually supporting one another. Both were generally believed to be under divine guidance, led by the providence of God. Monarchs were anointed with holy oil in sacred ceremonies to signify that their kingly power was divinely ordained. Clergymen were supported by the state to show that their religious role was supported by civil power. True religion was widely understood to be a gift of God on whom the salvation of souls depended; it was also a disciplinary force to help keep sinful persons aware of their duties to God and to their fellows. In western civilization at that time it was almost universally accepted that people were inherently divided into superior and inferior ranks, some to rule but most to be ruled, lest anarchy and barbarism result. Hence the story of the beginnings of Christian churches in the New World is closely related to the political and economic aspects of colonial origins.

The Spanish, French, English, Dutch, and Swedish colonies in North America were outposts of European Christendom, intended to transplant the cultural milieus of the competing national states into a wilderness setting. The churches played an important role in this movement of peoples; in most of the colonies that dotted the edge of the continent in the seventeenth century there were official establishments of religion. Christian beginnings in North America were thus closely related to the efforts at colonization made by the European nations. Much of the drama in the story of the churches lies in the way the initial patterns were altered and transformed through the centuries.

The vast masses of land that later became the United States of America and the Dominion of Canada were known in a very hazy and incomplete way to the nations of Europe in the sixteenth century. Explorers claimed great stretches of territory in the name of the monarchs who sponsored them. Spain's claims rested on the voyages of Christopher Columbus, France's on the expeditions of Giovanni Verrazano and Jacques Cartier, and England's on the explorations of John Cabot. Fishermen soon found it profitable to risk the stormy Atlantic to work the rich fishing grounds offshore. European naval and trading vessels occasionally put in at various points along the wilderness continent.

The historic race for empire in the western hemisphere focused first on the south. The initial adventures of Spain in the Americas gave her an early lead in the competition for overseas possessions. The Spanish empire was based in the West Indies and Central and South America. Only on the northern boundaries of New Spain were a few permanent settlements founded which much later were to be incorporated into the United States. The territories further north remained shadowy to Europeans and were of only sporadic interest during that stormy century that was so indelibly marked by the religious explosion that was the Reformation and by expanding rivalries between the leading nations of Europe. During that period in Europe little attention was being paid to the distant lands on the rim of Christendom. The focus of concern was the advancement and prosperity of the mother countries and their churches.

The settlement of most of North America came after the Reformation. Out of that complex and seminal series of events emerged new visions, leaders, institutions, and understandings, making a decisive shift in human history. Though there had been important preliminary movements, it was the Reformation which dramatically broke the unity of European Christendom, precipitating the formation of Protestant churches. Many forces were at work in the tangled fabric of the Reformation—fresh apprehensions of the meaning of Christian faith arising from the compelling insights of Luther and the other Reformers, the developing self-consciousness of nations growing restless under the authority of the Roman Catholic Church, the new visions of human freedom and destiny suggested by the Renaissance humanists, the opportunities offered by the burgeoning cities and expanding universities. During the course of that wide-ranging movement large segments of the western Christian Church departed from the jurisdiction of Rome to become Lutheran, Reformed, Anglican, or Anabaptist. These transitions were marked by much turmoil and considerable fighting. The patterns of polarization that were to plague European life for centuries were drawn in blood. In some cases large political units went over almost intact to the new, as in the Lutheran states of Germany and Scandinavia, and the Reformed territories of Switzerland, the Netherlands, and Scotland. In other cases, devotees of what they believed to be the true and only way of faith found themselves in an unenviable minority position, as, for example, the Protestants of France (the Huguenots) and the Catholics in England. The changing fortunes of war in many areas brought much suffering and hardship. The problems and instabilities of religious multiplicity were beginning to appear.

The Reformation did sever many of the links with the past, but it also preserved many things, often in an altered but still recognizable form. Only a few persons challenged the value of the theories and practices of Christendom, in which the political and ecclesiastical institutions were closely interrelated for the propagation of Christian faith and the maintenance of order and authority in society. Though political and religious leaders often quarrelled bitterly over their prerogatives and priorities, they nevertheless worked together, for they assumed that general order and morality would collapse if the Christian Church were not maintained and supported by the power of the state. Those radicals who did challenge such assumptions and called for the separation of church and state in the sixteenth century were persecuted, often to the death, in both Catholic and Protestant lands. This 'left wing of the Reformation' was made up of many fluid minority groups which we know today under the generic name of Anabaptist. Their challenge to authority, combined with the extreme behaviour that marked the course of a few of them, tended to confirm the majority view across Europe that established churches were normative.

As the European nations developed their colonies, they assumed that the familiar patterns of Christendom would be continued abroad, and that the churches there would be intrinsic parts of colonial settlements, undertaking the conversion and nurture of souls. The colonies were planted for the glory of Christ and his Church as well as for the advantage of the mother countries. Most colonial leaders hoped that the particular church in which they believed would be established in territories they controlled, and intended that others should submit to it or stay away.

The prevailing concepts of Christendom meant that the religious reasons for colonization were inextricably interwoven with political and economic ones. The advancement of a Christian kingdom was also understood to be an advancement of the Kingdom of God. The converting and civilizing of the native Indian populations were seen as an important part of the whole colonizing effort, and many of the early explorers and colonizers took this work seriously. Catholics shuddered at the thought that indigenous populations might be won by heretical Protestants, who in turn saw their colonial ventures as saving the savages from bondage to the superstitions and tyrannies of the papacy. There was hope of economic gain and political advantage in the colonial ventures, for prosperity was regarded as a sign of divine favour, and each country felt sure that it had a special destiny. Yet as in most human enterprises, there were often great differences between theory and practice; between promise and performance. In many instances the greed of national and colonial leaders was more in evidence than concern for Christian faith and mission. A fateful example was the way the Africans who were brought over were systematically enslaved, and considered as candidates for conversion and baptism only when it was made clear that freedom did not follow.

The competition for empire among the nations was keen enough between those of the same general religious perspective, and was sharper still between the opposing Catholic and Protestant camps. The various rivalries among the nations of Europe spilled over into the race for lands across the sea, and were fought out in the New World as well as in the Old. The churches that were transplanted in the westward movement of Christendom soon took root in North American soil. Over the centuries their patterns have spread, multiplied, and changed in surprising ways.

I

CHRISTIAN OUTPOSTS IN THE
WESTERN WILDERNESS

FROM the beginning of permanent European settlement of lands which later became the United States and Canada to the middle of the seventeenth century, a variety of Christian churches were transplanted to the new continent. By 1650 five European nations had established colonies in North America, in each of which churches had been formed. In some of the colonies the religious multiplicity that was to become so conspicuous in North America was already in evidence by that time, but not in those northern outposts of the Spanish possessions which fall within the purview of this account.

The Northern Perimeter of Spanish America

Spain had taken the lead early in the building of colonial empires, for conditions at home combined in ways which were favourable to the imperial thrust just as the great opportunity for overseas expansion opened. In the late fifteenth century Spanish patriotism, inspired by an ardent Catholic faith which had been reinvigorated during the long period of domination by Islamic Moors, had led to new national unity and strength. Early in 1492, the same year that Columbus made his historic first voyage, the last Moorish stronghold in Spain, Granada, was captured. Spain emerged as the strongest Catholic state in Europe, and was in a good position to press the exploration and conquest of the newly discovered western world. Successful in getting Pope Alexander VI to favour Spanish claims in drawing the line of demarcation in 1493 and 1494 so that Portugal was shut out of all but the eastern segment of South America, Spain founded permanent colonies in the West Indies. From these bases the exploration and conquest of Mexico and lands to the south were launched by the ruthless, able *conquistadores*.

An integral part of the Spanish advance was the extension of the Catholic faith. The state assumed an extraordinary measure of control over the church—by 1508 with papal consent the Spanish government had to approve the founding of any new religious institutions and had the right to make nominations to ecclesiastical posts in the colonies. This strict governmental control provided occasions for many quarrels to erupt between state and church officials in the New World. But it also long guaranteed the continuation of the familiar patterns of Christendom in the Spanish possessions.

The traditional structures of diocese and parish under the 'secular' clergy for the nurture of the Spanish settlers were soon established. In 1511 pope and king agreed to the erection of two dioceses in Española (Haiti and Santo Domingo) and one in Puerto Rico, on which settlement had begun five years before, and which nearly four centuries later was to become a territory of the United States. In these Spanish possessions the native populations were to be won not by the secular clergy but by the labours of members of religious Orders who lived by a formal rule (*regula*, hence 'regular' clergy). They were not directly under diocesan structures. The heroism of many of these missionaries, a number of whom became martyrs, has properly won for them an honourable place in historical annals. Their efforts to keep Indian converts apart from the often degrading influences of the Spanish settlers shows how far below the ideal of Christendom the realities often were.

The European discovery of lands which were later to become part of the continental United States was made in 1513 by the governor of Puerto Rico, Juan Ponce de León. Sighting the mainland in the Easter season when flowers were richly blooming, he named it 'La Florida'. For a century the name signified the whole northern continent to the Spanish. Over the next half-century, six efforts to settle the newly discovered peninsula failed.[1] Some collapsed because supply lines could not be kept functioning, while others fell before Indian attacks. One of the most serious efforts was led by Hernando de Soto, who landed at Tampa Bay in 1539 with more than 600 men, including a dozen priests. Finding no gold, the company explored the peninsula and then marched north and west, reaching the Mississippi River. De Soto fell ill and died the next spring; after much difficulty the remnants of the expedition reached Mexico a year later.

The successful founding of the first permanent European colony came

---

[1] The whole story of Catholic settlement in Florida is told with both realism and reverence by Michael V. Gannon, *The Cross in the Sand: The Early Catholic Church in Florida 1513–1870* (Gainesville, 1965). See also John Tracy Ellis, *Catholics in Colonial America* (Baltimore, 1965), Part I.

about as part of the bitter rivalry among nations. In 1564 Huguenot adventurers built Fort Caroline near the mouth of the River of May (St. Johns) on the north-east coast of Florida. Strategically located at the northern end of the Bahama channel, the fort challenged Spanish claims, and provided a base of operations against their treasure-ships. Thereupon Philip II of Spain authorized Pedro Menéndez de Avilés, Captain-General of the Indies fleet, to build a permanent colony as a base for securing the territory and for winning the Indians to Catholicism. Menéndez's fleet reached the Florida coast on 28 September 1565, the feast day of St. Augustine. After a brush with the French ships, Menéndez landed at a site known to the Indians as Seloy, and named it St. Augustine. Well received by the Indians, the Spaniards erected defences. The four priests who accompanied the expedition founded a parish and a mission which was to serve for nearly two centuries.

Religion and military duty were closely interwoven in the fabric of Christendom, and Menéndez wasted no time in marching on Fort Caroline, capturing it, and slaying the entire garrison, sparing only women, children, and youths not under arms. Such was the custom of the times; in the victors' view limited supplies were not sufficient to provide for captives. Such merciless cruelty (which did trouble some of Menéndez's followers) invited reprisal, delivered in full measure three years later when a French force surprised and destroyed Fort Caroline (renamed San Mateo).

From their newly established centre at St. Augustine, the Spanish founded other settlements at San Mateo and Santa Elena (in what later became South Carolina). The pastor at St. Augustine, Francisco López de Mendoza Grajales, directed the work of a handful of diocesan priests who for a time undertook both to serve the Spanish population and to do missionary work among the Indians. They had some success at the latter in the northern fringes of the settlement. It was hoped that the arrival of Jesuit missionaries would speed the conversion of Indian tribes, for the Society of Jesus, founded a quarter of a century before by Ignatius Loyola, was one of the most powerful of the movements which carried the Catholic or Counter-Reformation spirit. Utterly committed to the Church and to the papacy, Jesuit missionaries had already compiled an enviable record. Their first experience in Florida, however, was inauspicious. At the landing among hostile Indians, the superior, Pedro Martínez, was murdered. Despite reinforcements, the mission did not go well—the migratory nature of the natives did not make it possible to gather them into settlements. A trip as far north as Virginia ended in martyrdom for a party of eight Jesuits in 1571. Discouraged, the Order withdrew the next year.

In 1573 the Franciscan fathers appeared in Florida to carry on the mission, but not for a generation did the Order of Friars Minor throw adequate resources into the effort to win significant numbers of natives. In 1595 a large group of missionaries arrived, led by Fray Francisco Marrón. The fathers spread out along the coast northward from St. Augustine, erecting simple mission buildings in the towns of the Rimucuan and Guale (Georgia) Indians. Revolt among the latter resulted in a number of martyrdoms, bringing the total number of priests and lay brothers who lost their lives in Florida to seventeen. Their sacrifices were not in vain. In 1606 when the first bishop to visit Florida arrived from Santiago de Cuba, he confirmed hundreds of Spaniards and nearly 2,000 Indians. A valuable contribution to Indian life and piety was made through the completion of a Timucuan dictionary and grammar and the preparation of instructional and devotional books by Francisco Pareja. These materials meant that many of the converts were well-instructed in the faith; indeed some observers reported that they compared favourably with the Spaniards in this respect. A feature of much North American mission work, both Catholic and Protestant, was prefigured here—the preparation of linguistic tools and a religious literature.

In the 1630s the friars moved into the province of Apalache, where the Indian population was centred upon what later became the city of Tallahassee. The Apalachees were rather primitive; once the chiefs were won to the faith, the tribes followed. The friars achieved their greatest influence in the northern reaches of Florida; they had little outreach among the tribes to the south, along the peninsula. By 1650 there were in all about 40 mission stations and about the same number of priests, with an estimated 26,000 Indians converted or seriously considering the Christian faith. Although missionaries in some parts of the world were too hasty or superficial in making converts, in Florida the evidence points to the long and careful preparation of candidates. The friars were trying faithfully to reproduce what they knew and loved—Spanish Catholicism, with its liturgical forms, intense pieties, and hierarchical traditions.

Among the Timucuans and Apalachees the Franciscans succeeded despite difficulties caused by the poverty of the Indians and the corruption of Spanish officials that diverted commodities intended for the mission for their own use. The military and civil authorities were often at cross purposes with the friars, the former requiring forced labour from the natives and meting out harsh punishments. The devotion of the friars overcame many obstacles in what was a significant missionary achievement in Florida, which reached its peak in the mid-seventeenth century.

In one other area which later was to be incorporated into the United States permanent Spanish settlement was initiated late in the sixteenth century. After the Spanish conquest of Mexico in the first decades of the century, explorers and missionaries continued to press forward into regions as yet unexplored by Europeans, some of them journeying into what later became the American south-west—and as far north as Kansas. The most famous and wide-ranging expedition was that led by Francisco Vásquez de Coronado in 1540–42. When the expedition returned to New Spain, some of the Franciscan friars who had accompanied it remained to carry on missions among the Quivira Indians. One of the fathers, Juan de Padilla, was martyred in Kansas, the first of forty-two Franciscans who were to give their lives in the province of New Mexico in the next 200 years. Later efforts to reach the natives in that area failed until Don Juan de Oñate's expedition formally took possession of New Mexico and founded Real de San Juan in 1598. Nine Franciscans under Fray Alonso Martínez began the work of instruction among the nearby Pueblos. Although the colony did not prosper because of the arid climate, nevertheless the missionaries felt that they could not abandon the several thousand Indian converts. Soon several other towns were founded, including Santa Fé, the new capital, in 1610. Despite some bitter conflicts between religious and secular officials the mission flourished, and by the end of the first quarter of the century some 10,000 Indians had been gathered into missions. Here they were instructed in both the faith and the culture of the Spanish. The imposition of both regular daily religious devotions and a disciplined agricultural work schedule (made possible by the introduction of irrigation) imposed double demands on the Indians. It provoked some discontent and some efforts at revolt which were sharply put down, but the seeds of later difficulties had been planted. By 1650 on the southern edge of the future United States there had been planted several Spanish colonies, in which the Catholic Church was ministering both to the European settlers and to the native populations.

The Origins of New France

From the dawn of the sixteenth century, French fishermen braved the North Atlantic to work the fishing banks off Newfoundland, often putting ashore to dry their catches on the beaches. Involved in their tasks and anxious to return home, they left the penetration of the interior of the islands and the continent to the explorers. In his voyages in the 1530s,

Jacques Cartier explored the Gulf of St. Lawrence, adventured up the river as far as what later became Montreal, and pioneered the fur trade with the Indians. There were other explorations and some unsuccessful attempts at colonization, but not until the early seventeenth century was there permanent settlement. In 1603 a charter was granted to a Huguenot merchant, Pierre du Gua, Sieur de Monts, to monopolize the fur trade in France's North American claims. King Henry IV had several things in mind in granting this charter—a permanent colony in the New World, an opportunity for the commercial interests of French Protestants (among whom Henry had once been numbered), and a missionary outpost among the Indians. Though the Huguenots could have their own pastors, for this was in the period of toleration following the Edict of Nantes of 1598, the mission to the Indians was to be conducted under Catholic auspices. A blending of religious, political, and economic concerns was evident in these beginnings of permanent settlement in New France. Previous attempts to establish Huguenot refuges in the south had been frustrated by the Spanish, but the new effort was to be far to the north, in Acadia (later Nova Scotia).

Both a Protestant minister and Catholic priests were aboard the ships that sailed in 1604. In view of the recent religious wars in France, it is hardly surprising that heated arguments raged between the clergymen. Samuel de Champlain (1567–1635), who had already been on a voyage to the St. Lawrence and who was to devote the rest of his life to New France, had his gifts of ingenuity and leadership tested during a difficult and disease-ridden winter on the island of Sainte-Croix on the river that later became the boundary between Maine and New Brunswick. The next year the group resettled at Port Royal, across the Bay of Fundy on the Annapolis basin. Here they were joined by Jean de Biencourt, Sieur de Poutrincourt, who was placed in charge of the young colony by de Monts. The latter's charter was revoked the next year, and Port Royal had to be abandoned. Poutrincourt was determined to return, however, and succeeded in getting his *seigneurie*, a feudal land grant, confirmed. With him on his return in 1610 was a secular priest, Jessé Fléché, who began missionary work among the Micmac Indians, a tribe of the Abnaki family of Algonquians, one of the several main national groupings of American Indians.

The affairs of the little colony were greatly affected by a struggle going on in French Catholicism between those ardent in their devotion to the pope and the Counter-Reformation and those who prized the 'Gallican liberties' of the French church. Neither Poutrincourt nor the Huguenot merchants were anxious to have those ardent papalists, the Jesuits, in New France. The rights of de Monts had been bought by a wealthy patroness who also financed Poutrincourt's return, and somewhat to the latter's annoyance, two Jesuit priests, Pierre Biard and Ennémond Massé, were sent to Port Royal. Tensions between Poutrincourt and the missionaries led to the decision that the fathers should launch a new mission in Maine. This brought a swift response from the English colony that had recently been planted in Virginia. Captain Samuel Argall attacked the French at Mt. Desert Island. In the struggle, a Jesuit lay brother, Gilbert de Thet, was slain; the priests were captured and taken to Jamestown, but eventually they found their way back to France. Argall then bombarded and destroyed Port Royal. The work among the Indians that had been started was never completely given up, however, and was renewed from time to time in the stormy years ahead.[2] In 1635 Port Royal was made the capital of Acadia, and the Capuchin fathers made it their headquarters, carrying on work among both the French and the Micmac Indians. The foundations of a tenacious Acadian culture were firmly laid in this period. Common schools for both European and Indian children were founded.

A by-product of the Acadian settlement which was to become historically more significant was the founding of Quebec by Champlain. After the loss of his Acadian charter, de Monts again obtained another monopoly on the fur trade for a year. Champlain urged him to base the new trade in the valley of the St. Lawrence River, and a trading station was established at Quebec in 1608. Champlain had a dream of a prosperous French Catholic empire which would civilize and convert the native populations. Though a Catholic, Champlain was at home among the Huguenot merchants who were so important in developing the fur trade. With de Monts's help, he was able to obtain support for his missionary strategy. He secured the co-operation of an Order popular in France for its social service—the Recollects, a reforming branch of the Franciscans.

Four Recollects began their mission in 1615, but their early efforts to reach roving bands of Algonquian tribes were not very successful, and they concluded that Indians who had grouped themselves into relatively settled communities would be more likely to respond. In many respects the most likely candidates for their outreach would have been the Iroquois, a major linguistic family made up of the 'Five Nations' (Mohawks,

---

[2] A good treatment of the religious aspects of New France can be found in H. H. Walsh, *The Church in the French Era: From Colonization to the British Conquest*, A History of the Christian Church In Canada, i (Toronto, 1966); see also Ellis, *Catholics in Colonial America*, Part I, and J. H. Kennedy, *Jesuit and Savage in New France* (New Haven, 1950).

Oneidas, Onondagas, Cayugas, Senecas) which inhabited the region later identified as central and western New York state. The French had already made alliance with the Hurons, however, who though linked by language to the Iroquois were their bitter enemies. In a scuffle with a band of Iroquois in 1609 Champlain killed a chief, heightening Iroquois wrath against the Hurons and their French allies.

A relatively sedentary group, the Hurons were settled in several large villages in an area between Lake Simcoe and Georgian Bay, near the 'great lake' that bears their name, hundreds of miles west of Quebec. One of the Recollects, Father Joseph Le Caron, in an early form of a debate that was to rage for several centuries, argued that the best way to proceed was to civilize the Indians first and thus to prepare them for conversion. Champlain, on the other hand, insisted that they should be made Christians first and Frenchmen later. Not many of the colonists from France were of a devout type which would make them fit to serve as models to support Le Caron's plan. The Hurons themselves grew suspicious of the missionaries; one priest, Nicholas Viel, was martyred. Realizing that greater resources than they possessed were needed, the Recollects supported a plan to have the stronger Jesuits brought into the mission, and six arrived in 1625. The resistance of the Huguenot traders to their presence was overcome two years later when Cardinal Richelieu, Louis XIII's powerful minister, disbanded the old Company of Merchants and formed the Company of One Hundred Associates. The new company was ordered to make Quebec an exclusively Roman Catholic colony. The new plan was just starting when it was interrupted by the English seizure of Quebec in 1629—an incident in the long struggle between the English and the French. Until 1632, when it was restored by treaty to France, Canada was held by the English. Champlain then returned as governor, and the Jesuit fathers Massé and Jean de Brébeuf were with him. Until his death in 1635, Champlain did much to intensify the spiritual life of Quebec, and insisted that the French settlements should provide a solid base for missionary outreach. A college was opened in Quebec in that very year.

The Jesuits were anxious to re-establish the mission among the Hurons, and with great anticipation de Brébeuf and others made their way to the distant shores of Georgian Bay. The Hurons had had some unfortunate contacts with fur traders in the meantime, and were increasingly alarmed at the incidence of European diseases among their people. They were understandably suspicious of the Black Robes, and it took all of de Brébeuf's tact and skill to allay their distrust. His successor as superior, Jérôme Lalemant, developed a body of lay auxiliary volunteers to do much of the routine and construction work necessary in the building and maintaining of the mission. A central house was erected; from here the fathers fanned out to reach other tribes, hoping to draw them into something of a 'model state' within the orbit of the Catholic faith and French culture.

The Huron people were declining in numbers, however, and could not stand the onslaught of the militant Iroquois. A number of the fathers, some of them influenced by a strain of mystical, idealistic piety then popular in France and which prepared them for martyrdom, were caught in the turmoil. On a mission with several lay brothers, Isaac Jogues was captured by a band of Mohawks, abused, and enslaved. With the help of a Dutch commander he escaped down the Hudson, and after spending several months in New Amsterdam he returned to France, where he was reverently received at a time when religious fervour was running high. He was soon back in New France, in time to play a leading role in arranging for an uneasy peace between the Indian enemies in 1645. The next year, however, he was captured again and treacherously killed by Mohawk fanatics. The peace was broken and the Iroquois, who were allied with the Dutch, crushed the Hurons. In all, eight Jesuits were martyred, some after brutal tortures. The Huronia project had to be given up, and the fathers sadly retreated to Quebec in 1651.

Their suffering only intensified the determination of the leaders of New France that it would be especially devoted to the *Regnum Dei*, the Kingdom of God on earth. The letters of the Jesuit fathers[3] stimulated gifts from the mother country, so that schools and missions, a college, an Ursuline convent, and a hospital (the famous Hôtel-Dieu) could be built at Quebec by mid-century. Other settlements were appearing, especially Montreal, founded in 1642. By 1650, though hopes for the mass conversion of an Indian tribe had failed, the French had established a firm base in the New World. In the latter half of the century, the French were to reach out from this base deep into Illinois country.

The Beginnings of English Colonization: Virginia

As in the case of Spain and France, for England there was also a long period between initial claims and the founding of permanent settlements. During this time several unsuccessful attempts at colonization were undertaken, and various writings urging settlement were produced. Sir Humphrey Gilbert and Sir Walter Raleigh sponsored ill-fated colonial expeditions. Richard Hakluyt, a clergyman of the Church of England,

---

[3] A definitive collection was edited by R. G. Thwaites, *The Jesuit Relations and Allied Documents*, 73 vols. (Cleveland, 1896–1901).

wrote for the Queen an important manuscript which was widely circulated, 'A Discourse on Western Planting' (1584). He argued that Englishmen should carry the glorious Gospel to the simple natives by planting colonies before it was too late—before Catholic 'superstition' pre-empted the territory. He then published what grew into a multi-volume work, *The Principal Navigations* (1589–1600), citing daring exploits of English adventurers and urging colonization for the sake of the true faith and England's glory.

During the years of struggle against Catholicism and Spain, Englishmen were being conditioned to think of their country as specially elected to serve as a holy nation before the world. England's destiny under God—so a generation steeped in Foxe's *Book of Martyrs* agreed—was to spread the knowledge of divine truth, under God's providential care. This motive for colonization was repeated in many sermons and writings, and the manpower to carry it out was becoming available. Social and economic conditions in England in the sixteenth century brought severe hardships to many of the lower classes, so that not a few were ready to join expeditions, often by serving a period of years as indentured servants in order to pay their passage.

Early in the reign of James I (1603–25), several commercial companies were chartered to plant colonies in North America. The first charter for Virginia, granted to the London Company, emphasized the importance of propagating the Christian religion, and of bringing the 'infidels and savages' to human civility and settled government. Religious beliefs and practices of the Church of England were to be maintained. The company was in the control of men of Puritan sympathies. They were neither Separatists from the Established Church nor did they reject episcopal polity, but they were strongly evangelical in piety and liturgical practice.[4]

With the first shipload of colonists to arrive at Jamestown in 1607 came a clergyman, Robert Hunt, who twice daily conducted prayers in accordance with Church of England usage, and preached several sermons each Sunday. Hunt shared the sufferings of that first terrible summer and winter when food was in short supply and disease was rife. The chaplain also faced the disasters that plagued the settlement when the crude church which had been erected burned with most of the other structures. More than two-thirds of those who arrived in those first difficult months died within the year.

---

[4] For treatments of the English situation and its bearing on colonization, see Wallace Notestein, *The English People on the Eve of Colonization, 1603–1630* (New York, 1954), and Carl Bridenbaugh, *Vexed and Troubled Englishmen, 1590–1642* (New York, 1968).

In 1609 the company, now reorganized as the Virginia Company of London, set forth three main purposes for its existence: to preach to and baptize into the Christian religion 'a number of poore and miserable soules', thus preparing for the Kingdom of Glory by actions as well as words; to build up the public honour and safety of the King and his estates by preparing a place to which surplus population could go; and to develop a colony where certain commodities unavailable in England could be produced. Religious, political, and economic considerations all had their place in this design.

Firm measures were taken in the second decade of the century to ensure the continuity and stability of the young colony, and to maintain its religious life. The strict code known as 'Dale's Laws' required all the settlers to frequent diligently morning and evening prayer; the stated penalties for absence were stiff. When Governor Thomas Dale arrived in 1611, Alexander Whitaker, a Cambridge graduate with Puritan sympathies, came with him. Whitaker helped to build Henrico, over fifty miles up the James River from Jamestown, and ministered to the church that was planted there. In a sermon which was soon published in England as 'Good News from Virginia', Whitaker showed little appreciation for the natives' religion, but exhibited considerable respect for the Indians as persons with an impressive communal and moral life. He did succeed in winning some converts among the natives before his untimely death in 1617, and helped to arouse a measure of enthusiasm in the mother country for increased missionary effort.

The Virginia colony proved that Englishmen could successfully colonize in the western wilderness, though the cost had been very great in human and material resources. The sponsoring company had made little profit. Dissension in 1619 led to the issue of a new charter which provided for an Assembly with an elective lower house. This recognized that Virginia was maturing into a stable society within the framework of a commercial company. By that date there were eleven settlements, which sent two burgesses apiece to the Assembly. That body endorsed the Church of England as the one officially authorized church in the colony.

The same year 1619 saw also the beginning of an American dilemma when a Dutch man-of-war brought twenty indentured blacks to the colony. Their service as field hands was so effective that the colonists in time yielded to the temptation of transforming the indenture system into lifetime slavery for the Africans. The hierarchical patterns of thinking by which it was assumed that there would be superiors and inferiors were now given a new twist. The Negroes, recently plucked by force from more primitive cultures, were held to be inferior. On this basis the germs of racism festered and spread. In the minds and practices of the whites, the colour factor grew to be the most visible way of separating superior from inferior. The African presence among European settlers thus began very early in North American history—a presence that was steadily to increase.

Three years later another American problem was intensified. The Algonquian-speaking tribes in the vicinity of the new colony enjoyed a relatively well-developed culture and were in a period of expansion. A powerful chief, dubbed King Powhatan by the English, held the tribes together. He probably saw the Europeans as potential allies in his own struggle to maintain and extend control over the various tribes, while at the same time viewing them as a source of weapons in his defence against enemy tribes further west.

At first, the Indians apparently were not very impressed with the foreigners who despite their big white-winged ships did not know how to live off the land. The Europeans did not seem at the outset to be a very serious threat. Yet each side found the other hard to understand and, from its point of view, unpredictable. There were various incidents of violence, especially as the English numbers steadily increased. A peace was established in 1614 and was continued under Powhatan's successor, but the pressure on land by the English increased. The tobacco crop was proving profitable; in 1618 to encourage immigration the company offered 50 acres of land for every person who would journey to the colony to settle. The Indians retaliated in a bloody uprising in 1622, when over 300 settlers were killed in a surprise attack on Good Friday. The natives were unprepared, however, for the fury of European vengeance that devastated their lands and slaughtered their people. As happened again and again over the centuries, the military resources of the invaders were too great for the natives when they met in direct confrontation.

The English sense of superiority, and their belief that the failure of the Indians to cultivate the land in accordance with their standards, provided them with the justification for pressing into 'unoccupied' lands as they felt they needed them. The bitterness of warfare with the Indians bred a hatred on both sides that had tragic consequences. On the Christian civilization they were seeking to advance the colonists placed an indelible blot which has been visible with varying intensity through the centuries. After 1622 the Virginia settlers found it hard to regain much enthusiasm for the mission to the Indians, though some of the English persisted in well-intentioned efforts.

In 1624 the internal difficulties of the company proved unresolvable, and Virginia became a royal colony. The Puritan element was now replaced by a more Anglican one, and the colonial legislature required that ministers explicitly conform to the practices of the Church of England. The laws and the institutions which were developed in the dozen years after 1624 set the patterns for the government of the Established Church in Virginia for the rest of the colonial period.[5] There was one conspicuous weakness—though the system was episcopal, no bishops were appointed. Hence certain episcopal functions were vested in the governor, such as receiving ministers' orders on their arrival, recommending them to parishes, inducting them formally to their charges, issuing marriage licences, and probating wills. There was a severe shortage of ministers, however, and at the parish level this contributed to the increasing strength of the vestry. The vestry, a board of laymen, traditionally twelve in number, exercised considerable control over the temporal affairs of a local parish, and carried on the work of the parish in the period when there was no minister. For many parishes, such periods were long indeed. In 1650, for example, there were only about half a dozen clergymen for the some twenty parishes.

By the mid-seventeenth century, Virginia had been far surpassed in population by the New England colonies, but it had become firmly rooted. As it grew, the 'Old Dominion' extended its version of Christian civilization with an Established Church tradition. The colony remained loyal to the Church of England during the turmoil of the Puritan Revolution and its aftermath in the mother country. Though weakened by the lack of a bishop and by the shortage of clergy, the colonial establishment in Virginia had succeeded in permanently transplanting the Church of England to the New World.

The New England Colonies

The Puritan party of the Church of England played a role in the founding of Virginia, only to be largely replaced when the colony became a royal province, while in most of the New England settlements Puritan groups long remained in dominant roles. Some of the Puritans there had been inclined toward Separatism, setting themselves apart from the Church of England, but the majority was clearly non-Separatist. They too sought a truer form of the church than they believed could be found in the mother country. With one significant exception, the New England colonies of

[5] See the detailed work by George Maclaren Brydon, *Virginia's Mother Church and the Political Conditions Under Which It Grew*, vol. i, 1607–1727 (Richmond, 1947); vol. ii, 1727–1814 (Philadelphia, 1952).

the seventeenth century adhered to the patterns of religious establishment and uniformity, with churches supported legally through official channels. The true visible church as it was generally conceived in the New England colonies was established according to congregational polity, not episcopal (as in England) or presbyterial (as in Scotland).

Little Plymouth colony was soon dwarfed and eventually merged in 1691 with her larger neighbour to the north, Massachusetts Bay. The tales of 1620, of the Pilgrim Fathers, the *Mayflower*, and Plymouth Rock have been told many times, for an important chapter in the history of a people was beginning. The first transplanting of what was soon to become (and for several centuries to remain) the largest denomination of North America, Congregationalism, was at Plymouth.

Most of those in England who can be called Puritans during the reigns of Elizabeth I and James I remained within the established Church. Only a few followed Robert Browne, the Separatist pioneer; some of them continued to remain outside the Church of England after he returned. Some of the Separatists paid with their lives for their adherence to a forbidden position, notably John Barrow and John Greenwood. Other Separatists found it expedient to flee to the continent, as did a group from Scrooby who in 1608 departed with their pastor for Amsterdam, and then settled in Leiden. Among the exiles in Holland were not only the Separatists, but also some Puritan nonconformists who did not believe in separation from the Church of England but who wanted to reform it into an association of Congregational churches of true believers gathered voluntarily. Conspicuous among these non-Separatists was Henry Jacob, who ended his days in Virginia, and the celebrated theologian William Ames. The pastor of the Scrooby group, John Robinson, seems to have moderated his strict Separatism in discussion with Jacob and Ames, and was more friendly toward the non-Separatist view by the time the Pilgrims sailed for the New World.[6]

The Leiden exiles yearned to be again in an English-speaking land, for they found that their children were drifting away from the ways precious to them, and they hoped for wider opportunities for making a living than Holland afforded them. They turned to the Virginia Company for permission to settle within that colony, and finally obtained it. The larger part of the church was not prepared to go when the opportunity arose, so Pastor Robinson remained behind. Apparently through miscalculation,

---

[6] An extensive literature about these matters has grown up. See especially Champlin Burrage, *The Early English Dissenters in the Light of Recent Research, 1550–1641*, 2 vols. (Cambridge, 1912), and Perry Miller, *Orthodoxy in Massachusetts* (Cambridge, Mass., 1933).

the Pilgrims arrived at Cape Cod in Massachusetts too late in the year to go on further south. Their patent for Virginia was of no value in New England, so the group from the Leiden church, actually outnumbered by the 'strangers' who had joined the party in England at the beginning of the voyage, subscribed to what has become known as the 'Mayflower Compact'—in form a church covenant, put to civic use. The settlers encountered many difficulties during the first savage winter. Ravaged by disease, about half of them died. The survivors were aided by several Indians who had learned English from fishermen; with their help a treaty of peace was made with the Wampanoag chief, Massasoit. The Plymouth settlers sought to be friendly and fair to the Indians, but were in no way intimidated by them. Much of their economic livelihood came from trading with the natives.

The main purpose of the colony according to the Puritan leaders was that God might be worshipped according to the Bible. On a hilltop above the town they erected a large square meeting-house where they gathered twice on the Sabbath. Lacking a pastor, they were led in worship by Elder William Brewster. The London merchants sent a clergyman in 1624, but he proved to be an Anglican interested in founding a rival colony and was dismissed. The Pilgrims had hoped to be joined by their fellow believers from Leiden with their beloved pastor, but by the time they had bought out the London merchants who had financed them and arranged for the rest of the flock to come, Robinson had died. Not until 1629 did Ralph Smith fill the pastorate. The colony grew slowly; as more land was needed other towns were founded—Scituate was incorporated in 1636, and Duxbury a year later. By 1650 there were ten towns, with a total population of about 2,500. In each town a church was gathered; in Scituate, because of a controversy, there were two.

In the decade following the founding of Plymouth, little independent farming and fishing towns began to dot the shores beyond the colony to the north. The political and religious character of the developing society there was shaped decisively by the great influx of Puritans to Massachusetts Bay in the 1630s. An association of English Puritan ministers and laymen had become interested in settling New England, both to improve their living conditions and to form their churches and society in conformity with the patterns they discerned in the Bible. In the England of Charles I, non-Separatists found they had little chance of advancement. William Laud, the Bishop of London, who became Archbishop of Canterbury in 1633, opposed the Puritan movement vigorously. Some of the ministers were disciplined, silenced, or driven out of their posts. A group of non-Separatist

Puritan leaders gained control of a commercial company which already had undertaken some settlement in New England, at Salem, under John Endecott. In 1629 a royal charter for 'The Governor and Company of the Massachusetts Bay in New England' was formed. The usual provision that such a company should have its headquarters in England was omitted from the document. The central figure in this enterprise was John Winthrop (1588–1648), a convinced Puritan layman, who saw that neither his religious, political, nor economic interests could be much improved at home. When the fleet he gathered sailed in 1630, the charter, the officers, and the stockholders of the company were aboard. Once in Massachusetts, the officers became the legislators, the stockholders became the electorate, and the charter became the 'constitution' of a virtually independent commonwealth.

The leaders of Massachusetts Bay had a clear vision of the kind of society they hoped to build. As Protestants of the Reformed tradition, they believed that the Bible offered plain laws for all spheres of life, in family, church, and state. The biblical injunctions were most specific as a guide to the life of the spirit and the organization of the church, but the common law was believed to be congruent with the biblical law, for in the Puritan mind the law of nature was also God's law. The New England Puritans felt that the progress of the Reformation had been arrested in their beloved homeland, placing on them a special mission to demonstrate before the world the right way to order church and society. In most of their customs and ways these Puritans were typical Englishmen of their time. Their schools, which they founded as quickly as they could, and their legal systems, were patterned after those they had known across the water. As farmers, soldiers, and businessmen these settlers conducted themselves much as other Englishmen did. Not all who came in the great migration of the 1630s were Puritans, and not all of the latter were as ardent in their faith as those who were in control during the first decades. The leaders of the colony were determined that theirs would be a Bible colony, and they took resolute steps to realize their dream.

The young colony was immediately faced with an influx of new arrivals. Perhaps 20,000 came in the 1630s, most recruited chiefly from among the lesser gentry and the yeomen. With them were a number of university-trained ministers to serve the churches which were soon gathered as the communities spread out around the hub at Boston. By mid-century, according to one estimate, there were about seven times as many ministers, relative to European population, in Massachusetts as there were in Virginia. To preserve the special character of the colony as envisioned by the determined leaders, in 1631 the 'company' was changed from an open corporation to a closed commonwealth by limiting the franchise to church members. The elect saints, a minority of the population, were in control of both church and state.

The Bay colony was not technically a theocracy, however, for the ministers did not exercise civil power. Church and state were understood to be separate but co-ordinate spheres. When the Puritan leaders in 1648 drew up the definite statement of their polity in the Cambridge Platform, they insisted that church government stood in no opposition to civil government, nor did it encroach on the authority of the magistrate. Rather church government strengthened the hands of the civil authorities. The magistrates were forbidden to force people to become church members, and church officers were not to meddle with the work of the magistrates. Even so the latter were charged with seeing that the Ten Commandments were observed, and with putting down such things as idolatry, blasphemy, heresy, Sabbath-breaking, and the disruption of worship. The laws of the colony were to be informed by the laws of God as those were made known through the Scriptures.

Though the line between civil and religious authority was clearly drawn, the learned clergy were still called upon from time to time to meet in synod to interpret God's law, which gave them an important lever in public affairs. While not identical, church and state were to work in co-operation. Only true Congregational churches as defined by the Puritan leadership were to be allowed; others were invited to stay away, or to risk being driven out.

The study of Puritanism in both Old and New England has attracted much scholarly attention. That dynamic movement with its religious intensity, intellectual power, and rich complexity has provided materials for hundreds of studies, and the quest for understanding continues. The various Puritan groups exerted a powerful influence in American life, one that has been both greatly appreciated and vehemently detested. Those Puritans who dominated the early life of Massachusetts and Connecticut held certain firm convictions in theology and ecclesiology which were soon under attack by others who held different interpretations. Challenges came from various quarters and produced sharp struggles. Dissident groups that left the colony or were ousted from it played important roles in founding some of the other New England colonies. The debates that marked the stormy course of New England history have been prolonged by the scholars in their continuing efforts to interpret the Puritan experience.

The religious and theological style which became dominant in Puritan church life in Massachusetts was already prefigured in the gathering of the church in Salem in 1629. As Francis Higginson, soon to serve as co-pastor of that congregation with Samuel Skelton, sailed from England he uttered the oft-quoted words that reveal the non-Separatist stance of these Puritan Congregationalists:

We will not say, as the separatists who were wont to say at their leaving of England, 'Farewel, Babylon!' 'farewel, Rome!' but we will say, 'farewel, dear England! farewel, the Church of God in England, and the Christian friends there! We do not go to New-England as separatists from the Church of England; though we cannot but separate from the corruptions in it: but we go to practice the positive part of church reformation, and propagate the gospel in America.'[7]

The theory behind non-Separatism had been carefully worked out by theologians like Ames and Jacob; Massachusetts provided the opportunity to put it fully into practice. As did all strict Calvinists at that time, non-Separatists believed that only the truly elect of God should be admitted to church membership, though all persons should be called upon to attend church worship. It might be God's plan to call sinners to conversion and knowledge of their election as they listened to the reading of the scriptures and the exposition of the Word in preaching. Puritan non-Separatists believed that each congregation that was properly gathered had all the marks of the true church, and did not need presbyteries or episcopacies to guide it. A true church should be in a sisterly relationship with other congregations, but not be subordinate to any but Christ. Yet the non-Separatists did not reject as false those churches of the Reformation which followed other polities. They knew that some of the elect were scattered among them too. Hence they would not condemn the Church of England, but claimed the freedom to follow what their study of the Scriptures convinced them was the better way. These leaders did not at all reject the familiar principles of Christendom regarding religious uniformity and establishment; they were convinced that their mode of establishment was the best and wanted to secure it through the proper use of civil powers, which also are ordained of God. As Nathaniel Ward put it cogently, 'He that is willing to tolerate any Religion, or discrepant way of Religion, besides his own, unless it be in matters merely indifferent, either doubts of his own, or is not sincere in it.'[8] The non-Separatists believed in a gathered

[7] As quoted by Cotton Mather, *Magnalia Christi Americana*, i (Hartford, 1853), 362.
[8] Nathaniel Ward, *The Simple Cobbler of Aggawam in America* (4th ed., London, 1647, reprinted Salem, Mass., 1905), p. 8.

church of the elect who joined it voluntarily, and they also claimed that their congregations were the sole legitimate form of the church in their commonwealth. Eventually these two affirmations could no longer be held together, but the political situation of the 1630s reinforced the non-Separatism of the Bay, for with Laud determined to crush the Puritans a strong common front was needed. Hence the differences between the Bay and Plymouth colonies were minimized, and the similarities stressed.

In both colonies church leaders believed that church membership was restricted to the elect, though in Plymouth the judgement was characteristically a little more charitable than in the Bay. Both groups of churches were dependent on the civil government for protection and support, though there was not so much haste in Plymouth for passing laws requiring the attendance of all at church services. There was also less tendency toward centralization in the smaller colony to the south. The Plymouth experience was useful to the founders of the Massachusetts churches, so that the two ways, not so very different at the outset, tended to converge even more as time went on. The churches of the two colonies quickly recognized their affinities in the face of possible moves against them from Laudian England.

There were a few stubborn Separatists, however, who had difficulty recognizing the logic of non-Separatism. When Roger Williams (1603?–83), a Puritan minister who had graduated from Cambridge, arrived in Massachusetts in 1631 he had become a strict Separatist. Consequently he refused to accept the position of teacher of the church at Boston because it was not clearly separated from the Church of England. He served instead on a voluntary basis in the ministry at Plymouth, and then after two years moved to the church at Salem, Massachusetts, which did not always agree with the Boston leaders. There he became an associate of Skelton, and was chosen as his successor on Skelton's death.

Williams challenged a number of the principles on which Massachusetts was based. For example, he declared that the magistrates did not have the right to enforce the 'First Table' of the Ten Commandments which deal with duties to God, insisted that the King of England did not hold title to the Indians' land and had no right to issue the charter, and that the unregenerate could not take oaths as that was an act of worship. Theologically, Williams was a high Calvinist, believing fully in predestination and irresistible grace, as can be seen from his later writings against George Fox, the Quaker founder.

But Williams drew different conclusions from the same basic biblical and theological principles employed by his fellow Puritans. He argued against establishment in religion and for full liberty in religious matters, spelling out his position in full in later years in a difficult book, *The Bloudy Tenent of Persecution for Cause of Conscience* (1644). The Massachusetts leaders were determined to remove the man who held views which so sharply challenged their vision of a Holy Commonwealth. He was brought to trial in October 1635 and ordered to be banished on religious and civil grounds. Learning that the authorities were about to arrest him before the time agreed upon for his departure, he slipped away in mid-winter and journeyed south.

Williams stayed for a time with the Narragansett Indians, then settled within the bounds of Plymouth colony. Unwilling to risk the anger of her northern neighbour, Plymouth asked Williams to move on. In 1636 he purchased land at the head of Narragansett Bay and founded Providence, beginning the settlement of what became the colony of Rhode Island. During the rest of his long life, he earned his living by farming and trading. He served the colony he founded in many ways, making two voyages to England to secure charters for the colony's protection. A friend of the Indians as trader among them and preacher to them, Williams wrote a pioneering work, *A Key into the Language of America* . . . (1643).

In 1639 some English Baptists who arrived at Rhode Island in search of refuge won his support for their principles, especially the baptism of only adult regenerate believers and the separation of church and state. Thinking that this was the pattern for the true church for which he had been seeking, he joined with them in the gathering of the first Baptist congregation in the New World. Williams soon despaired of finding the true Church of Christ on earth, however, and became a 'Seeker', awaiting a new apostolic dispensation from God which would restore the true church. Meanwhile, as a Seeker he carried on a prophetic ministry, preaching to colonists and to Indians without remuneration. He did hold firmly to the principles of religious freedom and the separation of church and state, and persuaded his fellow colonists to support them. He was a strongly opinionated and somewhat difficult man, and certainly did not hesitate to attack those with whom he disagreed—but only verbally. He was convinced that no one should be penalized for his religious views, however extreme they might be.

The tiny colony grew slowly, attracting other refugees and rebels, to the dismay of the more orthodox New England colonies. Rhode Island harboured not a few of those who had been banished for one reason or another from the other colonies. The most famous such refugee, Anne Hutchinson, arrived not long after Williams founded Providence. The Antinomian Controversy erupted over the interpretation of the fundamental theology of the Massachusetts Bible commonwealth, and gathering up other tensions into itself, threatened to disrupt the Bay colony. The Puritans who were in control subscribed to the covenant theology which had been learnedly presented by some of the most influential Calvinist theologians of the time. Protecting the major Calvinistic emphasis on the absolute sovereignty of God and the unconditional election of some to salvation and others to damnation, the federal or covenant theologians interpreted these doctrines in a somewhat moderated and very preachable way. In barest outline the covenant theology taught that God had entered a covenant of works with Adam, whereby if Adam would obey God's commandments he would receive eternal life. But Adam fell, violating the covenant, so God made a second covenant, the covenant of grace, with Abraham, according to which the Eternal promised to give Abraham and his seed grace to fulfil the covenant of works on the basis of faith in Christ's coming. Carefully rationalized from biblical materials, the covenant theology affirmed that God himself had initiated the covenant of grace and would call, justify, and sanctify those whom he had elected. Conversion was the recognition by the elect that he was utterly unworthy and that except for the gift of God's saving grace and faith he would be utterly damned. Faith necessary for salvation was often made known to the chosen one as he was praying, meditating, reading Scripture, or listening to the preaching of the Word. The federal theology thus provided inducements for men to strive toward salvation, to prepare themselves for the visitation of saving grace—though finally God chose whom he would. Calvinist theologians earnestly debated the deeper implications of the covenant theology, for too great a stress on preparation seemed to deny the key doctrine of predestination, but too great attention to the latter doctrine could lead to fatalism.

If the godly ministers, carefully trained in the Bible and theology, found it difficult to apprehend and state the careful balance of the covenant theology, lay persons might more easily go astray amid these thorny issues. Mrs. Anne Hutchinson, a competent, articulate woman who arrived in Boston with her large family in 1634, did have difficulty with the emphasis on preparation for salvation as preached by most of the ministers. In commenting on sermons of the clergy in her home, at first to women who could not get to services for one reason or another, but then to a wider circle, Mrs. Hutchinson found that many of the preachers were really teaching a covenant of works, not a covenant of grace. She said that only a few, like the eminent John Cotton (1584–1652), who had been her pastor in England, and her brother-in-law, John Wheelwright who arrived in 1636, were really preaching a covenant of grace. She became very popular, and her criticism took on political overtones when her friend and relative by marriage, Sir Henry Vane, was elected governor. As the controversy raged, Mrs. Hutchinson insisted that the Holy Spirit dwelt in a justified person, stressed the importance of grace only for salvation, and taught that good works could not be offered as evidence of justification.[9] She was labelled an Antinomian, because it was believed that she suggested that the moral law is not binding upon true Christians, who live under the law of grace.

The orthodox party, under Winthrop and the pastor of the First Church in Boston, John Wilson, was seriously threatened. Winthrop wrested the governorship from Vane, and in the summer of 1637 a synod of the churches was called. Anne Hutchinson was confronted by the clergy again and again as they sought to show her the error of her ways, but she stood her ground. The synod condemned the Hutchinsonian doctrines. Brought before the General Court in October, she seemingly claimed to base her faith on direct divine revelation, thereby denying the centrality of the Scriptures. She was banished, and with some of her followers settled in Portsmouth, south-east of Providence on the island of Rhode Island in Narragansett Bay. Mrs. Hutchinson soon moved on again to settle on Long Island sound near the site of Rye, New York, where in 1643 she and five of her children were slain in an Indian massacre.

The treatment of Cotton and Wheelwright by the authorities was equally important. Cotton was brought into line by pressure from his peers; he conceded that the Spirit manifests justification in two ways, sometimes in absolute promise, sometimes conditionally—leaving a place for striving and preparation. Wheelwright was expelled from the colony because of his defective views on this second point; he migrated northward and became pastor in Exeter, New Hampshire. The victory of the non-Separatist covenant theology in Massachusetts was complete. Several other towns in New Hampshire had already been founded, but in the 1640s they were annexed by Massachusetts, which granted them a measure of home rule and exempted them from the requirement that only church members could vote.

There were some others who did not find Massachusetts to their liking. John Clarke, for example, arrived in the colony in 1637; apparently he

---

⁹ See David D. Hall (ed.) *The Antinomian Controversy, 1636–1638: A Documentary History* (Middletown, Conn., 1968); for an interesting interpretation of Mrs. Hutchinson see Emery Battis, *Saints and Sectaries: Anne Hutchinson and the Antinomian Controversy in the Massachusetts Bay Colony* (Chapel Hill, N.C., 1962).

was a Separatist and, being somewhat sympathetic to Anne Hutchinson, participated in the founding of Portsmouth and then of nearby Newport. At Newport he became pastor of a church that later adopted the Baptist position; he became the most influential of the early Baptist leaders.

Williams, Hutchinson, Wheelwright, and some of their followers were ousted from Massachusetts Bay by threat of force; some other Puritans went of their own accord to found new settlements. Thomas Hooker (1586–1647), like so many of the Puritan ministers a graduate of Cambridge, was one of the most eloquent among them, and was in basic agreement with the Massachusetts Bay leaders on most theological points. He had been forced to leave his pulpit in England, and after a period in Holland migrated to America and was ordained as pastor over the church in Newtown (later Cambridge). The early settlements around Boston— Dorchester, Roxbury, Newtown, Watertown—had been planted close together, and settlers were restive under the tight control of the General Court, and felt the need of more land than their cramped situation allowed. News filtered in about rich lands to the south-west in the Connecticut River valley. The Dutch of New Amsterdam had claimed the area, and in 1633 planted Fort Good Hope near where Hartford was later to be built. Plymouth was also interested in the valley for fur trading, and in that same year fixed a trading post further north, at Windsor. The following year a vanguard from the Massachusetts towns seeking new lands settled at Wethersfield. Hooker petitioned the Massachusetts authorities for permission to leave with his people, claiming that they were too crowded where they were, and that there were friends in England who would join them if they had more space. After long debate, permission for departure was granted, and several groups from the towns around Boston migrated in 1635 and 1636. Those who settled at Windsor bought out the Plymouth interests; the Dutch abandoned their fort as the English population increased. There were some differences between Hooker and Cotton over the details of church polity, for Hooker distrusted the centralizing tendencies in Massachusetts. Hooker was an orthodox Calvinist Puritan with an intense evangelical interest in conversion. He saw that the requirement of church membership for voting privileges worked toward the dilution of membership standards. In the Connecticut towns the churches were legally established as they were in Massachusetts, but the franchise was related to social standing and property, not to church membership. In most other respects, the Connecticut Puritan system was parallel to that of the Bay state and the congregations were in mutual fellowship; Hooker was one of the moderators of the synod that examined Anne Hutchinson, and later wrote one of the definitive Congregational treatises, *A Survey of the Summe of Church Discipline* (1648).

The Connecticut towns along the river elected representatives who were to meet to take care of common needs, and in 1639 the 'Fundamental Orders of Connecticut', based on the model of Congregational polity, outlined the plan of government. Each year the freemen chose a governor and a court of assistants, and each town selected four deputies to meet with the governor to form a General Court. The differences between the religious and political systems of the two colonies were not great, and close relationships between Massachusetts and her new southern neighbour were maintained.

Though later merged with Connecticut, New Haven began separately. John Davenport, who had served at St. Stephen's Church on Coleman Street in London for nearly a decade, withdrew when Laud became archbishop, and after troubled periods in Holland and at home sailed with some of his former parishioners for Boston in 1637. Unable to find a good site nearby, the company settled at New Haven on Long Island sound the next year, and gathered a Congregational church. Their system closely paralleled that of Massachusetts Bay, including the requirement of church membership for voting. The colony prospered; satellite towns were soon founded and became associated with New Haven in government.

The leaders of Plymouth, Massachusetts, Connecticut, and New Haven were deeply concerned with education, and the requirement laid down in Massachusetts that every town of fifty families must maintain a teacher while towns twice that size must also establish a grammar school was soon followed in the other colonies. In 1636 steps were taken to found a college at Cambridge, and until the next century Harvard was the only functioning institution of higher learning in the English colonies. The Puritan system required both an educated clergy and a literate laity, and the college was soon fulfilling its function of preparing leaders for church and society.[10]

Another challenge to the Puritan leaders of Massachusetts came in 1646, while the Civil War was raging in the mother country. Dr. Robert Child, a Presbyterian Puritan, had tried unsuccessfully to organize several churches of that polity. Irked by the requirement that only Congregational church members could vote, he signed with others a Remonstrance asking that civil and religious freedom be granted to all Englishmen without qualification, and that members of England's National Church (by

[10] The whole story has been brilliantly retold by Lawrence A. Cremin in *American Education: The Colonial Experience, 1607–1783* (New York, 1970), esp. pp. 180–224.

that time Presbyterian) be admitted to communion. He threatened to appeal to Parliament; he was arrested and fined, and soon left. The Puritans' intention to set down their way definitively was further strengthened by the debates then raging in England between Presbyterians and Independents in the Westminster Assembly. Hence a synod was called; it met in Cambridge in 1646. All but one of the 29 churches of Massachusetts Bay were represented, while the other 22 congregations of the three other Puritan colonies sent only a few delegates. The synod was theologically sympathetic to the Westminster Assembly and accepted the doctrinal substance of the Westminster Confession of Faith. In polity, the synod set forth the standards for the Congregational churches of New England which were largely followed through the rest of the colonial period. The Cambridge Platform (1648) defined the Church Catholic as the whole company of those that are elected and called to salvation, and the militant visible church on earth as existing in particular congregations. These consist of 'a company of saints by calling, united into one body, by a holy covenant, for the public worship of God, and the mutual edification one of another'. The Platform gave the Congregational churches—there were nearly 60 of them in the colonies by that time, almost twice the number of Anglican churches—a common bond, while the struggles of the early decades had given them a high degree of self-consciousness. The Bible commonwealth seemed to be on its way to realization by mid-seventeenth century, especially in Massachusetts.

The New Englanders got along fairly well with the Algonquian tribes they encountered, and several serious efforts to win them to Christianity were undertaken. Because of the fury of later struggles between Europeans and Indians, both in the later seventeenth century in New England and then in later centuries on the western frontiers, this earlier experience has often been overlooked. Alden T. Vaughan thoroughly explored this matter and found that although the English regarded themselves as culturally superior to the Indians, there was little thought then of racial superiority. In general, the Indians openly accepted the English settlers, who in most cases were careful to purchase the lands they needed from the tribes. Though they justified their settlement on the ground that the Indians had not sufficiently improved the land to hold title to it, they normally paid a fair price for the land into which they moved.[11] The tribes near the coast had been much reduced by the great plague of 1616–17; they were often glad to have the new settlers as allies against the powerful

<hr />

[11] Alden T. Vaughan, *New England Frontier: Puritans and Indians, 1620–1675* (Boston, 1965), esp. pp. 105–13, 181–2.

interior tribes. Both Europeans and Indians were warlike peoples. The General Court of Massachusetts, for example, put great emphasis on military preparations in the early years, both against threats from other colonial competitors in the race for empire, and against attacks from natives. Possessing superior weapons, the English were usually fair but very firm in their dealings with the Indians. They assumed that their laws, based on the Bible and on centuries of European development, should prevail over non-Christian and uncivilized customs. They retaliated sharply when English lives were taken, as in the Pequot War of 1637. The Pequot tribe, which had only recently pushed its way into eastern Connecticut, was charged with killing a party of traders. In the resulting action (in which a number of other tribes supported the English) the Pequots were surprised in their stockade and slaughtered, so that only remnants of the tribe were left. The Puritans cited Old Testament precedent for putting so many to the sword. The thoroughness of the victory was not soon forgotten by the tribes. Rumour of Indian conspiracy was one of the reasons for the forming of the New England Confederation in 1643, though there was also concern about the French to the north and the Dutch to the west.

From the early days of settlement, some Indians were converted to Christianity. One of the most impressive early missionary efforts was begun by Thomas Mayhew on the islands of Martha's Vineyard (on which he settled in 1642), Chappaquiddick, and Nantucket. A man of great tact, skill, and energy, he taught his first convert, Hiacoomes, to preach to other natives in accepted Puritan style. A score of converts were counted by 1650, with many more under instruction. Only after careful preparation and clear evidence of a saving spiritual experience would a convert be accepted as a genuine Christian by the Puritans.

The most notable of the missionaries to the Indians was John Eliot (1604–90). Educated at Cambridge, he taught in England with Thomas Hooker, and after coming to New England was settled as teacher at the church in Roxbury in 1632. He was to serve that congregation for nearly sixty years, while also carrying on extensive missionary labours. In the 1640s, recognizing that although the conversion of the Indians was one of the professed reasons for English colonization about which too little had been done, he began to learn the Algonquian tongue. In 1646 he preached his first sermon in their language before the Nonantum (Newton) band of Massachusetts Indians, and answered questions. He then undertook to preach to the Indians every other week, usually on Thursdays. Converts were soon won, and other bands were attracted. In 1649, Parliament chartered 'The President and Society for the Propagation of the Gospell in New-England', which served to collect funds in the mother country to maintain and extend the missionary thrust. Eliot was convinced that civilization and Christianization mutually supported each other, and gathered his praying Indians into towns of their own. The first was founded at Natick in 1651; the buildings were erected chiefly by the Indians themselves. Though the work of this 'apostle to the Indians' was remarkable as it flowered in the next quarter-century, only a minority of the natives was affected. There was almost no Christian progress among the major tribes, such as the Wampanoags of southern Massachusetts, the Narragansetts of Rhode Island, or the Niantics or Mohegans of Connecticut. The efforts of Mayhew and Eliot were exemplary, however, and show one of the most attractive aspects of Puritan piety.

New Netherland and New Sweden

Though the Dutch colony in North America was later surrendered, the church brought by the Dutch and established in their colony survived the political changes to play an important role in American religious history. The Reformed Church had won a significant place in the affections of the Dutch people. During the long period in which they were struggling for independence from Spain in the late sixteenth century, the Reformed faith became an effective unifying force. A moving personal statement of Calvinism by Guido de Brès became in 1561 the Belgic Confession, a rallying point for Dutch Protestants in their battle for freedom. Two years later the irenic Heidelberg Cathechism, prepared in an effort to bring together Lutherans and Reformed in Germany, was also adopted by the Dutch Reformed Church. The northern provinces of the Netherlands claimed their independence in 1581, and effectively secured it by the early seventeenth century.

Long a commercial people, the Dutch used their hard-won freedom to build great fleets of merchant, fishing, and naval vessels. Their explorers and traders moved aggressively into colonial areas in the Far East and in South America, seizing areas from the Portuguese and the Spanish. A great proponent of Dutch colonialism was William Usselinx, whose passion for overseas empire was not only stirred by economic considerations but also by his determination to advance Dutch Calvinism at the expense of Spanish Catholicism. In 1609, Dutch merchants seeking good routes to the Indies dispatched an English navigator, Henry Hudson, on a voyage on which he explored the north-east coast of America and sailed up the river that bears his name. Fur trading was soon being carried on with the Iroquois, and a settlement planted at Fort Orange (later Albany) on the Hudson. The Dutch West India Company was founded in 1621; within three years it had placed colonists on Manhattan Island and at Fort Nassau on the Delaware River. New Amsterdam on Manhattan became the principal settlement; other communities were soon growing on Long Island, Staten Island, and in what later became New Jersey.

It was the joint responsibility of the Dutch West India Company and the Classis of Amsterdam to provide an adequate ministry for New Netherland. With the coming of Peter Minuit as director in 1626, several lay 'comforters of the sick' began religious ministrations. Several years later the first ordained minister, Jonas Michaëlius, arrived and organized the first Reformed congregation. Both Dutch- and French-speaking Walloons were in his congregation, and he occasionally conducted services in French. Like so many Europeans, Michaëlius reacted negatively to the Indians, believing them to be treacherous, stupid, and cruel.

Both the colony and its churches grew slowly; Holland was not over-crowded and there was not the clear incentive for migration that so many English had. The high Calvinist position marked the theological life of the congregations, for in the mother country a theological dispute over pre-destination had been settled in a rigorous way by the Synod of Dort (1618–19). The moderate Arminian party, known as the Remonstrants, had been forced out of the church. In government the colonial congre-gations followed the familiar patterns of pyramidal representative organiza-tion that characterize Reformed and Presbyterian churches. Each local congregation had a consistory made up of pastor (or pastors) with elected elders and deacons; a number of consistories were gathered into a classis, and the classes met together in the national synod. The American congre-gations were under the Classis of Amsterdam.

In 1643 an Indian War, which had started with the Dutch massacre of peaceful Indians, reduced a European population from an estimated 3,000 to about a third of that; it was during that struggle that Anne Hutchinson lost her life. By 1650 there were only three Reformed congregations, widely scattered at New Amsterdam, Fort Orange, and Newcastle on the Delaware. The most prominent minister of this early period was Johannes Megapolensis, who served first as minister on the vast landholdings of Kilian van Rensselaer. Under great difficulties he carried on some missionary work among the Indians, mastering the Mohawk tongue. It was he who was instrumental in the escape of Father Jogues from the Indians. By mid-century he was ministering in New Amsterdam. Here the new director-general, Peter Stuyvesant, was treating religious dissenters with less tolerance than they would have received in Holland. English Puritans fared quite well, but German Lutherans and Dutch Mennonites felt the weight of Stuyvesant's disapproval.

Two of the leaders conspicuous in the founding of New Netherland were also instrumental in the planting of New Sweden in 1638. William Usselinx had persuaded the Swedish monarch of the value of trade in North America, and Peter Minuit, who had left the service of the Dutch, led the first Swedish expedition which planted Fort Christina on land purchased from the Indians, where the city of Wilmington was later to arise. Some Finns joined with the Swedes in settling the small colony. A year after the founding a pastor, Reorus Torkillus, arrived and conducted services in the Lutheran tradition as established in Sweden. Thus worship in conformity with the Augsburg Confession of 1530, the principal Lutheran Confession, began in North America. Torkillus and many of his flock soon succumbed to an epidemic, and was succeeded by John Campanius, who erected the first Lutheran church building. In his years in New Sweden, Campanius learned the Delaware language and translated Luther's *Small Catechism* in the course of his missionary labours among the Indians. By 1650 there were three churches in the colony, although the total population was less than 200.

A Refuge for English Catholics—Maryland

The fact that one of the English colonies was founded by Roman Catholics was a considerable achievement in view of the hostility of both Anglicans and Puritans towards 'Romanists' in the seventeenth century. Especially after the Gunpowder Plot of 1605, Catholics were subjected to penal legislation. Any convert to Catholicism, such as George Calvert, a member of a substantial family, was jeopardizing his future. Calvert had been one of James I's secretaries of state, and had been involved at several points in colonial efforts, including the sending of an expedition to plant a settlement on Newfoundland. After he became a Catholic in 1624 he resigned his post, which the King accepted but at the same time raised him to the Irish peerage as Baron of Baltimore. Lord Baltimore devoted much of his energy to finding a haven for Catholics abroad. He obtained from Charles I a patent for lands around Chesapeake Bay to be named Maryland in honour of Queen Henrietta Maria, a Catholic. By the time the formalities were completed in 1632, the first Lord Baltimore had died, and the charter was issued to his son and heir, Cecilius Calvert.

Maryland was the first of the English proprietary colonies; the others up to that time had been of the corporate type, in most places controlled by a corporation chartered by the Crown. As proprietor, Baltimore held extensive feudal powers, including the right to appoint the governor and councilmen, who became the upper house of the Maryland assembly. The religious clauses of the Maryland charter were purposefully vague, and stressed the general liberties of Englishmen.

The second Lord Baltimore was anxious to establish a colony that would be economically viable as well as being a refuge for Catholics, so others were not dissuaded from participation in the colony's life. Indeed, of the nearly three hundred persons who sailed late in 1633 on the *Ark* and the *Dove* the majority were Protestants. Two Jesuit priests, Andrew White and John Altham, went with the settlers, but as 'gentlemen adventurers' without special support from the colonial government. Calvert appointed his brother Leonard as governor, with instructions that Catholics should exercise their religion as privately as possible, and should avoid getting into discussion with others on matters of religion.

The colonists arrived at their new lands in March 1634. Governor Calvert approached the Pawtuxent Indians and purchased territory on the western shore of Chesapeake Bay, where St. Mary's, the first capital, was built. Social and economic patterns followed aristocratic traditions, though representatives of the freeholders soon formed the lower house of the assembly. An ordinance of 1639 passed by the assembly allowed considerable religious and political freedom to the citizenry; the separate sovereignties of state and church can be seen in this legislation.[12] Since tobacco soon became the principal crop, the settlement did not have to go through the difficult struggle for survival that Virginia and Plymouth had experienced.

The priests ministered to Catholics in the colony and also won some converts among the Protestants and the Indians. In the 1640s tensions arose between the Jesuit priests and the lay Catholics who were directing the colony's development. The fathers had accepted lands from the Indians without reference to the proprietor, and carried on mission projects among the Indians without permission in each case. Baltimore's effort to displace the Jesuits by secular priests deepened the tension. On advice from the Order, it was the Jesuits who yielded on the main points.

The initial hopes for rapid Catholic advance were dimmed not only by the internal tensions, but also by epidemics which took the lives of a number of the clergy, and by the enmity of William Claiborne who had

---

[12] See Thomas O. Hanley, *Their Rights and Liberties: The Beginnings of Religious and Political Freedom in Maryland* (Westminster, Md., 1959), pp. 93–108, and Sanford H. Cobb, *The Rise of Religious Liberty in America* (New York, 1902), pp. 371–2.

settled on Kent Island before the founding of Maryland and whose claims overlapped those of the Calverts. News of the Civil War in England had given Claiborne an opportunity for making a bid for power. He appealed to the Puritans in Maryland, some of whom had come from New England by way of Virginia. In the mid-1640s Claiborne took control of the colony, forced the governor and some of the priests to flee to Virginia, and sent the remaining clergy back to England. Leonard Calvert fought his way back into power, but when he died in 1647, the proprietor named a Protestant, William Stone, as governor. The Puritan element increased. Determined to maintain the colony as a refuge, Lord Baltimore prepared the text of an important law to guarantee religious toleration, and Stone saw it through the assembly in 1649.

This 'Act Concerning Religion' legitimated what had become the accepted standard in Maryland. Designed primarily to minimize the threat of religious controversy in a Christian commonwealth, the act provided that such things as blasphemy against God, or denial that Christ is the son of God, or the repudiation of the Trinity were punishable by death. The use of controversial religious labels 'in a reproachful manner' toward another was punishable by fine, as was profaning the Sabbath. The part of the act that rendered it an important accomplishment in the history of religious freedom read as follows:

noe person or psons whatsoever within this Province, or the Islands, Ports, Harbors, Creekes, or havens thereunto belonging professing to believe in Jesus Christ, shall from henceforth bee any waies troubled, Molested or discountenanced for or in respect of his or her religion nor in the free exercise thereof within this Province or the Islands thereunto belonging nor any way compelled to the beleife or exercise of any other Religion against his or her consent, soe as they be not unfaithfull to the Lord Proprietary, or molest or conspire against the civill Governemt. established or to bee established in this Province under him or his heires.[13]

Provision was made for 'trebble damages' to those wronged or molested contrary to the act.

By 1650 there were five Roman Catholic parishes in Maryland—apart from the mission to the Abnaki Indians in Maine, all the Catholic work in the English colonies was there. There were also four parishes of the Church of England and a Congregational church in the colony—the patterns of religious pluralism were developing early. Like the Anglicans, Catholics did not have a bishop until after the Revolution.

[13] William H. Browne (ed.) *Archives of Maryland: Proceedings and Acts of the General Assembly of Maryland, January 1637–38–September 1664*, i (Baltimore, 1883), 246.

To sum up, by the middle of the seventeenth century colonies had been planted on the North American coast by the five nations of Spain, France, England, Holland, Sweden. The English colonies were increasing in size considerably faster than those of the other nations. In these outposts of European Christendom, churches were established in accordance with the accepted patterns of the mother countries. Catholic, Anglican, Congregational, Lutheran, and Reformed establishments were seeking to maintain as much uniformity as they could in their respective territories. The churches were basically European, upholding the customs and value structures of western civilization with their achievements in law, education, government, science, and economics. In all the colonies, the enduring foundations of Christian churches in the western wilderness had been laid—an impressive achievement. Already conflict between various churches and traditions had started, and in Rhode Island and Maryland states without any establishment of religion were being tested—an important step indeed. Significant beginnings in mission to the Indian populations had been made, though the history of armed encounter between Indian and European was already a long one. The rivalries between the nations had also been transplanted to the New World, and had already spilled over into some bloody encounters, a foretaste of many decades of strife to come.

II

CONFLICT AND DIVERSITY IN
COLONIAL CHRISTIANITY

(1650–1720)

THE seven decades from the mid-point of the seventeenth century to 1720 were marked by the termination of two of the smaller colonial efforts in North America and by the continuation and expansion on a vast scale of the rivalry between two of the other nations for domination of the continent. In these seventy years the English and French colonies grew in area and population, and the Christian churches within them also increased in size and scope. In the English colonies, religious groups that previously had had only a few if any representatives in the New World became quite visible, often posing threats of various kinds to the established bodies. Some of the great hopes that had inspired the founding of churches in the earlier period were fading, while the familiar methods of sustaining Christian life and mission were showing inadequacies in the unfamiliar conditions of North American life.

On the eastern edge of the continent, the political and religious map of 1720 was beginning to take on a form that would be recognizable to later generations. To the north, New France, centred in Quebec, had become a royal colony in 1663. Firm in their loyalty to Catholicism, the communities along the St. Lawrence River became the base for daring trading and missionary advances deep into the Great Lakes region and down the Mississippi to its mouth. The frontiers between French and English colonies were often scenes of desperate struggle as European wars were fought in part in the vastness of North America. The War of the League of Augsburg was known as King William's War (1689–97) in the colonies, and the War of the Spanish Succession as Queen Anne's War (1702–13). Outnumbered in these struggles, the French lost Hudson Bay, Newfoundland, and Acadia to the English by the Treaty of Utrecht (1713). Acadia was renamed Nova Scotia but the French long remained much more numerous than the British, and they retained Cape Breton Island in the north.

During these conflicts, the English colonies continued to grow. The colonial population of an estimated 200,000 in 1690 had more than doubled by 1715. The populated areas of existing settlements were extended, and new colonies were formed. New Hampshire, separated from Massachusetts in 1677, became a royal colony two years later. It continued to be influenced by its powerful southern neighbour, however, and the pattern of Congregational establishment in the towns set the religious tone. Massachusetts lost her precious charter in 1684 through legal proceedings in London. The new charter of 1691 dropped the religious qualification for voting, but granted the Bay many of its privileges and left the Congregational establishments secure. At the same time, Maine and Plymouth were merged with Massachusetts. Congregational churches also remained firmly established in Connecticut, which absorbed New Haven in 1665. Rhode Island, with its commitment to religious freedom, was finally secured by a royal charter of 1663 for which Roger Williams and John Clarke had worked hard in England.

In the middle colonies, where large areas had not been touched by European settlement until after 1650, the changes were more dramatic. Little New Sweden was captured by the Dutch in 1655, but many of the Swedish and Finnish settlers long remained faithful to their Lutheran traditions despite changing political fortunes. Nine years later Dutch fortunes were reversed as New Netherland surrendered without a struggle to the English. Thus Swedish and Dutch holdings in North America ended. The government of the new proprietor, the Duke of York, did not interfere with Dutch church affairs, but provided for freedom of worship in an area which was already religiously diverse.

New Jersey was part of the territory given to the Duke, but he granted it to two other proprietors who soon divided it. After a complex history, the colony was reunited as a royal province in 1702. Settlers of various religious backgrounds were coming into New Jersey, and no one religion was established.

Pennsylvania was given to William Penn by the Crown in 1681 as a proprietary grant. Penn saw his great tract, situated between the Duke of York's holdings to the north and Lord Baltimore's to the south, not only as a good investment but also as a refuge for oppressed peoples and for religious minorities. As happened in many cases, the boundaries were rather vaguely stated—the source of many disputes in later years. In addition to this vast grant, Penn also obtained from the Duke of York the land that later became the separate little colony of Delaware. In both colonies the pattern of religious freedom was fixed from the start, and religious heterogeneity became evident at an early stage.

In the southern colonies, Maryland, previously a refuge under a Catholic proprietary family, was made a royal colony as a consequence of the 'Glorious Revolution' of 1688, and the Church of England was formally established there in 1702. The colony was restored to the fifth Lord Baltimore in 1715, but the family had by then become Protestant. The Anglican establishments in Virginia were strengthened in this period, even though toleration had to be accorded to dissenting groups. The development of the Carolinas, granted originally to a group of proprietors in 1663, was rather slow, but in 1706 the Church of England was established in South Carolina and nine years later in North. Much of the religious life of these colonies was under the guidance of dissenting churches, however, and the establishments were very weak. The remaining English colony, Georgia, was not founded until 1733.

Florida was invaded by English troops during Queen Anne's War, but it remained Spanish in the final settlement. Although the English had failed to take St. Augustine, they did great damage to the city and raided other settlements and missions. Florida remained quite small in population.

Within the outlines of these geographical and political realities, the Christian churches sought to fulfil their mission. Those which had been transplanted to the western wilderness before 1650 all continued to grow: Catholic, Anglican, Congregational, Dutch Reformed, Lutheran, and Baptist. Some new groups appeared, such as Quakers, Presbyterians, French and German Reformed, and Mennonites. Organized Jewish life began, and an interesting feature of religious life in North America was foreshadowed in the appearance of an indigenous body, the Rogerenes (see p. 48).

The Expansion of New France

Spanish and English Catholicism in North America remained small and carried on under great difficulties in these decades, but in New France the Catholic Church flourished. Patterns of Catholic life that were to be decisive for the future of Canada were shaped under two remarkable bishops, Laval and Saint-Vallier, whose terms together spanned some sixty-six years. The progress was not always smooth, for the expanding French Catholic world in the latter half of the seventeenth century was torn by bitter controversies, some within the church and others between church and state.

The tensions within the church, especially between religious Orders, were in part a reflection of struggles going on in France between Gallican and Ultramontane groups. The Gallicans stressed the distinct character and particular customs of *French* Roman Catholicism; the Sulpicians, for example, favoured this cause. The Ultramontanes looked 'beyond the mountains' to Rome and the papacy; they worked for a centralized Catholicism. The Jesuits were leaders in this camp.

The society of Saint Sulpice, devoted especially to the education of priests, had been founded in 1641 by Jean Jacques Olier, who had been inspired by the revival in spirituality stimulated by Pierre de Bérulle. Olier had been instrumental in planning for the founding of Montreal, and educated clerics for New France at the Sulpician seminary in France. When a group had been prepared for service abroad, their leader, Gabriel de Thubières de Quéylus, was granted the powers of a grand vicar of New France by the Archbishop of Rouen, a convinced Gallican. So many ships had sailed from his archdiocese to the New World that he was often thought to have canonical jurisdiction there. The Jesuit superior at Quebec, Jean de Quen, was also a grand vicar. When rumours circulated that de Quéylus might be named bishop, the stage was set for sharp conflict between the two Orders, in which the tensions between Gallicans and Ultramontanes—and between Montreal and Quebec—played a part. After complicated negotiations, a former student of the Jesuits, François de Montmorency de Laval (1623–1708), was named vicar-apostolic of New France and was consecrated titular Bishop of Petraea *in partibus infidelium*. It was a victory for the Jesuits and the Ultramontanes, as was made clear when Laval, who arrived in Quebec in 1659, saw to it that de Quéylus was sent back to France. In later years the two were reconciled and the Sulpician returned to his beloved seminary at Montreal.

The aggressive Laval was soon embroiled in another controversy, this time over church–state issues. The struggle was precipitated by Laval's broad use of excommunication in an effort to check the sale of alcoholic beverages to the Indians. The governor insisted that this admittedly serious problem was a civil and not an ecclesiastical matter. Laval felt obliged to have the matter brought personally to the attention of Louis XIV himself. One consequence was that in 1663 New France became a royal colony in which a Sovereign Council replaced the old Council of One Hundred Associates. The new controller-general of finances for France, Jean-Baptiste Colbert, devoted great attention to the building of a commercial empire in Canada. He named Jean Talon as intendant to direct economic growth. The latter began by stimulating immigration and by encouraging large families—running somewhat counter to the stress of the religious on chastity. The colony prospered under the new policies, but many felt that the religious concerns were being subordinated to economic interests. Quarrels between the bishop, the governor, and the intendant continued, especially as Laval carried on his crusade against the sale of intoxicating liquors to the Indians.

Under Laval's firm hand, the institutions of the church flourished. There was opened in 1663 at Quebec a *Grand Séminaire*, which was not only an educational centre, but also a headquarters and home for the bishop and the priests. Laval was building a centralized system in which priests were moved freely at the bishop's order as the situation required. The seminary also handled many administrative details for the growing church. Before Laval's coming there had been considerable encouragement of lay participation in parish affairs through elected church wardens; the bishop sought to maintain the advantages of this development but to control it through the centralizing work of the seminary. The resulting ecclesiastical system proved to have much resiliency and strength in later times of testing. Laval's position was further consolidated when he was made Bishop of Quebec in 1674, the new diocese being subject directly to Rome. During his long term, the bishop established some twenty-five parishes and missions. The quality of Catholic life was significantly affected by the work of some other remarkable persons, notable among them Marie de l'Incarnation, superior of the Ursulines, a teaching Order of nuns. Her combination of mystical piety, practical skill, and writing ability gave her great influence over the patterns of church life for generations.

Though the quarrels between religious and civil officials continued, the growth of French Catholic civilization depended on both the ecclesiastical and the secular Orders, which were complementary. The way religious and political leadership together advanced the growth of New France was especially evident in the adventurous push to the west and down the Mississippi. In this epic endeavour, missionaries and explorers, traders and soldiers journeyed and laboured side by side, the priests seeking converts and the others new opportunities and routes for trade.

When a small group of French accompanied a band of Chippewas westward over the Great Lakes route in 1660, a Jesuit, René Ménard, went with them despite his delicate health. They travelled as far as the southern shore of Lake Superior. Hearing about a band of Catholic Hurons some-where further south-west, early the following year Fr. Ménard set out to find them, but disappeared into the wilderness. The Order named Claude Jean Allouez to replace him; he built a mission near what later became Ashland, Wisconsin. Until his death a quarter of a century later, Allouez travelled extensively in Wisconsin and Illinois country, baptized many Indian converts (though the figure of 15,000 is probably an exaggeration), and founded several other missions. Laval named him vicar-general for missions.

Familiar to students of western discovery is the story of Louis Jolliet, a young Canadian-born explorer who was chosen by governor and intendant to find the mighty river about which so many stories were circulating. With him went the devout Jesuit father, Jacques Marquette, veteran of the mission among the Illinois Indians at Kaskaskia. Proceeding along the western edge of Lake Michigan, the party reached the Mississippi and travelled down it as far south as the Arkansas River, near Spanish territory. The group then returned to winter near Lake Michigan, convinced that the Mississippi did in fact empty into the Gulf of Mexico and not into the Pacific as some had surmised.

The Franciscan fathers had returned to New France in 1670, and Fr. Louis Hennepin became associated with the expedition of 1679–82 to explore the upper Mississippi region under the leadership of René-Robert de La Salle and Henry de Tonty. Fr. Hennepin was taken captive in Minnesota by a band of Sioux. After being freed, he returned to France where he described his experience in vivid terms; indeed, he was soon charged with exaggeration and plagiarism. In 1682 La Salle journeyed all the way down the Mississippi to its mouth, and claimed the vast Mississippi valley for the King of France, naming it Louisiana.

On a visit to his mother country following his great achievement, La Salle aroused enthusiasm for his vision of a great empire in the vast valley, and gathered a fleet to undertake settlement. Sulpician and Franciscan missionaries went with the expedition, which somehow missed the mouth of the river and landed on the Texas coast in 1685. Torn by dissension, beset by hostile Indians and marauding Spanish, weakened by the murder of La Salle during a mutiny, the colony was finally wiped out by the Indians. After that the great western thrust of the French weakened and the missions declined. The Jesuits then reintensified their mission work in the St. Lawrence region, reaching down into Maine. Prominent in this latter effort was Sébastian Râlé, who arrived in Maine in 1694 and endeavoured to get the Abnakis along the Kennebec River to settle in communities.

By this time two significant events had taken place. Troubled by ill health, Bishop Laval resigned his see in 1688, though he remained active in Canadian affairs until his death in 1708. His retirement did not really take effect until his successor, Jean Baptiste de La Croix de Chevrières de Saint-Vallier, arrived in 1688. Saint-Vallier was an imperious, proud man who was involved in many controversies with opponents in ecclesiastical, colonial, and imperial governments. He headed the huge diocese of Quebec for more than four decades, though he was absent on several occasions—once for thirteen years. His famous work of 1702, *Le Catéchisme du diocèse de Québec*, a volume combining biblical, doctrinal, and devotional materials, provided an educational instrument that shaped generations of Canadian Catholics.

The other great event—really a series of events—was the coming of war between France and England—King William's War, followed by Queen Anne's War. The struggles, carried on over vast distances, were marked by some cruel massacres. Both sides used and misused Indian allies; both resorted to terror tactics. Religious forces on both sides regarded the opponent with hatred and identified the will of God with victory for their cause and defeat for the enemy.

Early in the wars, an act of treachery by French officials through which a group of Iroquois was enslaved inflamed that people once again against the French, and New France was endangered as the Indians joined with the English in attack. The crusty Louis de Buade, Comte de Frontenac, a Gallican sympathizer, returned for a second term as governor. He pursued war with relentless determination; the Schenectady (New York) massacre of 1690 was not soon forgotten by the English, nor were their reprisals by their northern enemies. The French knew they were fighting for their survival on the continent, and resolutely resisted a formidable siege of Quebec itself by a fleet which had been fitted out in Boston.

The long struggle pitted two cultures, French Catholic and British Protestant, in a gigantic duel. The centuries of rivalry between England and France met in particularly ugly ways in the forests, waterways, and frontiers of the New World. At the end of Queen Anne's War in 1713, French Canada was bereft of Hudson's Bay, Newfoundland, and much of Acadia; the hatreds that had been sown flared up again for a further half-century, and the memories of those generations of struggle live on in history, legend, and feeling.

Through all these years of conflict, the Catholic Church in New France was carrying on the double task of providing ministrations for the far-flung network of forts and trading posts and seeking the conversion of Indians through the missions. The work was advanced by the continuing heroism of many missionaries, but marred by continuing controversies between members of religious Orders and the secular priests from the Quebec seminary, and between the religious leaders and the military authorities. The focus of the Jesuit missions in the Great Lakes area was at Michilimackinac (later Mackinac Island), where the superior-general for the region customarily resided. The appointment of Antoine de la Mothe Cadillac as commandant in the west in 1694 troubled the Jesuits, for he was a resolute opponent; his interests were clearly more in trade than in religion. He recognized the strategic importance of Detroit, and began settlement there in 1701. The old battle between priests and governors over the sale of liquor to the Indians was resumed. Under Cadillac's policies the Jesuit missions declined; the Franciscans became the principal spiritual guides at Detroit.

In the Illinois country, however, Jesuit activity flourished, centring at Kaskaskia; here the tribe that gave its name to the region was converted. In the mission to the Tamarois, an Illinois tribe, the Jesuits were replaced by the seminary priests. A conspicuous leader in this mission was Jean Baptiste Mercier, a Canadian-born priest who arrived at Cahokia in 1718. He mastered the Illinois Indian tongues, and served faithfully both natives and colonists.

The Louisiana country, claimed by France on the basis of La Salle's explorations, was settled directly from France by way of the Gulf of Mexico with the intention of winning Indians to the faith and blocking English expansion. The area came under the ecclesiastical jurisdiction of the vast diocese of Quebec. A leading political figure in the young colony's life over four decades was a Canadian, Jean-Baptiste Le Moyne de Bienville, who had learned several Indian languages. Internally, life in the French outposts was torn by controversies between governor and commissary, the one charged with political and the other with economic concerns. As one student of Louisiana has remarked, 'Louisiana was as healthy as any normal two-headed infant could be expected to be.'[1] The involvement of the mother country in war seriously limited the care and resources needed for effective colonization.

Louisiana's religious life was rent by the familiar tension between Jesuits and secular priests, until Bishop Saint-Vallier acted so decisively in 1703 in favour of the priests that the Jesuit presence there ceased for more than two decades. Under the seminary priests there was little outreach among the Indians, although attempts were made to win the Natchez. By 1720, the Illinois country had been placed under Louisiana administration, and New Orleans, soon to become the capital, was founded. It is fair to conclude that the religious fervour that had marked the origins of New France was missing in Louisiana, for although the church's presence was pervasive it was not as powerful. By the 1720s the total European popu-

---

[1] Charles E. O'Neill, *Church and State in French Colonial Louisiana: Policy and Politics to 1732* (New Haven, 1966), p. 95.

lation of Louisiana was about 2,500, 10 per cent of whom were probably Protestants, though officially there were none.

Though they had lost parts of their over-all holdings as a consequence of war, the French in 1720 were claiming vast territories, and with a relatively small population were committed to maintaining a French Catholic civilization there. Devoted missionaries strove to convert the Indians to the Catholic faith, though controversies within the church weakened the effort, as did the example of traders whose chief concern with the Indians was profit. The enmity between the French Catholic and English Protestant cultures had been vividly heightened during the two wars and the incidents of violence that continued.

Religious Diversification in New England

The contrasts between Catholic church life in New France and the religious experiences of Protestants in New England were many and striking. In French Canada centralized government and church administration were maintained; in New England by the end of the seventeenth century there were four separate colonies, in three of which were established town churches of Congregational character. Throughout New France there was a high degree of religious homogeneity, but in the English colonies to the south other forms of the Christian Church had come to stay, despite the efforts of Congregational leaders. To the north the controversies were not about basic questions of theology but over matters of ecclesiastical jurisdiction or public morals; while such issues were debated in various ways in New England, sharp differences erupted over fundamental matters of doctrine and polity. The French empire spread over a vast geographical area in the latter half of the seventeenth century; the New England colonies did not increase so markedly in area but did increase in population. In both settings, the religious excitement and expectancy that had marked the beginnings of these transplanted European Christian commonwealths had faded somewhat by the early eighteenth century.

The ways in which the leaders of Puritan Congregationalism perceived and responded to changes going on about them contributed significantly to later trends in American religious history. A most important shift in Puritan perspective over these seventy years is reflected in two signal events in the relations between Congregationalists and Baptists, one at the beginning and the other near the end of the period 1650–1720. The early Baptists in England and the colonies shared many basic theological premises with other Puritans, but had drawn certain conclusions that challenged the firm commitments of most Puritans to religious establishment and to the baptism of infants. The New England Congregational leaders were constantly on their guard lest some in their ranks be attracted to Baptist views.

In 1651 John Clarke, the Rhode Island physician and minister from Newport, visited a blind Baptist, William Witter, in Lynn, Massachusetts. With him were two fellow Baptists, Obadiah Holmes and John Crandall. While worshipping privately in Witter's home, the three were arrested. Holmes was whipped; Clarke would have been similarly punished had not someone paid the fine for him. Clarke described the event fully in a book published the next year in London, *Ill Newes from New-England: or, A narrative of New-England's Persecution, Wherin is declared that while old England is becoming new, New-England is become old . . .*

Strikingly different was the event of 1718 in which Increase and Cotton Mather, the father and son who were at the very heart of established Congregationalism, participated in the ordination of a Baptist, Elisha Callendar, a Harvard graduate, at the Baptist church in Boston. In his sermon, Cotton Mather alluded to the persecutions of the past which were still fresh in Baptist memories, and said:

Good Men, alas *Good Men*, have done such *Ill Things* as these; yea, Few Churches of the Reformation have been wholly clear of the *Iniquities. New England* also has in some Former Times, done some Things of this aspect, which would not now be so well approved of: in which, if the Brethren in whose *House* we are now convened, met with any thing *too unbrotherly*, they now with satisfaction *hear* us expressing our dislike of everything that has look'd like *Persecution* in the days that have passed over us.[2]

Increase Mather had been a boy of 12 when the whipping incident of 1651 had taken place—his life spanned a period of a significant refocusing of the Congregational way.

Massachusetts had been simply unable to keep the Baptists out. A Welsh Baptist who had studied at Oxford, John Myles, had come to New England and settled at Rehoboth in 1663, where he gathered a Baptist church. Under pressure from Massachusetts, Plymouth colony refused to allow the dissenting church to continue in Rehoboth, but did allow it to move to the new town of Swansea on the Rhode Island border. Here the new sect would not be disturbing to the Congregational faithful, and the usual requirement for the support of a town church could be overlooked. It was not long before a Baptist church appeared in Boston itself.

---

[2] *Brethren Dwelling Together in Unity. The True Basis for an Union Among the People of God . . .* (Boston, 1718), p. 39.

Thomas Goold, a farmer and wagon-maker, was a member of the Congregational church at Charlestown. In the 1650s he came to the conclusion that baptism according to the New Testament was for believers only. Consequently, he refused to allow an infant daughter to be baptized. Despite various actions against him, Goold held private meetings, and in 1665 with eight others was baptized by immersion and gathered a new church. Disenfranchisement, fines, and imprisonment followed. The refusal of the Baptists to pay religious taxes for the support of the established ministry added to their difficulties.

The desire of the authorities to banish Goold and other Baptists was checked by a petition for their toleration, signed by a number of prominent Congregationalists. Meanwhile, Baptist sympathizers were appearing in other towns. Goold apparently took refuge for five years as a semi-exile on nearby Noddles Island. In 1674 he moved to Boston, and five years later a small Baptist meeting-house was erected. The authorities promptly boarded it up, but the Baptists, appealing to a letter from King Charles II proclaiming toleration for all Protestants, regained access to their building —the same one in which Cotton Mather was to preach the ordination sermon of 1718.[3] Because of both internal and external resistance, the Congregational leaders were unable to go to the lengths necessary to stop determined dissenters. The religious diversity so long feared by European Christendom was becoming a reality, and the Congregationalists were learning to adjust to it.

The Puritans used the power of execution to try to keep the Quakers out, until they were stopped by orders from England. The willingness on the part of convinced members of the Religious Society of Friends to face martyrdom for their convictions helped other dissenters to gain their freedom. The first Quakers to reach North America came as missionaries determined to witness to their faith in the centres of religious establishment by using tactics of confrontation and disruption. Quakerism was then a very young movement; its exponents were inspired by what had recently come to them as new truth. Only in 1646 had the founder, George Fox (1624–91) gained religious peace in the conviction that to each person is given from God a gift of divine Inner Light. Fox had been brought up in a humble Puritan household in England, but troubled by the contrast between what Christians professed and what they practised, he went through a period of spiritual depression and searching. His emphasis on

---

[3] The story is told in careful detail by William G. McLoughlin, *New England Dissent, 1630–1833: The Baptists and the Separation of Church and State*, 2 vols. (Cambridge, Mass., 1971), vol. i.

the Divine Light meant that for him revelation was no longer narrowly confined to the Scriptures. Fox turned against all outward ceremonies of faith, against establishments of religion and paid ministries, against the taking of oaths and the making of war. With his early followers, he had to face intense persecution, which only increased his zeal.

As part of the missionary thrust of this expanding new movement, Quakers first arrived in the New World when Mary Fisher and Ann Austin came to Boston in 1656. They were imprisoned and expelled, as were others who soon followed. But there were enough affinities between Quakers and Puritans to make some Puritans vulnerable to Quaker appeals to inward religion and the direct experience of God. The Massachusetts authorities passed a series of laws against the invaders, the harshest providing the death penalty for those who returned after banishment. Determined at any cost to make their witness to the truth as they had received it, Quakers returned again and again from their refuges in Rhode Island and Barbados. Four of them, including a woman, Mary Dyer, were finally hanged on Boston Common (1659-61).

The reaction was sharp. George Bishop published *New England Judged, Not by Man's, but the Spirit of the Lord* (1661), and Charles II, though certainly no friend of Quakers, ordered an end to the executions. Deprived of their ultimate weapon, the Puritan leaders continued to harass the Friends, but by 1665 they were allowed to go about their secular concerns without interference. In New Hampshire the Friends were persecuted at first, but by the 1680s had gathered a sizeable meeting in Dover. In New Haven in the late 1650s Quakers were whipped and branded. In adjoining Connecticut they were driven out whenever they appeared, but after 1675 in the united colony they were tolerated. Early in the eighteenth century a new law against them was passed, but was disallowed by the Queen.

The new effort against them in Connecticut had come about apparently because they had been confused with the indigenous dissenting sect of the Rogerenes. In 1674 John Rogers, a prosperous merchant of New London, was convinced by a group of Seventh-Day Baptists, an offshoot of Clarke's church which had been influenced by members of a Seventh-Day sect from Cromwell's England, that infant baptism was not sanctioned by Scripture and that worship should be on Saturday, the seventh day, as the true Sabbath. The new group adopted the practice of faith-healing and was pacifistic. Rogerenes were uncompromising radicals who refused to pay religious taxes. Members of this small revolutionary sect were frequently imprisoned, but they continued their agitation and made a contribution to the coming of religious freedom; however, they disappeared shortly before the revolutionary epoch.[4]

The original hope of the Puritan leaders for religious uniformity had to be qualified as dissenters secured footholds in every colony. The battle then shifted to a struggle over religious taxation, a fight that continued into the nineteenth century.

The embarrassments confronting those who cherished the ideal of an homogeneous holy commonwealth did not only stem from the dissenters, but came also from those who outwardly professed the early goals but no longer found them as appealing or compelling. There were internal theological problems, too. The assumption of the federal theology was that the children of the elect were included in the covenant with their parents, for God's covenant with Abraham had included his seed (Genesis 17:7). The expectation was that when they reached the years of discretion, these children of the elect would give a satisfying public statement of their conversion and be admitted as full members of the church. As the second generation of Puritan Congregationalists matured, however, some found that they could not make the required profession, or did not wish to do so. Were they then to be counted as church members? Could *their* children be baptized? Anomalies were appearing in a church system which insisted that its congregations were the only recognized and established churches, and which at the same time understood them to be gathered churches of the elect. There was increasing danger that those who were excluded from the privileges of the sacraments might be attracted to dissenting groups.

The immediate practical problem concerned the third generation children whose parents had not become full church members in their own right. The dilemma was a real one: to allow the children of saints to be counted as full church members without their own acceptable profession of regeneration was to dilute church membership, but not to allow them the right to have their children baptized was to deepen dissatisfaction with the whole system and to narrow its base of support. Controversy over the issue had been building up for years—it had been discussed at the Cambridge Synod, but no solution had been found. In 1657 an assembly of seventeen ministers from Massachusetts and Connecticut decided that the baptized children of saints, though not themselves full members, could under certain conditions have *their* children baptized. Such an uproar was created that in 1662 the General Court of Massachusetts ordered a synod of ministers and messengers from the churches to settle the issue. The

[4] Richard L. Bushman, *From Puritan to Yankee: Character and Social Order in Connecticut, 1690–1765* (Cambridge, Mass., 1967), pp. 164–7.

seventy delegates by an overwhelming 7-1 margin approved what was later called the 'half-way covenant'. Henceforth children whose parents (or one of them) had been in the covenant relation at the time of their baptism could have their children baptized, provided that they (the parents) understood and assented to the doctrine of faith, were not scandalous in behaviour, and owned the covenant of the church. Such children were not to be counted full members of the church until they could give an acceptable public relation; they were not to be admitted to the Lord's Supper nor could they vote for a pastor.

The issue was settled officially, but not all congregations accepted the decision, and a number of churches were split over the matter. Gradually, however, the half-way covenant was widely accepted in Connecticut and Massachusetts. An analysis of the controversy has come to this conclusion:

By 1690 the half-way covenant was an effective part of the new orthodoxy, but this was an orthodoxy without compulsion. Churches applied the principle as they saw fit; they used what they wanted and rejected what they found inapplicable. In the rapidly changing society of seventeenth-century Massachusetts, the autonomy of the individual congregation proved to be the undoing of religious uniformity.[5]

Original theory was thus changed in an important particular by the general acceptance of the half-way covenant. The Congregational establishments were less united in doctrine and practice after the controversy, though they retained their privileged positions.

Missionary work among the Indians, especially under Eliot and the Mayhews, was getting hopeful results in the third quarter of the seventeenth century. An Indian church was finally covenanted at Natick in 1660. Three years later Eliot's vast project to translate the whole Bible into Algonquian was completed—the first Bible to be published in a native tongue, and the first to be printed in any language in North America. It was a remarkable achievement, which won wide acclaim for its translator. At Harvard an Indian college was begun and a building erected. Only a handful of native boys attended, however, and only one graduated. In the early 1670s, Eliot and his associates extended the mission to the Nipmuc Indians in central Massachusetts. In all there were fourteen towns of praying Indians by 1674, with a total population of about 1,100. On Martha's Vineyard, Thomas Mayhew, Sr. carried on the mission when his son was lost at sea. By 1674 there were several native churches on the island, and most of the Indians had been won to Christianity. At Plymouth, the most

    5 Robert G. Pope, *The Half-Way Covenant: Church Membership in Puritan New England* (Princeton, N.J., 1969), p. 260.

extensive missionary outreach was under the direction of Richard Bourne among the Nausets on Cape Cod; by 1674 nearly 500 praying Indians had been gathered in eight centres.[6]

Then disaster struck. The missionaries had succeeded in reaching some of the weaker tribes near the English settlements, but they had been unable to get a foothold among the stronger tribes. The Wampanoag Indians of southern Massachusetts had worked peaceably with Plymouth, for Massasoit needed a counter-force against the powerful Narragansetts. But when that chief died in about 1661, he was succeeded in time by his second son, Philip. By then the English population significantly out-numbered the Indian, and the English were increasing their domination over the political, economic, and social life of southern New England. Philip resented this domination, which meant a lessening of his own authority. He was able to secure the assistance of three other tribes: his former enemies, the Narragansetts, the Nipmucs, and the Pocumtucks of west central Massachusetts. In June 1675 King Philip's War erupted as the Wampanoags raided Swansea. The militia struck back, and the war spread quickly throughout the New England frontier region. A number of towns were attacked in sudden raids that resulted in so much death and destruction that they had to be abandoned.

The militia had been schooled in European-style warfare, and at first were no match for the hit-and-run tactics of the Indians. They fell repeatedly into ambush. Even towns close to Boston were raided; Providence suffered heavy losses. Fortunately for the English, a number of the tribes (Mohegans, Pequots, Massachusetts, Nausets) supported them, while others (Niantics, Abnakis) remained neutral.

The Christian Indians were in a difficult situation. Most of the Nausets had gone over to Philip, but the Massachusetts Indians remained firm in their loyalty to the English. They sought to form an armed buffer between the hostile tribes and the Europeans, but so many of the latter came to identify all Indians as enemies that this was not possible, and grave in-justices were inflicted on those natives among whom Eliot and his colleagues had laboured. Some innocent victims were murdered. Despite heroism on the part of the Christian Indians in battle for the colonists, they were confined first to five towns, and then moved to a compound on Deer Island, where they faced cold, hunger, and disease. Yet they were instrumental in the final fall of Philip. Terrible reprisals were then visited

---

[6] See Vaughan, *New England Frontier*, chs. X & XI, and William Kellaway, *The New England Company, 1649-1776: Missionary Society to the American Indians* (New York, 1961), ch. V.

on the defeated forces by the English, and New England tribes were restricted to early forms of reservations. The extensive missionary empire of Eliot never fully recovered. The Christian Indians were restored to only four towns, all of which were absorbed by the white population by the late eighteenth century. The war had been costly in life and property for the colonists. The stereotypes of the 'pagan savages' which were to exist for centuries were fixed in many minds; they played their part in the unhappy story of the degradation of the American Indian.

Eliot carried on as best he could. When age prevented him from going on his missionary journeys, he gathered Negro slaves who lived in his vicinity for weekly spiritual instruction. There were only a few hundred slaves in New England in 1680; in the next century they did not become more than 3 per cent of the total population. Although they were treated like white indentured servants in some respects, the fact that their term was for life made a decisive difference. The courts decided that enslavement could be justified as a form of punishment and for captives of war, especially for 'strangers' and pagans. Thus the way was prepared for the rationalization of Negro slavery. There was one famous Puritan protest against slavery—Judge Samuel Sewall's *The Selling of Joseph* (1700). For the most part the churches did not challenge the institution of black slavery, which was not a very conspicuous part of the New England scene.[7]

The second generation leaders of Puritanism were deeply perplexed that the great dreams and expectancies of the 1630s were not being fulfilled. True, the colony was growing, and had enjoyed considerable prosperity. But that was part of the problem—from the point of view of the devout, too many minds were fixed on material rather than on spiritual things. The half-way covenant did mean that many who were not 'proved saints' were content to let their religion be more a matter of respectability than of regeneration. In the 1670s came a time of troubles: the terrible war, a smallpox epidemic, a great fire in Boston, and the continual pressure of a hostile Restoration government in England. The clergy had frequent recourse to a 'jeremiad' style of preaching designed to convince the people of their responsibility for the commonwealth's decline, and to call them to repentance for the sin and pride that had provoked the divine wrath. Like the prophet Jeremiah they called the populace to face their shortcomings and to return to the ways of God.

In the late 1670s nearly a score of the ministers of Massachusetts petitioned

[7] Winthrop D. Jordan, *White Over Black: American Attitudes Toward the Negro, 1550–1812* (Chapel Hill, 1968), pp. 66–71, 193–8.

the General Court to call a synod to look deeply into the existing evils and to propose suitable action. The synod gathered in Boston in 1679; a second session was held the next year. With a certain direct honesty, the delegates of the churches did not attempt to shift the blame to someone else, but asked first of all what were the evils for which they were responsible that led God into controversy with his people in New England. The detailed answer was in the form of an extended jeremiad complete with many references to Scripture. Condemned were 'spiritual and heart Apostacy from God', pride of spirit and in apparel, disobedience, contention, profaneness, sloth and sleepiness in public and family worship, Sabbath-breaking, gossiping, intemperance, lying, land-hunger, and lack of public spirit.

When they came to deal with the second question—what is to be done for reform?—the delegates were able only to reaffirm the original faith, for they were bound by the system of the first generation even though it no longer quite fitted the changing scene. They called, predictably, for strict adherence to church discipline, for enforcing the laws, for the renewal of the covenant. Though they had been asked to revise the Cambridge Platform, they did not do so, but simply reaffirmed it. They were unable to deal in an adequate theological way with the dynamic realities about them, and tended to view all change as decline.[8] Their inherited system had inconsistencies and contradictions, many of them growing out of the basic tension between gathered and established images of the church, which they were unable collectively to face. The jeremiad style continued to be frequently invoked into the eighteenth century, but the old system was not significantly renewed, and new ways which did emerge here and there seemed like apostasy to those who were clinging to a vision from the past.

Nor did the troubles cease. The charter of Massachusetts was revoked in 1684, and Anglican worship introduced in Boston soon after. After the Duke of York assumed the throne as James II in 1685, Sir Edmund Andros was given charge over the entire Dominion of New England, including New York. On Good Friday 1687, Andros required that the South Church be used for Anglican worship, while the Puritans waited in the streets outside until the long liturgical service was completed. To be sure, at the time of the Glorious Revolution, the Dominion collapsed and Andros was imprisoned, but Anglican worship continued in the heart of New England as King's Chapel was erected. The new charter of 1691

---

[8] This emphasis is central in Perry Miller's brilliant work of interpretation, *The New England Mind: From Colony to Province* (Cambridge, Mass., 1953).

forbade religious tests for the suffrage, and provided freedom of worship for all Protestants.

The witchcraft tragedy at Salem Village further added to Puritan difficulties. A vast literature has gathered around the witchcraft trials of 1692, in which the Puritan leadership was often blamed.[9] In the spring of 1692 the accusations of several young girls launched a search for instruments of Satan, and before it was halted a score of persons, all protesting their innocence, had been executed, including a minister. Actually, considered against the background of the persecution of witches in both New England and Old, the number of executions was not extraordinary. While the trials were on, with several exceptions the role of the ministry was in fact a rather cautious and restraining one. Yet in the compulsiveness of their search for divine signs and in their reiteration of the guilt of the people, the Puritan clergy had helped to set the conditions for the witch-hunt, its terrible conclusion, and the unrest that followed. The whole Puritan system was weakened by the experience.

In the 1630s the Puritan leaders had so firmly put down internal dissent that it was a long time before variant interpretations of covenant theology began to be openly expressed from within. It was difficult enough for those who were trying to be faithful to the vision of a holy commonwealth to have to tolerate other churches; to have to contend with significantly different interpretations from within the system was even more threatening. Solomon Stoddard (1643–1729), son of a wealthy Boston merchant, preached first at the church at Northampton in western Massachusetts in 1669.[10] The next year he was called to its pastorate, married the widow of his predecessor, Eleazer Mather, and soon rose to prominence in the Connecticut River valley. He organized the Hampshire Association and long remained the dominant figure in it. His book on conversion, *The Safety of Appearing at the Day of Judgment* (1687), dealt in a fresh way with topics long debated among the Puritans. Stoddard insisted that the sinners should prepare themselves for conversion, and should strive for the gift of grace—yet only when they realized that there was nothing of goodness or righteousness in them and gave up in utter humiliation might God be pleased to let the spiritual light into their souls. There is no infallible external sign of election, Stoddard taught, for it is surely known only by intuition to the elect person. This theology led

---

[9] e.g., see Chadwick Hansen, *Witchcraft at Salem* (New York, 1969).

[10] Thomas A. Schafer, 'Solomon Stoddard and the Theology of the Revival', in Stuart C. Henry (ed.), *A Miscellany of American Christianity: Essays in Honor of H. Shelton Smith* (Durham, N.C., 1963), pp. 328–61.

Stoddard beyond the half-way covenant. If there can be no real certainty as to who had received saving grace, on what ground can the sincere seeker be barred from the Lord's Supper? God may use it as a 'converting ordinance' to disclose his grace to the penitent sinner. 'Stoddardeanism' was put into practice at Northampton and some of the nearby churches, and bore a rich fruit of converts, especially during five particular seasons of 'harvest' in Stoddard's own ministry of nearly six decades. Stoddard's careful defence of the practice of receiving into membership those who professed belief in the main articles of faith and lived a moral life appeared in *The Doctrine of Instituted Churches* in 1700, and opened a long controversy with Increase Mather.

Stoddard was an annoyance to those Calvinists who were trying to hold to the original New England Puritan system, but he was in the western part of the colony, while there were even more threatening variations developing within the capital itself. The Puritans had put great stress on the role of reason in religion, always meaning reason under the Scriptures, reason as employed by the godly. By the late seventeenth century there were already flowing currents of thought soon to be gathered up in what is called the Enlightenment. Reason was beginning to be employed as a freeing force, and used to challenge long-accepted assumptions. At the very end of the seventeenth century, some prominent Bostonians organized the Brattle Street Church, calling as pastor Benjamin Colman, who had been ordained in London and hence did not have to stand the examination of the orthodox in Boston. The 'Manifesto' of those who founded the new church called for the 'dumb reading' of Scripture, that is, without the comments of the clergy—a move toward greater formality in worship, and one which also suggested that people were competent to make their own interpretations. Members were admitted in full standing if the pastor indicated his satisfaction with the spiritual state of candidates. This went beyond the half-way covenant on quite a different theological ground from that employed by Stoddard. The Manifesto defined the church as 'a society of Christians by mutual agreement'—a far cry from the Cambridge Platform's definition, 'a company of saints by calling, united into one body, by a holy covenant'.

Soon after, control of instruction at Harvard College fell to those who were accused of Arminian tendencies, of putting too much stress on the role of reason in religion and on man's place in the covenant. Increase Mather was ousted from the presidency, and the tutors William Brattle and John Leverett became the central figures, Leverett eventually becoming president. Consequently the Mathers favoured the step undertaken by the Connecticut clergy in 1701 to found a properly orthodox college, which later was named Yale and moved from Saybrook to New Haven.

The challenged leaders of Calvinism in Massachusetts conceived a plan to defend the faith as they understood it. Their 'Massachusetts Proposals' recommended that permanent associations of ministers be organized to advise on the ordination and placement of clergy in vacant churches. This was accepted by a number of the congregations. The Proposals also suggested that the churches in a given area send clerical and lay delegates to form standing councils to supervise the churches and to make binding decisions. This was a movement in a Presbyterian direction; it was inconsistent with the Cambridge Platform and had no serious chance of acceptance in Massachusetts. It provoked some resolute defences of the Congregational system, especially from the pen of a pastor in Ipswich, John Wise, *The Churches Quarrel Espoused* (1713) and *A Vindication of the Government of the New England Churches* (1717). Wise appealed not only to biblical arguments but also to the law of nature, implying that there was a direct link from man to God through natural reason. He showed familiarity with the political thought of Locke and Pufendorf; on the eve of the American Revolution his works were reprinted as a contribution towards independence.

Though rejected in Massachusetts, in Connecticut the Proposals were put into use. Tendencies towards Presbyterian church government had already displayed themselves in western Massachusetts and Connecticut, in part through the influence of Stoddard. A synod was called in 1708 in Connecticut; it prepared the 'Saybrook Articles' which provided that the neighbouring congregations in each county were to form 'consociations' to hear and determine without appeal all cases brought before it. A General Association made up of delegates from the consociations was to meet annually in this step toward Presbyterianism. The agreement did help to maintain Connecticut as a citadel of Calvinist orthodoxy. This modified form of Congregationalism long dominated Connecticut church life; under it dissenting groups encountered great difficulties. The struggle of the Rogerene sect has already been mentioned. A Baptist church gathered at Groton in 1704 won the right to exist only through an appeal to the Toleration Act; its members still had to pay taxes in support of the established ministry.

It is easy to overdramatize the difficulties of such learned defenders of the old Puritan way as Cotton Mather. Though he deplored many of the trends of his time, he welcomed and contributed to others. He had great scientific curiosity, made important contributions to science, and was elected to membership in the Royal Society of London. His work *The Christian Philosopher* (1721) marvelled at the wonders of Nature. His acceptance of religious toleration by preaching an ordination sermon for a Baptist showed considerable resilience. He anticipated many of the currents that were to be influential in the religious life of the eighteenth century—humanitarianism, moralism, and the use of voluntary societies for accomplishing Christian work. One of his most popular books was directed to this end: *Bonifacius: An Essay Upon the Good* (1710), usually known by its running title, 'Essays to Do Good'. Yet Mather remained loyal to the Calvinist covenant theology; his scientific and philosophical interests strengthened his fervent piety.

In 1720 the Congregational system in which the Mathers were a force was still viable in Massachusetts, Connecticut, and New Hampshire, even though the great hopes of earlier years had faded. Although much genuine piety was nurtured in and through the churches, many were aware that there was much formalism and lethargy in what was the largest denomination in the English colonies, with about 250 congregations in 1720.

Zones of Freedom: Rhode Island and the Middle Colonies

In Rhode Island and the colonies of New York, New Jersey, Pennsylvania, and Delaware the atmosphere in this period was quite different. Here were developing the patterns of religious liberty, pluralism, and denominationalism that were to be so characteristic of American religious life. In a setting unique in European civilization—territories without established churches—a number of communions found that they could survive and flourish. These experiments in freedom proved what few Christians then believed, that an orderly society could survive without governmental backing for a favoured religion. Not that it was easy, for there were many controversies as groups competed and clashed, having to learn to live and let live.

Quaker missionaries who had met with such intense persecution elsewhere found refuge in Rhode Island and the middle colonies. In Rhode Island the Quakers won converts to their cause, much to the irritation of Roger Williams, who did not hesitate to attack them by word (but never by the law) on the basis of his Calvinism. In 1661 the first Yearly Meeting met in Newport, and in time the Quakers dominated the colony politically.

In the 1670s the first period of spectacular Quaker witness and martyrdom gave way to a time of consolidation and colonization. Missionary work was continued largely through the growth of Quaker meetings and the witness of 'travelling Friends' who visited Quaker homes and meetings, giving the rapidly growing movement unity and morale. The visit of George Fox to the colonies in 1672–3 was a feature of this transition. In the year following his visit, West (really south-west) Jersey came under the management of Quaker proprietors for a dozen years, and in 1680 East (really north-east) Jersey was also guided by a group of proprietors in which Quaker influence was strong. William Penn's first close contact with North America came as a member of this group, and his spirit was evident in the provision for liberty of conscience, trial by jury, and taxation by representatives of the people elected by secret ballot. An extensive Quaker migration from England was encouraged; the Burlington Monthly Meeting was organized in 1678 and for a time it was the most important centre of the Society of Friends.

Penn, the son of Admiral Sir William Penn and a convert to Quakerism in 1667, had a vision of an even greater refuge, and through his friendship with the Duke of York and in payment of a debt he received a munificent grant which he named after his father. Provision in the 'Frame of Government' was made for freedom of religion and for certain democratic rights. The 'holy experiment' was advertised widely in the British Isles, in southern Germany, and among the Dutch. Settlers soon arrived in great numbers. In 1682, the year Penn himself came for a stay, some 2,000 arrived, the majority of them Quakers. Penn travelled in his vast domain, visited Quaker meetings, and negotiated agreements with the Indians which paved the way for decades of quite harmonious relationships.

Friends' meetings spread through the enlarging colony, though those of other persuasions were also welcomed. As can be seen in the work of the leading English Quaker theologian, Robert Barclay, *An Apology for the True Christian Divinity* (1676), there was much of Puritan thought and piety in the life of the Friends, and the evangelical and prophetic motifs were as important as the mystical. The distinctive Quaker emphasis on the Inner Light was clearly stated by Barclay and other writers. Inasmuch as the theology of the Puritans was much concerned with the doctrine of the Holy Spirit, the Friends had a powerful point of entry in appealing to them. The stress on a religion of experience that did not use a paid ministry won many to their support.

With the influx of Germans into Pennsylvania came representatives of some of the persecuted religious minorities of Europe. Conspicuous among them were Anabaptist groups which baptized adult believers only and which had preserved the radical Reformation tradition in the face of intense persecution. The influence of a pacifistic Dutch Anabaptist,

Menno Simons (1492–1559), was strong in the Anabaptist communities which extended across the Rhineland from Holland to Switzerland. Seeking to be faithful to Christ's commands, simply and literally understood, the Mennonites refused to take oaths, hold public office, or bear arms. An early group of them from Krefeld settled in Germantown, just north of Philadelphia, in 1683. Some of them were won to the Quakers, with whom they had much in common religiously, and for a time they worshipped together. By 1690 the Mennonites had formed their own congregation, selecting preachers from among their own ranks. The Krefelders made their living chiefly through weaving; the second wave of Mennonite immigration was made up primarily of Swiss farm families which settled in the fertile lands west and north of Philadelphia, especially in what became Lancaster county. Through natural population increase (Mennonites forbade marriage outside their ranks) and through further immigration, Mennonite groups continued to swell in the eighteenth century. These folk had paid a heavy price for following their principles. Once settled in North America they clustered together, holding firmly to their religious and cultural customs and to the German language, which developed into a characteristic 'Pennsylvania Dutch' dialect.

Presbyterian churches first appeared on the American scene out of the Puritan context. Theologically, early Congregationalism and Presbyterianism were closely related, both adhering to the Westminster Confession of Faith after it appeared and both emphasizing the federal or covenant theology. The differences lay largely in polity, as Presbyterians preferred the pyramidal, jurisdictional style of church government with sessions (which governed each congregation), presbyteries, synods, and general assembly. There were some Presbyterian tendencies in New England Congregationalism. John Eliot, for example, preferred the Presbyterian scheme but agreed to subordinate his views to the majority; in Connecticut the Saybrook Articles illustrated the Presbyterian drift. The fact that the Congregational churches of New England were established provided certain structures (the care of the magistrates, the calling of synods by general courts) which overcame some of the problems of relationship between the various congregations. But those Puritans who founded congregations outside New England did not have such assistance, and Presbyterian polity often seemed preferable. Most of the Puritan churches on Long Island (one was founded at Southampton in 1640), in New York, New Jersey, and further south gradually became fully Presbyterian.

The arrival of Scots from the British Isles furthered the formation of

Presbyterian churches. In the early seventeenth century the English government had tried to displace the Roman Catholic population of North Ireland by settling Scots there, most of them Presbyterian. Economic difficulties combined with efforts to strengthen the minority Anglican establishment in Ulster turned Scottish eyes to North America. By the late seventeenth century a few were beginning to make their way to the colonies, to be followed by greater numbers in the eighteenth century. By the beginning of that century, a few Presbyterian congregations had gathered in Pennsylvania and in the southern colonies, with the Puritan and Scottish streams blending.

The conspicuous organizer of American Presbyterianism was Francis Makemie (1658?–1708), an Irish-born Scot and a graduate of the University of Aberdeen. He reached the colonies in 1683, travelled widely, and participated in the organization of a number of congregations in North America and on Barbados. Under his leadership in 1706 seven ministers met and made plans for regular meetings of a presbytery in Philadelphia.[11] Three of these ministers were from New England and four were of Scottish or Scotch–Irish origins. Not formally related to any Old World body, the new presbytery arose out of the needs of the churches. It was intercolonial from the start, and received financial assistance both from New England Puritans and from the 'United Brethren', an association of Congregational and Presbyterian ministers in London.

Unexpected publicity came to the young church when Makemie was arrested in New York for preaching without a licence. He won his case on the ground that a document issued in Barbados in keeping with the Toleration Act was valid in the English colonies, but Governor Cornbury spitefully assessed the heavy costs of the trial on him. There was much admiration for Makemie's spirited defence of liberty; the New York assembly soon passed an act to prevent such an assessment again, and Cornbury was recalled in disgrace.

As the Presbyterian church became more visible, it was joined by a number of congregations of Puritan background in the middle colonies, and Scotch–Irish immigrants added to the growth. By 1716 it was found advisable to form a synod with three functioning presbyteries: Philadelphia, New Castle, and Long Island. Two years later a large body of Scotch–Irish arrived in Boston but were not very hospitably received. Some congregations were formed in Maine and New Hampshire, but in Worcester, Massachusetts, the attempt to do the same was frustrated by

---

[11] On early Presbyterianism, see Leonard J. Trinterud, *The Forming of an American Tradition: A Re-examination of Colonial Presbyterianism* (Philadelphia, 1949), Part I.

Congregational hostility. After that Scottish immigration from Northern Ireland focused on the middle colonies.

The Baptist churches also found their main centre in the middle colonies in this period. The first Baptist congregation in Providence had been Calvinist or 'Particular' (Christ died for the elect only) in orientation; in the 1650s the General (Christ died for all men) or Arminian Baptist position won considerable support. A group of these Baptist churches took the name 'Six Principle' (Hebrews 6: 1–2), stressing the laying-on of hands after baptism as a symbol of the reception of the Holy Ghost. The Six Principle group reorganized the Providence church and founded a new one at Newport. In 1670 the four General Baptist churches in Rhode Island formed the first Baptist Association in North America. By 1729 this association embraced some thirteen churches, some in other colonies.

The largest centre of colonial Baptist growth, however, was in Philadelphia, where Particular Baptist churches were gathered in the late seventeenth century. Baptist immigrants from Wales and Ireland were conspicuous in this development. Five of these churches from three colonies formed in 1707 what became generally known as the Philadelphia Baptist Association. It quickly became the leading centre of Baptist growth and vitality. It adopted the London Confession of Faith, which was essentially the Westminster Confession with certain alterations to be consistent with key Baptist convictions. Despite their differences in polity and mode of baptism, Baptists and Presbyterians had many theological similarities, and both had formed intercolonial organizations centring in Philadelphia at about the same time. Out of the conditions of religious freedom and pluralism, the characteristic American church form, the denomination, was evolving.

In the middle colonies several churches that had once been established had to learn to survive and grow as free churches. The eleven Dutch Reformed congregations in New York and New Jersey lost their favoured status when the English took over in 1664, but they continued to grow in number through the natural increase in the Dutch population. A pattern that was to be repeated many times began to manifest itself—a church serving not only the institutional function of expressing Christian faith, but also filling the need many had for the preservation of national values and ethnic heritages.

For a number of decades, the Dutch Reformed Church remained the largest in New York. After the Glorious Revolution, however, there was pressure from England for the establishment of its national church. Governor Benjamin Fletcher was finally able to gain from the Assembly in 1693 a ministry act which provided for the support of a 'sufficient Protestant minister' in four of New York's ten counties. It was not decreed that Church of England clergy were specifically meant, but that was the usual meaning of the phrase in England. The first two vestries elected under the provisions of the act had a majority of the Dutch on them, and it was not until the Reformed Church received a charter in 1696 which allowed them freedom of worship, the right to hold property and to choose their own ministers that the ministry act could be interpreted as its designers intended. The first Church of England parish, Trinity, was founded the next year; at the turn of the century it was the only Anglican congregation compared to twenty-nine of the Reformed. By 1720 there were nearly fifty Reformed congregations in the colonies, most of them in New York and New Jersey. Staunchly Calvinist and firmly Dutch, clinging to the use of the Dutch language, the church had continued to grow despite the loss of established status and the transfer of political allegiance.

There were also a few French Reformed churches in the colonies. The revocation of the Edict of Nantes in 1685 multiplied the difficulties of the Huguenots in France, some of whom came to the New World, settling especially in New York and in South Carolina. In their case they were not particularly anxious to remember their French background or to cling to their native tongue. Most of these churches in the vicinity of New York became absorbed by the Dutch Reformed; those in the south by the Church of England. There were about fifteen French Reformed churches in 1700, but the number then declined.

The Lutheran churches did not become numerous in the period under consideration, but there were a number of nationalities represented within Lutheran ranks. The several small Swedish churches which had been founded along the Delaware River continued under Dutch and then English flags, long retaining ecclesiastical ties with the church in Sweden. Dutch Lutherans in New Netherland, however, faced considerable harassment under Governor Stuyvesant. A congregation had been formed in 1649, but it was not until 1657 that a pastor, Johannes Gutwasser, was sent from Amsterdam. The Reformed pastors protested, and the young cleric was forbidden to hold services and was soon deported, as was his successor. Under the English, the congregation had greater freedom, and another was formed in Albany. But these small Lutheran beginnings were numerically dwarfed early in the next century by the influx of Germans from the Palatinate, the region between France and the upper Rhine which had been so repeatedly despoiled by the troops of Louis XIV. Some

German Lutherans settled along the Hudson and in New Jersey, while others were attracted by Penn's solicitation.

The first German Lutheran church in Pennsylvania was formed at New Hanover in 1703 under the leadership of Daniel Falckner. His brother Justus was ordained at about the same time under Swedish Lutheran auspices and became pastor of the Dutch Lutheran church in New York, serving there for a score of years and also reaching the German settlements in the Hudson valley. The Falckners, in common with most of the Lutheran immigrants of that time, were strongly influenced by the pietist movement of Philipp Jakob Spener and August Hermann Francke, and stressed warm, inner faith and practical religion. These settlers usually came as individuals or in small family groups and had few possessions. Clustering together in little agricultural communities, they were grateful for ministration in their native languages and in the liturgical and confessional forms with which they were familiar. Though in 1720 the great wave of German immigration was just beginning, there were too few pastors for the burgeoning population.

In the northern and middle colonies the Church of England was slow in getting a foothold. As late as 1700 there were only four Anglican parishes north of Maryland. The origins of the congregations in Boston and New York have already been mentioned; the other two were at Perth Amboy (then capital of East Jersey) and Philadelphia. There was also a rapid increase in the number of Episcopal parishes and missions in the middle colonies, primarily through the work of the Society for the Propagation of the Gospel. The S.P.G. was largely the result of the vision and persistence of Thomas Bray (1656–1730), a graduate of All Souls College, Oxford, who served in several English parishes before coming to America. After a brief period of service in Maryland as commissary, Bray won the support of the Archbishop of Canterbury, the Bishop of London, and others, and was able to secure a royal charter for the Society in 1701. Its purposes were to advance the cause of religion among English settlers in the provinces, and also to carry on missions among Indians and Negroes. In part, the charter read:

Whereas Wee are credibly informed that in many of our Plantacons, Colonies, and Factories beyond the Seas, belonging to Our Kingdom of England, the Provision for Ministers is very mean. And many others of Our said Plantacons, Colonies, and Factories are wholy destitute, and unprovided of a Mainteynance for Ministers, and the Publick Worshipp of God; and for Lack of Support and Mainteynance for such, many of our Loveing Subjects doe want the Administration of God's Word and Sacraments, and seem to be abandoned to Atheism and Infidelity and alsoe for Want of Learned and Orthodox Ministers to instruct Our said Loveing Subjects in the Principles of true Religion, divers Romish Priests and Jesuits are the more incouraged and draw over Our said Loveing Subjects to Popish Superstition and Idolatry.[12]

The anti-Catholicism was explicit, but the anti-dissenting note, though more implicit, was unmistakable, for the S.P.G., consistently quite high church in tone, devoted its major attention to the middle and New England colonies where ministers of other persuasions were hard at work, and which were not as 'wholy destitute' as the charter stated. The S.P.G. did strive to serve God and man effectively, and compiled an enviable record. Many prestigious clergy in England warmly supported the new venture, and a complex organization was quickly developed.

The Society sent as its agent to survey the New World field a former Quaker whose search for authority had finally brought him into Anglican orders. Scottish-born George Keith had lived in the colonies for about ten years, and had been a controversial and schismatic figure among the Friends. In his two-year term of service for the S.P.G., Keith travelled from New Hampshire to North Carolina, engaged in many controversies, especially with Quakers, made many converts, and planted the seeds that grew into Anglican missions and churches. Even before his missionary term was over, S.P.G. missionaries began to arrive—more than 300 had served by the American Revolution, most of them in the colonies where the Church of England was weak.[13] By 1720 there had been a significant increase in the number of Church of England congregations in the middle colonies and Rhode Island, and the work of missions under devoted clergymen supported by the S.P.G. was laying foundations for the future of the Episcopal Church in the colonies.

Though in the middle colonies there was much more freedom for all religious groups than in the colonies where there were establishments, anti-Catholicism was strong everywhere in the colonies and was intensified by the struggles with the French. For a brief time in the 1680s Catholic worship had begun in New York. Thomas Dongan, an Irish-born Catholic, arrived as governor of New York in 1683. At the first session of the legislative assembly, which included members elected by the freeholders, a Charter of Liberties and Privileges was passed. It included

---

[12] C. F. Pascoe, *Two Hundred Years of the S.P.G.: An Historical Account of the Society for the Propagation of the Gospel in Foreign Parts, 1701–1900*, 2 vols. (London, 1901), ii, 932.

[13] During Queen Anne's reign, the missionaries were distributed as follows: New England, 8; New York, 16; New Jersey, 4; Pennsylvania, 11; Maryland, 4; Virginia, 1; North Carolina, 4; South Carolina, 14. See John Calam, *Parsons and Pedagogues: The S.P.G. Adventure in American Education* (New York, 1971), p. 36.

a provision that no Christian believer should be molested or called into question in matters of religious concernments. Dongan hoped to have an English Jesuit mission among the Iroquois to counteract French influence. A small group of the fathers came, and a chapel and school were opened at Fort James. Too few priests had arrived to implement the plan for a mission to the Indians when the fall of James II brought it all to a halt. In the period that followed, the anti-Catholic spirit flared up again, the Jesuits were forced to flee, and the work they had started came to an end. By the early eighteenth century, Catholics were finding their greatest freedom in Pennsylvania, though they were barred from holding office there after 1705. Despite some complaints from England, Mass was apparently being openly celebrated in Philadelphia.

Corporate Jewish worship in North America began privately at New Amsterdam in 1654 with the arrival of a group of Sephardic (Spanish and Portuguese) Jews who had been expelled from northern Brazil when the Portuguese ousted the Dutch from the region. They were not allowed to worship publicly until the English period; by 1695 they were meeting in a rented room. The first synagogue building was erected in 1730. Another congregation, also Sephardic, had been gathered at Newport in the later 1650s, but had disappeared by the 1690s, to be revived later.

Establishment versus Dissent in the Southern Colonies

In the southern colonies, the most conspicuous feature in the religious history of the period 1650–1720 was the strengthening of the Church of England at the same time that religious diversity was also increasing. To the Anglican establishment in Virginia were added those in Maryland and both Carolinas. Though the institutional strength of Anglicanism was clearly on the increase, still the feature which an episcopally governed church needs especially—bishops—was not introduced.

The church establishment in Virginia remained generally oriented to the Book of Common Prayer during the Cromwellian period in the mother country, and some royalist clergymen continued in their parishes. There were also some Puritan leanings in the parishes, for the power of the vestry made such variations possible. Babette M. Levy has concluded that

the records, scanty as they are, indicate clearly that nominal nonconformists composed a strong minority in Virginia, Barbados, and Jamaica, and a scarcely disputed majority in Bermuda, Maryland, and the Carolinas during practically all of the century in which colonial foundations were being laid.[14]

[14] *Early Puritanism in the Southern and Island Colonies* (Worcester, Mass., 1960), p. 75; cf. also Brydon, *Virginia's Mother Church*, i, 117–206.

After the Restoration there was some effort on the part of colonial leaders to make sure that all clergymen were in valid orders; at that time a number of ministers who conformed were of Puritan spirit. The high churchmen were somewhat disillusioned by the neglect of both English and Virginian governments in this period.

Some efforts were made to overcome this lack. Henry Compton became Bishop of London in 1675, a post he held until his death nearly 40 years later, and though he lacked adequate authority and power, he tried to take seriously the rather vague responsibilities he held for the Episcopal churches in the colonies. As an expedient in the absence of bishops in the colonies, he sent 'commissaries' as his representatives. Their powers, not very precisely defined, had to do chiefly with the oversight of the clergy, and the holding of conventions and investigations.

Outstanding among the commissaries was a Scot, James Blair (1656–1743), who became rector of Henrico parish in 1685. Beginning in 1689, he added the role of commissary to his duties, serving in that capacity for more than half a century. A stubborn man who could be tactless, he handled some of his new responsibilities ably, but at others he failed. He was able to have clerical salaries raised and have ministers placed in vacant parishes. He did not succeed in getting many congregations to present their ministers for permanent induction by the governor—the vestries preferred to keep their clergymen in a year-to-year basis. His attempt to introduce ecclesiastical courts into Virginia was ill-conceived, and was halted by the House of Burgesses, but many of those with whom he had to work distrusted him thereafter.

Blair's greatest achievement was the founding of the College of William and Mary, which he served as president. The charter was granted in 1693; the buildings were begun at Williamsburg several years later. Blair moved to a parish at James City to be nearer to the college; later he became rector at Bruton parish at the capital. In its early years the college was little more than a grammar school; not until the second quarter of the century were sufficient funds and faculty gathered for it to fulfil early hopes and to play an important role in the life of the Old Dominion. The college never served as Harvard and Yale did as an important source of ministers for the churches; the commissary had to rely more on the recruitment of clergy from England.

In the latter half of the seventeenth century there was some renewal of interest in the Christianization of the Indians; a more sympathetic attitude towards them than had followed the wars of 1622 and 1644 developed. Care was taken that certain lands would be held for them, and reservations provided, some of which were to survive into the twentieth century. Some eighteen tribes were tributary to the English when a northern tribe pressed down on the colony's frontiers, providing the occasion for Bacon's rebellion in 1676. This revolt, primarily directed against Governor Berkeley because of his neglect of defences against Indian attacks, was fiercely put down.

After that, not much of significance emerged from several efforts to carry out missionary work among the Indians. Hopes for an Indian school at William and Mary bore little fruit. A school founded early in the eighteenth century by Governor Alexander Spotswood in a reservation community which he named Christ-Anna had some seventy pupils. In recognition of this achievement he was made a member of the S.P.G. Spotswood realized that the economic life of the Indians would have to be improved if they were really to be helped, but the greed of some English merchants—and perhaps the silence of Commissary Blair—destroyed the stock company he founded and in turn precipitated the closing of the school. A promising beginning was thus choked off.

By 1720 there were more than fifty parishes in Virginia, and though the church was handicapped by the lack of a bishop, it had developed relevant ways of ministering to the English population. The very size of the parishes caused difficulties, for some of them extended forty miles or so along a river—one indeed was more than a hundred miles in length. Probably a majority of the clergy carried on some kind of educational effort, teaching in private schools or conducting tutorial classes. The effort to perpetuate the patterns of orderly English life in Virginia was thus successful to a degree, but the shortage of clergy, some of whom were not particularly competent men, and the lack of clear lines of authority weakened what was the leading Anglican establishment in the colonies.

The second significant establishment was in Maryland. During the 1650s the colony was controlled for a time by a Puritan group, but at the Restoration it was returned to the Calvert family. The proprietary rule became increasingly unpopular, however; distrust of the 'papists' was often exploited for political purposes in a colony in which less than ten per cent of the population was Catholic by 1676. The Calvert government was overthrown during the Glorious Revolution and Maryland became a royal colony in 1691. Though the Church of England was very weak—there were only five active clergymen there at that time—efforts were made to establish it, and to provide for a tax on the citizens for the support of the ministry. Several acts passed by the assembly were disallowed in England. The successful passage of an act of establishment was largely the work of Thomas Bray, the principal founder of the S.P.G.

When Bray was first named commissary for Maryland by Bishop Compton in 1696, he tried to find recruits for the some twenty-five parishes into which Maryland was being divided, and discovered that those who might be candidates were without funds for necessary books. His search for money to secure libraries for those going abroad, soon extended to include the purchase of libraries for deaneries at home, led to the organization of the Society for the Propagation of Christian Knowledge in 1698. The S.P.C.K. became a permanent organization which soon focused its concerns for education and publication in England and Wales. Bray finally arrived in Maryland in 1700, visited parishes, pressed an establishment act through the Assembly and then returned to England to ensure its approval. The act was approved in 1702, though modified to allow freedom to Protestants in accordance with the Toleration Act. By 1720, a ministry had been settled in more than twenty of the parishes.[15]

An unhappy reversal occurred in the colony which had been founded as a Catholic refuge and in which toleration had been extended to others when a penal code against Catholics was passed. In 1704, for example, Catholic priests were forbidden to exercise their functions in any public religious service under penalty of a fine of £50 or 6 months' imprisonment; banishment was provided for a second offence. To discourage Catholic immigration, fines were imposed for importing Irish servants. Public office was closed to faithful Catholics in 1716, and two years later the ballot was denied them. Parents were to be fined £100 if they sent their children abroad for education as Catholics. These laws were not strictly enforced, yet they reminded Catholics of their inferior status and confined Catholic worship to private settings.

The lands south of Virginia, the Carolinas, were granted to eight high-ranking proprietors by Charles II in 1663. Their hope was to make money from their huge grant, to produce commodities not native to England or her other possessions, and to develop a rather hierarchical society, somewhat reminiscent of a benevolent feudalism. The influence of Anthony Ashley Cooper and his friend John Locke was seen in the 'Fundamental Constitutions' of 1669, which offered religious freedom, but provided that only the Church of England should have public support. The constitutions were never really applied, however, for they were rather abstract, and the original proprietary group soon began to dissolve. Small oli-

---

[15] Nelson W. Rightmyer, *Maryland's Established Church* (Baltimore, 1956).

garchical groups of wealthy colonists soon became central in the Carolinas. Charleston in the south became the first important centre; in the northern part the settlements in the Albemarle Sound area grew slowly. Thereafter the two parts developed separately. By 1700 South Carolina had several Anglican parishes; adherents of that church apparently formed about half of the population. In 1706 an act of the assembly provided for public support of the Church of England. It became a royal colony in 1719, when some thirteen established parishes were reported.

North Carolina was much more heterogeneous religiously. An establishment act, secured largely through S.P.G. influence in 1715, had little real effect. Though established, the Episcopal Church remained very weak in that colony during the colonial period.

While the Church of England was thus established by law in the southern colonies, dissenting Protestant groups were slowly winning certain rights. In Virginia, the Quakers were first feared as much as they were in New England, and a series of acts against them were passed in the vain hope that they could be kept out. After the Toleration Act, however, the laws which prohibited them from holding public services were dropped, but they were still suspected of disloyalty and could be fined for not taking part in the militia drills. Their evident spirituality attracted converts, and a number of Quaker meetings were formed. George Fox began his North American trip in 1672 in Maryland, visiting the burgeoning meetings there, and participating in a great general meeting that lasted five days. The Quakers were the first to undertake extensive missionary work in North Carolina, and for a quarter of a century were the only ones engaged in such effort. Along with other dissenters, they later kept the establishment from becoming a real force.

Presbyterians and Baptists also laid their southern foundations in this period. By 1720 there were three Presbyterian congregations in Virginia, while the influx of the Scotch-Irish into Maryland was just beginning, though most of them later conformed to the established Anglican parishes. In South Carolina there were enough Presbyterian churches by 1722 to form a presbytery. There was some evidence of scattered Baptist work in the south in this period; the first congregation was gathered in South Carolina in 1696, and some immigrants from England who settled in south-east Virginia in about 1714 introduced the Baptist witness there. In general, while many of the leading families in the south belonged to established churches, Quakers and Baptists won most of their followers from among the humbler sort, and the patterns of religious pluralism often approximated socio-economic configurations. The Episcopal establishments were limited not only by the lack of bishops, but also by the resistance of the dissenting bodies.

Yet the renewed interest in England for the church in the colonies, the work of the S.P.G. and of the commissaries had brought fresh vitality and had developed new ties among the churches in the various colonies. As Carl Bridenbaugh has stated:

Under the direction of such an aggressive Bishop of London as Henry Compton, in whose jurisdiction 'the colonial church' belonged, and backed by the awakened interest of such primates as John Tillotson and Thomas Tenison, the future growth and well-being of the Church seemed assured at the beginning of the eighteenth century.

This much at least was certain: henceforth Anglicanism, with all the appurtenances and traditional associations symbolized by mitre and sceptre, ceased to be a regional ecclesiastical activity; it became an intercolonial and a transatlantic institution.[16]

Despite the problems, the future of few colonial churches seemed more secure.

The practice of holding Negro slaves for life developed during the middle seventeenth century in Virginia and Maryland. At first black slavery may not have been greatly different from indentured servanthood among the whites, but by mid-century the distinctions between the two groups were being increasingly drawn. The growth of the institution of slavery and the spread of white concepts of Negro inferiority appear to have reinforced one another. The adaptability of slave labour to the growing of tobacco made slavery economically viable. In Virginia the number of Negroes increased from about 300 in 1650 to over 6,000 in 1700—and then 'the slave ships began spilling forth their black cargoes in greater and greater numbers'.[17]

The question as to whether the baptism of slaves set them free arose early, and the Virginia General Assembly adopted an act in 1667 which gave the accepted answer:

WHEREAS some doubts have arisen whether children that are slaves by birth, and by the charity and piety of their owners made partakers of the blessed sacrament of baptisme, should by vertue of their baptisme be made ffree; *It is enacted and declared by this general assembly, and the authority thereof,* that the conferring of baptisme doth not alter the condition of the person as to his bondage or ffreedome; that diverse masters, ffreed from this doubt, may more carefully endea-

---

[16] *Mitre and Sceptre: Transatlantic Faiths, Ideas, Personalities, and Politics, 1689–1775* (New York, 1962), pp. 54–5.

[17] Jordan, *White Over Black*, p. 82; cf. pp. 71–85, 179–87.

vour the propagation of christianity by permitting children, though slaves, or those of greater growth if capable to be admitted to that sacrament.[18]

Even after this was made clear, many slave-owners were little concerned about having slave children in their plantations baptized, some out of indifference, others not wanting to assume obligations of sponsorship, or feeling that conversion would make them poor slaves. Some feared that the christianization of the blacks would minimize the differences between master and slave, and increase the potential for rebellion.

In South Carolina, slavery developed quickly in the late seventeenth century. The Fundamental Constitutions, despite their idealism, granted to the freemen 'absolute power and authority over his negro slaves, of what opinion or religion soever'. In the 1690s, the strict slave code of Barbados was introduced there in an effort to keep slaves under tight control. Occasionally a voice was raised in favour of a more intensive effort to christianize the slaves, as in a pamphlet published by a minister of Virginia and Barbados, Morgan Godwyn, *The Negro's and Indian's Advocate*, but, like Sewall's, his was a lonely voice.

Florida remained in Spanish hands in this period, but the extensive missions to the Indians declined sharply in the last quarter of the seventeenth century. Both the Timucuan and Apalachee Indians rebelled in 1656, for they were overworked by the civil authorities, and some of them were enslaved. The Franciscans retained their good relations with the Indians, braving tensions with the governmental authorities against whose treatment of the Indians they protested. Catholic life, both at St. Augustine and among the natives, suffered from lack of adequate support by the Crown; the colony remained poverty-stricken and did not grow significantly.

An extensive visit to Florida was made by the Bishop of Santiago de Cuba in 1674–5; he found the missions in a quite flourishing condition at that point and was able to confirm some 13,000 persons. He also noticed a certain loss of enthusiasm in the church and the Orders, and was able to make some corrections. But Florida was not made into a diocese, nor were attempts to have an auxiliary bishop there over an extended period successful until 1735. For the Catholic as for the Episcopal church, the lack of bishops was a handicap in the colonial period.

In view of a lack of vigorous support by Spanish officials for their colony in Florida, the increasing pressure from the English and their Indian allies was difficult to resist. In 1661, for example, the Westoe

---

[18] Brydon, *Virginia's Mother Church*, i, 186.

Indians, armed by Virginians, attacked the northern coastal missions, and with the settlement of Carolina the number of attacks increased. As more soldiers were brought into Florida to protect it, the number of missionaries decreased. During Queen Anne's War, the raids of James Moore, governor of Carolina, were devastatingly cruel. A siege of St. Augustine failed to capture the fort but did much damage to churches and missions. The discredited Moore resigned as governor, but in 1704 raided Apalachee country, laying waste to eight of the fourteen *doctrinas* or mission stations. By 1708 the Florida missions were no more; according to one estimate perhaps 12,000 Indians had been carried to Carolina as slaves. With the end of the war, hopes that the missions could regain some of their former effectiveness were frustrated by lack of support by the Crown and the discouragement of the few Franciscans who did come. Though Florida had been settled before the French and English had launched their colonies, it remained a remote outpost of the Spanish holdings in the New World.

The Spanish missions in New Mexico also fared badly in this period. In 1680 there was a violent uprising by the Christian Indians, some of whom were secretly involved in pagan practices, and who were troubled by raids by the militant Apaches. Some 400 Spaniards, including a score of friars, were slain in the revolt. The missions were destroyed and traces of their work annihilated. The Spanish settlements were later recaptured and in time some mission work was again undertaken, but not to the extent that had marked the initial effort.

Summary: Churches in Colonial Cultures

From 1650 to 1720 the Christian churches in North America had increased greatly in number and size, and played significant roles in their cultural settings. As the religious situation was steadily growing more diversified, over-all generalizations about it become more precarious, for it is hard to make statements that apply at once to the Diocese of Quebec, the Congregational churches of New England, the various movements of the middle colonies, the parishes of the Anglican establishments, and the Spanish outposts to the south. The religious bodies were still predominantly European churches, many still with governmental ties to mother churches, others independent but identifying themselves as part of continuing Christian traditions across the Atlantic. For the most part churches allied themselves without question with the empires of which they were a part in the struggle for the continent; the bitter hostility between Catholic and Protestant intensified the conflicts between English and French, English and Spanish. Save for a few prophetic voices, churches accepted the growth of slavery. Though there were some impressive missionary efforts among the Indians and considerable Christian concern for fair treatment of the natives, the churches supported the contention of the European invaders that as carriers of a superior civilization they could rightfully possess the land. In the bitterness of the struggle with the Indians, especially with those allied with one's enemies, the martial spirit of western Christendom—with the exception of the Quakers and some of those of Anabaptist background—manifested itself in very cruel ways.

In the earlier period of the European settlement of North America, those who initiated Christian life often exhibited a determination to provide fresh models of true Christian commonwealths. Some of that spirit still manifested itself in the later seventeenth century, as in the 'holy experiment' of Pennsylvania as a new place of freedom and opportunity for whoever would come. But the difficulties of maintaining renewed churches and a recognizably Christian culture amid the conditions of life in the New World were becoming evident, and serious efforts to overcome them were made. The Quebec seminary, the half-way covenant, the Saybrook Articles, and the S.P.G. were such efforts. Yet, although the churches continued to multiply, early dreams were hardly being fulfilled. Christian leaders in every section were protesting against the shift in interest from things of the spirit to realities of the market place.[19] The traditional territorial parish, modelled on the European experience, was not working as well as had been expected. In part this was because of the vast expanse of land—in New France the priests had little control over the freedom-loving *coureurs de bois*, in New England the development of outlying farm homes broke up the pattern of centralized town life, and in Virginia the vast parishes made effective ministry difficult. The growing strength of some of the dissenting religious movements further contributed to the weakening of the parish structures, especially of the established churches. In the middle colonies, indeed, the parish system was not really viable; congregations gathered their constituencies from the general population so that memberships overlapped.

Church life also showed the effect of class differences. In very broad terms, there was a widening gap between the wealthier, aristocratic groups gathered largely in the seaboard centres in places of political and economic power, and the poorer orders of society—small farmers, shopkeepers,

---

[19] Many studies have traced this shift; see, e.g., Bernard Bailyn, *The New England Merchants in the Seventeenth Century* (Cambridge, Mass., 1955); Frederick B. Tolles, *Meeting House and Counting House: The Quaker Merchants of Colonial Philadelphia, 1682–1763* (Chapel Hill, 1948); Richard L. Bushman, *From Puritan to Yankee*.

artisans, minor tradesmen. They lived in humble circumstances for the most part; leisure and educational opportunities were rarities for them. The newly arrived Germans and Scotch–Irish normally found themselves in such limited circumstances; many were shunted to the hinterland where the struggle for subsistence was both difficult and dangerous. At the bottom of the social structure were the indentured servants, who could hope to rise when their term was over, and the Negro slaves, who could not. These social differences showed themselves in church life: in New England where seating in the meeting-house was by rank, in Virginia by the self-perpetuation of the vestries by the upper classes after 1660. Dissenting groups often made their chief gains among the middling and poorer classes. Too much should not be made of this point, however, for the evidence shows that the established churches did retain the allegiance of many of the humble folk, and some rather well-placed persons could be found among Presbyterians, Baptists, and Quakers, especially in the colonies without establishments. Yet class tensions were certainly not unknown in church life, to the discomfort of some of the devout.

A good many European settlers were not effectively in touch with any church in the New World. For example, when Governor Dongan reported on religious conditions in New York in 1687, he said,

Every town ought to have a minister. New York has, first, a Chaplain belonging to the Fort, of the Church of England; secondly, a Dutch Calvinist; thirdly, a French Calvinist; fourthly, a Dutch Lutheran. Here bee not many of the Church of England, few Roman Catholicks; abundance of Quaker preachers, men and Women especially; Singing Quakers; Ranting Quakers; Sabbatarians; Anti-Sabbatarians; some Anabaptists; some Jews: in short, of all sorts of opinions there are some, and the most part of none at all.[20]

The phenomenon of religious multiplicity should not hide the point of the last phrase—'the most part of none at all'. In New England the percentage of support for church life was apparently relatively high, but in the middle and southern colonies a majority seems to have been effectively out of touch with church life. Some could not easily find a congregation of familiar language or confessional pattern, others were located far from any congregation. For those who were indifferent or hostile to religion, the conditions of growing toleration gave them freedom to stay away.

In the English colonies there were signs that most of the denominations were developing intercolonial perspectives. Quakers were in touch with

[20] As quoted by E. T. Corwin, *A History of the Reformed Church, Dutch* (New York, 1895), pp. 87–8.

each other through the travelling Friends; the Philadelphia Baptist Association began with members from three colonies and soon spread wider; the first Presbyterian synod was a rallying point for a scattered but burgeoning communion. Though the twentieth-century student of religious history looking back can see the outlines of the denominational system of free, voluntary churches in competition, at the time the breakdown of the familiar patterns of European Christendom constituted a threat in the eyes of the majority of Christians. The structures for maintaining common patterns of morality and values seemed to be decaying. To many of the devout in both establishment and dissenting congregations, spiritual lethargy and indifference appeared to be undermining the Christian destiny of the New World in which there had been such high hopes.

III

THE ERA OF THE
GREAT AWAKENINGS IN
COLONIAL AMERICA
(1720–75)

THE Great Awakenings were dramatic and formative events in the history of Christianity in the thirteen English colonies which were to become the United States. These happenings, which began in the 1720s and continued in certain areas into the era of the Revolution, had an unequal effect on the many strands of American religion; some groups were profoundly affected while others were lightly or even negatively influenced. Yet the whole religious scene was so altered by the Awakenings that this period in the history of Christianity in America can take its name from them, provided that the complex picture is not oversimplified.

An important part of the story of the colonial revivals concerns their opponents, and the controversies which arose between them and the defenders of the Awakenings. Some of the polarities that have since long plagued the American religious mind were intensified in those stormy decades. A striking feature of the Awakenings was that they took place at the same time as the impact of the Enlightenment was deepening. That seminal and many-sided movement in human thought and action with its concern for reason and order was critical of religious enthusiasm. The relationship between these two powerful developments was by no means simple, however, for the Awakeners drew in quite varying degrees on Enlightenment assumptions and viewpoints even as they resisted many of its characteristic emphases. Within the churches, the perspective of the Awakening was more widespread and decisive than that of the Enlightenment, though the influence of the latter was felt directly in certain sectors of church life, and its indirect influence was widely pervasive.

During the five decades in which the currents of Awakening were flowing, the thirteen colonies were slowly forming closer ties among themselves and were beginning to think and feel as a nation. The struggle between the French and the English for control of the continent continued through much of this period, coming to its climax in 1763. The common effort against the French and their Indian allies helped to bring the English colonies closer to each other. With their many intercolonial aspects, the Awakenings played a role in the emergence of a national spirit. The distinctive development of Christianity in the American colonies will be the theme of this chapter, while the quite different history of the churches in Canada in the parallel (but somewhat longer) period will be discussed in the next.

Though religious Awakenings impressive enough to be called 'great' appeared with dramatic suddenness in various places and at various times, they arose on prepared soil. Concern for the authority of the Bible and for the personal appropriation of religious truth had been part of Protestant life in America since the early seventeenth century, and the Awakeners who dramatized these themes often found ready response. The great attention paid by Puritan preachers to such themes as conversion, the new birth, and sanctification was echoed in the exhortations of the preachers of the revival.

The religious excitement that swept across the colonies had distinctively American characteristics, yet they were also influenced by revival movements in other parts of the Christian world, and in turn had an impact on those movements. The various Evangelical Awakenings in the British Isles, the Pietist movements on the continent, and the American revival reinforced one another. News of Awakening in one place travelled quickly; the leaders of revival read each other's writings and entered into correspondence. The greatest itinerant evangelist of the eighteenth century, George Whitefield (1714–70), was renowned on both sides of the Atlantic for his impassioned preaching. The continuities of colonial revivalism with certain previous and contemporary trends elsewhere in Christendom were indeed significant—yet the Great Awakenings were distinctively related to the particular contexts, problems, and opportunities of organized religion in America.

It would be easy to overstate the 'decline' of the churches prior to the emergence of the Awakenings, as leaders of that movement, and subsequent interpreters of it, have sometimes done. In fact, numerically the number of churches and of professed Christians was increasing throughout the colonial period, albeit unevenly and often not in proportion to a population which was expanding rapidly through immigration. Yet among those deeply concerned with religion in the early eighteenth century there was a sense of decline, a feeling that something was wrong.

Especially in New England, but not only there, religious leaders often insisted that in many quarters material concerns were replacing the spiritual ones that had been so strongly stressed in early colonial days. Ministers had frequent recourse to jeremiad preaching, berating their listeners for the sins and failures of the people.

Though it would not be seen clearly until later, the cohesion of colonial Christendom was weakening. In many areas the organization of parish life along geographical lines was proving inadequate in the face of the vast space and growing religious multiplicity of the new land. The religious practices of many ethnic churches seemed to be devoted more to the preservation of the language and culture of the mother country than to the professed aim of faithfulness to the gospel of Christ. The undercurrents of Enlightenment thought were making familiar religious assumptions and vocabularies seem antiquated among certain sections of the population, especially among the educated, so that feelings of devout loyalty to inherited church traditions had diminished somewhat by the second quarter of the eighteenth century. The existence of large numbers of the unchurched posed a sharp challenge both to the churches and to the culture, steeped as it was in the premisses of Christendom.

In this partial spiritual vacuum, revival was ardently desired by many of the devout, and the appearance of heightened religious interest was greeted with high expectations. News of Awakenings often served as a stimulant to renewal elsewhere. As the Awakenings began to reach their peak, many of the difficulties that had caused the loss of direction and morale in the churches were met, at least for a time. Yet in other places they were hardly touched.

Certain signs of the later high tides of revival began to appear in the 1720s. In Connecticut, for example, local Awakenings arose simultaneously in several towns, whereas previous 'harvests' had been isolated and scattered. Revivals became generally conspicuous first in the middle colonies, then in New England, and finally in the southern colonies. Though for the sake of clarity the various sections will be treated separately, in fact the movements overlapped to a considerable extent and were interrelated.

Awakening in the Middle Colonies

An early challenge to what he considered to be perfunctory orthodoxy in the Dutch Reformed Church was expressed by the newly arrived pastor of four New Jersey churches in 1720. Theodorus J. Frelinghuysen (1691–1748?) had been educated under Dutch Calvinist auspices at the University of Lingen, and was schooled in the writings of English Puritanism and Dutch Evangelicalism. It seemed to him on arrival that his new parishioners in America had slipped into a rather external, formalistic observance of Christianity and that they were using religion primarily to preserve their Dutch heritage. A somewhat difficult and contentious man, Frelinghuysen insisted that only penitent, upright, and believing persons should be admitted to the communion. His efforts to carry out a programme of reform through church discipline and the broad use of the powers of excommunication stirred up a bitter, long-drawn-out controversy in the Reformed Church. Both sides in the dispute appealed to the Classis of Amsterdam; a reconciliation between the two parties was finally effected in 1734. That Frelinghuysen spoke as many Awakeners did against formality and externality in religion and that he did make converts there is no doubt; that he also was the centre of a revival in the Dutch Reformed Church has become a matter of controversy among historians.[1] He was cited by some other leaders of the Awakenings (Whitefield, the Tennents, Edwards) as one who was deeply concerned about the conversion of sinners and who had helped to prepare the way for the full tide of revival in the middle colonies in the later 1730s. The tension between the Awakening and the more traditional theological perspectives intensified the quarrel between those who favoured the adjustment of the church to its changing culture and those who wanted to maintain strict Dutch patterns. The former group wanted a greater measure of independence from the mother church in Holland, but only after years of effort did the Classis of Amsterdam agree in 1747 to the organization in America of a Coetus (classis) which provided a measure of self-government for the colonial churches, including the right to ordain ministers under certain conditions. Frelinghuysen and those committed to the revival supported this development, but the strict, high Calvinist party, centred among the older ministers of New York, organized a counter-movement, the Conferentie. Thus for several decades the communion was divided by two well-defined parties; not until 1771–2 was reconciliation effected. During the separation the Coetus group took steps to found a college. The charter was granted in 1766, but not for five more years did Queen's College, later Rutgers, commence its work in New Brunswick, New Jersey.

The impact of the Awakening among the Presbyterian churches of the

---

[1] The evidence is examined by Herman Harmelink III, 'Another Look at Frelinghuysen and His "Awakening" ', *Church History*, 37 (1968), 423–38. He has concluded that there is little factual basis for the view that a significant revival did occur under Frelinghuysen's ministry, though much for seeing him as a fomenter of dissension. For another view, see James Tanis, *Dutch Calvinistic Pietism in the Middle Colonies: A Study in the Life and Theology of Theodorus Jacobus Frelinghuysen* (The Hague, 1967).

middle colonies was considerably greater, and it directly contributed to a formal schism within that communion, a break that lasted for nearly two decades. Central roles in the spread of the revival were played by members of the Tennent family. William Tennent, a graduate of the University of Edinburgh, served Presbyterian churches in Scotland and Ireland before becoming a priest in the (Anglican) Church of Ireland. Later disenchanted with the episcopacy and Arminianism of that establishment, Tennent migrated to North America in 1718, soon becoming affiliated with the Presbyterian synod. He served for some years in a parish in New York; in 1727 he moved to Neshaminy, just north of Philadelphia in Pennsylvania. An effective scholar and teacher, Tennent educated not only his four sons but also a group of others for the ministry, later erecting for his pedagogical purposes a rough building which his enemies derisively called the 'Log College'. Tennent and those under his influence, in particular the graduates of the Log College who entered the Presbyterian synod, preached a forceful, evangelical Calvinism that emphasized the conversion of souls to Christ.

During the 1720s Presbyterianism was torn by controversy over the issue of whether or not all candidates for the ministry should subscribe to the Westminster Confession of Faith. The Scottish and Scotch-Irish clergy, who were largely centred in Philadelphia, were greatly concerned that the ministers should hold correct doctrine, and stressed the necessity of subscription to the Confession. The Presbyterians of Puritan background—some from Old, others from New England—were centred in the New York–New Jersey area; while not neglectful of doctrine they were especially interested in the personal piety of candidates for the ministry, and felt that subscription should be to the Word of God itself, not to an interpretation of it. The principal spokesman for the antisubscription party was the eminent pastor at Elizabethtown, New Jersey, Jonathan Dickinson, a graduate of Yale.

A compromise between the two parties was reached in 1729 with the passage of the Adopting Act by the synod. This required ministers to declare their agreement with the Westminster Confession and catechisms, but gave them the freedom to state any conscientious scruple with any article or articles of the confessional statements at the time of subscription. If such scruples were judged by the presbytery or synod to be about 'articles not essential and necessary in doctrine, worship, or government', the candidate was to be recognized. The Adopting Act of 1729 allowed the church to contain the tension that characterized its life, but quarrels as to interpretation of the Act soon arose.

The Tennent group did not play a large role in the subscriptionist controversy. William Tennent and his eldest son, Gilbert, who had received an honorary M.A. from Yale, stated whatever scruples they may have had along with the other ministers at the time of the passage of the Adopting Act, and found themselves to be in agreement on major matters. Gilbert Tennent (1703–64) was maturing into a powerful preacher who soon became the real leader of the Tennent group. Called to minister in New Brunswick, he was greatly influenced by Frelinghuysen, who administered a well-designed rebuke to the younger man at a strategic moment in his development. Along with his father, brothers, and other young ministers connected with the Log College, Gilbert Tennent stressed the necessity of a work of humiliation, or conviction of sin, in order to achieve a sound conversion. His preaching was aimed especially at the 'presumptuous security' of those who were content with a merely 'historical' or formalistic form of Christianity instead of seeking its present power and life. By the beginning of the 1730s a revival had been stirred by his evangelical preaching, while a similar movement was arising in nearby Freehold under the ministry of his younger brother John, who was succeeded by William Tennent, Jr. following the former's early death.

The evangelical style of preaching and the concern for assurance through experience that characterized the Tennent party was bitterly opposed by the Scottish ministers who put so much stress on correct doctrine, for their views were often criticized sharply by the revivalists. The old pro-subscriptionist party now added the anti-revival cause to its concerns. The disquiet was greatly increased as congregations responded to the preaching of the Tennents and their allies with sobs, cries of terror, and even lapses into coma. The revival preachers derided things prized by the Scotch-Irish party, for they declared that orderliness, doctrinal precision, and good works were useless for salvation unless accompanied by the pain and ecstasy of the experience of regeneration. Yet the Tennents did not encourage the outbursts of emotion that often were generated by their intense preaching, and sought to guide those so influenced into calm and firm faith.

In 1736 the pro-subscriptionist, anti-revival party was in a majority at the meeting of synod, in part because so many of the Awakeners were carrying on itinerant ministries. The majority seized the opportunity, and modified the Adopting Act to require the adherence to the Westminster Confession without the least variation or alteration.[2] The next year the

---

[2] The story is told in considerable detail by Trinterud, *The Forming of an American Tradition.*

synod moved against the practice of ministers preaching to congregations other than their own without permission of the presbyteries involved. This made things more difficult for the revivalists, who were broadening their base of support through their itinerant practices. In 1738 they did secure from the synod permission to set up the New Brunswick presbytery, which gave them the opportunity to ordain candidates to the ministry congenial to their Awakening tastes. Their opponents then prepared to gather their forces to control the new presbytery through their strength in synod, and it looked as if they would succeed.

The balance was dramatically shifted, however, as a result of the un-announced and unplanned work of 'the grand itinerant', George White-field, the eloquent evangelist who was instrumental in bringing the Awakening to its apogee in the early 1740s. More than any other one person he served to link the Awakening movements at various places into a 'Great Awakening'. A graduate of Oxford where he had been intimately associated with the Wesleys, the Holy Club, and the beginnings of the Methodist movement, Whitefield took Anglican orders in 1736. On a visit to the newly founded colony of Georgia on a mission of mercy two years later, his marvellous homiletic gifts were displayed as he took steps to found a home for orphans. The next year in England he found pulpits closing to him because of his commitment to the controversial Evangelical Awakening, and he resorted to preaching in the open air. At first this distressed John Wesley, but it proved so effective an expedient that he adopted the practice too. Thus a great renewal movement which was to continue in nominal connection with the Church of England for half a century began.

On his return to the colonies in 1739, Whitefield, now an ordained priest, put in at Philadelphia for what had been planned as a brief stop on his way back to Georgia. The spectacular preaching of the young man achieved such a response that he was invited by the Presbyterian Awakening leaders to preach in many of their churches. The elder William Tennent called on him, and he met and worked with Gilbert and the younger William Tennent. The experience contributed to Whitefield's deepening commitment to Calvinism, which later led to a rift between him and Wesley. Gilbert Tennent's zeal and theological views especially made an impression on the itinerant Awakener. His preaching tour on ground prepared by the Log College men spread the revival widely and brought it to new peaks as thousands gathered to hear his messages. Opposition to him was arising too, especially when he censured ministers who opposed the exciting business of revival.

The revivalist Presbyterians gained much strength through the success of the evangelistic work of Whitefield and the others. Emboldened by this and by Whitefield's example, Gilbert Tennent delivered at Nottingham, Pennsylvania early in 1740 a stinging sermon on 'The Danger of an Unconverted Ministry'. He scorned those who stressed merely academic training for the ministry, calling them Pharisee-teachers. Only those who had truly gone through a conversion experience, he declared, could claim to have a genuine call to the ministry. He urged those who distrusted the ministry of unconverted men to leave their churches and to go to worship under a pious minister—a clear illustration of how the Awakening undermined the geographical parish.

By April 1740 Whitefield was again in Philadelphia, riding the crest of the wave of popularity, openly supporting the Tennents, and helping to bring Presbyterianism in the New York area into closer relationship to the Log College men in what became identified as the 'New Side' party. The gulf between the two main factions in the church widened greatly; harsh language was used on both sides as the battle between the two groups was fought out in pulpit, Press, and judicatory. The New Side insisted on the right of a presbytery to control its own internal affairs; the Old Side magnified the role of the synod, hoping to retain its control over the church in that way.

The climax came in the meeting of the synod in May 1741 when the New Brunswick presbytery was excluded. The reasons given for this drastic action showed how far apart the two parties had grown. New Brunswick was accused of holding heterodox and anarchical principles of government, ordaining candidates in opposition to the act of synod, intruding into congregations without following proper procedures, condemning those who disagreed with them, teaching subjective views of the call to the ministry, preaching the terrors of the law, and holding too rigid views of assurance.[3] Attempts by the New York presbytery under Jonathan Dickinson to reconcile the parties failed, and in 1745 the New Side merged with the New York presbytery to form the Synod of New York, which followed the original Adopting Act of 1729, endorsed the revival, and sought to maintain good relations with the rival Synod of Philadelphia. Both the creativity and the disruptiveness of the Awakening were richly illustrated in these events. On the one hand, the evangelical appeals gathered thousands of converts and launched various missionary

<hr>

[3] The relevant documents for this and other matters dealing with Presbyterian history can be found in Maurice W. Armstrong, Lefferts A. Loetscher, and Charles A. Anderson (eds.), *The Presbyterian Enterprise: Sources of American Presbyterian History* (Philadelphia, 1956).

and revivalistic thrusts that made the new synod dynamic and growing; on the other hand it provoked much sharp controversy and divided a denomination into two.

By the time the new synod was formed, the dramatic peaks of the Awakening in the middle colonies had passed—the vast crowds, the general excitement, and the sense of expectancy had all ebbed. But the methods and the theology of the Awakening continued in the work of many pastors and congregations of the New Side. Though the 'Great' Awakening was over, its practices and results had been institutionalized in an effective way. The evangelistic and missionary spirit continued to mark the life of the Synod of New York, and it flourished. When the elder William Tennent closed the Log College shortly before his death in 1746, Presbyterians chartered the College of New Jersey and opened it in 1747 with Jonathan Dickinson as president. The New Side spirit was strong in the college, which was soon drawing students across colonial lines and preparing many of them for the ministry. The New Side leaders were also involved in planting academies; outstanding among them were Fagg's Manor Academy and Nottingham Academy, both conducted by students of William Tennent.[4] Presbyterian churches on Long Island so increased in number that a new presbytery was formed there in 1748, while New York's presbytery remained the largest and strongest in the church.

While the New Side was increasing, the Old Side failed significantly to grow, though it too sought to win supporters, and also built academies. A telling comparative index of vitality is the number of active ministers. The Old Side in 1741 had 27, but the number had fallen to 23 by 1758, the year of reunion. The New Side had 22 ministers in 1745; the number had increased to 73 by 1758.[5] Efforts at reconciliation, which had been going on for some years, succeeded under the pressures of the French and Indian War, the slow subsiding of passions stirred by the Great Awakening, and the irenic stance of some (including Gilbert Tennent) who had once been unyielding. The reunion of 1758 returned essentially to the Adopting Act of 1729, requiring adherence to the essentials but not to every letter of the Westminster standards. Examination and ordination of ministerial candidates was left to presbytery, and it was agreed that accusations against others would be made in the regular channels, and that ministers would not trespass into another parish without invitation. Yet the following sentence

[4] The story of the Presbyterian academies has been perceptively treated by Douglas Sloan, *The Scottish Enlightenment and the American College Ideal* (New York, 1971), esp. ch. II.

[5] Trinterud, *The Forming of an American Tradition*, p. 150.

from the Plan of Reunion shows how much of the Awakening spirit was retained in the reunited church:

As the late religious appearances occasioned much speculation and debate, the members of the New York Synod, in order to prevent any misapprehensions, declare their adherence to their former sentiments in favour of them, that a blessed work of God's Holy Spirit in the conversion of numbers was then carried on; and for the satisfaction of all concerned, this united Synod agree in declaring, that as all mankind are naturally dead in trespasses and sins an entire change of heart and life is necessary to make them meet for the service and enjoyment of God; that such a change can be only effected by the powerful operations of the Divine Spirit; that when sinners are made sensible of their lost condition and absolute inability to recover themselves, are enlightened in the knowledge of Christ and convinced of his ability and willingness to save, and upon gospel encouragements, do choose him for their Saviour, and renouncing their own righteousness in point of merit, depend upon his imputed righteousness for their righteousness before God, and on his wisdom and strength for guidance and support; when upon these apprehensions and exercises their souls are comforted, notwithstanding all their past guilt, and rejoice in God through Jesus Christ; when they hate and bewail their sins of heart and life, delight in the laws of God without exception, reverently and diligently attend his ordinances, become humble and self denied, and make it the business of their lives to please and glorify God and to do good to their fellow men; this is to be acknowledged as a gracious work of God, even though it should be attended with unusual bodily commotions or some more exceptionable circumstances, by means of infirmity, temptations, or remaining corruptions; and wherever religious appearances are attended with the good effects above mentioned, we desire to rejoice in and thank God for them.

The agreement went on to warn against visions, voices, and faintings as a sign of conversion unless there were also 'the Scriptural characters of a work of God above described'.[6]

The reunited church was able to carry on mission work in the west and south, and to maintain its growing college at Princeton and a number of important academies. By the eve of the Revolution, it had become one of the leading churches in the colonies, one significantly shaped by the Great Awakening.

Baptists too increased impressively in the middle colonies in the era of the Great Awakenings. The Philadelphia Baptist Association, firmly Calvinist in its theological orientation, became the main centre of colonial Baptist life in these years. Revivals swept through the congregations

---

[6] *Records of the Presbyterian Church in the United States of America* ... [*1706* ... *1788*] (Philadelphia, 1841), pp. 287–8.

in the 1740s and 1750s, and missionaries sponsored by the Association travelled from Maine to the Carolinas, holding meetings and gathering churches.

The Association's swift growth raised organizational problems; Benjamin Griffith was asked to undertake a definition of its proper powers. His 'Essay on the Power and Duty of an Association of Churches' was adopted by the Association in 1749. It affirmed that the Association could not interfere in the government of the particular congregations, but it could 'declare and determine the mind of the Holy Ghost' and 'decree the observance of things supported in Scripture'. Churches not accepting such determinations could be excluded from the Association. Thus the Philadelphia Baptists conjoined their congregational polity with an associational principle in a way that proved to be well adapted to the colonial setting. By 1760 the Association included in its membership churches from seven colonies from Connecticut to Virginia, and was a model for several new associations organized in New England and in Virginia. Though the Baptists did have some eminent persons in their congregations, many of those who joined were from the middle and lower ranks of society. In both theology and piety, the Baptists were much like the New Side Presbyterians.

Awakening in New England

Some of the leaders of middle-colony revivals were also conspicuous in the Great Awakening in New England, but that region too produced its share of notable evangelists, with the brilliant, many-sided Edwards towering over them as exponent, defender, and critic of the revival. As elsewhere, there were preparatory movements—the 'harvests' of Stoddard at Northampton have already been mentioned, as have the stirrings in Connecticut in the 1720s. Something more portentous occurred in 1734–5, when an Awakening in western Massachusetts attracted wide attention and brought fame to its central figure.

Jonathan Edwards (1703–58), son of a Congregational minister, Timothy Edwards, and of Esther Stoddard, daughter of the eminent pastor of Northampton, graduated from Yale in 1720. He continued there for several years in preparation for the ministry, served for about eight months as pastor of a Scottish Presbyterian church in New York, and then returned to Yale as tutor. Both intellectually and religiously he came to maturity early, probing the writings of such Enlightenment thinkers as Locke and Newton and committing himself to a devout, reasoned Calvinism. He left the tutorship to become associated with his grandfather in the ministry at Northampton early in 1727, and assumed full charge there when Solomon Stoddard died two years later.

There was much curiosity in Boston about this young Yale graduate who had been called to succeed the great Stoddard, and in 1731 Edwards was invited to give a public lecture in Boston. He displayed his theological prowess and homiletical ability in a ringing appeal for a rigorous Calvinism that permitted no dilution of the doctrines of the absolute sovereignty of God and the unconditional predestination of human beings to salvation or damnation. 'God Glorified in the Work of Redemption' was a forceful call for a consistent Calvinism and a rejection of theological modifications of that position. The young pastor had stood up to the test and had laid down the doctrinal position he defended all through his career as evangelist and theologian.[7] Edwards is an important exception to the generalization that revivalism tends to press in an 'Arminian' direction, towards some emphasis on a person's role in salvation. Edwards repudiated Arminianism—a term he used broadly against theological trends he disliked—and adhered to a firm Calvinist position. When revivals came in response to his preaching, he believed them to be truly the work of God, a divine blessing on the truth preached.

He expounded his understanding of the gospel in imaginative ways, as in the sermon 'A Divine and Supernatural Light, immediately imparted to the soul, by the spirit of God, shown to be a spiritual and rational doctrine'. Delivered in 1733, the sermon was so impressive to his congregation that he was asked to publish it, so that others could read his message that the spiritual light immediately imparted by God to his elect gave 'a true sense of the divine excellency of the things revealed in the word of God, and a conviction of the truth and reality of them thence arising'. Under such preaching, late in 1734 the signs of a serious revival of interest in religion appeared in Northampton, and in the following spring and summer the Awakening tide swept high. As Edwards explained in a letter to Benjamin Colman which was then expanded and published in London and Boston as *A Faithful Narrative of the Surprising Work of God in the Conversion of many Hundred Souls* . . . (1737), 'a great and earnest concern about the great things of religion, and the eternal world, became universal in all parts of the town, and among persons of all degrees, and all ages. The noise among the dry bones waxed louder and louder'. The revival spread

---

[7] The sermon, 'God Glorified in the Work of Redemption, by the Greatness of Man's Dependence upon him, in the Whole of it', has been brilliantly analysed and the circumstances under which it was delivered reconstructed in the book that initiated a period of new interest in its subject, Perry Miller's study *Jonathan Edwards* (New York, 1949). On Arminianism, see below, p. 106.

to other towns in the Connecticut River valley, and down into Connecticut, but it did not move very far east. The 'frontier revival' ran its course and was largely over by the end of 1735; in part the banking of the fires of revival began with the suicide of a melancholic relative of Edwards, Joseph Hawley. The *Faithful Narrative* ran through many printings and editions. It played a role in many later revivals in both Europe and America; it had an immediate impact, for example, on John Wesley and the Evangelical Awakening in Britain. Also, collections of sermons by Edwards and others helped to maintain the expectancy of a great work to come.

In New England, the moment came in September 1740 with the visit of George Whitefield, who preached to thousands in Boston and the neighbouring towns day after day, often outdoors when the crowds could not be accommodated in the largest buildings. In October Whitefield travelled west to stay with Edwards, where he was greatly impressed by the spirituality and gifts of Sarah Pierrepont Edwards.[8] As Whitefield continued on his way into Connecticut, preaching from town to town to vast crowds, people of all denominations and of none came, many to find the flame of faith kindled or revived in them as they listened to his persuasive, free-flowing eloquence. His Calvinism was sincere but he did not press it with the logical rigour of an Edwards; his messages invited the listener to respond by actively seeking God. Many preachers endeavoured to copy the master's style; C. C. Goen has observed that 'in the last analysis it is not Edwards the theologian but Whitefield the preacher who founded the revival tradition'.[9]

Other itinerants helped in the work—soon after he left New England, Whitefield persuaded Gilbert Tennent to go to Boston in order 'to blow up the divine fire lately kindled there'.[10] Tennent did succeed in that, but protests against the revival, barely audible in the excitement of Whitefield's first New England tour, also began to spread. But in 1742 the New Light fire was still in the ascendancy; not only did other travelling evangelists emulate Whitefield and Tennent, but many pastors adopted the Awakening style in their own ministries. There were hundreds of inquirers and dozens of converts in place after place. The large majority of

---

[8] Elisabeth D. D. Dodds, *Marriage to a Difficult Man: The Uncommon Union of Jonathan and Sarah Edwards* (Philadelphia, 1971).

[9] *Revivalism and Separatism in New England, 1740–1760: Strict Congregationalists and Separate Baptists in the Great Awakening* (New Haven, 1962), p. 15.

[10] Whitefield to Jonathan Belcher, 7 November 1740, *The Works of the Reverend George Whitefield, M.A. . . .*, 6 vols. (London, 1771–2), i, 221. On the general course of the Awakening, see Edwin S. Gaustad, *The Great Awakening in New England* (New York, 1957).

the established clergy supported the revival, which was felt in all ranks of society and among persons of most religious persuasions; it was truly a 'great and general' Awakening.

Many Indians were won over during the Awakening. Special mission stations were served by Congregational and Presbyterian ministers; Indians also attended and joined regular churches. In Rhode Island and Connecticut there were Awakenings among the Niantic and Narragansett Indians. Some of the natives became missionaries to their people. John Sergeant reported evangelistic advance among the Housatonic Indians at Stockbridge, Massachusetts, where he had been labouring since 1736. David Brainerd effectively ministered among Indians in Pennsylvania and New Jersey despite illness and depression; his daily journal, edited for publication by Jonathan Edwards, became an inspiration for others. Under the intense preaching of James Davenport, Samson Occam, a Mohegan, was converted. He became New England's first ordained Indian missionary after receiving his education at a school at Lebanon, Connecticut, conducted by Eleazer Wheelock. Moor's Indian Charity School, as the institution came to be known, was later moved to New Hampshire and evolved into Dartmouth College, chartered in 1769.

While the revival was at its peak, Edwards preached a rather untypical sermon which presented the revival message in its most uncompromising form. At Enfield, Connecticut, he delivered the sermon 'Sinners in the Hands of an Angry God'. Even in such a sermon, where he pictured sinners dangling over the fiery pit by a single fragile thread, Edwards was always rational and controlled in his intensity, but others who took up itinerant evangelism were not always so. James Davenport, a direct descendant of New Haven's founder and a graduate of Yale, became an admirer of Whitefield and Tennent. In the summer of 1741 he took leave from his Congregational pulpit on Long Island to undertake a preaching tour in Connecticut, where his long, ranting, unprepared discourses were studded with invective and with condemnations of many of the leading ministers as unconverted men and blind guides. In the spring of 1742 he returned again to Connecticut; this time his behaviour was wilder than before. He claimed that he could distinguish at a glance the elect from the damned. The courts at the time believed him to be irrational and under the influences of enthusiastical impressions and impulses—whether his mental distress stemmed from a physical disorder or from an unusual doctrine of the Holy Spirit or both has never been satisfactorily settled. In June he reached Boston, feared now by both friend and foe of the revival. Despite his extravagances and crudities—perhaps in some cases because of them—he had his followers, but he alarmed the leaders of church and colony. He was jailed, declared *non compos mentis*, and returned to Long Island. Later he came to his senses and confessed to labouring under misguided zeal, published his *Retractions*, and entered the Presbyterian ministry. But great damage had been done to the revival in that burst of fanaticism.

The Awakening had been controversial from the beginning; an undercurrent of opposition was felt even during that first remarkable tour when Whitefield was carrying all before him. But his account of the New England trip, published in 1741, contained some charges against the decay of vital religion among the ministers and in the colleges, the light of which, Whitefield feared, had become darkness. Opposition to the Awakening was further stirred by Tennent's zeal, of which Boston people were reminded by the reprinting there of the Nottingham sermon in 1742. Although even Tennent repudiated the extremism of Davenport, it gave the opponents of the revival a lever which they did not hesitate to use. Thus while the Awakening was still running free the opposition against it was becoming vocal, and the house of New England Congregationalism was being divided. One of the figures thrown briefly into prominence as he plunged into an itinerant ministry was Samuel Buell, a recent graduate of Yale, who earned this entry for 29 March 1742, in the journal of a revivalist minister: 'The world full of Mr. Buel's [*sic*] preaching at Concord. In the judgment of some, great success; in the judgment of others, great confusion.'[11] The emergence of more emphatic criticism was one factor in the decline of the revival, and by 1744 the Great Awakening in New England had largely passed. But the rift that had been made in the churches persisted. New Light and Old Light parties continued to argue for decades over whether the Awakening had been a work of God or not. The battle was fought out in sermons, pamphlets, and books for the rest of the century as the parties solidified, but the two great champions, so close to each other in 1741, had moved steadily in opposite directions and soon produced works of defence and attack.

Jonathan Edwards early took the lead in a careful defence of the Awakening at Yale in a 1741 commencement sermon, 'The Distinguishing Marks of the Spirit of God'. Not denying flaws, Edwards provided criteria for his belief that the revival was a genuine work of God. As the excesses of the revival multiplied and the attacks grew sharper, Edwards enlarged his defence into a major work, *Some Thoughts Concerning the Present Revival of*

[11] Ebenezer Parkman, cited in Joseph Tracy, *The Great Awakening: A History of the Revival of Religion in the Time of Edwards and Whitefield* (Boston, 1842), p. 206.

Religion in New England (1743). He admitted that the revival had some features which were not of God and which ought to be purged.[12] With great thoroughness he then marshalled the evidence that the revival was genuine. He claimed that it brought an increase in concern for eternal things, improved moral behaviour, awakened consciences, cultivated soberness among youth, increased strictness in Sabbath observance, developed closer attention to the Bible, won many converts, helped in the gathering of the Indians, and speeded the advancement of Christ's Kingdom. In the light of all the evidence, he asked, who could doubt that for the most part the revival was really the work of God?

Those who were not convinced by such arguments found their leading spokesman in the pastor of First Church, Boston, Charles Chauncy (1705–87). In the autumn of 1743 he published *Seasonable Thoughts on the State of Religion in New-England*. Written with emotion, the book identified the Awakening with enthusiasm, Quakerism, and antinomianism. It examined the excesses of the revival in detail, and found that it did not deserve to be called a work of God. What Edwards had dismissed as accidental accompaniments of a good work, Chauncy insisted were clues to its basic error: over-emphasis on the affections at the expense of understanding and judgement.

Once the gates of criticism had been wrenched open, objections to the Awakening came from many quarters. When Whitefield returned to New England for a second visit the tide had turned against him. Few pulpits were available, and the Harvard faculty, seconded by Yale, censured him. The bickering among the clergy was a factor in the decline of the revival, as was the outbreak of King George's War in 1744. Attention was shifted to other matters, such as the successful attack on the great French fortress at Louisbourg on Cape Breton Island, conceived and carried out under the direction of the governor of Massachusetts, William Shirley.

When Edwards's final document in defence of the Great Awakening appeared in 1746, it was too late to save the movement. But the *Treatise Concerning Religious Affections* was much more than a reply to Chauncy—it was a sustained effort to define religion and to deal with fundamental issues in religious psychology and philosophy. It proved to be one of his greatest contributions. Emphasizing that true religion consists in holy affections, Edwards concluded his tightly reasoned, probing work by arguing that the truly gracious affections arise from the special work of the

[12] A critical text of those works, with some related pieces, has been edited by C. C. Goen, *The Great Awakening*, The Works of Jonathan Edwards, vol. iv (New Haven, 1972).

Spirit. This is not experienced by natural man but is visibly evident in the lives of true saints.

Great as the book was, it did not help its author when he challenged a long-standing practice of his congregation. Edwards had for years gone along with 'Stoddardeanism', the arrangement instituted by his grandfather which admitted to communion any respectable person consenting to the articles of faith. Edwards had finally become convinced that the original New England Puritan practice of admitting only proved saints to communion was scriptural, but was not able to persuade enough of his congregation of that to save his pulpit. He prepared a careful defence of his views, *An Humble Inquiry Into the Rules of the Word of God Concerning the Qualifications Requisite to a Compleat Standing and Full Communion* (1749), but to no avail. Rejected and dismissed, he finally accepted the missionary post at Stockbridge left open by the death of Sergeant, and settled there in 1751, preaching to both whites and Indians.

Though the Awakening faded as a matter of consuming general interest, the theology and practice of the revival continued to exert considerable influence and to excite continuing controversy within the churches. Many Congregational pastors continued to be identified with the New Light position; the uneasy rift between them and the Old Lights long persisted within the one church system.

In Connecticut, where Congregational affairs were more centralized in the hands of the Old Lights because of the Saybrook Platform, there were many splits, and a number of Strict or Separate Congregational churches were formed, especially following Whitefield's Connecticut tour of 1745. The Separates believed that only the truly regenerate should be admitted to church membership; they resisted the centralized control of the churches and the compulsory religious taxes. The New Lights who became Separates—and they included persons of all classes—often felt the sting of persecution and were subjected to extensive litigation over taxes. Separate churches were formed through the 1740s and 1750s in various ways: by factions pulling out of established congregations to found new ones, by the withdrawal of entire churches from consociations, and by gathering New Light believers from various congregations. The Separate congregations often chose and ordained as pastors laymen who lacked formal theological education. The bulk of the Separate churches were in Connecticut, though there were some in other New England colonies. In all, nearly a hundred were formed.

The Separate movement soon declined, however, for a number of reasons. The Separates were mercilessly harassed for non-payment of religious taxes to support the regular ministry; anything of value, including kitchen utensils and tools needed for livelihood, could be seized and sold by the tax-collector. Vitality was often dissipated in the long-drawn-out litigation and imprisonments. The Separates did play a part in the coming of religious freedom, but it was a sacrificial role, for relief came too late to save them. Their difficulties were not all external, however, for Separate congregations were never able to band together for any length of time. The angular individualism of these stubborn folk made it impossible for them to build a denomination; even their congregations were often torn by sharp inner conflicts. Some of the Separate churches returned to the establishment, in which the gradual abandonment of the half-way covenant and the ministries of some New Light pastors made mediation possible. The chief cause of the decline of the Separates was the spread of Baptist sentiment among them—in at least nineteen instances whole congregations adopted Baptist principles, and henceforth would baptize only professed believers. The Separate Baptist movement that developed was at first quite distinct from the older Baptist churches.

Most of the Baptist churches in New England in 1740 were Arminian in theology, and resisted the revival which in New England was Calvinistic in tone. After the great public excitement of the Awakening had passed, however, the number of Baptists of various orientations increased significantly. The few Baptist congregations that were Calvinistic shared in this growth, and developed closer ties with the Philadelphia Baptist Association. Disaffected Congregational New Lights, in part attracted by the Baptist commitment to freedom, often found a home among them. Most of the Separate Baptist churches that arose soon affiliated themselves with the main body of Baptists. The renewed vigour of that denomination made possible the founding of Rhode Island College (later Brown University) in 1764, and the organization of the Warren (Rhode Island) Baptist Association three years later. Both of these events were much influenced by James Manning, a Princeton graduate who ensured that the new association followed the Philadelphia model and who served as the first president of the new college.

In both its sweeping impact in the early 1740s and in its protracted after-effects, the Great Awakening transformed much of New England church life. When it was over, not only had the number of congregations significantly increased—it has been estimated that 150 new Congregational churches were founded as a result of the Awakening—but also the New Light theology was continued by a major theological party which had arisen within the established churches. The Baptists had also been much influenced by the Awakening spirit and were growing rapidly.

Awakening in the Southern Colonies

The Awakenings in the south were not unrelated to those of the other sections, but they followed a quite different path. There was not a period of such intense general excitement comparable to the years of 1739–42 in the other colonies. Whitefield did preach to great throngs in the southern colonies as elsewhere. Without the preliminary work of such persons as the Tennents and Edwards, however, the ground was not prepared for reactions like those of the north. Though Whitefield was an Anglican, the establishments of the southern colonies were cool to him and to his style of churchmanship. The southern Awakenings were consequently more episodic, reaching their peaks in different denominations at varying times. The total time-span was longer—beginning in the 1740s, they continued into the Revolutionary period.

The first stirrings appeared when a group of laymen in Hanover county, Virginia, hearing about the revivals elsewhere gathered in each other's homes to read such devotional literature as Whitefield's sermons and Luther's commentaries.[13] Serious religious feelings were expressed at these meetings, which soon became too large for private homes, so that reading-houses were built. This development diminished attendance at the established Anglican parishes. When the leaders of the new movements were brought before the authorities they claimed to be Lutherans and won toleration. In 1743 William Robinson, a Log College graduate who had been sent out as a missionary by the New Brunswick presbytery, visited the Hanover group and won them to Presbyterianism. Other New Light itinerants laboured to extend the revival. Samuel Davies (1723–61) took charge of the work at a number of points, soon numbering seven, in five counties. A good many Church of England people were attracted to his eloquent preaching. Colonial officials made various efforts to halt his work, but he persistently and at last successfully battled for the recognition of the Toleration Act of 1689 as applicable in Virginia. In 1755 the six congregations that had been founded as a result of the Awakening formed the Hanover presbytery, the first in the south. During the French and Indian War Davies preached such sermons as 'The Curse of Cowardice', which emphasized the necessity of resisting a threatening enemy. When he left to

[13] The story has been told by Wesley M. Gewehr, *The Great Awakening in Virginia, 1740–1790* (Durham, N.C., 1930).

become president of Princeton, Presbyterian foundations in the south had been solidly laid.

The next phase of the southern Awakenings was introduced by a pair of New Englanders, Shubal Stearns and Daniel Marshall. Both had been born in 1706, had been Congregationalists awakened by Whitefield's 1745 Connecticut tour, and had moved successively from Separate Congregationalism to become Separate Baptists. The two men accompanied by some others settled at Sandy Creek in central North Carolina in 1755. A church was gathered and a meeting-house erected; scattered residents of the area, many of them with no church connections, were drawn by the enthusiastic preaching of the Baptist Awakeners. Stearns and Marshall were soon itinerating widely, eastward to the coast and northward into Virginia, winning some General and some Particular Baptist churches to their Separate position.

The Sandy Creek Association was formed in 1758; the work then expanded in all directions, reaching down into South Carolina.[14] The next year the 'father' of the movement, Shubal Stearns, died, but the movement had developed deep roots and continued its remarkable growth. Marshall carried it into Georgia in the following year. Evangelical Calvinism with its emphasis on the new birth, the authority of the Bible, and the direct guidance of the Holy Spirit was eminently preachable in a simple, pungent style. It appealed to many of the meagerly educated, hard-working people of the frontiers. Blacks were also gathered up in the revival thrust—the Awakeners sought to save the souls of whomever they could reach, and some slaves were numbered among the new congregations.

There was tension between the Separate Baptists and the older Calvinistic Baptists, who had begun their work in North Carolina in 1729 and who were drawing strength in the Awakening years through the renewed missionary enthusiasm of the Philadelphia Baptist Association. These churches adopted the name 'Regular' when they founded the Ketockton (Virginia) Regular Baptist Association in 1765; the Kehukee (North Carolina) Regular Baptist Association was organized four years later. Certain differences in theology, practice, and social level kept the Separate and Regular groups apart until after the Revolution. The Separate Baptists were a denomination really created by the Awakening; its life was revivalist to the core, and it set its unmistakable stamp on the whole Baptist movement in the south with which it eventually became identified. The

[14] The story has been summarized by William L. Lumpkin, *Baptist Foundations in the South: Tracing through the Separates the Influence of the Great Awakening, 1754–1787* (Nashville, 1961).

rapid increase of Baptists in the south, when added to their growth in the other sections, meant that the total number of Baptist churches had increased from about ninety in 1740 to more than four times that in 1776. In number of churches, the Baptists had become the third largest denomination in America by the Revolution, surpassed only by the Congregationalists and the Presbyterians. The burst of energy that had planted so many Baptist churches in the south was checked by the excitement of the Revolution, by changes in the patterns of migration, and by the emergence of another revivalistic group in the 1770s which was in competition.

The lateness of Methodist beginnings in the New World is surprising—not until the 1760s did some Methodist immigrants form societies, in Maryland under Robert Strawbridge and in New York under Philip Embury. In 1769 the first of the eight lay missionaries Wesley named for America arrived. As in England, the Methodist societies operated within the general framework of the Church of England; they undertook to deepen the religious life of whomever they could reach without forming new churches.

Methodist work in Virginia was helped at first by an evangelically minded Anglican, Devereux Jarratt (1733–1801). Awakened himself under Presbyterian and Whitefieldian influences, Jarratt went to England for episcopal ordination, there meeting Wesley and Whitefield. Settled in 1763 as rector at Bath, he preached a rousing message with stress on the new birth. He gathered whom he could into special meetings for prayer, and itinerated into the surrounding territory. He drew such large crowds to his three churches that outdoor meetings became necessary.

When the Methodists began to work in Virginia in the early 1770s, Robert Williams, a lay preacher who had come on his own to the colonies, assured Jarratt that the Methodists were not separatists and that they intended to work with the ministers of the Established Church on whom they depended for the sacraments. Jarratt then merged his own evangelical labours with the Methodists in the third and final phase of the southern Great Awakenings.

When the first Methodist conference in America met in 1773, it assigned four lay preachers to Virginia. The next year Williams organized the first Methodist circuit there. The travelling preachers followed one another at two-week intervals on the circuit which took some six weeks to complete, for it extended into North Carolina. Jarratt was a participant in the burgeoning movement. At times he was disturbed by emotional excesses, but he found comfort in Edwards's writings on the subject. Many blacks pressed into the Methodist gatherings, some of which were held at night, and in which revival songs effectively supplemented the preaching. The alliance between the Methodists and Jarratt provided the leadership for the impressive revival of 1775–6 during which the membership of Methodist societies in Virginia grew spectacularly from less than 300 (1774) to nearly 2,500 two years later, plus hundreds more in North Carolina. New circuits were being developed as the revival spread.

The approach of the Revolution slowed the revival work as interest in political questions diverted public attention. Wesley's opposition to the Revolution and the Methodist connection with the Church of England, though largely nominal, raised hard questions in the minds of many who had been awakened but who favoured colonial independence. Most of the officially appointed lay missionaries returned to England at this time, and the Awakening was over. Yet the Methodist movement nurtured by this last phase of the southern Awakenings was firmly grounded, and the shock of war did not long slow its growth.

Religious Life Outside the Main Currents of Awakening

While the Great Awakenings were surging through some of the leading colonial denominations, there were other bodies which did not participate in the main stream of revival yet which did contribute in certain ways to the pietistic tone of eighteenth-century Protestantism. In differing degrees, the various German-speaking churches contributed to the emphasis on an inward, personally experienced, evangelical Protestantism. Cut off from the central movements of Awakening by language barriers and by the harsh judgements of some of the Calvinistic revivalists concerning German piety, various German groups nevertheless had certain affinities with the theologies and practices of the Awakenings, and contributed to the general shift in colonial Protestantism towards a pietistic, evangelical orientation.

The extensive German immigration after 1720 transformed Lutheranism as the Swedish and Dutch groups were vastly outnumbered. Some of the Lutheran pastors who laboured among the German immigrants were aligned with the pietism of Halle. The great leader of colonial Lutheranism was Henry Melchior Muhlenberg (1711–87). Educated at Göttingen, Muhlenberg taught in the orphanage at Halle, served in a pastorate in Germany, and then accepted a call to Pennsylvania. Arriving in 1742, he took charge of Lutheran affairs with a firm hand. In addition to serving as pastor of four churches, he travelled extensively through the colonies, preaching, teaching, founding churches and schools. In 1748 he organized what later became the Ministerium of Pennsylvania, the first permanent Lutheran synod in America. His detailed reports to Halle won support for his work. Theologically, Muhlenberg held in creative balance Lutheran orthodoxy and warm-hearted pietism. By the time of the Revolution, over eighty churches were under his watchful care, and the foundations of Lutheranism in America had been laid.

Though the largest group of German immigrants were Lutheran, there were some who were Reformed, chiefly from the Palatinate. Their first significant leader, John Philip Boehm, began as a lay reader while farming in Pennsylvania after his arrival in 1720. He was then called to serve as pastor of three congregations, and was ordained by the anti-Awakening Dutch Reformed ministers of New York. In a quarter-century of leadership, he founded thirteen congregations. The Dutch continued the oversight of these German Reformed congregations, sending Michael Schlatter, a Swiss, to organize a Coetus in 1747. Within this synod there developed two parties, somewhat analogous to the Old and New Side groups in the Presbyterian Church. The parts of the German Reformed denomination which clung to the German language and were largely isolated from contacts with others adhered to pure doctrine and the ancient traditions. In other places, as awareness of the religious needs of the heterogeneous middle colony population became known, the Reformed pietism which had spread in the Rhineland was more influential, and personal piety as well as sound learning in the ministry was more emphasized. The most prominent member of the latter party was Philip William Otterbein (1726–1813). Born in Germany, reared in pietist circles, and educated at the Reformed seminary at Herborn, Otterbein arrived in the colonies in 1752 and served parishes in Pennsylvania and Maryland. In the early 1770s Otterbein worked with Francis Asbury, the most prominent of the lay missionaries sent by Wesley, and the one who remained active on the American scene through and after the Revolution. By the outbreak of war the evangelical party was strong in the Coetus, and formed one of the strands in the broad pattern of pietistic Protestantism in colonial America.

The German Baptist Brethren, often popularly known as the Dunkers or Dunkards and much later as the Church of the Brethren, arose in Germany in the early eighteenth century as a pietist movement. Alexander Mack (1679–1735) grew discouraged with what he felt to be the deadness and formalism of the German Reformed tradition in which he had been raised. Fleeing to Schwarzenau in Hesse-Cassel, he came into contact with a pietist circle. In 1708 the group resolved itself into a new congregation committed to inner religion of the heart; it adopted the practice of baptizing believers three times face down in running water as an expression of its intense devotion. Other small congregations joined the new movement. In the face of persecution, often visited on such dissenting groups, some of the Brethren migrated to America, beginning in 1719. Four years later the first American congregation was gathered at Germantown; biblical practices of the washing of feet during service and of the exchange of the holy kiss were adopted. The remnants of the movement in Europe soon disappeared; Mack came to the colonies in 1729, and the church became located wholly in America. It remained small in the eighteenth century—there were only about fifteen congregations by 1770. In emphasizing plainness of dress and speech the Brethren were much like the Quakers and others of the 'plain people' among the Germans. Ministers were chosen from among the people and were not formally prepared for their tasks. Non-credal in emphasis and congregational in polity, the German Baptists stressed a simple, Bible-centred, warm-hearted religion. A Lutheran observer in the early nineteenth century reported that the Brethren in the middle eighteenth century had led the 'first ardent awakening to cause great excitement' among the Germans.[15]

A number of small new movements arose out of the various German sects of Pennsylvania, one of the most interesting of which centred upon Johann Conrad Beissel. He arrived in Pennsylvania in 1720, was baptized by the Brethren, and served a church at Conestoga. He withdrew in 1728 to form the German Seventh-Day Baptist group, which observed Saturday as the sabbath. Out of this movement there emerged four years later a communal settlement at Ephrata, Pennsylvania. Great communal cloisters (restored in part in the twentieth century) were erected; those who lived there accepted the way of celibacy under Beissel's leadership. A special feature of the Ephrata community was its choir; an important contribution to church music was made by this semi-monastic order. A printing-press spread the teachings of the community, which declined and eventually disappeared after the founder's death in 1768.

Another small German group which came with immigrants from Germany comprised the followers of Caspar Schwenckfeld, a lay contemporary of Martin Luther who stressed the immediate guidance of the Holy Spirit and put less emphasis on the Bible than the Reformers did—and was branded a heretic. His followers knew much persecution; seeking freedom they began migration to the New World in 1734. They continued their

---

[15] As quoted by Donald F. Durnbaugh, *The Believers' Church: The History and Character of Radical Protestantism* (New York, 1968), p. 129.

distinctive form of spiritual worship, but did not formally organize as a church until after the Revolution.

The importance of pietism among the Germans was heightened by the evangelistic and missionary labours of the Unity of the Brethren (Unitas Fratrum), or Moravians. This movement had risen in Bohemia in the fifteenth century among the followers of Jan Hus. They spread quickly in Bohemia and Moravia, but during the Thirty Years War were driven underground or into exile, and largely disappeared. Early in the eighteenth century, some remnants of the church took refuge on the estates of a Saxon count, Nicholas Ludwig von Zinzendorf (1700–60). Here they mingled with some German pietist refugees, and built a closely knit community, Herrnhut. Zinzendorf, who had been educated at Halle and Wittenberg, was an ardent pietist and an ecumenical pioneer who believed that the Moravians could serve as a disciplined order among genuine Christians wherever they could be found without disturbing their formal church connections. The Moravian leaders, however, were determined to continue their ancient episcopal church order, and reconstituted their church as The Renewed Church of the United Brethren in 1727. For many generations both aims were fulfilled; Moravians not only built up their own church but influenced Christians of other persuasions through their 'diaspora'.[16] Zinzendorf symbolized this twofold aspect of the life of the Unity of the Brethren, for he was ordained as a Lutheran pastor but also became a Moravian bishop.

The Moravians were devoted to missionary effort. In the 1730s they planted outposts in the West Indies, Greenland, South Africa, and North and South America. They began missionary work among the Indians in Georgia in 1735. The land they had secured proved to be swampy and undesirable, and their pacifism made their position in a buffer state between English and Spanish territories difficult, so with the aid of Whitefield they turned northward to Pennsylvania. Here they founded Nazareth and Bethlehem—the latter settlement named by Zinzendorf on Christmas Eve 1741. At these communities there arose a carefully regulated existence called the 'General Economy' which provided the base for missionary thrusts into new areas, especially in North Carolina.

Zinzendorf hoped to bring together the various German pietist groups in a spiritual association to be called 'The Church of God in the Spirit'. A series of seven conferences was held. The other bodies did not really understand the Moravian diaspora tradition and feared they would be

---

[16] Gillian Lindt Gollin, *Moravians in Two Worlds: A Study of Changing Communities* (New York, 1967); John Weinlick, *Count Zinzendorf* (New York, 1956).

taken over. Zinzendorf's strong hand and aristocratic ways often got in the way of his irenic intent, and the plans failed. More successful was his work among the Indians, for his journeys strengthened the foundations of a fruitful mission. The most famous of the Moravian missionaries was David Zeisberger, who laboured first among the Iroquois and then among the Delawares. A number of settlements of converted Indians were founded in Pennsylvania and Ohio—towns much like Eliot's communities of praying Indians in the previous century.

In the late 1740s in both Europe and America the Moravians went through a period of theological excess in focusing on the blood and wounds of Christ, employing sensuous images of union. Known as the 'sifting time', this period of emotional intensity was checked in America through the leadership of Bishop August G. Spangenberg.

The Mennonites increased in this period chiefly through Swiss immigration, which introduced a division among them. A split arose among the Mennonites of Switzerland in 1693 as the followers of Jakob Ammann followed old customs rigidly, sought to avoid worldliness, and were very strict in avoiding or 'shunning' excommunicated members. Individual Amish arrived early in the eighteenth century, but the first Amish congregation was formed in the 1730s. Though the split was overcome in Switzerland, it proved to be permanent in America. Largely isolated from the currents of the Awakening by their distinctive customs and language, the Mennonites continued to be guided by their literalistic reading of the Bible. By their stress on simple, inner religion they strengthened the pietistic aspects of American Protestantism.

The Society of Friends continued to be one of the leading denominations of the colonial period. The life of their disciplined meetings maintained a high degree of self-sufficiency and morale. In the first half of the eighteenth century, the Friends exhibited little concern for converting others. They studied to avoid worldliness, opposed marriage outside their own circles, and prohibited attendance at the religious services of other bodies. Their separateness kept them out of the Awakenings, yet they were indirectly affected. As Rufus Jones, the leading Quaker philosopher and historian of the early twentieth century, once put it: 'As a rule, the Quakers, although perhaps unconsciously, felt the influences pervading all classes of society; and the fresh breath of what has since been known as the "*Great Awakening*" swept even into the quiet atmosphere of the Quaker meeting.' Yet it was a very gentle breath, for only a handful of Quakers were pulled into the revival inasmuch as 'the majority were by this time so thoroughly insulated from contact with other religious bodies that the waves of religious enthusiasm that boiled all about them scarcely touched the hems of their garments'.[17]

Renewal among the Friends did come, however, in a characteristically Quaker way. In the 1750s a distinctively Quaker revival manifested itself in efforts to bring about conformity to early Quaker standards of spirituality and morality. There was an increased emphasis on the plain dress and speech that had long characterized the Friends, and an intensified stress on rigorous pacifism. The leading preacher of the Quaker revival was a travelling English Friend, Samuel Fothergill, who itinerated widely in the colonies in the middle 1750s. He related his work somewhat self-consciously to Whitefield's, and visited many of the places where the great evangelist had been. Like him, Fothergill spoke against pride, greed, and worldliness, and endorsed practical piety and good deeds. The Quaker reformer's mission was only to his own people.

Fothergill and those associated with him sought to get Friends who were active in the public affairs of Pennsylvania, where members of the Society still dominated the Assembly, to follow the pacifist position, but as Sydney V. James has noted, 'no provincial policy could alter the geography of the imperial conflict between France and England'.[18] The hostilities of the French and Indian War had begun in 1754; the formal declaration that opened what in Europe was known as the Seven Years' War came two years later. Over the issues of preparation for military action, however, the Friends divided. Some resigned from the Assembly, while the moderate Quakers compromised with the militants, so that the Quaker political domination of Pennsylvania came to an end. The moral renewal movement that had stirred Quaker life meant that those who had compromised could not again be conspicuous in Quaker leadership.

One of the significant developments within the Society in these years was a deepening opposition to slaveholding. The lonely pioneers in the anti-slavery movement among the Friends, in particular Ralph Sandiford and Benjamin Lay, suffered much for espousing an unpopular cause early in the century, for there were a number of slaveholders among the Quakers who saw no harm in what was a widespread practice. It was John Woolman (1720–72) in co-operation with Anthony Benezet (1713–84) who were chiefly responsible in winning the Society to an anti-slavery commitment, releasing forces that in time contributed to the elimination

---

[17] *The Quakers in the American Colonies* (London, 1923), p. 410; Frederick B. Tolles, *Meeting House and Counting House*, pp. 233 ff.

[18] *A People Among Peoples: Quaker Benevolence in Eighteenth-Century America* (Cambridge, Mass., 1963), p. 183.

of slavery in middle and northern colonies. Woolman, a devout Quaker who supported himself by serving as shopkeeper and clerk, by tailoring and teaching, was awakened to the evils of slavery when he made out a will involving a slave in 1742. Troubled by the transaction, he resolved never to participate in such a thing again. He travelled through the colonies to study the slave system close at hand. An essay, 'Some Considerations on the Keeping of Negroes', was approved by the Publication Committee of the Philadelphia Yearly Meeting in 1754.[19] It was thoughtfully and powerfully written, and presented a deeply spiritual argument against slaveholding, noting its evil effects on the master as well as on the slave. Benezet, a teacher, worked closely with Woolman and wrote prolifically against the practice. Both had an influence on the development of the anti-slavery crusade in England. Woolman was on a missionary journey among English Friends when he died of smallpox. Benezet was widely read in England, among others by John Wesley whose *Thoughts on Slavery* drew much from his writing. The Quaker stand against slavery was important to the passage of gradual abolition acts in Pennsylvania by 1780.

The one conspicuous colonial Protestant communion to align itself with only a few exceptions against the Awakenings was the Anglican. Most of the clergymen of the Church of England in the colonies opposed the Awakenings, and the congregations followed. Devereux Jarratt was the most prominent Anglican supporter of the revival, and he pulled back when the Methodists moved toward separation.

The period had begun quite auspiciously for the Church of England congregations. The Society for the Propagation of the Gospel was supporting missionaries in many places. In 1722 came a dramatic turn in Anglican fortunes, for the rector of Yale College, Timothy Cutler, along with Samuel Johnson, the Congregational pastor at West Haven, and several others declared their conversion to Anglicanism. They chose the occasion of the Yale commencement in September to make their startling disclosure, and soon were on their way to England for ordination. Cutler and Johnson returned as S.P.G. missionaries, the one to serve Christ Church in Boston, the other to take the lead in the erection of the first Episcopal church building in Connecticut, at Stratford.

In the next decade Anglican work was begun in Georgia with the help not only of the S.P.G. but also of another society inspired by Thomas Bray. Late in his life he received a substantial bequest, and created Dr.

[19] This essay, with several others and with a definitive edition of Woolman's famous *Journal*, has been edited and introduced by Phillips P. Moulton (ed.) in *The Journal and Major Essays of John Woolman* (New York, 1971).

Bray's Associates for the purpose of founding a colony for the good of the poor and the instruction of Negroes. General James Oglethorpe took the lead in securing a land grant where these purposes could be carried out; England's desire to have a colony to check Spanish advance northward from Florida opened the way for the founding of Savannah, Georgia, in 1733. At first slaves were prohibited in the new colony. Among the early settlers were debtors from England and refugees from Salzburg. John Wesley served in Georgia as an S.P.G. missionary for several years, and Whitefield built an orphanage there. The idealistic hopes for the colony were soon shaken by the realities of New World settlement. In 1752 Georgia became a royal colony, and later in the decade the Church of England was established by law—a rather nominal act.

Whitefield was an Anglican, but as an Awakener he played down denominational distinctions. He professed to be theologically a Calvinist, which served to ally him more with Congregationalists and Presbyterians, with Reformed and Baptists than with Anglicans, many of whom tended towards Arminianism. The Anglicans generally did not see the Awakenings as an interdenominational movement of renewal and revival, but viewed them in the light of historic British controversies concerning polity, liturgy, and theology. From these perspectives the Awakenings seemed like an attempt of enthusiastic dissenters to destroy the Church of England, with Whitefield contributing to the undermining of the church of which he was a minister. It has been said that 'Colonial Anglicans rejected and opposed the Awakening because George Whitefield's conduct convinced them that the revival was an instrument of antagonistic dissent'.[20] Though the Anglican churches did not generally participate in the Awakenings, their number was roughly doubled during the period, largely through the work of the S.P.G., which supported more than 300 missionaries in the colonies during the eighteenth century. The missionaries not only conducted divine worship, but many of them also carried on educational activities. For example, schools for Negroes were founded in four cities, and missionaries worked among blacks, teaching and baptizing.

The era of the Great Awakenings continued to be a difficult time for Roman Catholics. The penal legislation against them, though not strictly enforced, remained on the books and reminded them of their disabilities. The general anti-Catholicism of British Protestantism was not softened by the evangelicals, who often included 'papalism' among the errors the revival was intended to overcome. The largest group of practising

---

[20] Gerald J. Goodwin, 'The Anglican Reaction to the Great Awakening', *Historical Magazine of the Protestant Episcopal Church*, xxxv (1966), 369.

Catholics continued to reside in Maryland, carrying on without such civil rights as voting or office-holding. Chapels had to be built on private estates, and their small schools were illegal and had to be operated on something of an undercover basis. Maryland Catholics apparently were never more than 10 per cent of the population in this period—perhaps there were about 10,000 adult Catholics in 1770. The Jesuit priests who travelled among the faithful as itinerant missionaries were supported principally by their estates. To help their parishioners who were employed on the farms of Protestants, they were able to secure exemptions from observing most holy days of obligation from May to October.

Throughout the colonial period, Catholics continued to be most free in Pennsylvania. A Jesuit, Fr. Joseph Greaton, journeyed there in the 1720s. Eventually he took up residence in Philadelphia. In 1733 he opened a chapel—at the time the only one in the colonies where mass could publicly be celebrated. Some Catholics arrived in the German immigration; in 1741 several German Jesuits entered the colony to work among their countrymen.

There were only scattered groups of Catholics elsewhere in the colonies; most of them had no access to priestly ministrations. An untold number of Catholics who arrived in the various seaport cities were lost to the church, often through lack of opportunity for them to practise their faith. The distrust of Catholics increased with the outbreak of the French and Indian War, and the effort to relocate the forcibly uprooted Acadians from Nova Scotia further increased the tension. The ending of French rule in Quebec, followed by the intensification of political unrest in the colonies did ease the situation for Catholics and they encountered a more tolerant spirit.

The Jews continued to be a much smaller minority. They clustered largely in the seaport cities. In New York a synagogue was erected in 1730. By mid-century, congregations had been gathered in Savannah, Philadelphia, and Charleston. The Newport, Rhode Island, congregation was revived at about this time, and in 1763 the beautiful synagogue still in use in the late twentieth century was built. For a small group of people (by the first federal census in 1790 they were counted at 1,243) these achievements were impressive.

Theological Tensions: Awakening and Enlightenment

The Great Awakenings ran their course as Enlightenment thought became increasingly dominant in the intellectual life of the colonies. The many-sided movement called the Enlightenment, with its stress on reason and order, had considerable impact upon the life of the churches, especially as the 'New Learning' it fostered became known in the colonial colleges. The trends toward emphasizing the role of reason in religion were often labelled as Arminian. Most of the Awakeners were vehemently opposed to rational religion, but they could not help but be influenced to some extent by the Enlightenment itself. The keenest among the revivalists sought to use the weapons of the Enlightenment against it. The struggle between Awakeners and rationalists widened a rift within the Protestant mind and spirit which has reappeared in various forms again and again.

In New England the perspectives of the Enlightenment began to appear in the writings of some of the Puritan leaders, as, for example, when John Wise appealed to the natural rights philosophy as well as to the Bible in his defence of congregational autonomy early in the eighteenth century. The Puritan divines had long insisted on the role of reason in religion, but had meant reason yoked to the Scriptures and interpreting its revelation. In the later seventeenth century the scientific and philosophical advances made by such thinkers as Locke and Newton brought new prestige to human reason, and the New Learning that grew out of those achievements began to displace the older scholastic methods. Even the leaders of Puritan thought who remained firmly oriented to special revelation in the Bible were affected by the new intellectual currents. Cotton Mather's *The Christian Philosopher* (1721) showed a remarkable openness to scientific knowledge and to natural theology, though he struggled to contain the new forces within the framework of trinitarian orthodoxy.

There were others, however, who believed that the new discoveries in science and philosophy required fresh patterns in theology. Those ministers who introduced new perspectives in theology usually did so very cautiously, disavowing any serious departure from the familiar and accepted norms. Often they denied being what their opponents called them—Arminians. That label itself was being stretched broadly to cover a wide range of opinions, from those who believed that man is not wholly passive in his regeneration to those who believed that man contributes to his salvation. Originally associated with the moderate Calvinism of Jacob Arminius (1560–1609), whose interpretations of Calvinism were put down at the Synod of Dort (1618–19), by the eighteenth century the term was being used in a pejorative way by the orthodox against those who were emphasizing man's active role in his salvation. The spread of such views in the colonies was stimulated by the arrival from England of the writings of those who were drawing theological consequences from Enlightenment teachings, such books as Daniel

Whitby's *A Discourse . . . [on] Election and Reprobation* (1710, 1735) and John Taylor's *The Scripture Doctrine of Original Sin Proposed to a Free and Candid Examination* (1738) in which central doctrines of Calvinism were questioned. One reason that the defection of the Congregational leaders to Anglicanism in 1722 in Connecticut was so disturbing to the Standing Order was because it was feared that the way might be opened for the advance of Arminianism.

Equally upsetting to the Calvinist Congregationalists, however, was the appearance within their ranks of those who had no intention of departing but who were moving in an 'Arminian' or 'liberal' direction.[21] Following his role as the leading Old Light opponent of the Great Awakening, Charles Chauncy engaged in a long period of intense study of the Bible. Using insights derived from the New Learning, he questioned the orthodox theories of the fall, and discussed the formation of character necessary to inherit eternal life. Toward the end of his long life—he served Boston's First Church for sixty years—Chauncy espoused a universalist view, anticipating the salvation of all men.

A young friend of Chauncy, Jonathan Mayhew (1720–66), also a graduate of Harvard, was considerably more outspoken on theological issues. He repudiated the orthodox doctrine of original sin, and stressed the place of reason in religion. In Mayhew's view, reason is called upon to test whatever is put as revelation, to decide if its claim to be revelation is supported by clear external evidence and by internal consistency. He declared that salvation depended more upon a person's moral life than upon his beliefs, and repudiated the idea that the sin of Adam could be imputed to his children.

While men like Chauncy and Mayhew were spreading such views in New England Congregationalism, rationalist currents were also flowing within Episcopal churches. In the south, lay readers often used the sermons of John Tillotson, former Archbishop of Canterbury. His fundamental theological position was rationalist, but he recognized that natural religion must be supplemented by revelation, for human weakness requires a divine sanction for morality. Within Anglicanism, Arminianism did not have the negative connotations it had within the Calvinist bodies, and its patterns, usually somewhat closer to orthodoxy than the rational supernaturalism of a Tillotson, were spreading. The permeation of these liberal theological views within the southern establishment can be discerned in a multi-volume work published in 1722 by Commissary James

[21] The story is told in detail by Conrad Wright, *The Beginnings of Unitarianism in America* (Boston, 1955).

Blair of Virginia, *Our Saviour's Divine Sermon on the Mount,* a collection of 117 sermons. He was cautious in drawing theological conclusions; much more like Chauncy and Mayhew in this respect was Samuel Quincy, an S.P.G. missionary who arrived in Georgia in 1733 and who later settled in South Carolina. His *Twenty Sermons* of 1750 reflected the rationalistic positions of Locke and Tillotson. He did not reject revealed religion, but insisted that absurdities and also doctrines contrary to the light of nature should be given up. Reason, he declared, was the only basic guide for humanity in the search for truth.

An important figure in the intellectual life of Anglicanism was Samuel Johnson, who as a student at Yale in the early part of the century was exposed to the traditional Calvinist answers to theological and philosophical questions. His reading of such thinkers as Bacon, Locke, Boyle, Newton, and Whitby won him over to the New Learning while still a student. After his conversion to Anglicanism, Johnson became acquainted with George Berkeley during the latter's period of residency in Newport. His adoption of Berkeleian idealist philosophy helped him to remain oriented to revealed theology, but like many Anglicans he was a convinced Arminian who affirmed that humans had the ability to respond to the offer of salvation and who attacked Calvinism.

Most of the leaders of thought who were imbued to a greater or less degree with the Enlightenment spirit were opponents of the Awakening. They rarely went to a full Deist position as did Benjamin Franklin (1706–90), but swung to an Arminianism or on to rational supernaturalism.

These liberal positions were being set forth with much greater openness and self-consciousness by mid-century. Two colonial colleges founded at about that time—the College of Philadelphia (later the University of Pennsylvania) and King's College (later Columbia University) were hospitable to the rationalist trends in religion. In 1755 William Smith, an Anglican minister who had been educated at Aberdeen, transformed an academy into the College of Philadelphia and became its first provost. He was assisted by Francis Allison, an Old School Presbyterian who relied on the work of the Scottish moral philosopher, Francis Hutcheson. The college developed a broad curriculum which emphasized both the classics and science. The institution was non-sectarian in its origins—Benjamin Franklin was one of its moving spirits. He would have liked to secure Samuel Johnson as provost, but Johnson had gone as president to the new King's College in New York the year before. At King's, founded under Anglican auspices, a certain breadth and urbanity prevailed. In these two institutions Enlightenment thought and Arminian views were openly presented.

The more able of the Calvinist leaders learned how to turn the weapons of the Enlightenment against itself; they used reason against rationalism in religion. The conspicuous example is Jonathan Edwards, one of the most influential thinkers of his own and later times. While still in college he read the essays of Locke with higher pleasure 'than the most greedy miser finds, when gathering up handfuls of silver and gold, from some newly discovered treasure'.[22] From his own probings he knew the dangers that lay hidden in Enlightenment thought for those of weak theological principles—they might get swept away from the grand vision of the majestic and sovereign God, choosing whom he would to be saved. He believed that Arminian principles were lurking in the minds of the enemies of the Awakening, and indeed within the enemies who drove him from his pulpit in Northampton to the frontier mission at Stockbridge.

He determined to strike the Arminians at a vulnerable spot, and at the same time to give Calvinism an effective defence against the formidable opponents it faced. Those influenced by what he classified as Arminianism were arguing that if a person is not free to will and to do, then that person is not responsible for his acts, and if condemned, is condemned unjustly, and God is not just. Edwards set out to show that God is fully sovereign and hence that man is determined (predestined) as to his eternal destiny, yet is still responsible for his acts. The full title of what is often referred to as the *Freedom of the Will* (*Treatise on the Will* is more apt) is *A Careful and Strict Enquiry into the Modern Prevailing Notions of that Freedom of the Will which is Supposed to be Essential to Moral Agency, Virtue and Vice, Reward and Punishment, Praise and Blame* (1754). No brief summary can do justice to his lengthy, learned argument. On the basis of the postulate commonly accepted in his time that every event must have a cause, he explained that acts of will must also have causes, which are motives. The will is determined by the strongest motive; the idea of freedom cannot be applied to the will, for it is the *person* who has the power of choosing, not the will itself which has that power. There are, however, two kinds of necessity out of which a person acts, natural and moral. Natural necessity arises out of physical compulsion or restraint, but moral necessity arises out of the bonds of duty and conscience. As long as a person is free to do as he wills, then he is responsible for his acts, even if he is not free to will as he wills.

[22] *The Works of President Edwards: with a Memoir of His Life*, 10 vols. (New York, 1829), i, 30.

Edwards labelled the Arminian idea of the free will as self-contradictory, as either implying an effect without a cause, or as leading to a series of infinite regressions which becomes absurd. Argued with relentless intensity and precise logic, the *Treatise on the Will* gave Calvinism a new arsenal of intellectual weapons and a new lease on life.

Edwards then turned his attention to a defence of the doctrine of original sin, so criticized by various kinds of rationalists. In *The Great Christian Doctrine of Original Sin Defended* (1758), Edwards argued that no other understanding of man's situation except one that affirmed original sin is adequate to the facts of human life and history, or to the Bible. The evidence of history and of Scripture shows that natural man is totally depraved, Edwards declared. God was not the author of sin, but at the fall he withdrew his sustaining grace, permitting man to fall into sin. Adam's sin is imputed to all, the consequence of a divinely constituted personal identity between Adam and his posterity.

Edwards died prematurely in 1758 of a voluntary inoculation for smallpox soon after he had taken a new post as president of the College of New Jersey at Princeton. At his death some writings intended to become parts of a larger work or works were posthumously published, among them *The Nature of True Virtue*, apparently written in 1755 in 'dialogue' with Hutcheson and Shaftesbury. The aesthetic side of his work is shown in this piece, which suggests that for Edwards the idea of beauty was a more inclusive idea than either truth or goodness. True virtue consists in benevolence to being in general, in supreme love to God. True virtue, Edwards declared, is of the affections and the dispositions; its excellence can be perceived only by those who have received the gift of grace.

The works of Edwards were in time republished in a number of nineteenth-century editions, and in a renewal of interest in this profound thinker in the second half of the twentieth century his works are being printed again in definitive editions, including his largely unpublished notes or 'Miscellanies'. Since his time, many who have had little sympathy with his theology have nevertheless found his work challenging and intriguing.

An Edwardsean school, the 'New Divinity' or 'New England Theology' grew out of his work, but the Old Calvinists who had opposed the Awakenings and who were uncomfortable with some of Edwards's insistence on a 'consistent Calvinism' also drew much from him. The first principal figure in the Edwardsean school was Joseph Bellamy (1719–90) who had studied with Edwards, and who in 1750 wrote a work that was to be widely read in New England and beyond: *True Religion Delineated, or Experimental Religion, Distinguished from Formality on the one hand, and*

Enthusiasm on the other, set in a Scriptural and Rational Light . . . Bellamy extended the influence of Edwardseanism as he trained some ninety candidates for the ministry in his Connecticut home. Another leading representative of the New Divinity was Samuel Hopkins (1721–1803), who had also studied with Edwards and who became his literary executor. A rather prosaic, bookish man, awkward as a speaker, Hopkins summarized and modified the Edwardsean position in a two-volume *System of Doctrines* (1793).

Summary: The Significance of the Era of the Great Awakenings

The Great Awakenings were instrumental in the general redirection of Protestantism in the American colonies. All parts of American Protestantism were not equally affected, and those that were affected varied in the way their patterns of thought and life were altered by the revivals. The Awakenings did stir some intense controversies—Presbyterianism was governmentally divided for nearly two decades. Congregationalism was internally polarized, Baptists were arrayed in competing associations. After the great days of the Awakenings had passed and the controversies had cooled, the theologies and styles of piety and churchmanship encouraged by the revivals persisted and permeated increasing numbers of congregations and denominations. The evangelical parties of the various communions, though they had their own distinctive characteristics and intensities, often saw themselves as allies in the one Kingdom of Christ. The churches that felt this basic unity of evangelical experience tended to view as cold and lacking in vital piety any interpretation of Christianity that stressed too strict doctrinal precision or a formal catechetical approach. Certainly the Awakeners were concerned about doctrine—many were Calvinists who had no intention of neglecting theology or the Confession—but they were also concerned about the personal appropriation of religious experience as a throbbing, living force. The layman could experience this as well as the learned divine, and lay Christians were accorded a higher role in revivalistic Protestantism than had often been the case in older styles of churchmanship.

Though the Awakenings did strengthen a good many established parishes in New England, they also multiplied the number and deepened the life of many congregations which not only were not established but which opposed the legal recognition and support of religion. Separate Congregationalists, Baptists, Presbyterians, and Methodists were often in tension with leaders of establishments against religious taxation and for freedom. By significantly increasing the number of unestablished churches, the Awakenings hastened the day when church and state would be separated. America's religious diversity was significantly increased in this period.

The Awakenings, especially in the south, also brought some black members into the churches. 'By clearing an avenue down which Negroes could crowd into an important sector of the white man's community', wrote Winthrop Jordan, 'the Awakening gradually forced the colonists to face more squarely the fact that Negroes were going to participate in their American experience.'[23] There was opposition to this development, to be sure, yet the equalitarian strain in Protestantism was strengthened by the Awakenings, for the undercurrent in much revival doctrine was that the blacks were the spiritual equals of whites because they possessed immortal souls. This spirit played some role in the broadening humanitarianism and developing anti-slavery feeling of the time. Significantly, it was the most conspicuous of the Edwardseans, Samuel Hopkins, who in 1776 wrote one of the most forceful of the early tracts against slavery to be penned by an orthodox churchman, 'A Dialogue Concerning the Slavery of the Africans'.

Seventeenth-century Protestantism in the colonies had been cast largely in the familiar forms of European Christendom; the eighteenth-century Awakenings were important events in the indigenization of religion, in the development of American patterns of faith. The generalization can easily be overstated, for the Awakenings were related to analogous patterns of revival in Europe. Yet the patterns of perceiving and transmitting Christian faith that were shaped in part out of the tensions between the various revivalist movements and those who opposed them had some distinctive characteristics, as observers from abroad sometimes noted.

The denominational concept of the church, that each communion was a distinctive member of a larger whole, was advanced in many ways by the revival. The roots of that concept lay in seventeenth-century English church history, and it was being elaborated there with the growing of denominations of Puritan and evangelical background.[24] The full shaping of the American denominational tradition was a long process with some important developments to follow during the revolutionary and early national periods, but the crucible of the revival was instrumental in

---

[23] *White Over Black*, p. 214.
[24] Winthrop S. Hudson has written much on this theme, e.g. in *The Great Tradition of the American Churches* (New York, 1953), chs. I–III; *Religion in America*, 2nd edn. (New York, 1972), pp. 81 ff., and especially *American Protestantism* (Chicago, 1961), pp. 33–48.

bending much American church life in this direction. The churches that resisted paid the price of being left behind as popular churches; for example, Gerald Goodwin has concluded that 'the colonial Anglicans' rejection of evangelicalism in the Great Awakening sealed the Church of England's fate as a minority church in America.'[25] This happened despite some of the devoted work done by the several hundred S.P.G. missionaries.

Wherever the Awakenings swept, they brought renewed vigour to the churches, which was expressed through many channels. There was a resurgence of concern for the conversion and civilizing of the Indians. Heightened humanitarian concern often accompanied the work of religious renewal, as is evidenced by the founding of such institutions as Whitefield's orphanage, and by the formation of academies and colleges. The founding of Princeton can be ascribed directly to the Awakenings, while more indirectly they contributed to the rise of Brown, Rutgers, and Dartmouth. Lawrence A. Cremin has analysed the Awakenings as educational movements and found that they 'transformed the churches as teaching institutions'. The force of the Awakenings 'was to enhance the educational influence of the churches and through them to strengthen the role of Christian teaching and works in the everyday life of the colonists'.[26] Some of the revivalist groups were little concerned with education, especially the Separate Congregationalists and Separate Baptists. The authority and solidarity of the clergy were diminished somewhat by the rise of groups which did not stress the necessity of solid education and high ordination standards for the ministry.

The Great Awakenings were primarily religious movements, concerned with bringing sinners to conviction of sin and into a dependence on the God who alone could save. They nevertheless had important political as well as social and educational consequences. The intercolonial character of the movement, with its patterns of itineracy as evangelists moved from colony to colony, did much to spread common interests and loyalties among a people who had been largely isolated from one another. Many of the bonds of national feeling that later helped to give a sense of unity to a people were first forged in the warmth of religious renewal. By stressing the universality of sin and the possibility that any person might find salvation, and by elevating the place of the common man in church and society, however unevenly, the Awakening did contribute to the spread of

[25] 'The Anglican Reaction to the Great Awakening', 371.
[26] *American Education: The Colonial Experience*, pp. 316, 320. See also Douglas Sloan (ed.), *The Great Awakening and American Education: A Documentary History* (New York, 1973).

the democratic ideal. Other forces were moving in this direction too, of course, but the undergirding of democratic tendencies by evangelical religion is a major part of the whole story.[27]

The Awakenings did much to realign American Protestantism, but they did not quite revolutionize it. Especially among the Congregationalists and Presbyterians, the concern for order reasserted itself, and the excitement diminished. But not before real changes had occurred; as Richard Hofstadter has said, 'we may regard these movements as a second and milder Reformation' which affected 'what America was to become by intensifying what it already was: in religion the most Protestant of Protestant cultures, and in morals the most middle-class country of the emergent bourgeois world'.[28] The stress on religious feeling that accompanied the Awakenings, often at the expense of the intellect, laid an important foundation of the anti-intellectualism that has plagued American life.

The Awakenings did stress individual morality, but they also offered visions of a people under God dedicated to the right. Awakeners often promised that the visions would be fulfilled. Not only was there a dream of glorious things to come, but the millennial affirmations that were so often a part of the revivals declared that the dreams would become realities in God's good time—which might not be long deferred. As Jonathan Edwards, the greatest theologian of the Awakenings, expressed it:

America has received the true religion of the old continent, the church of ancient times had been there, and Christ is from thence: but that there may be an equality, and inasmuch as that continent has crucified Christ, they shall not have the honor of communicating religion in its most glorious state to us, but we to them. . . . When God is about to turn the earth into a Paradise, he does not begin his work where there is some good growth already, but in a wilderness, where nothing grows, and nothing is to be seen but dry sand and barren rocks; that the light may shine out of darkness, and the world replenished from emptiness, and the earth watered by springs from a droughty desert . . .[29]

What Edwards put cautiously, other revivalists put more simply and directly, instilling into American souls a sense of special destiny for the

27 For fuller treatments of this theme, cf., e.g., Clinton Rossiter, *Seedtime of the Republic: The Origins of the American Tradition of Political Liberty* (New York, 1953), esp. ch. 2; Ralph H. Gabriel, *The Course of American Democratic Thought: An Intellectual History Since 1815* (New York, 1940), esp. chs. 2, 3.

28 *America at 1750: A Social Portrait* (New York, 1971), pp. 217, 290. See also Hofstadter's *Anti-Intellectualism in American Life* (New York, 1963), Part II, 'The Religion of the Heart'.

29 *Thoughts on the Revival of Religion in New England*, in *The Works of President Edwards*, 4 vols. (New York, 1868), iii, 314—15. For a recent critical edition of this treatise, see *The Works of Jonathan Edwards*, iv, *The Great Awakening*, C. C. Goen (ed.), (New Haven, 1972), 289–530.

New World nation. The millennial expectancy and the messianism it bred was later to be explicated in many ways and to be put to many purposes, but at the time it instilled new hope in the hearts of a people on the edge of a vast wilderness facing formidable odds. It lifted and sustained morale for the tasks of Christianizing and civilizing a continent. The Awakenings were not the sole source of the American sense of destiny, but they made it convincing to masses of men and women, and they often intensified the feeling in the soul of a people. Reinforced by later revivals, some religious and some secular, that sense of destiny has at once guided, inspired, haunted, plagued, and misled the American people.

The Awakenings took place as Enlightenment thought was spreading, and thus contributed to an abiding tension in American religious life. By the eve of the Revolution, the evangelical-revivalistic way of apprehending and communicating the Christian tradition and the Enlightenment-rational style of understanding and transmitting the same heritage were sharply diverging. This was especially evident in New England, where the two parties were uncomfortably yoked in one established system of church government. Emerging as they did in the age of the Enlightenment, the Awakenings intensified a serious and persisting tension within the Protestant mind and soul.

The era of the Great Awakenings was marked by decisive changes in both church and national life. As Christian faith was effectively brought to the attention of masses of people who had not previously taken it seriously, new styles of piety and fresh patterns of religious organization were introduced. In a culture that was so strongly Protestant, the consequences of the Awakenings extended well beyond the churches and are woven into the fabric of American history.

IV

THE CLASH OF CULTURES:
FRENCH CATHOLICISM AND BRITISH
PROTESTANTISM IN
EIGHTEENTH-CENTURY CANADA
(1720–1800)

DURING the eighteenth century the struggle between Catholic France and Protestant Britain for political control of Canada was decisively settled in favour of the latter. The French Catholics of Quebec were determined to maintain their cultural identity, however, and succeeded so convincingly that the bicultural, bilingual pattern of the future Dominion was indelibly etched. After 1763 the two peoples with their own distinctive histories and religious perspectives had to work out their destinies in one political framework. The dramatic events of the period 1720–1800 are of decisive importance for understanding Canadian religious history.

Problems of a Colonial Catholic Establishment

At the conclusion of Queen Anne's War in 1713, France surrendered Hudson's Bay, Newfoundland, and much of Nova Scotia to the English. She determined to hold on more firmly to the vast possessions that remained to her—no small task, for the holdings stretched from the mouth of the Gulf of St. Lawrence westward along the river valley into the Great Lakes country, and down the Mississippi to the Gulf of Mexico. France retained Cape Breton Island (later part of Nova Scotia), calling it Ile Royale, and erected a fortress at Louisbourg. Although the Illinois-Louisiana region was made into a separate colony, Catholic life there continued to be supervised by the Bishop of Quebec.

New France enjoyed steady growth; the population of nearly 25,000 in 1720 had grown to 55,000 by 1755, largely by natural increase. The number was small, however, compared with the English population in the colonies to the south, where about 1,500,000 were living by mid-century. To protect a vast but unpopulated empire, the French constructed a line of forts stretching from the St. Lawrence to the Gulf of Mexico.

Despite periodic friction between civil and religious leaders and unseemly strife among the religious Orders, the French Canadians remained loyal to the Roman Catholic Church. Throughout the century, the Catholic faithful continued to build on the foundations which had been laid by Bishop Laval and Bishop Saint-Vallier, often facing obstacles from within provincial life as well as threats from the outside.

Saint-Vallier himself confronted some of these internal difficulties in his later years. Bitter quarrels erupted among both political and ecclesiastical leaders. Strongly devoted to the fixed location of resident priests in their parishes, in 1721 Saint-Vallier, in co-operation with civil officials, redesigned the boundaries of 82 parishes in which settled curacies were planned. No less than 50 of these parishes had been founded by the bishop —a testimony to his industry and determination. Actually there were nowhere enough priests to fulfil this ambitious design, and many parishes continued to be served by missionaries from the Orders. There were few resources for education; illiteracy was widespread in the rural parishes. Burdened by his many responsibilities, Saint-Vallier asked for an assistant—a coadjutor bishop who would one day succeed him. He planned to send this helper to Louisiana to administer Catholic affairs. The priest who was named, however, Louis Francois Duplessis de Mornay, accepted the revenue but never left France, disliking the long and dangerous voyage.

When Saint-Vallier died on Christmas Day 1727, he had earned a reputation not only for forceful leadership but also for holiness and sanctity. Something of the spirit of intense piety that had informed the religious life of New France in the early days of the previous century survived in him, but by the time of his death religious apathy had penetrated deeply into the life of the Gallican church at home and abroad. Immediately after his passing, the tension between religious and civil authorities exhibited itself in some sharp conflicts, intensified by a concern for wealth among both laity and clergy. A quarrel over the funeral arrangements for the late bishop, for example, revealed the bitterness between governor and intendant, and between the clergy from France as opposed to those of Canadian birth.[1] To the Canadian-born *curés* it seemed as though the leading posts always went to those of French birth.

[1] On this and related points, see the documents as cited, e.g., in Cameron Nish (ed.), *The French Régime* (Scarborough, Ont., 1965), pp. 136–41, cf. also Walsh, *The Church in the French Era*, ch. X.

Although strong episcopal leadership was much needed, it was long in coming. In the fourteen-year period following Saint-Vallier's death, New France was without a resident bishop nearly half of the time. When de Mornay succeeded as Bishop of Quebec, he still remained in France, naming as his coadjutor Pierre-Herman Dosquet, a former Sulpician who had seen service in Montreal. The coadjutor angered the Canadian clergy soon after his arrival because he did not support the appointment of fixed *curés*, and located French-born priests between parishes served by Canadians as a check on them. He soon found he lacked both the authority and the resources to deal with the troubled situation, and returned to France. His complaints resulted in the resignation of de Mornay and in his own advancement. Returning as Bishop of Quebec, Dosquet undertook the merger of the Seminary at Quebec with that at Montreal, incensing the Canadian clergy who were devoted to their beloved institutions. Pleading ill health, the bishop returned to France in 1735. Four years passed before a successor was chosen to replace him, but then the new incumbent died of the plague soon after arriving in Quebec.

In the autumn of 1741, a new era began with the arrival of the sixth Bishop of Quebec, Henri-Marie de Breil de Pontbriand (1708?–60). He had studied at the Jesuit college at La Flèche before continuing his education at the Sulpician house in Paris, becoming a doctor of the Sorbonne. The scholarly bishop was deeply disturbed by the degree of illiteracy in his diocese, and insisted on the catechetical method of instruction. His determination had a lot to do with the preservation of French Canadian culture at a time when religious vitality was in decline and Enlightenment thought was threatening Christian teachings. Monseigneur de Pontbriand also proved to be a skilful administrator, making some wise appointments. A strength of his episcopate was that he sincerely appreciated the qualities of the Canadian clergy and ordained about one hundred of them in his nearly twenty years as bishop. He was also able to reduce tensions among the religious Orders.

Considerable resources continued to be devoted to mission work from Île Royale to the Great Lakes and down the Mississippi Valley to the Gulf. Outpost communities, some with neighbouring settlements of Indians, were maintained, and missionaries from the Orders carried out their ministrations faithfully though without conspicuous success in the face of Indian mobility and indifference. At Michilimackinac, for example, the Jesuit mission was weakened as the Indians were attracted to the Detroit area, where they were subjected to the corrosive effects of a frontier commercial centre. In the middle decades of the century the half-dozen villages in the Upper Mississippi region enjoyed their most flourishing period; from these centres the Jesuit fathers continued to reach out to the declining Indian population.

Following a bloody Natchez Indian uprising in 1729, Louisiana was made a royal colony, but enjoyed little significant growth. Religious life was marked by sharp tensions between Jesuits and Capuchins, and by the difficulty of communication with Quebec. This was especially true during the unsettled period between the episcopates of Saint-Vallier and Pont-briand. It was not until near the end of his bishopric that Pontbriand was able to get the Jesuit vicar-general he had placed in charge of the Louisiana mission fully recognized. The lack of a bishop in the region seriously hindered the development of normal Catholic life, with suitable educational institutions. The efforts of the Jesuits to reach the Arkansas, Yazoo, Choctaw, and Alibamon Indians were not successful. The internal struggles among the French, the indifference of soldiers and traders, and the effects of drink on the natives conspired against significant achievement.

In Quebec, the French Canadian faithful were enthusiastic about their bishop's church-building projects, but felt that he gave in too often under the pressure of the civil authorities, especially in reducing the numbers of festivals of obligation that fell on weekdays, thereby cutting down their holidays. Pontbriand's penchant for co-operation with the governor led him into conflict with the native-born foundress of the Grey Nuns, Madame d'Youville. A widow who had conducted a store in Montreal following her husband's death, she gave herself tirelessly to the care of the poor and unfortunate, aided by a few associates who were at first laughed at as they begged from door to door for their charitable causes. She became superior of the Confraternity of the Holy Family, which took over the management of the deteriorating General Hospital at Montreal, soon restoring it to great usefulness. In 1748 a new intendant, François Bigot, attempted to merge the hospital with that of Quebec, securing the bishop's approval. With the support of the Sulpicians, the Grey Nuns appealed to the throne, were sustained, and were formally designated by Louis XV as a new religious Order, destined to play an important role in French-Canadian Catholic life.

Meanwhile, the final series of events that led to the fall of New France had begun. The expanding English population pressed increasingly on French territory in the Ohio-Mississippi basin. Early in King George's War (the North American aspects of the War of the Austrian Succession, 1744-8), the leaders of the fortress at Louisbourg planned to recapture Acadia. This was countered by a successful seige of Louisbourg by a New

England expedition. Though adjudged impregnable from the sea, the fort had not been properly secured on the landward side. A dramatic expression of the clash of the two cultures occurred when Protestant leaders destroyed Catholic images in the citadel's chapel—what seemed from the one point of view to be the suppression of the trappings of a hated superstition was seen from the other side as the desecration of a sacred place.

The northern colonies were unsuccessful in their efforts to conquer Canada by invasion through the interior. The Treaty of Aix-la-Chapelle (1748), based primarily on European considerations, restored all conquests, which meant that Louisbourg was once again in French hands. This was deeply resented by the New Englanders, who felt their sacrifices had been taken too lightly.

Tension remained high after the peace. There were sporadic outbursts of violence and the extension of fortifications on both sides. To strengthen their hold on Nova Scotia, the English founded Halifax in 1749, for the first time giving serious attention to the colony. The French-speaking Acadians in the western part of the peninsula were caught between the contending forces. They were urged to take an oath of allegiance to England if they wished to retain their lands and to practise their Catholic religion freely, but they objected to this lest they be called to fight against the fatherland. They also refused to take an oath of loyalty to France, wishing to be left alone on their Acadian farms.

Though most of the priests urged prudent neutrality, a missionary to the Shubenacadie Indians, the Abbé Le Loutre at Beauséjour on the Bay of Fundy with the help of Indians used guerrilla tactics against the English. A force from New England captured Beauséjour in 1755 in one of the early skirmishes of the French and Indian War (the Seven Years' War, formally declared the following year). With war impending, the acting governor of Nova Scotia, Colonel Charles Lawrence, determined to remove the Acadians as a security risk since they refused to take the required oath to Britain. In 1755–6 about half of the approximately 12,000 Acadians were rounded up and distributed among various English colonies. Lands and provisions were lost; family life was disrupted in the forced move. The remainder of the Acadian population fled to the forests, some resettling in New Brunswick or on the Island of St. John. The farms they were forced to leave were offered for sale to New Englanders.

In Quebec, the French were weakened from within by the scandalous profiteering of Intendant Bigot and others. In 1758 Louisbourg fell again, this time to a British fleet, opening the St. Lawrence for an attack on the city of Quebec. In the following year the historic battle on the Plains of Abraham was fought. The generals on both sides were mortally wounded, Wolfe in victory and Montcalm in defeat. The fall of Quebec was followed in 1760 by the capitulation of Montreal, foreshadowing the end of all French possessions on the North American continent.

French Catholicism under the British

Under the Treaty of Paris (1763) France ceded to Great Britain all claims to Cape Breton, Acadia, Quebec, and almost all of Louisiana east of the Mississippi. All territory west of that river had been ceded to Spain, so that at that point France no longer held any possessions in North America (two small unfortified islands near Newfoundland were retained as fishing bases). The treaty stated that His Britannic Majesty's new Catholic subjects in Canada could worship according to the rites of the 'Catholic, Apostolic, and Roman Religion' as far as the laws of Great Britain allowed. Since Roman Catholicism was restricted under English law, this provision left much to be clarified later.

At the time of the conquest, there were about 180 priests in Canada, and it was to the Catholic Church that the British turned as they faced the responsibilities of administering their new territories. Shortly before the surrender of Montreal, Bishop Pontbriand had died, leaving the church without its head at a critical juncture. The nuns of Quebec and Montreal were permitted to continue their work, but the Jesuits, Recollects, and Capuchins were not. Thus were brought to a close certain efforts extending over a century and a half to win Indians to the faith—efforts that had been marked by much heroism but by few lasting results. Yet by 1800 the great majority of the Indians of the Maritimes and Quebec were at least nominal, and in some cases fervent, Catholics.

When the English conquered New France, there were some 4,000 slaves in the population, less than one-third of them Negroes, the rest Indians. Although the Catholic Church condoned slavery, ecclesiastical law tended to soften its harsher effects. There was probably some increase in the number of Negro slaves in the first decades of the British period; then slavery gradually disappeared through a confluence of economic factors and anti-slavery sentiment.[2]

The instructions issued to the first British governor of the Province of Quebec, General James Murray, provided for the toleration of 65,000 Roman Catholics but looked toward the establishment of the Church

[2] See the remarkably complete work by Robin W. Winks, *The Blacks in Canada: A History* (New Haven, 1971).

of England in due course. The law did not permit the formal recognition of a Catholic bishop in Quebec. Faced with the pragmatic task of governing a conquered colony, Murray, sympathetic to the French Canadians, privately encouraged arrangements whereby the vicar-general who had been named by Pontbriand, Jean Olivier Briand (1715–94), was consecrated in France as Bishop of Quebec. Officially recognized only as 'Superior of the Clergy', Bishop Briand arrived in 1766. Murray had just returned to England, but the new governor, Sir Guy Carleton, was also willing to co-operate with the Catholic Church as a defence against the rising republicanism of the colonies to the south. In many ways, as it somewhat ironically turned out, the church was freer from government interference under the English than she had been when French officials of Gallican stamp had interfered in ecclesiastical affairs. The law officers of the Crown ruled that lands acquired by conquest were legally different from those colonized by British immigration, giving justification for co-operation between the government and a church which at home was still under legal disabilities.[3]

Briand led his people in facing some difficult tasks. Churches and other buildings needed restoration, especially at Quebec City where there had been much destruction. An adequate body of priests had to be enlisted, for the number had seriously declined, in part through the suppression of the male religious Orders. The morale of a proud people now living under alien rule had to be improved. Though it took time and patience, Briand made progress in all three areas. Some parishes had been vacant for years, but in all Briand was to ordain about ninety priests in his eighteen years of activity. He encouraged the movement which glorified the original customs of New France, yet guided his flock to accept their new rulers, and to co-operate with the English merchants who commenced undertakings in the two major cities.

This conciliatory policy paved the way for an important landmark in continental history, the Quebec Act, passed in 1774 by the British Parliament. The Act reversed the earlier plan to undertake to anglicize Quebec, and allowed the French Canadians to retain their old semi-feudal system and civil law even as it introduced the English criminal law. It also included within the boundaries of Quebec the old northwest (from which territory the states of Ohio, Indiana, Illinois, Michigan, and Wisconsin were later carved). The Act's provisions admitted Roman Catholics to citizenship and to eligibility for public office, and allowed the church to

[3] The relevant documents are quoted in a useful work edited by John S. Moir, *Church and State in Canada, 1627–1867: Basic Documents* (Toronto, 1967), pp. 77–91.

retain its right to tithe the faithful. In effect, parts of the system of New France were restored under British sovereignty, with controls actually lighter than under the French Crown.

Bishop Briand was convinced that the French Canadians were better off under the British than they would be under the Americans, for he was aware of the long-term hostility of the New England Puritans to Catholicism. When Continental Congress sent a committee (including Benjamin Franklin and John Carroll) to try to win support for the American Revolution in Canada, their efforts failed. Briand forbade his clergy to receive Carroll. During the war, most French Canadians remained neutral, often against the urging of their religious leaders that they support Great Britain more visibly. Very few Canadians joined the Americans, whose efforts at invasion had only limited success. The French Catholics gained a more secure place in British North America as a consequence of the Revolution. The enlarged boundaries of Quebec could not be retained, however, for the old north-west became part of the United States by the Treaty of Paris (1783).

Briand resigned in 1784 just as some 6,000 Loyalists were coming into Quebec, especially into the western parts of the province. Predominantly Protestant and English-speaking, these were the 'Tories' of American revolutionary history who remained loyal to the British Empire. Many had fled from their homes or had been driven out, usually with heavy losses of property and possessions. Uncomfortable with the French Catholic cast of Quebec, especially in matters of law, education, and the lack of representative government, they petitioned Carleton (now Lord Dorchester) for a division of the province so that they could have their own space. The Constitutional Act of 1791 was the result of their activity.

The Constitutional Act modified but did not repeal the Quebec Act. It left the status of the laws and the position of the Roman Catholic Church in Quebec untouched, but authorized the division of Canada (which then did not include Newfoundland or the Maritime provinces) into Lower Canada (the eastern portions with population centres along the lower St. Lawrence—Quebec) and Upper Canada (later Ontario) with the boundary running roughly along the Ottawa River. Thus Quebec, or Lower Canada, remained predominantly Catholic and French, with some English enclaves, chiefly in the major cities. The high birth-rate of the French Canadians was primarily responsible for the rapid increase in the population of Quebec. An estimated 65,000 persons at the time of conquest had increased to about 160,000 by 1791. The 1791 Act also made provision for the setting-aside of land for the endowment of the 'Protestant clergy' as areas were surveyed and opened. These 'Clergy Reserves' were to become a major religio-political issue in a few years.

Newfoundland was long neglected in the matter of religion. A Catholic priest took up residence there in 1770. Fourteen years later, when perhaps three-quarters of the population of about 25,000 were accounted Catholics, James Louis O'Donel, an Irish Franciscan, was named Prefect Apostolic. A Catholic chapel was built—the first since the French had ceded the island 170 years before. Before the end of the century, O'Donel had been elevated to episcopal status.

On the whole, Canadian Catholics were opposed to the French Revolution; only a few showed sympathy with its aims. Some French *emigré* priests settled in parishes in Lower Canada. The impact of the Revolution tended further to cement French-Canadian loyalties to Great Britain as it fought revolutionary France.

The Growth of Protestantism in the Maritime Provinces

The planting of Protestant churches in Canada began in earnest well over a century after Catholic foundations. Though Protestant services had been conducted in Canada from time to time in the seventeenth century, as in Newfoundland, no churches were founded until the latter half of the eighteenth century. Anglican chaplains conducted services on a regular basis following British military successes in Nova Scotia in 1710, but not until the founding of Halifax in 1749 were permanent congregations gathered. An Anglican church, St. Paul's, was soon erected. The population of the new city grew quickly, and was religiously diverse, for it included a few Jews and Catholics as well as several varieties of Protestants. To the original group of about 3,000 English 'adventurers' was soon added nearly as large a group of 'foreign Protestants' from Germany and Switzerland, and also many New Englanders. Missionaries supported by the S.P.G. laboured among the heterogeneous population, for the original hope of the founders had been that most would be attracted to the Church of England.

The growing population soon spread out into new communities; many of the foreign Protestants, for example, settled in Lunenburg, southwest of Halifax. In time many of them did affiliate themselves with the Anglican Church. The expulsion of the Acadians in 1755–6 opened the way for the resettlement of lands near the Bay of Fundy, especially by New Englanders. When the first provincial legislature met in 1758, it established the Church of England, but provided for religious freedom for Protestant dissenters of all kinds, including exemption from religious taxes levied in support of the establishment. Catholics, however, were denied the right to vote or to sit in the legislature, nor were priests allowed to exercise any ecclesiastical jurisdiction whatever.

To attract more New Englanders, in 1759 Governor Lawrence issued what has been called 'the charter of Nova Scotia'. It provided that the township and court systems familiar in New England would be adapted to supplement the legislature and the colonial administration. By 1775 there were nearly 18,000 persons in the province (which then included New Brunswick). Many Congregationalists were in the new immigration, and with the increase in dissenters the privileges of Anglicans were soon curtailed. Town meetings rather than parish corporations became the disseminators of public charity, and eventually the right to perform marriages had to be shared with the clergy of other denominations.

In 1769 the Island of Saint John (thirty years later to be renamed Prince Edward Island) became a colony in its own right with governor and legislature. An Anglican priest, Theophilus Des Brisay, was appointed by royal warrant in 1774 to serve the parish at Charlottetown, which long remained the only Anglican parish on the island. Des Brisay served for nearly half a century, supported in part by public funds. Toleration was extended to Roman Catholics (who had built a church on the island in 1722) and to Protestant dissenters. By the turn of the century Presbyterians, Methodists, and Baptists were carrying on missions.

Nova Scotia was officially aligned with the mother country during the American Revolution, though there was considerable neutralist sentiment among the people. During, and especially immediately after, the struggle the province was flooded by an influx of Loyalists. Some 30,000 in all came, many of them very ill-prepared for the arduous and unfamiliar tasks of settlement in the largely undeveloped lands set aside for them. Some went on to England. Many founded settlements along the St. John River west of the Bay of Fundy; in 1784 New Brunswick was separated from Nova Scotia. This 'Loyalist Province' was considerably more homogeneous than the parent colony, and the privileges of the Church of England were considerably less qualified by concessions to dissenters. At the first session of its legislature in 1786 the Church of England was established and dissenting clergy were brought under the direct control of the governor. Six Anglican parishes were erected in the larger communities by 1800.

The Anglican Loyalists were especially anxious to have bishops; the long experience of Episcopal parishes in the American colonies without bishops had not been very satisfactory from the point of view of convinced supporters of the Church of England. Eighteen Loyalist clergymen, determined to secure strong foundations for their church in the British colonies in North America that remained, met in New York in 1783 to plan for the naming of a bishop for Nova Scotia. Four years later Dr. Charles Inglis (1734–1816), Irish-born former rector of Trinity Church in New York City, was consecrated in London. His diocese at first included all of the Maritimes, Newfoundland, Quebec, and Bermuda. He set out to build a strong Episcopal Church as a defence against the levelling principles of republicanism, which he thoroughly distrusted because of his experiences in New York. He had to struggle not only against the pioneering conditions that characterized Canadian life for so long, but also against the spiritual lethargy of late eighteenth-century Anglicanism. The lack of qualified clergy handicapped his efforts. On one occasion he remarked. that 'of eleven clergy, four are diligent useful clergymen, three are indifferent neither doing much good or harm; as for the remaining four, it would be happy for the Church if they were not in her orders'.[4]

Inglis resolutely travelled through much of his vast diocese, preaching, confirming, and administering. At the time of his first visitation in the Maritimes in 1788, Anglican services were being conducted at 10 communities in Nova Scotia, at 6 in New Brunswick, at 4 in Newfoundland, and at 1 on Prince Edward Island. Inglis saw that schools were opened at Windsor and Halifax, and obtained the promise of a royal charter for King's University. The desired patterns of an established Anglicanism, however, were difficult to work out amid the realities of a frontier culture and in the face of mounting religious diversity, for even other religious bodies were active in the Maritimes by 1800. In Nova Scotia especially a spirit of co-operation among the denominations was evident, although the multiplication of dissenters led to the curtailment and later to the end of establishment.

Patterns of co-operation among Protestants were evident from the early days of Halifax's history, for the Congregationalists in the New England migration were aided by the government in building Mather's Meeting House. As more Congregationalists came into Nova Scotia after 1759 and took the lead in working with Presbyterians and Baptists in contending against the centralizing policies of Halifax in favour of the more decentralized township system, ecclesiastical tensions heightened. By the eve of the American Revolution there were ten Congregational

[4] As quoted by Philip Carrington, *The Anglican Church in Canada: A History* (Toronto, 1963), p. 46.

churches in the colony. The difficulties of calling and keeping qualified ministers for these churches of Puritan tradition increased with the outbreak of hostilities, and left them ill prepared to resist a movement that disrupted them.

During the years of war there erupted a remarkable 'Great Awakening in Nova Scotia', largely among the working people of the farms and fisheries. As in Connecticut decades before, indeed in direct historical continuity with the Separate Congregational movement there, separatist New Light churches were formed. As before, they did not prove to be long lasting, but contributed significantly to the multiplication of Baptist churches.

Henry Alline (1748–84), born in Newport, Rhode Island, came as a boy with his family to Falmouth, Nova Scotia. The struggle for survival there was not easy; the necessity of labour on the family farm cut the boy off from further education. Reared in a Puritan atmosphere, Alline went through a protracted religious crisis, largely on his own, for there was no settled ministry in his vicinity. His conversion experience was quite typical of evangelical Puritanism, for he was familiar with accounts of the work of divine grace in the soul in the tradition of John Bunyan and David Brainerd. The steps in the Puritan pattern of conversion—knowledge, examination, humiliation, grace, assurance—were well known to him. The joyous last experience of assurance came to him as he wandered in the fields in 1775, and was followed immediately by a call to preach. The theology he worked out to support the itinerant evangelical ministry that gradually opened before him was distinctively his own, for it combined certain mystical tendencies stemming chiefly from his reading of William Law (1686–1761), Anglican devotional author, with his anti-Calvinist, anti-authoritarian, and egalitarian notes. Like many of those to whom his intense, other-worldly, self-assured preaching appealed, he sought to remain neutral in the revolutionary struggle. His doctrine of the church was decisively influenced by Separate Congregationalists, a number of whom had migrated from New England to Nova Scotia. Alline's early efforts at preaching were in the vicinity of his home, but as military threats lessened and home responsibilities lightened, in 1779 he was ordained by delegates of three recently gathered churches, two New Light Congregational and one Baptist. His own influence had been strong in the formation and life of these congregations.[5]

[5] On Alline and the Awakening, see Maurice W. Armstrong, *The Great Awakening in Nova Scotia, 1776–1809* (Hartford, Conn., 1948), and J. M. Bumsted, *Henry Alline, 1748–1784* (Toronto, 1971).

Alline then set out on preaching tours that in a few short years carried him along both sides of the Bay of Fundy and south to Yarmouth at the southern tip of the peninsula. His eloquence stirred great excitement and won many converts. He appealed to restless and economically deprived persons in a time of great public tension; he focused attention on the glories of the other world where God is all in all and where the soul finds a joyous, endless rest. In all, six New Light churches arose out of the Awakening he inspired. He wrote a doctrinal work, *Two Mites on Some of the Most Important and Much Disputed Points of Divinity* (1781), some sermons, and hundreds of hymns. After he died of tuberculosis on a preaching tour in New Hampshire, the Awakening long continued to shape the piety of dissenting groups in the Maritimes.

For the next generation, outport and farm were kept in a state of religious fervour by itinerant New Lights, Methodists, Baptists and dissenting Presbyterians. Though politically mute during the last quarter of the eighteenth century, the folk of hinterland and seacoast underwent a religious experience as sustained and exalted as anything in the history of the Canadian church. In the eyes of the thousands of men, women and children won to grace, their leaders were like the prophets and patriarchs of the Old Testament (indeed, among the Baptists, the founding preachers were styled 'fathers').[6]

Though Alline's own distinctive theology largely passed with him, the Awakening itself was carried on by others for many years. The New Light churches which arose chiefly out of his inspiration also proved to be ephemeral; with the intense focus on conversion and their anti-institutional thrust they soon dissolved or were reconstituted as the Baptist churches, like those of New England, reaped the harvest of the Great Awakening.

Baptists had come to Nova Scotia in the New England migration before the days of Alline. Several small, short-lived congregations had been gathered; Alline had been partly responsible for the renewal of the one at Horton in 1778. An English Baptist, Nicholas Pierson, was then ordained as pastor. Although the Horton church later disagreed, Alline did not think that the issue of baptism of infants versus that of believers was important enought to lead to the breaking of evangelical fellowship. A number of the 'fathers' of the Baptist movement were originally associated with Alline. Thomas Handley Chipman, for example, had been converted by Alline and baptized by Pierson. He served as pastor of an 'open communion' church at Annapolis for nearly three decades. Most of the New Light preachers eventually espoused the Baptist position after

6 S. F. Wise, in W. L. Morton (ed.), *The Shield of Achilles: Aspects of Canada in the Victorian Age; Le Bouclier d'Achille: Regards sur le Canada de l'ère victorienne* (Toronto, 1968), p. 38.

passing through an 'open communion' stage. The trend to a strict Baptist polity and a more Calvinistic theology was clear by the time of the formation of the Nova Scotia Baptist Association by nine churches in 1800, one of which was the pioneer Baptist congregation in New Brunswick, at Sackville. As elsewhere, Baptists were ardent believers in religious freedom and opposed establishment and its privileges, especially those of the Anglican clergy respecting marriage.

Several diverse streams of settlers brought Presbyterianism into the Maritimes. Among the Americans who moved into the Acadian lands were those who petitioned the New Brunswick, New Jersey, presbytery for a minister. The Rev. James Lyon arrived in 1764 and served about eight years, until his sympathy with the cause of American independence led to his departure. Meanwhile immigration from Scotland, Ulster, and New England was bringing in Presbyterians, some of whom were associated with the Church of Scotland while others belonged to various bodies which had separated from the Scottish establishment. The Rev. James Murdoch was sent by one of the latter groups in 1766 to begin a ministry that lasted more than thirty years. Lyon and Murdoch joined with several Congregational clergymen to form a temporary presbytery which ordained a fisherman, Bruin Romkes Comingo, for the German Reformed settlers at Lunenburg. A man of deep piety, though lacking formal theological education, Comingo ('Mr. Brown') served diligently for half a century. Congregationalists and Presbyterians also co-operated at Mather's Meeting House in Halifax, which eventually became Presbyterian and was renamed St. Matthews. In 1791 Bishop Inglis helped to secure governmental support for the pastor of that church, the Rev. Andrew Brown, a Church of Scotland minister.

A new phase of Presbyterian history began in 1786 when the Rev. James MacGregor arrived to serve Scottish settlers in the region around Pictou on the Gulf of St. Lawrence. Presbyteries representing different secessionist strands of Scottish Presbyterianism were formed in 1786 and 1795; next century was to see the gradual unification of these diverse beginnings.

The presence of Methodists in the Maritimes began in 1772 with the arrival of a group from Yorkshire at the Isthmus of Chignecto (which linked Nova Scotia and New Brunswick). Nominally they were related to the Church of England, but they held private meetings of their own in the Wesleyan tradition. In the spring of 1779 a revival swept the group; among the converts was a young Yorkshireman, William Black (1760–1834). As the revival waxed, class meetings were organized, and zealous laymen visited nearby communities in nascent circuits. Black began an itinerant lay ministry at this time. In their enthusiastic style and insistence on the new birth these Methodist Awakeners were similar to the New Lights. They welcomed Alline when he came among them in 1781, and rejoiced with him in the high peak of revival. A non-denominational New Light church was gathered in Cumberland, but soon the Methodists became disturbed by Alline's brand of enthusiasm. When Black returned from a missionary journey during which he had laid foundations for Methodist societies at Windsor and Halifax, he found that Alline had disrupted the Cumberland church. He gathered the Methodist faithful into new classes, stressing the importance of careful discipline in spiritual matters.

Black emerged as the most prominent figure in Methodism in the Maritimes. He travelled to the organizing conference of American Methodism at Baltimore in 1784. In response to his appeal, the conference sent Freeborn Garrettson and James Cromwell to itinerate in Nova Scotia. When the first informal Canadian Methodist conference met at Halifax in 1786, it stationed the six preachers on four circuits. Garrettson's ministry was outstanding; Wesley would have liked to have appointed him superintendent of Canadian work, but Garrettson was unwilling to assume these responsibilities in a world unfamiliar to him. Black himself was ordained by Bishop Coke and Bishop Asbury in 1789, and became presiding elder of the growing Wesleyan movement in Nova Scotia until 1800. By that date, the efforts of some twenty preachers had laid the foundations for Methodist advance in the Maritimes.

In 1791 Black went on a journey to Newfoundland in response to a request by Wesley, and was able to dispel the factionalism that had marred the Methodist movement there since the middle of the previous decade. A spontaneous revival was stirred up by his preaching, but the absence of an effective continuing ministry left the movement weak and scattered. The Wesleyans of the Atlantic provinces (the Maritimes and Newfoundland) were generally Loyalist in sympathy, and many were not unfriendly to the Church of England. The trend towards full independence from the Church of England that had taken place in the United States and was then occurring in England was reflected in the decision taken by Maritime Wesleyans 1792 to hold their meetings during 'church' hours. The circuit system proved its usefulness in British North America as elsewhere. Most of the preachers, however, became attached to given areas and the system did not attain the flexibility it had in some other places. The strongly American tone of Methodism evoked considerable dissatisfaction; when the Methodist Episcopal Church withdrew its preachers, Black journeyed to England to enlist new helpers. By 1800 circuits centred in eight of the larger communities; the preachers who travelled them carried a warmly evangelical gospel to whomever they could reach.[7]

Several other Protestant bodies entered the Maritimes in this period, but remained small in number. Lutherans came with the 'foreign Protestants' early in Halifax's history. A church, St. George's, was formed, but it eventually became Anglican. At Lunenburg, however, Anglicanizing tendencies were resisted, and under the pastors Frederick Schultz and John Schweisser, the Zion Lutheran Church flourished—the only such church founded in the eighteenth century in the Maritimes to survive. Though German Lutherans settled at other points, lack of pastoral leadership is given as the chief reason why most of their churches dissolved or became Anglican. Some isolated Lutherans remembered their tradition, however, and contributed to its resurgence in the nineteenth century.

Some Quaker groups came into the Maritimes in the last half of the eighteenth century, but they slowly dissolved. Several groups came from Nantucket Island off Massachusetts primarily in connection with the whaling industry, and when that means of livelihood declined, the communities faded. A Quaker Loyalist group from Pennsylvania settled at Pennfield on the southern edge of New Brunswick, but after a hard struggle under primitive conditions the group scattered as a result of a disastrous forest fire. Though these early groups did not form permanent meetings, the Quaker presence through individuals continued.

The Moravians had begun missionary labours among the Eskimos in Greenland in 1733, and felt called to extend their work to Labrador. After several preliminary attempts failed, small missionary settlements were planted at Nain, Okak, and Hopedale (1771–82). There was a hard struggle for survival, and only a few converts were won—100 in the first thirty years. The turning-point came when Tuglavina, a leader among his people, was converted and became a lay preacher.[8] In the next century, the fruits of the seeds that had been planted at heavy cost were harvested.

[7] The story has been well told by Goldwin French, *Parsons and Politics: The Rôle of Wesleyan Methodists in Upper Canada and the Maritimes from 1780 to 1855* (Toronto, 1962), esp. pp. 29–53. The work of Black's leading associates, especially John and James Mann and Duncan McColl is briefly discussed.

[8] John R. Weinlick, *The Moravian Church in Canada* (Winston-Salem, N.C., 1966), pp. 11–14.

The numbers of Roman Catholics also increased, despite the legal disabilities they faced at first. Though the French-speaking Acadians had been expelled in the 1750s and the restrictive legislation made it difficult for the English-speaking Catholic minority, Acadians filtered back and Irish immigration increased. Governor Lawrence persuaded the only surviving French Catholic missionary in Nova Scotia, the Abbé Maillard, to continue his work among the Micmac Indians, hoping that they might be reconciled to British rule. Maillard and his successor, Abbé Charles Bailly, extended their ministries to the Acadians, too, helping them to adjust to the new conditions. In 1773 Abbé Bourg, a priest of Acadian origin, came as the grand vicar of the Bishop of Quebec; he also worked to pacify the Indians who were being stirred to rebellion by American influence during the Revolution. As the number of English-speaking Catholics increased through immigration, they petitioned for their rights, and in 1783 were legally permitted to own land and have their own clergy, though they did not secure the franchise for another six years. By 1786 under Abbé Bourg, the French and Irish priests had formed a small hierarchical group to direct Catholic life in the Maritimes.[9]

The influx of the Loyalists brought some Negro slaves into the region, and several thousand free Negroes were part of the migration. Though slavery was stoutly defended at first, the economic conditions were not suited to its continuation and it slowly died out. The free black settlements were not very successful both because of economic difficulty and the incidence of prejudice, and several groups left these colonies to try their luck elsewhere. Baptist, Methodist, and Anglican missionaries worked among the blacks. The persistent educational work of the Church of England's Associates of Dr. Bray was helpful to both slave and free Negroes.

Protestant Beginnings in Quebec and Ontario

Not until the Loyalist migration swept into Quebec were the Protestant communities large enough to build churches there. Church of England clergymen were soon at work among the Loyalists. John Stuart, for example, had been a missionary among the Mohawks; he followed remnants of his scattered flock to Montreal in 1781, and in the next ten years this 'Father of the Anglican Church in Upper Canada' ministered among the

---

[9] Much information about Catholicism in Canada is presented by Dominique de Saint-Denis, *L'Église catholique au Canada: Précis historique et statistique*, sixième édition; *The Catholic Church in Canada: Historical and Statistical Summary*, 6th edn. (Montreal, 1956); see p. 71 on the Catholic Church in Nova Scotia.

Loyalists in lands set aside for them west of Montreal. He continued to work among the Indians, who built the first Protestant chapel in the colony at Grand River in 1785. At the end of the decade Bishop Inglis came into Quebec, visiting churches that had been built in four centres along the St. Lawrence. He named Stuart as commissary for the western districts. When the Constitutional Act of 1791 provided for the division of Quebec into Upper and Lower Canada, there was considerable hope that there would be some form of establishment for the churches of England and of Scotland.

In 1793 Jacob Mountain, a Cambridge graduate and examining chaplain to the Bishop of Lincoln, was consecrated Bishop of Quebec. Designated 'Lord Bishop'—a dignity not granted to Inglis, from whose diocese the new one was divided—Mountain was to become a member of legislative and executive councils in both Canadas. He had a difficult struggle in obtaining funds from the government and the S.P.G. to support his clergy. He visited the parishes of Upper Canada, working closely with Stuart. In the early 1790s that province was a vast wilderness in which the growing population (30,000 by 1796) was concentrated along the upper St. Lawrence and in the vicinity of the Bay of Quinte, Niagara, and Detroit. In Lower Canada, the Church of England was very much the church of a minority, despite official backing. A man with less determination than Mountain might have given up the fight in the face of the great difficulties. Though he never obtained his major objective of building a Church of England established in principle and practice, the fruits of his early labours were to be realized later—by the end of his long episcopate in 1825 the number of clergymen in his vast diocese had increased from nine to sixty.

Other Protestant bodies were just beginning to be visible in the Canadas by the turn of the century. A Scottish military congregation was functioning in the city of Quebec soon after its capture by the British in 1759; it was the forerunner of St. Andrew's Church, founded six years later. A congregation was founded in Montreal in 1786 by John Bethune, a minister of the Church of Scotland, though he soon moved into Upper Canada to minister among the Loyalist communities. The first effort to form a presbytery failed because of the distances involved, but in the 1790s it was successfully reconstituted. Mission work carried out by the Dutch Reformed Church in the United States resulted in the formation of churches which ultimately became Presbyterian—another illustration of the complex origins of Canadian Presbyterianism.

Despite the resistance to Methodism by Bishop Inglis and Bishop

Mountain and by government officials like Governor Simcoe of Upper Canada, itinerant Methodist preachers from the United States were winning followers by their fiery preaching. In 1790 a young American Methodist, William Losee, journeyed through Upper Canada, visiting little isolated communities which had only rudimentary institutional development. A number of former Americans had moved into such settlements—and a number that would later increase as part of the westward migratory surge. As the circuits in Upper Canada multiplied, they were organized into a separate district of the New York Conference in 1794. From 1790 to 1812 no less than seventy-six missionaries were sent to Canada from the United States, most of whom lacked formal education. But they were well disciplined and deeply in earnest, and won many of the pioneer settlers with concern for their salvation in the world to come. Such a message had a powerful impact on a people who faced the uncertainties of frontier existence with its hard labour, long hours, disease, and disasters. The Methodist genius for organization was effective amid these trying conditions of life, and helped to lay the foundation for the later success of Methodism in Upper Canada.

Several other denominations trace their origins back to this period. A few German Lutheran congregations were formed; as with the Methodists, the jurisdictional ties were with synodical bodies in the United States. While some Baptist lay folk were among those who settled in the newly opened lands of Upper Canada and perhaps gathered in one another's homes, not until the turn of the century did that tradition begin significantly to grow, aided by missionaries from the States and by the arrival of Scottish Baptists. The number of Catholics in the vast domain was slowly increasing: in addition to those in the old French settlement near Detroit, others came with the Highland Scots in the Loyalist influx.

By 1800 the political map of the eastern half of the future Dominion of Canada was taking a shape that would be recognizable to the twentieth-century eye. The religious map was also showing patterns of diversity, with concentrations of certain churches in particular areas that were to be determinative for Canadian religious history. In the eighty years that have been scanned, the French Catholicism that had long screened out heretics and dissenters saw Protestant bodies appearing to the east and to the west, and also arising in the province where Catholics retained some of the privileges of establishment. The Catholic future of Quebec was secure, for the church provided a principal key to the continuing identity of the French-speaking people. Though many types of Protestantism were already represented on the Canadian scene by 1800, serious tensions between churches with hopes for strong establishment and the other denominations had appeared. The diversities among the Protestant bodies were to show themselves more sharply as the problem of the Clergy Reserves loomed large early in the next century.

V

REMOULDING THE CHURCHES
IN THE
AMERICAN REVOLUTIONARY EPOCH

(1775–1800)

THE ideal of freedom in human life was strongly upheld during the American revolutionary epoch and was applied, in combination with other ideals and realities, to political, economic, social, and religious affairs. Convinced that British attempts to fulfil the needs of the nationalist and mercantile system of the Empire were leading to an overriding of their interests and rights, colonial leaders undertook a movement of resistance that escalated into a war for independence. In addition to the economic and political factors, there were also religious forces in the rise and acceptance of the revolutionary viewpoint and in its translation into action.

Religion and Revolution

Most dramatic among these religious influences was a determined opposition to renewed attempts by Church of England leaders to secure bishops for the American colonies. The three old denominations of England (Congregational, Presbyterian, Baptist) and their American counterparts remembered the history of the Puritan revolution and its failure in the Restoration of 1660, and were watchful lest hard-won rights and freedoms be jeopardized by Episcopal aggressiveness. The growth of Anglican establishments in six colonies, the advance of the S.P.G. missionaries, and the efforts of some of their leaders to play a stronger role in higher education troubled members of other churches. But it was the drive to have bishops appointed for the colonies that especially fed dissatisfaction with the mother country. In England, bishops fulfilled roles in civil as well as ecclesiastical government; it was feared that if bishops came to the colonies they would snatch away liberties and reverse gains that had been made by other churches. Even though devout churchmen claimed that bishops were needed for purely spiritual and ecclesiastical purposes, as long as establishments persisted these protests did not seem very convincing.

In the 1760s the question of bishops was sharply debated. Jonathan Mayhew was one of the most prominent and forceful opponents, warning that if bishops came, freedom in the colonies would be seriously delimited. Missionaries of the S.P.G. were quite naturally in the vanguard of the campaign for bishops, but they heightened the alarm of others by arguing that such dignitaries would link the colonies more closely with the mother country. The agitation over bishops intensified colonial resistance to the hated Stamp Act (1765), for it was argued that if Parliament could fix a tax without reference to colonial assemblies, it could also establish the church and send bishops.[1] The debate broadened as conventions of Episcopal clergy campaigned for bishops and were countered by joint Congregational-Presbyterian conferences held annually from 1766 to the outbreak of war. The feelings aroused by the controversy over episcopacy thus played a considerable role in the intensification of the revolutionary spirit.

The passage of the Quebec Act of 1774 further spread alarm in the colonies and heightened determination to resist the mother country. The deep prejudices against 'Romanists' and fears of the loss of freedom at the hands of the Pope's followers were aroused. There was much resentment against the placing of the North-west Territory within Canadian boundaries, blocking western advance, and bringing hated Catholic influence close to American frontiers. When the first Continental Congress met soon after the passage of the Quebec Act, it issued an 'Address to the People of Great Britain' which condemned Parliament for countenancing a religion 'fraught with sanguinary and impious tenets' and responsible for disbursing 'impiety, bigotry, persecution, murder and rebellion through every part of the world'.[2] Small wonder that subsequent appeals for support for the Revolution among the inhabitants of Quebec failed.

In various ways religious factors were woven into the chain of events that caused the American Revolution. In his famous speech before Parliament calling for conciliation with the Americans shortly before hostilities erupted, Edmund Burke stated that the religion most prevalent in the northern tier of the thirteen colonies was 'the dissidence of dissent, and

[1] Bridenbaugh, *Mitre and Sceptre*, esp. ch. IX, 'Bishops and Stamps'.
[2] Charles H. Metzger, *Catholics and the American Revolution: A Study in Religious Climate* (Chicago, 1962), pp. 43 ff.

the protestantism of the protestant religion'. It existed under a variety of denominational forms, he observed, 'agreeing in nothing but in the communion of the spirit of liberty'.[3] And, as Burke knew, many constituents of the southern colonial establishments shared fully in that love of liberty, as illustrated in the opposition many of them publicly showed to a colonial episcopate.

In general there was solid support for the revolutionary cause among the churches, but facile generalizations can be misleading, for the 'clergy and laity of every denomination were in confusion as to their patriotic and religious duties'.[4] The sharpest tensions were felt within the Episcopal churches. In the south the majority, both laymen and clergy, supported the struggle for independence. Probably two-thirds of those who signed the Declaration of Independence were affiliated with the Church of England. In the northern colonies the influence of the high church S.P.G. missionaries was strong, and there the majority opposed the Revolution—many to join the Loyalist migration to Canada. Both because of the tides of feeling against the Church of England as the church of the enemy, and because of the way the destructiveness of war hit some areas heavily, the Anglican churches emerged from the struggle seriously weakened and isolated, so much so that some feared for their recovery.

Certain of the smaller religious bodies were also thrust into a delicate position by the outbreak of hostilities. The Methodist societies, burgeoning in the south in the last phase of the Great Awakenings as the fighting began, faced serious difficulty when John Wesley finally came out in opposition to the Revolution. Only one of his lay missionaries remained active in the colonies—Francis Asbury. Unable to take an oath of loyalty to Maryland because of his religious principles, which included non-combatancy, Asbury could not exercise leadership for several critical years. The movement was then led largely by native lay preachers who favoured independence and guided the societies under their care in that direction. The Lutherans of the middle colonies also faced painful tensions, for many had appreciated the toleration they had enjoyed under Britain and sought to remain neutral, as did their eminent leader, Muhlenberg. Yet several of his sons openly supported the American cause, and so finally did the majority of Lutherans. Churches which historically opposed war—Quakers, Moravians, Mennonites, Dunkers—clung to a stance of neutralism and non-resistance. In a revolutionary struggle

[3] *Old South Leaflets* (Boston, n.d.), viii, 486.
[4] Edward F. Humphrey, *Nationalism and Religion in America, 1774–1789* (New York, 1924, 1965), p. 19.

which divided neighbourhoods and families, and in which passions ran high, the pacifist position was often misunderstood, and the churches which supported it suffered harsh indignities. The Moravians, for example, were distrusted, though a very effective mission among the Indians of Ohio under David Zeisberger helped to keep their converts from warring on the colonists. Yet when a band of pacifist Indian Moravians was at last allowed to return home after having been driven from their lands by the British, they were deliberately slaughtered by a company of American militia.

The churches of the Reformed or Calvinist tradition were predominantly supporters of the cause of independence. A very important contribution to the shaping of the revolutionary spirit was made by those strongly influenced by Calvinist political philosophy. With its stress on obedience to God rather than man, the political teaching of Calvinist leaders justified the right of resistance to tyranny, especially by the lesser magistrates as guardians of the liberties of the people. Particularly as it developed in the British context in the seventeenth and eighteenth centuries, this important religio-political tradition favoured a theory of government in which democratic and aristocratic elements were combined in a system of checks and balances. John Locke, the 'philosopher of the American Revolution', drew on the political capital of the Reformed tradition in his seminal essays. Therefore many Calvinists could accept his political philosophy, even though his theological views were tinged with Enlightenment thought.[5]

It was against this background that the Congregational clergy of New England preached and wrote voluminously on behalf of the rebellion. Bernard Bailyn provided rich documentation for his statement that 'a major source of ideas and attitudes of the Revolutionary generation stemmed ultimately from the political and social theories of New England Puritanism, and particularly from the ideas associated with the covenant theology'. Channelled into the mainstream of eighteenth-century political thinking by generations of preachers, this body of thought was 'received, with minor variations, by almost the entire spectrum of American Protestantism'.[6] The Congregational leadership matched word with

[5] e.g., see George L. Hunt (ed.), *Calvinism and the Political Order* (Philadelphia, 1965), esp. the chapter by Winthrop S. Hudson, 'John Locke: Heir of Puritan Political Theorists', pp. 108–29.

[6] Bernard Bailyn (ed.), *Pamphlets of the American Revolution, 1750–1776*, 2 vols. (Cambridge, Mass., 1965), i, 27. In a heavily documented work, marred somewhat by oversimplifications, Alan Heimert has shown that the 'evangelical Calvinists' in the Edwardsean tradition more than the emerging liberal Calvinists embodied and inspired the thrust toward

deed during the struggle, providing chaplains, officers and men, and material support for the revolutionary armies.

Closely allied in theology and political philosophy to the Congregationalists in the 'spectrum of American Protestantism' were the Presbyterians; indeed, the two denominations were often mentioned together under the latter name. In Presbyterian ranks were many of Scotch-Irish background who blamed England for the troubles that had led to their migration across the Atlantic. Presbyterian bodies properly debated the issues of the war, but the outcome was predictable. The Synod of New York and Philadelphia endorsed the Continental Congress, and the Hanover presbytery in Virginia was the first church group officially to accept the Declaration of Independence. The most influential Presbyterian of the time, John Witherspoon (1723–94), had come from Scotland to be president of the College of New Jersey in 1768. Rising quickly to prominence in state affairs, this former leader of the evangelical 'popular party' of the Church of Scotland was chosen as a delegate to the Congress, and became the only active clergyman to sign the Declaration of Independence.

The Dutch and German Reformed churches also stood close to the Congregationalists and Presbyterians in theological and political thought. The Dutch were quite consistent in backing the Revolution, for they harboured resentment against the English since the conquest of New Netherland the century before. A minority of the German Reformed, who were centred chiefly in Pennsylvania, sought to remain neutral or were openly pro-British, but the majority shared in the Calvinist consensus for independence.

The Calvinist heritage was strong among the Regular Baptists, less so among the Separates. This denominational family was already the third largest in size by the time of the war, but with so many poor and uneducated people in its membership it was lacking in prestige, and in many places was regarded as a menace. Committed as they were to freedom in both religious and civil affairs, Baptists usually favoured the Revolution. Also deeply devoted to the cause of religious freedom, they persistently agitated for broader liberty for all, and for the separation of church and state.

As war neared, the dilemma of the small body of Roman Catholics became acute, for they had been victims of religious prejudice on both sides of the Atlantic. When the Declaration of Independence forced

independence; see *Religion and the American Mind: From the Great Awakening to the Revolution* (Cambridge, Mass., 1966).

a choice, the majority backed the Revolution, in the belief that greater civil liberty would also mean wider religious freedom. Led by several well-known Catholics such as Charles Carroll of Carrollton, a signer of the Declaration, and his cousin John Carroll (1735–1815), a Maryland-born priest and former Jesuit, Catholics served in combatant and non-combatant roles. It was not quite unanimous; a small regiment of Catholic volunteers was raised for the other side during the British occupation of Philadelphia. The role the majority of Catholics played in the Revolution did serve to win for them a larger measure of freedom and acceptance, while the alliance with France brought new prestige and recognition. When in 1779 a priest in a Catholic chapel to which members of the Continental Congress had been invited could speak in celebration of 'that glorious revolution, which has placed the sons of America among the free and independent nations of the earth', and have the event widely reported in the Press, a new day for Catholics was dawning.[7]

The termination of hostilities in 1781, followed by the Treaty of Paris two years later, which set the western boundary at the Mississippi and included the North-west Territory as part of the United States, provided the stage for the revolutionary generation to work out its ideas in the face of perplexing political and economic realities. As the Articles of Confederation proved too weak, a new constitution was drafted in 1787, ratified and put into effect two years later, with the important first ten amendments becoming operative in 1791. State constitutions were also redrawn during the revolutionary epoch. All these changes meant that organized religion was facing a much altered situation in which its ministries were to be exercised. The way the churches dealt with these transformations established patterns of thought and life that long persisted.

One of the most serious contradictions to the achievement of freedom within the new nation was the continuation of slavery, a contradiction that was reflected in the life of the churches. During the revolutionary epoch, slavery seemed to many to be inconsistent with the ideals of liberty and equality. A number of anti-slavery societies were founded. Most of them were gradualist in orientation; some believed that freed Negroes should be returned to Africa. In the 1780s, state laws in some southern states restricted or prohibited the slave trade, though such laws

[7] The sermon by Seraphin Bandol, chaplain to the French minister plenipotentiary, is reprinted in H. Shelton Smith, Robert T. Handy, and Lefferts A. Loetscher, *American Christianity: An Historical Interpretation with Representative Documents*, 2 vols. (New York, 1960–3), i, 448–50.

proved difficult to enforce and some were later repealed. In the northern states, provision was made for the gradual abolition of slavery, though the freed blacks were discriminated against in many ways. When slavery was debated in the Constitutional Convention, the reaction against earlier idealism was evident, and the view of slaves as property dominated the compromises that were made: not for twenty years could a law prohibiting the slave trade be passed. In the churches, especially among Methodists and Presbyterians, moderate anti-slavery sentiments continued to be expressed in sermons and at religious gatherings, but views of Negro inferiority persisted. Only the Quakers made slaveholders choose between their slaves and church membership.[8]

Religious Liberty

Prominent among the developments of the revolutionary epoch was the triumph of religious freedom at the national level. Religious liberty had been in the making for generations, and the process was not completed until later, for three states retained their forms of establishment until the next century, and certain forms of restrictions on religious minorities were stipulated in some state laws. But the provision in Article 6 of the Constitution that 'no religious Test shall ever be required as a Qualification to any Office or public Trust under the United States' and the provision of the First Amendment that 'Congress shall make no law respecting an establishment of religion, or prohibiting the free exercise thereof' set major landmarks in the history of religious liberty. These provisions meant that the churches would increasingly become wholly voluntary institutions, dependent on their ability to reach and persuade free people to join and support them, and that religious pluralism would markedly increase.[9]

Religious toleration and religious liberty are different, for the former grants limited rights to certain groups as a matter of expedience or sufferance, while the latter means that individuals and groups are equal before the law in matters of religion. Historically, however, the two have been closely related; the rise of toleration has often played an important role in the triumph of freedom. The broadening of toleration in the mother country bore some fruit in the colonies. In his massive study of the rise

[8] H. Shelton Smith, *In His Image, But ... Racism in Southern Religion, 1780–1910* (Durham, 1972), chs. I and II.

[9] e.g., see the standard works by Sanford H. Cobb, *The Rise of Religious Liberty in America*, and Anson Phelps Stokes, *Church and State in the United States*, 3 vols. (New York, 1950).

of toleration in England, Wilbur K. Jordan concluded that as early as 1660 the centre of gravity of opinion in the mother country 'had conceded the case for religious toleration, with very few reservations'. It was an 'intensely revolutionary decision', arising out of the conviction that 'had gained strength in English thought that the ends of national life . . . in the modern world could not be attained until the divisive and destructive energies of religious conflict had been tamed by toleration'.[10] The consequences of this important development sometimes affected the colonies in dramatic ways, as when the execution of Quakers on Boston common was halted by the Crown, presaging growing toleration. More often its meaning was exhibited in the more routine business of empire, as when the Lords of Trade in England protested against the persecution of the Awakening leader, Samuel Davies: 'With regard to the affair of Mr. Davies the Presbyterian, as Toleration and a free exercise of religion is so valuable a branch of true liberty, and so essential to the enriching and improving of a Trading Nation, it should ever be held sacred in His Majesty's Colonies.'[11] As toleration slowly broadened, the establishments could no longer effectively stop determined minorities, some of which advocated religious freedom as a matter of principle. There were other reasons for the weaknesses of the establishments, of course, such as the emergence of internal theological differences as in New England, and the failure to secure bishops for Episcopal churches, but their decline led to spreading toleration and an increase in religious pluralism.

Toleration's role in the rise of religious liberty was preparatory, but direct contributions were made by some religious minorities which stood for freedom out of their biblical and theological convictions. Groups stemming from the left wing of Puritanism, especially Separatists, Baptists, and Quakers, not only advocated religious liberty on the basis of Christian principle, but founded colonies in which religious freedom was upheld and in which no church establishments were maintained. Challenging the habits and prejudices of fourteen hundred years in the history of western Christendom, they demonstrated that a peaceful state could survive without state churches. Roger Williams and William Penn, founders of Rhode Island and Pennsylvania, were doubly important—not only as theoreticians of freedom, but as practitioners who put principles to work. In all, four of the thirteen colonies had no religious establishments:

10 Wilbur K. Jordan, *The Development of Religious Toleration in England*, 4 vols. (London, 1932–40), iv, 467.

11 Letter from William Dawson to the Bishop of London, 16 August 1751, in William S. Perry (ed.), *Historical Collections Relating to the American Colonial Church*, 2 vols. (Hartford, 1870), i, 380.

Rhode Island, Pennsylvania, Delaware, and New Jersey. To these refuges came other groups which believed in freedom, especially the Mennonites, children of the radical Reformation, and the German Baptist Brethren or Dunkers, children of radical pietism. Sometimes too much has been claimed for the contributions of these freedom-loving groups, but their witness, often made in the face of pressure and persecution, was important in the final triumph of religious liberty.

Important roles in the rise of religious freedom were played by those who spoke and acted out of the perspectives of the Enlightenment. The principles advocated by eighteenth-century philosophers that the practice of religion should be directed by reason and conviction and not by force or violence, and that therefore its exercise should be free, were accepted not only among the professed Deists and rationalists, but also among growing numbers of those who held to more traditional religious orientations. The position was classically expressed in Thomas Jefferson's famous Virginia Bill for Establishing Religious Freedom. The key passage declared 'That no man shall be compelled to frequent or support any religious worship, place, or ministry whatsoever, nor shall be inforced, restrained, molested, or burthened in his body or goods, nor shall otherwise suffer on account of his religious opinions or belief; but that all men shall be free to profess, and by argument to maintain, their opinions in matters of religion, and that the same shall in no wise diminish, enlarge, or effect their civil capacities'. Characteristically, Jefferson was appealing to as broad a range of opinion as he could.

Rationalists in religion often made common cause with evangelical pietists and sectarians of various persuasions in the pursuit of freedom. Leadership in several of the critical contests for disestablishment at state level was supplied by the rationalists, while popular support came from the others. Despite the vast theological differences between these two main orientations, there was sufficient agreement to make working alliances possible. Both were influenced by an ethical-subjectivist interpretation of religion that was quite different from the objectivism of classical orthodoxy. Both tended to concur that religion was a matter between the individual and his God, that churches were voluntary organizations, that clerical authoritarianism was to be rejected, and that true Christianity should remain close to the simple moral teachings and example of Jesus Christ. These agreements provided enough ground for co-operation in working towards a specific objective.

The ever-increasing religious diversity was probably the single most important factor in the attainment of religious freedom. No communion had anywhere near a majority of the church members at the time the Constitution was framed. The Awakenings had served to increase the number of the disestablished groups. In the country as a whole the majority of the population were not members of any church at all—the most favourable estimates do not suggest that more than ten per cent of the people were church members by 1790. To be sure, church discipline and membership requirements were much higher then than they later came to be, and most congregations had constituencies far larger than their memberships, but still the majority had no significant connection with any religious organization. Their sympathies were generally against the continuation of establishment when the choice was given.

The many forces working for freedom in religion and for the separation of church and state combined in various ways in crucial battles in the states. One of the most important contests was in Virginia, seat of the strongest southern establishment. The stipends for the clergy had been halted during the war, and dissenting ministers were granted the right to officiate at marriages. As happened in other cases, an effort was made to compromise with a 'multiple establishment' in which taxes for religious purposes would be divided among the denominations, but the eloquence of Patrick Henry was not enough to stop the determined drive led by James Madison for disestablishment. Jefferson's Bill for Establishing Religious Freedom was finally passed in 1786. Church of England establishments in other states were terminated in the same period. In the New England states of Massachusetts, Connecticut, and New Hampshire, however, where both orthodox and liberal Congregationalists defended the patterns of establishment, they were retained, with provision for other Protestant denominations to obtain a share in the taxes for their own ministers. By 1791, when the First Amendment became effective, the struggle for religious freedom had been won at national level and in many states, while in the others the direction of change was evident in the recognition of minority rights and the sharing of taxes.

Reorganizing the Churches

The newly won independence of the United States necessitated the reorganization of religious bodies which had had formal ties with institutions in the mother country—Church of England, Methodist, and Roman Catholic. It also provided an occasion for some other churches to reshape their national structures with a view to improving their ministries under the changed conditions—Presbyterian and Reformed bodies carried out such restructuring. Thus while the nation and the states were drafting new constitutions, so were many of the churches.

Anglican churches were almost destroyed during the revolutionary epoch. Organizational patterns, not too effective anyway, were disrupted as the supervision of the Bishop of London, his commissaries, and the missionaries of the S.P.G. were withdrawn. Many of those who had been adherents departed, some because of the disruptions of military activities, others because it seemed unpatriotic to remain in a church with such close connections with England. Some of those who left joined the Methodists, some went to Canada with the Loyalists, while others, influenced by rationalist religious currents, apparently drifted away from church life. The historic tensions between high churchmen and low among those who remained made it difficult for the shattered communion to find a new name and build a new organization.

An important step toward rebuilding came in a gathering in Maryland in 1780. Here low church and lay emphases were strong; in the meeting were twenty-one laymen and three clergymen. A state organization was formed to hold the properties and serve the needs of the church. In this gathering the name 'Protestant Episcopal' was first formally used.

Strikingly different was the first meeting for reorganization in Connecticut three years later, for it was made up of clergymen only, and from its high church viewpoint the first task was to elect a bishop. Samuel Seabury (1729–96), former S.P.G. missionary and British chaplain, was chosen. The English bishops were not able to consecrate him, however, not having the consent of the state, nor being able to waive the oath of allegiance to the Crown. The Scottish non-juring bishops (successors to the bishops who had not been able conscientiously to accept William III as monarch of England in 1689) did not have these constraints, and consecrated Seabury as the first American Episcopal bishop in 1784.

Meanwhile, a mediating position was being developed under the leadership of William White (1748–1836), rector of Christ Church, Philadelphia, and chaplain of Continental Congress. His low church views appeared in an anonymous pamphlet, *The Case of the Episcopal Churches in the United States Considered* (1782), in which he argued that under the circumstances it would be proper for clergy and laity together to elect a titular episcopacy without waiting for succession through other bishops—an event which at that point looked as though it would be long years away. When the Treaty of Paris opened the way for negotiations with the English bishops, however, White withdrew these proposals, and joined with others in calling for the first General Convention of the

Protestant Episcopal Church in the United States of America to meet in Philadelphia in 1785.[12]

Lay and clerical representatives from seven states met at the General Convention, but none was from New England as provision had not been made for a bishop to preside. Seabury was the only possible candidate. The convention called for the election of bishops by the state delegations, and opened negotiations with the English bishops, sending a proposed constitution and a liturgy. Meeting again the next year, the convention learned that it had won the consent of the archbishops of Canterbury and York to make the necessary arrangements in England for the consecration of bishops for the United States. Their constructive criticisms of the proposed documents led to some redrafting. Seabury still remained out of the convention; in a forceful gambit to secure his co-operation it was decided that ministers he ordained would not be accepted in other dioceses as long as he refused to co-operate. Meanwhile, White and Samuel Provoost (1742–1815), rector of Trinity Church in New York, who had been strong proponents of the Revolution, were consecrated in Lambeth chapel in 1787.

The organizational work was completed in the summer of 1789, when the General Convention met again. To meet the objections of Seabury and others, the constitution was amended to provide for a House of Bishops and a House of Deputies in the convention, the latter house including both clergy and laity. By this bicameral arrangement, the tensions between high church and low, between laity and clergy were reasonably handled. The convention then adjourned until the autumn, when Seabury at last came. The constitution was put into final form, providing for regular triennial meetings. A body of canons was prepared, and a revised Book of Common Prayer issued.

For a church which had been so hard hit by the Revolution, this constitutional achievement was considerable. The communion that was to grow on these foundations was quite different in self-understanding from the colonial establishments. As Leonard Bacon later tersely summed it up

[the new Episcopal frame of government] was quite consciously and confessedly devised for the government of a sect, with the full and fraternal understanding that other 'religious denominations of Christians' (to use the favorite American euphemism) 'were left at full and equal liberty to model and organize their respective churches' to suit themselves.[13]

[12] The story is summarized here very compactly; for a fine detailed account see Clara O. Loveland, *The Critical Years: The Reconstitution of the Anglican Church in the United States of America, 1780–1789* (New York, 1956).

[13] Leonard W. Bacon, *A History of American Christianity* (New York, 1900), p. 211.

That a church so recently established could affirm such views points to a significant transition in church life during the revolutionary epoch. Not for some time, however, did the Episcopalians know how durable was the work they had done in the 1780s. At first, the growth was very slow—by 1800 there were only about 12,000 communicants. Discouraged, Bishop Provoost resigned the following year, convinced that the church would die out with the old colonial families.

At the close of the war the Methodists were still only a religious society dependent on the Church of England for the sacraments. In the hands of Asbury and the native preachers the movement continued to thrive through the war, doubling to about 10,000 by 1781. The swift decline of the Episcopal churches sharply reduced sacramental opportunities for the Methodists. With the end of the war, John Wesley in England resumed his authority, and begged the Bishop of London to ordain at least one of his lay preachers for service in the United States, but in vain. Therefore, on the basis of his belief that bishops and presbyters in the ancient church were of one order, and following the example of the Alexandrian church in which for several hundred years presbyters did ordain, in 1784 Wesley joined with James Creighton, like him a presbyter of the Church of England, to set apart Dr. Thomas Coke (1747–1814) as superintendent for America and to ordain Thomas Vasey and Richard Whatcoat as presbyters (or elders) for America. Coke was to serve with Asbury in the oversight of the new church in the United States. Wesley also prepared a liturgy, a hymnbook, and twenty-four doctrinal articles, adapted from the Thirty-nine Articles of the Church of England.

When Coke met with Asbury at Barratt's Chapel in Delaware, Asbury explained that the American preachers would have to approve all these plans. Neither Wesley nor Coke had foreseen this, but in the new nation the 'consent of the governed' had become important in religious as well as in civil affairs. Therefore on Christmas Eve in 1784 the founding conference of the Methodist Episcopal Church was convened at Baltimore. Coke and Asbury were duly elected as superintendents. Asbury was ordained as deacon, elder, and superintendent on successive days, while a dozen others were ordained as elders. A *Form of Discipline* with rules for ministers and members was prepared by the Christmas conference, and one doctrinal article was added to those which Wesley had selected. The governmental plan that was put into effect was highly centralized; the itinerant ministers met regularly in conferences, while Asbury travelled restlessly, overseeing the whole.

The new church was intensely evangelistic and grew with surprising rapidity, especially in the south. By 1790 over 57,000 members were reported. The direct approach of the Methodists evoked the commitment of enthusiastic young preachers, whose zeal for souls gathered little flocks in classes under local leaders at many points on the vast circuits. The 'engagement clause' to follow the commands of the ageing Wesley in matters of church government was set aside by the conference of 1787, though the church had been virtually autonomous since the Christmas conference. Asbury and Coke soon began to call themselves bishops, much to the annoyance of Wesley, but the usage was made official in 1787. Coke actually did not spend much time in America, but travelled among Methodist conferences and missions in various parts of the world. Though this young church arose out of a society within the Church of England, it had such strong indigenous elements from its early days in the colonies, that it had a strong appeal to many Americans.

Roman Catholics emerged from the Revolution still very small numerically but with the older inhibiting and humiliating penal legislation largely removed. They were now recognized as citizens, though strong prejudices against them still flowed through the essentially Protestant culture. Jurisdictionally Catholics had been subject to the vicar-apostolic of London, but that tie was no longer appropriate under independence. In the interim, the elderly Father John Lewis continued as vicar-general, giving what supervision he could to some twenty to twenty-five priests, members of the Jesuit Order until it was suppressed in 1773. Recognizing the need for a stronger administration, John Carroll worked out a Plan of Organization which led to the adoption of a constitution for the body of priests in 1784. Meanwhile, a petition was sent to Rome to request that Lewis be named as superior with certain episcopal powers, especially for confirmation, the blessing of altar-stones and chalices, and the granting of faculties to newly arrived priests. The priests stated that they did not want a bishop set over them, for they feared the reaction of public opinion to the idea of foreign control. Partly because of the advice of Benjamin Franklin, in 1784 Rome named Carroll as superior of the mission in the United States. Carroll was troubled because the decision was made in Rome without proper consultation with the American priests. He carefully sought their advice before accepting the appointment.

As superior, Carroll travelled among his scattered flock, and soon ran into a problem that was long to trouble him and his successors. Perhaps because of the contact with Protestant practices, some of the lay trustees of the newly erected St. Peter's Church in New York claimed the right to appoint parish clergy, but became violently divided over rival candidates.

The problem of 'trusteeism' in that and other situations was complicated by troublesome and inadequate priests, some of whom, it later turned out, had been suspended abroad. At the new Church of the Holy Cross in Boston, in which city mass was first publicly said in 1788, priestly rivalries seriously affected the work. Carroll and others saw the need for broader powers to deal with the mounting problems. Hence at the second meeting of the body of priests in 1786 the Pope was petitioned to appoint as bishop one who would be elected by the American priests. The American Catholics were convinced that a missionary vicariate would not be suited to the situation, for it might bring foreign and poorly informed oversight. They were convinced that a diocese immediately subject to the Holy See was needed for the proper exercise of an informed authority that would be generally acceptable in the new nation. On the advice of the body at Rome responsible for missions, the Congregation for the Propagation of the Faith, Pope Pius VI agreed to the request, and allowed the priests to choose the seat of the new diocese and 'as a special favour and for this first time' to elect the bishop.

Carroll was the obvious choice; he was consecrated at Lulworth Castle in England in 1790; the phrase *exterminare haereticos* was omitted from the episcopal oath. Baltimore became the cathedral city; it was approximately the centre of the vast diocese whose boundaries were coterminous with these of the nation. Carroll proved to be an able leader who laboured to found Catholic institutions and to secure religious Orders. He played an important role in the development of Georgetown College, which opened its doors in 1791, and in the founding that same year of the first Catholic seminary, St. Mary's, staffed by French Sulpicians, who were in need of a refuge outside France because of revolutionary disturbances.

At the first synod of the clergy in Baltimore in 1791, the foundations were laid for the discipline of Catholicism in an effective fusion of Catholic principles with American circumstances.[14] As with other church traditions, there was a blend of faith and culture, and the particular combination of the 1790s, so formative in American Catholic history, was to be challenged many times in the next century by incoming tides of Catholics who were products of other religio-cultural settings.

The choice of Carroll proved to be a particularly good one, for he became a respected figure in American life, and was a sincere believer in liberty who frequently spoke of his 'earnest regard to preserve inviolate

[14] Thomas T. McAvoy, *A History of the Catholic Church in the United States* (Notre Dame, Indiana, 1969), p. 69.

forever in our new empire the great principle of religious freedom'.[15] Though Catholics still had to confront much prejudice, their church emerged from the revolutionary epoch with much greater freedom, a centralized organizational structure, and the developing institutions needed for full Catholic life. For more than a century it was to continue as a missionary church under the general supervision of the Congregation for the Propagation of the Faith.

The development of an independent status and a national organization for the Reformed Dutch Church was largely the work of one man, Dr. John H. Livingston, who had been instrumental shortly before the Revolution in healing the schism between the contending Coetus and Conferentie parties. Native-born but Dutch-educated, Livingston was elected as professor of theology just after the war, and began to give instruction to candidates for the ministry. In time his work developed into the nation's first regular theological seminary at New Brunswick. A few years later the doctrinal and liturgical symbols of the church were translated into English, though the full transition to the use of English in the church was not completed until the nineteenth century. A new constitution to guide an independent church was prepared by a committee under Livingston's leadership by the device of adding explanatory articles to the Articles of Dort on Church Order. Inasmuch as the church had already become largely autonomous, there was no reaction from Holland when the first General Synod of the fully independent communion met in 1793. This strongly Calvinist church remained quite small, and was long centred in New York and New Jersey among those of Dutch ancestry.

The German Reformed Church had also been under the care of the classis at Amsterdam, but the tie was largely formal, relating to the examination of candidates for the ministry. The natural affinities were more with the Lutherans (with whom they jointly founded Franklin College in 1787) and other German groups. After various preliminary steps, in 1793 the Synod of the German Reformed Church in the United States met for the first time and declared its full independence. The transition to the use of English was slower than in the case of the Dutch Church.

Communions that were already independent before the Revolution (Congregational, Presbyterian, Baptist, Lutheran, Quaker) did not need

---

[15] Letter from Pacificus to Mr. Fenno (Publisher), 10 June 1789, in *Gazette of the United States*, 10 June 1789, p. 65, col. 3; cited in Peter Guilday, *The Life and Times of John Carroll*, 2 vols. (New York, 1922), i, 368.

to go through a constitution-making process, but the Presbyterians, characteristically concerned about proper governmental structures, did seize the opportunity to reorganize. The Synod of New York and Philadelphia, created by the reunion of 1758 which healed the schism caused by the Great Awakenings, was really a presbytery of the whole, which all ministers were expected to attend, and to which all churches were to send lay elders. Attendance declined, and the structure proved to be more and more inadequate for an expanding communion. As new presbyteries were erected, some far from Philadelphia where synod usually met, the difficulties increased. Accordingly, under the leadership of Witherspoon and Dr. John Rodgers, pastor of the First Presbyterian Church of New York, a process was begun that ended with the adoption of carefully drawn standards for the doctrine, government, discipline, and worship of the Presbyterian Church in the United States of America in 1788. In reordering their standards, the Presbyterians were guided by the Reformed systems of doctrine, discipline, and order as developed in Europe, but they adapted them for their own purposes—the Westminster Confession, for example, was adapted in certain ways, especially concerning the relationship of the civil magistracy to the church. The particular historical development of the church from simple to more complex structures, from congregations to presbyteries, then to synods and finally to an assembly over the span of many decades left its mark. The rights to license and ordain ministers remained with the presbyteries. This allowed the communion to grow administratively even as it remained divided theologically, as the major theological parties entrenched themselves at presbytery level.

The first General Assembly met in 1789 and annually thereafter; four synods and sixteen presbyteries were authorized. Though perhaps not quite as large numerically as the New England Congregational churches with which it had close affinities, Presbyterianism was geographically more widespread, and having so strongly backed the Revolution seemed to be in an especially strategic position in the new nation.

The Lutheran churches had no jurisdictional ties abroad, and a sense of the autonomy of the local congregations was strong. Less than half of the congregations were related to the synod which Muhlenberg had organized in 1748 and which later became the Ministerium of Pennsylvania. A separate organization for the churches of New York was set up in 1786; then the Pennsylvania Ministerium reorganized itself, admitting lay delegates to the annual meetings. New efforts at national organization did not begin until the next century.

Facing the Challenges

The various moves towards reorganization that have been surveyed took place during a difficult period for religion. Not only had the war brought destruction and scattered congregations, but the general cultural atmosphere in the revolutionary epoch was somewhat unfriendly to 'revealed' religion. The sufferings and brutalities of the war, combined with a concentration of public attention on political questions, had served to weaken concern with spiritual and ecclesiastical questions. The increase of interest in rational and natural religion was often at the expense of the churches, and a militant Deism was being actively if sporadically promoted. The popularity of the thought of the Enlightenment was heightened through the presence of French military officers. In the colleges especially a Deism which was anticlerical and anti-establishment in tone was widespread. In 1784 Ethan Allen, who had won fame as the hero of Ticonderoga, issued *Reason the Only Oracle of Man*, the first book published in the United States openly to attack Christianity. Elihu Palmer, Dartmouth graduate and former Baptist minister, crusaded through the land organizing little deistic societies, while Tom Paine's *The Age of Reason* (1794) caused much discussion. His earlier achievements as a pamphleteer of the Revolution helped to win readers for his book, which was written primarily in response to counter-revolutionary forces in France. In the early days of ferment following the war, the ideas and trappings of revealed religion seemed in many quarters to be quite archaic, at a time when there was a strong cultural tendency to look ahead to the triumph of reason and natural religion in the new age of freedom. Though religious revivals were reported at various places during the last quarter of the eighteenth century, especially in the south, they did not then merge and swell into a general Awakening.

These trends presented the churches with their major challenge, and not until the 1790s did the outlines of an effective response appear. The excesses of the French Revolution, and the blood-bath of the guillotine produced a startled reaction—and gave the exponents of revealed religion a needed opening. They pointed to the Reign of Terror in France as the outcome of deistic religion which would inevitably lead to infidelity and brutality. Though they saw the need of a new awakening of religion, the leaders of the Congregational and Presbyterian churches especially remembered with some discomfort the excesses and disorders of the Great Awakenings and were not anxious to let them emerge again. Yet serious illness demands strong medicine; church leaders felt they could use the methods of religious revival in an orderly way in the interests of informed faith against the destructive dangers of militant Deism.

A conspicuous leader in working out the new revivalism was Timothy Dwight (1752–1817), grandson of Jonathan Edwards, Congregational pastor, former chaplain in the revolutionary army, poet, and educator, who in 1795 became president of his Alma Mater, Yale. Dwight's approach was to mount a frontal attack on the deistic enemy. In such bold addresses as *The Nature and Danger of Infidel Philosophy* (1797) and *The Duty of Americans at the Present Crisis* (1798), Dwight contrasted Christianity and infidelity, depicting one in a very favourable and the other in a very unattractive light—and then called for decision. Both among the major Calvinist churches and the smaller, more pietistic bodies this approach commended itself, and the first wave of a new outpouring of revivals, the 'Second Great Awakening', was just breaking into national prominence at the turn of the century. In the new atmosphere of freedom in which churches were to survive through voluntary means, persuasion, and action, many Protestant leaders were convinced that the enemies in the way of Christian advance—apathy and infidelity, Deism and the devil—could best be met by using the ways of revivalism. They were seeking a course between the emotional excesses of the Great Awakenings and the spiritual deadness that allowed Deism and infidelity to spread, and they believed they had learned the lesson and could keep the new revival under firm control.

This reaction against 'infidelity' led to an important shift in alignments, significant for the understanding of American religious history ever since. The co-operation of rationalists with pietists had been in part responsible for one of the major religious developments of the eighteenth century—the triumph of religious liberty. But, as Sidney E. Mead brilliantly explained, that alliance was largely broken, and a new one between orthodox and pietists developed in the crisis of the 1790s, as the view that deistic teaching led to social disorders and disasters was industriously promulgated. 'With the realignment of pietist-sectarians and traditionalists against the rationalists', wrote Mead, '. . . came the second major development in this period, the birth of the new revivalism'.[16] The new alignments were not often formalized, perhaps were not often fully recognized, but they displayed themselves in the way the various groups went about their tasks. The new wedding of interests was largely a matter of expediency, for the theological and ecclesiological differences were not seriously probed in depth, but were bypassed in the excitements

---

[16] *The Lively Experiment: The Shaping of Christianity in America* (New York, 1963), p. 52.

and oversimplifications of crusading. The new arrangements were possible because both traditionalists and pietists had changed during the revolutionary period, the older orthodox churches facing up to the meaning of religious liberty and voluntaryism, the more sectarian bodies recognizing the importance of contributing to the maintenance of the moral and social order. In general, churches and sects were taking on some of the characteristics of each other and were both becoming denominations. Differences persisted, of course, but similarities increased.

A challenge of a different kind lay before the churches in the rapid opening of vast new western territories to be saved from barbarism and superstition, and their growing populations to be won for Christ. Following the Revolution came a press westward across the barrier of the Appalachian Mountains. In 1790, some 5 per cent of the total population of about 4,000,000 had already settled on the other side of the mountains, especially in the western parts of Pennsylvania and Virginia, and in what soon became the states of Kentucky (1792) and Tennessee (1796). Though the magnitude of the westward thrust was soon to dwarf all that had gone before, already by the dawn of the new century the patterns of Protestantism were being put to the test. Those denominations that took seriously the challenge of the west and developed methods of meeting it were to become the giants. The churches that confidently accepted religious freedom and the voluntary style, that employed the message and methods of revivalism, and that exhibited a sense of mission, grew dramatically, especially as they were inspired by a renewed expectancy in the coming of the millennium.

The war and its outcome had again raised millennial hopes. Manifestly God had been guiding his chosen nation, so many preachers declared, and soon he would bring about that glorious new day so long foretold. As one of the pulpiteers put it during the first flush of victory, it would be

A *day* whose evening shall not terminate in night; but introduce that joyful period, when the outcasts of Israel, and the dispersed of Judah, shall be restored; and with them, the fulness of the Gentile world shall flow to the standard of redeeming love: and the nations of the earth, become the kingdom of our Lord and Saviour. Under whose auspicious reign holiness shall universally prevail, and the noise and alarm of war be heard no more.[17]

The millennial hope was expressed in various ways, for the biblical materials

[17] George Duffield, *A Sermon Preached in the Third Presbyterian Church* (Philadelphia, 1784), pp. 16–18, as quoted by Perry Miller, 'From the Covenant to the Revival', in James W. Smith and A. Leland Jamison (eds.), *The Shaping of American Religion* (Princeton, 1961), p. 348.

from which all drew could be interpreted in differing ways. However it was expressed, it helped the Protestants through difficult times, revived their enthusiasm to do battle with unbelief and infidelity, to press into the western wilderness in search of souls, to redouble their missionary efforts in an effort to prepare the way for the Lord's coming.

Some of the denominations planted the missionary concern deep into the life of their churches—the Methodist circuit system was a conspicuous example. It was one reason why that young church grew so rapidly as circuits multiplied in the western territories, even as they moved steadily forward into the older sections where they had not previously existed. Methodist preachers reached Kentucky as early as 1784, moving along the trail cut by Daniel Boone. In a quite different way, the Baptist churches had learned to blend their Calvinist and revivalist heritages effectively. Joint efforts of Baptists of differing sections and heritages in the struggle for religious freedom helped in that process; in 1787, for example, the Regular and Separate Baptists of Virginia merged. From 1780 to 1800 not a year went by without the gathering of a new Baptist association somewhere in the land—by 1800 there were nearly fifty of them. The Baptists lacked the centralized system of the Methodists, but they had a remarkable flexibility, for Baptist churches could be quickly gathered wherever their people went. Qualifications for ministry focused on a deeply felt personal call, so that many a layman without formal training was ordained by his congregation, thereafter to combine preaching with farming or some other means of livelihood. As population moved westward, crude church buildings appeared, often by stretches of water suitable for the baptism of believers by immersion.

The missionary thrust of Methodists and Baptists won growing numbers of blacks into their ranks during the revolutionary epoch. Because of their willingness to accept blacks as preachers and their emphasis on congregational self-government, the Baptists especially attracted both enslaved and freed Negroes. The first black Baptist congregation on record was gathered at Silver Bluff, South Carolina, by eight slaves on the eve of the Revolution. Other congregations were formed by 1800, while a number of benevolent and mutual aid societies in the cities of the north-east were really quasi-churches. Slaves also became members of older churches; some southern congregations had a large percentage of black members.

Among the Methodists, Richard Allen, who had purchased his own freedom in the year of his conversion, 1777, won the favourable attention of Francis Asbury. When the St. George Church at which he and other blacks worshipped in Philadelphia determined to segregate them and pulled them from their knees during prayer, they withdrew. Allen organized and dedicated the Bethel Church in 1794, and was later ordained by Asbury. At first this church, and others like it, was part of the Methodist Episcopal Church; later such congregations formed an independent African Methodist Episcopal Church. In a parallel way, a black separation from the John Street Methodist Episcopal Church in New York in 1796 was the seed out of which the African Methodist Episcopal Zion Church was to grow. By 1800 perhaps 50,000 blacks—about five per cent of their total number, and also about five per cent of the estimated total number of church members—had been converted to the Christian faith. Despite the persistence of racialism among most white Christians, the gospel had become an effective bearer of life and meaning for growing numbers of black Christians.

Toward the end of the revolutionary epoch the new missionary concerns were being implemented through the organization of missionary societies. Some of these were denominational in character—in 1798, for example, the General Association of Connecticut voted also to become the Missionary Society of Connecticut, and sent out ministers on short tours to frontier regions and among Indians. Other missionary societies were non-denominational—in 1796, the New York Missionary Society enjoyed the support of Presbyterian, Reformed, and Baptist bodies. The dream of a larger unity of Protestants in evangelistic and missionary efforts was part of the millennial hope; by the 1790s the co-operation of Christians of diverse backgrounds seemed to be a sign of promise. Alan Heimert observed that 'it was during the imperial crisis that the evangelical mind glimpsed the bright prospect of uniting the people of America in affectionate union'; in the period just after the war steps toward realizing that prospect could be undertaken.[18]

In this period missionary efforts were continued for the conversion of the Indians, of whom there were an estimated 250,000 in the nation in 1790. The S.P.G. and the New England Company could no longer operate when the ties with Britain were severed, and the Boston group that had co-operated with the Society in Scotland for Propagating Christian Knowledge chartered a new Society for the Propagation of the Gospel among the Indians and Others in New England. Missionary efforts among Indians had to operate within the realities of the national determination to press into western territory. The government operated on the principle that the Indian tribes owned the lands on which they lived,

18 *Religion and the American Mind*, p. 398.

and made treaties with them to clear the way for white settlement. It was hoped that the Indians would become 'civilized', and missions were to play an important part in this process. For the missionary movement, conversion and civilizing were seen as parts of one process, and conversion meant a transformation of native existence into accommodation to western ways. But the flood of land-hungry settlers swept over treaties and good intentions, and new tragic chapters were added to the story of conquest and displacement. Some tribes were backed by the Spaniards or by the British in their continued resistance to American advance; the Tennessee militia had subdued the tribes on its frontiers by 1794, the same year that the Indians in the Ohio region were decisively defeated at the Battle of Fallen Timbers. Missionary work was difficult under those conditions, yet devout missionaries were able to communicate the gospel in some of the tribes.

The Roman Catholic minority accommodated itself with growing effectiveness to the atmosphere and the opportunities of the young nation. In McAvoy's words, 'Somehow the notion was accepted that the United States was a Protestant country in which the small Catholic group had full legal freedom'.[19] As the new freedom was being enjoyed, ways of maintaining Catholicism through voluntary support and missionary outreach were being tested. Early in his administration, Carroll sent priests, most of them refugees from the French Revolution, to continue the old missions in the north-west, and dispatched Stephen T. Badin (1768–1853), the first seminarian ordained to the priesthood in the United States, to Kentucky.

To glance quickly at the continental setting, Catholics in other areas which were eventually to fall within the boundaries of the United States— Florida, Louisiana territory, the Pacific coast—were then under Spanish administration, and were suffering under the decline that had overcome that empire. In distant California, however, a famous chain of missions was being stretched under the leadership of a remarkable Franciscan friar, Junipero Serra (1713–84). Beginning at San Diego in 1769, and extending northward to San Francisco he established nine missions, which gathered Indians under their paternalistic care. After Serra's death, his successors continued to add a dozen more missions to this impressive thrust. It was part of the effort of Spain to counter the Russian advance in the North American continent. Following the explorations of Vitus Bering, Russian traders in Alaska were reaching down the west coast. Extensive Eastern Orthodox missions among Eskimos and Indians waited

---

[19] *A History of the Catholic Church in the United States*, p. 74.

until the arrival of ten Russian Orthodox monks on Kodiak Island in 1794. Thus the third main branch of Christianity entered the North American scene.

New Religious Movements

The number of denominations increased during the revolutionary epoch. Dramatic increase in the number of denominations was to come later, but the future was already prefigured. One of the most distinctive groups, popularly known as the Shakers, had antecedents in a French inspirationist sect which took refuge in England and there was influenced by former Quakers. A convert, Ann Lee Stanley (1736–84), claimed that during a stay in prison it was revealed to her that the 'mystery of iniquity' lay in sexual intercourse. Acknowledged by the Shakers as their spiritual mother in Christ, she with some of her followers were driven by persecution to America in 1774. Settling near Albany, New York, Mother Ann Lee undertook preaching tours and won new converts to the Shaker way of withdrawal from the world, celibacy, and perfection. In 1787, after her death, the Millennial Church, or the United Society of Believers in Christ's Second Appearing, was formally organized under an Eldership. It was affirmed that Mother Ann had been the second appearance of Christ, the second incarnation of the Holy Spirit in which the female element in the Godhead continued the work begun by Jesus Christ. A communal style of living was adopted; soon ten communities were flourishing, as converts were won in the wake of local revivals. Under the leadership of Elder Joseph Meacham rules for a regulated existence were prepared, and the characteristic ritualistic dance, the source of the group's popular name, became standard practice.

There were certain similarities between the Shakers and a smaller and shorter-lived group that gathered around Jemima Wilkinson (1752–1819), the 'Publick Universal Friend'. Following an illness, she took her distinctive title and began an itinerant ministry in her native Rhode Island. Her Quaker background with some New Light overtones was evident in her mystical preaching, which attracted a following in southern New England, leading to the formation of several congregations. Celibacy was encouraged but not required. In the late 1780s she left New England, allowing her movement there to decline, to build a community at Jerusalem in western New York, where she lived out her days.

Two new denominations in which the influence of Enlightenment thought was evident made their first appearance in this period. John Murray (1741–1815), an Englishman who had been inspired by both

Whitefield and James Relly, an advocate of universal salvation, came to America in 1770. In New England, where already universalist sentiments had been expressed within the Congregational churches, he gathered several congregations that claimed the name Universalist. The movement expanded when a former Baptist, Elhanan Winchester, independently espoused the Universalist position. In 1785 and 1790 conferences of Universalist churches were held. Originally Trinitarian in emphasis, early in the next century the growing denomination moved theologically closer to Unitarianism.

Though the great expansion of Unitarianism was to come in the next century when the Congregational churches divided, the first congregation to become formally Unitarian was King's Chapel, which had been the first Anglican church in New England. Under the leadership of a youthful lay reader from Harvard, James Freeman, references to the Trinity were dropped from the liturgical forms. Both of these liberal trends were institutional manifestations of a rationalist and anti-Calvinist spirit, which was gaining strength in the closing years of the century.

Various reasons were given for some other schisms. Anti-Calvinism also played a role in the emergence of the Free Will Baptists in 1779 in northern New England under the leadership of Benjamin Randall. He was influenced by the writings of Henry Alline, the Awakener of Nova Scotia, and was especially emphatic in rejecting the doctrine of the perseverance of the saints. During the Revolution, a Mennonite split occurred over whether or not war-taxes could be paid, while a group of Quakers who argued that armed resistance was justifiable under certain conditions left the main body of Friends to form the 'Free Quakers', which survived well into the nineteenth century. A serious setback for the rapidly growing Methodists came when James O'Kelly, one of those ordained at the Christmas conference, argued at the General Conference of 1792 that a preacher dissatisfied with his appointment by the bishop had the right of appeal to the conference. When his reform was rejected, he and thousands of followers in Virginia and North Carolina withdrew to form the Republican Methodist Church, soon renamed simply The Christian Church. Thus the organizational diversity of Christianity in America was increasing, in part through schisms within denominations, so that the term 'denominational family' becomes useful to identify a tradition divided into more than one organizational entity.

By the dawn of the new century, the Christian churches, after a period of difficulty and decline, were again on the upswing—indeed, on the edge of a great period of revival. The once vast differences between the more traditional, orthodox churches and the pietistic and left-wing sects had narrowed as both were becoming denominations. Though the denominations were in general agreement in their resistance to militant Deism, they lived in a nation in which the philosophy of the Enlightenment had been influential in guiding a revolution and in shaping national self-understanding. The churches accepted more of the perspectives of the Enlightenment than they knew or were willing to admit. For despite the great differences between Enlightenment philosophy and revealed theology, the two did have certain things in common: concern for the moral order, for an orderly society, for the translation of ideas into practice, and for the continual elevation of humankind in a glorious future. An America at once secular and religious was emerging; liberal democracy and religious piety were found to be compatible. A democratic society in which religious bodies would have no official preference or support seemed to offer a successful way of dealing with a variety of churches. Churches were discovering that they could relate to the spread of democratic ideas, not only by external adjustment but internally by taking the ideas and practices of representative democracy into themselves in their new constitutions. Indeed, they found that the rise of popular government made it all the more important that they do their work well, so that the body of the people be properly influenced by religious and moral sentiments. Between secular and Christian America were to be many tensions, but growing numbers of Americans grew up in both worlds with little sign of strain. The pragmatic quality of American life stems in part from the partnership between democracy and the churches struck during the revolutionary epoch.

VI

CRUSADING FOR AN AMERICAN
PROTESTANT COMMONWEALTH
(1800–60)

FROM the beginning of the nineteenth century up until the decade of the Civil War, the United States expanded spectacularly in area and in population. In 1800 the nation's main western boundary was at the Mississippi River, but within half a century the Louisiana Purchase, the acquisition of Florida, Texas, and Oregon, and the cession of much of the south-west by Mexico increased the geographical extent of the nation more than two and a half times. In the years from 1800 to 1860, the population increased from about 5 million to more than 31 million. The natural increase was supplemented by immigration, chiefly from the British Isles, Germany, and Scandinavia. The great migration to the west that had begun soon after the Revolution increased markedly. Indian tribes were pushed back, and many of them were forced into reservations. New states were carved out and admitted to the union; by 1830 more than a third of the population lived in the nine states west of the Allegheny mountains. In the context of this expansion in territory and population, there occurred many dramatic and tumultuous events of American religious history, which led to realignments in the nation's religious forces.

The Second Great Awakening

No more than 10 per cent—probably less—of Americans in 1800 were members of congregations. In most parts of the country there were too few churches to provide for the religious needs of the population. The central task before the churches was to win new converts and to found new congregations. Within many Protestant bodies, the revival spirit of the pre-Revolutionary days was kindled again in what is often called 'the Second Great Awakening'. Building on the Evangelical Awakenings of Britain and of colonial America, nineteenth-century revivalism focused theology and practice on the experience of the new birth and on the gathering of converts into churches. In certain respects similar to the older Awakenings, the new revivalism was much more self-consciously controlled as its leaders concerned themselves with methods of securing believers for their particular apprehensions of the Christian faith. The Awakeners were convinced that the authority for their work lay in the Bible, and that their view of the church as a voluntary society of the saved for which the primary task was to save others was indeed biblical. The new Awakenings precipitated significant shifts, schisms, and realignments in the denominational patterns of American life, and initiated a period in which revivalistic Protestantism deeply influenced the mind and heart of the nation.

Some denominations had few, if any, reservations in embracing the revivalistic, pietistic way of understanding and transmitting Christian faith. The churches which accepted the new evangelicalism grew with surprising rapidity—but were themselves changed in the process. With its direct, forceful appeal for decisions, revivalism neglected many traditional theological concerns and stimulated sharp controversies. Some of the older denominations divided, and new ones committed to the revival were founded.

The patterns of revivalism varied somewhat in detail from denomination to denomination, and from section to section. There were great differences between the intense but orderly Awakenings in New England and the spectacular camp-meeting revivals of the western frontiers, yet they both played major roles in the resurgence and realignment of Protestantism in the new century. In the older communities of the east and south as well as in the areas of the west just being opened, revivals were ardently sought in order to counter the presumed threats of Deism and infidelity, of moral decay and spiritual lethargy—and to build up the households of faith.

Scattered signs of renewal had begun to appear in New England in the 1790s. The leaders of the churches remembered not only the ingatherings of the Great Awakenings, but also the excesses, the threats to order, and the ensuing divisions. The Congregational ministers who stood in the Edwardsean, 'new divinity' tradition worked for revival, striving to keep it within the orderly patterns of churches still established by law and committed to historic Calvinism. In town after town, especially in Connecticut and Massachusetts, signs of revival appeared in the closing years of the century. Following the examination of the state of the soul required by tradition, hundreds professed conversion. Then, just as the excitement of Awakening began to wane in the churches, revival occurred on the campus of Yale College, winning a quite considerable number of students by 1802. Yale's president, Timothy Dwight, had laboured for this harvest ever since taking his post there in 1795. He presented his whole theological system—one that supported the revival emphasis—in a four-year cycle of sermons in the college chapel.[1] Dwight also trained some of his ablest students to carry on the crusade, especially Lyman Beecher (1776–1863), a great organizer; the biblical scholar and teacher, Moses Stuart (1780–1858); and Nathaniel William Taylor (1786–1858), pastor of New Haven's Center Church and later first professor of didactic theology at Yale's new department of theology (1822).

Old Calvinist and Edwardsean theological parties joined forces to support the Awakening. Two Massachusetts pastors, Jedediah Morse (1761–1826), also famous as the 'father of American geography', and Leonard Woods (1774–1854) worked out an alliance between the two groups that led to the opening in 1808 of Andover Theological Seminary, which quickly assumed a major role in the education of Protestant ministers. Leaders of both parties fully intended to maintain the Calvinism of their inherited system, yet the new attention to the revival contributed to certain shifts in theological perspective. Taylor sought to be faithful to the Calvinist tradition in his restatement of it, but in his debates with the Unitarians who were then capturing some of the prominent New England congregations, he conceded that human free agency had not been wholly lost in the fall, and encouraged the wise use of freedom in matters of religion.[2]

Some saw that an important theological shift was taking place. The famous evangelist Asahel Nettleton, for example, was temporarily dislodged from his roots in Old Calvinism, and was willing to let some of the old distinctiveness lapse. As he wrote to Beecher, 'Why not take this ground with Unitarians? We feel no concern for Old Calvinism. Let them dispute it as much as they please: we feel bound to make no defence. Come home to the *evangelical system* now taught in New England.'[3] Even in its cautious, controlled New England form, revival practice encouraged theological modification; the 'evangelical system' was recognizably different from the older Calvinism. While some were pleased with the shift, interpreting it as an advance in keeping with the mood of the times,

[1] Published posthumously as *Theology: Explained and Defended, in a Series of Sermons*, 5 vols. (Middletown, Conn., 1818–19).
[2] See Sidney E. Mead, *Nathaniel William Taylor, 1786–1858, A Connecticut Liberal* (Chicago, 1942). The rise of Unitarianism will be discussed in the next chapter.
[3] Charles Beecher (ed.), *Autobiography, Correspondence, &c. of Lyman Beecher, D.D.*, 2 vols. (London, 1863), i, 491–2.

others opposed it sharply. Some of those most disturbed by the new trends founded in 1833 a new theological seminary which eventually was located at Hartford, Connecticut. The founders viewed the new institution as necessitated by the changes at Yale, as earlier those who founded Yale had been reacting against the 'liberalization' of Harvard.

Similar patterns of Awakening also appeared in the other seaboard states and in the old north-west. As New Englanders migrated into New York state, some moving further west into Ohio, they carried the forms of churchmanship to which they had become attached. The close historic relationship between Congregationalists and Presbyterians, strengthened now by the Plan of Union, contributed to the spread of the revival spirit among Presbyterians. The Plan of Union was initially an agreement between the Presbyterian General Assembly and the Congregational General Association of Connecticut in 1801 to provide for intimate collaboration in the planting of new churches, especially in New York and the old north-west. By 1830 the Congregational associations of the other five New England states had accepted the plan, and provided ways for the two communions to merge their forces in forming congregations in new settlements. A supplementary 'Accomodation Plan' of 1808 allowed a Congregational association to be received as a constituent branch of a Presbyterian synod, while its local churches retained the Congregational name and practices. As a result, many persons of Congregational background entered Presbyterian structures. A number of problems eventually emerged, but in the early decades the Plan of Union was an important factor in spreading the Awakening. Andover and Yale men carried the revival into Presbyterian churches of both east and west.

Methodists and Baptists in New England also welcomed the Second Awakening, gaining numerous converts and gathering many congregations. While the more spectacular growth of these bodies was on the frontiers, they were also expanding in the eastern states, in part by drawing from other churches. For example, the Methodists had formed their New England Conference in 1796; in the next several decades they industriously organized new circuits across the region. William G. McLoughlin has compared the numerical advances of Baptists and others in the two Awakenings, concluding that 'between 1795 and 1820 the Second Great Awakening produced an equally rapid growth among the Baptists and other dissenters at the expense of the Congregationalists, but in this movement the Baptists had to share a larger number of the converts with the Methodists and Universalists'.[4]

---

[4] *New England Dissent*, ii, 699.

The most tumultuous and controversial aspects of early nineteenth-century revivalism were in the south and the old south-west. Some preliminary movements prepared the way for the major revivals that were to follow. In 1787 at Hampden-Sidney College and Washington College in Virginia, both of Presbyterian orientation, revivals of religion occurred. In the early 1790s local Awakenings were influential in North Carolina. Many of the leaders and converts of these episodes later moved west, sowing seeds that were to bear much fruit.[5] The social setting of frontier revivalism was quite different from that of the east, however, for life on the frontier was often hard, lonely, and dangerous. The civilizing amenities of the older sections were usually at a minimum. When crowds gathered at some appointed place, the preachers knew that it might be some time before most of the listeners had another opportunity to hear the gospel preached, so that the call for decision seemed especially urgent. In such settings, revivals sometimes reached peaks of undisciplined emotion. Presbyterian, Methodist, and Baptist leaders laboured among the growing number of settlers in Kentucky and Tennessee, often working together in the effort to gather folk from a large area to a central place for several days of services. The frontier camp-meeting arose out of these joint endeavours.

James McGready (1758?–1817), a fiery, Scotch-Irish Presbyterian who migrated to Kentucky in 1796 and took charge of three churches, prayed and preached for a revival of religion. In 1800, in co-operation with other ministers, a four-day 'sacramental meeting' was held at McGready's Red River Church. The shouted exhortations were matched by the sobs and screams of those convicted of sin, many of whom went on to the joy of conversion. Plans were speedily made to gather another revival during the last week in July at another of McGready's churches, Gasper River, the participants to camp out around the building. When the worshippers were far too many to be contained inside, a space outside was hastily cleared and fitted with a rough platform and simple log benches. A Methodist preacher, John McGee, delivered an especially vivid sermon, toward the end of which the cries of the distressed almost drowned out the exhorter. Revival-minded preachers of various traditions quickly seized on the camp-meeting and co-operated in arranging for other such affairs in Kentucky and Tennessee.[6] The most famous of all such gatherings took

---

[5] John B. Boles, *The Great Revival, 1787–1805: The Origins of the Southern Evangelical Mind* (Lexington, Ky., 1972).

[6] Charles A. Johnson, *The Frontier Camp Meeting: Religion's Harvest Time* (Dallas, 1955), pp. 25–40.

place in August 1801 at Cane Ridge, Kentucky, under the leadership of a McGready convert, Barton Warren Stone (1772–1844). Here thousands congregated as simultaneous preaching went on from various stands about the camp grounds; many, including some who had been sceptical unbelievers, were plunged into anguish over their soul's state and then brought to confession of faith amid shouts of joy.

At Cane Ridge, as at other camp-meetings in the early years of the century, there appeared such physical manifestations as falling, jerking, rolling, dancing, barking, and laughing. Opponents of the revival dwelt on these extremes in their criticism of the exciting events. The 'bodily exercises' did soon diminish, though the camp-meetings themselves went on for decades. Some immoral behaviour did take place as critics were quick to charge, but the evidence indicates that the camp-meetings generally improved the moral tone of the frontier.

The two bodies which soon became (and have remained) by far the largest Protestant denominational families in North America capitalized on the power of the revivals. The Methodists were immediately drawn to the camp-meetings, and worked them into their carefully supervised system. They skilfully joined advance planning and spontaneity with a preachable theology which affirmed that free grace was available to all. Francis Asbury was a great believer in the camp-meetings and urged their use in the north and east as well as in the south and west—his journal describes one not far from New York City. The key figures in the Methodist advance were the circuit riders, devout, courageous, enthusiastic young men. They covered their long routes perseveringly, stirring up revivals where they could, and following up their converts in remote places.

The Baptists made full use of frontier evangelism in quite different ways. They lacked the strong central organization of the Methodists, their great rivals, but had an advantage in that congregations could be quickly formed around a small handful of convinced believers who then could call and quickly ordain a gifted layman as preacher. Through the week such a man would normally earn his living as did other members of the flock, but on Sunday, making up by sincerity what he lacked in formal training, he exhorted his congregation, using images and idioms fully understandable to the people. Baptist doctrine remained clearly Calvinistic, but with some tolerance in many places for the 'general' view that Christ died for all men. Baptist churches sprang up quickly in new settlements as they appeared, and new associations of churches provided some ties with the over-all movement. Though the Baptist preachers co-operated in camp-meetings with other revivalists, they withdrew for the sacramental occasions, and insisted strictly on the baptism of believers by immersion. There were many points of similarity in the evangelical spirit and teachings of Methodists and Baptists, but there was also intense competition.

Presbyterian ministers who were conspicuous in the revivals were often regarded with suspicion by their colleagues, both because of the emotionalism of the camp-meetings and because of their purported Arminian theological tendencies. In their overriding concern for the salvation of souls, the Awakeners were not deeply concerned about the traditional educational standards for ordination. One of the most effective among them, Richard McNemar (?–1839), was accused of theological error. When his case was being brought before the Synod of Kentucky in 1803, he and four others (including Barton Stone) protested and resigned to form the independent Springfield Presbytery. They resolved to follow only the teachings of the Bible, and rejected man-made patterns in their religious lives. In less than a year these 'New Lights' dissolved their new presbytery to take simply the name 'Christian'. When McNemar moved on to Shakerism, Stone became the leader of the new Christian movement, and his growing number of followers was gathered into congregationally governed churches.

Soon after the New Light schism, the Synod of Kentucky had to deal with another group of its members who believed deeply in revivalism, among them some of the most conspicuous of the camp-meeting leaders. They had gained control of the Cumberland Presbytery, and needing ministers to keep the revival going and to care for converts, put field ability ahead of full formal education in ordaining Finis Ewing and others. Censured by the synod, the majority of the presbytery formed themselves into an unofficial council and appealed to the General Assembly. When that failed, they organized themselves in 1810 into the independent Cumberland Presbytery, which expanded into the Cumberland Presbyterian Church. These several schisms dampened the enthusiasm of the main body of Presbyterians for frontier revivalism, and that communion was soon outdistanced numerically by her Methodist and Baptist rivals.

Another schism, whose significance only became evident much later, was not from the main Presbyterian body but from the conservative Seceder Presbyterians. Thomas Campbell (1763–1854) became troubled by the exclusive spirit of his church soon after coming from Ireland to western Pennsylvania. Gathering his followers into an independent 'Christian Association of Washington' in 1809, he prepared a 'Declaration and

Address' to explain that the new association hoped to avoid partisan theological strife by promoting 'simple evangelical Christianity'. In quest of the 'restoration of primitive Christianity', Campbell chose as a watchword of his new movement, 'Where the Scriptures speak we speak; where they are silent we are silent.' It was hoped that the various branches of Christendom might be reunited by the restoration of primitive apostolic patterns.

Leadership in the new movement was taken by Thomas's son Alexander Campbell (1788–1866) after his arrival from Scotland in 1809. Two years later the followers were gathered into the Brush Run Church. Scriptural study led to the acceptance of the baptism of believers by immersion, and hence the new congregation joined the Redstone Baptist Association in 1813. The younger Campbell grew uncomfortable with the Calvinism and associationalism of the Baptists. By the late 1820s the 'Reformers', now deployed in many congregations, were again moving toward independence. Stressing the authority of the *New* Testament, Campbell repudiated such things as missionary societies and the use of organ music in worship for they were not specifically warranted in Scripture.

His spirited delivery in debate attracted many followers, among them Walter Scott (1796–1861), a graduate of the University of Edinburgh who became a travelling evangelist for the Campbellite movement in 1827. Scott insisted that there was an objective plan of salvation in the gospel, which he effectively summarized in a famous 'five finger exercise' stressing faith, repentance, baptism, remission of sins, and the gift of the Holy Spirit. This blend of rationalized simplicity and the revivalist spirit proved to have great popularity on the western and south-western frontiers, and attracted converts from other evangelical churches.

In 1832 despite certain differences the two 'Christian' movements of Campbell and Stone merged in Lexington, Kentucky, to form the Disciples of Christ, a denomination which stressed congregational polity, the baptism of believers by immersion, and the weekly observance of the Lord's Supper. Originally made up of about 8,000 Stonites and 5,000 Campbellites, by mid-century the movement claimed nearly 120,000 members. This largely indigenous religious development, destined in time to produce several major denominations, grew out of and long perpetuated the revivalist spirit of the west.

A similar spirit was operative in the formation of two German-speaking evangelical bodies which took shape in the early nineteenth century. The pietistic role of Philip William Otterbein among the German Reformed has already been mentioned; he and Martin Boehm, a pastor of

Mennonite background, found themselves preaching a similar gospel and recognized each other as 'brethren' in their evangelical work. Although they both greatly admired Francis Asbury and the theology and polity of the Methodist Episcopal Church, they recognized that it made no real provision for German-speaking peoples. As a result, in 1800 Otterbein and Boehm joined with others to form The United Brethren in Christ, a church which flourished especially in Ohio, Indiana, and Illinois. A somewhat similar church arose out of the work of Jacob Albright (1759–1808), a German of Lutheran background who also came under Methodist influence. In 1803 Albright gathered little groups of his followers into an independent Evangelical Association, later the Evangelical Church. Throughout the nineteenth century these two groups helped to spread the fervent revivalism of the Second Awakening; in the twentieth century they were to merge with each other (1946) and then with the Methodist Church (1968).

A German evangelical body of quite different background and orientation developed in Missouri and neighbouring states. In 1840 German pietistic immigrants of both Reformed and Lutheran backgrounds who were committed to the ideal of union formed the Evangelical Church-Union of the West. Their irenic and warm-hearted spirit was shown in an Evangelical Catechism of 1847. In later years this group merged with others to become the Evangelical Synod of North America. In the twentieth century they merged with the German Reformed Church (1934) and then with the Congregational Christian Churches to form the United Church of Christ (1957).

The evangelistic impulse also proved to be congenial to many Quakers, both in England and America. Though the emphases on biblical authority and on human depravity that so often characterized revivalism were resisted in Quaker tradition, the attention to personal religious experience was attractive. In England the 'evangelical' Quakers were strongly influenced by Joseph John Gurney (1788–1847). An opponent of this trend was Elias Hicks (1748–1830) of Long Island, New York, who believed that the new directions were inconsistent with the traditional Quaker emphasis on the Inner Light. The two parties confronted each other in the Philadelphia Yearly Meeting, which divided in 1827 into 'Orthodox' and 'Hicksite' yearlies, followed by divisions in many other yearly meetings. As in so many schisms, factors other than theological ones were involved. Many rural Quakers distrusted what they believed to be the worldliness and sophistication of urban Friends, among whom the evangelical style with its Bible study groups and Sunday Schools had considerable appeal. When Gurney arrived in the United States in 1837 for a three-year visit, he travelled extensively, strengthening the orthodox meetings and also contributing to the anti-slavery cause. Toward mid-century disruption again cut into Quaker life as the followers of John Wilbur (1774–1856), a moderate who opposed the 'creaturely activity' of the Gurneyites, separated from orthodox meetings in Philadelphia and elsewhere.

The revivalism of the Second Awakening thus brought great changes into American Protestant life—under its influence some denominations burgeoned into giants, others were brought into promising existence, while still other churches divided under the strain.

The New Measures and the Voluntary Societies

Though there were real differences between the quieter, more ordered revivals of the east and the tempestuous affairs of the frontier, they did both play important roles in the emergence of a dominant evangelical strain in nineteenth-century Protestantism. A theology of revivalism, eclectic enough to blend and systematize the two types, was articulated by Charles G. Finney and his school. Born in Connecticut, Finney (1792–1875) grew up on the frontier of upstate New York. After an academy education, he tried his hand at school-teaching, and then worked in a law office in Adams, New York. While he was serving as choir director at the local Presbyterian Church, the efforts of the pastor, George W. Gale, combined with those of Finney's fiancée, prepared the way for an intense religious experience in 1821. He later described it as a 'mighty baptism of the Holy Ghost'.[7] Immediately he resolved to undertake evangelistic work. Though they disagreed on many theological matters, Finney studied with Gale, but refused to attend a theological seminary. He became an agent of the Utica Female Missionary Society and was ordained as a Presbyterian minister. Spectacular results followed his evangelistic crusades in the cities of central New York—Troy, Rome, Utica, Auburn. This area became known as the 'burned-over district' because the 'fires' of revival swept back and forth across it. There was a directness and sincerity about Finney that was convincing; it was said that 'never was a man whose soul looked out through his face as his did'.[8]

---

[7] *Memoirs of the Rev. Charles G. Finney, Written by Himself* (New York, 1876), p. 20. On Finney and his evangelicalism, see William G. McLoughlin, *Modern Revivalism: Charles Grandison Finney to Billy Graham* (New York, 1959).

[8] As quoted by Whitney R. Cross, *The Burned-over District: The Social and Intellectual History of Enthusiastic Religion in Western New York, 1800–1850* (Ithaca, N.Y., 1950), p. 151.

Gifted with a wonderful, clear voice of great range, he never lost the ability to speak in the idioms of the people, or to use earthy, effective illustrations in his intense appeals.

A man of great self-confidence, Finney set out deliberately to stir up revivals wherever he went. He developed the system of 'new measures' to accomplish this. Services were called at 'unseasonable hours' and were often 'protracted' over a period of days so that a resistant congregation could be 'broken down'. Prayer-circles, inquiry sessions, cottage-meetings, and personal instruction went along with the main services, helping to create an atmosphere conducive to the desired decision for Christ. Prayers were usually highly emotional, direct, and uttered with particular sinners in mind. Women were invited to pray aloud in mixed assemblies— a radical step at the time. The evangelist did not hesitate to use harsh and colloquial language, believing that such means were justified in the effort to save resisting souls. Of particular effectiveness among the new measures was the 'anxious bench' or 'mourners' seat', where those in deep spiritual distress about their eternal destiny were gathered directly under the Awakener's hypnotic eye.

Taken singly, none of the new measures was really new—what was different was the way in which Finney combined and systematized them. He provided a theology to undergird his practices in such books as *Lectures on Revivals of Religion* (1835) and *Lectures on Systematic Theology* (1846–7), which blended Calvinist, Methodist, and Arminian elements. Some of the features of western revivalism were thus adapted to the mushrooming towns and cities of the east, for the protracted services had some of the aspects of the camp-meeting. At first the eastern leaders were suspicious. In 1827 at New Lebanon, New York, Lyman Beecher and Finney and their respective followers met in a nine-day session to see if they could resolve their differences, but at that point the gulf was too great. Beecher, at the time a pastor in Boston, warned Finney to stay away—but four years later invited him into his pulpit, and praised him afterwards. For by then the great Rochester revival of 1830–1 had given Finney a national reputation. Here the new measures showed their effectiveness in a controlled, dignified but intense way as the evangelist gathered hundreds of converts, including some of the city's leading citizens. A year later 'the father of modern revivalism' settled in New York City as pastor of a Free Presbyterian Church; several years after that he became a Congregationalist as pastor of the Broadway Tabernacle, a church built up around him. In 1835 he also accepted a teaching post at the new Oberlin College in Ohio, hoping to combine the two positions, but the distance was too great, and soon his activities centred at Oberlin for the rest of his long life.

Finney was such a powerful, articulate figure that it is all too easy to focus on him and not to pay sufficient attention to the many other evangelists and pastors of various denominations who adopted similar methods and theological emphases. His ideas and practices were utilized not only among the evangelical denominations of British background, but also among some of Lutheran and Reformed alignment. By the 1830s, the revivalism that blended aspects of the eastern and western Awakenings became a recognizable style, with its characteristic—though denominationally diversified—devotional piety, low churchmanship, and activist programmes. During the middle years of the nineteenth century, new-measures revivalism was a conspicuous and powerful force in Protestantism.

In calling persons to commit themselves to Christian faith and service, revivalism aroused great enthusiasm and released much energy that was then put to use in efforts to extend Christian influence in society. 'Saved for service' was a popular evangelical emphasis, and converts were enlisted in the tasks of carrying on the revival, of seeking converts, of building churches, and of doing works of benevolence among the people. A favourite way of channelling the energies generated by revival was through the use of voluntary societies, free associations for the accomplishment of selected benevolent objectives. A particularly effective example of how voluntary societies could be put to Christian use was provided by English evangelicals in the British and Foreign Bible Society (1804). The models of association provided by Christians of the United Kingdom were often followed as Protestants in America built their own 'evangelical united front' in the nineteenth century.[9] In one sense, of course, all churches were 'voluntary societies', for the last establishment (Massachusetts) was voted out in 1833. Each denomination had its own distinctive tenets and practices to maintain, yet those denominations which had been influenced to a greater or less degree by the revival experienced a certain kinship and shared in the mission of making their country more fully a Christian nation. New ways of permeating society with Christian values were needed—and the voluntary societies provided effective channels for common Protestant action without compromising the particularities of each communion, or violating the principle of the separation of church and state.

---

[9] Charles I. Foster, *An Errand of Mercy: The Evangelical United Front, 1790–1837* (Chapel Hill, N.C., 1960), tells the story for both lands in considerable detail.

Some of the voluntary associations were made up wholly or largely from the constituencies of a given church, but many others were non-denominational, composed of individual members from many traditions. Societies were founded to advance some specific purpose, such as the promotion of missions, the distribution of the Bible, the publishing of religious tracts, the planting of Sunday schools, the care of the handicapped, and the sponsoring of moral and social reform crusades. Associations for such causes arose locally in many parts of the country, and then were brought into affiliation in overarching state and national societies. Among the conspicuous national agencies were the American Board of Commissioners for Foreign Missions (founded in 1810), the American Education Society (1815), the American Bible Society (1816), the American Colonization Society (1817), the American Sunday School Union (1817–24), the American Tract Society (1825), the American Temperance Society (1826), the American Home Missionary Society (1826), the American Peace Society (1828), and the American Anti-Slavery Society (1833). Prominent ministers and laymen often served on the boards of a number of these agencies, so that the whole general movement has been called a 'benevolent empire' controlled by 'interlocking directorates'. It has often been observed that many of the most influential leaders were Congregationalists or Presbyterians, occupants of leading pulpits and managers of successful businesses. Though support came from evangelicals of many denominations, the central directives issued from a largely eastern group of educated, well-placed clerical and lay leaders. Conspicuous among them were Arthur Tappan (1786–1870) and Lewis Tappan (1788–1873), wealthy New York Presbyterian merchants, close friends of Nathaniel William Taylor of Yale.

The sequence of annual anniversary meetings of the societies in Philadelphia, New York, and Boston in the late spring gathered the leaders of the evangelical united front together. When they were at their peak in the 1830s the May anniversaries provided a vivid sense of growing evangelical power. Something of the enthusiasm and hope that the rise of the voluntary societies engendered was reflected in a typical anniversary sermon delivered by Heman Humphrey, president of Amherst College, in 1831:

And who can look at these great benevolent institutions, which are the glory of the present age, without being struck with the simplicity of their principles; with the unparalleled extent and efficiency of their operations? How much more is done to enlighten and save mankind, than the world ever dreamed of, till the current century, and with how little comparative cost. It is sufficient, here, just to name the American Bible Society, the American Tract Society, and the American Sunday School Union, which now holds its seventh and brightest anniversary. Who would have believed, thirty years ago, that so many denominations of Christians could ever be brought to meet on common ground, in any such great Society; or that so many millions of people could be furnished with the means of improvement in knowledge and piety, with so much ease, and so little expence?[10]

As such societies burgeoned, evangelicals thought they had found a way to win the nations of the world for Christ by these voluntary means, with none of the disadvantages of establishment.

Before the victory of Christian civilization could come, however, there were several domestic enemies to be put down. Evangelical leaders believed that in the principle of association they had discovered how to deal with the forces that threatened their evangelical empire. They feared that the crudity of life on the frontiers was eroding the moral standards they prized, and that the candle of civilization might flicker out in the west and lead to national ruin. Lyman Beecher, their eloquent spokesman, called for a flood of human and financial resources for the preservation of religion and culture against the inroads of barbarism in *A Plea for the West* (1835) and other writings. But the dangers were not all from the west—many of the new immigrants from Germany and Ireland were Catholics, who did not accept all of the details of Protestant moral codes. Evangelicals customarily thought of them as being bound to superstitious practices and unreformed moral standards. When Horace Bushnell (1802–76), Congregational pastor and theologian, spoke out on the threats to the future in *Barbarism the First Danger*, he insisted that only true religion could save the state before barbarism ruined it. The second great danger he described was Romanism, whose designs must be defeated. Rhetorically he stated what many believed:

To save this mighty nation; to make it the leading power of the earth; to present to mankind the spectacle of a nation stretching from ocean to ocean, across this broad continent; a nation of free men, self-governed, governed by simple law, without soldiers or a police; a nation of a hundred millions of people, covering the sea with their fleets, the land with cities, roads and harvests; first in learning and art, and all the fruits of genius, and, what is highest and best of all, a religious nation, blooming in all the Christian virtues; the protector of the poor; the scourge of oppression; the dispenser of light, and the symbol to mankind, of the ennobling genial power of righteous laws, and a simple christian faith—this is

10 *The Way to Bless and Save our Country: A Sermon, Preached in Philadelphia, at the Request of the American Sunday School Union, May 23, 1831* (Philadelphia, n.d. [1831]), pp. 6 ff.

the charge God lays upon us, this we accept and this, by God's blessing, we mean to perform, with a spirit worthy of its magnitude.[11]

No other duty is comparable to that of saving the country, he explained, appealing for an outpouring of Christian concern for the frontier. Yet the salvation of the nation was not only for its own sake—it was also for the good of all nations.

Those who led and believed in this effort to win as many as they could to Christ and to christianize a nation were dedicated to the methods of persuasion. They were sure they were right, and assumed that all persons of goodwill would recognize that. They felt themselves fully justified in summoning the power of public opinion against those who resisted their aims, which they believed to be righteous. They identified as enemies to the Christian cause those who did not accept their evangelical premises and moral codes. They resisted Roman Catholicism and certain immigrant groups, fearing that they would undermine both true religion and free government. The marked increase in Irish immigration in the 1840s intensified evangelical fears, and in 1842 a non-denominational American Protestant Association was formed to co-ordinate resistance.[12] In the anti-Catholic spirit of the mid-nineteenth century, which several times spilled over into violence, the limitations of Protestant claims to believe fully in freedom and voluntaryism were apparent.

Missionary, Educational, and Reform Impulses

Throughout the Protestant world there were great upsurges of missionary interest from the closing years of the eighteenth century through the nineteenth, the 'Great Century' of missions.[13] The movement had been launched in England through the zeal of William Carey (1761-1834), a shoemaker turned Baptist preacher, whose writings and sermons led to the organization of the Baptist Society for Propagating the Gospel among the Heathen (1792). While he was serving as its first missionary, his letters helped to stir others to action, and in 1795 the interdenominational London Missionary Society was formed. The British example was soon followed by the Americans. In 1796 the New York Missionary Society was founded with the support of Presbyterians, Reformed, and

---

[11] *Barbarism the First Danger: A Discourse for Home Missions* (New York, 1847), p. 29.

[12] The story is told in full by Ray A. Billington, *The Protestant Crusade, 1800-1860: A Study in the Origins of American Nativism* (New York, 1938). For a fuller discussion, see below, pp. 216-20.

[13] The term used by Kenneth Scott Latourette to characterize the nineteenth century in 3 of the 7 volumes of *A History of the Expansion of Christianity* (New York, 1937-45).

Baptists. Denominations also undertook fresh missionary endeavours—in 1798 the General Association of Connecticut voted to become also the Missionary Society of Connecticut. At first, such agencies sent ministers on short missionary tours, but it was soon found better to send persons regularly ordained as evangelists for full-time service. The early missionary societies were concerned chiefly with carrying the gospel to settlers and Indians on the frontiers, but an awareness that much of the world had not yet heard about the Christian faith was increasing as American ships pushed further and further in the search for trade. An impetus toward organizing for outreach overseas came from a group of 'awakened' students at Williams College, a Congregational institution in western Massachusetts. Meeting for prayer in the shelter of a haystack during a summer thundershower in 1806, they resolved to become missionaries to the heathen. Some of them went on to study at the new Andover Seminary, where their dedication to foreign missions under the leadership of Samuel J. Mills (1783–1818) precipitated the founding in 1810 of the American Board of Commissioners for Foreign Missions (A.B.C.F.M.). Basically Congregationalist, the board also enjoyed the support of Presbyterian and Reformed churches. A national missionary organization of Baptists arose when two of the original group of missionaries sent to India by the American Board became convinced during the voyage that the baptism of believers by immersion was in accord with New Testament teaching. Adoniram Judson (1788–1850) and Luther Rice (1783–1836) appealed to the Baptists for support, and in 1814 the General Missionary Convention of the Baptist Denomination in the United States of America for Foreign Missions was formed, providing that congregationally ordered tradition with a national organization.

Many other denominational and non-denominational societies for home and foreign missions were founded, and streams of missionaries were sent to the frontiers and overseas. In 1820 the Presbyterians exulted that missionary co-operation was replacing the old denominational rivalry: 'The Missionary spirit is another distinguishing characteristic of the age. Dissolving the worst rigours of sectarian bigotry, the spirit of missions, which is emphatically the spirit of heaven, has directed toward the miseries of perishing millions, that zeal which had been worse than wasting itself in contests between the members of Christ.'[14]

The evangelical leaders hoped also to win the Indians to the faith and to Christian civilization. In the first half of the nineteenth century,

[14] *Extracts from the Minutes of the General Assembly, of the Presbyterian Church, in the United States of America, A.D. 1820* (Philadelphia, 1820), p. 319.

various societies sent missionaries to work among many tribes: Oneidas, Wyandottes, Ojibways, Tuscaroras, Potawatomies, Winnebagos, Chippewas, Cherokees, Choctaws, Chickasaws, Creeks, Osages, Cayuses, Nez Perces, and Sioux.[15] There was some effective evangelical and educational work done, and Indians who exhibited genuine fruits of the Spirit professed the Christian way. Yet the facts of the seizure of Indian lands and the removal of tribes to reservations or to undeveloped land to the west, coupled with the prejudices of whites toward Indians, set up barriers that prevented the missions from becoming the triumphs of which evangelical leaders had dreamed. The missionaries combined the converting and the civilizing of Indians, which meant that their native existence would be totally transformed. Thus, as Robert F. Berkhofer, Jr. explained in a careful study, 'no matter how pious and exemplary the Indian Christian became, the white population still considered him a savage and an inferior'. The missionaries usually consented to Indian removal, where they would be 'beyond the blighting influence of lower class white civilization'.[16] When missionaries did protest against the removal of Indians from their lands, they were often reprimanded by their superiors for interfering in political affairs. In the case of the removal by Federal forces of Cherokees from their lands in the southern states along the 'trail of tears' to Indian territory beyond the Mississippi, protesting missionaries were ruthlessly imprisoned by the authorities of Georgia, for President Andrew Jackson refused to enforce a Supreme Court decision in their favour.

Sometimes missionary efforts failed because of the resistance of the Indians. The most conspicuous example was the fate of the A.B.C.F.M. mission among the Cayuse Indians at Waiilatpu in Oregon territory. Marcus Whitman (1803–47), a physician, was the leader of a group that settled there in 1836; he became an elder in the first Protestant church west of the Rockies. In 1847 rumour spread among the Cayuses that Whitman was responsible for epidemics among them. In the massacre which followed, the doctor, his wife and a dozen others were slain. Though the effort to evangelize the Indians did elicit selfless and sacrificial service, and did lead to the founding of permanent religious and educational institutions, it was not in itself very successful, handicapped as it was by cultural prejudices which it too often shared.

[15] See Clifton E. Olmstead, *History of Religion in the United States* (Englewood Cliffs, N.J., 1960), pp. 274–7.

[16] *Salvation and the Savage: An Analysis of Protestant Missions and American Indian Response, 1787–1862* (Lexington, Ky., 1965), pp. 123, 100. See also R. Pierce Beaver, *Church, State, and the American Indians* (St. Louis, 1966), p. 94.

The growth of missionary organizations with their developing bureau-cracies and financial interests did not go unchallenged, especially among the Baptists. In the west and south in the 1820s an anti-mission movement spread. Certain local leaders were resentful of the educated, professional-ized agents of the eastern-based societies who seemed to minimize the work of ordinary pastors. Men like Daniel Parker and Alexander Camp-bell (during his Baptist phase) failed to find scriptural bases for missionary societies. Many persons affected by the anti-mission movement became members of Primitive Baptist congregations and associations, while others insisted on a strict definition of congregational autonomy as they remained in the mainstream of Baptist life. The Baptist family was developing a number of branches as the nineteenth century wore on.

Methodism also experienced internal resistance to its centralization of authority. The protest came primarily not from the frontier but from Maryland, and was not anti-mission in spirit. As the Methodist Episcopal Church was enjoying such rapid growth that it claimed some half a million members by 1830, the bishops and superintendents made decisions that often seemed arbitrary to those in the congregations. Reformers pressed for the election (rather than the appointment) of presiding elders and sought the representation of laymen in the conferences. When these requests were refused by the General Conference of 1828, the dissidents withdrew two years later to form the Methodist Protestant Church of some 100,000 members.

The principles of voluntary association, so useful in missions, also worked effectively in church educational enterprises. For elementary schooling the Protestant churches relied chiefly on the common schools. It was in this period that the drive for universal, compulsory, free, tax-supported public elementary education was largely won. Horace Mann (1796–1859) and the other leaders in this educational achievement were determined that the common schools should be non-sectarian, and yet should unmistakably inculcate the general moral and religious teachings on which most Protestants agreed. With a few exceptions, Protestant leaders were convinced that the public educational institutions could be trusted to play a general role in the moulding of a Christian nation, and that the building of extensive church elementary school systems was therefore not necessary. Ministers and home missionaries often were involved in teaching classes, or took time off from their regular ministries to superintend growing public school systems.

The support Protestants gave to public education was in their minds wholly consistent with their great enthusiasm for the Sunday school, in which the Bible and the plan of salvation were specifically central in all that was done. The roots of the Sunday school run back into the previous century in both England and America. While English efforts long remained centred on educating the children of the poor, the American Sunday schools soon became inclusive. By 1830 the evangelical leaders seized on the Sabbath school as a way of spreading the gospel, elevating the moral level, and planting congregations across the frontier. The American Sunday School Union resolved to establish 'a Sunday school in every destitute place where it is practicable, throughout the Valley of the Mississippi'.[17] With the willing co-operation of other national voluntary societies, the Union started many Sunday schools from the Alleghenies to the Rockies, and equipped them with teaching materials and small libraries. The leaders of the benevolent empire were hoping to forestall both the growth of Roman Catholicism and the spread of Andrew Jackson's Democratic forces which threatened the alliance of conservative Whig politics and middle-class Protestant morality. In a number of localities the Sunday schools served as surrogates for common schools until the latter could be established. Many congregations grew out of the Sunday schools. Some of the missionaries who founded Sabbath schools became celebrities; the most famous, self-educated Stephen Paxson, founded over 1,200. Though denominations also moved into the field of Sunday school development, the movement long retained a semi-autonomous character, devoted to inculcating a broad evangelical faith and morality. The popular, Bible-centred Protestantism so strong in American culture in the nineteenth century found one of its most characteristic expressions in the thousands of Sunday schools it scattered across the land.

Even as Protestants became ardent supporters of public elementary education, they dominated collegiate education in this period. A few state colleges had been founded at the end of the previous century, but the great expansion of such institutions was not to come until after the Civil War. Meanwhile, hundreds of denominational colleges were founded, as the aspirations of the churches and the ambitions of communities wanting an institution of higher learning coincided. Though some of these colleges did grow into significant and permanent ventures, the majority, often hastily erected in poor locations without adequate resources because of the enthusiastic spirit in local communities, later went out of existence. The American Education Society (its original name had been

[17] Quoted from the American Sunday School Union, *Sixth Annual Report* (1830), p. 3, by Robert W. Lynn and Elliott Wright in *The Big Little School: Sunday Child of American Protestantism* (New York, 1971), p. 18.

The American Society for Educating Pious Youth for the Gospel Ministry)
aided in the development of church colleges, especially by providing
scholarships for young men who hoped to enter the ministry but who
needed monetary assistance. After the financial panic of 1837, a number of
colleges faced continuing fiscal difficulties; as a consequence, the Society
for the Promotion of Collegiate and Theological Education at the West
was founded in 1843. The control of these societies was in the hands of
the Congregationalists and Presbyterians, but assistance was given to
colleges of other denominations. These agencies also played a role in the
growth and improvement of theological seminaries; by the time of the
Civil War more than a score had been founded.

Among the many societies proliferated by the evangelical empire were
those concerned with moral reform. Essentially the same premises and
methods that informed the missionary, tract, and education societies also
guided those which conducted reforming crusades—and they envisioned
the same goal of a Christian America. As he so often did, Lyman Beecher
showed the way in a sermon of 1812, 'A Reformation of Morals Practical
and Indispensable'. He called for 'local voluntary associations of the wise
and the good' to form public opinion which would render violations of
the law disgraceful as well as dangerous.[18] The idea caught on as the
Connecticut Moral Society was founded the next year. Similar agencies
soon appeared across the land. The evangelicals had stumbled on a way
of securing some of the advantages of establishment, even to influencing
legislation and enforcing the law, without its liabilities. The full christianization of America seemed possible, within the framework of religious
freedom, by energetic use of the means of persuasion.

Conspicuous among the reform causes which fired evangelical imagina-
tion was that of temperance. At the beginning of the century there had
been little Protestant objection to the consumption of alcoholic beverages,
as long as it was not excessive. The intake of spirits was rising noticeably,
however, and was accompanied by problems of increasing poverty and
crime. Evangelical crusaders began to move against the consumption of
drink. They applied the methods of the revival, characteristically over-
simplifying the decision into a choice between a clear good and an
obvious evil. This tendency led them to interpret 'temperance' as total
abstinence from alcoholic beverages, for it seemed to them that the surest
and safest way to be temperate was never to touch a drop. Not only did
the revivals influence the temperance crusade, but that cause also proved
to be useful in promoting revivals, as Charles Finney demonstrated in the

[18] *Sermons, Delivered on Various Occasions*, vol. ii, *Beecher's Works* (Boston, 1852), p. 95.

famous Rochester Awakening. A local paper at the time noted that temperance had become 'a "new measure" for the promotion of revivals', and a presbytery noted 'that the Temperance Reformation and the Revivals of Religion have a peculiarly intimate relation and bearing upon each other'.[19]

The direct link between revivalism and reform enabled the American Temperance Society to spearhead a movement which did effect a long-lasting change in the drinking habits of a majority of American Christians. In the 1830s hundreds of tracts and thousands of sermons argued for the complete avoidance of alcoholic beverages. Characteristic was the conclusion of an address by an evangelical Episcopal bishop, Charles P. McIlvaine: 'The deliverance of this land from its present degradation, and from the increasing woes attendant upon this vice, depends altogether upon the extent to which the principle of total abstinence shall be adopted by our citizens.'[20] By 1834 the A.T.S. reported that it had some 5,000 affiliated local societies with a total membership of one million. Later in the decade the movement declined somewhat, in part because of tensions between moderates and absolutists in the movement. The position of the absolutists was strengthened in the early 1840s by the Washington Temperance Society, founded by reformed drunkards who launched an intensive campaign to get others to take the pledge. Though secular in approach, the Washington movement was based on religious ideas and appeals. Temperance forces, in which women reformers became very active, worked for legislation which would curb the sale of alcoholic beverages; the first state-wide prohibition act was passed in Maine in 1846. By 1860, fifteen other states, chiefly across the north, had passed some kind of restrictive law, not all of which were effective or permanent.

The various agencies of the benevolent empire aided one another in their crusades—the publication of millions of pieces of temperance literature by the American Tract Society is an illustration. The evangelicals were much concerned about maintaining patterns of strict Sabbath observance. An Act of Congress in 1810 which provided that the mail should be delivered daily including Sunday evoked angry protests from the Protestant world. The organization of a spate of societies devoted to the preservation of the 'Puritan Sabbath' followed. In 1828 a General Union for Promoting the Observance of the Christian Sabbath was

[19] As quoted in Cross, *The Burned-over District*, p. 169.
[20] 'Address to the Young Men of the United States on Temperance', *The Temperance Volume; Embracing the Temperance Tracts of the American Tract Society* (New York, n.d.), No. 244, p. 7.

formed in New York, with the ubiquitous Arthur Tappan as treasurer. For the evangelicals, strict Sunday observance had both symbolic and practical value. As long as it was maintained, they had strong evidence that the United States was still a Christian nation, and at the same time their principal base of support—the two main Sunday services of worship of the congregations across America—was protected against threatening competition.

The temperance and Sabbath causes were widely supported by Protestants; some of the other causes tended to draw smaller, but equally devoted, constituencies. Prison reform was significantly advanced by the evangelical empire. As with a number of humanitarian causes, other groups in society, especially those linked with Enlightenment thought, had been working towards reform. They now gained powerful allies, who threw their weight into certain causes—often redirecting and reshaping them as they did so. The Reverend Louis Dwight, for example, formerly an agent successively of the American Tract, Education, and Bible societies, became aware of the inhuman conditions in the prisons in which he distributed Bibles. He became an ardent advocate of prison reform, and was a driving influence in the replacement of the old Pennsylvania system of solitary confinement and labour by the Auburn system of cell blocks and group labour—a forward step at the time.

In the early years of the young republic very few occupations were open to women, and in legal status they were often treated as servile and incompetent. The churches generally supported the cultural conventions of the time concerning women, and interpreted strictly the dictum of the Apostle Paul that they should keep silence in the churches. It took much courage and determination on the part of the pioneering leaders of women's rights to lift their voices against long-standing customs of society and church. Important breakthroughs came in the field of education; one pioneer was Emma Willard (1787–1870), the founder of Troy (New York) Female Seminary in 1821. Catharine Beecher (1800–78), one of the remarkable children of Lyman and Roxana Beecher, led in the establishment of Hartford (Connecticut) Female Seminary, which became a significant model and example. Mary Lyon (1797–1849) combined deep religious concerns with high educational objectives in the founding of Mt. Holyoke (Massachusetts) College in 1836–7. Meanwhile, the place of women in the churches was slightly improved by the new measures of Finney, for they were at least permitted to pray aloud in mixed assemblies.

The missionary movement was much strengthened by the labour and sacrifices of women, who formed their own supportive voluntary societies.

Foreign missions especially drew their attention; by 1839, of some 1,600 auxiliaries related to the A.B.C.F.M., 680 were Ladies' Associations. Most of the denominational mission boards were similarly supported by a network of auxiliaries, yet they were denied significant participation in the making of missionary policy. The first women in missions were the wives of missionaries; they carried an important load in overseas work yet were granted little official recognition. Their sacrificial services were celebrated by the women at home.[21]

Single women encountered a persistent reluctance on the part of the boards to appoint them for service abroad. Though some were active in Indian missions from 1820 onwards, and though the British and Foreign School Society sent M. A. Cook to Calcutta that year, the resistance to the appointment of unmarried women long continued. A widow, Charlotte H. White, was named for service abroad by the Baptist board in 1815; however, she soon remarried. Betsy Stockton, born a slave and largely self-educated while in the service of the president of Princeton, went to Hawaii as a domestic assistant, but while there conducted a well-run school for several years. The first unmarried woman missionary sent abroad in a missionary capacity was Cynthia Farrar, who in 1827 sailed for India under the A.B.C.F.M. and served as a teacher in the Marathi Mission for 34 years. She was the first of what became a sizeable and significant group of missionaries of many denominational backgrounds. Resistance to their appointment persisted for a long period, and consequently they were often assigned to conventional tasks, usually in education.[22]

At home women also played important roles in the reform crusades, including those for women's rights and equal educational opportunities. Oberlin was the first co-educational college, but only as a result of great persistence was Antoinette Louise Brown (1825–1921) admitted to the theological school. She completed her work in 1850, but was not graduated. Three years later she was ordained a Congregational minister, the first woman so recognized by a major denomination. The two most notable leaders of the women's rights movement of the mid-nineteenth century were deeply religious persons, Elizabeth Cady Stanton (1815–1902) and Susan B. Anthony (1820–1906), both of whom were also outstanding figures in the temperance crusade.

The peace movement never became as popular as most of the other

---

[21] R. Pierce Beaver, *All Loves Excelling: American Women in World Mission* (Grand Rapids, Michigan, 1968), ch. II.

[22] Ibid., ch. III.

crusades. Reaction to the war of 1812 precipitated the rise of local societies devoted to the abolition of war. A wealthy retired merchant, William Ladd (1778–1841) devoted his energies to that cause and was the central figure in the organization of the American Peace Society in 1818. Much literature was produced, but like the other reform societies, the Peace Society was torn by tension between the moderates and the ultraists. It was also typical of the movement that 'women made up the rank and file of the peace crusade and carried on extensive correspondence with women of other countries in the United States, in England, and in European countries'.[23]

The Churches and Slavery

The crusade for the abolition of slavery was the most controversial of the humanitarian reform movements of the nineteenth century. It focused insistently on the disparity between the American profession of freedom and democracy and the demonstrable facts of human bondage. It played a role in the division of several of the leading denominations and was a major factor in precipitating the Civil War in 1861.

The enslavement of blacks had virtually disappeared from the north by 1830; the philosophy of the American Revolution, the opposition of religious groups (especially the Quakers), and economic conditions not too favourable to slaveholding worked together to that end. In the south the 'peculiar institution' was deep rooted, yet there was considerable anti-slavery feeling in the early decades of the century. There were many local and state anti-slavery societies, and a number of journals devoted to the cause—most of them, however, based in the upper rather than in the lower south where the plantation system was strongest. Within the churches there was ambivalence on this point. Some strong statements against slaveholding were made by individuals and reform groups, yet most denominations compromised by receiving slaveholders into their membership and even into the ministry. Only the Quakers refused to allow slaveholders into their active fellowship.

One of the strongest anti-slavery statements made by a national church body in the early century was issued by the General Assembly of the Presbyterian Church. A declaration that slavery was 'utterly inconsistent with the law of God' was voted unanimously, by southern as well as northern commissioners. The report went on to say, however, that immediate emancipation would bring great hardship to both masters and

[23] Alice Felt Tyler, *Freedom's Ferment: Phases of American Social History to 1860* (Minneapolis, 1944), p. 428.

slaves. It urged Presbyterians to support the American Colonization Society, to provide religious instruction for slaves, and to prevent all cruelty of whatever kind in the treatment of slaves—especially the cruelty of separating family members. This was clearly a gradualist approach which assumed the continuation of the slave system for several generations.

The American Colonization Society was formally organized early in 1817 with the support of many persons highly prominent in civil and religious life, many of whom were slaveholders. Its purpose was to return free blacks, with their consent, to Africa. It received widespread publicity, but its results were rather minimal, with only 12,000 slaves actually freed and colonized, primarily in Liberia. The venture was predicated on the view that blacks were inferior, could never attain equality in white America, and hence should be encouraged to leave. Understandably, most blacks resisted this approach; at a protest meeting in Richard Allen's Bethel Church in Philadelphia soon after the founding of the Colonization Society the nation was reminded of its principles of freedom and justice by prominent black leaders who pledged themselves not to be separated from their brothers in bondage.

The moderate southern anti-slavery movement had virtually collapsed by the early 1830s. A new, radical, militant and immediatist abolitionism was proclaimed by William Lloyd Garrison (1805-79) in his vitriolic *Liberator* which commenced publication in 1831. His bold challenge to colonization and gradualism alarmed the south, and all forms of anti-slavery sentiment fell under sharp attack. Moreover, the fear of slave uprisings was greatly increased in 1831 when many lives were lost during a slave rebellion in Virginia under Nat Turner. The most important factor in the shift of opinion was probably the deepening southern conviction that its economic future was based on the production of cotton by the plantation system with its slave labour. The south's anxiety was further intensified by its growing minority status in the nation; as slavery was excluded in many of the western territories the south felt itself threatened.

Southern leaders of thought and action thereafter increasingly espoused 'positive good' theories of slavery as the best way of advancing civilization and controlling a race they assumed to be inferior—and which outnumbered whites in certain areas of the deep south. Prominent southern churchmen, both lay and clergy, many of them slaveholders, affirmed that inasmuch as the Bible did not condemn slavery, it was therefore permitted by divine authority. As early as 1822 Richard Furman, president of the South Carolina Baptist State Convention, argued that 'the right of holding slaves is clearly established in the Holy Scriptures, both by precept and example', and so 'in proving this subject justifiable by Scriptural authority, its morality is also proved; for the Divine Law never sanctions immoral actions'.[24] Christian pro-slavery spokesmen argued that the advance of an orderly, prosperous Christian civilization in the south depended on slavery, and encouraged masters to treat their slaves with justice and humanity, and to be concerned with their religious instruction. As southern opinion hardened against abolitionists, who were usually pictured as radicals and atheists, southern anti-slavery figures were driven out or silenced, or, like James G. Birney, the Alabama planter, became discouraged and moved north. Although the south became a closed society, not all opposition to slavery was totally crushed. As Clement Eaton has concluded:

from the Southern ministry came a larger portion of outspoken critics of slavery than from any other professional group. Such a group of insurgents, isolated though they were, indicate that perhaps the strongest force in producing free lances was moral conviction.[25]

In the north, however, abolitionism was a growing but highly controversial movement in the early 1830s. Many local and state societies were founded, and in 1833 the American Anti-Slavery Society was organized in Philadelphia as one of the major channels of the benevolence crusade. Arthur Tappan was chosen to be president. The principle of immediate abolition, popular because of the great British achievement of ending slavery in the West Indies, was affirmed but redefined to mean the immediate beginning of the process of eliminating slavery. Both the New England abolitionists around Garrison and the evangelically minded followers of Finney co-operated so that the new society expanded quickly and mounted an aggressive programme. A central figure in the vigorous crusade was Theodore Dwight Weld (1803–95), a Finney convert and reformer who entered Lane Seminary in Cincinnati in the autumn of 1833 to complete his theological education. Lyman Beecher, the first president of this new Presbyterian institution, soon found his school torn by controversy as Weld won the student body over to the abolitionist cause. When the trustees objected to the anti-slavery activities that were undertaken, most of the students left, many to enter the recently founded Oberlin College in Ohio. Weld went on to become one of the most

---

[24] *Rev. Dr. Furman's Exposition of the Views of the Baptists, Relative to the Coloured Population of the United States in a Communication to the Governor of South Carolina* (Charleston, 1823), as quoted in Smith, Handy, Loetscher, *American Christianity*, ii, 184–5.
[25] *Freedom of Thought in the Old South* (Durham, N.C., 1940), p. 271.

competent field agents for the cause of abolition, using the techniques of revivalism to lead initially hostile audiences to see the sin of slavery and to pledge themselves to fight against it. He trained others, given the biblical name 'the seventy', to carry on the crusade, and penned some of the most influential manifestoes of the movement: *The Bible Against Slavery* (1837) and *Slavery As It Is* (1839). In answer to the pro-slavery Christians, the abolitionists pointed to the differences between the bondage of biblical times and the chattel slavery of America, and insisted that the whole tenor of biblical teaching, especially of the New Testament, was against slavery.

Many free blacks played an important role in the American Anti-Slavery Society, half a dozen serving on its board of managers. When the strife-torn society divided, eight blacks, all of them clergymen, were active in the founding of the American and Foreign Anti-Slavery Society in 1840, notably Henry Highland Garnet (1815–82), a prominent, out-spoken Presbyterian pastor. Black abolitionists had a double concern: to eliminate slavery and to elevate freemen. They rightly felt that most of the white abolitionists, among whom views of black inferiority often persisted, were not sufficiently concerned about this second point.[26] Free blacks played important roles in the famous 'underground railroad' along which thousands of fugitive slaves came to freedom in the northern states or in Canada. Especially outstanding among the operators of this secret network, which included many Quakers, was Harriet Tubman (1821?–1913), a former slave who journeyed many times from her refuge in Canada to guide groups of slaves out of bondage.

The northern anti-slavery leaders struggled against much opposition in the 1830s, and often had to face the wrath of angry mobs. A courageous Illinois editor, Elijah P. Lovejoy, was assassinated in 1837 while defending his press. The immediate abolitionists were opposed by many prominent churchmen who were committed to moderate and colonizationist views, and who sought to keep their communions from any association with the 'extremists'. The General Conference of the Methodist Episcopal Church, for example, passed a resolution in 1836 declaring that 'they are decidedly opposed to modern abolition, and wholly disclaim any right, wish, or intention to interfere in the civil and political relation between master and slave as it exists in the slave-holding states of this union'.[27] With each passing year, however, feeling in favour of abolition spread rapidly in the churches, despite the factionalism that weakened the national anti-slavery

---

[26] Benjamin Quarles, *Black Abolitionists* (New York, 1969).
[27] *Journals of the General Conference of the Methodist Episcopal Church, i, 1796–1836* (New York, 1855), p. 447.

movement. Abolitionism had become part of the reforming currents of evangelical church life in the north, and found both political and ecclesiastical expression in the late 1830s and the 1840s. It was chiefly from the regions where revivalism and the benevolence movement had prepared the way that there came the flood of petitions that kept the issue alive on the national political scene.[28]

A number of prominent advocates of women's rights identified themselves with abolitionism, notably Sarah Grimké and Angelina Grimké Weld, Lucretia Mott, Lydia Maria Child, Sojourner Truth, and Elizabeth Cady Stanton. Active in the general anti-slavery societies as well as in their own, the women found in the petition campaigns an effective channel for their zeal and commitment. The most notable contribution by a woman to the cause of emancipation was made by Harriet Beecher Stowe (1811–96), who learned about slavery at first hand while her father was president of Lane. She inspired the anti-slavery forces and spread their message in the time of discouragement following the Compromise of 1850 with its hated Fugitive Slave Law. Her novel, *Uncle Tom's Cabin* (1852), one of the most influential ever written, made vivid and unforgettable the misery and cruelty that accompanied human bondage. She touched many consciences.

The conflict between pro-slavery and anti-slavery Christians—both insisting that their views were based on biblical teachings and were theologically justifiable—came to its most dramatic climax in the division of the two largest Protestant denominations in the mid-1840s.[29] The abolitionists in the Methodist Episcopal Church were long frustrated in their efforts to move their communion towards an anti-slavery stand. Even though there were perhaps 50,000 abolitionists in that denomination by 1840, they were blocked at every turn in their efforts to introduce anti-slavery measures at the General Conference of 1840. Three years later one of the most vocal of the anti-slavery Methodists, Orange Scott, formed with others the Wesleyan Methodist Connection of America, a body which rejected episcopacy and refused membership to slaveholders. Threatened with a still larger break, the General Conference of 1844 could no longer avoid a showdown. The debate centred on the question whether Bishop James O. Andrew of Georgia, a slaveholder, could

[28] See the important work by Gilbert H. Barnes, *The Antislavery Impulse, 1830–1844* (New York, 1933, 1964). The literature on anti-slavery is vast and growing; see, e.g., Dwight L. Dumond, *Antislavery: The Crusade for Freedom in America* (Ann Arbor, Mich., 1961), and David Brion Davis, *The Problem of Slavery in Western Culture* (Ithaca, N.Y., 1966).

[29] For a very careful study of this and related topics, see H. Shelton Smith, *In His Image, But . . . Racism in Southern Religion*, pp. 94–128.

continue to serve his episcopal functions; by a vote of 110 to 68 it was concluded that he could not. It was decided somewhat amicably to divide the church along sectional lines, and in May 1845 at Louisville, Kentucky, the Methodist Episcopal Church South was organized with about half a million members. The northern church later repudiated the plan of division, and great bitterness was engendered.

Anti-slavery sentiment among the Baptists arose first in New England and then spread across the north, despite the opposition of many of the denomination's prominent figures. The national ties of the congregationally oriented Baptists were in the General Missionary Convention and the American Baptist Home Mission Society, so it was in these agencies that the division of the denomination was fought out. The moderate and pro-slavery factions were able to resist the abolitionists' efforts to have these churches take a stand against slavery until 1844, when the Home Mission Society refused to appoint a slaveholder. The board of managers of the Missionary Convention also declared it would not be party to any arrangement which would imply approbation of slavery. Thereupon the southerners called for a gathering at Augusta, Georgia, in May 1845 and organized the Southern Baptist Convention. The new denomination stressed the autonomy of the local congregation, but also proved to be an effective centralizing agency as it carried out missionary and benevolent purposes on behalf of the congregations. Its initial membership of some 350,000 had nearly doubled by the time of the war.

Some of the evangelical denominations escaped division because their memberships were largely sectional.[30] The Congregationalists were strongest in New England and in the mid-west. The Disciples of Christ were less centralized than either the Congregationalists or Baptists, and were located largely in the border states where the direct conflict of the more extreme groups was minimized.

Hopes Deferred

Those who led and supported the revivals, missions, and crusades of evangelical Protestantism were usually confident of victory despite all difficulties. They shared in the optimistic, expectant spirit so pervasive in the first half of the nineteenth century among the free citizens of the new nation. Many rejoiced in the conviction that the stranglehold of superstition and tyranny that had so long tormented humanity was at last being loosened. The hope in evangelical hearts was intensified by the assurance that the millennium, the time of God's direct rule on earth, was

[30] The complex divisions of Presbyterianism will be treated below, pp. 192–4.

indeed at last at hand. The expectation of the imminent appearance of the long-promised Kingdom of God was one of the sources of the more secular idea of progress, which millennialism indirectly encouraged. For the evangelicals, the millennial theme was doubly attractive, since it was rooted in the Bible, and proved to be effective in promoting and sustaining revivals. As articulated by many notable preachers, the doctrine was already being given a gradualist, progressive interpretation.[31] Alexander Campbell, for example, changed the name of his journal to the *Millennial Harbinger* in 1830, noting that it 'shall have for its object the development, and introduction of the political and religious order of society called THE MILLENNIUM, which will be the consummation of that ultimate amelioration of society proposed in the Christian Scriptures'.[32] During the century a marked increase in the number of sermons, tracts, and treatises devoted to millennialism testified to its growing strength and popularity. Leaders of many denominations representing various theological positions lent their talents to the elaboration of the theme. They differed in details, to be sure, but were united in the expectation that the glorious millennial dawn was near. The benevolent societies were described as 'moral machinery' which would directly contribute to the long-desired consummation.[33] Until that great moment arrived there was much to do to prepare for it. The evangelicals ardently believed that they were called to be co-workers with God, and that he was using them as agents of his will. As a Presbyterian statement piously put it,

Not a finger shall be lifted, nor shall a devout aspiration heave the bosom of a single son or daughter of man, to contribute to the advancement, or plead for the glory of the kingdom of the Messiah, that shall not be met with the smiles and crowned with the blessing of God.[34]

The sense of anticipation was so high that it did not seem that the promised rewards would be long deferred. Hence the inducement to throw one's energies and substance into the glorious work of evangelism and reformation could be presented to the faithful in emotionally powerful terms.

[31] Ernest L. Tuveson, in *Redeemer Nation: The Idea of America's Millennial Role* (Chicago, 1968), p. 34, calls this group of interpreters the 'millennialists', and calls those who expected a physical return of Christ to usher in the thousand years of peace as the 'millenarians', terms he finds preferable to the more familiar 'postmillenialists' and 'premillennialists'.

[32] Quoted from the *Millennial Harbinger*, i (January 1830), by David E. Harrell, Jr., *Quest for a Christian America: The Disciples of Christ and American Society to 1866* (Nashville, Tenn., 1966), p. 44.

[33] e.g., see William Cogswell, *The Harbinger of the Millennium* (Boston, 1833), p. iii.

[34] *Extracts from the Minutes of the General Assembly, of the Presbyterian Church in the United States of America, A.D. 1819* (Philadelphia, 1819), p. 178.

The remarkable growth and dynamism of the voluntary societies was an important outcome. Their vitality was further increased by the assurance of Anglo-American evangelical leaders that God had chosen their people to play a special role in the forthcoming triumph of Christianity in the world. In the light of this sense of destiny, even a humble role in the life of the church and its agencies could be invested with great meaning. Thus the energies of the saved were poured into the intricate, hungry channels of the voluntary system.

Towards the late 1830s, however, the evangelical programme began to encounter some serious difficulties. The financial panic of 1837 weakened the fiscal basis of the voluntary societies. The tensions between the moderates and the absolutists or 'ultraists' in the crusades slowed them down and in several conspicuous cases led to schism. The schism in 1837-8 of the Presbyterian Church, which had provided much support for the benevolent empire, was devastating, for the slightly larger Old School branch repudiated connections with the whole voluntary movement.

The co-operative arrangements between Presbyterians and Congregationalists through the Plan of Union and the voluntary societies had in fact worked to the numerical advantage of Presbyterianism. Many migrating New Englanders of Congregational background found their way into Presbyterian structures, and the largest number of the 'Presbygational' churches formed under the Plan of Union eventually became Presbyterian. Those who entered the denomination in this manner strengthened the New School party which had its roots in the Puritan tradition. As this element grew in size and power, the Old School party, still largely based in the Scottish and Scotch-Irish groups in the church, became increasingly alarmed.

There were important theological differences between the Presbyterian parties in matters of theology, practice, and churchmanship. The Old School held firm to a strict interpretation of the Westminster Confession's doctrine of original sin, for example, while the New School, influenced by the New England theology, especially as interpreted by Nathaniel William Taylor, held milder views on the depravity of man. The parties disagreed in their attitude toward Finney revivalism. A Presbyterian minister who returned to the United States in 1835 after a four-year absence found that he was in another world religiously from the one he had left. He reported that

the Presbyterian and Congregational denominations of Christians, to which I had ever been attached, seemed to me, to a very great extent, lying under the blighting desolation of the new and extravagant measures, by which religious excitements had been attempted and managed on the one hand, and of endless and bitter theological controversy of the other.[35]

In matters of churchmanship, the Old School granted greater authority to the church courts, and was increasingly restive as the life of the denomination was influenced by agents and missionaries in the service of the voluntary societies and not under the control of their judicatories. Presbyterian support of the American Board of Commissioners for Foreign Missions and the American Home Missionary Society was increasingly resisted in favour of direct connection with the mission boards directly under Presbyterian control.

An effective opponent of the voluntary societies was Charles Hodge (1797–1878), professor at Princeton Theological Seminary and a strict Calvinist. He argued that the societies, in which lay influence was strong, were encroaching on the rights and duties of the ecclesiastical courts and were diluting the theological integrity of Presbyterianism.

The two parties also disagreed about slavery, though that was not formally discussed at the time of schism. The New School had its strength primarily in New York and other northern states and was generally more favourable to anti-slavery. The Old School was more evenly distributed in both sections, and hence had far more southern members, many of whom were pro-slavery.

At the meeting of the General Assembly in 1837, the Old School was in a majority, and proceeded not only to abrogate the Plan of Union, but made it retroactive, thus disowning the four synods—three in New York and one in Ohio—formed under the plan. The New School elements in the remaining synods, now vastly outnumbered, joined with the excluded synods in an unsuccessful effort to rejoin the parent church in 1838. They then regrouped into a separate church of about 100,000 members—approximately four-ninths of the previously undivided church.[36]

The New School church continued its ties with the benevolent empire, which had been seriously weakened by the upsurge of denominational spirit. By 1852 the Congregationalists, who were steadily developing a sense of denominational identity, terminated the Plan of Union with

[35] Calvin Colton, *Thoughts on the Religious State of the Country with Reasons for Preferring Episcopacy* (New York, 1836), p. 23.

[36] For a detailed analysis of differences between Old and New School Presbyterianism, see George M. Marsden, *The Evangelical Mind and the New School Presbyterian Experience: A Case Study of Thought and Theology in Nineteenth-Century America* (New Haven, Conn., 1970).

the New School, and societies that had enjoyed multidenominational support, such as the American Board and the American Education Society, soon became Congregational. The New School was further torn over the slavery issue—it harboured many abolitionists, but the presence of some southerners kept its assembly from strong anti-slavery pronouncements for many years. There were some withdrawals into free church movements, especially into the Free Church Synod in 1847. Ten years later the southern wing withdrew from the New School church, but the Old School did not divide until the war actually came.

The schisms over slavery were especially damaging to evangelical plans for winning the nation. The division of the leading denominations over a major moral issue cast a heavy shadow over their hopes to lift the nation into a great Christian commonwealth, for those who were to prepare the way had broken ranks. The benevolent empire was now limited chiefly to the north. The religious ties that had been shaped during the Great Awakenings and that had helped to bring a nation together, ties that had been strengthened in the Second Awakenings to the point that the Kingdom seemed close were now rudely broken. The separations not only foreshadowed the political division but prepared the arguments by which each section would claim its cause as God's cause.

Another development in the 1830s and 1840s added to the difficulties of the evangelicals. Though the millennium was often referred to in sermons and writings, Protestant leaders did not normally undertake to set the date of its coming. But that was done by William Miller (1782–1849), a former Deist who had been received as a convert in the Baptist church at Low Hampton, New York, in 1816. Troubled by the charge that the Bible was inconsistent, he found the solution of the difficulties in the millennial prophecies, especially of the books of Daniel and Revelation. When he announced his conclusion that Christ would return to earth in 1843, he discovered that there was great interest in his message, and found that millenarianism was an effective revivalistic measure. Receiving a licence to preach in 1833, he soon became famous and engaged in considerable travel, illustrating his predictions with a huge chart. Many thousands from various denominations flocked to his meetings.

Several specific dates for the return of the Lord were set and passed—finally all was staked on 22 October 1844. Disillusionment followed—some returned to their churches, others lost interest in religion, while a few remained faithful to the Adventist or millenarian cause, believing that somehow an interpretive error had been made. An Adventist general conference was held in Albany in 1845, but the movement, torn by controversy, proliferated into a number of bodies, such as the Advent Christian Church and the Church of God (Adventist). One stream of the movement adopted the Seventh-day (Saturday) observance of the Sabbath and eventually became the Seventh-day Adventist Church. A biblicistic, revivalist spirit marked these continuing Adventist bodies as a new denominational family was added to the widening spectrum of American religion.

Despite the many difficulties that dimmed evangelical hopes, revival theology and practice did not decline in the middle decades of the century, but were resurgent in the evangelical denominations. After careful study of the evidence, Timothy L. Smith concluded 'that there can be no doubt that the popularity of revival men and methods surged forward in the major segments of American religion between 1840 and 1860'.[37] The revival fervour became a dominant mood in urban as well as in rural Protestant life. The voluntary system which was based on the revival proved to be quite resilient and remained a continuing force through the turmoil of sectional and civil strife—indeed, a number of the national societies lived on into the twentieth century.

The way revivalism had permeated Protestantism became evident during the great revival of 1857–8. Against the background of a financial panic and deep anxiety over the slavery issue, a noon day prayer-meeting in New York rather suddenly began to draw sizable audiences, and was widely publicized. Then, with seeming spontaneity, 'prayer-meeting revivals' erupted in other cities and towns in many parts of the land. Ministers and laymen gave conspicuous leadership—the latter were especially in evidence. The Press devoted much space to the Awakening. Before it had run its course, tens of thousands of converts had been won, their energies often enlisted in the benevolent enterprises. Though at the time many were especially impressed by the wide, swift spread of revival, the way had actually been prepared over many decades as the revival theology and style had become generally accepted in most of the leading denominations.

The percentage of church members in proportion to the population had been steadily increasing throughout the period, as denominations in which revivalism was strong surpassed the others in size. In 1780 the Congregational churches had about 750 congregations, the Presbyterians nearly 500, the Baptists just over 450, and the Episcopal Church slightly over 400. By 1860 the Methodists, who did not form an independent

[37] *Revivalism and Social Reform in Mid-Nineteenth-Century America* (New York, 1957), p. 59.

church until 1784, had nearly 20,000 congregations, the Baptists over 12,000. The two leading denominations of 1780, in both of which were significant elements opposed to the revival, grew much more slowly— by 1860 the Congregationalists claimed about 2,230 congregations and the Presbyterians 6,400. The Episcopal churches were then about 2,150 in number, while the more recently formed Disciples of Christ movement had only about 50 fewer congregations.[38]

A significant realignment of Protestant strength had taken place; the patterns of revivalism and its concomitants left their mark in church and society. By 1860 many of the prestigious figures in national life were outspoken supporters of evangelical faith. Protestant ideas and perspectives were disseminated in the culture not only through the institutions of religion but also through those of education and reform. The middle years of the nineteenth century were in many respects more of a 'Protestant age' than the colonial period with its established churches. This was the time in which the Protestant denominations which had embraced most fully the system of the revival grew to massive size and influence.

[38] Edwin S. Gaustad, *Historical Atlas of Religion in America* (New York, 1962), pp. 4, 43.

VII

OTHER KEYS TO THE KINGDOM: THE WIDENING SPECTRUM OF RELIGION IN AMERICA

(1800–60)

EVEN as the evangelical empire expanded in size and prestige in the first sixty years of the nineteenth century in the United States, some strikingly different forms of religion were also spreading. Certain of the denominations in which revivalism was a major force also harboured movements of quite different types; in some cases schism was a result. While most of the Protestant groups which resisted popular revivalism did not increase spectacularly as did the vast evangelical bodies, they survived, some laying solid foundations for later growth. Most communions which ministered to the needs of immigrant groups expanded markedly—the Roman Catholic Church grew from one of the smaller churches to become the largest single denomination by mid-century. Then there were small groups which dissented sharply from the mainline traditions and experimented in novel ways. Some of these groups were ephemeral, but others became permanent. As the religious spectrum widened, bitter controversies emerged, testing the nation's commitment to religious liberty. Persons whose religious visions differed from those of the confident evangelicals insisted that their ways of faith also had a future in the new land of promise, but some tragic clashes occurred before their rights to freedom were honoured.

The Advance of Liberal Religion

At the same time as the theology and practice of the Second Awakening was spreading among the Congregational churches, another quite different movement was quietly gaining strength in the same denomination, especially in Massachusetts. Many graduates of Harvard had been schooled in the liberal religion of the Enlightenment, and their interpretation of the Calvinist heritage of the Congregational way was influenced by Arminian,

rationalist, and anti-Trinitarian churches.[1] Leaders in the liberal stream of
thought were not anxious to make public their divergences from orthodoxy. They believed that the contribution of the churches to the common
good would be weakened by too much controversy. They accepted the
patterns of religious establishment which were then still operative in parts
of New England, and sensed that a frank facing of theological issues might
show how wide the gulf within the establishment had become and threaten
its already questioned continuation.

The Old Calvinists and Edwardseans of various stripes, especially the
rigorous followers of Samuel Hopkins, were troubled by the spread of
liberal views. They believed that their great Puritan Calvinist heritage was
being undermined, yet they were divided and weakened by disagreements
among themselves. The leader in the long fight to expose the liberals was
Jedidiah Morse, a Yale graduate who before becoming a pastor in Charlestown, Massachusetts, in 1789 had won early fame as the 'father of American geography'. He was greatly alarmed when the Hollis chair of divinity
at Harvard was filled in 1805 not by an orthodox or even a moderate
Calvinist, but by a recognized liberal, Henry Ware. Morse was now able
to get the threatened Old Calvinists and Hopkinsians to join forces. A
new orthodox journal, *The Panoplist* (1805), and a new seminary, Andover
(1808), were early fruits of the alliance.

This new united front was especially encouraging to those Congregationalists who had become active in the Second Awakening, for they
now had the support of most of the Calvinist parties. The widening gulf
between the orthodox and liberal perspectives was becoming more visible
through the growing practice of excluding representatives of one party
from the pulpits of the other. But there was little public alarm until
Morse, seeking to dramatize the extent of the polarization in the hope of
driving the liberal party into the open, finally found the instrument he
needed. In Thomas Belsham's *Memoirs* of Theophilus Lindsey, the father
of English Unitarianism, was a chapter on the progress of Unitarianism in
the United States. By that time most English Unitarians were stressing
the unity of God and the *simple* humanity of Christ, while the Christo-
logical views of most American liberals were closer to familiar Trinitarian
positions. Belsham obscured that difference, linking the more radical
English definition of Unitarianism with the American liberals. As leader
of the anti-liberals, Morse was delighted with Belsham's claim, and had his
bold chapter republished in 1815 as *American Unitarianism*. In the *Panoplist*

[1] For a careful study of this complex history, see Conrad Wright, *The Beginnings of
Unitarianism in America.*

he expounded on this evidence of a wide theological gulf and called for a division of the Congregational house.

The issue had eventually to be squarely faced, and a pamphlet war erupted. The most effective Unitarian spokesman to emerge was the pastor of the Federal Street Church in Boston, William Ellery Channing (1780–1842). A native of Newport, Rhode Island, Channing had often heard the preaching of Samuel Hopkins, and though he reacted against that theologian's strict Edwardseanism, he was deeply impressed by his stress on benevolence. As a Harvard student Channing had developed a rational interpretation of Christianity based on Enlightenment motifs. A man of great dignity and moral power, he delivered in 1819 the sermon regarded as the Magna Charta of an emerging new denomination, 'Unitarian Christianity'. He stressed the importance of the Scriptures as records of God's successive revelations—but to be interpreted as other books are, with the use of reason. He declared that the sacred book so interpreted affirms the doctrines of the unity of God and of his moral perfection. It pictures Jesus Christ as a unified being distinct from and inferior to God, yet nevertheless sent by the Father as a Saviour to effect a moral or spiritual deliverance of mankind from sin. Virtue, Channing taught, has its foundation in the moral nature of man, in conscience and the sense of duty. The moral faculties are the grounds of responsibility and the highest distinctions of human nature. The preacher's own moral passion breathed life into his doctrine. The emerging denomination was crystallized by this clear statement, which ran through eight editions in four months.

Struggles over the control of local church properties had already begun. In 1820 a decision in the historic Dedham (Massachusetts) case found that all contributors to the parish or religious society related to a church had the right to vote in the calling of a minister and the allocation of church property, even though they might outvote the communicant members of the congregation. Inasmuch as many non-communicants had been required by law to pay religious taxes, situations arose where churches did go Unitarian though most of the full members were orthodox. In such cases, the Trinitarians often withdrew to form new congregations; in others it was the Unitarians who had to start afresh.

In 1825 the American Unitarian Association was formed with 125 congregations, four-fifths of them in Massachusetts. The new denomination appealed especially to the cultured, prosperous people who found the Calvinist emphasis on human depravity quite alien. Harvard was the intellectual centre of the new denomination, and its divinity school, just taking shape during those years of division, fell under liberal control. Many of New England's prominent literary figures such as Lowell, Longfellow, and Holmes were Unitarians. Though the new church was centred in Boston and its environs, important congregations were founded in other major cities, especially in the south, and for a time it looked as though the movement might capture a large national following. Jefferson, for example, rejoiced in the early promise of Unitarian advance. But the liberals were no match for the evangelicals in popular appeal; the Awakeners turned the power of their revivals against the new movement. A few Unitarian leaders did show effectiveness in conducting religious Awakenings, but the tide went overwhelmingly against them, checking the early promise of the liberal thrust and confining its main strength largely to eastern Massachusetts.

The young denomination was soon torn by inner tension. Unitarianism had arisen in part as a reaction against Calvinism, and consequently was characterized by a somewhat negative, rational spirit which was not satisfying to some of its younger leaders. They were influenced by the currents of Romanticism then flowing in Europe, especially as mediated by Samuel Taylor Coleridge and Thomas Carlyle.

Notable among the new voices was Ralph Waldo Emerson (1803–82), who engaged in school teaching and divinity study following his graduation from Harvard, and then served several years as a Unitarian pastor. In 1832 he resigned from his pulpit, troubled over the use of the material elements in the Lord's Supper, and by the customs of public prayer. He travelled in Europe, talked with prominent leaders of Romanticism, and on his return published his foundational book, *Nature* (1836). That same year he became the central figure in the famous Transcendental Club. Active in the group were a number of younger Unitarian ministers, including Orestes A. Brownson, William Henry Channing, James Freeman Clarke, Frederic Henry Hedge, Theodore Parker, and George Ripley. The older philosophic tradition which had synthesized Locke and 'common-sense' philosophy was rejected in favour of the more dynamic philosophy of German Idealism. The Transcendentalists read avidly the writings of Schleiermacher and the German biblical scholars. They remained convinced of the Unitarian emphasis on the oneness of God and of his benevolent character, but stressed a radical doctrine of divine immanence, the intuitive perception of truth, a rejection of external authority, and a radical social ethic. The familiar distinctions between revealed and natural religion, employed often by both the orthodox Trinitarians and the earlier Unitarians, were denied. The fame of the Transcendental Club was increased by the brilliance of talented lay participants, especially Bronson Alcott, Henry David Thoreau, Margaret Fuller, and Elizabeth Peabody. A group of articulate individualists, the Transcendentalists' expositions of their views varied considerably in detail.

The Transcendentalist challenge to long-accepted views was powerfully expressed by Emerson's famous 'Divinity School Address' at Harvard in 1838. Informed by an idealistic metaphysical monism, he viewed the world as the product of one will and mind everywhere active and with which individual infinite souls could make direct contact. From this perspective, he criticized historical Christianity sharply. First, instead of stressing the doctrine of the soul, traditional religion dwells 'with noxious exaggeration about the *person* of Jesus. The soul knows no persons. It invites every man to expand to the full circle of the universe, and will have no preferences but those of spontaneous love'. Second, instead of seeing revelation as the present, continuing introduction of God himself 'into the open soul', traditional Christianity speaks as though revelation were wholly past—'as if God were dead'. He concluded with a paragraph that showed the Transcendentalist interest in other religions, and its basic attitude toward the Bible:

I look for the hour when that supreme Beauty which ravished the souls of those Eastern men, and chiefly of those Hebrews, and through their lips spoke oracles to all time, shall speak in the West also. The Hebrew and Greek Scriptures contain immortal sentences, that have been bread of life to millions. But they have no epical integrity; are fragmentary; are not shown in their order to the intellect. I look for the new Teacher that shall follow so far those shining laws that he shall see them come full circle; shall see their rounding complete grace; shall see the world to be the mirror of the soul; shall see the identity of the law of gravitation with purity of heart; and shall show that the Ought, that Duty, is one thing with Science, with Beauty, and with Joy.[2]

Andrews Norton, the leading Unitarian biblical scholar, attacked Emerson's position as 'the latest form of infidelity'. As controversy intensified, Theodore Parker defended Transcendentalism in a sermon, 'The Transient and Permanent in Christianity', in which he defined Christianity as 'absolute, pure morality; absolute, pure religion'—a religion which would

[2] There are many reprints of the Address, see, e.g., Sydney E. Ahlstrom (ed.), *Theology in America: The Major Protestant Voices from Puritanism to Neo-Orthodoxy* (Indianapolis, 1967), pp. 293–316. Compact treatments of Transcendentalism can be found in Ahlstrom, *A Religious History of the American People* (New Haven, 1972), pp. 583–609, and in Smith, Handy, Loetscher (eds.), *American Christianity*, ii, 119–66; fuller treatments are in William R. Hutchison, *The Transcendentalist Ministers: Church Reform in the New England Renaissance* (New Haven, 1959), and Perry Miller (ed.), *The Transcendentalists: An Anthology* (Cambridge, Mass., 1950).

stand even if it could be shown that the gospels themselves were fabrications and that Jesus of Nazareth had never lived. Parker's fame was increased by his effective and fearless work as a social reformer.

The Unitarian ranks were deeply divided. There was no formal schism; after the Civil War many Transcendentalist views became acceptable to Unitarians as the earlier biblical emphasis grew fainter. The denomination as a whole tended to espouse the new position as it moved slowly away from the ground staked out by Channing.

The history of Universalism paralleled in a general way the Unitarian story. The first Universalist churches in the later eighteenth century had been Trinitarian in doctrine, but with the emergence of Hosea Ballou (1771–1852) as the dominant thinker, the transition was made to a Unitarian theology. Ballou stemmed from a Calvinist Baptist background and had little formal education; he began to preach Universalism in 1790, first as an itinerant and then as a settled pastor. Influenced by Ethan Allen's *Reason the Only Oracle of Man*, Ballou became prominent in 1805 as author of *A Treatise on the Atonement*. While Unitarianism had its following largely among the élite and the cultured, Universalism had its appeal among the common people, and was much more successful in the rural areas. By 1860 the Universalists had well over twice as many churches as the Unitarians; according to one count there were 264 Unitarian churches and 664 Universalist churches.[3]

The Unitarian schism heightened the resistance of Congregational leaders to certain liberal trends in theology, and helps to explain why such a storm of controversy swirled around the mediating efforts of a Congregational pastor, Horace Bushnell (1802–76), to restate certain central Christian affirmations in the light of Romantic and idealist patterns of thought. A graduate of Yale Divinity School, Bushnell was dissatisfied by the blend of revival theology and common-sense realism taught by Nathaniel Taylor. He found inspiration in Coleridge's *Aids to Reflection* and Schleiermacher's discussion of the Trinity. In 1833 he became pastor of the North Church of Hartford, Connecticut, serving there until his early retirement because of ill health in 1859. His theological work was not systematic but apologetic, often coming to clearest expression in sermons, addresses, and essays. Aware of both the values and limitations of most theological positions, he was seeking a larger, more comprehensive uniting truth. Early editions of *Christian Nurture*, his most influential

[3] Gaustad, *Historical Atlas of Religion in America*, pp. 43, 126–31. On Universalism, see Ernest Cassara (ed.), *Universalism in America: A Documentary History* (Boston, 1971), and George H. Williams, *American Universalism* (Boston, 1971).

book, appeared in 1847. Troubled by the individualism that was so much a part of revivalism, Bushnell stressed the organic nature of family, church, and community. From this perspective, conversion and the Christian life could be seen from a developmental and contextual viewpoint. In place of the revivalists' understanding of the new birth as normative for all Christians, Bushnell stressed the importance of the spiritual nurture of the child, who 'is to grow up a Christian, and never know himself as being otherwise'.[4] Reprinted many times, the book later became a manifesto of the religious education movement.

Bushnell's foundational *theological* work was *God in Christ* (1849). In the impressive Preface, 'Preliminary Dissertation on the Nature of Language as Related to Thought and Spirit', he argued forcefully that theological language was not scientific and logical but symbolic and poetic. Theological words were not only imprecise, but they also always conveyed something contrary to the truth intended. Hence theological subjects were best approached from many sides—the insufficiencies of words could thus be largely transcended. The Gospel of John, Bushnell found, was probably the most contradictory book in the world, and for that very reason contained more and loftier truth than any others. It follows that creeds should be held in a spirit of accommodation as badges of consent and understanding. *God in Christ* was composed chiefly of three addresses Bushnell had given at Harvard, Andover, and Yale on the issues between the orthodox party and the Unitarians, in which he dealt with the fundamental themes of Christology, Trinity, and atonement. The preacher's Christocentrism came through clearly as he affirmed Christ to be the centre and goal of history—indeed, Bushnell had difficulty affirming the full humanity of Christ, quite the opposite of later liberals who claimed him as their inspiration but who had trouble asserting Christ's full divinity.

Bushnell sought to blend objective and subjective views in his treatment of the atonement, affirming both what God accomplished in Christ's death on the cross and what that meant to the believer. In stressing the way Christ's sufferings express the unconquerable love of God's heart, however, he asserted a subjectivist, moral-influence theory of atonement which brought intense criticism. He returned to this theme in the major work of his retirement, *The Vicarious Sacrifice* (1866–74). Meanwhile, he had produced his most systematic work, *Nature and the Supernatural, as Together Constituting the One System of God* (1858). Viewing nature as a

---

[4] As quoted by H. Shelton Smith (ed.), *Horace Bushnell*, A Library of Protestant Thought (New York, 1965), p. 379.

subordinate, humble member of the cosmic system, one distorted by sin into a condition of 'unnature', he asserted that a supernatural work of redemption to restore the original unity was an intellectual necessity. Bushnell felt that this book was his most significant contribution; later liberal theology was to draw heavily on his reconciliation between the doctrines of the divine immanence and transcendence.

Many other themes were touched in his varied addresses and writings, but like most mediators he was the focus of criticism from both sides. He was an irenic thinker who did not want to cause schism in the Congregationalism he was defending, yet intense controversy greeted his labours. At one point his own congregation withdrew from its association to protect him from a heresy trial. His seminal work did provide avenues for thought and change for opponents as well as for followers; the emerging schools of evangelical or Christocentric liberalism found his work especially informative.

High Church Movements

Even as the evangelical system with its characteristic voluntary, low doctrine of the church and its commitment to co-operation through non-denominational societies was confidently advancing, counter movements with a high church emphasis were also renascent. The individualism, subjectivism, and voluntaryism that characterized the popular revivalistic movements were criticized by those who felt the need for a more centralized church that possessed intrinsic authority. The high churchmen drew ideas and inspiration from Romanticism, that many-sided movement of thought and feeling that had also nourished the Transcendentalists. Romantic thought characteristically focused attention on the genesis and growth of things, hence on historical study. It stimulated Christians of various communions to a new interest in their own ancient traditions, and to a fresh attention to the 'catholic' aspects of their past. Currents of concern with high doctrines of the church flowed to some degree among most of the European churches; these movements became known to their American branches through publications and through immigration.

An early, forceful advocate of high church views was John Henry Hobart (1775–1830), who grew up in an Episcopal church in Philadelphia and was educated at Princeton. After serving parishes in New York, he became assistant bishop and then bishop of the diocese. His interests were strongly practical rather than speculative, but he drew inspiration from early church history, resisted evangelical and low church emphases within the Protestant Episcopal Church, opposed Anglican participation in the voluntary societies, and magnified the importance of the liturgy. He stressed especially the importance of the threefold ministry of bishops, priests, and deacons in apostolic succession from the early church through the bishops, denying the validity of non-episcopal ministries. He was an indefatigable organizer of institutions to support his communion, especially the General Theological Seminary in New York, opened in 1819, at which he taught pastoral theology. His writings were designed chiefly to strengthen and enrich the spiritual life and worship of the congregations. Hobart was not alone in his energetic efforts; other bishops such as John Stark Ravenscroft in North Carolina advocated similar positions, and a high church party began to take shape.

Though there was little use of the techniques of revivalism in the Episcopal Church, there was a strong evangelical party. In the same year that Hobart was consecrated (1811), Alexander Viets Griswold (1776–1843) was consecrated bishop of a diocese that covered much of New England. An exponent of experiential Christianity, Griswold was aided by other militant evangelical bishops. Though the rift between the parties remained, the general liturgical trend throughout the century was in the high church direction. This trend was encouraged in the late 1830s by the impact of the Oxford or Tractarian movement of the Church of England, with its emphasis on episcopal succession and its search for a *via media* between Rome and the Reformation. The impact of the Oxford movement was intensified by an American edition of the Tracts. A number of bishops supported this project, but after the appearance of the famous and final Tract Ninety in which John Henry Newman sought to interpret the Thirty-nine Articles in a fully Catholic sense, the movement became highly controversial. General Seminary continued as a centre for high church and Tractarian emphases; some of the students took a dramatic step and entered the Roman Catholic Church. After the uproar had subsided somewhat, General and some of the other seminaries, especially Nashota House in Wisconsin (1841) continued an Anglo-Catholic emphasis within the Protestant Episcopal Church. The tension between the evangelical and high church parties became sharp as some parishes and dioceses identified themselves with one camp or the other, but a shared loyalty to the Book of Common Prayer provided a point of unity. The communion, so weak at the opening of the century, did not enjoy rapid growth, but was gaining in numbers by mid-century, especially among the upper and middle classes in the urban centres. The Episcopal dioceses generally reflected the predominant sentiment of their sections concerning slavery, more often than not on the conservative side, and the matter never became decisive in the triennial meetings of the General Convention.

A theologically and liturgically creative high church movement developed in the seminary of the German Reformed Church at Mercersburg, Pennsylvania. The forerunner was Frederick Augustus Rauch (1806–41), a German whose lectures at Mercersburg during the 1830s aroused enthusiasm for philosophical idealism, Romanticism, and continental theological developments. The central figures in shaping the Mercersburg theology were John Williamson Nevin (1803–86) and Philip Schaff (1819–93). Nevin was educated at Princeton and had taught at Western, a Presbyterian seminary. In 1840 he began work at Mercersburg, accepting the call to serve as theologian of the much smaller German Reformed Church. One of his early efforts at Mercersburg was to oppose Finney's new measures. He believed that the new revivalism was not only disrupting Reformed congregations but was undermining the classical Reformation heritage. The German Reformed Church was losing members both to the German Methodist bodies and to the groups influenced by John Winebrenner, a former German Reformed minister who in 1830 was the central figure in founding the General Eldership of the Church of God, a congregationally ordered body which adopted the baptism of believers. Nevin's *The Anxious Bench* (1843, 1844) sharply challenged the system of the new measures as having no affinity with the life of the Reformation, especially as embodied in the Heidelberg Catechism, the standard of the church he was now representing.

Nevin's greatest work, *The Mystical Presence*, appeared in 1846. In it, as in many important articles in *The Mercersburg Review*, he argued for a return to the full classical Reformed or Calvinist doctrine of the Lord's Supper, with its affirmation that '. . . the believer communicates not only with the Spirit of Christ, or with his divine nature, but with Christ himself in his whole living person, so that he may be said to be fed and nourished by his very flesh and blood'.[5]

Philip Schaff, a native of Switzerland who had been educated at Tübingen, Halle, and Berlin, gave strong support to his new colleague when he came from Europe to take a post at Mercersburg in 1844. Schaff was a gifted, irenic, rather eclectic theologian and historian. His inaugural address, elaborated into *The Principle of Protestantism*, offered a developmental view of church history as theodicy—a demonstration of how God patiently works out his purposes. Schaff believed that in principle Protestantism was

[5] *The Mystical Presence: A Vindication of the Reformed or Calvinistic Doctrine of the Holy Eucharist* (Philadelphia, 1846), p. 109.

operative through the entire history of the church. Accordingly he interpreted the Reformation not as a revolutionary separation from the Catholic Church but as its greatest act, '... the full ripe fruit of all its better tendencies, particularly of the deep spiritual law-conflicts of the Middle Period, which were as a schoolmaster toward the Protestant doctrine of justification'.[6] Schaff's views were highly controversial, for they contradicted traditional Protestant affirmations that the 'pure' gospel had existed unchanged through the centuries. Schaff elaborated his position—one of the central affirmations of the Mercersburg theology—in another book, *What Is Church History? A Vindication of the Idea of Historical Development* (1846), in which he disclosed his own debt to the philosophical work of Johann Gottfried von Herder and to the historical researches of Augustus Neander, with whom he had studied in Berlin.

The Mercersburg theologians presented their 'evangelical catholicism' with spirited passion and immense learning, but at a time when revivalism and anti-Catholicism were powerful, their work was highly controversial, and their circle of followers small. The movement declined in the early 1850s when Nevin went through a double crisis—his health failed, and his theological pilgrimage brought him to the verge of Roman Catholicism. He resigned from his various offices in the church and her institutions, and went into semi-retirement. By the time he recovered his health and settled the religious issue by remaining in the Reformed Church, the force of the movement had been broken. The excitements of the Civil War, during which Schaff left for New York, further contributed to the fading of the movement. Yet the Mercersburg theology had encouraged serious reflection on the nature of the church and ministry within and beyond its own tradition, especially on Lutheranism, and had specifically contributed to a revival of liturgical interest, chiefly through the publication of the *Liturgy or Order of Christian Worship* in 1857.

In a radically different context a distinctive type of high church movement appeared in the strongly revivalistic and characteristically low church Southern Baptist Convention. Feeling the need for a clear and authoritative doctrine of the church, a core of leaders proclaimed an apostolic succession through a continuous chain of true congregations from New Testament times to the present. A minister of great oratorical ability, James R. Graves, argued that only congregations in an unbroken succession of local congregations through the centuries were true

6 From a synopsis of *The Principle of Protestantism*, thesis 33, as reprinted in James H. Nichols (ed.), *The Mercersburg Theology*, A Library of Protestant Thought (New York, 1966), p. 129.

churches—all others were merely religious societies with which there should be no fellowship. It followed that only those ordained in the Baptist congregational succession were valid gospel ministers, and that only the baptism of believers by immersion in the true churches could be recognized. The familiar Baptist emphasis on the autonomy of the local congregation was also strongly affirmed, both through a rejection of mission boards and an insistence that only members of any given local church had the right to partake of the Lord's Supper there—even those from a church of the same faith and order were not invited.

In 1851 Graves gained a victory for his views in the 'Cotton Grove Resolution', passed at a mass meeting in Tennessee. The movement drew its name from a pamphlet by James M. Pendleton, *An Old Landmark Reset* (1854). With great dependence on the writings of an English Baptist minister, G. H. Orchard, the 'true' succession was traced across the centuries through a long line of heretical sects to the emergence of Baptist groups in the Reformation. Landmarkism won a considerable following in the denomination, causing much controversy for half a century. Though it never succeeded in capturing the convention, Landmarkism left a lasting impression, and caused a small schism in the early twentieth century when Landmarkers in Arkansas withdrew.

Protestantism among the Blacks

The number of Christians among the black people greatly increased in the period from the turn of the century to the Civil War, from an estimated 5 per cent of about a million to somewhere between 12–15 per cent of an estimated four and a half million, of which about four million were slaves. Students of black religion debate about the degree to which vestiges of the African past were preserved within the adopted Christian framework, but clearly many blacks made that framework their own, pouring into it their own deep feelings about life and death and their longing for deliverance. Their spirituals were powerful instruments of piety and communication among a largely illiterate people. Based in part on black folk music, they combined elemental religiousness, authentic Christian experience, awareness of the reality and pain of bondage, and hope for liberation in this world or the next.

Slaves who were converted to Christianity found a new orientation for their lives which provided an interpretation of their experience of bondage and offered them hope of salvation. Only a minority of slaves ever became formally Christian—many never had a chance to hear the gospel, and others resisted what to them was a white man's religion in which words of love and justice were not reflected in deeds. The gospel was presented to the slaves in various ways—some masters regularly took their slaves to their own churches, where they customarily were seated in a segregated gallery. Others invited evangelists, both black and white, to preach to the slaves on the plantations, and some maintained chapels for them. Sunday schools for slaves operated irregularly and intermittently in the south. There were several conspicuous efforts by denominations to conduct missions for the slaves; at the high point in the 1840s the Methodists had eighty missionaries at work among them.[7] Some masters thought that Christian influences made the blacks more manageable, while others feared that any religious instruction might increase slave restlessness.

The black preachers, some remarkably gifted in their ability to make the Bible come alive in a powerful way, exercised their gifts both within the recognized channels and also in secret gatherings of slaves. Living within a system marked by coercion and fear that regulated and oppressed their lives and kept most of them illiterate, slaves who were converted could not openly develop a church life of their own. Some became members of the mainline congregations; indeed, some of the leading churches of the south had a large majority of black members. There were some separate black churches whose activities and properties were supervised by whites. Beyond that there was an underground 'invisible institution' of faith which met late at night, often in the woods, where the black preachers brought inspiration and solace to their oppressed flocks.[8] By the eve of the Civil War over 200,000 slaves were Methodists and some 175,000 were Baptists, but many others had heard and received biblical faith through the informal channels of black life.

In the north free blacks were able to develop their own congregations. Their freedom was seriously restricted; as Lawrence N. Jones has observed, '. . . the freedman had some prerogatives denied to the slave, but he was seriously proscribed by custom, by law, by judicial decision, and by his previous condition of servitude'.[9] Many free blacks would have liked to have been members of the regular white churches and some were, but were rarely treated with true respect, love, and concern. The 'nigger pew' dramatically symbolized their inferior status in most white churches;

[7] Donald G. Mathews, *Slavery and Methodism: A Chapter in American Morality, 1780–1845* (Princeton, 1965), p. 70.

[8] See E. Franklin Frazier, *The Negro Church in America* (New York, 1964), esp. ch. 1, 'The Religion of the Slaves'.

[9] 'They Sought a City: The Black Church and Churchmen in the Nineteenth Century', *Union Seminary Quarterly Review*, 26 (1971), 262.

hence many preferred their own congregations and denominations. The separations that had taken place in the late eighteenth century from the Methodist Episcopal Church in Philadelphia and New York[10] grew into full-scale denominations. The African Methodist Episcopal Church was formally organized with Richard Allen as first bishop in 1816, and the African Methodist Episcopal Zion Church four years later with James Varick as bishop. In doctrine and polity these denominations were much like the parent church. They devoted considerable attention to improving the lot of their members through mutual aid societies and the development of educational institutions. Baptist congregations were gathered in northern and mid-western towns and cities in the early nineteenth century; the first association of their churches was the Providence Baptist Association in Ohio (1836), soon followed by others. Some black congregations, especially Presbyterian, continued a relationship with the major denominations, in which their pastors struggled for the social and political rights of their people.

The Impact of Immigration

A churchly renewal that largely reshaped the Lutheran tradition in the United States was in part a reaction to the advancing tide of voluntaryism and revivalism, but was more directly related to the way immigration affected that denominational family. The Germans arrived in significant numbers in this period, nearly 450,000 in the 1840s and more than twice that in the following decade. Many of them were Lutherans from diverse backgrounds. The ethnic complexity of Lutheranism was further heightened by the great increase of migration from the Scandinavian countries toward the middle of the century. A good many of these new Lutherans were troubled by the Americanization of their co-religionists who had preceded them. Both immigrant and native Lutherans were influenced to some extent by certain high church currents flowing in the continental churches—movements associated with such figures as Ludwig von Gerlach in Prussia (from whom Schaff had learned much), Wilhelm Loehe in Bavaria, and Theodor Kliefoth of Mecklenberg. Mercersburg also had some effect; Nevin and Schaff were deeply concerned over the proper interpretation of the Reformation, Lutheran as well as Reformed.

In the early part of the century, the descendants of colonial Lutheranism were in various stages of accommodation to the English-speaking culture, and a strictly Lutheran consciousness and confessionalism were on the decline in many places. Until 1820 the congregations were grouped in

[10] See above, pp. 156-7.

territorial bodies; in that year the General Synod was formed with the synods of Pennsylvania, North Carolina, and Maryland-Virginia supporting it, though Pennsylvania soon withdrew and stayed out for thirty years. New York did not join until 1837, and the Ohio and Tennessee synods became a viable organization—though largely advisory—through the able leadership of a young Maryland pastor, Samuel Simon Schmucker (1799–1873), a graduate of Princeton. He persuaded the new West Pennsylvania Synod to join the General Synod in 1825, and the next year he led in the founding of a seminary at Gettysburg, Pennsylvania, becoming professor of theology and president. Although he stressed the importance of confessional standards in his teaching, he was progressively drawn into co-operation with the non-denominational voluntary societies and with other churches. He became the central figure in the movement for an 'American Lutheranism'. His text on systematics of 1834, *Elements of Popular Theology*, was somewhat critical of confessionalism and of the traditional Lutheran doctrines of the Lord's Supper. His irenic attitude toward other churches was evident in his *A Fraternal Appeal to the American Churches, with a Plan for Catholic Union on Apostolic Principles* (1838), a pioneering ecumenical book. Other champions of his 'American' emphasis arose, and new institutions and journals were founded to advance that cause.

Then came the increasing floods of German immigrants; in 1837, for example, the New York Ministerium went back to the use of German as its official language after thirty years. New synods were being formed, many in the west, some of them stressing strict confessional standards. Oriented theologically to the European scene, great numbers of the new arrivals asserted the confessional character of Lutheranism against the Americanist tendencies toward co-operation with other churches and with revivalism. This reassertion of 'normative' Lutheranism made itself felt in the General Synod, especially when the Ministerium of Pennsylvania returned in 1853, determined to stand for the confessional principle. The leaders of the American movement made an effort to sustain their position by circulating in 1855 a 'Definite Synodical Platform' which proposed a rather drastic revision of the beloved Augsburg Confession, eliminating such central Lutheran affirmations as baptismal regeneration and the real presence of Christ's body and blood in the communion. A period of sharp controversy followed this daring move. Some of the regional synods associated with the General Synod—by then there were more than twenty—approved in whole or in part this development, but eight disapproved. The most conspicuous leader in the confessional resurgence was Charles

Porterfield Krauth (1823–83). Originally aligned with American Lutheranism, this son of a professor at Gettysburg had been won by the arguments of the other side while serving in the pastorate. His own studies, summarized in his book *The Conservative Reformation and Its Theology* (1871), put great emphasis on the doctrine of the real presence of Christ in the Eucharist, and interpreted Luther as a conservative Reformer who resisted the errors of both the Anabaptists and the Reformed.

After some preliminary separations, the major break between the two parties came when the General Synod accepted into its membership the Franckean synod of western New York in which the revivalist style of Charles Finney was strong. The Ministerium of Pennsylvania then withdrew, founded a new seminary in Philadelphia, at which Krauth became professor of systematic theology, and joined with ten other synods to form a new General Council in 1867. This second effort at national Lutheran unity took the Unaltered Augsburg Confession as its standard. It included such important bodies as the New York Ministerium and a Swedish synod, Augustana, recently consolidated in 1860. A number of the regional synods divided in great bitterness, one side affiliating with the older General Synod, the other with the new General Council. Krauth played a central role in shaping the character of the council, writing its fundamental principles of faith and polity and serving as president in the 1870s. His scholarship was well recognized outside his communion— from 1868 until his death he also taught as professor of philosophy at the University of Pennsylvania. His liturgical and sacramental emphases paralleled those of John Nevin.

Some of the very conservative synods did not become members of either of these two unitive efforts. The most conspicuous of these synods developed out of an immigrant group which had reacted against the rationalism and lethargy of the Church of Saxony. Combining a devotion to Lutheran confessional orthodoxy with an intense piety, these immigrants settled in Missouri in 1839, and came under the powerful leadership of C. F. W. Walther (1811–87), a graduate of Leipzig and an outstanding preacher, editor, and theologian. He served as first president of the Evangelical Lutheran Synod of Missouri at its formal organization in 1847, and also became professor of theology at the synod's Concordia Seminary in St. Louis. The Missouri Synod grew rapidly, spreading into other states. Walther's personal influence extended into other conservative and independent synods, such as Buffalo, Wisconsin, and Iowa. In the latter the work of the Bavarian high church leader, Wilhelm Loehe, who put great emphasis on the apostolic succession, was prized.

The whole story of Lutheran organization in the nineteenth century is very complex, for various immigrant groups from Germany and Scandinavia founded bodies which grew, divided, and combined in differing ways, but with a few exceptions these churches were asserting their confessional and churchly character in their new home. The strength of Lutheran organization lay in the territorial and ethnic synods, and in the synods the slavery issue was dealt with largely in sectional terms. The General Synod did express some strong anti-slavery views, but its role was largely advisory and it was not inclusive, so that the matter was not directly confronted nationally.

An influx of immigrants from Holland towards mid-century provoked a schism in Dutch Reformed ranks. That church had already suffered a small schism in 1822 with the departure of a group which believed that lax disciplinary standards and a lack of proper stress on the doctrines of election and predestination had gone too far. Among the new Dutch immigrants were many who had been part of a Separatist movement in the Netherlands in 1834. At first they joined with the existing Reformed Church in America, but in 1857 there came a break. The protesters, troubled by what they felt to be a neglect of the Heidelberg Catechism and the singing of hymns instead of psalms, formed the Christian Reformed Church, a conservative Calvinist body centred in Michigan, which the remnants of the 1822 schism later joined.

Among the floods of immigrants that so deeply affected American religious life were increasing numbers of Jews, especially among the Germans, so that the Ashkenazic (German) Jews soon vastly outnumbered the Sephardic (Spanish and Portuguese). In 1840 the Jewish population was about 15,000, but in 1860 there were ten times as many. Jewish life was largely under lay control—the first regularly ordained rabbi arrived only in 1840, when there were just eighteen formally organized synagogues, a number that quadrupled in the next decade. Accepted as full citizens, Jews were free from the legal restrictions which forced them to live in isolation in many parts of Christendom.

In their American setting, a number of Jews began to question certain traditional laws and customs that seemed outdated. A conspicuous figure in the effort to strengthen Jewish life was Isaac Leeser (1806–68), who introduced the English sermon into the Sabbath service, and translated the Hebrew Scriptures and Prayer Books into English. He saw that some ancient customs had to be modified, but tried to have this done conservatively and with a concern for continuity. Others, however, wanted more thoroughgoing changes. In the 1840s synagogues in Baltimore and

New York introduced such reforms as the use of organs and mixed choirs, seating by families, and the greater use of English in worship. Where sympathy for reform slowly spread, the authority of the Talmud was questioned, the observance of the dietary laws relaxed, and the return to Israel no longer expected. Indigenous patterns of reform were strengthened by the arrival of leaders who had been in touch with the reform movement of Germany, especially Isaac Meyer Wise (1819–1900) and David Einhorn (1809–79). The formal division and 'denominalization' of American Judaism did not take place until after the Civil War.

Roman Catholicism: Growth and Tension

The church that gained by far the largest number from immigration was the Roman Catholic. One of the startling developments in the young nation was the growth of that church from about 50,000 members of a single diocese in 1800 to become the country's largest denomination of more than two million in forty-four dioceses by 1860. The chief reason for such a rapid increase was the arrival of Catholics from abroad, but there were such other factors as the natural increase of Catholic population, the addition to the United States of territories containing Catholics, and the winning of converts. In responding to the organizational challenges thrust on her by the aggregation of persons of so many different backgrounds in the face of a largely hostile social and cultural environment, the Roman Catholic Church in the United States was decisively reshaped. The distinctive character of this giant among American churches was moulded as it simultaneously faced anti-Catholicism from the outside and the conflict of nationalities from within.

As the church grew slowly but steadily in the early century under Bishop Carroll, he effectively encouraged the building of Catholic institutions. The number of religious Orders increased, some from across the water, others indigenously formed. In 1808, a long-desired reorganization of the church was effected when Pope Pius VII established dioceses at Boston, New York, Philadelphia, and Bardstown, Kentucky, and made Baltimore into the metropolitan see. The new diocese of Bardstown was vast, covering most of the area from the Appalachian Mountains to the Mississippi. The veteran missionary Benedict Joseph Flaget reluctantly became bishop, superintending Catholic life and growth in the Indian missions and the white settlements. The new archbishop—Carroll received the pallium, symbol of his high office, in 1811—retained jurisdiction over the seaboard states from Maryland to Georgia, and was also given the administration of the combined dioceses of Louisiana and Florida.

(Florida remained in Spanish hands until 1821; four years later it was linked with Alabama and made a vicariate apostolic.) The larger dioceses were redivided as numbers warranted.

Carroll's later years were saddened by turmoil over the old question of the role of lay trustees. In New York, Baltimore, Philadelphia, and Charleston, South Carolina, he had to insist that though lay trustees might hold church property, in keeping with American practice, this did not give them any claim to spiritual power or the right to call, dismiss, or reject properly appointed pastors. The trusteeism controversy was intensified by the desire of certain congregations made up largely of a particular national group to manage their own resources and to have a congenial priest. Trustees often believed that they were affirming the rights of the people against the aristocratic ways of the hierarchy.

Carroll's successors as archbishop, Leonard Neale (1815–17) and Ambrose Maréchal (1817–28) had to deal with a number of difficult trustee situations, in some of which schisms arose. Especially unhappy struggles developed at Norfolk, Virginia, Charleston, and Philadelphia.[11] In Charleston, which was made a diocese in 1820, the first bishop, John England (1786–1842), relieved the tension by preparing a constitution which defined the way ecclesiastical discipline was to be separated from the regulation of temporal affairs, and provided for a convention with two houses of lay and clerical delegates. This successful democratic approach did not win wide support elsewhere, however, and was not maintained after England's death.

The more typical solution to the problem of trusteeism was at Philadelphia, where in 1827 a firm stand from Rome strengthened the hands of the bishop against the lay trustees. By the time the First Provincial Council met at Baltimore in 1829, trusteeism was largely under control by the bishops, though there were some later eruptions. At the council, actions to regularize the administrative life of the church were passed, and the bishops took pride that their church now had some 200,000 members, 11 dioceses, 9 colleges, and 37 communities of religious Orders.

As tensions over trusteeism diminished, however, others intensified as increasing numbers of immigrants arrived especially from Ireland. They resented the dominance in the church of the English, French, and American clergy. During the era of the French Revolution, nearly a hundred

---

[11] For details, see McAvoy, *A History of the Catholic Church in the United States*, ch. V. A brief interpretation can be found in John Tracy Ellis, *American Catholicism* (Chicago, 1956), pp. 44–6.

emigré priests took refuge in the United States, among them members of the Society of Saint Sulpice, which was concerned with higher education. The French clergy in America, among whom was the scholarly Maréchal (1764–1828), an *emigré* Sulpician, generally co-operated with the older Anglo-American Catholics of relatively high social status who were centred in Maryland and Virginia. Maréchal, however, lacked Carroll's irenic spirit, and there were some sharp conflicts among the bishops. As the number of French clergy declined, those of English and native background continued to dominate the hierarchy; Maréchal's successors at Baltimore were James Whitfield (1828–34), born in Liverpool and educated at Lyons, and Samuel Eccleston (1834–51), an American of English ancestry who had studied at the Sulpician seminary in Paris. During their administrations, the addition of vast numbers of immigrants, especially from Germany and Ireland, brought about radical changes in the Catholic constituency. The newer groups wanted an increasing share in church leadership, and sharp tensions between the nationality groups were experienced.

The influx of newcomers also provoked and intensified anti-Catholic feeling which spilled over into unfortunate episodes of violence. About 200,000 Irish arrived in the 1830s, though not all of them were Catholics. Nearly four times that number came in the next decade, and even more in the 1850s—the terrible potato famine and its aftermath was one of the main reasons for the great migration. Large numbers of those who came were poorly educated, impoverished, and distrustful of Anglo-American ways, but ardently Catholic. Lacking means or preparation to settle on farms or on the frontiers, most clustered in the seaboard cities. Some very able clergymen gave leadership to the Irish, notably Bishop England, John Hughes (1797–1864), who was later to become Archbishop of New York, and Francis Patrick Kenrick (1796–1863), destined to become Archbishop of Baltimore—all natives of Ireland. Among the immigrants were also great numbers of Germans; many of the Catholics among them made their way to rural communities in the south and mid-west. By 1850 the majority of American Catholics were immigrants. The centre of gravity in the church was shifting from the older, acculturated groups led by the Anglo-American and French clergy to the newer groups, especially the Irish, who were determined to make themselves fully at home in their new land. The shift was marked by acute tension within the church, and also by increased conflicts between Catholics and Protestants.

The historic antipathy between Roman Catholicism and the Reformation traditions that had emerged so decisively in the sixteenth century was periodically re-emphasized in times of crisis. An anti-Catholic spirit lived on in the Protestant bodies, especially those of Puritan and evangelical cast. Although the Enlightenment had stressed the importance of religious toleration, it characteristically viewed Catholicism as a form of superstition and despotism. Yet in the early years of the new nation's life, the acceptance of religious freedom opened a new era for Catholics in a country of predominantly Protestant heritage, as in state after state laws that kept the Roman Catholics from full equality were lifted. Though Protestants praised religious liberty highly, they were determined to use opportunities of freedom to capture the mind and the heart of the nation for 'true' Christianity. They had been able to look with benevolent condescension on the Roman Catholics when the latter were in a small minority which in time might be 'liberated'. But when the number of Catholics began to grow so swiftly, chiefly because of the hordes of illiterate foreigners who crowded noisily into the cities—and into their political structures—the reactions were sharp and in some cases violent. Protestants who wrangled among themselves over denominational differences could readily make common cause against the old threat of 'popery'. Many were convinced that the Catholics, bound to a hierarchical and authoritarian system, could never fully accept democracy, and in a time when Rome was reacting so negatively against the French Revolution and its consequences, various particulars could be cited which gave credence to such charges. The increase in the number of Catholic schools—the Provincial Council of 1829 had urged all parishes to build parochial schools—troubled many citizens who feared the power of alien elements, unschooled in fully American ways of thinking and acting. The Catholics threatened two groups: the native workers who saw themselves being undercut economically, and the middle and upper classes who had to pay for increased social services. Many antipathies and fears were roused by the swift increase of Irish immigration after 1830, and touched off new manifestations of an ugly anti-Catholicism.

The incidents of violence were usually carried out by mob action and were deplored by responsible Protestant leaders, yet their sermons and writings helped to set the conditions out of which overt hostilities emerged. In Boston, strife between Irish and Yankee workers erupted early in the 1830s, and ministers often spoke on the Catholic issue in their sermons. In August 1834 a mob burned the Ursuline convent and girls' school near Charlestown. Though regret over this unfortunate occurrence was widely expressed, anti-Catholic literature and organizations multiplied. Fraudulent and inflammatory books appeared, such as Rebecca Reed's *Six Months in a Convent* in 1835 and Maria Monk's *Awful Disclosures of the Hotel Dieu Nunnery of Montreal* the following year. Respectable leaders also stressed the anti-Catholic theme—Beecher's famous *Plea for the West*, for example, pointed to the spectre of a Catholic conspiracy to capture the west for popery and reaction. Voluntary societies designed to halt the Catholic threat were founded, important among them the American Protestant Association in 1842. Such organizations linked Protestantism, Americanism, democracy, and nativism in the struggle against what to them was the Catholic menace to Protestant freedom and American democracy.

Ten years after the Charlestown burning a riot was touched off in Philadelphia when Francis Patrick Kenrick, then Bishop of Philadelphia, asked the Board of Controllers of the public schools not to require Catholic children to read the King James version of the Bible. Protest meetings against his intervention got out of control and two Catholic churches were burned, and over a dozen persons were killed and many more injured. In New York Bishop Hughes took strong action to prevent similar destruction. There Catholics attempted to secure a share in the common school fund, for only about a third of their children were in church-directed schools. Hughes insisted that the institutions maintained by the Public School Society, which in fact was a quasi-Protestant philanthropic agency, were not at all neutral in religion. The hold of the Society over the city's schools was broken, but the state legislature provided that no state aid could be given to religiously controlled schools. During the peak of the controversy in 1844, nativist groups roamed the streets, and Hughes stationed armed guards around the churches to keep them from harm.

Catholic leaders fought against the anti-Catholic spirit in various ways. Papers and journals were founded—the pioneer was Bishop England's *The United States Catholic Miscellany*, the first American Catholic newspaper. The example was soon followed elsewhere.

After the storms of 1844 the situation outwardly quieted somewhat. The growth of the church went on steadily, many schools and other institutions were founded, and mission work was carried on. Efforts to convert Indians continued, especially through the missionary labours of Pierre-Jean de Smet, a Jesuit who wrote extensively about the tribes. For the whites on the frontier, the church spread its organizational network as quickly as it could—sometimes before political futures were decided. The first bishop was appointed for California, for example, in 1840, for Texas the next year, and a vicariate-apostolic appointed for Oregon in 1843. Three years later Oregon was made a metropolitan see, at first related to the Canadian Church, until the boundary was fixed. In the next several years St. Louis, New Orleans, New York, and Cincinnati also became archdioceses. The latter two were strongly Irish in tone, and the significance of their growing strength was mirrored in the selection of Francis Patrick Kenrick as Archbishop of Baltimore in 1851.

Now that there was not one but a number of archdioceses, the period of the provincial councils was succeeded by that of the plenary councils at which the multiplying number of provinces and dioceses was represented. When Kenrick presided over the First Plenary Council in the spring of 1852, the church was made up of six metropolitan and twenty-seven suffragan sees, and had over a million and a half members. (The following year yet another archdiocese, San Francisco, was erected.) Though the church had grown to be the largest in the land, it was prevailingly a church of immigrants—of the thirty-two prelates at the First Plenary, only a quarter were native-born. That council devoted much attention to regularizing the patterns of organization and discipline, and to encouraging the development of schools and seminaries.

The 1850s were marked by a new surge of nativism. The decline of the Whig party left a political vacuum which the nativists sought to fill. A secret Order of the Star-Spangled Banner accepted as members only native Protestants who promised to oppose foreigners and Catholics in political office. The 'Know-Nothings', as they were nicknamed, gained political power in a number of states in the 1850s. The public image of the Catholic Church was tarnished in an already difficult time when Archbishop Gaetano Bedini came to the country in 1853 as a papal representative to report on the conditions of religion and to deal with certain administrative difficulties, some relating to the continuing problems of trusteeism. Bedini's role in the suppression of liberalism in Italy in 1848 made him an obvious target for criticism, which was sensationally applied by a former priest, Alessandro Gavazzi. Demonstrations confronted the archbishop, who proved to be an embarrassment to the American bishops. The Know-Nothings gained at the polls, but their surge did not last long. The movement rather quickly declined as the issue of slavery, on which it compromised, grew in importance, and the new Republican party quickly swept past it. But before it was over, there had been a number of nativist riots, especially at Louisville in 1855 where there were a score of deaths. The whole affair tended to increase the isolation of the Catholics, who assiduously developed their own network of institutions. It did not drive them out of politics, however, for they remained active, especially in the Democratic party.

The Catholic Church did not take a stand on the slavery issue, for the practice was not in violation of its official teaching on divine and natural law. Individual Catholics held a variety of positions on both sides; Bishop England, for example, though he expressed a personal antipathy to slavery, wrote that it was not contrary to Scripture. The hierarchy was divided, chiefly along sectional lines. Faced with so many other pressing matters, it was not expedient for them to confront such a divisive problem.

Though many Catholics left or drifted away from their church for various reasons, many others were won as converts. Early in the century, Elizabeth Bayley Seton (1774–1821) became a Catholic, and later founded a teaching Order, the Sisters of Charity. A number of high church Episcopalians entered Roman Catholic ranks towards the middle of the century. One of the most famous converts of all was Orestes A. Brownson (1803–76), who after a long religious pilgrimage which included Presbyterian, Universalist, atheist, Unitarian, and Transcendentalist positions, came to rest in Catholicism in 1844. A prolific journalist and writer, he was a highly independent and stubborn man who made many enemies through his criticisms of the parochial schools and of the Irish tendency toward isolation. This creative thinker anticipated the Christian social thinkers of a later period at many points. During his own pilgrimage, he influenced Isaac Hecker (1819–88), a former Methodist of German ancestry whose wanderings brought him into contact with Transcendentalism and, also in 1844, into Catholicism. Hecker became a Redemptorist priest, but in order better to accomplish his goal of winning American Protestants, he was given permission to leave that Order to found the Congregation of Missionary Priests of Saint Paul the Apostle in 1858. Devoted both to Catholicism and to democracy, Hecker and his Paulist Order helped many Catholics to regard the American scene in a more appreciative light. Many of the ideas so important in the general culture—individualism, perfectibility, equality, progress—Hecker adapted for the Catholic context, and dreamed of an America that would one day find fulfilment of its ideals in Catholicism.

Communitarianism and Experimentation

The religious hungers whetted by the intensities of revivalism were not always adequately satisfied by the patterns of life within the denominations. The Awakeners called for direct experience of God, and the living of a holy life moving towards perfection. The faithful were exhorted to prepare for the coming of the glorious millennium of God's rule on earth, for as they saw it many signs pointed to the promised fulfilment. There were indeed great numbers who found that the continuing religious services, meetings, and causes of the evangelical churches and the patterns of Bible-reading, prayer, Sabbath observance, and good works which they cultivated were generally satisfying. But there were those whose religious needs were not fully met; some found peace in the more churchly movements, while others longed to live in religious communities wholly subordinate to the spiritual vision, communities in which all the details of daily life would be religiously ordered. Conditions were favourable for the development of communal societies: religious freedom opened the door of opportunity, while the existence of open land in a nation of growing resources provided the material base. Well over a hundred communities in which property was held in common were inaugurated. Some were small and had only a fleeting existence, while others grew in size and significance.

There is no easy way to characterize the many 'communitarian' movements, for they varied greatly. Some were predominantly religious in pattern, while others were more secular or Utopian in origin. The Shakers or United Society of Believers in Christ's Second Appearing had founded a dozen communities before the beginning of the nineteenth century.[12] A great period of expansion followed the Second Awakenings, especially on the frontiers of Ohio and Kentucky. Several prominent revivalist leaders, notably Richard McNemar, were converted to the United Society, and devoted their powers to building up the disciplined, celibate communities designed to match the individual search for perfection with a truly Christian corporate existence—an example of the perfect society. At their peak before mid-century, there were some 6,000 members of Shaker societies, deployed in about twenty communities. They saw themselves as a people who regarded biblical and millennial teachings with complete earnestness, and who were overcoming the evils of individualism and secularism. They attracted great attention, both because of their distinctive patterns of belief and worship, and because of the impressiveness of their architecture and the ingenuity of their agricultural and mechanical inventions.

Their history was marked in the late 1830s and early 1840s by a period of intense religious excitement inspired by belief in communications with spirits. Trances and physical manifestations reminiscent of early campmeetings broke out, and got so out of control that services were closed to

[12] See above, p. 159.

the public. When the excitement finally passed after a few years, the fear of further undisciplined enthusiasm, combined with a worldliness that crept in with prosperity, led to a loss of zeal, and a long, steady decline began.

A number of the communities were planted by sectarian groups from Germany seeking opportunities to work out complete patterns of Christian living, usually under the inspiration of some charismatic leader. The followers of George Rapp, devout pietists who stressed millenarianism and celibacy, founded Harmony and Economy in Pennsylvania and New Harmony in Indiana. Disrupted by troublemakers, the Rappite communities declined rapidly after the founder's death. Some seceders from the movement joined another German-born leader, William Keil, in founding Bible-centred communities in Bethel, Missouri, and (when some of the members got 'Oregon fever') in Aurora, Oregon. Both communities were economically prosperous, but dissolved after Keil's death. Another settlement of German pietist immigrants was at Zoar, Ohio; faced with poverty, they adopted communal ownership of property and, temporarily, celibacy. Their economic difficulties passed with the opening of the Ohio Canal, but characteristically they disbanded with the passing of their beloved leader, Michael Bimeler. Some of the communitarian groups have survived in some form into the late twentieth century—a few Shakers, and the descendants of the Amana Society, or Community of True Inspiration, pietists with charismatic beliefs who finally settled in Iowa.

One of the most distinctive of the communitarian movements arose indigenously in an atmosphere prepared by revivalism and perfectionism under the leadership of John Humphrey Noyes (1811–86), who had been converted during the Finney revivals. A graduate of Dartmouth, Noyes studied divinity at Andover and at Yale, where he adopted extreme perfectionist views, claiming that true conversion meant that one could live free from sin. He also reacted against the individualism so widely accepted in his time, adopting socialistic views. The little perfectionist group that gathered around him in Putney, Vermont, adopted in 1846 the practice of 'complex marriage', whereby each woman in the group was the wife of every man, and each man was the husband of every woman. The reaction of the neighbourhood to this experiment in religious adultery was so negative that Noyes led his group to Oneida, New York, where in relative isolation a large central 'Mansion House' was erected for the burgeoning community. Complex marriage was continued, but a rule of 'male continence' was followed, with propagation permitted only by community decision. The economic life of the community was based on farming, logging, and, especially, the manufacture of animal traps and silverware. Life was strictly regulated; through the practice of 'mutual criticism' Noyes maintained internal discipline and kept control. Children were brought up in nurseries, and were well educated. The community flourished for thirty years, but internal restlessness, combined with growing resistance from the neighbourhood, brought the experiment to a close. Complex marriage was abandoned in 1879, and communal ownership abandoned soon after.

The famous but short-lived Hopedale, Brook Farm, and Fruitlands experiments in Massachusetts were inspired by liberal and Transcendentalist philosophies, and became widely known through the concerns of renowned religious and literary figures with their aims, difficulties, and failures. Still other communitarian groups were formed on Utopian socialist principles. Robert Owen, the industrialist who had treated his employees in an exemplary way in his Scottish factories, purchased the Rappite colony in Indiana to establish his New Harmony experiment in 1826. Internal dissension frustrated his dream of presenting a model for the ideal socialist society; a score of other Owenite communities were developed in this same period but soon ended, their idealist theories inadequate to meet the stubborn realities of economics and human nature. Then in the 1840s nearly fifty 'phalanxes' were founded in the effort to work out the Utopian teachings of Charles Fourier—Brook Farm went through a brief Fourieristic phase. On the whole, the communities centred in religion proved longer lasting, but though they attracted considerable attention, they did not seriously influence the dominant patterns of denominational life. They do illustrate, however, the depth of religious feelings and the longing for closer contact with divine power in a close fellowship.

In several of the communitarian groups there was an interest in spiritism or spiritualism, the quest for direct communication with the world of spirits, a reflection of the growing interest in such matters in the wider culture. A writer who in a general way contributed to an upsurge of interest in the world beyond the senses was the famous Swedish scientist, author, and seer, Emmanuel Swedenborg (1688–1772). Claiming that he was in direct communication with the spirit world and had been divinely directed to explain the spiritual sense of the Scriptures, Swedenborg produced many volumes in presenting a monistic religious interpretation of the universe that affirmed human freedom and perfectibility. His philosophy appealed to some intellectuals, and also to some unconventional folk. His influence went far beyond the small groups of Sweden-borgian followers who in the early nineteenth century formed the 'New Church' or the Church of the New Jerusalem. The Swedish thinker's works were but one of the forces that heightened interest in phenomena of the spirit in this period—other teachers and writers contributed to the growing popular interest in the subject.

In 1848 a decisive new stage in spiritualist history was reached when strange rappings at the home of John D. Fox of Hydesville, New York, were interpreted by his two younger daughters as having come from the world of departed spirits, with which they had established communication. Soon they were holding public seances; other mediums sprang into prominence, periodicals were issued, and a chaotic movement, in which the motifs of religion and entertainment were mixed, spread with surprising swiftness. Forty years later the Fox sisters explained that they had produced the rappings by cracking their toe joints, but that did not seriously check the spread of the movement. By the end of the century the National Spiritualist Association of Churches was in effect a small, very liberal denomination, the first of several such bodies.

Latter-Day Saints

By far the largest of the indigenous denominational families to arise in the United States, Mormonism, combined Puritan, evangelical, Campbellite, churchly, democratic, and communitarian elements with some very unique features of its own in its origins and growth. Joseph Smith (1805–44) moved with his family when he was 10 from New England to the 'burned-over district' of upstate New York. The excitements of revivalism aroused spiritual hungers within him, but he was troubled by the denominational rivalries which swept through the neighbourhood and into his own family. The claims and counter-claims of the churches led him to distrust all churches and to seek divine guidance as to the true path. As he later described it, in 1822 he was led by the angel Moroni to a place where were buried golden plates written in strange hieroglyphics, and was given special spectacles which enabled him to translate them. In 1830 Smith published what he claimed was a translation of the golden plates, which an angel then swept away.

The Book of Mormon tells of the wanderings of the good Nephites and the evil Lamanites, descendants of a lost tribe of Israel who inhabited the American continent in biblical times. Crushed by the Lamanites, the surviving Nephites, Mormon and his son Moroni, buried the plates in the fourth century A.D. Their disclosure to Smith was, he claimed, a sign of the coming Last Judgement. Written in a style much like that of the King James version of the Bible, some of which it repeats and to which it was considered a supplement, *The Book of Mormon* provided answers to many of the perplexing religious and theological questions then being so hotly debated. Critics quickly pointed out that the work showed internal marks of recent authorship by the way it referred to places, ideas, and events of modern times. But to believers in the prophet's testimony, the book offered a satisfying world-view and provided convincing answers to ultimate questions. The problems which had troubled Smith as to what church to join were decisively solved by the founding of a new one, interpreted as the restoration of the one true Church of Christ, in Fayette, New York, in 1830. In a few years the official name was taken: The Church of Jesus Christ of Latter-day Saints.

Joseph Smith claimed that the age of revelation was not over. At the first meeting of the new church, for example, he announced that it had been revealed that he was to be called prophet, seer, apostle, and elder in the new movement. The Mormon theology that continued to develop from his teachings and revelations was optimistic in tone, and stressed the eternality of matter, a self-made, finite deity, and a church that balanced individual striving with strong central authority. It spoke convincingly to many persons caught in the religious and political turmoils of the time in both America and Europe.

Though many strands of contemporary religious life were woven into the fabric of Mormonism, its distinctive elements set it apart, quickly evoking sharp hostility which deepened the Saints' sense of isolation and particularity. Hence the move was made to Kirtland, Ohio, early in 1831, under the influence of an early convert, Sidney Rigdon, a former Baptist who was a preacher of the Disciples of Christ. At Kirtland the Mormons, growing steadily as converts were won, gathered for a time in a semi-communal society, largely because of economic necessity. Under the guidance of the founder and prophet who was maturing into an effective and inspiring leader, outposts were developed in Missouri, first near Independence, envisioned as the place where the promised city of Zion would be built.

A feature of the life of the growing church was the development of an ordered hierarchy of priests which included all male members of good standing—a non-professional, lay ministry which incorporated certain democratic aspects, yet which bound the participants to the decisions of the top leadership in a system of consent. The publication of Smith's continuing revelations as *The Doctrine and Covenants* in 1835 gave authoritative patterns for the burgeoning internal structures of Mormon life.

The centre of the movement shifted westwards to Missouri, largely because of difficulties at Kirtland during the financial troubles of 1837. There the resistance of the 'gentiles' forced the resettlement of the Saints northward to Far West, Missouri, and then as hostilities erupted in the 'Mormon War' of 1838 they moved again, back across the Mississippi to found Nauvoo, Illinois. Chartered as a 'state within a state' in 1840, Nauvoo soon became the largest city in the state. The growth of the church was augmented by the success of missionaries in England's factory towns—more than 4,000 converts from abroad arrived during the Nauvoo period.

Once again, this distinctive religion based on new and continuing re-velations evoked the ire of surrounding populations, especially as it was becoming a force at the polls. The prophet's revelations stressed such novel doctrines as the plurality of gods, the baptism of the dead, and marriage for time and eternity. In 1843 Smith had a revelation authorizing polygamy, and as the news leaked out, the enemies of the movement had a powerful weapon. Smith then announced his candidacy for the presidency of the United States; he was also growing increasingly autocratic in his control of his people. When a printing press in Nauvoo belonging to the opposition was destroyed following a sham trial, the combined forces of a mob and the militia compelled Smith and his brother Hyrum to surrender. They were promised a fair trial, but instead were brutally murdered in the Carthage jail by the mob, which then took Nauvoo.[13]

The leader who emerged as the new prophet, seer, and revelator was an early convert, Brigham Young (1801–77), a superb organizer who early in 1846 led the Saints out of Nauvoo westwards on a trek beyond the boundaries of the United States as they then were into Mexican territory to found the Provisional State of Deseret in the basin of the Great Salt Lake. A number of schismatic movements developed after Smith's death, only one of which proved to be of permanent significance. A small group that did not go west but moved into Iowa (and later also back into Missouri) founded the Reorganized Church of Jesus Christ of Latter-day Saints, and won the support of the original prophet's family. It has con-tinued as a small church, much closer to the patterns of conservative, pietistic Protestantism than the larger, more distinctive body that relocated in the west.

[13] See Thomas F. O'Dea's penetrating study, *The Mormons* (Chicago, 1957). On Smith, see Fawn Brodie, *No Man Knows My History: The Life of Joseph Smith* (New York, 1946).

Under Young's forceful leadership, the Salt Lake City Mormons spread their empire across the great western basin; before the leader's death over 350 Mormon settlements, chiefly agricultural, were established. The overseas mission prospered, with the Scandinavian countries proving to be a source of converts second only to England. An emphasis on the gathering of the Saints in their western Zion in anticipation of the millennium helped to draw those won by the missionaries to Mormon territory.

As a result of the Mexican War the Mormons again found themselves in American territory. Instead of maintaining an independent state they had to become part of the new territory of Utah, of which Young was elected governor. An old story was repeated; as 'gentiles' moved west tension again erupted into another Mormon War in 1857. Peace was soon made, for the Mormons recognized the legitimacy of civil government, and felt secure in their own centralized, highly activistic church. By 1860, three decades after the founding in Fayette, the Mormons had established their predominance over the western inter-mountain area, and were well on the way to becoming the nation's largest indigenous church. The Church of Jesus Christ of Latter-day Saints had many recognizable ties with the historic Christian tradition, but it also had some distinctive departures and surprising innovations. In its blend of continuity and discontinuity it showed in magnified form certain major tendencies of American religion, such as activism, optimism, pragmatism, a missionary spirit, and a sense of destiny.

The first six decades of the nineteenth century in the United States were thus marked by an impressive series of Awakenings in the evangelical churches, movements that helped some of them to mushroom into giants, divided others, and helped bring some new ones into being. The patterns of piety and morality in these denominations were sufficiently uniform to enable them to make a powerful impact on the culture of their time through the use of the voluntary societies, and to move measurably toward their goal of making America a 'Christian nation'. Yet churches and movements of very diversified orientations that resisted or rejected the evangelical way also gathered strength over the same span of years, some primarily because trends of immigration from Europe favoured their causes. Though many of the movements that opposed the evangelical sweep remained small, some did lay permanent foundations so that the fundamental patterns of American religion had become far more diversified and the spectrum of beliefs much wider by the outbreak of the Civil War than they had been at the beginning of the century.

VIII

GROWTH, CONFLICT, AND
CANADIANIZATION IN THE
BRITISH ERA

(1800–67)

THE story of the Christian churches in British North America in the first
two-thirds of the nineteenth century is one of impressive growth, sharp
conflict, and the emergence of certain definitive patterns of freedom and
voluntaryism in institutional religious life as a nation came into being.
In this period the separate and diverse provinces under British rule slowly
worked out political arrangements for national unity. At the outset the
colonies were thinly and unevenly populated, separately supervised from
London, and largely isolated from each other. In 1867 the four provinces
of Nova Scotia, New Brunswick, Quebec, and Ontario confederated to
form the Dominion of Canada; they were soon joined by Manitoba,
British Columbia, and Prince Edward Island. During these years the
population was steadily expanding to about three million by the time of
Confederation, with considerable movement into the undeveloped lands.
Churches and missions went with the people, both with those who moved
into newly opened areas of the older provinces and with those who ventured into the vast frontiers of the north and west. As the denominations
responded to the challenges before them, many religious and educational
institutions were planted and nurtured. The great bulk of the population
continued to be identified with the churches—a rather impressive achievement in view of the vastness of the task.

The growth of the British provinces and their churches was often accompanied by competition and conflict. The tensions in Canadian life,
most of which had a religious component and some of which centred in
religion, came from many complex sources. In addition to the massive
differences between French Catholics and English Protestants, political
and religious tensions often appeared among competing groups of English, Scottish, Irish, German, and American origin. An intense struggle

went on between those who wanted some form of religious establishment and those committed to religious liberty and the voluntary support of churches. Walls between communions were generally high, and a polemic note was often sounded in religious discourse and literature. Within the churches, contentions among the various parties often became acute, in several cases leading to schism. Religious differences played a role in the political conflicts of the period, which occasionally boiled over into riot, and in 1837 into rebellion. By mid-century the growing strength of those who espoused a secular creed of liberal nationalism was in part a reaction against bickering among and within the churches. Quarrels between the religious groups often became especially vociferous over educational issues, which so often were the focus of religious, ethnic, and cultural differences.

Out of the various political and religious conflicts emerged certain compromises and arrangements that cleared the way for Confederation. The struggle of certain sincere leaders to maintain patterns of establishment and privilege for their churches was defeated; freedom, voluntaryism, and diversity in religious affairs came to be generally accepted. Provision for the maintenance of separate educational institutions, often with some governmental assistance, permitted various groups to adjust to each other. Although church and state did become separated in this period, the American image of a 'wall of separation' did not seem relevant and was not invoked; in Canada religious institutions were not so sharply differentiated from the other major institutions of the culture. The churches were in various stages of developing their own national organizations as Confederation was achieved, and hence the patterns of their 'Canadianization' varied considerably in detail. Certain heritages from across the Atlantic were modified and influences from south of the border were resisted or adapted as the churches addressed themselves to their mission in the steadily enlarging Canadian scene. The way in which patterns of religious life and organization were shaped as churches expanded amid trying conflicts and growing freedom provides the central theme in the history of Christianity in Canada in this era.

Growth and Consolidation in the Atlantic Colonies

The term 'Atlantic colonies' refers to the Maritime provinces (Nova Scotia, New Brunswick, Prince Edward Island) plus Newfoundland, which was only recognized by the British Parliament as a colony in 1824 (and which did not enter the Dominion until 1949). In these eastern areas the Church of England, as the Established Church of the mother country, enjoyed certain initial advantages. Bishop Charles Inglis of Nova Scotia, whose vast diocese included all the Atlantic colonies and Bermuda, drew a government salary which was increased in 1807, the year before he was named to serve on the appointive legislative council of Nova Scotia. An annual parliamentary grant for that province administered by the S.P.G. reached a high point of £13,000 by 1830, while certain other funds and grants of land aided the Church of England.[1] Although Inglis desired to cultivate good relations with other religious groups, trouble arose when a commission in England ruled that King's College in Windsor must have a wholly Anglican faculty and that its students must subscribe to the Thirty-nine Articles. The efforts on the part of the home government to use the arms of the Church of England in the colonies as bulwarks of imperial loyalty were resented and resisted by dissenters, and added to the troubles of the bishop and his successors.

When Inglis died in 1816 he was succeeded briefly by a man who soon returned to England, and Inglis's son took resident leadership as commissary. Deeply concerned about the development of schools and the training of teachers, John Inglis introduced a branch of the Society for the Promotion of Christian Knowledge. In 1825 he became bishop in his own right, and secured four archdeacons to aid in the work of administring the vast diocese with its increasing population. After a visitation of his diocese, though he failed to reach Newfoundland, Inglis reported that he had confirmed more than 6,700 persons and that there were 163 churches in his domain.[2] He devoted much effort to building educational institutions. In 1828 a school in Fredericton, New Brunswick, that had been basically Anglican, was granted a royal charter as King's College. Although all members of the college council had to be Anglicans, others could serve on the faculty.[3] The S.P.G. and Dr. Bray's Associates long maintained some schools for blacks who had come with the Loyalist migration, but they tended to join other churches.

Other denominations, though lacking the privileges of the Church of England, were growing stronger in these years. Presbyterian strength increased markedly in the early nineteenth century as immigration from Scotland brought members of the Church of Scotland and the two secessionist churches which had broken with the Established Church in the eighteenth century. The secessionist presbyteries flourished. The

---

[1] John S. Moir (ed.), *Church and State in Canada*, pp. 49–71.

[2] John S. Moir, *The Church in the British Era: From the British Conquest to Confederation*, A History of the Christian Church In Canada, ii (Toronto, 1972), p. 130.

[3] D. C. Masters, *Protestant Church Colleges in Canada: A History* (Toronto, 1966), p. 21.

devoted leadership of James MacGregor (1759–1830), the father of Presbyterianism in the Maritimes, and Thomas McCulloch (1776–1843), who assumed an important role in education, was especially conspicuous. The distinctions between the Presbyterian bodies that had caused the separations in Scotland did not loom so large in North America, and in 1817 the first of what were to be many church unions took place as the self-governing Synod of Nova Scotia was formed with three presbyteries and twenty-nine congregations; a fourth presbytery for Prince Edward Island was soon added. Though all three strands of Scottish Presbyterianism participated, the secessionist spirit was dominant. The largest Protestant church in the Maritimes was brought into being by the union. Deeply concerned about higher education, the Presbyterians founded an academy at Pictou under McCulloch; because King's College was open only to Anglicans Pictou provided instruction in theology.

The Synod of Nova Scotia included most but not quite all of the Presbyterian ministers and congregations. Over the years, a number of Church of Scotland ministers who did not co-operate with the synod entered the region, usually with the backing of the Glasgow Colonial Society (founded in 1825). In 1833 ten of these ministers founded a competing Synod of Nova Scotia, adding two years later another synod in New Brunswick. These bodies claimed to represent the original Scottish Reformed tradition. Not only were efforts to unite the competing synods unsuccessful, but in the 1840s further splits occurred. They were related to the Disruption of the Church of Scotland in 1843 on the issues of the control of patrons over congregations and the control of Parliament over the established Church of Scotland. The Free Church of Scotland, evangelical and missionary in spirit, broke with the establishment. This dramatic event had immediate repercussions in the Maritimes. In Nova Scotia the newer synod went over almost unanimously to the Free Church side, while in New Brunswick the opposite occurred, with the majority of ministers adhering to the established 'Auld Kirk' of Scotland. In the Maritimes as a whole it was the Free Church bodies which moved ahead in missionary and educational activity.[4]

These divisions within the Presbyterian family were deeply disturbing to a people traditionally concerned about the unity of the church, and with the passage of time changed attitudes opened the way for union negotiations. There were some important differences to be overcome: the Free Church of Nova Scotia at first did not reject the principle of establishment

[4] Neil G. Smith, Allan L. Farris, H. Keith Markel, *A Short History of the Presbyterian Church in Canada* (Toronto, n.d.), pp. 143–8.

as long as the proper rights of the churches were respected, but the Presbyterian Church of Nova Scotia with its secessionist background emphasized voluntaryism in religion. The latter view gradually prevailed, in part because of a resurgence of anti-Catholicism in the 1850s, and opened the way for the union of the two bodies as the Synod of the Lower Provinces in 1860. The Free Church of New Brunswick joined six years later. Despite their tangled history of division and union, the Presbyterians vigorously witnessed to their version of the faith in the Atlantic provinces.

The Baptist churches of Nova Scotia, reaping the late harvest of the Alline revival, formed an association of churches in 1800. It was soon torn by controversy over the question of whether unimmersed Christians could be admitted to communion. The predominant trend in Baptist circles in Britain and the United States at the time was toward closed communion, and in 1809 the association withdrew fellowship from congregations that did not abide by the strict rule. When that issue was settled, numbers greatly increased, especially as the fruit of revival. As in evangelical churches elsewhere, missionary enthusiasm swept through the denomination, leading to the organization of a missionary society in 1814, and later to the publishing of the Baptist Missionary Magazine. By 1821 the association was strong enough to divide along provincial lines, with sixteen churches left in the Nova Scotia Baptist Association as thirteen were gathered into a new one in New Brunswick. The first Baptist congregation on Prince Edward Island was formed in 1827, but within six years half a dozen more were gathered. Close relationships with Baptists in the United States were maintained during these decades; common interests in promoting full religious liberty were shared. The growing strength of this Free Church tradition was reflected in the founding of two educational institutions. The opening of an academy at Horton (later Wolfville) in 1829 was aided by a group of evangelicals from Halifax who found a home among the Baptists after leaving the Anglican fold. Supported in part by public funds, the school became Acadia College in 1841. Three years later a gift from the Baptists of England helped to make possible a Department of Theology. Meanwhile, the Baptists of New Brunswick, shut out of the new King's College, opened a co-educational seminary at Fredericton in 1836.[5]

Not all Baptists belonged to churches related to the large associations which tended to be Calvinistic in theology; small groups of Free Will

[5] George E. Levy, *The Baptists of the Maritime Provinces, 1753–1946* (Saint John, N.B., 1946), p. 121.

Baptists gathered in the 1830s. In 1846 the two major associations formed the Baptist Convention of Nova Scotia, New Brunswick, and Prince Edward Island. Boards to promote missionary and educational work were set up, and the associations were subdivided to make more workable units. Baptists were strong supporters of movements for temperance and for Sabbath observance. By the time of Confederation, Baptists had gathered or revived over a hundred congregations, and had erected more than that number of buildings. John Moir concludes that the Baptist fellowship was 'the most dynamic religious force in the Maritimes during the three decades before Confederation'.[6]

Baptists launched a missionary effort among the Micmac Indians of the Maritime provinces. Silas T. Rand (1810–89), a pastor skilled in languages, including three Indian tongues, undertook a mission among the Micmacs, many of whom were nominal Catholics, while he was serving a congregation on Prince Edward Island. In 1850 he joined with other Protestants to found the Micmac Missionary Society, and then combined missionary labours with translating the Scriptures into Indian languages. Settling in Hantsport, Nova Scotia, Rand travelled widely among the Indians of the Maritimes in an extensive evangelical and social ministry, although he was not rewarded with large numbers of converts. Rand was troubled by the 'abominable and unreasonable ideas of caste' held by many of the whites.[7]

The Baptist way gathered greater support among the blacks than did any other Christian tradition. Slavery had largely disappeared in the Maritimes by the time the British Parliament passed the act in 1833 which abolished it throughout the colonies. Many of the Negroes who had been brought with the Loyalist migration became Baptists, while the majority of the refugees who came fleeing slavery in the United States were already Baptists. Some of the black congregations at first joined the existing Baptist associations, but in 1854 Richard Preston, a former slave who had escaped from Virginia and had been ordained in London, gathered a dozen churches into the African Baptist Association of Nova Scotia. As happened elsewhere in North America, discrimination against blacks deprived them of equal educational and economic opportunities.[8] By the time of Confederation, about half the blacks of Canada lived in the Halifax area, the majority of them Baptists.

At the opening of the nineteenth century, Methodists were a small

6 *The Church in the British Era*, p. 150.
7 Levy, *The Baptists of the Maritime Provinces*, p. 168.
8 Winks, *The Blacks in Canada*, pp. 139–41.

group, numbering less than a thousand. A decisive shift in direction took place as the nominal supervision of the Methodist Episcopal Church in the United States was replaced by the increasing role of the English Wesleyan Conference. William Black, the Nova Scotian who had emerged as the forceful indigenous leader of the Methodists, returned from England in 1800 with four preachers who had volunteered for service in the provinces. The organization in the mother country of the General Wesleyan Methodist Missionary Society for the raising of funds and the advancement of work abroad was instrumental in drawing Methodists in the Maritimes closer to the English orbit. By the 1820s many of the preachers were relatively recent arrivals from England. They were zealous evangelicals, but reflected the growing moderation of English Methodism, and stressed strict discipline in the societies.[9] Pietistic in their teachings, the Methodists in the eastern provinces were in the main politically conservative and did not question the privileges of the Anglican church. Growth was steady but not spectacular; the sense of dependence on the Missionary Society inhibited local initiative. In 1826 separate districts for Nova Scotia and New Brunswick (the latter including Prince Edward Island) were created, and in the decade that followed membership tripled. Revival meetings had been prohibited in 1820, but in 1836 protracted meetings, usually lasting four days, were held. As a result of their caution the Methodists were still not expanding as fast as their co-religionists to the west—and to the south —were doing.

In 1843 the institution which came to be known as the Mount Allison Wesleyan Academy was opened in Sackville, New Brunswick, with financial aid from public lands as well as by private donation. Fifteen years later it became a college. Although formal theological training came afterwards, some of its earlier students entered the ministry. Only after considerable prodding from England did the Wesleyans of the Maritimes assume a measure of self-government with the formation in 1855 of the Conference of Eastern British America, which included Bermuda and claimed about 13,000 members.

The story of the emancipation of Roman Catholics in the Atlantic colonies is complex. The General Emancipation Act of the British Parliament in 1829 finally brought the rights of voting and office-holding in places where they had not previously been secured (especially Prince Edward Island). There were three distinct national traditions among Catholics: the Acadians, grouped largely in New Brunswick, Prince Edward and Cape Breton Islands, the Irish in Halifax, and the Scottish in

9 French, *Parsons and Politics*, pp. 54–63.

eastern Nova Scotia and Cape Breton (which was annexed to Nova Scotia in 1820). Rivalries between these groups, especially the latter two, deepened Catholic difficulties in a Protestant environment. The remoteness of the region from Quebec and the turmoil of the Napoleonic period long frustrated efforts to provide adequate ecclesiastical supervision. Finally, in 1817 Edmund Burke was named vicar-apostolic for Nova Scotia, and two years later Angus Bernard MacEachern was similarly appointed for Prince Edward and Cape Breton Islands. Catholic life in Newfoundland was handicapped by a lack of priests; after serving effectively in the face of heavy odds as vicar-apostolic for many years, in 1847 Michael Anthony Fleming finally became bishop of the newly created see of St. John's.

Catholicism in the Atlantic colonies gained from the steady growth of population, and shared in the general prosperity of mid-century. By 1860 no less than seven dioceses had been created for the region; the year before Halifax had been made a metropolitan see with the right of supervision over neighbouring dioceses. In this period of growth important centres of higher education were founded. A seminary matured in 1866 into St. Francis Xavier University at Antigonish, Nova Scotia—a source of priests for the Maritimes. A *petit séminaire* at Memramcook in New Brunswick developed into St. Joseph's College, focus of a revival of Acadian culture. New religious Orders further strengthened the life of the growing church.

In the 1850s the good relations between Protestants and Catholics were broken by a series of anti-Catholic incidents. In part, these were byproducts of an emotional reaction to the restoration of the hierarchy in England by Rome in 1850. The fact that the hierarchy had been outlawed for 300 years meant to many Protestants that its restoration could only be an illustration of 'papal aggression', an insult to both the Crown and to Protestantism.[10]

Because of the growth of the Presbyterian, Baptist, Methodist, and Catholic churches, combined with changes in the status of the Established Church in England during the years of reform, the privileged position of the Church of England in the colonies came to an end. The Anglicans had shared in the growth of the region too, as was reflected in the division of the original huge diocese of Nova Scotia. New dioceses for Newfoundland and Bermuda and for New Brunswick were erected in 1839 and 1845 respectively. But as early as the 1820s, questions had been raised in

[10] Dominic of Saint-Denis, *The Catholic Church in Canada*, pp. 70–4; Moir, *The Church in the British Era*, pp. 135–8, 144–7.

England about the appropriation of parliamentary grants through the S.P.G. for the support of a minority tradition in the colonies. In the following decade the sums were progressively reduced. Such Anglican privileges as the sole authority to perform marriages in the western colonies had to be shared with the clergy of other denominations. Then in 1851 when the new Bishop of Nova Scotia, Hibbert Binney, sought a seat in the legislative council he was refused. This signalled the end of the politically preferential position of the Church of England. Six years later the Bishop of Fredericton, John Medley, resigned his seat on the legislative council of New Brunswick under political pressure, marking the end of establishment there. Another sign of the change was the founding of Dalhousie College in Halifax in reaction to Anglican exclusiveness at King's. Though the beginnings of the new college can be traced back to 1818, not for twenty years did teaching at college level begin under Thomas McCulloch, who came from Pictou to lead in the development of Dalhousie. Officially non-sectarian and publicly supported, the college was dominantly Presbyterian for many years.

The Anglican churches had to develop new ways of financing and maintaining their work in the face of their loss of privileges; they had to learn the ways of voluntaryism. Bishop John Inglis took a bold but necessary step in urging the formation of 'Church Societies' of laymen and clergy under episcopal presidency; they were formed in all the Atlantic colonies between 1837 and 1843. These diocesan societies supplemented the moneys coming from English sources for the support of missionaries, the building of churches, and the conduct of schools. The trend toward autonomy was assisted by contributions from the Colonial Bishoprics Fund, raised in England under the auspices of the S.P.G. to provide endowments for the overseas dioceses which were then being formed in many parts of the world. Bishops supported by the new endowments were usually high churchmen, such as Binney of Nova Scotia, Medley of Fredericton, and Edward Feild, second Bishop of Newfoundland. These leaders were not interested in reviving the old dream of establishment for they distrusted governmental aid; they preferred to build their church through the use of societies and synods of laity and clergy. Feild plunged into his work with great energy, building a cathedral, developing a theological college, and encouraging much educational and charitable work.[11] Thus the Church of England made the difficult transition from privileged institution to voluntary denomination.

The Congregational churches had virtually disappeared from the

---

[11] Carrington, *The Anglican Church in Canada*, pp. 91 ff., 101 ff.

eastern provinces by 1800, but a considerable resurgence of that tradition occurred in the 1840s, with the help of the London Missionary Society and the travels of a dynamic Congregational preacher from Montreal, Henry Wilkes. The gains did not last, however—in a few years decline again set in as members were lost, primarily to the Presbyterians.

By the time of Confederation in 1867 the significant transition to religious freedom, with the denominations treated as equals before the law, had generally been accepted. The churches held a secure place in the affections of the people, however, and in the life of a society that was widely understood to be Christian. The denominational schools and colleges usually received some financial assistance from public funds. In Newfoundland, the general school system developed along denominational lines—a distinctive pattern for British North America. In all the eastern colonies, a Christian world-view informed the course of life, morality was undergirded by church teaching, and strict patterns of Sabbath observance were followed. Though religious establishment was a thing of the past, the Christian character of the Atlantic provinces seemed firmly secured.

Conflict in the Canadas

In Lower (Quebec) and Upper (Ontario) Canada the expanding Christian churches frequently found themselves in contention with each other in this period with their differences entering into several major political crises. The two settings were quite different, for the Catholic Church dominated the older, larger, French-speaking Lower Canada, while various denominations were still laying their foundations in the new communities of English-speaking Upper Canada.

In Lower Canada the Catholic Church was pressing for full recognition of its rights and for freedom from British supervision. The central figure in this drive was Joseph-Octave Plessis (1763–1825). Born and educated in Quebec, he possessed great administrative and diplomatic skills. Appointed coadjutor to Bishop Pierre Denaut of Quebec shortly before the beginning of the nineteenth century, Plessis took effective charge of many diocesan affairs. The Catholic leaders were resisting a plan that was being proposed by the Anglican bishop, Jacob Mountain, to offer the Catholic Bishop of Quebec legal and financial recognition of his status by the government in exchange for royal control of the appointments of parish priests. The French Catholics much preferred their freedom to this kind of supervised recognition, even if the latter did provide some of the advantages of establishment. The imperial government perhaps hoped to assert its supremacy over the Catholic Church before allowing Plessis to follow Denaut as Bishop of Quebec, but when the latter died in 1806, an elderly administrator of Lower Canada, who happened to be married to a French-Canadian woman, permitted Plessis to take the oath of allegiance as Roman Catholic Bishop of Quebec.[12] Mountain was troubled, but the possibility of war with the United States made it undesirable for the government to jeopardize Catholic loyalty by any effort to undo what had been done.

When the war of 1812–14 did come, Plessis was active in guiding his church to support Britain. Reward came in the form of increased salary, and in his being named to the legislative council in 1817 as 'Bishop of the Roman Catholic Church in Quebec'. With his hand thus strengthened, the bishop had opportunity to press for a much-needed division of the huge diocese. Two years later Rome named vicars-apostolic for Prince Edward Island and New Brunswick (MacEachern), for Montreal (Jean-Jacques Lartigue), for Upper Canada (Alexander Macdonell), and for the North-west (Joseph-Norbert Provencher). Thus the diocese of some half a million souls was reorganized into five districts. The shortage of clergy continued, placing heavy burdens on the overworked *curés* as they struggled to maintain French Catholic culture in the face of many difficulties. The devoted, self-giving service of various Orders of nuns in schools, hospitals, and other institutions was of great help to church and people, and was widely praised.

The forceful Plessis died in 1825, and was succeeded by the aged, moderate Bernard-Claude Panet. Much of his patience and skill was needed in restraining as premature Bishop Lartigue's ambitious plan to have his Montreal district named as a diocese. The blunt Lartigue was an early spokesman in Canada for ultramontanism, with its resistance to liberal and Gallican ideas and its commitment to papal infallibility and ecclesiastical centralization. Not until 1836, however, after Panet had been succeeded by Joseph Signay, did Rome and London finally approve the elevation of Montreal into a diocese. By this time the British authorities were treating the Roman Catholic Church as a body independent of the state, but which drew some financial assistance from the land set aside as Clergy Reserves.

In the 1830s considerable republican sentiment spread among the French Canadians, under the leadership of the reformer Louis-Joseph Papineau, whose followers consistently held a majority in the elected assembly. As demands for the rights of the French-Canadian people

[12] Moir (ed.), *Church and State in Canada*, p. 128.

against the oligarchical control of the English-dominated appointive legislative council grew sharper, the Catholic authorities resisted the radical
shift and supported the government. The tension exploded into rebellion.
Actually the rebellion of 1837 in Lower Canada was not simply a battle
of French versus English, for some rebels were English-speaking while
the great majority of French Canadians remained loyal. In simple terms,
the rebellion was led by those who claimed to speak for the rights of the
masses against the oligarchical minorities of officials and merchants. On
a stage set by crop failures and financial panic the dissidents fought for
a parliamentary government responsive to the wishes of the electorate,
an elective legislative council, and control of revenue.[13] The rebels drew
on precedents from both American and French revolutions, and threatened
to invite American annexation. When fighting broke out in November, the
rebels faced troops under English command. The rebellion was decisively
put down. The constitution of Lower Canada was suspended by the
British Parliament, and Lord Durham was named governor-general and
high commissioner to investigate grievances. His famous *Report on the
Affairs of British North America* led to the Union Act of 1840, which provided that Upper and Lower Canada were to be united under a single
government with one governor, an appointive legislative council, and
an elected assembly with equal representation from the former separated
provinces that were popularly known as Canada East and Canada West.
The French Catholic leaders did not like this move, for the political
merger of the two disparate regions threatened the continued independence of their church and the future of their people. The Act further
outlawed the official use of French and provided for the remodelling of
the French-Canadian legal system.

A wave of French-Canadian emigration, chiefly to New England,
followed these events. French-Canadian ultranationalism originated in
the turmoil of 1837 and in reaction to the Durham Report and its consequences. Papineau came to be honoured by many of his followers as
the first great French-Canadian nationalist. The trend toward responsible
parliamentary government in Canada was generally favoured by the
French Canadians, but the union with the predominantly English and
Protestant Canada West was a move away from the prized autonomy
they sought, and it nurtured a lasting sense of injustice and resentment.
Though politically cautious, the church identified itself with the distinctive culture of the French in Canada.

In Upper Canada Catholic life since the beginning of the century had

[13] Mason Wade, *The French Canadians, 1760–1945* (London, 1954), pp. 152–62.

developed under the watchful eye of Alexander Macdonell (1762-1840). A former British army chaplain—the first Catholic in such a post since the Reformation—he arrived in Glengarry County in 1804. The Colonial Office had granted lands for the Highland Scots gathered by Macdonell, who also received a small government salary and later became a member of Upper Canada's legislative council. He did much to improve relationships between the Catholic minority and the Protestants, many of whom were strongly anti-Catholic. In 1824 Macdonell was recognized as bishop of Upper Canada, subject to Bishop Plessis of Quebec. By then the Catholic population had reached about 17,000. In the 1830s the church grew steadily through immigration, with the Irish outnumbering the Scots. When he died in 1840, the number of Catholic churches had increased from the three he found on his arrival to forty.

The Anglican Church in the Canadas was also growing significantly throughout this period, but was not given the official recognition and support her leaders expected. The hopes of Bishop Mountain for the full establishment of the Church of England were dashed by the recognition given by British officials to the Catholics. The political and religious realities of the situation did not permit the building of the effective Anglican establishment of which Mountain had dreamed. The Catholic rather than the Anglican Church came closer to being the established church in Lower Canada. The right of the Episcopal Church to collect tithes was not allowed, for it was expected that money from the Clergy Reserves—about 675,000 acres in Lower Canada—would provide sufficient funds. But the lands were only developed slowly and for years barely provided enough to cover administrative expenses. As they did begin to produce more significant revenues towards the end of Mountain's life, representatives of the congregations of Church of Scotland background were demanding a share, opening a debate that was to grow increasingly complex and angry as it was fought out politically. Though bitterly disappointed by these difficulties and defeats, the aged bishop continued his arduous labours and travels. When he died in 1825 the number of clergy had increased from nine to sixty. His successor, Charles James Stewart, who had long served as a missionary in Canada, had a better understanding of the difference between British and Canadian scenes, and was anxious to recognize the rights of other denominations. As one who had been deeply influenced by the evangelical movement within the Church of England, Stewart could sympathize with many of the other Protestant groups in a way his predecessor could not.

The expansion of the Church of England in Upper Canada was guided by a leader of iron will and fierce loyalties—John Strachan (1778–1867). A native of Scotland, Strachan served as a private tutor on his arrival in Kingston in 1800. He was soon drawn to Anglicanism, and after ordination founded a grammar school in Cornwall. Later, while serving a church at York (Toronto), his resoluteness in defending the rights of the population during the American occupation in the war of 1812–14 added to his growing prestige. He was a vigorous spokesman for Anglican privilege and aristocratic government, and was a central figure in the so-called 'Family Compact', an élite group including many of his former students which long directed affairs in Upper Canada. He became a regular member of the executive council in 1817 and of the legislative council three years later—both appointive bodies. An uncompromising champion of the ruling group, he vehemently opposed both reforming political elements and dissenting religious groups. S. F. Wise has declared that

the ruthlessness and intolerance of his political style derived from the absolute belief that the prescriptions he defended in church, state and society were part of the providential order, that Upper Canada had a special mission to preserve them in North America, and that any opposition to them was a sign of the grossest and most blasphemous infidelity, and of a dangerous sympathy for the condemned revolutionary society of the United States.[14]

As the extensive diocese of Quebec increased in numbers of churches and communicants, administrative help for the bishop came through the appointment of several archdeaconries in central locations. In 1827 Strachan became Archdeacon of York (given its Indian name of Toronto in 1834), which deferred his hopes of becoming bishop for Upper Canada, where his communion was already stronger than in Lower Canada. That same year he brought back from England the charter for King's College, York, which provided that he would be the first president and that all the professors were to be Anglicans. No religious tests were required of students—a surprisingly liberal concession—but the provision for control by a minority church stiffened the resistance of other denominations to the privileges and financial advantages of the Church of England.

Presbyterianism in the Canadas was steadily gaining in numbers, chiefly because of Scottish immigration, though the American presence was still felt. In 1818 ministers of evangelical and secessionist backgrounds formed themselves into the independent Presbytery of the Canadas. This later divided along geographical lines, with the United Presbytery of Upper Canada in the better position to take advantage of demographic

[14] 'God's Peculiar Peoples', in W. L. Morton (ed.), *The Shield of Achilles*, p. 56.

trends. There were other Presbyterian ministers in the region; those of Church of Scotland background were especially resentful of the fact that funds from the Clergy Reserves and other official sources flowed so heavily to the Anglicans. They insisted that inasmuch as in Scotland their church was established, and as the Canadas were British and not only English dependencies, they should get their share of support. In 1831 nineteen ministers formed the Synod of the Presbyterian Church of Canada in Connection with the Church of Scotland; it had four presbyteries, one in Lower Canada. That name was retained when, after long negotiations, the two Upper Canada synods merged. An important fruit of the union was the opening in 1842 of Queen's University in Kingston, the first active university in the Canadas. This rapidly growing denomination was characterized by an ardent missionary spirit and strong loyalties to the Reformed heritage.

The patterns of Methodist growth in the Canadas were quite different. At the beginning of the century American Methodists viewed Upper Canada as a field white for the harvest. It was estimated that by 1812 eight of ten persons in that province were of American origin. Between 1790 and 1812 seventy-six missionaries had been sent from the United States. With their ardent, simple but intense faith, the Methodist preachers won growing numbers of settlers, so that by 1810 there were ten circuits in operation, grouped in the Upper Canada District of the Genesee (New York) Conference. Camp-meetings were introduced in 1805, and the sights and sounds of revivalism became familiar.[15]

The war of 1812–14 brought dramatic changes to Methodism in Upper Canada. Communication across the border was cut off, and the flow of ministers from the south virtually ceased. The invading forces from the United States caused much devastation, disrupted the circuits, and upset the life of many societies. With the resurgence of the anti-American spirit, the old Loyalist attitudes came alive again. During the struggle, many Americans left the province; when it was over, immigration came predominantly from the United Kingdom rather than from the United States. When the Genesee Conference resumed its work, with separate districts for the two Canadas, care had to be taken to avoid offending Canadian sensibilities by unwise appointments to circuits. By 1817 a revival was in full swing, and some ground that had been lost was won back. By that time, however, the British Wesleyans were sending ministers into the Canadas, and they charged the American preachers with being ignorant, uncouth, and even

[15] French, *Parsons and Politics*, pp. 42–7; Arthur E. Kewley, 'The Beginning of the Camp Meeting Movement in Upper Canada', *Canadian Journal of Theology*, x (1964), 192–202.

disloyal. In 1820 a truce between the conflicting Methodist forces was reached, whereby Lower Canada would be left to the Wesleyans, while Upper Canada retained its ties with the Genesee Conference.

During the decade that followed, however, the Canadian Methodists of Upper Canada pressed for their independence, wanting to be free of control either by the Americans or the British. The Canadian Conference was finally granted its autonomy by the American General Conference in 1828. Attempts to fill the episcopate for Upper Canada failed, and the office of bishop was later abolished, so that the English rather than the American practice was followed thereafter. Talented young Canadians began to fill the positions of responsibility. Outstanding among them were the sons of Joseph Ryerson, five of whom entered the Methodist ministry, three rising to places of prominence. Egerton Ryerson (1803–82) emerged into public view in a reply to a sermon by Strachan which belittled the other churches in insisting that the government must strengthen the Church of England. Ryerson argued against such claims and defended the loyalty and religious contributions of his Methodist brethren.

This was only the opening round. In pursuing a plan to sell off some of the Clergy Reserves and use the income only for his own church, Strachan presented an inaccurate 'ecclesiastic chart' which contrasted Anglican numbers with those of other bodies to the disadvantage of the latter. Ryerson responded with counter-claims, attacked establishment as inimical to political freedom and true religion, and argued for the equality of all religious groups before the law. His brethren made him editor of what quickly became an influential weekly, the *Christian Guardian*, in which he presented a rather cautious brand of liberal thought. Reacting also against the Anglican dominance at King's College, Methodists founded Upper Canada Academy, the future Victoria University.

In the early 1830s the agreement which confined the British Wesleyans to Lower Canada broke down, for they claimed that the new independence of the Canadian Methodists outdated the previous arrangements. They were also anxious to extend their missions among the Indians and, encouraged by the government, re-entered Upper Canada as champions of respectability and loyalty. The Canadian Methodists did not relish the idea of losing their recently won autonomy, but neither did they want their witness clouded by divisive controversy. A union of the two groups offered certain advantages: it would help to overcome the lingering suspicion of Americanism, and would also open the way for some financial assistance from Britain and the Upper Canada government. Despite controversy, the Canadian Methodists agreed in 1833 to accept

Wesleyan forms and placed their missions under the Wesleyan Missionary Society. Egerton Ryerson was instrumental in working for the union. His innate conservatism now emerged in his writing, to the dismay of some who had championed his earlier defence of freedom and equality. Because of the union, the 'local preachers' lost certain rights to the full-time itinerant ministers; a few broke from the merged Wesleyan Methodist Church and took the old name, the Methodist Episcopal Church.

The growth of the Baptists in the Canadas in the early years of the century, like that of the Methodists, was at first much aided by missionaries from the United States, as various associations despatched ministers on preaching tours. The Shaftesbury Baptist Association, which had churches in Vermont, Massachusetts, and New York, was especially active in this mission. The agents urged the development of associations of churches; the first was the Thurlow Association, formed in the Bay of Quinte area of Lake Ontario in 1802. The Niagara peninsula was also visited by travelling evangelists. The war of 1812–14 shook these foundations, depleted ministerial ranks, and weakened the small, struggling congregations. The emergence of indigenous associations followed the war; in 1818 the Shaftesbury Association dismissed its five churches in the western parts of Upper Canada to become part of the Clinton Conference which took on the responsibilities of an association. To the east the Thurlow Association was reorganized as the Haldimand Association (1819). The Particular Baptist tradition as reflected in the Philadelphia Confession of Faith was influential as the congregations of Upper Canada took charge of their own affairs, with some financial help coming from the American Baptist Home Mission Society for many years.[16] In the Ottawa Valley and in Lower Canada, the Baptist cause was strengthened by Scottish immigrants who had been much influenced by the evangelical revival in Scotland under James and Robert Haldane. By the mid-1830s the Baptists were the fifth largest denomination in the Canadas, but were much smaller than the four leading denominations.[17]

There was also a range of smaller bodies of various kinds. Congregationalism had a considerable renaissance after Henry Wilkes became pastor of Zion Church in Montreal in 1836, four years after its founding. Lutheran congregations persisted throughout the period, but synodical

[16] Stuart Ivison and Fred Rosser, *The Baptists in Upper and Lower Canada before 1820* (Toronto, 1956), pp. 56–63.

[17] The census of 1842 listed church statistics in the Canadas as follows: Roman Catholic, 637, 742; Anglican, 151, 318; Presbyterian, 129, 076; Methodists, 98, 747; Baptist, 20,474. All other bodies were under 10,000. (H. H. Walsh, *The Christian Church in Canada* (Toronto, 1956), p. 149.)

structures were not formed until after mid-century. The Quakers brought three monthly meetings of Upper Canada into a Half Year's meeting under the New York Yearly Meeting in 1810. The Canadian Friends were later torn by the same Hicksite-Orthodox schism that fragmented the meetings to the south; some divided and others went out of existence. The Moravian Indian settlement at Fairfield was plundered and burned by American troops during the war of 1812–14; the next year the missionaries returned and gathered some of the scattered Indian flock to begin again across the river at New Fairfield. The first Jewish synagogue in Lower Canada had been formed among Spanish and Portuguese Jews in the eighteenth century, but in this period Jewish communal life in the Sephardic tradition also began in Toronto. There were close ties with American Jewry. Other small bodies were also to be found: Disciples, Mennonites, Mormons, Primitive Methodists, Methodist New Connection, and Bible Christians. Though individually tiny in number, together they represented a noticeable part of the Christian population, especially when questions regarding church and state had to be resolved.

In the 1830s the controversies over the Clergy Reserves increased in intensity, especially in Upper Canada, where 2,400,000 acres were involved. In 1827 an act was passed which allowed the sale of portions of the reserved lands, the proceeds to go for religious purposes. Reformers in the Upper Canada assembly were anxious to have the lands used for the advantage of all denominations, or secularized to be used for education and internal improvements. Leaders of the Church of England wanted to retain control of the lands and of funds accruing from them, while Presbyterians of Church of Scotland background sought a significant share in these resources as an established church of the empire. Most of the other churches wanted either a general sharing in the advantages of the Reserves by all denominations, or their disposal for the general good. A small advance toward religious equality was made in 1831 when all clergy received the right to perform marriages, but Strachan and other Anglican leaders were determined to hold the Reserves primarily for the advantage of their communion.

The pages of the religious and secular Press and the halls of government in both the provinces and the mother country reflected the growing bitterness of the debate over the Reserves. Mismanagement and inefficiency in the handling of the lands intensified the opposition. A reform majority in the Upper Canada legislature in 1834 voted to devote the proceeds from the sale of the Reserves to education, but the proposal was defeated by the legislative council. Tension was greatly increased when the lieutenant-governor, Sir John Colborne, erected forty-four Anglican rectories in the last hours of his administration in 1836, endowing them with 400 acres each. Political reformers and spokesmen from other churches joined in the clamour against this action, but despite two decades of controversy and judicial test cases it was never reversed.

Resentments against the Reserves and the rectories were among the reasons for the rebellion of 1837 in Upper Canada, though the prime causes were economic and political. Earlier associations between such Methodist leaders as Egerton Ryerson and political Reformers under the leadership of William Lyon Mackenzie, a Presbyterian layman, had cooled, in part because of the irreligion and radicalism of some who supported the reform cause. When the rebellion began, the churches rallied to the support of the government, and the revolt was quickly put down. But when some executions, imprisonments, and excessive harrassments followed, the Methodists reacted, and resumed their protests against the Reserves and the rectories in the name of 'loyal' reform. With the support of other religious groups, they participated in the struggle for constitutional government and the equality of religious groups before the law.

In his report about the uprising and the conditions that caused it, Lord Durham criticized the virtual monopoly of the Reserves by a minority church (actually the Church of England comprised about a fifth of the population). In 1839, after much wrangling, the two legislative houses in Upper Canada agreed to sell the Reserves with the proceeds to go for religious purposes. This was disallowed by the law officers of the Crown. Strachan, who that same year was at last named Bishop of Toronto, was in England protecting his church's interests. An imperial statute then decreed that the Church of England in Canada would receive 42 per cent of the Reserves, the Church of Scotland (which was about the same size numerically) 21 per cent, with the rest to be divided among other denominations, including Roman Catholics and Methodists.

This arrangement did little to ease the contention among the churches, and was unpopular with those who felt that the Reserves should be used for the benefit of all the people. Sharp differences of opinion over the development of an adequate school system further intensified the religious and political controversies in the united province. In Canada East (Lower Canada—Quebec) the denominational basis for schools was continued, but in Canada West (Upper Canada—Ontario) there was agitation for a single common system. A compromise was worked out under Egerton Ryerson, who was named superintendent for education in Canada West in 1844. Two years later the School Act provided for common or

mixed schools in which the rights of religious minorities would be protected, and allowed for separate schools under certain restricted conditions
at the expense of the dissenters. The Board of Education included clerical
and lay representatives of six denominations, with the Roman Catholic
Bishop of Toronto, Michael Power, as first chairman. Ryerson argued
persuasively for a generalized Christian tone in the common schools,
sounding very much like Horace Mann in the United States, on whose
ideas he drew heavily. Anglicans and Roman Catholics (especially after
Power's death during the terrible plague of 1847) became increasingly
unhappy with these arrangements.

Efforts to secure public aid for denominational colleges was an even
more controversial question in the 1840s. Political reformers had long
been hoping to secularize King's College. This did not happen until the
ministry of Baldwin and Lafontaine moved towards 'responsible government' whereby an administration had to be accountable to the elected
assembly. In 1849 King's College was transformed into the secular University of Toronto, with the denominational colleges cut off from public
funds.

To the disappointment of those who had great hopes for the reform
ministry, however, there was no move to settle the question of the Clergy
Reserves. Radical reformers formed the Clear Grit movement, devoted
to nationalism, secularism, and democracy, and to the final settlement of
the Reserves. Not until 1853 did the British Parliament pass an enabling
act so that the matter could at last be settled in Canada. Then a coalition of
Liberal-Conservatives under John A. Macdonald, elected in a campaign
in which the Reserves were a major issue, took the decisive action. The
statute 18 Victoria Cap. 2 (1854) provided that the sale of the Clergy
Reserves was to continue to provide life income for those dependent on
them, the rest to go for municipal public works. The Act indicated the
desirability of removing 'all semblance of connexion between Church
and State'.[18] The rectories, however, were not dissolved. The Act also
provided that individual clergymen could commute the estimated total
lump sum due them to their communions, from which their salary would
be provided. The Church of England and the Church of Scotland received sizeable sums by this means, the Methodist and Catholic churches
much smaller ones.[19] Though the Act did not satisfy the more extreme

[18] Cited in Moir (ed.), *Church and State in Canada*, pp. 243–5.

[19] £381,971 was thus commuted, with the Church of England receiving 65 per cent, the
Church of Scotland 28 per cent, the Roman Catholic Church 5·4 per cent, and the Metho-
dists 2·6 per cent. (Alan Wilson, *The Clergy Reserves of Upper Canada: A Canadian Mortmain*
(Toronto, 1968), p. 216.)

separationists, a vexing public issue that had long brought bitterness into religious and political life was at last concluded. With the exception of the lump-sum settlement, which became less significant as the decades passed, all churches would have to rely on voluntary support to continue their ministries effectively. A troubled chapter in Canadian history closed with the triumph of voluntaryism; special privilege had fallen before popular pressures.

Church Reorganization in Canada East and Canada West

In the atmosphere of contention over the political union, the Clergy Reserves, and the educational systems the churches had to work out new programmes and patterns of organization for a changing situation. For the Anglicans, the challenges were formidable. As the flow of money from public sources diminished, and as the secularizing trends in government rendered ecclesiastical arrangements based on English precedents less and less applicable to the Canadian scene, that formerly privileged communion had to develop its own sources of voluntary support. Of great help was the forming of church societies to raise the needed funds by general appeal. This practice was brought from the Maritime provinces by George J. Mountain, the son of the first bishop, who became Bishop of Quebec in 1836.

A further step towards the development of suitable structures for a fully autonomous church was taken in 1851 when Strachan invited laymen to participate in church government in his diocese. A few months later five of the seven Anglican bishops in British North America met to recommend that functioning synods of bishops, clergy, and laymen be formed for each diocese. Suitable legislation authorized this, and the resourceful Strachan presided over the first official diocesan synod in 1856. The following year the synod elected a bishop—a new event in Anglican history—for the Diocese of Huron, created in the western portions of Canada West by the division of the Diocese of Toronto. In 1861 the eastern portions were separated as the Diocese of Ontario, and five years later still another division became the Diocese of Niagara. These moves enabled the communion to make a difficult transition quite creatively.

The final step toward the self-government of the Episcopal Church was the appointment by the Crown of Francis Fulford, Bishop of Montreal, as metropolitan (or presiding bishop) for the Canadas. A 'provincial synod' that included all of the dioceses in the province was created, so that the church was no longer dependent on England. The name 'The Church of England in Canada' was chosen—not until 1955 was the name

'The Anglican Church in Canada' adopted. In 1865 the provincial synod suggested to Canterbury that a 'Pan-Anglican Conference of Bishops' be held, which led to the calling of the first of a series of regular Lambeth Conferences of Anglican Bishops in London. The Canadian Episcopalians have rightly been proud of their role in launching this pioneer gathering of a world confessional body in 1867. That same year, Bishop Strachan died after sixty-four years of active ministry. His early hopes for his adopted church had been defeated despite his tenacious and resourceful resistance, but instead a growing, autonomous, 'Canadianized' church was learning to fulfil its ministry within the voluntary system.

The Roman Catholic Church also experienced reorganization and renewal. The ecclesiastical province of Canada, projected in 1817, was finally created in 1844; Quebec became the metropolitan see and Signay an archbishop. There were three suffragan bishops, for Montreal, Kingston, and Toronto. Three others were added three years later, for Newfoundland, Ottawa, and the North-west. When the first provincial council was called in 1851, delegates came from all the provinces of British North America (including the Maritimes), representing a total constituency of over a million persons. A resolution calling for a Catholic university led to the founding of Laval University in Quebec.

The morale of the church, especially in the French-speaking area, was raised by renewal movements in the 1840s under the leadership of Bishop Ignace Bourget, successor and spiritual son of Lartigue at Montreal. He was founder of two indigenous religious congregations, and was instrumental in getting other Orders to undertake work in Canada: the Oblates, the *Dames du Sacré-Coeur*, the Sisters of the Good Shepherd, and (once again) the Jesuits.[20] The surges of ultramontane piety and of French-Canadian nationalism supported each other. Lord Durham in his *Report* had spoken of the French Canadians as a people with no history and no literature. The angry reaction to this attitude, which was shared by many of English background, sparked a cultural renaissance. The Roman Catholic Church played an important role in that renewal and gained increased strength from it. The historical writings of François Xavier Garneau and the poetry of Octave Crémazie were important in the movement. Politically, the ultramontanist concerns expressed themselves through co-operation with reforming elements in Canada West, for an astute political leader, Louis-Hippolyte Lafontaine, rightly saw that 'responsible government' in which an administration would be accountable to the electorate, would provide increased opportunities for

[20] Moir, *The Church in the British Era*, pp. 168–70.

French Canadians to manage their own affairs. The ministry of Lafontaine and Robert Baldwin secured the passage of the Rebellion Losses Bill which favoured long-standing French-Canadian claims but led to the sacking and burning of the legislative building by rioters with English sympathies. The opposition gradually subsided, however, and the governor-general's acceptance of the provincial cabinet's advice marked Canada's full achievement of responsible government. Though the extreme nationalist minority did not support the co-operation with English-speaking Canadians represented by Lafontaine and later by the 'dominant figure in Canadian public life from 1855 to 1867', George-Etienne Cartier, the conservatives were willing to collaborate while firmly adhering to their own distinctive language, institutions, and customs.[21]

In both Canadas the development of Roman Catholic schools continued in varying patterns through the 1840s despite the opposition of Protestants and secularists who hoped for one common school system in the united province. By the later 1840s separate Catholic and Protestant school commissions were permitted in Canada East, while in Canada West Bishop Power's successor, Bishop Charbonnel, laid the foundation for separate schools thanks to French-Canadian political support. In 1855 an act removing most restrictions from the founding and support of Catholic schools was pressed through the legislature. The Catholic population was growing rapidly in Canada West, especially through Irish immigration; one indication of the increase was the creation of the new dioceses of London and Hamilton in the middle 1850s. Though still under the Congregation for the Propagation of the Faith (until 1908, as in the United States), the Roman Catholic Church had moved a long way towards administrative maturity.

As in the Maritimes, so in the Canadas those Presbyterians who had recently united were torn apart again as a consequence of the Disruption of 1843 in Scotland. The Free Church quickly sent Robert Burns, who as one-time secretary of the Glasgow Colonial Society had done much for Church of Scotland interests in the provinces, on a tour to gather support for the new denomination. Most of the societies' former missionaries favoured the Free Church. Burns was especially successful in the more recently settled parts of Canada West. At Kingston, the newly founded Queen's College was disrupted, as almost all of the students moved to the new Knox College in Toronto. The Free Church exhibited great missionary concern, and by mid-century had surpassed its rival in numbers. Though the Free Church in Scotland did not object in principle to the

21 Wade, *The French Canadians 1760–1945*, p. 308; cf. pp. 210–317.

state support of religion, the Canadian Free Church quickly adopted voluntary principles. One reason for this was the powerful influence of an energetic layman, publisher, and politician, George Brown; another was the desire for union between the Free Church and the smaller United Presbyterian Church. When this union took place in 1861, Scottish, Irish, and American elements were brought together in the flourishing Canada Presbyterian Church, soon the largest Presbyterian body in all the provinces. Trends toward union and voluntaryism thus characterized the Canadianizing of the Presbyterian tradition.

In Methodism there was a parallel pattern of division and unification. After seven years of union between the Upper Canadian and English Wesleyan conferences, there began in 1840 seven lean years of separation because of differing attitudes towards church establishment. The English party counted on government grants to help finance its missionary work among Indians, while the Canadian Conference swung again toward voluntary principles. The resulting competition and strife harmed the cause, and the sects gained at Methodist expense. In 1847 the two conferences merged again as the Canadian Wesleyan Church; both sides were tired of controversy and a fruitful compromise was struck. Seven years later the Methodist work of Canada East and West was amalgamated. Methodism resumed its familiar pattern of growth with these unitive moves. The intense evangelical fervour of earlier years moderated somewhat as a longing for peace was widely felt and as the stability of the church as an institution became an increasing concern of its leaders.[22]

The evangelical Calvinist witness of the Baptists was carried on with characteristic energy in the 1840s, but efforts to find effective agencies of unity were long frustrated among this independent and congregationally oriented people. There were several causes for the continuing tension. The traditions of the Scottish Baptists (strongest in Canada East and the Ottawa Valley) and those who retained American patterns (much of Canada West) often came into conflict. The old controversy over whether communion should be open only to immersed believers cut across this difference, for the east was more inclined to open communion and the west to closed. Colleges, periodicals, and unions established in the face of these tensions were usually short lived. Not until mid-century did the controversies abate sufficiently to enable the Regular Baptist Missionary Convention of Canada West (1851) to be formed with broad support; seven years later a similar convention for Canada East was founded. In 1857 the Woodstock Literary Institute was organized under the leadership

[22] French, *Parsons and Politics*, pp. 250–9.

of Dr. R. A. Fyfe; it eventually evolved into McMaster University at Hamilton.

Like most of the Protestants of the period, Baptists were deeply opposed to Roman Catholicism, and became the principal backers of one of the most notable missionary efforts to convert French-Canadian Catholics to evangelical views. Its origins were in French-speaking Switzerland, where Madame Henrietta Feller learned of those in Canada who spoke her language, and resolved to carry on evangelical labours among them. Settling finally at St. John, south of Montreal, she founded in 1836 the Grande Ligne Mission, which sought to work constructively in evangelism and education among Catholics, avoiding offensive attacks.

The other denominations were small compared to the five that have been mentioned, but they also illustrated the trend toward organizational consolidation. Henry Wilkes of Montreal continued to be the central figure in Congregationalism, serving as the head of a college and promoting the organization of a Congregational Union for the Canadas in 1853. Wilkes was instrumental in developing lines of co-operation with other communions, and was the principal founder of the non-denominational Canada Foreign Missionary Society (1854). Lutherans also achieved synodical organization in this period, with the help of the Pittsburgh Synod. The aid was secured through the determined efforts of 'Father' Adam Keffer, a Lutheran elder, who was sent by the churches of the Markham-Vaughan parish, west of Toronto, to implore the American synod for assistance. In successive years Keffer walked to the place where the synod met—over a thousand miles in all. At last the synod responded by sending to Canada in 1850 Charles Frederick Diehl, a young pastor who had been born in Strasburg and educated at Gettysburg Seminary. Soon other missionaries came; in 1853 they formed the Canada Conference of the Pittsburgh Synod of the Evangelical Lutheran Church. Between then and 1861, when the autonomous Evangelical Lutheran Synod of Canada was founded with the blessing of the mother synod, some eighteen new congregations came into being, meeting the religious needs of many who had arrived with the German immigration of the 1850s. On the eve of Confederation Lutherans had some twenty pastors at work in more than sixty congregations and preaching stations.[23] Some other denominations began their work in the Canadas in this period, especially the Disciples of Christ and branches of the American German Methodist groups, Evangelicals, and United Brethren.

Though the numbers have frequently been overestimated, many blacks

[23] Carl R. Cronmiller, *A History of the Lutheran Church in Canada* (n.p., 1961), pp. 130–50.

entered Canada in this period. Robin Winks estimated that at the most generous accounting, 40,000 entered Canada West, about three-quarters of them fugitive slaves. Canadians were generally sympathetic to the anti-slavery cause; some ministers were especially vocal on behalf of the slaves. The Presbyterians were critical of their fellow religionists in the United States who did not clearly state their opposition to holding others in bondage. The Baptists were the first to speak out clearly against slavery. More of the blacks joined Baptist churches than those of any other tradition. Originally interracial, by the 1840s separate congregations for blacks were increasing. The reluctance of white congregations to treat blacks as equals was a major reason for this development. Black Baptist congregations formed their own Amherstburg Association. In 1851 a small, non-denominational Anti-Slavery Society of Canada was founded; George Brown, editor of the *Globe*, was the most conspicuous Canadian abolitionist. In his definitive work, Winks asked—and answered—an important question:

What had the Negro settlements, the missionary societies, and the churches accomplished? Much and little—fugitive slaves had been cared for across more than a decade, and some had acquired a stake in Canadian society, land, a sense of belonging, and the courage to show pride. Canada had acquired a substantial if passing Negro population, an opportunity to show itself above prejudice—which it missed—and a chance to give reality to its insistence upon institutional equality—which it grasped.[24]

Once the Civil War broke out, Canadians tended to be anti-northern, reluctant to support a struggle to maintain the Union that had threatened them so often, and largely lost interest in the former slaves. The bulk of the fugitives returned to the United States after the war, some discouraged by the difficulties they had faced.

The Challenge of the West

The story of the pioneer efforts of the churches to carry Christian faith into the little-known territories to the west and north of the main centres of population is one of adventurous determination and self-sacrifice. Back in the days of New France, Catholic missionaries had ventured north to Hudson's Bay and west as far as the Lake of the Woods, but the British conquest brought those ventures to an end. Trappers and traders were soon moving across the great spaces north to the Arctic and west to the

[24] *The Blacks in Canada*, p. 231; cf. chs. 6–8.

Pacific, but permanent settlement did not begin until the nineteenth century.

One of the most interesting chapters in the history of the western settlements began in Scotland, where a wealthy landowner, Lord Selkirk, was unwilling to turn his tenants off the land when it became economically unprofitable for them to remain. He devoted much of his time and resources to settling those displaced persons across the Atlantic. After several preliminary undertakings, in 1812 he placed an agricultural colony, Kildonan, on the Red River, on land purchased from the Hudson's Bay Company. Traders employed by the rival North West Fur Company, chiefly the Métis, a people who had arisen out of the intermarriage of Scottish and French with the Indians, felt themselves threatened by the 'invasion' and intimidated many of the new settlers into leaving. A fresh influx of colonists in 1815 brought renewed strength to the settlement. An encounter between the rival groups was precipitated at Seven Oaks in 1816; a score of colonists were killed. Selkirk returned with Swiss mercenaries to ensure the continuation of the effort on the site of what later became part of the city of Winnipeg. Many of the colonists were Presbyterians, who carried on their traditions for decades under lay leadership. It was not until 1851 that a congregation was formally organized, when John Black, a recent graduate of Knox College, was persuaded to settle in Kildonan.

The Catholics in the area received ordained leadership much sooner. Selkirk had urged Bishop Plessis to provide priests for the French Canadians and Swiss soldiers in the area, and in 1818 Joseph-Norbert Provencher took charge of the mission on the Red River, soon becoming Bishop of Juliopolis. A church, schools, and an Indian agricultural colony were founded. In the early 1830s a mission exclusively for Indians was established nearby, the first of a series of mission stations which were planted as missionaries arrived. Their role proved to be difficult, for the Indians were nomadic and their standards of food and sanitation were inadequate by western standards. Provencher had difficulty keeping his priests in such a difficult and discouraging field, and welcomed the help of the French Order of Oblates of Mary Immaculate in 1845. With them came a novice, Alexandre-Antonin Taché, who was later to succeed Provencher. In the 1850s and 1860s the Oblates, aided by lay brothers and Gray Nuns, carried their mission work among the Indians and Eskimos along the rivers to the Arctic and the Pacific, an impressive spiritual and institutional achievement. The extensive missionary journeys and accomplishments of a Belgian Jesuit, Pierre-Jean de Smet, became known through his writings. Associated with him for a time was another of the pioneer priests of the Red River, Modeste Demers, who eventually became Bishop of Vancouver Island.

Anglican missionaries were assisted in their effort to evangelize Indians by the support of the Church Missionary Society, which had been founded by evangelical churchmen in England in 1799. This agency provided a grant for building schools in the Red River settlement to the Hudson's Bay Company chaplain, John West, in the 1820s. He laid foundations for the education of Indians, which he believed was the best way to christianize them, in addition to ministering among settlers of French and British background. West and his successors, especially David T. Jones and William Cockran, planted schools and missions along the Red River Valley.

As the work of education and evangelism prospered, the missionaries extended their work further into the west. Bishop Mountain of Quebec visited the Red River settlement in 1844 and recommended that a diocese be formed; five years later David Anderson was named Bishop of Rupert's Land. His frontier diocese called for long journeys; in 1852, for example he journeyed to the James Bay region to ordain John Horden, who had been sent to that northern area by the Church Missionary Society. Not all the work was on the frontiers; an academy that had been founded at Red River grew into St. John's College, around which the University of Manitoba was later to grow. Anderson ordained a number of local people for his diocese, including some Indians. Under his supervision, adventurous missionaries pressed west and north from the Red River base into the Mackenzie River basin and on into Yukon territory, undertaking the work of evangelizing and civilizing Indian tribes. Notable among the missionaries was Robert McDonald, who began a remarkable effort among the Tukudh or Loucheux Indians at Fort Yukon in 1862.

As early as 1836 an Anglican missionary had reached the Pacific coast to serve employees of the Hudson's Bay Company. The discovery of gold on the Fraser River led to the Cariboo rush of 1858, stimulating the rapid influx of population and the organization of British Columbia as a Crown colony. The next year George Hills was consecrated as Church of England bishop for the new colony. There was considerable competitiveness between Anglican and Catholic missionaries who with a similar sacrificial spirit were carrying their faith along the same waterways of the northwest.

Methodist entry into the west to evangelize the Indians was made in 1840 under the leadership of the English Wesleyan Conference. Four missionaries were dispatched to work at strategic locations, one far to the west in the foothills of the Rocky Mountains. Notable in this work was James Evans of Norway House, at the outlet of Lake Winnipeg. He invented a system of phonetic characters for Indian languages, and using scrap materials he designed a press to print verses of scripture and hymns for the use of the Cree Indians. His 'Cree syllabic' writing was adapted to other native languages and came into standard use in the Canadian Arctic. He also built a mission community for Indians at Rossville, near Norway House. These ambitious beginnings were not fully sustained. In the second half of the century the Canadian Wesleyan Methodist Church accepted control of the western mission. George McDougall was named superintendent for the west; from his headquarters at Victoria on the North Saskatchewan River he injected new life into the missionary work among the tribes. By the end of the decade, four missionaries had been sent to work in British Columbia, chiefly among the white population.

The record of the missionaries in exploration and in initiating religious work is impressive. They succeeded in holding many people of European background within the orbit of the church, and won many Indians to the faith. But, as Moir has observed, 'it was beyond the ability of the missionaries or the society of that era to make much improvement in the quality of life of these nomadic stone-age people'.[25] That had to await the Confederation and the building of the railroad across the west.

The Churches and Confederation

The 1850s and 1860s were a troubled time in the religious and political life of the provinces. The tensions of the 'fiery fifties' relating to the Clergy Reserves and their settlement have already been discussed. But the polarizations so deeply rooted in the vast united province surfaced again and again as Protestant and Catholic, English and French, religionist and secular nationalist contended with each other in complex and shifting ways. The province was kept in turmoil by the struggle between the strong French Catholic Canada East and the predominantly English Protestant Canada West. The tension was heightened when the ugly quarrel in England over 'papal aggression' spilled over into the provinces. In his editorials George Brown, for example, sharply criticized Catholic interference in Canadian politics. In the resulting war of words the Orange Order with its ultra-Protestant slant joined in the outcry against French Catholic political power. The tension erupted in violence following the lectures of Alessandro Gavazzi—the same man who was so critical of

[25] *The Church in the British Era*, p. 212.

Archbishop Bedini's visit to the United States in 1853. In Montreal, after the former priest had spoken against the papal resistance to the drive of the Italian liberal nationalists for the unification of their country, a tragic massacre occurred when troops unaccountably fired into the departing crowd. Other indignities followed. The angry feelings that had been aroused flared up again and again over the school issue, especially as Catholics in Canada West pressed hard to strengthen their separate schools through legislation. It became widely evident that some other political solution than the forced union of two peoples in one province would be preferable.

Though religious considerations played a part in the move for a new political arrangement, the Confederation was largely the work of politicians and railroad promoters on the basis of economic and political realities. Officially the churches had little to say about the movement for Confederation, but the religious Press, reflecting general opinion in the churches, discussed it thoroughly and almost entirely favourably. Protestants of various traditions in Canada West wanted to continue British imperial interests to avoid piecemeal annexation of provinces by the United States, a very undesirable alternative. The population of Canada West was shown by the census of 1861 to have reached about 1,400,000, almost 300,000 more than Canada East, yet each had the same number of seats in the legislature. What had originally been designed to protect a minority now served to inhibit it as a majority! On the more positive side, many Canadians did catch a vision of a federation of provinces which would form a Christian nation extending across the entire continent. George Brown lent his talents and pen to the cause of Confederation, for he envisioned 'a government that would "endeavour to maintain liberty, and justice, and Christianity throughout the land"'.[26] There were some resistances to be overcome in Protestant ranks, especially relating to the possible plight of minorities in a separated Quebec.

Catholic support for Confederation was articulated by several prominent bishops. The coadjutor of Trois-Rivières, L. F. Laflèche, explained that by separating the Canadas and allowing them to join in federal union with the other provinces the political stalemate would be ended. A particularly outspoken advocate was Thomas Louis Connolly, Archbishop of Halifax, who saw the move as necessary in view of the expansionism of the colossus to the south. Important Catholic laymen were active in the cause of Confederation, especially the eloquent D'Arcy McGee,

---

[26] John W. Grant, 'Canadian Confederation and the Protestant Churches', *Church History*, xxxviii (1969), 330.

spokesman for the Irish and member of the legislature. Such leaders helped to overcome Catholic opposition to Confederation, voiced especially by those who feared that the French-Canadian province might be at a great disadvantage in a union with those of predominantly English and Protestant cast.[27]

The work of a great French-Canadian political leader, George-Etienne Cartier (1814–73), was crucial in the final outcome. A collateral descendant of Jacques Cartier, as a young man he had participated in the rebellion of 1837 and for a time had to leave the country. Later rising to power, Cartier helped to solve the issue of the Clergy Reserves, and was chiefly responsible for the abolition of seigneurial tenure, the codification of Quebec law, and judicial and administrative reforms. One historian concluded that 'Confederation owed more to him, perhaps, than to any other single man'.[28] He was determined that union should be federal rather than legislative. It was his political skill that brought French Canadians to support Confederation by a slim majority.

With the general but not official support of the Christian churches, Confederation was finally consummated. Following important conferences at Charlottetown and Quebec in 1864, at which the details were worked out, Cartier joined forces with John A. Macdonald to win a decisive vote in Canada. This paved the way for the British North America Act of the imperial Parliament, enabling the provinces of Nova Scotia, New Brunswick, Quebec, and Ontario (formerly Canada East and Canada West) to form the Dominion of Canada on 1 July 1867.

Summary: A Comparison

An attempt to compare the Christianity of these two North American lands in the mid-nineteenth century has many subtle difficulties, for in certain ways the Canada of 1867 at the beginning of Confederation was parallel with the United States at 1789 as its Federal Union was formed. Obviously there were many similarities; sister churches in both lands were facing the problems of bringing the faith to steadily expanding populations pressing into the untamed spaces of the west. But Canadian Christianity on the whole was more conservative and adhered more closely to European religious traditions than did the American. A Catholicism that preserved beloved traditions of the past and that had rejected the French Revolution was the binding force of French Canada—a

---

[27] John A. K. Farrell, 'Roman Catholic Influence Supporting Canadian Confederation', *The Catholic Historical Review*, lv (1969), 7–25.

[28] Wade, *The French Canadians 1760–1945*, p. 303.

Catholicism that had been well entrenched long before Protestant denominational life had begun. The early British provinces welcomed waves of Loyalists at crucial times in their histories—Loyalists who had rejected the American Revolution. There was a much greater emphasis on continuity with the past in Canadian than in American religion, less experimentation, less willingness to take fresh starts and make new departures in religion.

The denominational spectrum was smaller in Canada than in her neighbour; the great bulk of church membership in the Dominion in 1867 was in the five major denominations (but it must be remembered that the Canadian population at that point was still less than that of the United States in 1789). Canada was a rather 'churchly' nation in 1867 with the overwhelming majority of the population claimed as members or constituents of its denominations, while the America of 1789 had less than a tenth of its population as church members. In another connection, Moir remarked that

Canada has preserved churchism to preserve itself. Whenever military, economic, political or cultural absorption by the United States threatened, as in 1776, 1812, 1837, 1911 or even 1957, Canada has turned to its counter-revolutionary tradition for inspiration. And ecclesiasticism is a traditional part of that tradition.[29]

The religious tone of these two 'Christian nations' in the nineteenth century was quite different, for Canada was more cautious, traditional, and church-oriented than the United States.

Despite the strength and vitality of the Christian churches in nineteenth-century Canada, the basic religious duality of French Catholicism and British Protestantism prevented the emergence of a universally acceptable religious interpretation of the new Dominion and its destiny. Though the religious diversity of the United States was greater, the Protestant denominations, especially those influenced by Calvinism and evangelicalism, were dominant, and helped to provide the context in which 'the Americans, those new men, came to look upon themselves as a peculiar, a chosen people, set apart by God to serve a peculiar purpose in the history of mankind—a purpose that would be fully revealed in God's good time'.[30] But in Canada the churches could not agree 'on a single providential interpretation' of Canadian destiny, and hence no 'generally acceptable religious interpretation of national purpose', no

[29] 'Sectarian Tradition in Canada', in John W. Grant (ed.), *The Churches and the Canadian Experience: A Faith and Order Study of The Christian Tradition* (Toronto, 1963), p. 132.
[30] Mead, *The Lively Experiment*, p. 80.

overarching myth 'sufficiently powerful to serve as the focus of a new nationalism' emerged.[31] While Americans, whatever their church affiliation or lack of it, customarily invested certain religious feelings in the nation, increasing its dynamism, optimism, sense of destiny, and buoyant self-confidence, Canadian religious feeling was contained much more within church boundaries. In Protestantism an effort was made to interpret Canada as a Christian and Protestant nation, largely ignoring Catholicism, somewhat analogous to similar efforts in the United States. Within one's camp a religious vision of the nation could be elaborated, but one could not expect it to win appeal on the other side.

In both countries religious freedom and the separation of church and state had come to be widely accepted. Yet in Canada the Jeffersonian image of a 'wall of separation' so popular in the United States was not acceptable. The separation of church and state in Canada was not rigidly interpreted, and allowed for flexibility, especially in the way public and private schools were regarded and funded, a resolution not possible in the United States. Though the Canadian practices varied according to locality, denominational educational institutions usually received some financial assistance from public sources. These differences lay in the distinctive histories and situations of both nations, but one factor seems especially important. In the United States, the influence of the Enlightenment has been significant, especially on the concepts and definitions of religious liberty and the separation of church and state. In Canada, the influence of the Enlightenment in both religion and politics was largely suppressed. Both the American and French revolutions were rejected, and, as H. H. Walsh put it

perhaps even more significant in creating a basis for a common Canadianism was a third rejection, that of the Enlightenment. The closest either of the Canadas came to the Enlightenment, which has played such a prominent role in shaping reform movements in the rest of the new world, was during the rebellious era of the 1830s.[32]

The much less significant impact of the Enlightenment in Canada as compared to the United States accounts in part for the quite different understandings of the nature of religious freedom and the separation of church and state.

The differences between the religious styles and structures of the two

---

[31] Goldwin S. French, 'The Impact of Christianity on Canadian Culture and Society before 1867', *Theological Bulletin, McMaster Divinity College*, No. 3 (January 1968), p. 34.

[32] 'A Canadian Christian Tradition', in Grant (ed.), *The Churches and the Canadian Experience*, p. 146.

North American nations are evident, yet the similarities and parallels must not be minimized. Despite the anti-Americanism that has been part of Canadian life, the interrelationships between churches of the two lands continued with few interruptions. Fraternal delegates were exchanged, students crossed the border, ministers served in both commonwealths.[33] With the increase in Canadian national consciousness as one consequence of Confederation, the churches entered a period of consolidation and nationalization, in some respects reminiscent of the nationalization of the American churches after the Revolution.

[33] John S. Moir, 'American Influences on Canadian Protestant Churches before Confederation', *Church History* (1967), 440–55.

IX

AMERICAN EVANGELICAL PROTESTANTISM: GROWTH AND CONFLICT

(1860–1920)

THE churches of the United States were plunged into a steadily changing milieu in the six decades from the outbreak of the Civil War to the close of World War I. Massive and unanticipated alterations in the patterns of thought and action in the nation and in the churches took place in those years of turmoil. The most conspicuous initiator of change was war—four terrible years of civil strife, a series of engagements with Indian tribes, the short but decisive Spanish–American War, and the 'great crusade' of the war that was to end war and to make the world safe for democracy. The churches generally became deeply involved in the justification, support, and interpretation of these struggles; along with other institutions in the culture they had to live with the many and complex consequences of war periods.

Another major source of change was immigration—not a new factor except for its increased magnitude and complexity. In the 1860s and 1870s over five million immigrants entered the country—more than had entered in the previous four decades. In the 1880s there was a remarkable increase in arrivals, with a much larger percentage coming from central, southern, and eastern Europe. Their languages and customs seemed strange and threatening to those more familiar with immigrants from western and northern Europe. As many newcomers entered in that ninth decade as had in the previous two decades, in part a consequence of major population shifts in Europe. In the 1890s only about two-thirds of that number immigrated, but then the first decade of the twentieth century reached an all-time high level with nearly nine million. In all, more than twenty-eight million immigrants arrived in the period 1860–1920, during which the total population of the nation increased from about thirty-one and a half million to well over one hundred and five million. The religious preferences of those who entered brought marked changes in the relative size of the denominations.

The internal migration of people on the North American continent was also not new, but it increased in scope as unprecedented numbers swept into vast open spaces in the western half of the nation. The growth of the railroad network—a trans-continental link was completed in 1869—speeded the process of settlement. Homestead laws made land readily available to enterprising settlers, and, despite the limitations of such laws and their exploitation by commercial interests, they did serve to excite interest in the west and to draw people to the frontiers. Indian tribes fought this invasion of their lands which deprived them of their livelihood; for three decades a series of costly Indian wars beat the tribes into submission and forced them into reservations. Drawn by the opportunities for farming, cattle raising, mining, and railroading, whites settled the area rapidly. Between 1860 and 1912 fifteen new states were added to the Union.

Not all the migration was to the west. Some of it was from rural areas to the swiftly expanding cities, the growth of which was important in altering patterns of thought and life in this period. Winthrop S. Hudson observed that

during the three decades from 1860 to 1890, the population of Detroit and Kansas City grew fourfold, Memphis and San Francisco fivefold, Cleveland sixfold, Chicago tenfold, Los Angeles twentyfold, and Minneapolis and Omaha fiftyfold and more. Even such previously major centers as New York, Philadelphia, and Baltimore more than doubled in population.[1]

In many of the cities, streams of immigration from abroad merged with currents of migration from rural areas. These patterns continued in the early twentieth century; a significant addition was the movement of blacks from southern rural areas to the cities, at first in the south but then, especially during World War I, to the great metropolises of the north. All this meant that churches long accustomed to dealing primarily with rural and small town constituencies had to adjust to startling new contexts for ministry. A pioneer sociologist of religion in America stated that urbanization gave the church 'the greatest inner revolution it has ever known'.[2]

Closely linked with the rise of the cities was the rapid industrialization of the nation, a process greatly accelerated by the Civil War. Technological development greatly increased the ease and speed of communication and transportation. Thousands of miles of telegraph and telephone

[1] *Religion in America*, p. 293.
[2] H. Paul Douglass, 'Religion—The Protestant Faiths', in Harold E. Stearns (ed.), *America Now: An Inquiry into Civilization in the United States* (New York, 1938), p. 514.

wires and railroad tracks linked the growing industrial centres. The great natural resources of the land were freely exploited by industrial leaders who were favoured by the political climate and protected by legislation. The amount of money invested in manufacturing plants increased a dozen times in the last forty years of the nineteenth century and the number of employed workers doubled more than twice as the United States became by 1890 the first manufacturing nation of the world in the quantity and value of many products. Vast railroad, steel, oil, and meat-packing empires were created. The regimentation of industrial workers, their difficulties during times of business decline, and their sense of being exploited by employers raised human problems for which the solutions of an earlier agrarian age were increasingly inadequate.

Another major source of change in American life in this period was the intellectual revolution that cut through familiar ways of thought and perception. In the earlier part of the century the churches had been able to deal with the challenges of rationalism, romanticism, and idealism in varied but widely accepted ways. The authority of the Bible was generally assumed. The prestige of scientific and evolutionary thought had been rising, but had not generally become a serious threat to faith. Then came the impact of Charles Darwin's *Origin of Species* (1859). His extensive research gave the theory of evolution plausibility and clarity, while his later writings more directly challenged traditional views of human origins. Intense debates ensued, and a rift opened between those who accepted evolution in some form and those who rejected it. Evolutionary thought also encouraged critical approaches to historical and literary study, which had an impact on the study of the Bible. The arguments in the churches over evolution had been sharp enough; those that emerged a decade or two later over the critical study of the Bible were even fiercer. Many Christians found that the historical approach to the Bible—viewing it as a collection of writings gathered over a long period of time—was liberating, allowing them to separate its spiritual message from an outworn cosmology. Others found this method an impious mistreatment of the divine and authoritative Word of God to men. The controversies divided the churches into opposing camps which have been in tension ever since. Some felt themselves obliged to choose between science and religion, while others found ways to mediate between the two.

The intellectual ferment of the time penetrated most areas of human thought. Of particular importance for the churches was the questioning of the widespread philosophy of individualism that had become so prominent. The increase of poverty and the lack of concern for the weak by many of the strong in the era of the robber barons led some bold thinkers to stress the corporate and social dimensions of human life, and to call for public concern for individuals in need. Yet many clung resolutely to the familiar gospel of individualism which had been closely identified with Christian teachings. The *laissez-faire* philosophy justified those who were piling up wealth in a rapidly expanding economy, and they often viewed those who fell behind in the struggle as lazy, incompetent, or immoral. A number of prominent churchmen lent their support to the popular 'gospel of wealth' with its characteristic doctrines of the free individual, unlimited competition, the acquisition of wealth by hard work and disciplined saving, and the stewardship of the competent. This socio-economic view was widely popular, and devoutly believed by many who had been little rewarded with the wealth for which they laboured. Yet the world in which unqualified individualism could go unchallenged was rapidly passing with the spread of giant corporations, vast cities, and governmental power. Such controversial movements as socialism, populism, and progressivism were endeavouring to come to terms with the new realities. As some religious leaders espoused new patterns of social thought and action, especially in the latter half of the period, others sharply resisted. Hence new controversies over the relationship of Christianity to the social order emerged even as the issues over evolution and biblical authority continued to be sharply debated.

The actual numbers of church members increased tenfold in these sixty years, through the nurture of the young, the power of the revival, and the flood of immigrants. Growing numbers of immigrants, however, were not affiliated with Anglo-American Protestantism but with such movements as Lutheranism, Roman Catholicism, Eastern Orthodoxy, and Judaism. Though it was not really seen until later, sociologically the easy dominance and relative importance of the English-speaking, evangelical denominations were being slowly undermined. Despite vast changes, however, the evangelical churches were flourishing and growing, and they remained in their own and in others' minds the 'majority'. At the end of the period as at its beginning, they were still confident of the future and of their continuing central role in American life.

Evangelical Protestantism in Civil War and Reconstruction

The religious forces of the land were caught up in support of their sections during the Civil War of 1861–5, yet that fratricidal strife was in many important respects a war between evangelicals, north and south.

Conspicuous leaders and interpreters of the combat on both sides were products of Anglo–American Protestantism, and freely cited its concepts and sanctions on behalf of the Union or the Confederacy. As the crisis unfolded, the pulpit and the church Press hastened to interpret the dramatic events. Abraham Lincoln, the compromise candidate of the young Republican party, won the election for the presidency with about two-fifths of the popular vote in 1860 on a platform which was understood to be hostile to the further expansion of slavery. This was the signal to many southerners, including the clergy, to demand secession from the Union. Before the inauguration on 4 March 1861 seven states from South Carolina to Texas had withdrawn to form the Confederate States of America. While the new President struggled to preserve the Union, Fort Sumter in Charleston harbour was captured by southern forces. Four more states joined the Confederacy, and the war was on.

With a few exceptions, the evangelical leaders of the warring sections interpreted the cause to which they were committed as holy and righteous. The sectional self-consciousness of the south had been growing long before the crisis of 1861. The two largest Protestant communions, Baptist and Methodist, had divided along sectional lines fifteen years before, and the New School Presbyterians split in 1857. When the war came, most of the other churches with national memberships also divided, in fact if not always formally.

On both sides the imagery of holy war was freely invoked as the faithful were assured that God was on their side. 'God cannot afford to do without America', cried the eloquent Matthew Simpson, a northern Methodist bishop,[3] while the northern Old School Presbyterians resolved 'in the spirit of Christian patriotism which the Scriptures enjoin' to 'acknowledge and declare our obligation to promote and perpetuate, so far as in us lies, the integrity of these United States, and to strengthen, uphold, and encourage, the Federal Government in the exercise of all its functions under our noble Constitution . . .'[4] In the south, one of the forceful voices to defend the Confederate cause as God's was an Episcopal bishop, Stephen Elliott. Defining the sacred objects for which the south was contending, he declared that 'we are fighting to drive away from our sanctuaries the infidel and rationalistic principles which are sweeping over the land and substituting a gospel of the stars and stripes for the gospel of

---

[3] As quoted by James E. Kirby, 'Matthew Simpson and the Mission of America', *Church History*, 36 (1967), 301.

[4] *Minutes of the General Assembly of the Presbyterian Church in the United States of America*, 1861, pp. 329–30.

Jesus Christ'.[5] In a section in which, according to one scholar, 'the church was the most powerful organization influencing the lives of men and women', clergymen were 'quite successful in helping the people to identify God, the right, and the destiny of history with slavery, the Confederacy, and the war'.[6] So both sides felt themselves to be divinely led, and the Christian imagery employed was often strikingly similar. Late in 1861 Bishop Elliott declared in a sermon 'we are moving in the light of God's countenance; and the waving of His hand and the flashing of His eye are almost visible to us'.[7] Gilbert Haven, a northern Methodist preacher and abolitionist, declared two years later that if his section remained faithful to God victory would surely come, and 'then shall other nations behold the image of the transfigured Christ shining in our uplifted face, that will glow, like that of Moses, with the radiance of his divine countenance'.[8] Guided by such convictions, many ministers served as chaplains in the contending armies; officers of many ranks frequently supported their work, and services were generally well attended. In the series of revivals that swept through both armies thousands were converted, and in the midst of the carnage men found both religious power and renewed assurance of the righteousness of the cause for which they fought. The work of the chaplains was aided by civilian volunteers, clergy and lay, who also carried out ministries of preaching, healing, comfort, and practical assistance to the soldiers. In the north, such service was organized through several voluntary agencies, especially the United States Christian Commission which co-ordinated the efforts of more than 5,000 volunteers. The older voluntary societies and the various denominational agencies on both sides worked among the armies.

Lincoln's avowed purpose as president was to save the Union; when he became convinced that by declaring the slaves in Confederate territory to be free the end of the war would be hastened, he issued the Emancipation Proclamation at the beginning of 1863. As Federal troops moved into the south, thousands of slaves were freed, a number of whom entered the northern armies. Some of the established voluntary societies and many new ones took on the task of aiding and educating the freed blacks. The American Missionary Association especially took the lead in founding schools and colleges for Negroes in the south.

[5] *God's Presence with the Confederate States. A Sermon, Preached in Christ Church, Savannah, on Thursday, the 13th June*, . . . (Savannah, Ga., 1861), p. 21, as quoted by Smith, *In His Image, But* . . . , pp. 192–3.

[6] James W. Silver, *Confederate Morale and Church Propaganda* (Gloucester, Mass., 1964), p. 93.   [7] *Ibid.*, p. 49.

[8] *Sermons, Speeches and Letters on Slavery and Its War* (Boston, 1869), p. 359.

When the numerical and industrial superiority of the north finally prevailed in April 1865, hopes for early reconciliation were cut short by the assassination of Lincoln, for which the north blamed the south. In the ensuing wave of anger, the words with which the slain president had concluded his Second Inaugural Address only a few weeks before were largely forgotten:

With malice toward none; with charity for all; with firmness in the right, as God gives us to see the right, let us strive on to finish the work we are in; to bind up the nation's wounds; to care for him who shall have borne the battle, and for his widow, and his orphan—to do all which may achieve and cherish a just, and a lasting peace, among ourselves, and with all nations.

Lincoln was not a church member, though he often attended services, but his reflections on the war during the course of that historic address were deeply theological:

Fondly do we hope—fervently do we pray—that this mighty scourge of war may speedily pass away. Yet, if God will that it continue, until all the wealth piled by the bondman's two hundred and fifty years of unrequited toil shall be sunk, and until every drop of blood drawn with the lash, shall be paid with another drawn with the sword, as was said three thousand years ago, so still it must be said 'the judgments of the Lord are true and righteous altogether'.

Other interpreters of the war also saw it as one in which the guilt of the whole nation was judged for its involvement in slavery. Such spokesmen as Horace Bushnell and Philip Schaff viewed the war as a sacrifice out of which could come national unity and regeneration, for in their view without the shedding of blood there could be no atonement.[9] But instead of reconciliation there followed a period of northern reprisal and southern resistance that long delayed genuine national unity. During the war some northern churches had seized the opportunity to advance their mission programmes at the expense of the southern churches by co-operating with the invading Union armies. The Methodist Episcopal Church was especially active in this effort, so that many northern ministers were placed in pulpits in occupied territories, to the deep resentment of the southern congregations. After the assassination of Lincoln, the northern churches generally supported the Radical Republicans in Congress. They viewed the southern states as conquered territories to be thoroughly 'reconstructed' and only then to be readmitted to the Union. The northern

[9] William A. Clebsch has studied the matter in detail; his conclusions are summarized in his book *From Sacred to Profane America: The Role of Religion in American History* (New York, 1968), pp. 193–200.

branches of the Methodist, Baptist, and Presbyterian communions had some fleeting hopes of pressing into the south and replacing the southern branches, but they only aroused the ire of the Christians there, who rallied to their own institutions.

During the period of Reconstruction, 1865–77, the northern religious forces that supported the anti-slavery cause favoured efforts to secure the rights of the freed. The Thirteenth, Fourteenth, and Fifteenth Constitutional Amendments, which abolished slavery, forbade the abridgment of any citizen's privileges and immunities, and guaranteed the right to vote, were notable achievements of Reconstruction. Blacks played some important roles in the governments of southern states during the time of Federal occupation and Republican rule. While such regimes were marred by some corruption and extravagance, they also were marked by significant accomplishments, especially in public service and education.

In their determination to end northern influence and black participation in their state governments, some southern whites resorted to such terroristic secret societies as the Ku Klux Klan to keep blacks and other opponents from the polls. Then as northern interest in the plight of the former slaves faded, the Reconstruction governments came to an end and the victory of white supremacy in the south was assured. The great bulk of the four million freed persons suffered economic discrimination whether they turned to agriculture or to industry.

One of the significant achievements of the whole post-war period was the continuing work of the northern churches in evangelizing and educating the newly freed blacks. In a careful study one scholar has concluded that 'the northern mission to freedmen marks one of the finest chapters in the history of American Protestant benevolence'.[10] The American Missionary Association, certain of the denominational agencies, and various aid and relief societies, especially the American Freedmen's Union Commission (1865), took the lead in this effort. Such important colleges as Atlanta, Hampton, Fisk, Lincoln, Morehouse, Paine, Spelman, Talladega, and Tougaloo, which played prominent roles in preparing black preachers, teachers, and other leaders, were helped through lean and difficult years by the Christian philanthropy of both blacks and whites. Great personal contributions were made by the missionary teachers and educators who left safe homes and adequate livings to face misunderstanding, isolation, and hostility in the south as they laboured among the new citizens. Many of the latter assumed leading roles in these educational efforts.

10 Smith, *In His Image, But . . .*, p. 217.

When the war ended, southern white Christians had to accept the fact that the country was reunited and that slavery was no more, but with few exceptions they continued to insist that slavery had not been wrong and that secession was a constitutional right. 'The great majority of the Southern people had emerged from the War with their dislike of Yankees increased and their devotion to Southern principles intensified', wrote Hunter D. Farish. 'They were unwilling to recognize any but the unmistakable accomplishments of the War, the emancipation of the slaves and the restoration of the Union.'[11] Most of them also believed firmly in white supremacy, resisted black participation in politics, and accepted the spreading patterns of segregation. These views were largely shared by southern Christians, the majority of whom were in the three leading evangelical denominations: Baptist, Methodist, and Presbyterian.

The Methodist Episcopal Church, South, was at a low ebb at the end of the war but quickly revived. A General Conference was convened in 1866, and over the next two decades Methodists grew rapidly with membership doubling to more than a million, drawn predominantly from middle- and upper-class whites. As for the Baptists, they too 'refused to admit that secession and slavery were wrong in any way, constitutionally or morally, and denied any responsibility for causing the war. Because God had overridden their views through the instrumentality of war, they would accept his will, but they would change none of their views'.[12] There was little interest in reuniting with Baptists in the north; only slowly did minimum co-operation develop. They devoted themselves primarily to evangelical and missionary tasks, and grew rapidly in membership to well over a million by 1890. Southern Presbyterians were much fewer in number—not quite 200,000 by 1890—but they exerted great influence because of their educated ministry, tight organization, high morale, and hold on many prominent leaders of southern thought and action. Old and New School branches merged in 1864, and soon adopted the name Presbyterian Church in the United States. In his study of Southern Presbyterians, Ernest Trice Thompson said:

Ministers who had lived through the war years continued throughout their lifetime to defend the cause of the South. They readily acknowledged that they were well rid of slavery, and would not have it back; but slavery itself, they

---

[11] *The Circuit Rider Dismounts: A Social History of Southern Methodism, 1865–1900* (Richmond, Va., 1938), p. 111.

[12] Rufus B. Spain, *At Ease in Zion: Social History of Southern Baptists, 1865–1900* (Nashville, Tenn., 1967), p. 20.

insisted to their dying day, was no sin, being sanctified by God's Holy Word. Secession, they maintained, had been constitutionally proper.[13]

Presbyterian spokesmen advanced a doctrine of the 'spirituality of the church' which restrained them from speaking on social and political issues —hence by silence supporting the triumph of white supremacy in the south.

Still smaller numerically were the southern Episcopal dioceses, which also contained strong evangelical elements. The healing of the formal breach with the northern dioceses was accomplished in such a way that southern viewpoints were not challenged. Representatives from the south were welcomed back at the national Triennial Convention of 1865; the presiding bishop, John Henry Hopkins of Vermont, had long been sympathetic to the southern cause and had prepared the way for the return.

The continued independence of the three larger southern bodies, however, contributed to the deepening isolation of the defeated section. The common experiences of the loss of the war and the consequent humiliation of a proud people set them apart. Poverty followed a war that had destituted great sections of the land, and industry spread relatively slowly compared with the north, so that the south remained strongly rural. The patterns of revivalistic, Bible-centred Protestantism that had spread so widely before the war now became even more fixed as white southern Christians idealized their pre-war past and felt themselves to be the truest exponents of biblical faith. To the end of the period there was but little change in these attitudes; social, rural, and religious conservatism reinforced each other for the majority of southern whites.

The Expansion of Black Protestantism

As soon as the war was over, the black denominations burgeoned rapidly. They had been largely kept out of the south before the war, but now they spread swiftly as black congregations proliferated across the south. The first significant public institutions that could be completely under the control of the blacks were the churches. Here the freedmen were unimpeded in moulding the centres to meet the religious and social needs of a newly emancipated but much disadvantaged people—the traditions of religious freedom and the separation of church and state worked to their advantage. Especially as political hopes faded with the end of Reconstruction and as patterns of oppression persisted, the church became the chief arena for the exercise of black leadership. In the white churches the Negroes were customarily treated as inferior, and were expected to keep

---

[13] *Presbyterianism in the South*, ii, *1861–1890* (Richmond, Va., 1973), 113–14.

their place on the margins of church life. With few exceptions, the southern white congregations really did not want blacks in their memberships any longer, but preferred them to have their own churches. There was little inclination to stop the black Baptists who poured out of the mixed congregations, about 150,000 in number. Associations of black churches were quickly formed, and then gathered into state conventions. National boards for home and foreign missions were organized; they merged in 1895 at Atlanta to form the National Baptist Convention, with which the great majority of the congregations affiliated.[14]

Nearly 200,000 black members of the Methodist Episcopal Church, South, had left by 1870. Some became members of black congregations related to the northern Methodists, but the great majority entered the African Methodist Episcopal and the African Methodist Episcopal Zion churches, whose membership increased rapidly in the later 1860s. In 1870 the remaining black members of the Methodist Episcopal Church, South, left by mutual agreement to form the Colored (later Christian) Methodist Episcopal Church.

The piety of the expanding black churches had certain similarities with that of the white evangelical churches, for it was revivalistic and Bible-centred, emotional in tone, simplistic in theology, at home in lay-led Sunday schools and missionary societies. Until their national bodies developed sufficient strength, the black churches (especially Baptist) used the general denominational publications. The religious tone of the churches of the blacks was affected by their aspirations and needs as an economically and educationally underprivileged people who found in the gospel both prophetic vigour and solace. Patterns of faith took on a distinctive cast, and spiritual resources that sustained a frustrating pilgrimage towards freedom were fed by the enthusiastic preaching, praying, and singing of the congregations. The fact that these churches were the primary centres of community and social life in the post-war period brought them especially close to the life of the people. 'For the Negro masses, in their social and moral isolation in American society,' wrote E. Franklin Frazier, 'the Negro church community has been a nation within a nation.'[15] Preachers with notable talent for leadership dominated these communities; under their guidance periodicals were founded, books written, schools and colleges built despite limited resources, and the morale of a people sustained.

---

[14] Owen D. Pelt and Ralph Lee Smith, *The Story of the National Baptists* (New York, 1960), pp. 79–96.

[15] *The Negro Church in America*, p. 44.

By the last quarter of the century it became grimly clear to black leaders that many of the earlier hopes for equality and full citizenship were not being met, but that their plight was actually getting worse. The earlier concern of many northerners for the rights of the freed slaves faded perceptibly after the compromise of 1877 brought Reconstruction to an end. Northern and southern whites slowly groped their way toward a sense of unity—but it was at the expense of the blacks. Many Yankees came to believe that the southern white leaders knew best how to manage their section. The result was a wave of 'Jim Crow' laws which effectively set the Negroes in a separate and subordinate position in public accommodations, transportation, and education, and which largely deprived them of the franchise—various means were used to that end, including terror tactics. 'That he has been treated as a brute instead of a human being—robbed of his liberty and of his honest wage, scourged and harassed as was the blind Samson—is an ineffaceable blot upon the humanity and the religion of the white man, and no reflection whatever upon him', stormed T. Thomas Fortune in the leading black magazine of the time. 'In society, in State, in Church, in commerce, the universal verdict is that a black face is a bar to advancement, to equal justice, to equal Humanity!'[16] Within the safety of their own institutions, blacks could be frank in their assessment of white Christianity, but their criticisms were rarely listened to in white churches and gatherings. Though the black religion which had been largely invisible to whites before the war was now channelled largely into public institutions, there was little interchange in either section between these two kinds of evangelicals—so alike in so many ways, yet so distinctively different.

Faced with such realities, many black leaders counselled moderation, and urged their people to strive to improve and advance within the system. An effective advocate of this position was Booker T. Washington (1859?–1915), who by the last decade of the century had become the most conspicuous black figure in the nation. Born in slavery and brought up a Baptist, he was educated at Hampton Institute, where he accepted the teachings of its founder, General Samuel C. Armstrong. Both believed that physical labour could be a spiritual force, and offered a way for Negroes to win a place in society by providing useful services. Taking over the direction of Tuskegee Institute in 1881, Washington set the students to work in building, gardening, and cooking as well as studying. He urged them to co-operate with the white community and to perform the tasks it needed. As his fame spread, he tirelessly urged his people to

[16] *The A. M. E. Church Review*, viii (July 1890), 3.

advance economically by hard work in agriculture and industry. A realist, he outwardly did not challenge the social customs of the south, and won the confidence of white leaders in all sections. His message was influential in the black churches and colleges. There were some prominent preachers who did not accept his accommodationist stance, notably African Methodist Episcopal Bishop Henry M. Turner (1834–1915), who angrily protested against the unjust treatment of his people. He advocated a return to Africa, though with little success. August Meier concluded that 'Negroes never abandoned their emphasis upon the Christian and humanitarian and democratic elements in the American tradition', and observed that 'their outlook never became as secular as that of many of their fellow Americans'.[17] This is a real tribute to the work of the black churches in the difficult decades following the Civil War.

The Evangelicals and their 'Empire'

After the war many northern evangelicals felt that the main work of liberation had been done with the emancipation of the slaves. Often influenced to some extent by racist thinking themselves, they were increasingly ready to let their southern brethren settle their own affairs. In ways that did not affect the largely rural south for many decades, the northern churches had to deal with the impact of scientific and critical thinking on faith, the realities of the expanding cities with their spreading slums and labour unrest, and the development of the west. They entered the post-war period with great confidence. The Union was saved, slavery was ended, and their missionary and revivalistic heritage offered the means to enrol in ever greater number persons committed to the goal of winning America—and the world—for Christ.

The denominations expressed a renewed concern for planting churches in the west by expanding their home mission and church extension agencies. By the 1880s Protestant mission and extension societies were raising four million dollars a year for planting churches in new territories, doubling the sums raised at the beginning of the period. As permanent communities developed along the spreading rail lines, the Methodists, Presbyterians, Congregationalists, Baptists, and Disciples were frequent rivals in the founding of new congregations. Several energetic missionaries rose to particular prominence because of their determination and resourcefulness in church extension work—and their knowledge of how to publicize the evangelical advance. Sheldon Jackson (1834–1909) served

---

[17] *Negro Thought in America, 1880–1915: Racial Ideologies in the Age of Booker T. Washington* (Ann Arbor, Mich., 1963), p. 23.

Presbyterians well as he travelled widely in the west, founding churches and arranging for the shipping of prefabricated church buildings to prairie states where lumber was scarce. In 1877 he visited Alaska, which had been purchased from Russia ten years before, and devoted the last twenty-five years of his active life to that territory. He played a major role in its religious and educational development, and befriended the Eskimos, introducing the reindeer which was a great boon in their economic life.

During this period hundreds of missionaries laboured among the Indian tribes of the west. They won sizeable minorities to at least a nominal acceptance of evangelical Christianity. The work was difficult, for the defeated Indians, forced into reservations and dependent on governmental assistance, were reluctant to adopt the customs of the invaders. Their numbers were slowly increasing—from an estimated 225,000 in 1860 to about 265,000 fifty years later. Much effort went into educational work, especially under the 'peace policy' begun under President Grant whereby the bulk of public agencies of service to the Indians were put into denominational hands, both Protestant and Catholic. There was hope that the missionary forces could succeed in winning the natives to accept white civilization. But by the end of the century, contention over the sectarian nature of the reservation schools terminated the co-operation of government and missions in education. Though much good was accomplished through the well-meaning and devoted services of many missionaries, the disintegrating effect of American life on Indian cultures, combined with a general apathy and indifference to the needs of the natives, meant that many of the tribes had to survive under very limited cultural and economic advantages. There was some resurgence of Indian religions in this period.

Missionary zeal was focused not only on the west, but also on the burgeoning cities of the east and mid-west. By 1900 about two-fifths of the nation's people were in urban areas, and more than half by 1920. The great leader of urban evangelism was Dwight L. Moody (1837–99), a Congregational layman who became an independent city missionary in Chicago in 1861. He worked through the channels of the Young Men's Christian Association, and soon became the central force in the Chicago Y.M.C.A. Founded in England by George Williams in 1844, the Y.M.C.A. was introduced to North America soon after mid-century, and provided a congenial and Christian atmosphere for boys and young men flooding into the cities to make their living. Intensely evangelistic all through this period, the Y.M.C.A. effectively worked with the churches to carry the gospel to those who were often not reached by congregational life. In much the same spirit, Young Women's Christian Association work began in New York in 1858, and soon spread to other cities in North America.

Moody's first notable success as an urban revivalist occurred not in Chicago but in London in 1872, and was followed by a vigorous campaign across the British Isles in which the lay evangelist, assisted by the singer Ira D. Sankey, was heard by millions. Returning to his native land, Moody carefully systematized his revival methods and achieved spectacular results in city after city. He was deeply sincere in his simple, uncomplicated faith, and skilled in using scriptural materials to prepare messages for a generation steeped in the Bible. He called people back to the familiar religious commitments from which many had been diverted by the novelties and mobilities of the time. Though his famous revivalistic campaigns did win previously unchurched people to Christian faith, many of those who responded to his invitations had been brought up under church influence.[18] Optimistic, confident, sentimental, and sweet-spirited, Moody adapted for urban audiences the evangelical motifs and methods that had been so effective earlier in the century. His energies were poured out in other channels, too, especially in the founding of schools for boys and girls at Mt. Hermon and Northfield, Massachusetts, and in the Moody Bible Institute in Chicago.

The churches rallied under the banners of revivalism, and continued to grow at a faster rate than the population. Moody was but the most famous of the many evangelists of the period; Sam Jones is remembered as the colourful 'Moody of the south', while B. Fay Mills stressed organizational efficiency, developing meticulously the use of advance teams which prepared the way for intense campaigns of many weeks in which the churches of a city were caught up in intricate patterns of organization. There were many lesser figures; a journalist looking back from the 1920s could say, 'If collected in one volume with only a paragraph apiece, the revivalists of the past fifty years would form a book that would dwarf an unabridged dictionary.'[19] The climactic exponent of mass evangelism in this period was William Ashley Sunday (1863–1935)—Billy Sunday, a former professional baseball player who continued his showmanship on the revival trail, exhorting his audiences by pulpit antics and the use of colloquial and vulgar language. The high watermark of his career was in the

[18] McLoughlin, *Modern Revivalism*, ch. V; see also James F. Findlay, Jr., *Dwight L. Moody, American Evangelist, 1837–1899* (Chicago, 1969).
[19] Grover C. Loud, *Evangelized America* (New York, 1928), p. 257.

ten-week campaign in New York in 1917, during which nearly a hundred thousand 'converts' responded to the altar call.

The work of Moody was one of the factors in the intensification of foreign missionary interest in the latter decades of the century. The primary channels for recruiting, sending, and supporting overseas missionaries were the denominational societies, assisted by a number of non-denominational agencies. Y.M.C.A. and Y.W.C.A. branches on college campuses were contributing significantly to the popularizing of foreign missions under the energetic leadership of Luther D. Wishard. This work was further intensified as a result of a conference of college men called by Moody at Mt. Hermon in 1886. The participants were challenged to commit themselves to overseas Christian service, and one hundred did so. Following the gathering, Robert P. Wilder, born in India of missionary parents, toured American campuses, enrolling more than two thousand volunteers for foreign service, a quarter of them women. In 1888 the Student Volunteer Movement for Foreign Missions (S.V.M.) was formally organized.

John R. Mott (1865–1955), a Methodist layman who was entering on an eventful career as the secretary of the American–Canadian Intercollegiate Y.M.C.A. movement, was chosen as the first chairman of the S.V.M., an office he was to hold for three decades. Another layman, Robert E. Speer (1867–1947), served as travelling secretary for the Volunteer Movement before beginning his association of fifty years with the Presbyterian Board of Foreign Missions, during which time he became one of American Christianity's great missionary statesmen. Under such leaders as Mott, Wilder, and Speer, the S.V.M. brought much excitement and challenge to college campuses, and thousands—a conservative estimate puts the number at over 20,000 by 1945—did serve abroad, typically as representatives of their denominational societies. The Movement adopted a motto which soon became famous: 'the evangelization of the world in this generation', by which was meant that the Christian message should be preached to all the world's peoples within a few years.

The resurgence of missionary interest in the evangelical churches was heightened as the century drew to a close by a growing feeling that Protestant Christianity was rapidly becoming the most important religious force in the world. There were many statements of this by individuals and groups; a Congregational theologian, for example, declared in 1890:

Today Christianity is the power which is moulding the destinies of the world. The Christian nations are in the ascendant. Just in proportion to the purity of

Christianity as it exists in the various nations of Christendom is the influence they are exerting upon the world's destiny. The future of the world seems to be in the hands of the three great Protestant powers—England, Germany, and the United States. The old promise is being fulfilled; the followers of the true God are inheriting the world.[20]

A decade later William Newton Clarke (1841–1912), a Baptist who won fame as a leading liberal theologian, insisted that 'Christianity deserves possession of the world. It has the right to offer itself boldly to all men, and to displace all other religions, for no other religion offers what it brings. It is the best that the world contains'.[21] Guided by such confident expectations of world spiritual conquest, American and Canadian Protestant foreign missionary forces went over the seven thousand mark in the first decade of the twentieth century. North America was then supplying about a third of the total world Protestant missionary staff and almost half of the financial backing for the whole enterprise.

Though the primary conscious motivations for the missionary thrust were spiritual and theological, they became tinged with imperialistic overtones, for the missionary and imperialist thrusts did tend to support one another. Convinced of the superiority of their religion and civilization, missionaries sailed in the confident hope that many converts would be won both to Christianity and to western culture, which seemed to them to be so closely related. As witnesses of the gospel fanned out into Africa, Asia, and the islands of the Pacific, they wanted to bring not only the good news of salvation through Christ but also to help people burdened by ignorance, superstition, and primitive patterns of life. Therefore in addition to preaching stations they established schools and hospitals in which the standards of the west were maintained and encouraged. Those who were 'won' often forsook both their inherited religion and their traditional culture to settle within the orbit of a western Christian outpost. In ways that were quite contrary to their own conscious intentions and self-understanding, missionaries were often seen by many in the lands to which they went as closely associated with western imperialism. For example, in the Hawaiian Islands missionary activity during the nineteenth century was one of the forces which prepared the way for their annexation by the United States in 1898. As Paul A. Varg wrote in a probing study of the advance of the churches into China,

Granted that a Christian sense of oughtness inspired the missionary, it is also true

[20] Lewis French Stearns, *The Evidence of Christian Experience* (New York, 1890), p. 366.
[21] *A Study of Christian Missions* (New York, 1901), p. 19.

that the missionary movement and imperialism were wheels driven by the same explosive energy generated by a sense of superiority, moral duty, and the ego satisfaction to be gained in developing the underdeveloped areas of the world in the image of one's own society.[22]

Both movements hoped to 'save the world'.

The achievement of the missionary movement, in which American Protestantism had become so deeply involved, was a major event in Christian history. In many parts of the world churches were planted where they had not been before—institutions which later became strong and independent, able to restate the faith in indigenous terms. The movement also did much for educational, medical, and social service, making contributions to human welfare that were often later copied by new nations as they took shape in the twentieth century.

Both missionary and imperialistic interests were involved in the American decision to engage in the war with Spain in 1898. Though some quite prominent Protestants were opposed to the imperialistic war, a number of influential church leaders, including members of the Catholic hierarchy, became convinced that the Spanish government was cruelly mistreating the Cuban rebels, and enthusiastically supported the short but decisive struggle. Many religious interpreters viewed the victory that so quickly came as clear evidence of God's blessing on America, and favoured the acquisition of Puerto Rico, Guam, and the Philippine Islands (where Dewey had destroyed the Spanish fleet) as evidence of the growing importance of their Christian nation in world affairs. Though most of the Protestant anti-imperialists were also opposed to the annexation of territories—especially the Philippines—they nevertheless soon reconciled themselves to the opportunities for Christian expansion once the annexations had become a fact. Some saw in the situation a chance to weaken the hold of Catholicism on Spanish-speaking peoples. Ernest R. May observed that 'practically every American scholar who has studied the record has come to the same conclusion—that the taking of these new territories was a result of a temporary emotional upswell among the public'.[23] One important ingredient in that surge of feeling was the evangelical sense of special destiny for their cause and for their nation.

Confident of their own special role in history, white evangelicals naïvely assumed that other races would be benefited by finding a subordinate place in their civilization, and would be grateful for the blessings it offered. Josiah Strong, prolific author, speaker, and secretary of the

---

[22] *Missionaries, Chinese, and Diplomats* (Princeton, N.J., 1958), pp. 81–2.
[23] *From Imperialism to Isolationism, 1898–1919* (New York, 1964), p. 31.

American Evangelical Alliance, was voicing convictions widely shared among white Protestants when he said

We have seen that the world is evidently about to enter on a new era, that in this new era mankind is to come more and more under Anglo-Saxon influence, and that Anglo-Saxon civilization is more favorable than any other to the spread of those principles whose universal triumph is necessary to that perfection of the race to which it is destined; the entire realization of which will be the kingdom of heaven fully come on earth.[24]

Inspired both by religious vision and by a sense of destiny, Protestant missionary intensity did not slacken in the first quarter of the new century. John B. Sleman, Jr., a Presbyterian layman, was so moved by the zeal of young people attending the meeting of the S.V.M. in 1906 that he helped in the founding of the Laymen's Missionary Movement. This crusading effort sponsored vast, well-publicized mass meetings across the continent and was successful in generating heightened interest in and securing increased financial resources for the world outreach of the churches. The facts seemed to support a claim made in 1911 that 'during the last quarter century there has been the most advance in the Kingdom of God that the Church has ever witnessed, surely surpassing any that was accomplished in the centuries that preceded'.[25] It was indeed a time of great excitement and hope. Looking back on that period, one who had lived through it spoke of the first fifteen years of the twentieth century as an age of crusades. 'There were a superabundance of zeal, a sufficiency of good causes, unusual moral idealism, excessive confidence in mass movements and leaders with rare gifts of popular appeal.'[26]

The black churches, so largely cut off from participation with their white fellow evangelicals, were much more sober in their expectations; their concerns were focused heavily on the needs of their segregated people, many of whom were finding in Christianity a sense of worth and direction, and spiritual resources for a hard struggle. The black churches did have extensive missionary work at home and abroad; they were especially active in the West Indies and Africa. By 1916 the number of adult black Baptists went well over the two million mark, while almost a million and a half were members of one of the Methodist bodies. At that point, the percentage of blacks who were church members had surpassed that of the white population.

---

[24] *The New Era, or the Coming Kingdom* (New York, 1893), p. 81.
[25] J. Ross Stevenson, *The Student Volunteer Movement After Twenty-five Years* (n.p., n.d. [1911]), p. 46.
[26] Gaius Glenn Atkins, *Religion in Our Times* (New York, 1932), p. 156.

The National Baptist Convention went through some acute organizational difficulties. When the Foreign Mission Board offices were moved from Virginia to Kentucky, leaders in Virginia protested, and formed the Lott Carey Missionary Convention, named after a pioneer black missionary in Liberia. A more serious split occurred in 1915 mainly over the conduct of the Publishing Board. The larger and continuing group became incorporated, while the unincorporated group became known as the National Baptist Convention of America.[27]

Sunday Schools and Public Schools

The churches' ability to adapt their channels of outreach and to create new institutional forms in the process is illustrated not only in revivalism and missions but also in education. Early in his career, Moody saw the possibilities of remoulding the Sunday schools and was instrumental in enlisting people to do the job, especially Benjamin F. Jacobs, an energetic Chicago businessman. A group set to work with determination to turn informal local and state conventions of Sunday-school workers into an efficient organization which became the International Sunday School Association—international because Canada was included. A voluntary network was developed to serve all the evangelical churches on the continent. The lay influence was strong in the actual operation of the local Sunday schools, in the county and regional meetings, and in the vast triennial International Sunday School Conventions, the first of which met in 1875. The clergy also participated in this new drive to improve the Sunday schools and to mould them into instruments of evangelism. A young Methodist minister, John H. Vincent (1832–1920), was concerned about the confusion and lack of standards in the average class. He started training institutes for teachers, and proposed that all evangelical denominations follow a uniform lesson plan, so that classes of all ages and denominations across the land would be focusing on the same theme at the same time, for which printed materials would be prepared in advance.

Jacobs and Vincent showed great organizational skill in guiding their growing movement to accept the uniform—or International—lesson system. The move not only brought increased efficiency and order into the educational programmes of local churches, but it significantly increased the sense of fellowship across denominational lines. 'Uniform lessons, for a time,' historians of the movement observed, 'gave evangelical Protestantism in the English-speaking world a common language, a Protestant version of the Roman Catholic Latin Mass of pre-Second

[27] Pelt and Smith, *The Story of the National Baptists*, pp. 100–5.

Vatican Council days.'[28] The lessons were also carried abroad, and were translated into many languages for overseas use. Adults studied them too—some classes for men and women regularly drew hundreds and in a few cases thousands. Training institutes for teachers flourished—one founded by Vincent at Lake Chautauqua, New York, became especially famous as it developed into an elaborate, varied, summer programme.

Almost forty years after the decision to adopt the uniform lesson plan, when the Thirteenth International Sunday School Convention met in San Francisco in 1911, the general secretary, Marion Lawrance, reported that the movement was reaching regularly about 15,000,000 persons in 173,000 Sunday schools in the United States and Canada. But 'the supreme thing' of which he was most proud was that 'we have great occasion to be thankful to the Heavenly Father for one million one hundred and ninety-three thousand conversions in the Sunday Schools during the last three years'.[29] The Sunday schools were not only the principal training ground of the Protestant laity but also a major recruiting ground.

Included among the 173,000 schools were about 35,000 black Sunday schools, which for many of those freed during and at the conclusion of the war had been 'their primary school, their academy, their seminary and their college all in one'.[30] Many of these ventures had adopted the International lesson plan, and despite limited resources followed the programme of teachers' meetings, state conventions, and record-keeping. The Sunday school—north and south, black and white—was everywhere a vital partner in the life of the evangelical churches.

The basic educational interests of the churches did not end with their Sunday schools. A few denominations operated parochial schools, but all were convinced of the importance of the public, tax-supported elementary and secondary schools. Because of the principle of the separation of church and state, the relationship could not be direct. Nevertheless, in a culture in which evangelical values were strong, the indirect ties were effective. In his massive study of the United States in the first quarter of the twentieth century, Mark Sullivan explained the paradox of school systems which operated under legal requirements separating church and state but which were clearly oriented to Protestant values:

What happened was that the States carried on a system of education in which

---

[28] Lynn and Wright, *The Big Little School*, p. 66.
[29] *Organized Sunday School Work in America, 1908–1911, Triennial Survey of Sunday School Work including the Official Report of the Thirteenth Official Sunday School Convention* (Chicago, 1911), p. 159.
[30] *Ibid.*, p. 521.

practically all the traditions and most of the influences were religious. . . . So deeply embedded was the spirit of religion in the common schools of America that nothing short of a revolution, or a trend immensely long, could have uprooted it.[31]

To be sure, there were certain challenges to the dominance of the spirit of evangelical religion in the public schools. One was the emergence of naturalistic and secular trends of thought in the culture, but such currents were often roundly criticized by leaders of both religious and public education. Though they were making headway in some institutions of higher education, such trends made little advance in the public schools. A more direct threat was the criticism of the common schools by the rapidly growing Roman Catholic Church and the expansion of its own parochial school system.

Though anti-Catholic feeling had subsided somewhat during and after the Civil War, in the later nineteenth century there was some resurgence of it. The American Protective Association was founded in 1887 in an effort to curb immigration and to keep parochial schools from securing public funds. On the whole the Catholic objections to the public schools strengthened the determined Protestant support of them. As the National Council of the Congregational Churches once put it, 'We cannot abandon our public-school system on account of the difficulties with infidels or with Roman Catholics.'[32] Calendars and customs in the common schools were largely shaped by the Protestant consensus; pupils from evangelical backgrounds found familiar moral standards taught in the classroom.

Sabbath Observance and Temperance

Protestant leaders found themselves in a quandary as the nation became more pluralistic. Dedicated to the separation of church and state, they also desired to continue to dominate their culture and make America a Christian (by which they meant a Protestant) nation. To that end, they wanted to maintain strict patterns of Sabbath observance. They sought to escape from a difficult predicament by keeping clear the difference between the religious and the civil Sabbath. They agreed that Sunday as a holy day, which they wanted as an uninterrupted time for church and family observances, could not be enforced by law if religious freedom were to mean anything at all. But the civil Sabbath as a day of rest was so essential for the health and morale of the people, they believed, that it could be

---

[31] *Our Times: The United States, 1900–1925*, vol. ii: *America Finding Herself* (New York, 1932), p. 85.

[32] *Minutes of the National Council of the Congregational Churches*, 1877, p. 24.

defended on humanitarian grounds and should be maintained by law. They therefore sought to maintain strict Sunday observance by appealing to the civil tradition of a day free of work and the regular pressures of the week. Yet Sunday customs were changing, in part because of the immigration of those from cultures not familiar with the Puritan Sabbath. In spite of themselves, evangelicals were being carried along with the cultural tide—especially when the twentieth century brought the motor car. Reports at denominational gatherings lamented the slow decline of Sabbath observance and tried to urge the faithful to maintain them. For example, in 1900 the Methodist bishops cried that 'the decay of religion is inevitable if the Church does not abide in the right use of the holy day', and a Presbyterian committee told the General Assembly that 'when the people who should be in the pews in the sanctuary are absorbed in the pursuit of pleasure or business on the Lord's Day, the Church and the Lord's treasury are the immediate and inevitable sufferers'.[33] Though the patterns of strict observance of Sunday were eroding, more quickly in some areas of the country than in others, Sunday 'blue laws' often remained on the books, keeping stores closed and limiting public amusements.

If the crusade to maintain a rigorous Sabbath was slowly being lost, the period ended with a great evangelical victory for another of its crusades—prohibition. The Civil War had interrupted the pre-war temperance movement, and in some of the dozen states legislation which had restricted in various ways the sale and traffic of liquor was withdrawn. Following the war, curbs on the use of alcoholic beverages were advocated by such new organizations as the Prohibition Party (1869) and the Woman's Christian Temperance Union (1874). The W.C.T.U., especially under the long presidency of the noted feminist, Frances Willard (1839–98), became associated with many of the progressive reform movements of the time. The English-speaking Protestant denominations across sectional and racial lines gave nearly unanimous support to the cause of temperance, and formed and strengthened their own agencies of reform in this area.

As before, the evangelicals found it hard to draw a line between light, moderate, and heavy drinking, and usually concluded that the safest way was to press for the complete avoidance of alcohol. 'We rejoice that the word temperance is coming more and more to designate total abstinence', reported one denomination's committee on temperance, 'and is aiming, not only at the reformation of the drunkard and the right of education for

---

[33] *Journal of the General Conference of the Methodist Episcopal Church*, 1900, p. 75; *Minutes of the General Assembly of the Presbyterian Church in the United States of America*, 1900, p. 30.

the young but also at total suppression of distillery, saloon, brewery and bar.'[34]

A new turn in the drive for prohibition came in 1895 with the formation of the Anti-Saloon League, which utilized non-partisan political channels in its drive for a constitutional amendment to end the sale of intoxicating beverages. Beginning as a coalition of temperance groups, the League soon developed an efficient national structure of its own, broadly based on church constituencies. In 1905 nearly 20,000 congregations were co-operating with the League; in ten years the number doubled. Methodist, Baptist, Presbyterian, and Congregational churches were in the forefront. Even the Southern Baptists overcame their resistance to political action and to co-operation with northerners to join this great crusade. 'In view of the historical tendency of Baptists to avoid "entangling alliances", the aid which they rendered the League was little short of revolutionary', a social historian of the Southern Baptist Convention declared. 'State Conventions authorized collections for the League's support, publicized its literature, and appointed messengers and delegates to the national meetings of the League.'[35] By combining rural, small town, middle-class, and progressive interests (in all of which Protestants were deeply involved), the League was able to secure the ratification of the Eighteenth Amendment. It resorted to the techniques of pressure politics in accomplishing its purpose.

The struggle for prohibition can be seen as one attempt to secure Protestant value orientations in the nation against the challenges of pluralistic and secular currents. One interpreter of the temperance movement declared that the Eighteenth Amendment 'established the victory of Protestant over Catholic, rural over urban, tradition over modernity, the middle class over both the lower and the upper strata'.[36] At the time the struggle was understood in similar terms; one reformer in 1915 insisted that 'our nation can only be saved by turning the pure stream of country sentiment and township morals to flush out the cesspools of cities and to save civilization from pollution'.[37] As the prohibition amendment went into effect in January 1920 the evangelicals rejoiced in a great victory; a crusade that had begun a hundred years before had been won. Though the churches had not accomplished it alone, it never could have been done without them.

[34] *Minutes of the Twentieth Quadrennial Session of the General Conference of the African Methodist Episcopal Zion Connection,* 1896, p. 255.   [35] Spain, *At Ease in Zion,* p. 195.
[36] Joseph R. Gusfield, *Symbolic Crusade: Status Politics and the American Temperance Movement* (Urbana, Ill., 1963), p. 7.
[37] As quoted by James H. Timberlake, *Prohibition and the Progressive Movement, 1900–1920* (Cambridge, Mass., 1963), p. 151.

Theological Tensions

While outwardly flourishing, the evangelical denominations were troubled by deepening internal theological tensions between those who accepted to some significant degree certain results of the revolutions in thought that marked the period and those who largely rejected them. The churches of British Protestant background in the north were especially vulnerable to the new currents of scientific thought and historical criticism of the later nineteenth century. These trends intensified a widening inner division between liberal and conservative movements in evangelical bodies.

For a number of generations the researches and speculations of scientists and scholars had been raising certain questions about traditional supernaturalistic world views. In their responses to the challenges of Enlightenment thought in the first and second Great Awakenings, evangelical leaders had often pushed doubts and questions into the background without fully facing them. These habits persisted when critical questions were raised again in a more telling way by geologists and evolutionary thinkers in the later nineteenth century. Great numbers of Protestants continued to affirm the concepts of the creation of the world and the human race by God in six days a few thousand years ago in accordance with what they believed to be the teaching of the divinely inspired and inerrant Bible.

Then came remarkable changes in the intellectual apprehension of human origins as evolutionary and developmental thought matured and spread. The impact of Darwin's *Origin of Species* was somewhat delayed in the United States because of the crisis of the Civil War. By 1870 the new views were being vigorously debated; the next year Darwin's *The Descent of Man* more directly challenged traditional views of creation. While many Protestant leaders continued to reject the new views, some conspicuous mediators entered the debate at an early stage, finding that it was possible to interpret evolutionary theory in theistic terms. Prominent among the mediators were Asa Gray, distinguished scientist and devout layman; George Frederick Wright, a young pastor who later taught science and religion at Oberlin; James McCosh, Scottish-born president of Princeton; and John Fiske, popularizer and apologist of evolution who penned the often quoted words, 'Evolution is God's way of doing things.'[38] Such leaders of thought clearly had great respect for the methods and conclusions of scientists and urged that their investigations be encouraged; they also believed that essential Christian doctrines might not only be

[38] For a compact discussion of this, see Ahlstrom, *A Religious History of the American People*, pp. 763–84; for a more extended treatment with documents, consult William R. Hutchison (ed.), *American Protestant Thought: The Liberal Era* (New York, 1968).

interpreted in developmental terms, but might be more fully understood in that context. As evangelicals were exposed to the new trends of thought, often through college experiences, many came to believe that there were several ways to truth, and that the analytical approach of the scientists could shed light on the mysteries of the universe while the reflections of modern philosophers could help in clarifying the new understandings of reality.

The problems presented by natural science were difficult enough for those steeped in traditional supernaturalistic views of the universe, but the perplexities deepened when new critical ways of researching and reinterpreting religious pasts became more familiar. In the decades following the Civil War a number of American students went abroad for further work, getting first-hand exposure to the complex debates raging among European scholars of various points of view who were examining sacred writings and theological doctrines in the light of their histories. To those reared in an atmosphere in which the Bible was taken to be the infallible Word of God, it was upsetting to approach it like other books. Many found their inherited views of the Scriptures weakened, and accepted liberal theological perspectives, especially as interpreted by the German theologian, Albrecht Ritschl (1822–89), and his school.

Similar shifts of thought were occurring in America, even in the denominations in which the evangelical counter-offensive to Enlightenment and Unitarian views had enthroned doctrines of biblical infallibility. For example, a well-educated young Baptist pastor, William Newton Clarke, was typical of his generation in believing that the Bible was 'so inspired by God that its writers were not capable of error. I did not feel myself at liberty to dissent from its teachings, to doubt the accuracy of its statements, or to question the reality of its reasonings'. Difficulties arose as he became more aware of the historical nature of the Bible from reading the commentaries, but more especially when a study of conflicting notions of the millennium forced him to the conclusion that some New Testament writers expected the Lord's return in their time—obviously they had been mistaken, and therefore all biblical statements were not literally true. Clarke remained a staunch evangelical, believing that Christ had indeed come to save sinners and was the only way to salvation, but he also became an advocate of the 'new theology', committed to rethinking basic traditional views in the light of critical study of Bible and theology. He also realized that church practice was being affected by the changing doctrinal currents; as an illustration he reported that women were playing an expanding role in church life. 'They knew all about the argument for reading Paul's prohibition [of women speaking in church] as local and temporary, at least the Corinthian one, and so had no fear that they were sinning against the Scriptures.'[39] Clarke was called to teach theology at Colgate University, and wrote a widely read liberal text on systematics, *An Outline of Christian Theology* (1894).

There were many other routes to an evangelical or Christocentric liberal theology. At Andover Theological Seminary in Massachusetts the members of a distinguished faculty marched into the 'new theology' under the banner of 'progressive orthodoxy'; by the turn of the century a number of the leading seminaries had accepted liberal perspectives. Some of the young scholars who had studied in Europe emerged as influential teachers, such as Lewis French Stearns at Bangor Seminary in Maine, Borden Parker Bowne at Boston University, Shailer Mathews at Chicago, and Arthur C. McGiffert and William Adams Brown at Union Theological Seminary in New York. Liberal theology was also presented with genuine power by a number of renowned preachers: Phillips Brooks and George A. Gordon of Boston, Theodore T. Munger and Newman Smyth of New Haven, Washington Gladden of Columbus, David Swing of Chicago, and especially Henry Ward Beecher of Brooklyn and his successor, Lyman Abbott. Beecher (1813–89), one of the famous children of Lyman, was the most prominent pulpiteer of his time. An eloquent, sensational speaker, he dramatically presented a blend of evangelical religion, modern thought, and middle-class values. One of his interpreters has reported that his 'great achievement was to amalgamate Romanticism, religion, and science—the epistemology of Kant, the Gospel of Jesus, the teleology of Spencer'.[40] A proud, self-centred, outspoken man, he had many ardent admirers, and some bitter enemies.

The whole liberal movement had many strands within it, for while some were struggling with questions posed primarily by scientists or biblical critics, others were wrestling with ethical and social questions, or with philosophical considerations. Yet they agreed on a number of central issues. With variations in detail, the evangelical liberals linked an insistence on loyalty to Jesus Christ as the final principle for the interpretation of ultimate reality with acceptance of the evolutionary hypothesis, the historical approach to the Bible, and certain insights of modern psychology, sociology, and philosophy. In their doctrine of God, they sought

[39] *Sixty Years with the Bible* (New York, 1909), pp. 42–3, 153. See also Daniel Day Williams, *The Andover Liberals: A Study of American Theology* (New York, 1941).

[40] William G. McLoughlin, *The Meaning of Henry Ward Beecher: An Essay on the Shifting Values of Mid-Victorian America, 1840–1870* (New York, 1970), p. 4.

to keep a balanced emphasis on both transcendence and immanence, yet often they came down harder on the latter as they stressed continuity between God and the world. They also preached that humanity arose from divine creative action, and that human personality was to be highly valued and reverenced. Yet they believed that human life was marred by the reality of individual and corporate sin, and that deliverance was available through the unique divinity of Jesus Christ. As more persons and groups were brought into the sphere of redemption, they affirmed that the Kingdom of God, the all-embracing goal of history, would be realized progressively. William Adams Brown, a major liberal systematic theologian, declared that the Kingdom of God meant 'that society of redeemed personalities, of which Christ is at once the ideal and the mediator, the union of whose members, one with another and with God in the community of holy love, progressively realized in history, constitutes the end for which the world exists'.[41]

The liberal synthesis of Christian faith and modern thought exerted great influence within Protestantism for several generations. Strong liberal parties arose in Congregationalism, in the northern branches of the Methodist, Baptist, and Presbyterian churches, and in the Episcopal and Disciples traditions. The Congregational and Methodist communions were most deeply influenced. In the former the role of Bangor, Andover, Yale, and Chicago seminaries was strategic. In the latter the contribution of Boston University's Borden Parker Bowne (1847–1910) was significant; he provided a philosophical basis for evangelical liberalism in an idealistic 'personalism' which was especially influential and persisting. By the outbreak of World War I, liberalism was confidently growing, and optimistically looking forward to the coming Kingdom of God on earth. An influential weekly journal, *The Christian Century*, edited by Charles Clayton Morrison, gave the movement an important channel of influence.

Resistance to these efforts to mediate between evangelical faith and modern thought was not long in coming, and from several directions. From inside the liberal camp there were those who shifted the very locus of authority to scientific and historical method, and who in retrospect have been called 'modernistic liberals' or 'scientific modernists'. A relatively small though articulate group, they were less interested in preserving the Christocentric heritage than the evangelical liberals, and found many theological traditions not worth preserving in the light of fresh knowledge about the universe and in view of increased awareness of the relativities of historical religions and their doctrines. Their interests swung to empirical

41 *Christian Theology in Outline* (New York, 1906), pp. 182–3.

theologies and to comparative religion; they could appreciate and identify with the pioneering liberalism of Enlightenment, Unitarian, and Trans-cendentalist figures. A conspicuous centre of such thought in the early twentieth century was the Divinity School of the University of Chicago under such leaders as Shailer Mathews, who studied Christian doctrines in the light of their socio-economic backgrounds, theologian George Burman Foster, and philosopher Edward Scribner Ames. Some of the members of the 'Chicago school', especially Mathews himself, remained strong churchmen, but their theological drift beyond evangelical liberal-ism weakened their mediatorial efforts.

Much more formidable resistance to the liberal synthesis came from the outside. Even as theological liberalism gathered strength in the last quarter of the nineteenth century, evangelical conservatism was also renascent in most of the denominations. In part, the movement to the theological right emerged in reaction to liberal acceptances of evolutionary hypotheses and biblical criticism. While some of the conservative attacks on Darwinism were very superficial, there were a few serious responses, as by Charles Hodge, the formidable Princeton theologian who rejected 'natural selection' as inconsistent with Christian faith in *What is Darwin-ism?* (1874). Hodge, and especially his successors Archibald Alexander Hodge and Benjamin Warfield, developed in careful detail what they believed was a biblical doctrine of the inspiration of the Bible. In their view, the Scriptures claim to be inspired and inerrant, and believers must accept that on the credibility of the apostles as teachers of doctrine. Though they agreed that there might be copyists' errors in transcribing the 'original autographs', they insisted that these did not invalidate the inerrancy of the Bible as a whole. The learned, scholastic arguments of the Princeton theologians greatly comforted those who believed in an infallible Bible, and provided much ammunition for those who set themselves against historical criticism.

Increasingly pervasive in many conservative circles was the influence of a millenarian, 'dispensationalist' strand of thought and piety that stemmed largely from the work of John Nelson Darby (1800–82), leader of the fragmented Plymouth Brethren in England who travelled extensively in the United States and Canada. The dispensationalists interpreted the Bible as teaching that all history was divided into a series of periods or dis-pensations soon to climax in the Second Coming of Christ and the pro-mised Millennium. Many prominent evangelists and preachers found this approach congenial, and supportive of their belief in an inerrant Bible.

The various lines of resurgent conservatism mutually reinforced each other in a series of non-denominational 'prophetic' and Bible conferences. The Believers' Meeting for Bible Study met in Chicago in 1875; its later annual gatherings were often at Niagara-on-the-Lake, Ontario, and became popularly known as the Niagara Bible Conference. It was the mother of a number of other similar meetings at which the literal interpretation of the Scriptures was emphasized in long periods of study. Some noted preachers were active at these conferences, for example Baptist Adoniram Judson Gordon of Boston, and Presbyterians James Hall Brookes, a St. Louis pastor, and William G. Moorhead, professor and later president of the seminary in Xenia, Ohio. The Niagara Conference was in part based on English models as was the Bible and Prophetic Conference called in New York in 1878 at Holy Trinity Episcopal Church. Many of the Niagara leaders were on the platform, from which millenarian themes were forcefully proclaimed. The religious and secular Press gave wide coverage to the gathering. In 1886 and 1895 similar conferences were held at Chicago and Philadelphia, while on a smaller scale many other such meetings were held in various cities. As many of the theological seminaries were moving in a liberal direction, resurgent evangelical conservatism founded another series of institutions—Bible colleges and seminaries in which central doctrines precious to conservatives were strongly emphasized: the reliability of the biblical text, the virgin birth and deity of Christ, the substitutionary atonement, and Christ's physical resurrection and bodily return.

Few of the ministers directly or indirectly influenced by such currents as Princeton theology and dispensationalism left their denominations to join one of the Plymouth Brethren groups; in Ernest R. Sandeen's words, 'they could not bring themselves to drop out of their churches'. But they preached and led their congregations in quite distinctive ways: 'In an age in which American pulpit oratory reached its zenith with such fashionable ministers as T. De Witt Talmage, Henry Ward Beecher, Joseph Cook, and Phillips Brooks, the Bible teacher conceived of himself not only as teaching a different gospel, but as teaching it in a wholly contrasting fashion.'[42] He made no effort to be eloquent or magnetic, but told his simple story in a straightforward way, staying close to the biblical text as he understood it.

Conservative parties thus gained strength in the same denominations in which there were strong liberal movements. Though Presbyterians and Baptists in the north were especially affected, the increase of inner

---

[42] Ernest R. Sandeen, *The Roots of Fundamentalism: British and American Millenarianism, 1800–1930* (Chicago, 1970), pp. 136–7.

theological tension was also felt in the Congregational, Methodist, Disciples, and Episcopal churches. Conflict emerged within many local congregations. At denominational and transdenominational conventions and assemblies the bickering between the parties often became sharp and bitter.

As the theological debate intensified, there were some dismissals of liberal ministers and professors from pulpits and chairs. The most famous of the 'heresy trials' of the period involved Charles H. Briggs (1841–1913) of Union Theological Seminary, New York. He was suspended from the ministry by the Presbyterian General Assembly in 1893 because of an address in which he criticized certain concepts of verbal inspiration and the inerrancy of Scripture as barriers that kept people from actual encounter with the Bible. The seminary severed all its ties with the denomination and retained Briggs, who became an Episcopalian. Henry Preserved Smith, a professor at Lane Seminary who came to Briggs's defence, was also suspended; he became a Congregationalist and later served Union as librarian. Arthur C. McGiffert (1861–1933), a rising young historical theologian, also forsook Presbyterianism for Congregationalism to avoid the storms of another heresy trial when charges were advanced against him.

In the isolated south, devotion to conservative views was strong, and certain scholars who seemed to be advancing unsound views were ousted from their posts, notably Alexander Winchell from Vanderbilt University (Methodist) in 1878, James Woodrow from the Presbyterian seminary at Columbia, South Carolina, eight years later, and Crawford H. Toy and William H. Whitsett from the Southern Baptist seminary at Louisville, Kentucky, in 1879 and 1898. The continuing influence of Landmarkism[43] accentuated the conservative cast of Baptists in the south. Another illustration of the conservative mind of much southern and south-western Protestantism was provided when a significant minority of the churches of Disciples of Christ background refused to associate with the denomination's conventions, societies, and mission boards, and rejected as non-apostolic and modernistic such things as instrumental music, Sunday schools, and over-all denominational co-operation as they sought to restore what they believed were authentic New Testament patterns. By 1906 these 'Churches of Christ' were recognized as having wholly withdrawn from the Disciples; eventually they were to rival the parent body in size.

Though there were some sharp clashes between the various theological

---

[43] See above, pp. 207–8.

parties, they also had much in common, and in missionary, Sunday school, and temperance movements all but the extremists continued to work together in this period. Probably a majority of evangelicals thought of themselves as moderates, not strongly identified with either conspicuously liberal or militantly conservative leadership. Evangelical liberals, for example, were prominent in foreign missionary work, but were motivated more by concern for social change, moral improvement, and the advance of Christian civilization than by the older passion for saving souls from hell's fires. Liberal interest in missions was illustrated and heightened by the publication of a massive work by James A. Dennis, who presented impressive statistical evidence to back his claim that 'Christian missions have already produced social results which are manifest, and that society in the non-Christian world at the present time is conscious of a new and powerful factor which is working positive and revolutionary changes in the direction of a higher civilization'.[44] Both conservative and liberal evangelicals rejoiced in the progress of missions; those great lay leaders, Mott and Speer, were conservative in their own religious and social views, yet were not preoccupied with the niceties of doctrine and had the ability to bridge theological gaps. At the Ecumenical Missionary Conference in New York in 1900, at which representatives of Protestant missionary organizations gathered from around the world, Speer admitted that 'considerations of future destiny now occupy less place in the thought of men than considerations of present duty' but reported that the gathering clearly 'demonstrated the essential unity of the evangelical churches'.[45] The crusade for a Christian America and a Christian world helped to keep most of the evangelicals working together.

The co-operation continued into the early twentieth century, but the distance between theological groups to the left and right was increasing. In 1903, for example, the Religious Education Association was founded in Chicago, an organization which did much to integrate the insights of progressive education into liberal Christianity—a development that slowly began to permeate denominational education and Sunday school boards. The dominating leader of thought in the new movement was George Albert Coe (1862–1951), who dwelt on ideas of divine immanence and evolutionary development in stressing 'Salvation by Education'.[46] A

---

[44] *Christian Missions and Social Progress: A Sociological Study of Foreign Missions*, 3 vols. (New York, 1897–1906), i, 31.

[45] *Ecumenical Missionary Conference, New York, 1900* . . ., 2 vols. (New York, 1900), i, 63.

[46] The title of one of his seminal essays, published in *The Religion of a Mature Mind* (Chicago, 1902), pp. 293–396.

number of colleges and universities historically associated with the evangelical denominations moved clearly in a liberal direction, some eventually cutting all formal ties.

A portent of a coming storm was a counter-attack on the liberal programme in the publication of a series of twelve small volumes of essays, *The Fundamentals* (1910–15), which presented the conservative case for biblical inerrancy as put by an influential group of British, American, and Canadian writers. Conservative but scholarly contributions were mingled with dispensationalist articles in the somewhat uneven series, which was distributed widely across the continent. Copies were sent to lay and clerical leaders in an effort to swing Protestantism away from liberalism. Though *The Fundamentals* did not halt the liberal trend, by rallying conservative forces the series widened theological gulfs within the churches. Despite growing inner tension, however, the outward prestige and strength of Protestantism and her institutions seemed secure in the first two decades of the twentieth century.

Evangelical Dissenters

Agreeing on many points with the larger evangelical denominations but self-consciously separated from them by certain distinctive emphases were a number of smaller bodies, most of them very conservative theologically. The Adventist churches that had stemmed from the Millerite excitement and disappointment of the 1840s continued to multiply in the post-Civil War period. The Seventh-day Adventists had a remarkable leader in the prophetess Ellen Harmon White (1827–1915), whose spiritual visions and concerns about matters of diet and health set their mark on a steadily growing church. In the twentieth century, Seventh-day Adventist mission, stewardship, and publication efforts were impressive for so relatively small a denomination.

A more spectacular group of Adventist background arose around Charles Taze Russell (1852–1916), a Congregational layman who was won over to millenarian views. A vigorous preacher and voluminous writer, he declared that inasmuch as the Lord's Second Advent had in fact occurred in 1874, the prophesied end of the world would soon come. His growing band of followers took as their official name the Watchtower Bible and Tract Society, but later became more familiarly known as the International Bible Students Association and then as Jehovah's Witnesses. Believing that the culture and religions of the world were doomed, the Russellites sought to gather converts who would be saved from the oncoming catastrophe, for, according to a favourite motto, 'millions now living will never die'. The Witnesses were tightly controlled by their colourful leader, who bitingly criticized traditional Protestant theology and church life, and shaped a distinctive position focused on the imminent Second Coming of Christ. When the founder died, a leader of strong organizational abilities, Joseph Franklin Rutherford (1869–1942) gained control of the highly disciplined, intensely zealous movement. Because conscientious objector status was claimed for all active members, the group was persecuted during World War I. Rutherford and other prominent leaders were imprisoned for nine months. The movement emerged from the war period stronger than ever; 'Kingdom Halls' became an increasingly familiar sight, not only in America but overseas as well.

A number of new extremely evangelistic denominations arose in this period out of the stimulus of the Holiness and Pentecostal movements. Their emergence was marked by controversy—often they proclaimed that they were reclaiming true Christianity, all but lost in the major denominations. Their distinctive understandings of what was vital in Christianity often set them apart from each other and from the older denominations, which they often repudiated as apostate. The latter in turn often looked down on the new groups as marginal or aberrational sects. They greatly increased the organizational diversity of Christianity, not only in America but also across the world, for most of them were strongly missionary-minded.

The Holiness movement as it emerged after the Civil War drew on the earlier perfectionist currents of Finney and Mahan at Oberlin and of the Wesleyan tradition. Characteristic evangelical emphases on industry, honesty, and thrift helped many of the faithful to grow prosperous, and with an increase in goods and position there followed what many regarded as spiritual laxity and an accommodation to the world. The emphasis on the search for Christian perfection lost its general appeal in the churches of the gilded age, to the distress of those who yearned for the doctrine. Some who were deeply committed to Wesleyan and Oberlin forms of perfection-ism brought these teachings into their revival work.[47] In 1867 a National Association for the Promotion of Holiness was organized in Vineland, New Jersey. It disavowed any separatist intent as it sponsored camp-meetings to promote the work of entire sanctification. A number of local Holiness associations were formed. Though Methodist people were

[47] Cf. Timothy L. Smith, *Revivalism and Social Reform in Mid-Nineteenth Century America*, pp. 135–47, and James L. Peters, *Christian Perfection and American Methodism* (New York, 1956), pp. 133–80.

especially prominent in the upsurge of Holiness efforts, Baptists and others also participated. In their non-denominational associations, revivals, camp-meetings, and periodicals the Holiness leaders stressed both justification and entire sanctification as two gifts of the Holy Ghost.

Then resistance came—a number of Methodist leaders criticized the limited theological horizons and the 'come-outer' spirit of the Holiness movement. The enthusiasts for the new movement responded that they were being driven out of their own denominations, where they no longer felt at home because of the emergence of alien liberal theological and social currents. In the last two decades of the nineteenth century while some of the Holiness people remained in their denominational homes, others organized separate churches.

One of the earliest independent groups was founded by Daniel S. Warner, whose own background was in the General Eldership of the Churches of God in North America, a small, revivalistic frontier denomination. Somewhat like the leaders of the 'Christian' churches in the earlier nineteenth century, Warner became convinced that sectarianism was wrong, and in 1881 separated himself both from his denomination and from a non-denominational Holiness association in which he had been active in order to lead a 'Church of God Reformation Movement'. An old story repeated itself—a movement determined to be free of all human creeds and party names and to follow primitive apostolic pattern slowly grew into a new denomination, the Church of God (Anderson, Indiana). In 1917 the establishment of a General Ministerial Assembly marked a major step towards a conventional denominational bureaucracy.

Another institutional development, this one stressing holiness, divine healing, and missions, was led by a former Presbyterian, the Canadian Albert Benjamin Simpson (1844–1919). The Christian and Missionary Alliance was organized in New York in 1887 as a non-denominational fellowship; in time it became virtually a new denomination, with a special focus on urban evangelism.

One of the most conspicuous of the Holiness groups to withdraw from its denominational home evolved rather quickly into a new church, the Nazarenes. The First Church of the Nazarene was organized in Los Angeles in 1895; central in its development was Phineas Bresee (1838–1915), a prominent Methodist minister of southern California who left his church to carry the Holiness message to the young and poor. In co-operation with a wealthy Methodist layman, J. P. Widney, M.D., president of the University of Southern California, the Church of the Nazarene was formed as 'a simple, primitive church, a church of the people and for the people. It has no new doctrines, only the old, old Bible truths'.[48] The congregation grew swiftly, and many satellite churches were formed. The revivalistic services conducted by the new congregations invited intensely emotional responses. A General Holiness Assembly met in Chicago in 1901; at this gathering the desire to form a new denomination was patently felt. The founding of schools and colleges furthered the growth of this missionary and evangelistic movement as Nazarene congregations and associations were gathered in all sections of the country. A series of unions, culminating at Pilot Point, Texas, in 1908, brought the Church of the Nazarene officially into being as a conservative, revivalistic, perfectionist body, its Methodist ancestry evident in its doctrine and polity. In its early years, the new Holiness denomination developed a strong superintendency and extensive educational and foreign missionary channels. Already by 1910, its reported membership was 10,000, and was increasing rapidly. Like most of the Holiness denominations, the Church of the Nazarene stressed a rather strict code of personal ethics, and frowned on member participation in dancing, theatre-going, card-playing, and ostentatious dress. Most such groups drew much of their membership from the older evangelical denominations. The growth of the large, popular churches was not seriously affected, but there was considerable concern over the new threat.

While most of the new Holiness groups arose indigenously, the Salvation Army, which combined perfectionist doctrine with particular concern for the urban poor, was founded in England by William Booth (1829–1912) in 1865. His wife, Catherine Booth (1829–90), author of books on sanctification, was influential in the movement. In 1880 the Army was introduced into the United States and grew rapidly; when the founder visited the country, the work was already well rooted. Like many of the Holiness groups, the Salvation Army set out to be a recruiting agency for the churches among the depressed city masses, but in time it grew into another denomination. It carried out a variety of activities to aid the poor and win them to the faith, attracting them with its street preaching and band music, and by sending slum brigades into the most dangerous areas in the metropolises. General Booth's son Ballington led the Army in America with great vigour for about a decade before leaving it in 1896 to found the rival Volunteers of America. Evangeline Booth (1865–1950), the founder's daughter, assumed direction of the work early in 1904 following an eight-year term in Canada. A dramatic and

[48] As quoted by Timothy L. Smith, *Called Unto Holiness: The Story of the Nazarenes: The Formative Years* (Kansas City, Missouri, 1962), p. 111.

eloquent speaker, she led the movement to new heights of recognition and service as national commander for thirty years.

In the early twentieth century the modern Pentecostal movement erupted. A number of its early leaders had been active in Holiness churches; conservative biblicism, expectancy of Christ's imminent return, strict moral emphases, and interest in faith-healing marked both movements. But the distinctive Pentecostal doctrine—emphasis on the descent of the Holy Spirit as evidenced by *glossolalia*, the speaking in tongues, quickly set the new development apart, and it in turn proliferated into a range of new denominations. An early prominent figure in guiding Pentecostal or 'full gospel' revivals in Kansas, Missouri, and Texas was Charles F. Parham (1837–1937), who influenced a black preacher of Baptist and Holiness background, William J. Seymour (d. 1923). Under Seymour's unpretentious leadership in a former Methodist church on Azusa Street in Los Angeles in 1906 came the impetus that escalated Pentecostalism into a world-wide phenomenon. During a series of largely unplanned revival meetings at the Apostolic Faith Gospel Mission, many received what they ardently believed was the baptism of the Holy Spirit. Seekers and sceptics came to Azusa Street; from both groups came converts who spread the Pentecostal movement across the land and the world.

A rift between Parham and Seymour led to the former's withdrawal from the movement he had helped to found but had begun to criticize. He felt it was becoming extremist and encouraging people to roll in the aisles in emotional response to religious experience; the nickname 'holy roller' was often given to participants at Pentecostal meetings. But there were many others, caught up in the Pentecostal excitement as it spread especially among dispossessed and poorer elements across the land, who moved into positions of leadership. The freedom, informality, excitement, healings, and *glossolalia* of the Pentecostal services brought joy and assurance to many who took part in them.

At first Pentecostalism had strong non-denominational aspects. But it faced growing opposition from those within both the mainline evangelical denominations and the newer Holiness churches to whom the new movement seemed disruptive and parasitic. To resist such criticism and to maintain their distinctive emphases, Pentecostal leaders rather quickly adopted denominational ways. In 1906, for example, A. J. Tomlinson took the lead in the founding of the Church of God (Cleveland, Tennessee), and a year later Charles H. Mason formed the Church of God in Christ, eventually to become the largest black Pentecostal church in the world. Sharp differences of doctrine and practice soon appeared in this movement which put high priority on spontaneity and freedom in the spirit, and a variety of Pentecostal churches were founded. One of the early major controversies within the movement arose when some so stressed the importance of Jesus that they 'denied the trinity of persons in the Godhead, maintaining that while God is a threefold Being, Father, Son, and Holy Ghost, there is but one Person and that one is Jesus'.[49] This 'Jesus Only' emphasis led to a division of the first Pentecostal church to attain national dimensions, the Assemblies of God, a fusion of a number of local and regional bodies in 1914 at Hot Springs, Arkansas. This fast-growing missionary-minded body, soon the largest in the total spectrum of Pentecostal churches, affirmed its trinitarian position in 1916, whereupon the 'unitarians' withdrew to form Pentecostal Assemblies of the World, originally an interracial body that later became wholly black. The Assemblies remained overwhelmingly white. A smaller body of similar theological emphasis was founded in 1916 in Mobile, Alabama, under the leadership of W. T. Phillips, a former Methodist preacher, as the Ethiopian [later changed to Apostolic] Overcoming Holy Church of God. In its early stages the Pentecostal movement was 'completely interracial', but within two decades it became racially divided.[50] Black Pentecostal congregations and denominations appeared in the north in increasing numbers as migration from the south was greatly accelerated during World War I.

Social Christianity

To return to the mainstream evangelical churches, the tensions between the conservative and liberal trends within evangelical Protestantism were further heightened in this period by varying reactions to the many social problems that were coming into prominence. The individualistic *laissez-faire* social philosophy that seemed so familiar and right to Protestants reared in rural and small-town middle-class America offered few resources for dealing with the social ills of the spreading slums or with the needs of the swelling ranks of inadequately paid working people. Confronted with the reality of human suffering because of wretched housing, high medical costs, and economic insecurity, many Protestants became aware that there were serious maladjustments in the society they prized so highly. Sensitivity to certain serious problems was heightened by growing acquaintance with trends in Christian social thought abroad, especially those of Great Britain associated with the names of Thomas Chalmers,

[49] John T. Nichol, *Pentecostalism* (New York, 1966), p. 90.

[50] Vinson Synan, *The Holiness-Pentecostal Movement in the United States* (Grand Rapids, Michigan, 1971), p. 168; cf. pp. 166–84.

Frederick Denison Maurice, Charles Kingsley, John R. Seeley, and Henry Scott Holland. In academic circles, the theories of economic individualism were being criticized by such thinkers as Lester Frank Ward, John Bascom, and Richard T. Ely. But the decisive factor in shaking the complacency of many Protestants was a series of major labour conflicts, especially the railroad strike of 1877, really a minor rebellion, the strife of 1886 climaxed by the Haymarket riot in Chicago, and the bitter Homestead and Pullman strikes of the early 1890s. Though numbers of religious people condemned such strikes as brutal and anarchistic, these actions nevertheless gave 'the old, powerful insistence that all was well . . . a devastating rebuttal' as Henry F. May has put it. 'With a sudden shock, comfortable citizens, religious leaders among them, realized the meaning of slums and unemployment . . . The movements of social Christianity, developing as early as any American response to industrial crisis, became in turn a strong influence on all varieties of American social opinion.'[51]

Many Protestant leaders attempted to deal with the social question in essentially conservative terms. They urged cautious reforms of a voluntary type and resisted socialism in any of its forms. Characteristically, they sought to help the victims of social maladjustments as individual cases, especially through the development of the relief programmes of city mission societies, the founding of rescue missions where homeless men could be fed and cared for, and the shaping of extensive parish programmes in which the poor and unfortunate could be aided. In certain cities Unions for Christian Work were formed so that such efforts could be accomplished more effectively and with some coordination. Y.M.C.A.s and Y.W.C.A.s expanded their programmes to take account of the victims of unemployment. Persons of many denominational and theological alignments participated in such programmes, which tended to be conservative both religiously and socially.

The social gospel was developed by those who felt that such remedial measures were simply not enough. For the most part the proponents of the social gospel came from the ranks of the evangelical liberals, and they challenged the individualistic 'clerical *laissez-faire*' perspective by emphasizing the social concerns they found in the prophets of the Old Testament and in the Saviour of the New Testament, and in the various Christian reform movements over the centuries. Washington Gladden (1836–1918),

[51] *Protestant Churches and Industrial America* (New York, 1949), pp. 159–60. See also C. Howard Hopkins, *The Rise of the Social Gospel in American Protestantism, 1865–1915* (New Haven, 1940), and Robert T. Handy (ed.), *The Social Gospel in America, 1870–1920: Gladden, Ely, Rauschenbusch* (New York, 1966).

a Congregational minister who had been much influenced by Horace Bushnell, became an outspoken advocate of the right of labour to organize during a long pastorate in Columbus, Ohio. He was also a champion of liberal theology, advocating the historical approach to the Scriptures and preaching the coming of the Kingdom of God in history in the near future. Often called 'the father of the social gospel', he developed a Christian version of progressive economic and social views that by the turn of the century was a rising force in the churches.

Other prominent leaders of the social gospel were the Episcopal layman and economist, Richard T. Ely (1854–1943), and Josiah Strong, the Congregational minister who advocated social Christianity as secretary of the Evangelical Alliance, a post which he resigned when his social views became too advanced for his constituency. The outstanding prophet of the social gospel was a Baptist, Walter Rauschenbusch (1861–1918), who saw the human costs of industrial and urban growth while he was pastor of a German Baptist church on the edge of New York's 'hell's kitchen' from 1886–97. His social views were matured through travels in England and Germany, and by participation in an informal fellowship, the Brotherhood of the Kingdom, which annually brought together prominent figures in the movement. A book published in 1907, *Christianity and the Social Crisis*, written to discharge a debt to his former parishioners after he had become a seminary professor, became a best seller, and brought the social gospel to national attention. In later books he drew on many of the themes articulated by the reformist, progressive, and socialist thinkers of his time, always relating them to Christian faith. It was his belief that 'the Kingdom of God includes the economic life; for it means the progressive transformation of all human affairs by the thought and spirit of Christ'.[52] *A Theology for the Social Gospel* (1917) was his effort to provide a sound theological basis for the movement, which indeed did show tendencies to become so concerned with practical reform that its religious origins were often slighted. In the first few decades of the twentieth century, the social gospel won a large following in those denominations which had contingents of evangelical liberals. Seminaries added courses on social ethics, a number of denominational and interdenominational social service commissions were formed, and many preachers and writers dealt with social issues in pulpit and Press.

Even when presented by persons of evangelical spirit like Rauschenbusch, the social gospel was not congenial to conservative Protestants; their ideas of the Kingdom of God were more often predicated on a

[52] *Christianizing the Social Order* (New York, 1912), p. 458.

literal reading of the books of Daniel and Revelation. Their primary concern was to save individual souls, leaving the problems of society (to them less important) to those whose profession it was to deal with them. They felt that too much reformist activity by religious leaders violated the principle of the separation of church and state. Troubled by the social gospel, they were even more repelled by the small group of radical social Christians, often called Christian socialists, who went on beyond the social gospel to advocate not only reform but the radical reconstruction of society. In the 1890s an Episcopal clergyman, W. D. P. Bliss, and a Congregational minister, George D. Herron, led small Christian socialist movements. In the twentieth century a newly organized Christian Social-ist Fellowship was committed to political socialism; a leading figure was a remarkable Episcopal lay scholar and writer, Vida D. Scudder. Radical social Christianity tended to pull the social gospel towards the left, and further broadened the evangelical Protestant spectrum.

The blending of liberal evangelical and progressive reformist motifs in the social gospel furthered somewhat the movement for women's suffrage. Churches in general were quite divided in their attitude toward the struggle of women to achieve full rights as citizens. Women found themselves kept out of power in church life even in such matters of deep concern to them as home and foreign missions. Therefore they formed their own national societies, both denominational and interdenomina-tional, and saw to it that more adequate provision was made for work with women and children in missions under their care. Between 1861 and 1900 41 foreign mission boards were formed by women in the United States and 7 in Canada. In the 1870s and 1880s Baptist, Congregational, Episcopal, Methodist, Presbyterian, and Reformed women developed their own national home mission boards, which co-operated with the general denominational boards but devoted particular attention to ministry and education for minority groups.

Growing support by evangelical churches for the right of women to vote was often a by-product of the temperance crusade, of which many church women were ardent supporters. Especially in the west, where the first state women's suffrage laws were passed, supporters of prohibition generally favoured the right of women to vote as a means of attaining their temperance goals. After the initial victories, the cause of women's suffrage lost momentum, until it caught on in the early twentieth century as one of the causes favoured by Progressivism, which in part was an effort of native-born élites to retain their political predominance in a time of increasing immigration. 'Not until the Progressive movement developed in 1910', Alan P. Grimes has concluded, 'would suffrage referendums be successful in other states'.[53] Along with such other goals of Progressivism as anti-trust laws, the limitation of immigration, election reforms, municipal ownership of public utilities, the control of interstate commerce, and the restriction of the liquor traffic, the drive to secure women's suffrage gained ground. Although their primary concern was for the rights of labour, social gospel leaders supported most of these causes. After decades of work, in which the major roles were played by determined women, the Nineteenth Amendment to the Constitution establishing the right of women to vote went into effect in 1920.

Unitive Trends

The period from the Civil War to World War I was one in which there was considerable interest in reunion among Christians. Much of what was expressed was vague and idealistic, but it helped to create an atmosphere in which certain moves towards greater unity could be made. One of the important approaches to union was outlined by an Episcopal rector, William Reed Huntington (1838–1918), who in 1870 published a volume entitled *The Church-Idea: An Essay Toward Unity*. He suggested that his own communion could serve as a reconciling centre with which other churches could merge on the basis of four minimum essentials: the Holy Scriptures as the Word of God, the primitive creeds as the rule of faith, the two sacraments ordained by Christ himself, and the historic episcopate as the key-stone to governmental unity. The bishops of his church adopted this four-point approach as a platform for discussing union with other bodies; in amended form the 'Chicago–Lambeth Quadrilateral' was adopted by the Anglican bishops of the world who met in England in 1888.

A quite different approach to union was taken by another Episcopalian, Bishop George Cummins. In 1873 he reacted against what he felt to be the 'high church exclusivism' of his own fold to form with others the small Reformed Episcopal Church. Their hope was that many Christians of evangelical background would gather in this new church, started by a small group of men who, 'in the innovative, science-minded nineteenth century, sought to purge their faith of denominational exclusiveness and "holy mysteries" '.[54] As a strategy of union it failed, adding another small denomination to the widening spectrum.

The only significant unions of denominations in this period were within

[53] *The Puritan Ethic and Woman Suffrage* (New York, 1967), p. 98.
[54] Paul A. Carter, *The Spiritual Crisis of the Gilded Age* (DeKalb, Ill., 1971), p. 184.

denominational families, as when two branches of southern Presbyterianism united in 1864 as the Presbyterian Church in the United States, to be followed by the reunion of the northern Old and New Schools in 1869–70 as the Presbyterian Church in the United States of America. When the latter church made slight modifications in its Westminster Confession of Faith in 1903, the way was opened for the return of the majority of Cumberland Presbyterians, who had separated a century earlier in the first flush of frontier revivalism.

Christians of many denominations continued to work together through the familiar method of gathering individuals in voluntary societies for particular causes. The formation of the American branch of the Evangelical Alliance, which had been founded in London in 1846, had been delayed by the slavery controversy until 1867. It became especially concerned with advancing religious liberty, countering infidelity and superstition, deepening fellowship among evangelicals, and resisting Catholic influence. The prominent church historian, Philip Schaff, who had become a Presbyterian and was much more receptive to American evangelicalism than in his Mercersburg days, was active in Alliance affairs. In 1893, in the last few weeks of his life, Schaff addressed the World's Parliament of Religions in Chicago on 'The Reunion of Christendom', urging a federal association of denominations. Each member would retain its own freedom and independence but recognize others as sister churches and co-operate with them in common tasks of mission and reform. The desirability for churches officially to sponsor such co-operation as a step toward the larger unity of Christians was widely felt. The concerns of mission, reform, and unity were converging in a new way.

The first official move came quietly in the same year that Schaff gave his memorable farewell address when 'sixty-eight officers and representatives of foreign mission boards and societies in the United States and Canada assembled in New York on January 12, 1893'.[55] The first gathering proved to be so helpful that it was continued on an annual basis and in 1911 was made permanent as the Foreign Missions Conference of North America. To help them in the task of conveying effectively their story to the churches, the mission boards in 1902 formed another co-operative agency which later was named the Missionary Education Movement of the United States and Canada. In 1896 the first Interdenominational

---

[55] Samuel McCrea Cavert, *Church Cooperation and Unity in America, A Historical Review: 1900–1970* (New York, 1970), p. 34. In this work and in *The American Churches in the Ecumenical Movement, 1900–1968* (New York, 1968), Cavert has provided detailed information on the many strands of co-operative and ecumenical endeavour in North America.

Conference of Woman's Boards of Foreign Missions of the United States and Canada met; in later years it settled into a regular annual session. Meanwhile, home mission leaders had also been meeting informally, and in 1908 the Home Missions Council was organized, winning the membership of the domestic missions agencies of Baptist, Congregational, Disciples, Episcopal, Lutheran, Methodist, Presbyterian, Reformed, and United Brethren churches. In the same year, representatives of eight national women's boards founded the Council of Women for Home Missions.

In the conduct of Sunday schools, denominational educational boards staffed by professionals working co-operatively were beginning to challenge the long domination of the International Sunday School Association. In 1910 the Sunday School Council of Evangelical Denominations was founded. Its leaders had learned from the progressive educators about the maturation process in humans and were pressing for graded lessons instead of the prevailing uniform lessons. The new council worked with the old association until they merged in 1922, taking the name International Council of Religious Education (I.C.R.E.) two years later.

These many co-operative agencies were formed by the appropriate boards of the churches, not by the communions themselves. Certain leaders were insisting that the social dimensions of Christian witness and work in modern society would be more effective when carried out along with evangelistic and missionary tasks in an official federation of churches. During his more than ten years as secretary of the Evangelical Alliance, Josiah Strong had called for such a federation so that the social tasks of Christianity could be more fully accomplished. Leadership in the drive to effect this was taken by Elias B. Sanford (1843–1932) and William H. Ward (1835–1916), both Congregational ministers. In 1905 an Inter-Church Conference on Federation met in New York at which delegates appointed by their communions drafted plans for the Federal Council of the Churches of Christ in America. It came formally into existence in 1908 with most of the larger and some of the smaller evangelical denominations in the membership—thirty-three in all. The Southern Baptist, Southern Presbyterian, and Protestant Episcopal churches did not join at that point, and of the Lutherans only the General Synod was included. Two large black denominations did join: African Methodist Episcopal and African Methodist Episcopal Zion.

The Federal Council had no authority over its members, but encouraged and provided channels for co-operation in evangelism, education, home and foreign missions, and social service. Without neglecting other evangelical concerns, the Council was in many respects an embodiment of the social gospel, for its founders believed that unless the churches worked together, they could not cope adequately with the problems of the new industrial order. At the founding meeting a report on 'The Church on Modern Society' was especially influential. It incorporated a statement which became known as 'the social creed of the churches', and which was adopted by most of the major denominations. Calling on Christians to concern themselves directly with certain practical industrial problems, the statement urged the churches to stand for such things as equal rights and complete justice for all, for the principles of arbitration in industrial dissensions, for the abolition of child labour, for the regulation of the conditions of toil for women so that the physical and moral health of the community be safeguarded, and for the most equitable division of the products of industry that could be devised.

The Federal Council represented the triumph of the co-operative over the organic principle of unity in American Protestantism. It did not challenge denominational sovereignty, and was consistent with the somewhat pragmatic style of American evangelical religion. Prominent among its leaders were those informed by liberal theology and the social gospel. Yet its member denominations encompassed vast groups—probably majorities in most cases—which were not centrally concerned about theological issues but whose religious sympathies leaned towards the conservative side. The new co-operative councils had to move somewhat cautiously to hold the loyalties of constituencies of so many denominational and theological backgrounds, but they soon became accepted structures with growing influence in the Protestant world. One of the fruits of the new co-operative advance was the Men and Religion Forward Movement of 1911-12, during which eight-day campaigns to win men and boys to Christ and the church were conducted in sixty cities, arousing great enthusiasm. The main themes of the movement brought together the evangelistic, missionary, co-operative, and social concerns of the Anglo-American churches.

The War to End War

Though the Civil and Spanish–American wars had been faced in a crusading spirit by the churches, many Christians supported the burgeoning peace movement in the buoyant, optimistic opening years of the new century. Denominational assemblies passed resolutions condemning war as unchristian and uncivilized. The American Peace Society doubled its membership; the Federal Council supported the cause of peace, and an interfaith Church Peace Union was founded in 1914.

With the outbreak of World War I that year in Europe, however, sentiments began to change. Despite early official neutrality, which helped to re-elect Woodrow Wilson as president in 1916, the majority of Americans favoured Great Britain and her allies, and the United States helped to finance and supply the Allied forces. Various patriotic organizations which stressed preparedness for war flourished, 'especially in the East among Americans of "Anglo-Saxon" descent, and they won increasing support from clergy of the denominations with strong and clear British rootage—Presbyterians, Congregationalists, Methodists and, most outspokenly, Episcopalians'.[56] The torpedoing of American ships by German submarines triggered Wilson's decision to ask Congress to declare war in April 1917. The son of a southern Presbyterian minister, the president interpreted the war as a crusade to bring peace and democracy to all the world.

With few exceptions, the churches backed the war effort with conviction. The vision of a world won to Christ had long guided evangelicals in their mission efforts; now many believed that through the events of war the way might be cleared for a fuller realization of that dream. A prominent editor, Lyman Abbott, dashed off a book entitled *Twentieth Century Crusade*, which stated on its title-page that 'a crusade to make this world a home in which God's children can live in peace and safety is more Christian than a crusade to recover from pagans the tomb in which the body of Christ was buried'. Pulpit orators invoked the imagery of holy war; some uttered expressions of unrestrained hatred of the enemy. The sensational revivalist Billy Sunday prayed in the House of Representatives early in 1918, 'Thou knowest, O Lord, that no nation so infamous, vile, greedy, sensuous, blood-thirsty ever disgraced the pages of history. Make bare thy mighty arm, O Lord, and smite the hungry, wolfish Hun, whose fangs drip with blood, and we will forever raise our voice to Thy praise.'[57] While there was much extravagant oratory and uncritical acceptance of stories of atrocity, there were also more sober voices, responsive to the basic imperatives of Christian faith, which did not give in to hatred.[58] Yet most of the churches supported the war effort, sending some of their

56 Ahlstrom, *A Religious History of the American People*, p. 883.
57 As quoted by Winfred E. Garrison, *The March of Faith: The Story of Religion in America Since 1865* (New York, 1933), p. 243.
58 e.g. compare Ray H. Abrams, *Preachers Present Arms* (New York, 1933) and John F. Piper, Jr., 'The Social Policy of the Federal Council of the Churches of Christ in America During World War I' (Ph.D. thesis, Duke University, Durham, 1964).

ministers abroad as chaplains and Y.M.C.A. workers, encouraging many of their young men to fight, and supporting their members' participation in the countless activities of a nation mobilized for war. A General Wartime Commission of the Churches under the leadership of theologian William Adams Brown co-ordinated the work of some thirty-five major denominations and their co-operative councils.

When the Great Crusade was victoriously over, many thrilled to Wilson's interpretation of what had happened when he returned from the peace conference in July 1919:

We answered the call of duty in a way so spirited, so utterly without thought of what we spent of blood or treasure, so effective, so worthy of the admiration of true men everywhere, so wrought out of the stuff of all that was heroic, that the whole world saw at last, in the flesh, in noble action, a great ideal asserted and vindicated, by a Nation they had deemed material and now found to be compact of the spiritual forces that must free men of every nation from every unworthy bondage.[59]

Disillusionment was to come later, but as the third decade of the century drew near the prospects of the mainline Anglo-American denominations seemed very bright indeed. Their membership figures were the highest ever. Of course there were differences among them, but they had developed effective instruments of co-operation, tested now in national crisis. There were serious problems in national life, but the churches had a social as well as an evangelistic programme—and national prohibition was coming into reality after decades of crusading. At long last a league of nations was coming into reality. The Kingdom of God on earth seemed to be approaching.

A Christian America, or Americanized Christianity?

The direction and mood of the evangelical denominations had long been shaped by their mission to win individuals to a commitment to Christ and to make America a Christian nation. From the Second Awakenings through the revivals of Finney and Moody to the social gospel and co-operative Christianity, these general goals remained. The work of local congregations, of church assemblies, and of interdenominational councils had these ends in view. For example, in 1911 the general secretary of the International Sunday School Association stated the central themes that united evangelical Protestants—though not all would agree with his wording—in proclaiming that

There should be no uncertain tone go forth from this great convention as to the fundamentals of our religion; the Bible as the all-sufficient Word of God and rule of life; the Church as God's appointed agency to do His work; the Sabbath to be kept lest our national life be undermined; temperance, righteousness and purity in personal life—these things we should stand for as a flint if America is ever to fulfil her God-appointed mission in the world.[60]

To win souls to Christ and to christianize a nation so that it might fulfil its destiny under God—these were the goals for which evangelicals laboured. They had visible ways of measuring progress toward the first objective: growth in the number of converts and church members. But how to measure the second? Inspired by their belief in God's guidance over the nation—some spoke of his providential care, others were more comfortable with the language of progress—they found evidence that the nation was indeed becoming more Christian. As they learned about 'barbarian' civilizations from their missionaries on furlough, the surer they were that their own culture had absorbed much of the spirit of Christianity and could ever more fully serve God's purposes. In the centennial year of 1876 the Methodist bishops spoke of their nation in religious terms, finding that

here the human spirit of Christianity has been signally exemplified in generous hospitality to aliens, in the mitigation of penal laws, in protection and opportunity given to woman, in care for the rights and interests of labor, in the overthrow of slavery, in war waged against intemperance, and in successful effort for international arbitration. Here have been added to the visible agencies by which the world shall be subjugated to Christ a free, great, and enlightened nation, and a Church vital with the missionary spirit of its Lord.[61]

The idea that the nation was a visible agency of divine purpose was widely shared, and it allowed evangelicals who were divided by denomination, section, and theological party to agree on an important point. The communions were actually a competing group of voluntary agencies, but their own roles were magnified by viewing them in relation to the nation as a carrier of divine activity in history. Denominational pluralities could be accepted comfortably because there was an overarching frame of reference provided by the nation which was confidently given a Christian interpretation. In the evangelical mind, the nation was carrying out God's purposes on behalf of all men.

[60] *Organized Sunday School Work in America, 1908–1911*, p. 120.
[61] *Journal of the General Conference of the Methodist Episcopal Church*, 1876, p. 407.

When the delegates of thirty-three denominations gathered in Philadelphia for the first meeting of the Federal Council of Churches, they were greeted by these words of William Henry Roberts, Presbyterian leader:

The essential spirit of our Nation is that of Jesus Christ, and it is the duty of the American Churches to make that spirit more Christian, to awaken yet greater national interest in the welfare of all earth's people, to provide men and means in increasing ratios for the work of spiritual salvation, and to hasten the day when the true King of Men shall everywhere be crowned Lord of all. This council stands for the hope of organized work for speedy Christian advance toward World Conquest.[62]

When the essential spirit of a nation was understood to be Christian, then Christianity and patriotism became mutual allies, and the virtual identification of Christian and American ways seemed natural, and was little criticized from within.

A few outsiders were aware of what was happening. With perhaps some exaggeration the philosopher George Santayana noted that

the churches, a little ashamed of their past, began to court the good opinion of so excellent a world. Although called evangelical, they were far, very far, from prophesying its end, or offering a refuge from it, or preaching contempt for it; they existed only to serve it, and their highest divine credential was that the world needed them.[63]

Some 'insiders' saw it too; black evangelicals knew from bitter experience the racist flaws in the idealized picture of America as Christian, and saw how many compromises the leading churches had made with the national ethos. A distinguished black church historian, Carter G. Woodson, said as he looked at those who were most confident that theirs was a Christian America

The North, then, if it ever wakes from its lethargy, will probably accept either the principles of Jesus of Nazareth as they have been preached and practised by the Negroes, or the Anglo-Saxon-chosen-people-of-God faith for which many misguided white communicants have jeopardized their own lives and have taken those of Negroes unwilling to worship at the shrine of race prejudice.[64]

Few whites, however, were seriously listening to their black evangelical brethren. Certain leaders of the denominations were aware of limitations in the religious life of the churches and were trying in various ways—some

[62] As quoted by Elias B. Sanford (ed.), *Federal Council of the Churches of Christ in America: Report of the First Meeting . . .* (New York, 1909), p. 323.

[63] *Character and Opinion in the United States* (New York, 1920), pp. 14–15.

[64] *The History of the Negro Church* (Washington D.C., 1921), p. 306.

quite contradictory—to do something about them. Evangelical styles had been evolving over a long period of time, and as a new era opened following the successful completion of the war the methods that had been developed seemed full of promise. The problems ahead seemed surmountable and were being faced in a confident, optimistic spirit.

X

ROMAN CATHOLIC, LUTHERAN, EASTERN ORTHODOX, AND OTHER CHURCHES IN AMERICA

(1860–1920)

THE realities of war, the patterns of immigration and migration, the growth of giant cities and industries, and the ferment of intellectual revolution in the period from 1860 to 1920 influenced not only the denominations of British Protestant background, but also strongly affected churches of other traditions. Several of America's major denominational families were so transformed, especially by immigration, that their situation was strikingly different by the end of World War I than it had been at the beginning of the Civil War. Meanwhile, a number of smaller churches carried on their distinctive witness, some new and quite unconventional groups emerged, and certain non-Christian religions, especially Judaism, became more visible on the American scene.

Roman Catholicism: Expansion and Crisis; Struggle for Unity

Already America's largest Christian church by mid-nineteenth century, the Roman Catholic Church continued to grow rapidly throughout this period. Like most Americans, Catholics generally aligned themselves with their respective sections during the Civil War. In the south, they usually regarded slavery as a political matter, and several bishops were outspoken in its defence. For example, Augustus Martin, Bishop of Natchitoches, Louisiana, affirmed that slavery, 'far from being an evil . . . is an arrangement eminently Christian by which millions pass from intellectual darkness to the sweet brilliance of the Gospel'.[1] In the north John Hughes, Archbishop of New York, wrote that his people, both native- and foreign-born, were willing 'to fight to the death for the support of the constitution, the Government, and the laws of the country'.[2] He was

---

[1] As quoted by Benjamin J. Blied, *Catholics and the Civil War* (Milwaukee, 1945), p. 25.
[2] As quoted by John R. G. Hassard, *Life of the Most Rev. John Hughes . . .* (New York, 1866), p. 437.

commissioned by Lincoln to travel in Europe to interpret the Union cause. Many Catholics who supported the federal government out of a sense of patriotic duty—especially the Irish workers of New York—were not enthusiastic over the emancipation of slaves, for they feared their competition in the labour market. When draft laws were passed in 1863, following the Emancipation Proclamation, they rioted, destroyed property, and killed blacks in their path. It took all of Archbishop Hughes's skill to quiet them and to halt what has been called 'the most disgraceful incident in American Catholic history'.[3]

Large numbers of Catholics served in the contending armies, some rising to positions of prominence. Priests served as chaplains in Catholic regiments. The work of nursing-sisters attracted favourable comment. The loyalty of Catholics to their states helped to reduce hostility to their religious tradition. The church never formally divided; the small Catholic minority in the south continued to adhere to the social and racial patterns of that region at war's end. In both sections, Catholics generally became more visible and active in political and community affairs following the war.

To help the church deal with the problems of discipline and organization in the post-war years, the Second Plenary Council was convened in Baltimore in 1866. There had been some important changes in leadership —Irish-born Archbishop Francis Patrick Kenrick had died in 1863, to be succeeded in Baltimore by the American-born Martin John Spalding, while the passing of Hughes in 1864 brought John McCloskey to the archdiocese of New York. The decrees of the council stressed the role of the *church* (not the pope) as an infallible agency, the importance of the basic doctrines of the faith, and condemned such 'errors' of the day as indifferentism, Unitarianism, Universalism, Transcendentalism, and pantheism. Rules for the internal administration of the church were stated, and each parish was urged to erect a school of its own. Work among the newly freed slaves was encouraged, either by providing separate churches or by welcoming them to mixed parishes when the bishop of a diocese considered that to be best.

Most of the American bishops attended the First Vatican Council when it opened in Rome late in 1869. There was considerable objection among the nearly fifty American prelates present to the proclamation of papal infallibility, the principal event of the council. Some felt that the doctrine was not certainly evident in Scripture and Tradition; others believed it was simply an inopportune time to declare what would alienate non-Catholics

---

[3] John Cogley, *Catholic America* (New York, 1973), p. 60.

and disclose disunity within the church. In his detailed account of the role of the bishops at Rome, James Hennesey concluded that '. . . the dominant motive of the American opposition was the fear that the definition would hinder conversions and embarrass the progress of the Church in Protestant countries'.[4] But the minority group opposed to the declaration of infallibility was outmanœuvered, and many of its members left Rome before the climax. When the final vote was taken on the constitution *Pastor aeternus* which defined papal infallibility on 18 July 1870, one of the two dissenting ballots (of 535) was given by Edward Fitzgerald, Bishop of Little Rock, Arkansas; but he submitted, as did all the bishops. The part played by the Americans at Rome signalled to the Catholic world the importance of '. . . a relatively new and different branch of the universal Church, with its own peculiar problems and hopes'.[5]

Spalding, whose health had been poor, did not long survive the council. When he died in 1872, he was succeeded at Baltimore by American-born James Roosevelt Bayley, former Bishop of Newark. The overwhelming problem and opportunity before the church continued to be the influx of immigrants of Catholic background. In the decade of the Civil War about 700,000 arrived, over half of them Irish. In the following decade the number of Catholic immigrants was about 100,000 less, with a greater percentage coming from Germany. By 1880 there were more than six million Catholics in the United States—but the number was to double by 1900. In these two decades immigration increasingly originated in central, eastern, and southern Europe, and often from strongly Catholic areas. Many of the new arrivals clustered in the urban centres of the east, where the variety of nationalities and tongues intensified the many problems of a church that was still often regarded as an intruder by great numbers of Americans. Internal resources were strained as new dioceses and archdioceses were erected, new churches and educational institutions built, and the network of religious Orders and auxiliary societies expanded. The financial burden fell heavily on people often ill-equipped to bear it. Some help came from Europe, but the main load was carried in the United States. The number of dioceses almost doubled in the years from 1860 to 1900, while the ranks of the priesthood swelled from a little more than 2,000 to 12,000. Inevitably, many tensions appeared in such a swift-growing church of diverse peoples, and the struggle to hold it together in an effective theological and institutional unity was long and difficult.

Catholics of Irish background dominated the leadership of the church

---

[4] *The First Council of the Vatican: The American Experience* (New York, 1963), p. 215.
[5] *Ibid.*, p. 170.

in the post-Civil War period. Those who had arrived during the two decades prior to the war were advancing in both church and society, and their growing power and influence were often resented by people of other nationalities. Becoming aware of the growing tensions, the authorities in Rome suggested to the Archbishop of Baltimore, the virtual though unofficial primate of the American church, that a Third Plenary Council would be helpful. In 1877 James Gibbons (1834–1921), who had been born in Baltimore of Irish immigrants and who had spent much of his boyhood in Ireland, had succeeded to that post. Under his guidance, careful preparations were made for the gathering of fourteen archbishops and fifty-eight bishops. That only about one-third of the seventy-two prelates were American born reflected the ethnic complexity of American Catholicism. The largest group of foreign-born prelates in the hierarchy was Irish, with Germans, French, and six other nationalities following. To forge the diversities of custom and culture into a working unity would be no easy matter. The general purpose of the council when it gathered in 1884 was to bring the American church under standard canon law practices; it was called at the insistence of certain bishops of the midwestern dioceses.

'Of all the matters presented to the Council', McAvoy has written, 'the most important were education, both of the clergy and of the faithful, methods of nominating candidates for bishoprics, and the establishment in the dioceses of a certain number of irremovable rectors.'[6] A very important provision of the council, one that originated in Rome, was that within two years there should be attached to all existing churches a parochial school. Catholic parents were required to send their children to the parish school unless they could provide for their Catholic education in other ways. It was also decided that a Catholic university should be founded.

The Third Plenary Council did not solve the problem of the church's inner unity; indeed the tensions were to increase and to precipitate a major internal crisis in the next fifteen years. Yet while the struggle that ensued deeply engaged ecclesiastical leaders, the Christian work of parishes and institutions went on in an impressive way. During the council's sessions, Bernard J. McQuaid (1823–1909), Bishop of Rochester, New York, celebrated the scope and quality of Catholic life in America in a sermon:

A Cardinal of the Holy Roman Church, the Most Eminent and Illustrious Archbishop of New York; an Apostolic Delegate, the Most Reverend and

[6] *A History of the Catholic Church in the United States*, p. 259.

Illustrious Metropolitan of the See of Baltimore; thirteen other archbishops, and coadjutor archbishops, and sixty-one bishops and vicars apostolic rule over God's Church in this republic; 6,835 priests, under the leadership of these successors of the Apostles, in 7,763 churches and chapels, feed their flocks with the bread of life and devotedly care for their souls. In 708 seminaries, colleges and academies, the higher education of clerics and of the youth of both sexes is carried forward by learned professors and accomplished nuns. Many thousands of brothers and sisters, of all the teaching orders and communities, assist these priests and perform a part that, without their services, would be left undone. Our orphans, the aged, the abandoned, are sheltered in 294 asylums, and our sick are nursed in 139 hospitals. The crowning glory of the church's work, however, is . . . [that] she now sustains 2,532 Christian schools, in which secular learning is imparted without sacrificing instruction in the belief and observances which the Lord commanded His Apostles and their successors to preach to the end of time. During the year 1883, 481,834 pupils frequented these Christian schools, built, fostered lovingly and supported for the people's children without aid from the state.[7]

The educational achievement of which McQuaid spoke would have been impossible without the competence and devotion of the various Orders of sisters. Through their influence over children during the impressionable years, the nuns' contribution to Catholic life was immense. They were also conspicuous in the hospitals and in social service activities. Significantly, the only American citizens so far to be elevated to sainthood (1946, 1975) were nuns, Italian-born Frances Xavier Cabrini (1850–1917), who founded convents, schools, orphanages, and hospitals in the Americas and in Europe, and native-born Elizabeth Bayley Seton (1774–1821), who had been especially prominent in education.

All was not as harmonious as McQuaid's picture suggests, however. As various important issues requiring settlement surged to the fore, two broad schools of thought emerged among church leaders. The distinctions between the two perspectives were not rigid—on a given issue a bishop usually counted in one camp might favour the other—but they were persistent. On the one side were the so-called Americanists, those who regarded the development of American democracy with its commitment to religious freedom in a positive way. They believed that a broadly tolerant approach to the problems arising out of the church's life in the American republic with its Protestant flavour would better disarm the church's

7 *The Memorial Volume: A History of the Third Plenary Council of Baltimore, November 9–December 7, 1884* (Baltimore, 1885), p. 169. The cardinal mentioned was John McCloskey (1810–85), the first American so honoured (1875). In part because of McCloskey's poor health, Gibbons was named by Rome to preside as apostolic delegate.

opponents and help in the assimilation of the floods of foreign-born Catholics. Generally favourable to the Americanist position was the tactful, irenic Gibbons, who in 1886 was made a cardinal of the church—for a quarter of a century the only one in the country. His rather cautious nature was reinforced by his responsibilities as the nominal head of the church in America, yet his stance and sympathies were usually on the Americanist side. An intensely patriotic leader, he urged his people of many national backgrounds to be proud both of their Catholic faith and their American citizenship. At a particularly high moment of tension between German and Irish groups in the church, at the installation of Archbishop Katzer in Milwaukee, he preached 'God and our country! This our watchword—Loyalty to God's Church and to our country!—this our religious and political faith.'[8] He believed that for the church to maintain a narrow, rigid line of defence would only intensify anti-Catholic feeling and give the church's enemies openings for their attacks. When the American Protective Association raised its alarmist cries about the dangers of 'Romanism', Gibbons insisted that American and Catholic ways were really not incompatible.

Less restrained than the cardinal was his energetic and eloquent Irish-born friend, John Ireland (1838–1918), the Archbishop of St. Paul, Minnesota, who ardently believed that Catholics of all backgrounds could be brought into sympathy with the spirit of the times and the ethos of their new country. He said, 'The Church of America must be, of course, as Catholic as even in Jerusalem or Rome; but as far as her garments assume color from the local atmosphere she must be American. Let no one dare paint her brows with a foreign tint, or pin to her mantle foreign linings.'[9] John J. Keane (1839–1918), who succeeded Gibbons as Bishop of Richmond soon after the latter went to Baltimore, was another important Americanist leader, as was Denis J. O'Connell (1849–1927), who long served Gibbons's interests in Rome as rector of the North American College.

On the 'conservative' side were those whose attitude to American ways was more qualified; they were mistrustful of the liberal and accommodationist tendencies of the Americanists. Some of them were Irish too, but retained more of their traditional opposition to Anglo-Saxon culture. The strong leaders were Michael A. Corrigan (1839–1902), a

[8] *A Retrospect of Fifty Years*, 2 vols. (Baltimore, 1916), ii, 152. A very detailed treatment of Gibbons's role is given by John Tracy Ellis, *The Life of James Cardinal Gibbons, Archbishop of Baltimore, 1834–1921*, 2 vols. (Milwaukee, 1952). See also Robert D. Cross, *The Emergence of Liberal Catholicism in America* (Cambridge, Mass., 1958).

[9] *Souvenir Volume Illustrated: Three Great Events in the History of the Catholic Church in the United States* (Detroit, 1889), p. 17.

former professor of dogmatics who became Archbishop of New York, Bernard McQuaid, who was regarded in Europe 'as the most conservative prelate in the United States',[10] and Frederick F. X. Katzer (1844–1903), a priest of German background who became Archbishop of Milwaukee in 1891. Katzer spoke for a national group of growing importance, and one that clung more tenaciously to its mother tongue than most other nationality groups. The German Catholics tended to gather in communities concentrated largely in what has been called the 'German triangle', an area marked out by Cincinnati, St. Louis, and Milwaukee.[11] Expanding rapidly through immigration in the 1860s and 1870s, the Germans often found themselves in dioceses dominated by clergy of Irish background. Despite tensions between them, these ethnic groups could make common cause at certain points against the Americanists.

Four issues were prominent in the contention between these two general orientations. One was the desire of Catholics of particular ethnic backgrounds to have their own national as opposed to territorial parishes and also a larger representation in the hierarchy. When grouped according to nationality background, the 69 bishops of 1886 numbered 35 Irish, 15 German (including Austrian and Swiss), 11 French, 5 English, and 1 each Dutch, Swedish, and Spanish.[12] In view of their rapid increase in numbers, the Germans felt that they were insufficiently represented. There were other than language differences between the two largest nationality groups. For example, their attitudes toward the temperance movement were quite different. Gibbons favoured temperance but not prohibition, while Ireland and Keane actively supported the Catholic Total Abstinence Union of America, founded in 1872. Among the German-American Catholics, however, even mild advocacy of the cause of temperance aroused ridicule and resentment.[13] Of particular annoyance to the German priests was their sense of being subordinated to English-speaking parishes and clergy. In St. Louis, for example, a number of German Catholic churches were kept under the jurisdiction of English-speaking parishes as succursal (subsidiary) churches or chapels of ease. Resenting their lack of full parochial rights, some German-speaking pastors and bishops sent Peter M. Abbelen of Milwaukee to present their case in a petition to the

---

[10] Felix Klein, *In the Land of the Strenuous Life* (Chicago, 1905), p. 97.

[11] Colman J. Barry, O.S.B., *The Catholic Church and German Americans* (Milwaukee, 1953), pp. 44–85; Philip Gleason, *The Conservative Reformers: German-American Catholics and the Social Order* (Notre Dame, Ind., 1968).

[12] Ellis, *Life of James Cardinal Gibbons*, i, 334.

[13] Paul C. Conley and Andrew A. Sorensen, *The Staggering Steeple: The Story of Alcoholism and the Churches* (Philadelphia, 1971), pp. 44–54.

Sacred Congregation of Propaganda in Rome in 1886. There O'Connell alerted Ireland and Keane, who responded sharply and emotionally raised the spectre of a German conspiracy to dominate the church in America. Gibbons's position was to insist that no distinctions based on nationality should be recognized in the government of the church. The Propaganda did allow separate parishes for different foreign language groups in the same neighbourhood. Pressure for separate nationality *dioceses* continued, however; the increase in the number of Catholics of Slavic origin meant that others were also anxious for this development. The Germans won a victory when Katzer was named as the Archbishop of Milwaukee, a strongly German archdiocese, in 1890.

A new stage in the dispute emerged soon after when representatives of European branches of the St. Raphael Society, which was devoted to the aid and protection of German and other emigrants, prepared a memorial for the pope in Lucerne. Declaring that the church had lost more than ten million immigrants abroad through neglect, the memorial called for the organization of separate dioceses along nationality lines, and for more parity among nationalities in the hierarchy. When Peter Paul Cahensly, a devout European layman, brought the memorial to the pope in 1891, Gibbons and others responded sharply, challenging the claims and aims of 'Cahenslyism', and Leo XIII refused to grant what was asked. On the occasion of the bestowing of the pallium on Archbishop Katzer, Gibbons seized the opportunity to preach against Cahenslyism—a bold move by the cautious cardinal. The danger of separate nationality dioceses on a large scale was forestalled, but the deeper tension long continued.

A second issue which divided Americanists and their opponents was that of elementary and secondary education. While the American bishops agreed on the desirability of Catholic schooling for the children in view of the secular character and Protestant tone of public education, differences appeared as to the attitude to be taken to the public schools and to Catholic parents who sent their children to them. The German Catholic communities of the mid-west were especially proud of their parochial schools, and they were prosperous enough to be able to sustain them comfortably — an advantage the generally poorer Irish crowded in the eastern cities did not enjoy. In some localities, among which Poughkeepsie, New York, became a famous example, parochial schools were operated by the public school board at a nominal rental, with Catholic instruction provided after regular hours. In an address before the National Education Association in 1890 John Ireland looked towards a time when all American schools would be supported and supervised by the state, with opportunities for religious instruction. Because of the situation of Catholics in the country, he agreed to the need for continuing parochial education in the meantime, but advocated a compromise between the systems by which secular education in the parochial schools would be paid for by the public authorities and be subject to examination by public officials. This view aroused a great outcry, intensified the following year when schools of his archdiocese at Faribault and Stillwater adopted the Poughkeepsie plan with his approval.

Support for Ireland and those similarly minded came from a professor of moral theology at Catholic University, Thomas Bouquillon, who published late in 1891 a pamphlet, *Education: To Whom Does It Belong?* He argued that the state as well as the parent and the church had a right to insist on the education of the child. The intense debate that followed attracted the attention of the secular and international Press; the tension between the parties in the church became acute. To Ireland's joy, the Congregation of Propaganda tolerated the Faribault-Stillwater arrangements in view of all the circumstances, but stated its consent in such an ambiguous way that the debate raged on.[14]

Another point of contention was the founding, location, and direction of the Catholic University of America. The Third Plenary had approved the project, in part because of eloquent pleas by the Bishop of Peoria, John Lancaster Spalding (1840–1916), who emphasized the importance of the sound intellectual formation of priests. Some felt that other needs were more pressing; others feared it would undercut other institutions of higher learning. A committee chaired by Gibbons located the new university in Washington, D.C. When Spalding refused the rectorship, Keane was chosen. Opposition to the new university continued, however, in part because of the objections of Corrigan and McQuaid, who felt it might become an Americanist centre. Ireland's determination to see the project succeed encouraged Gibbons to move ahead at a critical juncture. The formal opening was celebrated in November 1889—the centennial of the American hierarchy. Some of the new faculty members were from Europe, which meant that certain of the nationality tensions faced in many dioceses were directly felt on the campus. For example, Joseph Schroeder, professor of dogmatic theology, supported the German Catholics in their opposition to Ireland's educational views. Gibbons served the university as chancellor through some stormy days.

A fourth issue which precipitated debate between the Americanists and

[14] Ellis, *Life of James Cardinal Gibbons*, i, 653–707. Ironically, the controversy focused so much attention and hostility on the Faribault-Stillwater experiments that they were soon terminated by the public school boards.

their opponents was that of the secret societies. Though suspicion of such societies had long been widespread among many groups in western society, fraternal lodges were increasing in number in the later nineteenth century. The bishops generally opposed Catholic membership in such associations, both because of the secrecy of their aims and purposes and because some of the societies were believed to have semi-religious aspects. Yet Catholics were joining them—some of them had a special appeal for those of Irish descent. In agreement with the decrees of the Third Plenary, Gibbons was reluctant to let a given society be condemned unless it was clear that it made demands contrary to Catholic conscience; he preferred the methods of persuasion to the imposition of Catholic authority. After long discussion, the archbishops decided not to oppose Catholic membership in the Grand Army of the Republic or the Ancient Order of Hibernians.

A very distinctive and controversial 'secret society' case emerged with the growth of the Noble and Holy Order of the Knights of Labor. Organized in Philadelphia in 1869, the Knights spread to neighbouring cities and to the coal-mining regions, where they were active in support of working people. A Catholic, Terence V. Powderly, was elected head of the society ten years after its founding. Gibbons was a friend of labour; as a young man he had worked to support his widowed mother, delaying his education for the priesthood. He was generally sympathetic to the Knights of Labor. But the organization had also spread to Canada, where Archbishop Elzéar A. Taschereau of Quebec had asked the Holy See for a judgement concerning the Knights. It was adverse, and some of the conservative bishops of the United States wanted a similar judgement. Gibbons felt that the Knights offered no real danger to Catholics, of which sizable numbers had become members by 1886. Keane and Ireland were in Rome later that year and lent their efforts to prevent a condemnation of the Order. Gibbons himself went to Rome early the next year, and presented a memorial stating a strong case against condemnation, and indicating a keen understanding of the importance of labour and an awareness of general social issues. His views prevailed, and when the confidential memorial was leaked to the Press, his popularity greatly increased among many segments of the public at home and abroad. His reputation as a champion of the working man and a moulder of Catholic thought on social questions was established.[15]

Another incident occurred in New York, where a popular priest and

[15] *Ibid.*, i, 486–546; cf. Henry J. Browne, *The Catholic Church and the Knights of Labor* (Washington, 1949).

reformer, Edward McGlynn, supported Henry George, the champion of the single tax on land, in his campaign for mayor in 1886. Archbishop Corrigan suspended McGlynn temporarily, but the priest continued his advocacy of the unsuccessful candidate. This triggered a chain of events that led to his excommunication the following year. Then when Corrigan sought to have George's teachings condemned, Gibbons opposed the move, thinking it might only help to revive the reformer's declining popularity. In 1889, however, the Congregation of the Inquisition did decide that the works of George should be condemned, but that the decree need not be published. The breach between the two archbishops widened.

The tension between the Americanists and their opponents increased, seriously troubling the peace of the church, as these major issues were intensely debated. The pope proposed to name an apostolic delegate for the United States; Archbishop Francesco Sattoli, who had previously visited the country, was thought to be a suitable person. In preparation for the Chicago World's Fair of 1893, at which the 400th anniversary of Columbus's landing was celebrated, certain charts from the Vatican Library were requested; the pope sent them with Satolli as his personal representative. While he was in the country the archbishop was also to undertake to reconcile the opposing groups. Appearing before the meeting of the American archbishops late in 1892, Satolli helped to quiet the storm over the public school issue by offering propositions which favoured parochial education but declared that where there were no such schools, it was permissible for Catholic children to attend public schools with the bishop's approval. In no case, he declared, could a Catholic parent be excommunicated for sending children to public schools. A papal letter confirmed Satolli's views, but many felt that the archbishop had made a mistake. As papal ablegate, he was also authorized to settle the McGlynn issue. When the latter's views were found to be consistent with the teaching of Leo XIII's 1891 social encyclical, *Rerum novarum,* and on his promise to go to Rome to submit to the Propaganda, he was released from censure and later appointed as rector of another parish. The decisions made by the pope's representative generally favoured the liberals.

When Satolli was named as the first permanent apostolic delegate to the American hierarchy in 1893, things seemed to be going well for the Americanists. Their progressive spirit was displayed at the Catholic Columbian Congress in Chicago, as well as at the World's Parliament of Religions. Gibbons, Ireland, and Keane participated in both of them, despite considerable opposition to Catholic presence at the latter, for it seemed to some to put the Catholic Church on a level with other religious groups.

At about the same time, however, opposition to the progressive Americanist position increased in Rome. In 1894 three secret societies, the Knights of Pythias, the Odd Fellows, and the Sons of Temperance were condemned; the efforts of Keane and Gibbons to get the measure softened were unsuccessful. Then, early in 1895 the pope sent an encyclical to the Catholics of the United States, *Longinqua oceani*. The pope praised the American nation and the progress made by the Roman Catholic Church under the conditions of freedom, but added the warning that it would be erroneous to draw the conclusion that America provided the model for 'the most desirable status of the Church or that it would be universally lawful or expedient for State and Church to be, as in America, dissevered or divorced'. He also asked for the support of Catholic University, and encouraged the faithful to form their own societies for civic and social purposes.

By this time Satolli's views had decisively changed. Early in the decade, when he knew little English, he had been under the influence of Ireland and Keane, but by 1895 he had become more aware of the total American situation and switched sides. His change was indicative of the conservative trend in Rome. In April he defended the right of German Catholics to retain their language and customs. He requested and received a letter from the pope forbidding further Catholic participation in such international congresses as the World's Parliament of Religions. The tendency of Americanists to enter into conversation with non-Catholics about religious matters was checked. 'As the Vatican swung back to its traditionally conservative attitude toward America,' wrote Gerald P. Fogarty, 'it would find allies among the conservatives in the American Church and in Propaganda. Of this new alliance the first victim would be O'Connell.'[16] Under sharp criticism, the latter resigned as rector of the North American College. To keep him in Rome, Gibbons named him as vicar of his titular church, but the setback was real. Another blow followed in the autumn of 1896—by action from Rome, Keane was dismissed as rector of Catholic University. He was made an archbishop, but there was no disguising the conservative victory or Gibbons's unhappiness. The Catholic Press on both sides of the Atlantic published interpretations, often critical, of the liberal tendencies of Ireland and Keane. The drift was not all one way, however—the friends of Keane at the University succeeded in causing

---

[16] *The Vatican and the Americanist Crisis: Denis J. O'Connell, American Agent in Rome, 1885–1903* (Rome, 1974), p. 250.

the dismissal of Schroeder, whom they believed to have made the charges against their favourite.

The Americanist controversy then became involved in French ecclesiastical politics in a surprising way. A somewhat popular *Life of Father Hecker* by a Paulist priest, Walter Elliott, had been published in 1891. The founder of the Paulist Fathers had indeed been concerned about the relationship between the Catholic Church and the modern age, but a French edition of 1897 distorted Hecker's actual teaching. A preface by the Abbé Felix Klein interpreted the American convert as an attractive illustration of how the church and the age might be reconciled. The book was much discussed as part of an effort of certain French leaders to win support for Pope Leo XIII's policy of *ralliement*, by which French Catholics would be persuaded to accept a republican form of government. An intense debate erupted over the concept of 'Americanism'. Hecker was sharply criticized, especially in a work by the Abbé Charles Maignen. Gibbons sprang to the defence of Hecker's orthodoxy, writing 'to denounce the part of the book where it treats of Americanism, to protest with all the energy in my soul and conscience against the incriminating tendency brought against us . . .'[17] But French Catholic leaders opposed to the *ralliement* continued to criticize Hecker and other exponents of *Américanisme* as contributing to an erroneous and dangerous movement, and a barrage of publications for and against poured from the presses through 1898.

The question was further complicated by the dramatic American victory in the war with Spain, the most Catholic country of Europe. Here was Americanism of another type, but also threatening to conservative European Catholics. A protest by Gibbons to Leo XIII played an important part in preventing the condemnation of Hecker, but the pope was determined to settle the basic issue. Early in 1899, despite a fruitless trip to Rome by Ireland in an effort to delay or halt its publication, the papal letter *Testem benevolentiae* was sent to Gibbons. It spoke of the emergence of certain erroneous opinions, called 'Americanism' by some, concerning the nature of the Christian life, opinions based on such faulty principles as 'the Church ought to adapt herself somewhat to our advanced civilization, and, relaxing her ancient rigor, show some indulgence to modern popular theories and methods'. After spelling out certain doctrinal consequences dangerous for faith and morals in such views, the letter rather adroitly affirmed the following:

If, indeed, by that name [Americanism] be designated the characteristic qualities

[17] Ellis, *Life of James Cardinal Gibbons*, ii, 60.

which reflect honor on the people of America, just as other nations have what is special to them; or if it implies the condition of your commonwealths, or the laws and customs which prevail in them, there is surely no reason why We should deem that it ought to be discarded. But if it is to be used not only to signify, but even to commend the above doctrines, there can be no doubt that our Venerable Brethren the bishops of America would be the first to repudiate and condemn it, as being especially unjust to them and to the entire nation as well.[18]

Gibbons promptly replied that what was called Americanism was not to be found among American Catholics. Yet the warning did its work—the Americanists were rebuked, their efforts to interpret their church in American idioms checked, and the conservative cast of Catholicism in the United States was set for more than half a century. Gibbons and Ireland continued in their posts, though the latter never won the coveted red hat of a cardinal. Keane became Archbishop of Dubuque and O'Connell rector of Catholic University and later Bishop of Richmond. But the liberal, fraternizing movement they had furthered was over, and the church turned inward to focus on the tasks of consolidation and organization.

The Americanist movement had not been deeply concerned with theological issues; it was primarily an effort to show the compatibility of Catholic and American principles. Even among the Americanists there was no close parallel to the liberal and modernist theological movements of Protestantism. One scholar observed that the American Catholic clerical mind, when placed in contact with secular sciences, 'vacillated between granting the probability of evolution without fully accepting it and rejecting it without fully condemning it'.[19] One prominent priest and scientist, John A. Zahm of the University of Notre Dame, Indiana, did espouse evolutionary views in *Evolution and Dogma* (1896). After considerable controversy the Sacred Congregation of the Index demanded the withdrawal of the book. In the early twentieth century there were few signs of the theological modernism that was disturbing Europe. There was considerable intellectual vitality at St. Joseph's Seminary at Dunwoodie, Yonkers, New York; prominent figures were invited to lecture, including professors from Columbia University and Charles A. Briggs of Union Theological Seminary. A lively periodical, the *New York Review*, was launched; it published scholarly articles by leading European

[18] John J. Wynne (ed.), *The Great Encyclical Letters of Pope Leo XIII*, 3rd edn. (New York, 1903), pp. 442, 452.

[19] Michael V. Gannon, 'Before and After Modernism: The Intellectual Isolation of the American Priest', in John Tracy Ellis (ed.), *The Catholic Priest in the United States: Historical Investigations* (Collegeville, Minn., 1971), p. 314.

Catholic modernists. All this was brought to a halt in 1907 when the Holy Office issued the syllabus *Lamentabili sane exitu*, which listed sixty-five heretical propositions of modern thought. This was followed by the sharp encyclical of Pius X, *Pascendi Dominici gregis*, which condemned modernism as a conspiracy against Catholic truth, and attacked modernists in their roles as philosophers, believers, theologians, critics, apologists, and reformers. The condemnation of modernism was aimed primarily at certain European developments, and did not create much stir in the United States. A few priests resigned, and the *New York Review* was given up. The spread of an inquisitorial and suspicious spirit through the church was inimical to scholarly creativity and a rigid theological stamp was imposed on the church.

The main energies of Catholics were thus diverted from scholarly and intellectual pursuits and poured into the church's active work. The pastoral and administrative tasks before the rapidly growing church were indeed immense. Previous levels of immigration were topped as nearly nine million persons entered the land in the first decade of the new century, and well over five million in the second—a large percentage of them from Catholic backgrounds. The total claimed membership of the church jumped from about twelve million in 1900 to eighteen million twenty years later. The high tide of German immigration had passed, while the numbers from Italy, Austria-Hungary, and Poland were especially conspicuous. Not all of the immigration was from overseas; French Canadians contributed significantly to the growing Catholic strength in New England and New York, while Mexicans pressed into the south-west. With the great migration came certain Catholic minorities much concerned about retaining important aspects of their distinctive religious cultures. Not only were there such eastern European groups as Slovaks and Lithuanians, but such eastern-rite Byzantine Catholics as Ruthenians, Ukrainians, and Croats. These groups formed their own parishes and retained separate canonical disciplines, some with their own bishops.

A significant permanent schism from the American Roman Catholic Church occurred when a group of Poles, centred largely in eastern Pennsylvania, withdrew to form the Polish National Catholic Church. A number of Polish people had been troubled by the control of a largely Irish and German hierarchy over church property. A dispute between Francis Hodur (1866–1953), pastor of a parish in Scranton, and his diocesan authorities led to his excommunication in 1898. Six years later his congregation joined with others to form the new autonomous church; in 1907 Hodur was consecrated bishop in Utrecht by Old Catholic bishops, the heirs of an eighteenth-century schism. Though the church grew to be a significant body with some quarter of a million members by mid-century, the majority of Poles remained with the mother church, becoming one of the main ethnic groups.

Until the opening of the twentieth century, Catholic missionary interest had been focused not only on the immigrants, but also on blacks and Indians. At the close of the Civil War there were about 100,000 black Catholics, the majority in Maryland and Louisiana; the racial conventions of the culture were all too evident in church life. Some separate black congregations were formed. In 1871 a group of Mill Hill Fathers from England arrived to take up work among the blacks.[20] Gibbons actively encouraged their work, sponsored the opening of their St. Joseph's Seminary in Baltimore in 1880, and in 1891 presided at the ordination of Charles R. Uncles, the first black to be ordained to the priesthood in the United States. That same year Katharine Drexel founded the Sisters of the Blessed Sacrament for Indians and Colored People; an outstanding achievement of this community was the building of Xavier University in New Orleans, for decades the only Catholic Negro university in the land. There was one black bishop in this period: James Healy of Portland, Maine, born of an Irish father and a slave mother, and educated by the Jesuits of Holy Cross College and then by the Sulpicians in Montreal and Paris. The numbers of black Catholics grew slowly, but increased appreciably during World War I.

A number of religious Orders ministered and taught among the Indians, so that by the later nineteenth century the Catholic Church had more Indians in its charge than any other denomination. A Commissioner for Indian Affairs was named in 1874; five years later the office became the Bureau of Catholic Indian Missions. Under the 'peace plan' that had been started during Grant's administration, denominational schools among Indians received public funds, but this aroused the ire of anti-Catholic groups. When the plan came to an end at the close of the century, the schools continued to receive some appropriations from tribal funds.

A new interest in foreign missions emerged in the last decade of the nineteenth century. Long a recipient of missionary aid from Europe, the church was growing strong enough to reach out to others. This concern was further stimulated when the church found itself responsible for Catholics in the islands acquired as a consequence of the Spanish-American

[20] William A. Osborne, *The Segregated Covenant: Race Relations and American Catholics* (New York, 1967), pp. 23–4.

War—Puerto Rico, Guam, and the Philippines. Many Catholics had been troubled at the prospect of war with Spain, yet in general supported the military effort wholeheartedly once the declaration came—and were quite well satisfied when the new lands were retained. There were serious problems to be faced, especially in the Philippines where the Spaniards who had fled during hostilities had to be compensated for their land. The change from being a receiving to becoming a sending church was symbolized in 1908 when the mission status of the American church was formally terminated. Three years later two priests, Thomas F. Price and James A. Walsh, won the willing assistance of Cardinal Gibbons in founding the Catholic Foreign Mission Society of America and in building its seminary, Maryknoll, located near New York. A group of missionaries left for China in 1918, the first of what was to become a world-wide mission.

The reputation of the Catholic Church as the friend of labour, stemming largely from the work of Gibbons and Leo XIII's *Rerum novarum*, was increased in the twentieth century by the forceful writings and activities of a priest of the archdiocese of St. Paul, John A. Ryan (1869–1945), whose book *A Living Wage* (1906) won national attention. He became the best-known of a small group of clerics pressing for social reform; his acceptance in 1915 of a professorship in moral theology and industrial ethics at Catholic University widened his sphere of influence. His social progressivism was striking in view of his traditionalism on theological and church–state issues. Another prominent figure was Peter E. Dietz (1878–1947) of Cincinnati, a priest who also laboured at the task of bringing the church to recognize and support the cause of labour. He worked through the German Central-Verein, a lay-led federation of Catholic benefit and insurance societies which won the support of many of the Americanized younger members of the German Catholic community.[21] Dietz was instrumental in the founding of the American Federation of Catholic Societies in 1901, but his hopes that it might become a vehicle for a national programme of social reform were not fulfilled, in part because of internal dissension. At its peak it had some three million members and provided channels for education and social action. Another approach to social problems was the founding in 1910 of the National Conference of Catholic Charities, which helped to co-ordinate the vast network of social and charitable institutions, and to stress the need for trained professionals in social service. These various efforts at deepening Catholic

[21] David J. O'Brien, 'The American Priest and Social Action', in Ellis (ed.), *The Catholic Priest in the United States*, p. 436.

social concern and effectiveness were hindered by the diversities and tensions of Catholic life.

American entry into World War I proved to be an important turning-point in Catholic history, for in responding patriotically to the national crusade the church experienced a lessening of inner tensions and achieved a unity for which many had long hoped. Ethnic frictions were reduced in the common emphasis on national loyalty; immigrant groups that had been clinging to indigenous languages often yielded to Americanizing pressures. The tone was set by Cardinal Gibbons, who called for the loyalty of all citizens to their country, and went so far as to say that 'the members of both Houses of Congress are the instruments of God in guiding us in our civic duties'.[22] As many Catholic groups engaged in activities related to the war effort, a need for co-ordination was recognized, and in 1917 representatives of sixty-eight dioceses and twenty-seven national organizations formed the National Catholic War Council in Washington. It soon became an instrument of the hierarchy, providing a much more effective centralizing agency for the church than the yearly meeting of archbishops which had been instituted in 1889. Under N.C.W.C. leadership, Catholics participated energetically in the national cause as men flocked to the colours as soldiers and chaplains, while those at home maintained service organizations, and contributed to fund-drives and to the Red Cross. Actual service to the troops was provided largely through the Knights of Columbus, which maintained centres for recreation and worship at military and naval establishments. A dozen units of women service workers assisted in the task.

The agency proved to be so useful that it was retained after the war as the National Catholic Welfare Council. It was subject to the control of the bishops; when their first annual meeting gathered in 1919, of the 101 bishops 92 were present. The N.C.W.C. provided a channel for the expression of the social spirit. In 1919 Ryan drafted a statement which the Administrative Committee of the N.C.W.C. adopted. The Bishops' Program of Social Reconstruction, as it came to be known, spoke clearly as to the need for adequate wages, housing, and social insurance; it insisted on the right of labour to organize, and though it opposed socialism, it criticized the defects of the industrial system. In certain respects it was a parallel statement to the Social Creed of the Churches as approved by the Federal Council of Churches. Of the eight departments of the N.C.W.C., that for Social Action, organized in 1920 with Ryan as its head, soon became the best known. Early in 1922 the Council was

[22] Ellis, *Life of James Cardinal Gibbons*, ii, 239.

suppressed by Rome where it was feared it would be too autonomous, but through quick action it was restored with more limited powers as the National Catholic Welfare *Conference.*

By 1920, the estimated eighteen million members of the Roman Catholic Church in the United States comprised about 18 per cent of the population. The church had come through a time of rapid growth and sharp tension into maturity and stability under centralized leadership. Though anti-Catholic prejudice was still actively expressed in such movements as the revived Ku Klux Klan, Catholics were conscious of their record of patriotism and their identity as Americans. The feeling of alienation was fading, especially among the prominent leaders of the church. John M. Blum has observed that 'the separate definitions of the good life, the good man, and the good American of James Cardinal Gibbons, Archbishop John Ireland and Father John Ryan was essentially the definition also of Theodore Roosevelt and likeminded strong young men'.[23] The N.C.W.C. provided the church with an effective instrument of unity; as John T. McNicholas, then Bishop of Duluth, put it in 1921

We have coordinated and united the Catholic power in this country. It now knows where and when it can act and is encouraged by the consciousness of its unity. We feel ourselves powerful because our union has become visible. All our Catholic organizations report an increase of energy and we do not doubt that, thanks to the N.C.W.C., we can bring Catholic cooperation to its apogee.[24]

In the same year that that statement was made, the sole American survivor of Vatican Council I, Cardinal Gibbons, died. Ordained in 1861, his priestly life had spanned sixty eventful years that saw spectacular growth, sharp conflict, and organizational maturity for the nation's largest Christian church.

Lutheranism in America: Diversity and Unity

Like others, Lutherans supported the section in which they lived during the Civil War. The vast majority of Lutherans of German and Scandinavian origins were opposed to slavery, and their influence was very important in keeping Missouri aligned with the Union. Lutherans came to feel somewhat more at home in a country new to so many of them as they participated in the war effort and in such organizations as the United States Christian Commission.

Only a minority of them, an estimated 40,000 of somewhat more than

---

[23] *The Promise of America: An Historical Inquiry* (Boston, 1966), p. 81.
[24] As quoted in *The Christian Century*, lxi (July–December 1944), 1411.

250,000, were in Confederate territory. The southern synods that had formerly been members of the General Synod formed their own parallel body in the south by 1863, taking a quite conservative doctrinal stance. This trend was further intensified when a merger was worked out with the Tennessee Synod in 1886 to form the United Synod of the South.

The disruption of the General Synod and the emergence of the General Council in 1867 has already been described.[25] Thus the effort begun in the early nineteenth century to bring Lutheran churches and synods into greater national unity had divided into three parts at a time when unprecedented waves of immigration swept over Lutheranism and escalated it numerically into the third largest Protestant denominational family, surpassed only by Baptists and Methodists. From less than half a million confirmed members in 1870, the total came to well over two million forty years later. Yet the Lutheran churches were not very conspicuous on the American religious scene in these years of rapid growth. Though represented in most parts of the country, they were rather heavily concentrated in the rural areas of the north central states. Many Lutheran groups were cut off from other groups (and from each other) by differences of language—more than a score were in regular use in this period. The churches had to focus much of their efforts on meeting the needs of the newcomers, and in trying to find proper organizational forms for their sprawling, diversified, theologically strict movement. At one point there were more than sixty independent members of this one denominational family.

Shortly after the Civil War, immigration from Germany, which had been interrupted temporarily, swept in again, reaching a peak in the early 1880s. About half of the three million who came had had ties of varying strength with the Lutheran tradition. As they settled in cities and towns, especially in the mid-west, the home mission agencies of the synods laboured to reach them with effective ministries. A moving spirit in this work was William Alfred Passavent (1821–94), a minister who was also instrumental in founding hospitals and orphanages, and in introducing the first Lutheran deaconesses into the country. For the most part, the new immigrants who became active in church life favoured the confessional emphasis in the various synods. The very conservative Missouri Synod gained greatly in size, and in 1872 became the leading member of a federation of synods, the Synodical Conference. The central figure was Missouri's able C. F. W. Walther;[26] his hopes that the conference might lead to a still larger unity were frustrated when a bitter theological

[25] See above, pp. 211–12.   [26] See above, p. 212.

controversy over the doctrine of predestination erupted and led to the withdrawal of some of the participating synods.

In these same years more than 1,750,000 Scandinavians poured in, about half from Sweden, a third from Norway, a sixth from Denmark. Many of them settled in the farmlands of the upper Mississippi valley, especially in Minnesota. Most of them were of Lutheran background, which for some had been a rather unpleasant experience under state churches from which they were glad to escape. A number of independent synods were formed to provide for the religious needs of these immigrants, among whom were many of a strongly pietist orientation. Especially important was the Augustana Synod (1860), which became the leading Swedish synod. It associated itself with the General Council. Its dominant figure was Tufve Nilsson Hasselquist (1816–91), president of Augustana College in Illinois, seminary professor, and influential editor. Norwegians and Danes also formed several independent synods, as did the smaller Lutheran flocks from Finland, Iceland, and the Austro-Hungarian Empire.

The various bodies were active in missionary outreach at home and abroad. In the years from 1870 to 1910, for example, the General Synod founded more than 600 new congregations. Many of them were English-speaking as were the older congregations of the east, so that by 1910, only one-tenth of the pastors and congregations of the synod continued to use German. The missionaries of the General Council also fanned out across the west and into Canada; the Manitoba (1891), Nova Scotia (1903), and Central Canada (1908) synods were fruits of this effort. Only in the twentieth century were significant Lutheran ministries to Negroes undertaken. Overseas, fields in Asia and Africa were served by Lutheran missionaries from the United States.

Conscious of their many divisions, Lutherans worked with considerable success toward internal unification. Despite their ethnic and institutional diversity, they remained confessionally oriented and were largely undisturbed by the liberal and modernist movements that were influential in many other traditions. This gave them a 'homogeneous quality' which 'was most visible in the attitude that all the [Lutheran] church bodies assumed over against the new intellectual climate of the 19th century'.[27] These theological similarities were a positive factor in a series of Lutheran unions. After a long preparatory period marked by preliminary fusions and involved negotiations, three main mergers came to their climax toward the very end of the 1860–1920 period.

The first of these involved bodies of Norwegian background. It took

[27] E. Clifford Nelson, *Lutheranism in North America, 1914–1970* (Minneapolis, 1972), p. 10.

a good deal of patience to work out a theological position inclusive of those from both pietist and strict confessional orientations. Strong unitive bonds lay in the common nationality, and in the Norwegian hymnal that was in use across the theological spectrum. During the quadricentennial year of the Reformation, 1917, most of those of Norwegian background came together to form what was at the time called the Norwegian Lutheran Church of America.

The next year the divisions between the General Synod, the General Council, and the United Synod of the South were overcome in a union that quickly became the largest Lutheran body in America. An important step in this direction had been the preparation of a uniform liturgy by the predominantly English-speaking synods. Joint committees, drawing on the liturgies of the sixteenth century in the light of the liturgical renaissance of the nineteenth, prepared in 1888 a Common Service, which became widely popular. The acceptance by the General Synod of the historic Lutheran standard, the Unaltered Augsburg Confession, a conservative step, further prepared the way for union. Significantly, lay members, some of whom had participated in organizations that cut across synodical lines, pressed church leaders for the merger, which was consummated in November 1918. The United Lutheran Church in America committed itself to further unity among those submitting to the traditional confessional statements. The union brought together forty-five regional synods, many of which overlapped geographically. It took many years to get the necessary realignments made.

A third Lutheran merger was of four mid-western conservative synods of German background: Wisconsin, Michigan, Minnesota, and Nebraska. These bodies had previously formed a federation which had participated in the work of the Synodical Conference; in 1919 the four synods united organically as the Evangelical Lutheran Joint Synod of Wisconsin and Other States.

The popular revulsion against Germany during World War I brought some persecution of German Lutherans but the general support for the national cause speeded the Americanization process. As among Roman Catholics, an agency created to co-ordinate church outreach to those in military service was later transformed into a more permanent unitive agency. The National Lutheran Commission for Soldiers' and Sailors' Welfare was formed at the initiative of laymen of various synods to care for the religious and moral well-being of fighting men. Its success as the only general Lutheran organization suggested that a more broadly defined co-ordinating agency would be useful; in 1918 the National Lutheran

Council was formed. The newly merged Norwegian and United churches were members, along with a number of the smaller bodies, but the Missouri and Wisconsin synods did not join. About two-thirds of the Lutherans of America were included. Among the tasks of the new council were to speak for the churches, and to represent their interests in the larger scene.

Thus the churches of this tradition entered the post-World War I years vastly greater in numbers and in geographical area than they had been when the Civil War began. Though they were still somewhat divided along both national and theological lines, they had effected consolidation through three major mergers, and had founded an important co-ordinating council. The long isolation from other Christian churches, in part a result of language barriers, was beginning to fade as this third largest denominational family began to play a more conspicuous role in the American religious and social scene.

Eastern Orthodoxy in the Western World

The beginnings of Eastern Orthodox church life on the North American continent can be traced back to the arrival of ten Russian Orthodox monks on Kodiak Island in Alaska, then Russian territory, in 1794. The work was later nourished by a priest who has been described in these words:

An unusually capable missionary—John Veniaminov [1797–1879]—[who] labored for many arduous years in this vineyard (1822–1852), as missionary, the author of a grammar of the Aleutian language, the translator of the Gospels and the Byzantine liturgy into the same language, and then as bishop of an immense territory embracing the Kamchatka, the Kurile Islands, Aleutian Islands, and Alaska.[28]

In 1867—the same year that Alaska was purchased by the United States— he was called to serve as metropolitan of Moscow and primate of Russia.

As Russians in North America moved southwards down the Pacific coast, the cathedral city of the vast diocese, which then covered the whole of the United States and Canada, was moved from Sitka to San Francisco in 1872. After 1880, Russian immigration was largely through the eastern seaports and much increased, so that the diocesan centre was again shifted. Under the leadership of Tikhon Bellavin (1866–1925), a cathedral was built, seminary work begun, and the see formally established in New York in 1905. By 1916 there were about 350 parishes with a total constituency of approximately 500,000.

[28] John Meyendorff, *The Orthodox Church: Its Past and Its Role in the World Today*, translated from the French by John Chapin (New York, 1962), p. 185.

As the only Orthodox communion with a hierarchy on the continent at the time, the Russian Orthodox at first maintained a general supervision over various other Orthodox groups—Greeks, Serbs, Albanians, Bulgarians, and Ukrainians—which were also growing through immigration. The first permanent Greek Orthodox congregation was founded in New Orleans in 1864; following the Balkan Wars and the expulsion of Greeks from Turkey many more were founded. Greek immigrants often thought of themselves as temporary residents, but as the years passed they turned their energies to settling down and building institutions of their own in their new home. In 1918 an emissary of the Ecumenical Patriarch of Constantinople (Istanbul) took the first step toward the formation of the Greek Archdiocese of North and South America, an event completed three years later.

The impact of World War I and the Russian Revolution of 1917 resulted in a confused and agitated period of Orthodox reorganization. The Russian Orthodox people were divided over their attitude toward the new regime, but the main body insisted on autonomy in matters of church government while adhering to their historic ecclesiastical tradition. Various other Orthodox bodies which had been under Russian supervision became independent—for example, the Ukrainian Orthodox Church was organized in 1919, and the Serbian Orthodox Church in the United States and Canada in 1921.

The Orthodox churches continued their historic theological emphases and liturgical traditions in the New World, feeling that it was their mission to stand firm in their confident claim that the faith of the ancient and indivisible Church of the seven ecumenical councils lived on intact in their midst. By 1920 a new major denominational family with its membership located heavily in eastern, mid-western, and Californian cities had taken its place in the spectrum of Christianity in America.

Some Smaller Denominations, Old and New

These years were marked not only by the growth of the major Protestant, Roman Catholic, and Eastern Orthodox churches, but also by the continued life of some of the smaller denominations and by the rise of some unconventional new religious movements. Though the majority of the several hundred denominations in America were small, together they served the religious needs of a significant portion of the population, and often introduced ideas and practices that later became more general. The inner histories of the smaller denominations—some of which eventually became very large—are often complex and colourful.

Smaller churches of pacifist inclination which had been transplanted to America in the colonial period maintained their witness through these exciting decades, often growing modestly and making some adjustments to the changing cultural climate. The conservative Mennonite Church, predominantly of Swiss background, continued to be the largest of the various Anabaptist bodies. What became its closest rival, the General Conference Mennonite Church, was founded in 1860. Somewhat less strict in discipline, it grew in great measure when Russian Mennonite immigrants in the 1870s affiliated with it.

The German Baptist Brethren, a pietist body which had originated in the early eighteenth century, suffered several divisions; the continuing central body took the name Church of the Brethren in 1908, and remained the largest of the Brethren groups as it slowly made the transition from a largely rural constituency to one with a steadily growing number of its members in the cities, especially of the mid-west. It undertook mission projects in India and China, and later in Africa.

The divisions among the Quakers in the early nineteenth century have already been mentioned; in the latter part of the century most of the various Quaker Yearly Meetings participated in a series of advisory General Conferences. Out of these gatherings a 'Five Years Meeting' emerged as a consultative and administrative body. It carried on missionary, educational, and reform activities on behalf of the Friends.

Often called the 'historic peace churches', these small denominations upheld the pacifist position in a period marked by three wars. Many of their young men refused to bear arms and did alternative service as conscientious objectors. During World War I, under the leadership of the influential Quaker philosopher and mystic, Rufus Jones (1863–1948), the American Friends Service Committee was organized; it provided outstanding leadership in training workers for non-combatant service and provided effective relief in places of human need.

The small Moravian Church did not maintain its earlier pacifist emphasis. Though the General Synod which met in Herrnhut in Germany remained the final authority in Moravianism, the American church attained a large measure of self-determination in 1857. Mission work overseas and among North American Indians and Eskimos continued to be emphasized by this zealous pietistic church.

The older small liberal denominations, Unitarian and Universalist, also maintained their witness in this period, both reaching their peak in the number of congregations around the turn of the century, when the

Unitarians claimed 70,000 members and the Universalists about 60,000. Movements such as the Free Religious Association (1867) and Ethical Culture (1876), devoted to a religion of humanity, provided havens for those who no longer identified themselves with historic Christianity or Judaism. Some within the liberal denominations also no longer made specifically Christian affirmations. Within the Universalist churches there raged an intense debate about whether Universalism was to be understood as a branch of the Christian Church or as a more 'natural' religion which foreshadowed the future World Religion, with the trend moving slowly in the latter direction. Women were prominent in Universalist leadership; in 1863 Olympia Brown became 'the first denominationally ordained woman minister in the country'.[29] In the 1890s the Unitarian and Universalist churches began rather uncertainly to draw together, a pilgrimage eventually completed in the formation of the Unitarian Universalist Association in 1961.

The Latter-day Saints, especially the dominant Salt Lake City church, grew steadily in this period. There was a bitter struggle with the federal government over the practice of polygamy. The Morrill Act of 1862 made it illegal, a stand confirmed by the Supreme Court sixteen years later. The government finally moved decisively against the Mormons in 1887, dissolving the corporation of the church, confiscating property, and imprisoning offenders. In 1890 the church forbade plural marriages, which cleared the way for Utah to be admitted as a state in 1896. With that settled, legal opposition to the Saints slowly receded. Firmly guided by a President, his two Counsellors, and a Council of the Twelve Apostles, the church enlisted most of its male members in some rank of priesthood. Many young Mormons customarily devoted two years to spreading their 'restored gospel'. Membership swelled in the first two decades of the twentieth century to about 500,000, largely because of the effective work of missionaries at home and abroad.

In the later nineteenth century a range of religious bodies emerged out of a resurgence of interest in 'mental healing' and in the way a life of prosperity and abundance could be advanced by cultivating positive attitudes. The founder of what came to be broadly described as the New Thought movement was Phineas P. Quimby (1802–66), a clockmaker who experimented with hypnotism and healing. Late in life he settled in Portland, Maine, to devote all his time to curing the sick. He became convinced that 'disease is what follows the disturbance of the mind or spiritual matter . . . Disease is what follows an opinion, it is made up of

[29] Williams, *American Universalism*, p. 46.

mind diverted by error, and Truth is the destruction of this opinion.'[30] His teaching was cast in broadly Christian terms, for Christ for him was the founder of the science of healing. Some of those cured under Quimby's teaching became conspicuous in the spread of New Thought—Julius A. and Horatio W. Dresser, Warren F. Evans, and Mary Baker Eddy. The movement absorbed ideas from various strands of thought, and spawned a number of new churches and cults. In his famous Gifford lectures of 1901–2 William James analysed some of the elements that had gone into the movement that had by then become a significant religious force:

One of the doctrinal sources of Mind-cure is the four Gospels; another is Emersonianism or New England transcendentalism; another is Berkeleyan idealism; another is spiritism, with its messages of 'law' and 'progress' and 'development'; another the optimistic popular science evolutionism . . . and, finally, Hinduism has contributed a strain. But the most characteristic feature of the mind-cure movement is an inspiration much more direct. The leaders in this faith have had an intuitive belief in the all-saving power of healthy-minded attitudes as such, in the conquering efficacy of courage, hope, and a correlative contempt for doubt, fear, worry, and all nervously precautionary states of mind.[31]

One of the most distinctive of the new churches to arise was the Church of Christ, Scientist, or Christian Science. After a life troubled by much illness, Mary Baker Eddy (1821–1910) was helped by Quimby and studied with him in the early 1860s. Then, shortly after his death in 1866 and following a fall on the ice, she claimed that she was remarkably healed, and was led to the discovery of how to be in good health and how to cure others. The facts of Mrs. Eddy's cure, the source of her ideas, and the reasons for the spread of her movement have been much debated. Within a few years, a growing band of followers accepted her contention that her experiences had led her to a revelation of the divine law of life and to an original discovery of the deeper meaning of the Bible. In 1875 came the beginnings of organization and the publication of the first edition of her *Science and Health with Key to the Scriptures*. Within a few years, the 'mother church' in Boston became the authoritative centre of a movement that spread into many cities and towns, and also to other lands. Educational and publishing ventures added to the growing fame of Christian Science, and brought the curious to services in which the testimonies of those who had been restored to health helped to make new believers. The central

[30] As quoted by Charles S. Braden, *Spirits in Rebellion: The Rise and Development of New Thought* (Dallas, Texas, 1968), pp. 57–8.
[31] *The Varieties of Religious Experience: A Study in Human Nature* (New York, 1902), p. 93.

message of the foundress stressed that God is All, that whatever is not God is illusion, that matter is substance or error and hence, with all evil, sin, and disease, is unreal. Illness is false belief, she taught, and death a 'mortal illusion'. By the time of her death, Christian Science had about 100,000 members and was rapidly expanding.

Out of the same general body of ideas arose a series of other groups, some of them offshoots of Christian Science. They varied greatly in size and took many names, such as the Church of the Higher Life, the Church of the Higher Design, and the Church of Divine Science. Among the new bodies was the Unity School of Christianity, founded by Charles and Myrtle Fillmore in Kansas City, Missouri, in 1889. Both had had some :ontact with Christian Science, and had experienced a recovery of health under New Thought teaching. Seeking through a vast publishing programme to deepen the life of prayer and its healing power in the churches and in the larger society, Unity at first carefully avoided becoming a new church, but in time it did evolve slowly into denominational status.

As the New Thought movement proliferated organizationally, its leaders, including some who had remained in their traditional religious homes, met in various conventions. Several lines of development were brought together in 1915 in an over-all world organization, the International New Thought Alliance, following a conference in London. In 1919 the I.N.T.A. formally adopted a declaration of principles which included such statements as these:

Man is made in the image of the Good, and evil and pain are but the tests and correctives that appear when his thought does not reflect the full glory of this image . . .

We affirm the divine supply. He who serves God and man in the full understanding of the law of compensation shall not lack. Within us are unused resources of energy and power . . .

We affirm the teaching of Christ that the Kingdom of Heaven is within us, that we are one with the Father, that we should not judge, that we should love one another, that we should heal the sick, that we should return good for evil, that we should minister to others, and that we should be perfect even as our Father in Heaven is perfect. These are not only ideals, but practical, everyday working principles.

We affirm the new thought of God as Universal Love, Life, Truth and Joy, in whom we live, move and have our being, and by whom our oneness with Him means love, truth, peace, health and plenty, not only in our own lives but in the giving out of these fruits of the Spirit to others.[32]

---

[32] Braden, *Spirits in Rebellion*, pp. 95–6.

Many of the ideas and expressions of New Thought were carried far beyond the movement's own churches and organizations to other denominations and to the general public by such popular writers as Orison Swett Marden, Ralph Waldo Trine, Glenn Clark, and Emmet Fox. New Thought not only won members from the older churches, but also significantly influenced some who chose to remain within them. Not only did the spectrum of Christian churches broaden appreciably in this period, but some aspects of the growing diversity were reflected in the older congregations and denominations.

Non-Christian Religions

Although this book deals with the Christian churches, it is important to observe that up to this period, except for the small Jewish minority, non-Christian religions had made little impact on American life. In part as a consequence of the World's Parliament of Religions in 1893, where spokesmen of religions of the east had received a warm welcome, this began to change. A Vedānta Society to spread Hindu teachings was founded in 1894 by Swami Vivekananda, whose striking personality had made a great impression at the Parliament. He was convinced that there was a great opportunity for the dissemination of oriental religious philosophies in North America. Buddhism was taught by a Japanese priest who settled in San Francisco, to be followed later by others. Some groups of Islamic background also extended their work in this period. An American convert to Islam reported to the Parliament that a Muslim study-group was at work in New York, and the Baha'i movement had begun to win converts and to build an impressive temple in Winnetka, Illinois.

Of particular significance, however, was the rapid growth in these years of Judaism, with which the Christian churches have so long had an historic but often tragic relationship. At the time of the Civil War, there were perhaps 150,000 Jews in the country, the great majority of them of Ashkenazic (German) background. The trend toward Reform flowed strongly among them in post-war years as dietary laws were relaxed, English increasingly used in sermons, and Sabbath services often held on Friday evenings. A conference of Reform congregations was held in 1869—'the beginning of the great divide in American Jewish religious history'.[33] Under the leadership of Isaac Meyer Wise a permanent Union of American Hebrew Congregations was founded in 1873, and Hebrew Union College founded in Cincinnati two years later. In 1885 the

[33] Moshe Davis, 'Jewish Religious Life and Institutions in America', in Louis Finkelstein (ed.), The Jews: Their History, Culture, and Religion, i (New York, 1949), 378.

'Pittsburgh Platform' was prepared by a small group of Reform rabbis in an effort to modify traditional Judaism in the light of scientific and evolutionary thought. The Talmudic tradition was pushed into the background by this liberalizing, Americanizing thrust, and the messianic expectation was restated in terms of the doctrine of progress. A rabbinical assembly, the Central Conference of American Rabbis, completed the organizational structure of the Reform movement in 1889.

The pace of change was too fast for some Jews who nevertheless saw the need for certain adjustments to the times. The scholarly Isaac Leeser (1806–68) feared that the reformist trends were becoming reductionist and were severing important links with past traditions. He believed that changes should be made more cautiously, without cutting important links with the past. Historical or Conservative Judaism began to take shape under his guidance; after such episodes as one in 1883 when dietary laws were violated at a banquet honouring graduates of Hebrew Union, the Jewish Theological Seminary of America was founded in New York in 1886 and dedicated to the preservation of the knowledge and practice of historical Judaism as ordained in the law of Moses and expanded by the prophets and sages of Israel in biblical and Talmudic writings.

Meanwhile, beginning in about 1880 when the Jewish population was about 250,000, a vast new wave of immigration brought great transformations, so that by the outbreak of World War I the Jewish population had increased some twelve times. The great majority of the new arrivals were from eastern and central Europe, most of them poor, many fleeing the feared pogroms of Russia. Reared in ghettos in which identity was related to the traditions of close-knit Jewish communities, the newcomers were understandably suspicious of things modern. They were devoted to the use of Yiddish, a high-German dialect developed under Hebrew and Slavic influences and written in Hebrew characters, and often seemed to feel that the Torah could not be properly expounded in any other tongue. Not finding themselves at home in the synagogues they encountered— especially not Reform ones—they formed dozens of Orthodox institutions of their own. The total number of their synagogues leaped from about 270 in 1880 to about 1,000 in twenty years. The new Orthodox founded a theological seminary in 1896; in time it grew into Yeshiva University in New York. Two years later a Union of Orthodox Jewish congregations was set up, and four years after that a Union of Orthodox Rabbis of the United States and Canada was founded.

In the early twentieth century Conservative Judaism grew stronger, in part as a mediating force between the other two strands. Under the leadership of Solomon Schechter (1847-1915), Jewish Theological Seminary was built into a great scholarly centre, and an organization of Conservative synagogues, The United Synagogue of America, was founded in 1913, and the Rabbinical Assembly of America five years later.

The emergence of the modern Zionist movement at the turn of the century stimulated much controversy within Judaism. Reform Jews generally opposed it, believing that America was their Zion. Many Orthodox Jews believed that the Messiah, not political measures, would bring the restoration of Jews to Israel, while Conservatives more generally supported Zionism from its beginning.

In addition to the three Jewish 'denominations' and their organizations, which by no means enlisted the active support of all Jews in America, the Jewish community developed an elaborate network of benevolent, mutual aid, philanthropic, defence, and labour organizations. During World War I, a number of Jewish groups of various types worked together in such joint agencies as the Jewish Welfare Board (1917) in support of the war effort. As in the case of many Christian churches, the members of this denominational family discovered values of co-operation in time of national emergency.

In the latter part of the nineteenth century there developed an increase in anti-Semitism, related to its resurgence in other parts of the world. Fantasies of a Jewish international conspiracy to control the world's finances were spread by hatemongers. The search for a scapegoat in a time of rapid change and insecurity often ended with the Jews, who were spoken of in racial rather than religious terms. Restrictive covenants and 'gentlemen's agreements' created difficulties for this growing minority group. Some church people who felt that the growing religious pluralism was eroding the Christian character of their nation showed their resentment in such tactics. The anti-Semitism that had for so long stained Christian history found some expression in Christian publications and educational materials and in certain of the missions which singled out the Jews for conversion.

In the eventful decades from the beginning of the Civil War to the close of World War I, the Christian churches had increased greatly in membership, both because of the success of evangelistic and missionary efforts and because of the influx of immigrants of Christian background. There was also a marked increase in the variety of Christian churches, both because of the persistence of ethnic institutional patterns and because of the founding of new churches under the impact of such movements as Holiness, Pentecostalism, and New Thought. By the early twentieth century more than half of the adult population were at least nominal members of churches, while most of the others identified themselves however vaguely with one of the increasing number of religious bodies. Home and foreign missionary enterprises were flourishing in most denominations. America was generally considered to be a Christian nation, in a world in which the Christian forces seemed to be still in the ascendant.

XI

ALTERNATIVE VISIONS OF
A CHRISTIAN CANADA

(1867–1925)

THE Dominion of Canada was welcomed by the churches as it came into being in 1867. It increased quickly in geographical extent, but much more slowly in population. The vast North-west Territories were soon purchased from Hudson's Bay Company and taken over by the new government; Manitoba was constituted a province in 1870, British Columbia joined the Confederation a year later, and Prince Edward Island in 1873. Larger in area than the United States, Canada was much smaller in population; by 1901 it was about five and a third million, compared to seventy-six million for its southern neighbour.

The Christian churches felt secure in the new political arrangement, for 'membership in a particular denomination ranked high as a badge of personal identity' for Canadians and 'even the irreligious usually went to church on Sunday'.[1] In part because the churches had played an important civilizing role under frontier conditions and continued to deal with pioneering realities in the north and west, their influence was deeply felt in the patterns of family, community, and social life. Catholic parishes were central in the French-Canadian towns and villages, for the church was seen as essential to the preservation of French culture in the face of the British majority. But the Protestant congregations with their pro-gramme of activities also played a large role in the growing cities and towns of the expanding country. Now that the land stretched from ocean to ocean, Canadian churches thought and acted more and more in national terms. Though they respected the traditions of the mother churches in Europe, they tended to frame their decisions more in response to Canadian than to European or American realities. They laboured to win the unconverted to Christ and the church, to deepen the commitment

[1] John W. Grant, *The Church in the Canadian Era: The First Century of Confederation*, History of the Christian Church In Canada, iii (Toronto, 1972), pp. 1, 10.

of the faithful, and to make their vast dominion a Christian nation. The story of the expansion of the churches in the early decades of Confederation is dramatic and impressive.

The effort was handicapped, however, by the diverging interpretations of faith and church. These ranged from the basic differences between Catholic and Protestant through the well-marked denominational distinctions of Protestantism to the inner tensions between ethnic and theological parties within all communions. Often intensifying the conflicts among the witnesses to these alternative visions of the role of Christianity in Canada were the familiar differences between those who struggled to maintain great traditions and those who relished fresh insights and shaped new practices for ever-changing conditions. In given crises some Christians felt strongly the pull of tradition, while others responded more to the challenge of the contemporary. The six decades following Confederation were marked by strong Protestant movements towards union, first within divided denominational families and then among three of them. The drive for a church united across confessional lines—then a distinctive achievement in western church history—succeeded at the cost of an intense and emotional struggle and the painful division of one of the uniting churches. In the same period, Roman Catholic life was marked by tensions between liberal and ultramontane currents in Quebec, and between French and English-speaking Catholics in the country as a whole.

Not only were the churches faced with the problems of shaping national organizations and planting churches in vast unsettled areas, but soon they had also to deal with a changing intellectual climate, with the spread of industrial problems, with an influx of European immigrants familiar neither with British nor French cultures and traditions, and with the realities of overseas wars. The rapid and overlapping transitions from a predominantly agricultural civilization to an urban, industrial, pluralistic culture strained the inner resources of the churches and left their marks on their development.

An Era of Expansion and Organization

The Confederation of 1867 was designed to contain the racial and religious antipathies that lay at the heart of many of Canada's political difficulties. Though these tensions remained and sometimes produced conflict, there was in both French and English Canada 'a desire for nationhood so strong that even religious controversy was stilled in its presence'.[2] The churches

---

[2] Walsh, *The Christian Church in Canada*, p. 228.

played an important role in maintaining an atmosphere in which Dominion could succeed. As one observer put it,

the Churches in this respect were years ahead of most of the politicians and the people in the isolated British North American colonies. More than any other organized body, their very structure and their goals moved them towards preparing the way for the joining together of the colonies and the old Hudson's Bay Company territories which took place between 1867 and 1872, and to fostering that colonial Confederation as it grew to nationhood.[3]

Yet the churches themselves were rather slow in seeing the possibilities of the west and north-west. Until the very end of the century, economic conditions were not highly favourable to western growth. The completion of the transcontinental railway in 1885 helped to some extent, but more important for the churches' interest in the west was the missionary vision of some eloquent and energetic leaders. An important preliminary step for the religious institutions was the ordering of their own houses so as to be ready for the new opportunities.

The largest of the four major Protestant denominational families, which together claimed a following of a little more than half of the population in 1881, was the Methodist, which counted about 17 per cent of all Canadians in its constituency. Despite several previous mergers, Methodists were still grouped in four main bodies. The differences among them were administrative and temperamental rather than doctrinal; the largest group, the Methodist Church of Canada, followed British Wesleyan precedents, while the much smaller Methodist Episcopal Church wanted to maintain its episcopate, paralleling American Methodism. Two other still smaller bodies, the Primitive Methodist and Bible Christian churches, were concerned about maintaining lay representation. In 1884 the differences were worked out—the title of bishop was dropped, though superintendents were named, and the lay emphasis was recognized—so that the Methodist Church (Canada) came into being with a membership of 170,000. Strongly evangelical in tone, Methodists actively built up their churches across Canada, and were seriously concerned about the spiritual and moral improvement of the nation. An important fruit of the union of 1884 was the appointment of James Woodsworth (?–1917) as superintendent of missions. An optimistic activist, Woodsworth built solidly on the foundations that had been laid earlier in the century. Much of his energy was invested in working with Indian missions and schools, especially in northern Manitoba and Alberta. While approving much of

---

[3] William Kilbourn (ed.), *Religion in Canada: The Spiritual Development of a Nation* (Toronto, 1968), p. 33.

the 'civilizing' achievements of missionaries like Thomas Crosby, who brought important improvements to native villages in British Columbia, Woodsworth warned against too much paternalism and the neglect of the distinctively spiritual aspects of missionary work. He enlisted preachers from Great Britain who added to their ministries a concern to spread Anglo-Saxon institutions among the heterogeneous peoples who were beginning to move into the west. Methodists also developed an interest in foreign missions, opening fields in Japan and West China. Missions, both home and foreign, were greatly aided by the enthusiasm of Methodist women, who organized a network of missionary societies, and showed a particular interest in educational enterprises. In 1887 the Methodists borrowed from their American counterparts the idea of instituting orders of deaconesses, full-time workers who served first as social workers and urban evangelists.

Only slightly smaller than the Methodist family in the nineteenth century were the Presbyterians. They completed their national union about a decade before their rivals. The tangled history of Presbyterianism in the earlier nineteenth century had produced four main groups by the time of Confederation—separate bodies, one connected with the Church of Scotland and one not, in both the Maritimes and central Canada. In 1875 all four came together as the Presbyterian Church in Canada. Congregations often did not merge but carried on their older traditions. Those of 'Auld Kirk' or Church of Scotland background tended to include many political conservatives of well-established social standing. Those of Free Church orientation were more likely to be liberal in politics, middle-class, and more warmly evangelical in their religious enthusiasms.

One of the significant achievements of the newly united church was to appoint a superintendent for missions in the north-west—a new departure for a people who feared that the word 'oversight' in the terms of appointment sounded like feared episcopacy. James Robertson (1839–1902), educated at the University of Toronto and at Princeton and Union seminaries, had succeeded in the demanding role of Presbyterian minister, once described in these words:

For all Scotch folk, and for all folk of Presbyterian extraction, connection or leaning, the Presbyterian minister was the natural resort for all in need of advice, of guidance, of cheer, of aid financial and other, and the minister's home became a kind of Immigration Office, a General Information Bureau, an Employment Agency, an Institution for Universal aid.[4]

---

[4] Charles W. Gordon, *The Life of James Robertson, Missionary Superintendent in the North-west Territories* (New York, 1908), p. 148.

As pastor of Knox Church, Winnipeg, Manitoba, Robertson was familiar with western problems, and threw himself into the new work with great energy, exemplifying the activism he had learned in part through his American experiences. He travelled incessantly, recruited missionaries, started a Church and Manse Building Fund, created enthusiasm at General Assembly meetings by his intensity, and got things done by taking extraordinary powers on himself when he thought it necessary.

In part because they were late in reaching the west and did not have extensive missions among Indians, the Presbyterians now devoted their attention primarily to incoming settlers, many of whom were of Presbyterian background, with considerable success. The Presbyterians soon had a commanding lead in the west—Robertson had worked so thoroughly that growth continued after his death in 1902, so that by 1910 the western missions had doubled to about 500, and when the census was taken in the following year it was found that the Presbyterians had become the largest Protestant denomination in Canada. They also extended their foreign missionary work in this period, adding stations in Trinidad, Formosa, India, China, and later Korea. The year after the union of 1875 a women's national missionary society was formed, an autonomous organization that paralleled the official denominational missionary structures.

Anglicanism before Confederation had set up a diocesan organization for the west by creating the Diocese of Rupert's Land, which remained directly under the Archbishop of Canterbury and not under the Church of England in Canada until 1893. A remarkable leader, Robert Machray (1831–1904), became in 1865 second bishop of this vast diocese, which at that point covered northern and western areas from the Labrador coast to the Rockies, about three million square miles—roughly the size of the United States. A Scotsman of great intellectual and leadership gifts, educated at Aberdeen and Cambridge, Machray was an ecclesiastical statesman and empire-builder who 'sought to mobilize the resources of church and state for the formation of a new society that would be an outpost at the same time of Britain and of Christendom'.[5] Centring his work at Fort Garry (later Winnipeg), the frontier bishop took the lead in seeing that as the work spread, new dioceses were carved out of the original—finally a dozen in all. For example, the veteran missionary John Horden was consecrated as Bishop of Moosonee in the James Bay area in 1872; he reported four distinct races and languages in his charge: the Crees, the Ojibways, the Eskimos, and the Chippewyans. Two years later another veteran who had served among the Indians, William

---

[5] Grant, *The Church in the Canadian Era*, p. 51.

Carpenter Bompas, became Bishop of Athabasca; this 'apostle of the north' was later to head in turn the Mackenzie River and the Yukon dioceses. By 1875 the original Diocese of Rupert's Land had become an ecclesiastical province, with Machray as archbishop.

The most colourful and in many respects successful part of the work of the Church of England in the north-west was among the Indians and Eskimos. The Anglicans had more missionaries among the former than any other Protestant body, and the help of the Church Missionary Society of the mother country was considerable. Important work among the Eskimos along the eastern shore of Hudson Bay was led for nearly half a century by a former sailor, Edward James Peck, who found these natives responsive to the gospel and responsible in propagating their own religious community. The only other Protestant denomination involved in Eskimo missions was the Moravian.

The Anglicans were far less successful than their Protestant rivals in gathering English-speaking settlers into their western churches. In part this was because the western dioceses were related to England and not to their eastern counterparts, which showed little interest in Canadian missions. Hence the initial strength of Anglicanism in British Columbia was not long maintained. The controversy within the church between evangelicals and Anglo-Catholics also absorbed much energy and attention. The former were shocked by the colourful ceremonies and vestments introduced by the latter. Evangelical congregations had been accustomed to considerable autonomy, and were troubled by the claims to episcopal authority made by those influenced by the Oxford movement, and fears of 'Romanism' were raised. Conflict between congregations and their bishops became visible in various highly publicized incidents. For example, there was strife in Halifax between the high church Bishop Hibbert Binney and the evangelicals; in Victoria, British Columbia, a group dissenting from the tractarian tendencies of Bishop George Hills founded a branch of the Reformed Episcopal Church; in Toronto the evangelicals, troubled by the high church atmosphere of Trinity College, founded what was later named Wycliffe College for the education of their candidates for the ministry.

In this difficult situation which hindered missionary advance, Archbishop Machray was at last convinced that an over-all autonomous synod with a house of bishops and a house of delegates to represent both clergy and laity was needed for the whole of Canada. After long preparation, the General Synod of the Church of England in Canada first met in 1893; Machray was chosen as the first Primate of All Canada. It took another ten years before a unified missionary society could be organized. Meanwhile, foreign mission work had been undertaken in Japan. As in other communions, women were deeply interested in missionary work and formed auxiliary societies; distinctive among Protestant churches was the founding in 1884 of the Anglican Sisterhood of St. John the Divine, devoted especially to social and educational service. In part because of their slowness in responding to the missionary challenge and achieving national structures, by the turn of the century the Anglicans had declined in relative size, claiming the allegiance of about 13 per cent of the population.

The Baptists were much smaller than the three large Protestant bodies, serving about 6 per cent of Canadians during the last part of the century. They were planted in Ontario and Manitoba largely through the evangelical zeal of individuals and congregations, for deep-rooted fears of central organization long kept the Baptists from forming effective national agencies. In 1888, however, a single convention for Quebec and Ontario was organized. Much of the strength of Baptist life remained, as before, in the Atlantic provinces. In 1884 the Baptist Convention of the Maritime provinces admitted the African Association of seventeen churches on the same basis as the other associations; Baptists continued to be the largest religious grouping among the blacks. By the early twentieth century the long-standing theological differences between the Regular (Calvinist) and Free (Arminian) Baptists had lessened, and in 1905–6 they merged as the Maritime United Baptists, but an effort to bring all Canadian Baptists into union failed at that time. Foreign mission work had been undertaken by various Baptist groups in India, Burma, and Bolivia.

Lutheranism was the only other Protestant tradition to claim as much as 1 per cent of the population—and little more than that until the increasing immigration toward the end of the century promoted its growth. In general, throughout this entire period Lutherans retained organizational ties with American synods. Those in Nova Scotia organized their own Evangelical Lutheran Synod in 1903, separating from the Pittsburgh Synod but continuing in connection with the conservative General Council, the second major effort to gather the regional synods into a larger unity. The larger Evangelical Lutheran Synod of Canada remained predominantly German-speaking, so in order to care for English interests the Synod of Central Canada, also associated with the General Council, was formed in 1909. The two synods co-operated in the founding of a theological seminary which opened in 1911 in Waterloo, Ontario. In the west, work among Lutheran immigrants had increased to the point that in 1897 a Manitoba Synod was organized, which also opened a second theological college in Edmonton (1913).

The impact of World War I hastened the trend towards English, so that in 1925 the two central Canada synods merged, continuing as part of the United Lutheran Church in America, the result of the 1918 merger of the General Council and the General Synod. Though small, Canadian Lutheranism was ethnically complex: those of Norwegian, Danish, Icelandic, and Swedish background founded their own congregations, some related to parallel bodies in the south. The Missouri Synod also extended its work into Canada, and by 1925 had formed three separate districts. By that date, Lutherans had a following of about 3½ per cent of the population, and were steadily increasing.

Though the Protestant denominations were in many ways competitive, they did recognize that they were partners in an effort to christianize Canada, and their individual members often co-operated in mutual endeavours. The various evangelical elements in the denominations were especially aware of their common orientation, and worked together in revival and other undertakings. For example, Dwight L. Moody's mission to Toronto in 1885 was sponsored by all the leading Protestant bodies. Evangelical laymen of various backgrounds took the lead in spreading the Y.M.C.A. in many cities and towns 'as a distinctive lay organization of Christian men concerned with providing rooms, libraries, lectures and other resources in order that larger numbers of young men might be attracted and led to "a Christian view of life"'. Beginning in New Brunswick in 1870, women co-operated in founding Y.W.C.A. chapters across Canada, giving particular attention to residences for young women and to student work.[6] Evangelicals of many backgrounds supported the significant work begun in Labrador in 1892 by a young medical missionary inspired by Moody, Wilfred T. Grenfell (1865-1940). He built an effective network of hospitals, schools, and industries. Evangelical Protestants laboured to base the life of Canadians on the foundation of Christian moral principles, usually defined in very personal terms. They opposed profanity, tobacco, Sabbath-breaking, undesirable literature, and the consumption of alcoholic beverages. The temperance movement, especially among Methodists and Baptists, grew strong late in the nineteenth century; one consequence was a shift to the use of unfermented grape juice in communion.

[6] Murray G. Ross, *The Y.M.C.A. in Canada: The Chronicle of a Century* (Toronto, 1951), p. 36; Josephine P. Harshaw, *When Women Work Together: A History of the Young Women's Christian Association in Canada* (n.p., 1966).

By far the largest single denomination in Canada was the Roman Catholic Church—by 1891 the total membership was counted at just over two million, about 41 per cent of the population. The largest bloc of Catholics were the French Canadians, who composed about 31 per cent of the population through the latter part of the century. The numbers of Catholics were increasing in Ontario and Manitoba; indeed they were the largest group in Manitoba when it was admitted to the Dominion. A. A. Taché, Bishop of St. Boniface since 1853, hoped that Manitoba would become a French Catholic stronghold, a Quebec of the west. He had consolidated Catholic strength among the French Métis, gathering them into parishes and building educational institutions for them. Largely through the sacrificial ministry of religious Orders, especially the Oblates, effective French missions were conducted among many Indian tribes, and they were encouraged and assisted to gather into communities equipped with schools. In many parts of the west, as in British Columbia, missionaries who had come to work among Indians found themselves serving the Catholics among the white settlers. But despite the hopes of Taché, not many French Canadians were drawn to the west; in Quebec religious and political leaders preferred to encourage colonization on Quebec's vast unoccupied frontiers rather than migration either to the west or to the United States, where many had gone. One consequence was that as the west was settled, the percentage of Catholic population slowly declined. But in absolute numbers the church everywhere was growing, and more efficient and decentralized organizational structures were needed, for at the time of Confederation there was but one ecclesiastical province under the Archbishop of Quebec for the whole country west of the Maritimes. Consequently, Toronto and St. Boniface were made into metropolitan sees in 1870 and 1871, while in 1886 Montreal and Ottawa also became archdioceses; suffragan sees were created as needed.

The tone of Canadian Catholicism was set largely by the French hierarchy centred in Quebec. These bishops were much concerned about the preservation of French Canada. Some of them warmly supported an ultramontane party which sought to follow strictly Pope Pius IX's *Syllabus of Errors* of 1864. Significantly, at the Vatican Council of 1869–70 only Thomas Connolly, Archbishop of Halifax, was in the minority opposed to the proclamation of the dogma of papal infallibility—a sharp contrast to the American hierarchy, where the opposition was much stronger. In the 1870s the ultramontane party launched a vigorous *programme catholique* to rally the faithful to the support of the pope and to bring the state to help with church goals in education and public morals.

Lay-led, the *programmistes* had the warm support of Ignace Bourget, Bishop of Montreal (1799–1885), and Louis-François Laflèche, Bishop of Trois-Rivières (1818–98). Although the terms were freely used at the time, the European meanings of 'ultramontane' and 'liberal' hardly fit the Canadian scene. Mason Wade observed that 'French-Canadian ultramontanism had a strong nationalist and even racist bent more characteristic of gallicanism than of its historical opposite'.[7] The intense and eloquent Laflèche insisted that the loss of the French language would also mean the loss of Catholic faith, and that the French Canadians were indeed a nation, based on the solidarity of family, language, nationality, and faith. He believed that the slightest trend toward liberalism in religion or in politics would weaken the foundations of French Canada. But the French Catholic 'liberals' were not those described in the *Syllabus of Errors*; their leading figure was Elzéar A. Taschereau (1820–98), Archbishop of Quebec. A former rector of Laval University, he spoke for a scholarly and conservative tradition which recognized the difference between religious and political liberalism, and tolerated the latter in view of the delicate political balance that had made Confederation possible. It was he who later secured the judgement against the Knights of Labor.

The crusading ultramontanists attacked the *Institut canadien* of Montreal, which had been founded long before to enrich cultural life in Quebec. Persons of various views supported it, but it was dominated by liberals, both political and religious. Bourget secured a papal condemnation against it, and its members were excommunicated. At that point, late in 1869, a prominent member, Joseph Guibord, died. The church refused to allow his body to be buried in consecrated ground, whereupon Institute members carried out a well-publicized and successful five-year legal fight to have the decision reversed. On the day of reburial, however, Bourget declared that the particular plot in which Guibord's remains were interred was forever unconsecrated. The bizarre event demonstrated the intensity of feeling between the contending groups, and curbed a threat to clerical control.

The ultramontanes were merciless in their criticism of Taschereau, who opposed their programme, and were determined to secure their own Catholic university in Montreal, rather than to remain dependent for professional education on Laval, which they declared was too interested in science and modern progress. Appeals to Rome, where representatives of both parties were heard by Pius IX, led to a victory for Laval, which received a papal charter (1876) and permission to establish a branch in

7 *The French Canadians, 1760–1945*, p. 341.

Montreal. The ultramontanes persisted in their efforts, however, in the early years of the reign of Pope Leo XIII. The struggle was fought out in the political arena, too, for ultramontanes generally voted Conservative while Taschereau had ties with the Liberals. Rome cautioned against the confusion of religious and political liberalism, and against undue clerical influence in elections, but determined lay ultramontanes found a new party, the *Castors* (Beavers), which rejected all compromise in their 'holy war'. Rome spoke again in 1884, once more supporting Laval, and when Taschereau became the first Canadian cardinal two years later while Laflèche was passed over in the naming of two new archbishops, the Canadian ultramontane programme was decisively defeated.

Religious and Political Tensions and Adjustments

On the broader Canadian scene in these same years new tension between Catholics and Protestants emerged. Early in the life of the Confederation the government moved too quickly into territory formerly held by the Hudson's Bay Company, before the formal transfer of title. The French Métis felt that their power was threatened, and in the autumn of 1869 revolted under the leadership of Louis Riel, one of their number who had at one time studied for the priesthood. The rebels' execution of Thomas Scott, a settler from Ontario and a member of the militantly Protestant Orange Order, inflamed religious and ethnic hatreds. The revolt was put down early in the spring; the Manitoba Act of 1870 promised to maintain the educational rights of both Catholic and Protestant minorities, and to allow the use of both French and English in government. The English population soon came to outnumber the French, and the Orangemen kept alive the memory of Scott's execution. Although amnesty was finally extended to most of the rebels, Riel was banished. He became something of a hero in Quebec before he settled in the United States.

Catholic–Protestant tensions were sporadically heightened by clashes over the educational rights of minorities. The French Catholics looked to the schools to ensure the continuation of their language and traditions; in Quebec, where they were in a strong majority, they set up two autonomous school systems so that the children of English Protestants would have adequate educational facilities. Understandably, they were angered when similar policies were not followed elsewhere. But in New Brunswick in 1871 an act forbade the teaching of religion and the continuation of French as the language of instruction in tax-supported schools. There was much annoyance and a refusal to pay school rates before some compromises were effected. French Catholics resented Protestant attempts to carry out evangelization programmes among them, especially when a former French Catholic priest, Charles Chiniquy, conducted missions in French Canada, offering sensational exposés of alleged Catholic mal-practices. Some other programmes of French evangelization were less offensive, but were unquestionably aimed at winning converts from the one interpretation of the faith to the other. On the other hand, Protestants were alarmed by the forceful critiques of Protestantism and of liberal values by the *programmistes*, and in Montreal a Protestant Defence Association was organized.

Then came the dramatic reappearance of Louis Riel on the Canadian scene in 1884 as a champion of the French Métis who were convinced that their interests were being slighted by the government at Ottawa. Driven by a sense of mission and an intense religiosity, Riel led the North-west Rebellion of 1885, envisioning an independent Métis nation in the west. In the face of an Indian uprising that would aid the rebels, the authorities quickly brought in Canadian troops, including French Cana-dians, and the insurgents surrendered before their superior fire-power. But thirty-eight soldiers had died, and the feeling of English-speaking Canadians was so strong that after trial and conviction it was felt in-expedient to grant mercy to the leader, and Riel was hanged before the year was out. This inflamed the French Canadians; under the leadership of Honoré Mercier the *Parti National* gained strength in Quebec and swept him into power in that province. As Wade wrote,

A whole generation in Quebec was filled with emotional hatred for all things English by the Riel affair. Mercier, who had won power by invoking the gibbet of Regina at ninety political meetings and had built his government on Riel's grave, did much to further the division between French and English in 1885 and to make it permanent.[8]

Certain of Mercier's actions, such as the compensation of the Jesuits for property that had been confiscated more than a hundred years before, deeply annoyed some Catholics as well as angering Protestants.

Reactions were not long in coming. In Ontario, where Protestants were so clearly dominant, separate schools were constitutionally guaran-teed, but efforts to increase the limited funds available to Catholic schools brought sharp Protestant response. An Equal Rights Association was formed, and a militant Protestant leader, D'Alton McCarthy, gained a wide hearing by attacking the separate schools as furthering a dangerous racialism by their use of French. Acts of 1892 and 1901 put serious restric-tions on the separate schools and weakened church influence in Ontario's

8 *The French Canadians, 1760–1945,* p. 421.

educational system. McCarthy had also crusaded in Manitoba, where in 1890 the dual school system was replaced with an interdenominational structure which denied the right of instruction in minority languages. The French Canadians bitterly protested these denials of their rights. Archbishop Taché died in 1894; his successor, J.-P.-F. Laforce Langevin, carried the fight against the Manitoba decision to the Parliament, where the Conservative government promised relief.

At this point an irenic French-Canadian leader, a Liberal, Wilfrid Laurier (1841–1919), who for many years had been insisting that the organization of a Catholic party would force Protestants to organize one of their own and lead to religious war, argued that the overthrow of provincial autonomy would set a precedent dangerous for Quebec. He became Canada's Prime Minister in 1896, a post he was to hold for fifteen years. As opposed to Mercier, whose focus was on Quebec, Laurier's vision was national, and he devoted himself to racial reconciliation. He soon worked out a compromise with Manitoba officials so that French could be taught under certain conditions, and Catholic instruction given after hours. Many were dissatisfied with the settlement, and later school battles in the new (1905) provinces of Alberta and Saskatchewan kept the issue alive. But despite the outcries of militants on both sides, the majority saw that Canada's viability as a nation depended on a measure of compromise, as advocated by Laurier.

During these intense conflicts, Catholic parishes and institutions for both French and English were flourishing, especially as economic conditions improved late in the century. The awakening of the Acadian people continued; they pressed for more priests of their own background, and in 1912 an Acadian bishop was placed over a Maritime see. There was growing Catholic interest in foreign missions, especially among French-Canadian priests who often chose Africa as their field of service.

By the turn of the century, the six major denominations had constituencies covering well over 90 per cent of the Dominion's population, and all but the two smaller bodies, Baptist and Lutheran, had achieved national organizational structures. Despite the many tensions and controversies, the churches were clearly holding the loyalties of the vast majority of the people. All the churches were carrying out effective missionary enterprises at home and abroad. Missions among the Indians had brought more than three-quarters of them within the Christian fold; the relatively better treatment of the Indians in Canada as compared to the United States was to a considerable extent an achievement of the churches. The missionaries were convinced of the superiority of both their religion and their civilization, and often did seek to win Indians to white cultural ways, yet also sought to protect Indian rights.

Also by the beginning of the new century, a distinctive development in the way church colleges were related to the growth of state-supported higher education was being worked out. The period before Confederation was characterized by D. C. Masters as 'the Golden Age in the history of church colleges', but the emergence of the secular ideal in university education threatened the future of the church-related institutions. A significant pattern of adjustment was worked out in Manitoba in 1877 in which St. John's (Anglican), St. Boniface (Roman Catholic), and Manitoba College (Presbyterian) federated to form the University of Manitoba as a non-denominational, provincial but not state-supported institution. Common standards and examinations for degrees to be conferred by the new university were decided upon, but teaching was in the hands of the three colleges. As Masters has observed:

The establishment of the University was an important landmark in the history of church colleges in Canada. It meant that the component colleges were able to continue the liberal arts course in a church atmosphere, while sharing in the benefits of membership in a larger body. The unique Canadian achievement in higher education, the working out of a relationship between church colleges and higher education had begun.[9]

Later the Methodist college, Wesley, also affiliated with the university.

In Toronto the story was somewhat different, for hopes that the denominational colleges would federate with the university at its founding in 1849 were long deferred. In the 1880s limited federation with the University of Toronto was worked out by St. Michael's (Roman Catholic), and by three theological colleges, Wycliffe (Anglican), Knox (Presbyterian), and Toronto Baptist College, a forerunner of McMaster University. In 1886 Victoria University (Methodist) was authorized by the General Conference to federate, and in the following year the University Act provided that affiliating colleges would withhold their right to grant degrees except in theology, would turn over to the university instruction in certain (especially scientific) subjects, and would submit control of examinations to the university senate. State supervision in certain academic matters was accepted in return for state support. The high church Anglican Trinity College also came into the federation in 1904, after an amendment permitting it to provide for the religious instruction and worship of its own students was passed.

Not all the church colleges came into federation. Some dropped their

9 *Protestant Church Colleges in Canada*, pp. 29, 95–6.

formal church relationship—for example, Queen's University (Presbyterian) in 1877 and the University of Western Ontario (Anglican) in 1908. Others remained independent, such as the Baptist Acadia University in Nova Scotia, the Anglican Bishop's University in Quebec, and the Methodist Mount Allison University in New Brunswick, and a number of Roman Catholic institutions. The federation pattern, however, proved important for both church and society in Canada, for it embodied the principles that church institutions made significant contributions to higher education, and could avail themselves of the advantages of state resources for educational advance. It was an arrangement not possible in the United States because of the American understanding of the separation of church and state.

The churches entered the twentieth century in an optimistic and expansive mood. Economic prosperity had come at last, the gross national product was markedly increasing and many Canadians, especially those of British background, took pride in the confident imperialism of the British Empire of which they were a part. Though French-Canadian nationalism remained a force, the policies of the Laurier administration generally eased racial tensions nationally. The government's programme of attracting immigrants to settle the west came to rich fruition as a great influx added one-third to the population. In the decade 1901–11 more than a million persons came to Manitoba, Saskatchewan, and Alberta. Some of them were from the United States—reversing a long trend in the other direction —and Great Britain, but there also came increasing numbers of religious minorities from eastern Europe. Wherever these immigrants came—and they moved into the growing urban centres as well as on to the prairies— familiar balances in religious life were upset. Delicate adjustments between French and Irish Catholic leadership were altered by the newcomers. 'All Canadian churches had deep roots in national traditions', wrote John Webster Grant, 'and the preservation of ethnic patterns often took on quasi-religious connotations.'[10]

The leading Protestant denominations identified their mission with that of the British peoples, and hastened to 'Canadianize' the aliens. Chaplains were maintained at ports of entry, immigrant aid societies were formed, and pastoral work was extended to new groups. It was soon found that the best approach was through hospitals and schools, and through the diversified programmes of 'All Peoples' Missions', as pioneered by the Methodist J. S. Woodsworth (1874–1942), son of the superintendent of western missions. The goal of all this effort was boldly stated in

---

[10] *The Church in the Canadian Era*, p. 93.

a book issued under Methodist, Presbyterian, and Congregational auspices in 1917. 'When the Dominions, full grown, stand side by side with the Motherland, one in speech, one in their ideals of justice and freedom and one in their most holy faith, what will there be under God that they will not be able to do for the welfare of the Nations and the Kingdom of Jesus?' It was recognized that the French Roman Catholic minority would 'retard the unifying of our national life', and hence urged French evangelization 'to call people back to the foundation truths, to the Gospel as Christ gave it, unencumbered by the traditions of men, and thus get rid of all that stands between the soul and its Saviour'. These Protestants hoped a solution to the problem was 'to appreciate and cooperate with the best in their race and faith and, by sharing with them the blessings of our own, unite both in building up in Canada "His Dominion" '.[11]

Within Catholicism, the predominance of the French element in church and hierarchy was lessened as various minorities demanded a larger role. Newcomers who had to learn a new language generally found English preferable for it was more widely used. As hope for a French-Catholic west faded, bishops whose native tongue was English were named for prominent positions. In 1910 Neil McNeil (1851–1934) was called from Newfoundland to become Archbishop of Vancouver; two years later he was transferred to the metropolitan see of Toronto, where he especially interested himself in strengthening St. Augustine's seminary for the education of English-speaking priests. English-speaking prelates were also named for the diocese of Calgary, and for the archdiocese of Winnipeg, formed by the division of the archdiocese of St. Boniface.

In French Canada alarm was felt at Protestant expressions of a religious imperialism. French Canadians were even more troubled by the emergence of political imperialism, brought to the fore by Canadian participation in the Boer War at the beginning of the century. A political protégé of Laurier, Henri Bourassa, emerged as a critic of such participation and became the dominant hero of an intense French-Canadian nationalism, and its leading voice. The paths of the two men diverged; an alliance of the Conservative party with French nationalists led to the fall of the Laurier regime in 1911 and brought in as prime minister Robert L. Borden, whose political strength was based in Ontario. During World War I, after initial enthusiasm, French Canadians were not generally ardent supporters of the military effort, many believing that the war was Britain's problem which did not directly involve them. Enlistments from

---

[11] William T. Gunn, *His Dominion* (n.p., 1917), pp. 20, 157–8, 56. See N. Keith Clifford, 'His Dominion: A Vision in Crisis', *Studies in Religion*, ii (1973), 315–26.

Quebec lagged behind other parts of the country, and conscription was sharply opposed. Anti-draft riots broke out in the city of Quebec in March 1918; when a Toronto battalion charged the crowd with fixed bayonets, fuel was poured on a raging fire of resentment, checked only after some civilians were killed, many casualties suffered on both sides, and after church and Press called for truce. Behind the resistance of French Canadians to the war effort was continuing anger at the restrictions on Catholic schools and the use of French in Ontario; they repeatedly argued for the priority of correcting injustices at home. In the flush of victory in the autumn, English-Canadian bitterness toward Quebec softened, but French-Canadian nationalists long remembered the troubles of 1917–18. Under Abbé Lionel Groulx, a forceful interpreter of history from the viewpoint of French Catholic Canada, a new provincial nationalism which sometimes had separatist overtones emerged. A number of French Catholic labour and agricultural organizations were formed in the 1920s.

Liberal Theology and the Social Gospel

There was little parallel in Canadian Catholicism to the emergence of liberal theology among Protestants. By the late nineteenth century the universities, especially Queen's and Toronto, had developed high standards of academic excellence. Attention was given to evolutionary theory and biblical criticism, usually in a moderate way as students were guided toward a synthesis of inherited faith and modern thought. The theological colleges, many of them related to the universities, rather cautiously followed. Patterns of preaching, worship, and education in the Protestant churches were probably more widely affected by the historical study of Scripture and tradition than was the case in the United States. The missionary emphasis and moral concern of the older evangelicalism were combined with the newer perspectives in a confident Christocentric liberalism that won followers in all the major denominations. Especially in the growing urban areas, the rising economic standard of many of the faithful was reflected in the impressiveness of new church buildings, in the growing formality and decorum of services of worship, and in lessened insistence on doctrinal precision.

An example of the increasing tolerance on theological matters was the quite different result of controversies which erupted at Victoria University in 1890 and 1909. In the first instance, George C. Workman, professor of Old Testament language and literature, challenged prevailing views that Jesus of Nazareth was 'present to the thoughts of the prophets as they visualized the promised and coming Messiah'. He was attacked by the general superintendent of the Methodist Church, Albert Carman, among others, and was removed from the theological faculty. Nineteen years later George Jackson, a pastor of British background, gave a lecture in the Toronto Y.M.C.A. on Genesis, in which he insisted on the right of students to use scientific methods in an effort to interpret the records and discover the real meaning of biblical passages. He too was attacked by Superintendent Carman, but nevertheless was appointed professor of English Bible at Victoria. In 1910 an attempt to have such teaching condemned by the General Conference failed. The general effect of the controversy was 'a wholesome liberation of the thinking of that Church from a purely dogmatic approach, and to this extent tended to harmonize the search for Christian truth with the prevailing methods used in other phases of research'.[12] Somewhat similarly, at the Montreal Diocesan College, an Anglican institution, Frederick J. Steen had been forced to resign in 1901 from the chair of Apologetics and Church History because of his liberal views, yet opinions quite similar to his were soon to be offered by G. Abbott Smith, who introduced higher criticism into his lectures on the New Testament. And at McMaster University, I. G. Matthews was long under attack for his critical interpretation of Old Testament materials, but the right of scholars in that Baptist university to pursue their investigations freely was vindicated. The rising educational level and the growing sophistication of the times probably favoured the spread of liberal thought among Protestants.

Canadian Christians of all denominations in the nineteenth century showed concern for orphans, the handicapped, the aged, and the poor by erecting charitable institutions and missions to help unfortunate individuals. With spreading industrialization and urbanization towards the end of the century came an increase in the number of victims of unemployment and destitution, and a growing realization that there were moral and social evils that needed correction. Many Christians believed that the neglect of Sunday as a day of rest increased those evils, and most Protestant denominations officially supported the Lord's Day Alliance of Canada. Under the secretaryship of J. G. Shearer, a Presbyterian minister, an alliance of church and labour forces was built on the propositions that a life of uninterrupted toil is brutalizing and that leisure is necessary for cultural and spiritual development. In the face of considerable opposition from commercial interests and the Press, and with the co-operation of Roman Catholic leaders, the alliance succeeded in getting Parliament in

[12] J. H. Riddell, *Methodism in the Middle West* (Toronto, 1946), pp. 229, 290.

1906 to pass a uniform Lord's Day Act. This victory encouraged those who hoped to bring further reforms by legislation.

A still more popular cause among Protestants in the later nineteenth century was the war against alcohol, and the increasing power of temperance forces was exhibited in the passage of local legislation restricting or prohibiting the sale of liquor. The Methodist, Presbyterian, and Baptist churches, with some support from the Anglicans, backed the crusade for prohibition. In the early twentieth century the Roman Catholic Archbishop of Montreal, Paul Bruchési, supported the temperance crusade, but most Catholic clergy favoured voluntary abstinence and not legal prohibition. An Anti-Alcohol League of the Roman Catholic Church won a considerable following.

As social problems increased during the hard times of the 1890s and in the period of rapid industrialization in the following decade, the social gospel became widespread in Protestantism. The way had been prepared by the spread of evangelical liberal theology. Canadian leaders studied the social Christian movements of Britain and the United States. Among the Baptists, for example, the social gospel 'came from two main sources: the contact of some of the younger ministers with exponents of the Social Gospel in American theological schools, and the widely read writings of these same teachers, one of the most important of whom was Dr. Walter Rauschenbusch of Rochester Theological Seminary'.[13] Richard Allen has concluded that 'no major Protestant denomination in the nation escaped the impact of the social gospel, and few did not contribute some major figure to the movement'.[14] Methodists and Presbyterians were especially prominent in the new development, which was historically related to earlier campaigns for moral reform. Anglican social Christianity was more influenced by British than by American sources.

The leading Canadian interpreter of social gospel thought was Salem G. Bland (1859–1950), a Methodist who joined the faculty of Wesley College in Winnipeg in 1903. Though there were radical, progressive, and conservative strands in Canadian as in American social Christianity from its beginnings in the 1890s up to the outbreak of World War I, in Canada the movement remained remarkably cohesive. An influential practitioner of social gospel teachings was J. S. Woodsworth, superintendent of All Peoples' Mission in Winnipeg. He worked among newcomers to the country who were facing unemployment, inadequate housing and health services, and public neglect. His accounts of his experiences, *Strangers*

---

[13] Levy, *Baptists of the Maritime Provinces*, p. 299.
[14] *The Social Passion: Religion and Social Reform in Canada, 1914–1928* (Toronto, 1971), p. 15.

Within Our Gates (1909) and *My Neighbor* (1911) helped to popularize the growing movement. University settlement houses, promoted especially by Sara Libby Carson, a Presbyterian who had experience in settlement houses across the border, were important in the spread of reform sentiment. Youth fellowships sponsored by the churches and the Y.M.C.A. and Y.W.C.A. also contributed to the growth of the social gospel.

By the second decade of the century the social emphasis was strong in Protestant churches, but it had not had much effect on either the business community or the working classes. As in the United States, the social gospel was especially influential in the middle classes. A high point was the Social Service Congress in Ottawa in 1914, to which religious, community, labour, and government organizations sent representatives. Charles Stelzle and Graham Taylor, so prominent in the American movement, were speakers, as were forty Canadians, half of them clergymen. The social service chaplain for the Toronto Diocese of the Church of England in Canada concluded that 'the social conscience is awake as never before'.[15]

Catholic social thought and action in the same period drew its inspiration from a different source, Pope Leo XIII's social encyclical, *Rerum novarum*. In keeping with its concern for labour and for the development of a network of institutions under church influence, a series of Catholic unions were organized. In most of them clerical influence was present. By 1911 these unions had a membership of some 350,000 and had become involved in collective bargaining.

Most of those influenced by the Protestant social gospel favoured Canadian participation in World War I. Since the churches had been deeply involved in establishing values and norms for Canadian life, they quite uncritically identified themselves with the nation in a time of crisis. They threw themselves into the war effort vigorously, sometimes going to extremes in becoming agents of recruitment and in transmitting stories of atrocity about the enemy. The image of holy war was invoked, and Protestants generally supported conscription in 1917. But social gospel concerns were not a casualty of the war. The drive for prohibition, a cause dear to the hearts of social Christians, triumphed in all the provinces before the second decade was over. Often promoted as a patriotic measure, prohibition won support from all the churches, and from certain French-Canadian and labour interests. After this victory, the coming of the Kingdom of God on earth, so often envisioned by social gospel advocates, seemed near, and as the end of the war approached some strong statements favouring economic and social reform were made by responsible church

[15] *Ibid.*, p. 24.

bodies. The social emphasis was also strong in the Inter-Church Forward Movement, which was parallel to but more soberly planned than the Interchurch World Movement to the south. It marked a new high point in effective co-operation between the churches, and went well over its financial goal.

Even as these social gospel achievements during the years of the war and its immediate aftermath were recorded, certain tensions within the movement's leadership emerged. Some of the most prominent figures— William Irvine (Presbyterian), Salem Bland, A. E. Smith, J. S. Woodsworth, and William Ivens (all Methodists)—espoused a more radical, socialist programme of social reconstruction than the main body of social gospel moderates could accept. The radicals were critical of the conduct of the war, and Woodsworth and Ivens were also outspoken pacifists, at a time when that position was highly unpopular. These Christian socialists set their hopes on labour churches and on the causes of agrarian and urban working people. They supported the Winnipeg General Sympathetic Strike of 1919, which arose over the right of metal-workers to bargain collectively through agents of their choice. The strike was supported by many in other cities across Canada as a step toward 'One Big Union'. When the strike failed, Ivens and Woodsworth were among those arrested. The more moderate of the social gospel leaders were divided in their attitude toward the great strike, but were not as unqualified in their opposition as many others in positions of religious and political power. Even so, a decisive break in the movement had come; the radicals dropped out of denominational circles, and as their labour churches had difficulty gathering permanent constituencies and rather quickly declined, they turned to radical politics. Woodsworth and Irvine were elected to Parliament late in 1921, identifying themselves with the Progressive minority.

Despite this rift, social gospel leaders in the churches faced the 1920s in a confident mood. The Social Service Council of Canada, an affiliation of national religious and social agencies with provincial units, secured the foremost Presbyterian leader of social work, J. G. Shearer, as its executive, and enjoyed some co-operation with Roman Catholic leaders. In 1925, one of the favourite causes of the social gospel, church union, bore fruit in the formation of the United Church of Canada.

The United Church of Canada

In the last half of the nineteenth century in Canada as elsewhere in the Protestant world there was considerable discussion of Christian unity. When denominational reunions took place, they were interpreted as first steps towards a still larger union. The custom of the exchange of fraternal delegates at national denominational meetings provided opportunities for continued discussion of eventual church union. Many reasons for uniting were offered; in 1889, for example, the Presbyterian William Caven, principal of Knox College, declared:

The ideal of the unity of believers set forth in the Scriptures—especially in our Lord's Intercessory Prayer—while chiefly spiritual in its nature, can be fully represented in an undivided state of the visible Church, in which perfect fellowship shall be maintained throughout the entire body of Christ; and it is the duty of the Church, and of all its members continually, to aspire towards, and labor for, the completeness of this manifested union in the Lord.[16]

He made these remarks at a conference to discuss union at the invitation of the Provincial Synod of the Church of England in Canada. Presbyterian and Methodist representatives met with the Anglicans in Toronto in an atmosphere of great cordiality, but the Anglican stance on the historic episcopate—the Lambeth Quadrilateral had been adopted in 1888—was only one of the difficulties that forestalled the formulation of a basis of union.[17] Yet the dream did not die; in 1893 the General Assembly of the Presbyterian Church in Canada declared itself always 'ready to entertain the subject of union with other Evangelical Churches', and appointed a committee to confer with such other denominational groups as might be named.[18] There were other similar actions, but they had no concrete result; some voluntary union societies across denominational lines kept interest in the effort alive.

In 1902 there was an important breakthrough. The General Conference of the Methodist Church meeting in Winnipeg routinely received the fraternal delegates of the Presbyterian Church. The communion's moderator, George P. Bryce, spoke about how much the two churches had in common; the principal of Manitoba College, William Patrick, pointed to the need for a great national church and proposed a union; Charles W. Gordon, a Winnipeg pastor famous for his novels under the pseudonym Ralph Conner, called attention to the common foe of materialism facing both churches in the west. Patrick's proposal sparked much interest; over the next few days the subject of union was much in Methodist minds.

[16] As quoted by Kenneth H. Cousland, 'A Brief History of the Church Union Movement in Canada', in Thomas B. Kilpatrick, *Our Common Faith* (Toronto, 1928), p. 5.

[17] Claris E. Silcox, *Church Union in Canada: Its Causes and Consequences* (New York, 1933), pp. 106–10.

[18] *The Acts and Proceedings of the Nineteenth General Assembly of the Presbyterian Church in Canada . . . 1893*, p. 47.

Before the conference adjourned, the fraternal delegates from the Congregational churches asked that their churches be part of any union negotiations. Though they had a long history in Canada, the Congregationalists had been declining steadily in relative size through the nineteenth century, and at that point could claim the allegiance of only about a half per cent of the population—less than one-thirtieth the size of Methodists or Presbyterians. They were strongest in the Maritimes, and had not achieved a national organization. Although they maintained missions among some German and Swedish groups, they had not been very successful in the west, perhaps because of the liberalism and sophistication of their presentation of the gospel. But they were much interested in union. Before the Methodist Conference adjourned, it approved the naming of a Standing Committee and invited other denominations to do the same that together the feasibility of organic union could be explored.

Representatives of the Methodist Church, the Presbyterian Church, and the several Congregational Unions formed a Joint Committee on Union which met five times between 1904 and 1908, and proliferated a series of sub-committees as a Basis of Union was prepared. An effort was made to bring Anglicans and Baptists into the negotiations, but both declined. The former were bound by the Lambeth Quadrilateral to insist on the historic episcopate, while the latter found it necessary to maintain a separate existence to further their Baptist distinctives. During these years of preparation, the Congregationalists achieved their own national union in 1906, and the next year absorbed a very small Canadian church of American origin, the United Brethren in Christ.

The development of a satisfactory doctrinal statement as the first main part of the Basis did not raise serious difficulties. By the early twentieth century, practical and social concerns seemed much more pressing than theological matters. Biblical criticism and liberal trends eroded some of the older concepts of theological authority, and in all the churches there was impatience with detailed creeds—less in the Presbyterian than in the other two. The aim of the committee was to develop a brief new statement of faith which would bring together the characteristic theological features of each participating communion in a non-controversial way. Two Presbyterian documents were found helpful: A Brief Statement of the Reformed Faith, prepared by the Presbyterian Church in the United States of America (1902), and the Articles of Faith of the Presbyterian Church of England (1890). The first twelve of the Twenty Articles that were finally decided upon as the doctrinal basis for the United Church were directly based on the Brief Statement. The Articles brought together mild

Calvinism and mild Arminianism in a rather conservative short consensus. The Congregational delegation fought unsuccessfully for further simplification of the Articles, but in one crucial matter they gained their point. Arguing for the priority of Christian experience over creedal formulas, they succeeded in eliminating the requirement that ministers in the United Church should subscribe to the new standards. An introductory statement to the articles did acknowledge 'the teaching of the great creeds of the ancient Church. We further maintain our allegiance to the evangelical doctrines of the Reformation . . .'[19] The Twenty Articles reflected main Protestant doctrinal positions in quite traditional language, and did not seriously reflect the liberal and social movements that were then conspicuous in the negotiating churches.

Some of the practical questions of blending the three polities were long debated. It was finally agreed in rather general terms to allow the congregations to call ministers if they wished, but the right of appointment was vested in the settlement committees of the conferences. Though the autonomy of local congregations was respected, the Basis of Union proposed a connectional system of government, a pyramidal organization moving from the congregations at the base up to presbyteries, regional conferences, and a national General Council.

By the time the Basis of Union was completed and sent to the churches for consideration, much enthusiasm for the United Church had been generated. The vision of a national church was quite captivating. A book entitled *A National Church* had been published in 1898 by an American Episcopalian, William R. Huntington. Though written with the American scene in mind, the book never caught on in the United States. The Protestant picture there was considerably more diversified, and the approach to unity through the co-operation of autonomous denominations was widely favoured over church union. In Canada, the two leading churches in the negotiations for the United Church, Methodist and Presbyterian, had overcome their organizational divisions during the nineteenth century and each had become unified, while in the United States these denominations (among others) had suffered serious schisms, especially over slavery, and remained sectionally divided. Talk of a national church was premature; federation was the more feasible first step. Hence by the time the Canadian Basis of Union was essentially completed in 1908, the Americans were forming the Federal Council of the Churches of Christ. The parallel Canadian organization was not to be founded until 1944;

---

[19] As quoted by Randolph C. Chalmers, *See the Christ Stand! A Study in Doctrine in The United Church of Canada* (Toronto, 1945), p. 300.

in Canada the drive for organic Protestant unity took priority over the federative approach.

Huntington's book, *A National Church*, thus actually fitted Canada, where, in John Webster Grant's words, 'the phrase "national church" was a spectacular success'. It was even referred to in the preamble to the Basis, which declared that 'It shall be the policy of The United Church to foster the spirit of unity in the hope that this sentiment of unity may in due time, so far as Canada is concerned, take shape in a Church which may fittingly be described as national'.[20] The Congregational Union was clearly and strongly in favour of such a church. In 1910 the General Assembly of the Presbyterian Church approved the proposed Basis, and ordered the presbyteries to vote on the matter. The Methodist General Conference also declared its approval of the Basis, directing it to be submitted to the annual conferences for a decisive vote.

The responses were favourable to union. Fifty presbyteries voted to approve and twenty disapproved—the total individual vote was 793 to 476.[21] The Methodists had less division: ten conferences favoured the union and only one did not; 1,579 votes were cast in favour and 270 against. There were understandable reasons why only the Newfoundland Conference voted in the negative. On that island the two main churches were Anglican and Methodist, with very few Presbyterians or Congregationalists, so that there was little point to union there from a Methodist perspective. Furthermore, Methodist ties in Newfoundland, which did not come into the Dominion until 1949, were more with England than Canada, despite the formal relationship with Canadian Methodism.

The two large churches then submitted the question to their memberships. The Methodists voted overwhelmingly for the Basis of Union and reported themselves ready to proceed to union, but about a third of the Presbyterians voted against it, offering suggestions for its modification. The General Assembly voted to delay union, but urged further conference and discussion in the expectation that practically unanimous action could be secured within a reasonable time. Various groups opposed to union organized against it. Many of the opposition cited the loss of the requirement of subscription by ministers to the Westminster Confession of Faith in their reaction. One pastor observed that

it was indeed surprising that many ministers and elders voted in favour of the substitution of the doctrinal part of the 'Basis of Union' for the 'Confession of

---

[20] John Webster Grant, *The Canadian Experience of Church Union* (London, 1967), p. 30.
[21] The voting details are recorded in Silcox, *Church Union in Canada, passim*, and Appendix F.

Faith', seeing that there is wanting to it the virile Pauline doctrine of Predestination, that there is in it no reference to the covenant made with Adam, and that
particular election and particular redemption are not embraced in it.

Others objected to the proposed organization, and there was criticism
of the tactics used by the unionist majority. Undercurrents of dislike of
Methodist Arminianism and Methodist enthusiasms for temperance and
social gospel surfaced. Deep-rooted Scottish resistance to a tradition of
English origin could be observed; the pastor quoted above went on to
deplore the loss of 'the high doctrines of "Free-will and Fate", which Scottish artizans have been wont to discuss when they met at the street corner,
and which had not a little to do with shaping Scottish life and character'.[22]
Some of the objectors more diplomatically argued that federation, like
the recently organized Federal Council of the Churches of Christ in
America, would be preferable to organic union.

An important fact in the dynamics for union was the growing number
of 'local union' churches, especially in rural areas where small communities
had a handful of tiny, inadequate, competing congregations. As soon as
the Basis of Union was published, a number of local congregations merged
in anticipation of the coming United Church. Somewhat embarrassed
by this spontaneous local enthusiasm, denominational leaders were able
to persuade many such merged congregations to maintain ties with the
denominations. But a sense of unity among the new-style congregations
arose, and a General Council of Local Union Churches was formed in
1912 in Saskatchewan. This agency served to relate union congregations
to the denominations in matters of mission funds, ministerial standing,
and property tenure, and actually became a fourth member when the
United Church was finally founded. The presence of these and of other
types of union churches—some 3,000 in all by 1925—served to press the
denominations to union.

By the second decade of the century the Presbyterian Church had become the largest Protestant church in the land, and unionists hoped it
could be brought as unanimously as possible into the proposed merger.
But the vote on the slightly amended Basis of Union in 1915 showed that
fifty-three of the presbyteries approved (by then there were seventy-six
in all), but that in the popular vote the minority had increased to nearly
40 per cent, concentrated largely in the conservative east. Nevertheless,
the General Assembly at Winnipeg in 1916, acting as the supreme court
of the church whose decisions were final, resolved (406 to 90) to go ahead

---

[22] Robert Campbell, *The Relations of the Christian Churches* (Toronto, 1913), pp. 216-17.

with the union, appointing a committee to take the necessary legal steps and to report back to the second meeting of the Assembly following the war. The opposition then organized the Presbyterian Church Association and launched a determined effort to halt the union. The 1917 Assembly unanimously agreed to drop all controversy until after the war. The Congregationalists and Methodists, ready to proceed to union, showed signs of impatience. The matter came to vote again in the Assembly of 1921; by then it was clear that schism on one side or the other was inevitable. The decision (414 to 107) was to consummate the union; the drafting of the necessary legislation was authorized. There followed a crescendo of bitterness as the congregations had to decide with which side they would align.

At the heart of the controversy were irreconcilable views. The unionists insisted that a proper action had been taken through the specified channels of Presbyterian government and that the majority had clearly spoken for union. The non-concurrents were convinced that proper standards for the ministry had been neglected in the proceedings and that the unionists were in fact leaving the Presbyterian Church, which they were free to do, but not to move the whole church to a new foundation. Presbyterians traditionally have emphasized the unity of the church as the first principle of their polity, but one of the non-concurrents explained that 'this does not mean organic union within the church as over against uncontrolled individualistic movements. The idea was and is that of the church standing for authority as against rash or anarchic democracy'.[23] The conflict between these viewpoints came to its bitter conclusion in the 1920s.

The final battle was fought in the full glare of general publicity because enabling legislation concerning matters of property and funds had to be secured from provincial legislatures and from the Dominion Parliament. At every stage the opposition was intense and well organized. The climax before Parliament was dramatic in that the prime minister, William Lyon Mackenzie King, a Presbyterian, was the leading spokesman for the non-concurrents, while Arthur Meighen, former prime minister and leader of the opposition, championed the union cause, and is generally agreed to have made the decisive speech that paved the way for the merger. The needed bill received royal assent on 19 July 1924, to go into effect on 10 June 1925. Any congregation wanting to stay out of union had to vote

---

[23] E. Lloyd Morrow, *Church Union in Canada: Its History, Motives, Doctrines and Government* (Toronto, 1923), p. 199. An analysis of the various elements among the non-concurrents has been prepared by Allan L. Farris, 'The Fathers of 1925', in *Enkindled by the Word: Essays on Presbyterianism in Canada* (Toronto, 1966), pp. 59–82.

to do so; in the final struggle for the congregations the bitterness often became intense and emotional as many congregations, neighbourhoods, and families became sharply divided. The division of property by a neutral award commission caused further hard feelings; about 31 per cent of the church's general assets went to the continuing Presbyterian Church, including two theological colleges, Knox in Toronto with its fine new buildings, and the Presbyterian College in Montreal.

When the General Assembly met in Toronto just prior to union, seventy-nine commissioners laid a protest on the table, saying it would be lawful for them to continue in session for the continuance of the Presbyterian Church in Canada, maintaining the Confession of Faith and standards of the church as hitherto understood. Then, as the Assembly was about to adjourn on 9 June, Ephraim Scott, a minister and editor, rose to protest and was refused, but the seventy-nine gathered to reconstitute the Assembly as the organ blared. On the next day, the United Church of Canada came into existence. The statistics need considerable interpretation for local congregations varied greatly in size, but they show that the 4,797 Methodist, 3,728 Presbyterian, and 166 Congregational churches entered the union at the outset, while 784 Presbyterian (including some of the largest) and 8 Congregational did not. Perhaps slightly less than two-thirds of the Presbyterians entered the United Church on 10 June as three streams of tradition flowed together in one of the most significant church unions since the Reformation. The new church began with a membership of just over 600,000, while the continuing Presbyterian Church had about one-fourth of that number. The total number of 'adherents' of each church according to the census records was much higher; by 1931 the figure had passed two million for the United Church, about 20 per cent of the population, and had reached 860,000 for the Presbyterians.

The United Church of Canada was able to bring its three traditions into an effective whole rather quickly, in part because of the long period of preparation and testing. It did not deny its continuity with its three pasts, and became a member of the world confessional bodies of each, the Ecumenical Methodist Conference, the International Congregational Council, and the World Alliance of Reformed Churches Holding the Presbyterian System. It was also recognized by the Protestant churches of Scotland and Ireland. As the largest Protestant communion in the Dominion, it began early to fulfil some of the functions of a national church. Its thought and life were cast in the general patterns of evangelical liberal theology and the social gospel; its emergence was recognized as one of the major achievements of social Christianity. One of the strong units of the new church was its department of Evangelism and Social Service.

Yet the social gospel was already in decline by 1925. Its dreams for the speedy christianization of Canada were clouded by the many problems of the troubled twenties, of which the defeat of prohibition in Ontario in 1926 was one keenly felt by the churches. The criticism directed from various quarters at the liberal and optimistic theological premisses of the social gospel led to a loss of confidence and resiliency. And despite the hope that the United Church would pave the way for further union, the achievement of 1925 marked the end—a somewhat delayed end—of union enthusiasm for many decades. Coolness rather than a spirit of unity was characteristic of the years following 1925, illustrated by continuing rivalries between United and Presbyterian churches. The achievement of the United Church was a great one, but it came at a high cost.

A Broadening Denominational Spectrum

While major themes of the religious history of Canada from 1867 to 1925 are those of the unification of denominational families and the emergence of the United Church, another important development going on at the same time was the proliferation of smaller religious bodies, often regarded as sects or cults from the viewpoint of the larger churches. Some of the smaller groups had long been on the Canadian scene and simply continued on a modest scale; others were newcomers whose arrival was marked with controversy. No attempt will be made to list them all; some were very tiny yet had complex histories involving changes of name, schisms, and combinations.[24] Among the traditions which had a Canadian past were the Moravians, with missions among the Eskimos in Labrador and a small group of congregations centred in Alberta; the Friends, whose divided ranks were slowly dwindling; the Disciples of Christ who organized on a national basis in 1922; and the Latter-day Saints, who developed a community and built a temple in Cardston, Alberta. Some smaller Methodist bodies remained apart from the unionist trends; the Free Methodist Church, the Evangelical Church (located largely among Germans in Ontario), and small African Methodist Episcopal, African Methodist Episcopal Zion, and British Methodist Episcopal churches among blacks—half of whom lived in the Halifax area.

While Mennonites had first come to Canada in the late eighteenth

---

[24] For a careful study of one province, which shows clearly how complicated the history of smaller religious movements can be, see W. E. Mann, *Sect, Cult, and Church in Alberta* (Toronto, 1955), especially chapter II.

century, their numbers were much increased in 1874 when a group of these pacifist children of the radical Reformation migrated from Russia to Manitoba, and took to farming on the open prairie. Further Mennonites came from other sources, so that a complex organizational picture emerged, with half a dozen separate bodies, several of them parts of American denominations. Great tension between these independent folk and the Manitoba government appeared in the 1890s when denominational school systems were eliminated. The difficulties were later intensified in further disputes, especially during World War I when their private schools were closed and public hostility was directed against them. Some conservative Mennonites emigrated to settle in Central and South America. But other descendants of the Anabaptists came into the country at that time. Because of conscription and interference in their lives in the United States during World War I, the Hutterian Brethren, a very strict group which had preserved its traditions with remarkable fidelity since the sixteenth century, migrated across the border. A number of German-speaking communitarian colonies were soon planted in Alberta and Manitoba.

The most distinctive of the communitarian groups was the pacifist, vegetarian Russian sect of the Doukhobors ('spirit wrestlers'). As part of the national government's desire to settle the west, and with the help of the Russian novelist Leo Tolstoy and his followers, arrangements were made for the Doukhobors to secure holdings in Saskatchewan. A simple and largely illiterate agricultural people, some 7,400 arrived in 1899, settled in fifty-seven small villages, and formed the Christian Community of Universal Brotherhood. Religiously they were mystically inclined, rejected the authority of the Bible but treasured 'The Living Book', an orally transmitted changing collection of hymns and psalms. They submitted to the almost dictatorial powers of the hereditary prophetic leader, while resisting the authority of earthly governments. Their ruler, Peter the Lordly Verigin (1859–1924), arrived from Russian exile in 1902; he aimed for a pattern of life for his people that would be 'puritanical in morals and manners, pacifist in its behaviour to the outside world and the animal kingdom, and communistic in its economic organization, with, of course, the unwritten understanding that the traditional symbiosis of theocrat and sobranie [the Doukhobor meeting] would shape its political functioning'.[25] Some members of the group operated their own farms independently; a strict group which called itself the Sons of Freedom marched naked in protest against a growing laxness in the community. Conflict with

[25] George Woodcock and Ivan Avakumovic, *The Doukhobors* (Toronto, 1968), p. 153.

provincial law followed, and the hostility of the surrounding population was aroused. The troubles increased when the Doukhobors refused to take the oath of naturalization, in consequence of which much of their land was seized in 1907. Verigin then purchased land in the Kootenay and Boundary areas of British Columbia, and planted a second community to which many of his followers migrated. Tension arose again in this new home over the provincial determination to have the children attend school. This was resolved in 1915 when the Doukhobors agreed to build schools on their own land. When educational squabbles erupted again in the 1920s, the schools and other buildings were burned by arsonists, and Verigin himself was killed by a still unexplained dynamiting of a railway carriage. A troubled period of strife and terrorism lay ahead.

In the years following Confederation, a number of the new religious movements of Great Britain and the United States found their way into Canada. Among them were those with varying Adventist and millenarian views, such as Seventh-day Adventists, Jehovah's Witnesses, and Plymouth Brethren. Churches of the Holiness movement, for example the Church of the Nazarene, the Pilgrim Holiness Church, and the Christian and Missionary Alliance, established Canadian branches. There was also an indigenous movement of this persuasion. While a student at Victoria University, Ralph Horner spent much of his time in organizing perfectionist groups; in 1886 he refused to accept a circuit assigned to him by the Montreal Methodist Conference and became a travelling evangelist. His intensely emotional and well-attended revival services became highly controversial; in 1895 he was deposed from the Methodist ministry and founded the Holiness Movement Church in Canada, of which he became bishop. For a time it grew rapidly, but then was plagued with inner division and split in 1916, Horner siding with the new Standard Church of America. He died two years later, and both churches went into a period of decline.

Of the Holiness movements, the Salvation Army made the greatest impression. Introduced in 1882, it was for decades an aggressive, competitive revivalistic group that was especially threatening to the Methodists. The latter copied Army methods with their Gospel Bands, while the Anglicans organized a Church Army, but neither could quite match the followers of William Booth. The older churches had their main following among the middle and upper classes, while 'the rise of new religious movements such as the Hornerites and the Salvation Army indicated the failure of the traditional organization of religion to effectively act as . . . an agent of social solidarity' for the urban masses, among whom were many 'outside of and not really a part of society'.[26] The new movements won much of their following among the dispossessed and poorly educated groups, who found a congenial atmosphere, a new orientation for life, and a chance to exercise their talents for leadership. As in the United States, after a generation the Salvation Army became respectable and evolved into a generally accepted religious organization with a special role in social welfare.

As the Holiness churches were settling down in the early twentieth century, the Pentecostalists took their place as centres of controversy in the Protestant world, breaking with the Holiness groups to form their own—and also winning some sympathizers in the older churches. In 1919 the Pentecostal Assemblies of Canada were organized, and in time became the largest of the new range of groups. Pentecostalist growth did not reach an early peak and then become relatively static as the Holiness movement had done, but continued to climb—the membership of about 500 in 1911 had become 95,000 forty years later.

The drive for immigrants in the early decades of the twentieth century brought in adherents of Eastern Orthodox traditions, Russians, Greeks, Serbians, and Ukrainians. The latter were especially numerous, and reflected the troubled religious history of Galicia, the majority being Uniates who recognized the pope but kept many of their Greek Orthodox customs and rites. The Canadian Roman Catholic Church objected to their married clergy, and many Ukrainians protested. In the first decade of the century an Independent Greek Church was aided by the Presbyterians, but the movement proved unstable and was absorbed by the helping church. The naming of a Roman Catholic bishop of the eastern rite in 1912, and the placing of the Greek Catholic Church directly under Rome eased the tension within the Ukrainian community but did not end it. In 1918 the Ukrainian Greek Orthodox Church of Canada was founded, and served as a centre of identity for these eastern immigrants in western Canada.

Various of the religious movements inspired by New Thought opened missions and churches in the Dominion, for example Christian Science and Unity. Some non-Christian religions were introduced with immigration from across the Pacific; small numbers of Buddhists and Confucianists began to be counted in the census of 1901. The small Canadian Jewish community tripled in the first decade of the twentieth century, largely through Polish, Russian, and Lithuanian immigration, to include 1 per cent of the population by 1911. Orthodox, Conservative, and a few

Reform synagogues were founded, especially where Jewish population tended to concentrate, in Montreal, Toronto, and Winnipeg. A Canadian Jewish Congress was founded in 1919.

As the first quarter of the twentieth century closed, the identification of Canada as a Christian nation remained strong. The creation of the United Church was a major milestone in church history; it was the climax of a long trend towards unity. Yet the intense struggles between Protestant and Catholic, between Presbyterian and Methodist, between old denominations and rising sects, and between conservatives and liberals within denominations played their part in weakening somewhat the prestige of the churches. The secularizing trends in western culture were being felt in Canada, especially after World War I, but were not as evident as in the United States. Four major churches—Roman Catholic, United, Anglican, Presbyterian—dominated the Canadian religious scene in a situation quite different from that in the southern neighbour, where there were a dozen major denominational families, many of them subdivided into branches. But in both lands the diversity of the Christian tradition was increasing with the spread of new religious movements, and the growing mobility in the cultures was threatening homogeneous religious and ethnic enclaves. This was less true for the Dominion than it was for the States, for in Canada the image of a mosaic of peoples of various backgrounds fitting together without pressure for homogeneity was stronger than the concept of the melting-pot long popular in the United States. Yet the seemingly secure denominational structures, even that of the new United Church of Canada, had been shaped for expansion in a largely unsettled country and were now called to serve a country with growing industrialized areas in a time of transition and conflict.

XII

NORTH AMERICAN CHURCHES
AND THE
DECLINE OF CHRISTENDOM

THE American and Canadian churches entered the period following World War I devoted as they had always sought to be to the service of God and to the continuation of the patterns of western Christendom. Though divided among themselves and often within themselves regarding the means of fulfilling these purposes, they had long since come to believe that they could accomplish them better through voluntary ways of persuasion rather than through formal establishment. With very few exceptions, the churches were convinced that the civilization of which they were a part was superior to all others, and was rooted to a considerable degree in Christian teachings and values. They also recognized that their civilization only imperfectly embodied Christian principles and was confronted by both internal and external threats. The denominations longed to close the difficult gap between profession and practice in order to deal more efficiently with the dangers. Yet the churches remained generally confident of the basic soundness and superiority of western Christendom as they entered the post-war period, and their missionaries believed they were doing right in carrying both Christian faith and western practices to other cultures. Though there were doubters, agnostics, and dissidents—and an important Jewish minority—among them, the great majority of North American people identified themselves as Christians.

In the half-century following World War I increasing numbers of persons both inside and outside the churches came to believe that their civilization was no longer basically Christian and that Christendom was a fading reality. Some accepted this as liberating, as opening the way for a Christianity more free from cultural entanglements, others found it deeply disturbing and regrettable, while the majority was probably hardly aware of the basic changes in the relationship of Christianity to culture. But certain sharp challenges to the concepts and practices of

Christendom and to its religious ideas and institutions came during the 1920s and early 1930s, which hit the Protestant traditions with particular force. Then came a remarkable and many-sided revival of religion, beginning during the hard years of depression and World War II and reaching its peak in the 1950s. This was followed by another period of doubt, challenge, and decline, during which certain of the themes and moods of the 1920s reappeared again, but in a quite changed setting. Christian churches in Canada and the United States continued to show their characteristic differences which should never be minimized, yet the patterns in both lands for the fifty years following World War I had many similarities, and the stories can be interpreted together.

Through the troubles and crises that affected western civilization since World War I, there was surprisingly little change in the basic structures of Christian belief and organization that had been developing for three centuries in North America. This came about in part because the religious revival following World War II actually reaffirmed many of the older viewpoints and practices: tensions between liberal and conservative perspectives continued, a few denominational schisms and unions occurred, and the relative numerical ranking of certain groups shifted somewhat. As the decades passed, however, many found that familiar styles of belief and organization were becoming anachronistic and problematic, while others clung firmly to them.

From Prosperity to Depression in the United States

After a period of post-war economic adjustment, the 1920s became a decade of unprecedented prosperity. For many American families, incomes and standards of living were on the rise: the luxury of one year became the necessity of the next as advertising and mass production made the automobile, the radio, and the electric refrigerator increasingly available. The mass production of motor vehicles increased the mobility of the population, and suburban living came within the reach of growing numbers of people. Big business enjoyed mounting prestige. Newly enfranchised women played a more conspicuous role in society and—in part because of the necessities of the war—had gained a wider range of employment options. The growing popularity of motion pictures was one of the factors in spreading new appetites and interests. Patterns of home life changed as the radio increasingly became an important centre of interest. Science and technology attained great prestige, and when Charles A. Lindbergh completed the first solo non-stop flight across the Atlantic from New York to Paris in 1927 the possibilities of progress seemed unlimited.

Churches shared in the ebullient spirit of the time, and reflected its prosperity. Especially in urban settings, expensive new sanctuaries and educational buildings were erected. Radio ministries brought the voices of such famous preachers as S. Parkes Cadman and Harry Emerson Fosdick into many homes. In part because of the growing mobility of their members, denominations which had been largely regional began to think in national terms.

Nevertheless, the decade was a hard one for the churches, for familiar moral standards were being challenged and accepted religious values were under direct criticism by such prominent literary figures as Sinclair Lewis and H. L. Mencken. The 'great crusade' of the war had been a disillusioning and grim reality for many, and the idealism and reformism of the early century had largely evaporated. The 'noble experiment' of prohibition was still earnestly supported by many evangelical Protestants, but the refusal of many Americans to abide by the unpopular law contributed to the growing lawlessness and gangsterism of the time. The picture of religion presented by certain intellectual leaders was often quite negative. They drew on Freudian themes and were aware of the way moral codes reflected the relativities of history as they criticized institutional religion and harped on its repressive and old-fashioned morality. In university circles there was widespread rejection of religion. A professor of philosophy, William P. Montague, was stating a view well known to *avant-garde* intellectuals when he said 'there is today a widespread and increasing belief that the minimal essentials of Christian supernaturalism . . . have been rendered antiquated, false, and absurd by our modern knowledge'.[1] On a more popular level there was much indifference to organized religion, and the trend toward a frankly secular society was strong.

The churches responded in quite different ways to those currents in the cultural climate of the twenties that were so critical of religion. The Roman Catholic Church sharply resisted such trends, holding fast to the newly gained sense of unity that had come out of its experience in the war and through the instrumentality of the National Catholic Welfare Conference. A new self-confidence and an awareness of growing strength marked Catholic leadership. Though the realities were changing rapidly, Catholicism still did not feel fully at home on American soil. As the perceptive French observer, André Siegfried, noted as late as 1927, 'the

[1] *Belief Unbound: A Promethean Religion for the Modern World* (New Haven, 1930), p. 20.

civilization of the United States is essentially Protestant', and 'Protestant-ism is the only national religion'.[2] The continuing opposition of the Catholic Church to many aspects of the culture of its environment isolated the faithful from critical currents, especially as they were shep-herded into Catholic schools, societies, and unions. The decisive slowing of immigration in 1924 by legislation imposing quotas based on the popu-lation of 1890 was intended in part to reduce the influx of eastern and southern Europeans, many of whom were Catholics. The checking of growth through immigration, however, gave the church an opportunity to continue to assimilate its many nationalities, and it continued to increase numerically through high birth rates. The parochial school system was impressive in scope. In an historic Supreme Court decision of 1925, *Pierce* v. *Society of Sisters*, the right of parents to have their children educated in private schools was clearly upheld. Millions of Catholics were getting all of their schooling in church institutions, presumably protected from the secular critical and naturalistic forces that swept across the public schools and the influential private universities. As the children of immigrants moved up the economic scale, the church found the means to build many expensive churches and educational buildings. By 1928 there were more than 10,000 Catholic educational institutions (over 2,000 of them high schools), with a total enrolment of 2,500,000—a remarkable increase.

The unity of Catholic life was further strengthened by the use of the new codification of canon law which became effective in 1918. As Thomas McAvoy wrote,

Within a decade the new formulation of church law was being carried out in great detail. Sometimes the purpose of legislation seemed to be forgotten in the fulfillment of the law, and the distinction between the regulation and the moral law was sometimes obscured in the enforcement, but for the first time most of the clergy of the country knew clearly the legal aspects of their functions.[3]

The sense of Catholic unity was not only in externals but also in piety, as evidenced in an emphasis on frequent communion and in the observance of retreats and novenas. The liturgical emphasis was highlighted by the holding of the Twenty-eighth International Eucharistic Congress in Chicago in 1926—the first time such a gathering had been held in the United States. A dozen cardinals were present; up to 400,000 of the faithful attended some of its celebrations of the mass. It was a dramatic

---

[2] *America Comes of Age*, trans. H. H. and Doris Hemming (New York, 1927), p. 33.
[3] *A History of the Catholic Church in the United States*, p. 391.

illustration of the growth and strength of the Roman Catholic Church in North America. Although largely isolated from creative interchanges with other cultural streams in America, the church was nevertheless gaining in confidence and in inner unity.

Religion has often been held responsible for the defeat of Alfred E. Smith, first Catholic candidate for president, in the election of 1928. Later study has shown that a number of factors were involved; for example, Smith's lack of formal higher education, his opposition to prohibition against the commitment to it by his Quaker opponent, Herbert Hoover, and the continuing prosperity of the nation under the Republican administration. The last was probably the decisive factor.[4] Yet the religious issue had been sharply raised during the campaign, especially in the south, old fears of Romanism had been stirred, and the defeat seemed to many Catholics to be a reminder of their second-class status in Protestant America. Conversely, many Protestants interpreted Hoover's victory as an indication that America was still a Protestant nation.

Within Protestantism the relationship of the churches to the currents of the times was much more varied, for there was a wide spectrum of reactions all the way from determined opposition to an eager acceptance of most of the values and patterns of modernity. The issues were most clearly focused in theological battles between fundamentalists and modernists; in the heat of controversy the actual complexities and nuances of position became largely obscured in struggles for power. Deep differences had long been developing as to the way faith should be understood and presented to the modern mind, differences sometimes accentuated by class and cultural tensions. The liberal theological movements in the evangelical denominations had arisen as a way of restating the historic, Christ-centred faith of Protestantism in terms that would be understandable to persons familiar with modern concepts of scientific, evolutionary, and historical thinking. Inevitably, liberal theologies were themselves deeply influenced by the use of these approaches to truth. Some liberals moved farther than others in shifting the bases of authority from Bible, church, and tradition toward the methods of science, philosophy, and critical history.[5] Modernist theological programmes which put great emphasis on empirical methods were emphasized at Yale under

[4] See Edward A. Moore, *A Catholic Runs for President: The Campaign of 1928* (New York, 1956); Ruth C. Silva, *Rum, Religion and Votes: 1928 Re-examined* (University Park, Pa., 1962).

[5] See above, pp. 289–90.

Douglas Clyde Macintosh (1877–1948) and at Chicago under Henry Nelson Wieman (b. 1884) and others. So confident were they that scientific methods in the social and behavioural as well as in the natural sciences would lead to truth that they felt secure in turning from the stress on revelation and the supernatural that had long marked Protestant piety and theology.

The larger liberal movement wanted to conjoin old certainties with new methods, but by the 1920s it was being pulled somewhat unevenly toward the modernists. Moving well beyond the latter were those who gave up revealed religion to espouse a non-theistic humanist position. Though small in number, such humanists had some influential leaders, such as John Dewey and John H. Randall, Jr. of Columbia, and some who were on theological faculties, such as A. Eustace Haydon of Chicago. The humanists criticized what they regarded as the cautious stubbornness of the liberals, and prodded them to abandon rationally weak positions. It was not until 1933 that their position was clearly stated in the Humanist Manifesto, with its fifteen affirmations, beginning with 'Religious humanists regard the universe as self-existing and not created'.[6] Though many liberal preachers and teachers tried hard to hold their movement within redefined but historic evangelicalism, it proved increasingly difficult to keep some of their educated followers from sliding toward modernism and humanism.

The movement which had aroused much enthusiasm for reform before the war, the social gospel, lost some of its distinctive drive as its theological base in evangelical liberalism was eroded and as prosperity seemed to be overcoming economic problems. Social gospel leaders increasingly stressed the spread of democratic values and interpreted the Kingdom of God as a this-worldly Utopian possibility. The movement did some effective work in interpreting the labour movement to its largely middle-class constituency, and with somewhat patronizing overtones it began to address racial issues more directly. Along with much of liberal Protestantism, in reaction to the terrors of modern war it moved toward pacifism; some of its leaders committed themselves not to support war under any circumstances. The relationships between the social gospel and pacifism was illustrated when the Fellowship of Reconciliation, a non-denominational pacifist organization founded during World War I, took increasing interest in the whole field of social thought and action. Though the social gospel lost something of the dynamism and clear sense

---

[6] The Manifesto has been reprinted many times; e.g., see Smith, Handy, Loetscher, *American Christianity*, ii, 250–3.

of direction it had had before the war, it by no means disappeared, and remained an important influence, especially in many northern seminaries and denominational bureaucracies.

At the other end of the Protestant theological spectrum, however, there was a new burst of energy. Convinced that the liberal interpretation of Christianity was faulty and was getting further from the centre, conservative leaders of various denominations—Presbyterian and Baptist especially—took steps to try to save their churches from what they believed to be apostasy. In 1919 the World's Christian Fundamentals Association was founded in Philadelphia at a gathering of 6,500 people. Led by William Bell Riley, John Roach Straton, and Jasper C. Massey—all Baptist preachers—the Association 'launched a revivalistic campaign to recapture for orthodoxy the pre-eminent place in American life. Their plan was to disseminate fundamentalism through the distribution of polemical literature, public debate between modernists and fundamentalists, and Bible conferences conducted throughout the United States.'[7] These conservatives put great emphasis on the doctrine of the verbal inerrancy of the Scriptures, the virgin birth of Christ, his atonement on the cross for the sins of mankind as their substitute, and his imminent return miraculously to inaugurate the promised millennium. Fundamentalist fellowships were formed in several northern denominations in an effort to win them to a conservative stance and to resist the liberals. Southern churches were generally sympathetic to conservative views.

Fundamentalism's drive to emphasize its particular kind of orthodoxy within the various churches was assisted by some competent persons. A Presbyterian layman, William Jennings Bryan (1860–1925), three times unsuccessful Democratic candidate for the presidency and for a time Secretary of State in the Wilson administration, devoted his last years to the movement, using his great eloquence on its platforms and publishing a series of small books defending the infallible Bible and attacking the theory of evolution. The most effective theological leadership was provided by another Presbyterian, J. Gresham Machen (1881–1937), a biblical scholar trained at Johns Hopkins, Princeton Seminary, Marburg, and Göttingen. In his *Christianity and Liberalism* (1923) he argued forcefully that liberalism was a movement 'anti-Christian to the core' which was attacking from within true Christianity, a supernatural religion of redemption. Though admitting that not all liberals fully accepted the logical implications of their unitary system, he defined liberalism as

[7] Willard B. Gatewood, Jr. in the introduction to his documentary study, *Controversy in the Twenties: Fundamentalism, Modernism, and Evolution* (Nashville, 1969), p. 18.

radical naturalism. While the controversy raged, middle ground between the parties was largely cut away as the fundamentalists exercised leadership among conservatives and as liberals gravitated toward modernism.

Conflict between the parties soon became intense in northern Presbyterian and Baptist churches. In 1922, in an effort to defuse an explosive situation, Harry Emerson Fosdick (1878–1969), the leading pulpiteer of the time, a Baptist liberal on the faculty of Union Theological Seminary in New York, preached on the theme 'Shall the Fundamentalists Win?' at the First Presbyterian Church, where he was serving as guest minister. Attacking boldly what he perceived as the fundamentalists' apparent intention to drive those of liberal opinions out of the churches, Fosdick pleaded for a spirit of tolerance so that together Christians of various theological persuasions might address themselves to human needs. This attempt to hold middle ground was criticized sharply by both extremes, but those who sympathized with him were chiefly on the liberal side. Within the Presbyterian fold nearly 1,300 ministers signed the 'Auburn Affirmation' of 1924 which also called for toleration. It criticized as inconsistent with the Westminster Confession the 'five-point doctrinal deliverance of the Assembly of 1910, repeated in 1916 and 1923, which had declared that the inerrancy of the Bible, Christ's virgin birth, his offering up of himself as a sacrifice to satisfy divine justice, his physical resurrection, and his sharing of his power and love by working miracles were each "an essential doctrine of the Word of God"'.[8] The five-point statement was later given up, but meanwhile the Assembly of 1924 required that Fosdick either come under Presbyterian doctrinal standards or resign his Presbyterian post; he took the latter route and took a Baptist pulpit, later becoming minister of New York's Riverside Church. Housed in a magnificent edifice financed largely by the Rockefellers, this liberal church was built largely around the famous preacher, nationally known through his radio addresses and many books—and for his controversial role in the fundamentalist/modernist controversy.

In the Northern Baptist Convention the struggle between the parties was intense, and was fought out over issues related to denominational programmes of missions and education. The divisiveness of the controversy was heightened because the Baptist seminaries were controlled by boards of trustees which represented one side or the other; when some of the older institutions like Newton, Crozer, and Chicago inclined toward liberalism, conservative seminaries were founded: Gordon in

---

[8] Lefferts A. Loetscher, *The Broadening Church: A Study of Theological Issues in the Presbyterian Church Since 1869* (Philadelphia, 1954), pp. 117–18.

Massachusetts, Eastern in Pennsylvania, and Northern in Illinois. Though Presbyterian and Baptist churches were especially shaken by the controversy, it was also felt in other denominations, notably Methodist, Disciples, and Episcopal. The Lutheran churches were little touched, for their confessional standards kept them conservatively oriented, and they were just beginning to emerge out of their isolation from other streams of religious life in North America.

The southern churches were also not sharply divided by the controversy, for they regarded themselves as citadels of orthodoxy, and liberal theology had few prominent representatives. The south had long been plagued by poverty, and the educational level was generally lower than in the north. With conservative theological leadership in control in most places, the challenges raised for faith by modern scientific and historical thinking did not as seriously trouble the southern churches, either white or black. The focus of the fundamentalist/modernist controversy in the south was more in the legislatures and the courts, for laws to prevent the teaching of evolution were passed in Mississippi, Florida, Tennessee, and Arkansas. It was assumed that most taxpayers were Christians who were opposed to instruction in evolutionary theory and who had the right to ban what they understood to be anti-Christian teachings from the schools which they supported.

The Tennessee anti-evolution law of 1925 set the stage for the famous test case which fundamentalism formally won—but at the high cost of having its positions severely and publicly criticized and ridiculed, a blow which contributed to the movement's sharp decline. When a young high-school teacher, John Scopes, was brought to trial for teaching evolution, both sides brought in nationally famous figures, led for the defence by a prominent criminal lawyer, Clarence Darrow, and by fundamentalism's leading spokesman, William Jennings Bryan, in support of the anti-evolution laws. International attention was given to the trial which took place in July 1925 at Dayton, Tennessee. During the affair Darrow mercilessly laid bare flaws in Bryan's interpretation of the Bible. Scopes was found guilty and fined (a decision later reversed), but the notoriety accorded to fundamentalism in the general Press hurt its cause. Bryan died just after the trial, and the movement to which he had devoted his last years receded. It did not succeed in capturing any of the major denominations, but neither did it disappear. Fundamentalist congregations, parties, and educational institutions kept the cause alive, while some of the smaller denominations of literalist, pietist, Holiness, or Pentecostal orientation were often sympathetic to fundamentalism. Determined fundamentalists led groups out of their denominational homes into splinter bodies. Machen, for example, left Princeton Seminary in 1929 to organize a new one, and four years later he participated in the founding of an independent mission board. In due course he was suspended from the ministry of the Presbyterian Church in the United States of America, and joined with others to form a small new body which became known as the Orthodox Presbyterian Church. The Northern Baptists also suffered a schism in 1932 when a group of fundamentalist churches withdrew to form the General Association of Regular Baptist Churches.

Though the fundamentalist/modernist controversy was only one of the causes of a change in Protestant fortunes, by the middle of the 1920s a spiritual decline, noticed by a few observers at the time, was besetting the churches. Something of the general disillusionment and loss of morale that marked the decade swept into the churches. They had so identified themselves with certain transient aspects of American culture—liberals with optimistic views of progress through science and scholarship, conservatives with nineteenth-century hopes for a homogeneous nation— that they had lost much of the ability to act prophetically and independently. The bitter intensity of the fundamentalist/modernist controversy not only lowered the general prestige of religion, but also sapped the enthusiasm and commitment of many within the churches. The cause of missions, an important indicator of Christian vitality, was clearly suffering by the mid-twenties, as missionary-giving fell sharply—in a time of great prosperity—and as the number of candidates for missionary service declined noticeably.

The lessening of missionary zeal precipitated an interdenominational Laymen's Foreign Missions Inquiry. Its summary report, *Re-Thinking Missions: A Laymen's Inquiry After One Hundred Years* (1932), edited by Harvard philosopher William E. Hocking, exhibited a strongly liberal bias and was sharply criticized by conservatives for calling for the freeing of educational and philanthropic work from direct concern for evangelizing. The general loss of confidence in western leadership since World War I seemed to require new strategies for mission on the part of the churches, but a divided, troubled Protestantism lacked the vision and resiliency to respond with adequate effectiveness. Of course there were many individuals who made exemplary missionaries and who exhibited an heroic spirit in the face of difficulties, but at the home base the enthusiasm and self-confidence of the pre-war years had ebbed. There were many other evidences of Protestant decline: falling attendance at church services and Sunday schools, a lowering of ministerial prestige, an inability to maintain the power of the revival and the reform movements that had been such a feature of church life, and a general lessening in the quality of sermons and religious literature.

The stock market crash of 1929, followed by the terrible economic depression of the 1930s, deeply affected all of America's institutions, not the least the churches. Budgets were reduced, programmes of all kinds reduced or dropped, marginal churches closed, and clergymen displaced— some to join the ranks of the unemployed, which at one point numbered more than twelve million people. Yet most churches struggled through the difficult time of testing, providing solace and assistance for their followers. Social gospel emphases were revived as some pointed criticisms of the capitalist system were made by denominational and interdenomina-tional assemblies in the early thirties. At the other extreme, a few Protes-tant voices sounded anti-Semitic themes, notably the fundamentalist Gerald B. Winrod, the theosophically minded William Dudley Pelley, and the demagogic minister, Gerald L. K. Smith. While most responsible church leaders condemned their crusades, they did claim a considerable radio-following in the depression decade.

While the major denominations were having such a difficult time, some of the smaller churches whose ministries were largely among the poor and disinherited were growing spectacularly, some doubling or even tripling in size. Bodies of Holiness and Pentecostal origin illustrated this trend. Their sense of religious certainty, their resistance to upper- and upper-middle-class standards and customs, and their warmth and in-formality drew many members of the lower and lower middle classes into their orbits.

The churches of the Negro people continued to play a very important role in these difficult years, offering resources of strength for those who were often 'last hired and first fired', and serving as centres for the life of neighbourhoods and communities. Most of the larger denominations had some black members, customarily gathered in separate congregations. The great bulk of black Christians continued to be in their own Baptist and Methodist denominations, which were hard pressed in accommodating to the great migration to the cities.

The movement of coloured populations to northern cities that had been greatly accelerated during World War I continued in the next two decades as more than a million made the journey. Though most of the major black denominations became members of the Federal Council of the Churches of Christ in America, there was actually little meaningful inter-change between white and black Christians in local communities. With some exceptions, the black churches were conservative in theology, and their social concerns focused around the needs of an oppressed minority. The Federal Council established a Commission on Race Relations in 1921, and for a quarter of a century George E. Haynes (1880–1961), educator and sociologist, gave conspicuous service in helping his people in a difficult time and in trying to guide white churches into a deeper understanding of their fellow Christians. An analysis of the religious census of 1936 showed that the percentage of church members in the black population was higher than that of the white.[9]

As in white Protestantism, the fastest growing denominations among blacks in depression years were those smaller ones of independent and Pentecostalist background; literally hundreds of small store-front churches were founded in the ghettos of Philadelphia, New York, Detroit, and Chicago. Some very distinctive movements arose. The Father Divine Peace Mission sprang into prominence early in the depression years. The leader of this eclectic religious sect, George Baker, had taken the name Father Divine, claimed to be God, and provided generous feasts for his followers. When he was found guilty of creating a disturbance in his headquarters on New York's Long Island, the judge who sentenced him died three days later, attracting great publicity to Father Divine who reportedly said he 'hated to do it'. All through the depression years the Peace Mission flourished; there was an abundance of food and shelter for the faithful. Not all the members were black; indeed racial intolerance was strictly forbidden. The group continued after the depression years, and declined after the founder's death in 1965.

A rival group, the United House of Prayer for All People, was led by Bishop Charles E. 'Sweet Daddy' Grace, whose services showed some remnants of its Pentecostal origins.[10] Many other, less spectacular cults arose, most in the Christian tradition, others claiming an Islamic or Jewish background. Yet the older major black denominations also continued to grow in significant numbers during these difficult years, and their ministers played central roles in black community life.

With so many of its members in the working classes, Roman Catho-

---

[9] Admitting the problems of working with inaccurate statistics, Gunnar Myrdal reported that 'even if we make all the assumptions that work in the direction of under-enumerating Negro church membership, the Negroes still have a larger membership: 44·0 per cent of the Negro population are members of Negro churches, as compared to 42·4 per cent of the white population in white churches'. *An American Dilemma: The Negro Problem and Modern Democracy* (New York, 1944), p. 864.

[10] These and other groups are treated in a standard work by Arthur H. Fauset, *Black Gods of the Metropolis: Negro Religious Cults of the Urban North* (Philadelphia, 1944).

licism keenly felt the lash of depression, and invoked the social-ethical position that had been developing since *Rerum novarum* in criticizing the arrangements that had brought about economic disaster. As McAvoy wrote,

Probably for the first time in its existence in the United States the Church was in a position to speak to the nation and to point to a doctrine that was not formed just for the occasion but one that was already declared in the encyclicals and in the pastoral letters. And for the first time the people of the United States were really willing to listen to the voice of Catholicism.[11]

The Catholic concern for justice, so clearly evident in the Bishops' Program of Social Reconstruction in 1919[12] was reaffirmed on the 40th anniversary of *Rerum novarum* when Pope Pius XI issued the encyclical *Quadragesimo Anno* in 1931. This encyclical stated that both individual and social obligations went with the ownership of property, and upheld the right of a government to interfere for the common good. The Catholic Worker Movement arose in the depths of the depression as an influential 'unofficial' effort to work among victims of social injustice and gather them into a force for change. Led by a remarkable convert journalist Dorothy Day (b. 1897), the movement's writings articulated a broad programme of social reconstruction, while its houses of hospitality in many cities exhibited a direct and effective concern for those struggling with poverty and unemployment. The Catholic Worker Movement exerted a lasting influence far outside its own circles.

Tensions in Canadian Church Life

The 1920s and 1930s were marked by some sharp tensions in Canadian religious life; the increased bitterness between French Catholics and English Protestants during the war, and the conflict over the formation of the United Church of Canada have already been discussed. Another cause of strife was the impact of fundamentalism, felt especially in the Baptist churches, and in the emergence of independent religious movements, particularly in the western provinces. A prominent Toronto Baptist pastor who associated with American fundamentalist leaders, T. T. Shields, conducted a slashing attack on the leadership of the Baptist Convention of Ontario and Quebec and of his Alma Mater, McMaster University. He did not hesitate to assail his opponents at the personal level,

11 *A History of the Catholic Church in the United States,* pp. 406–7.
12 See above, p. 329.

and when he was censured by his convention in 1926 for his tactics, he founded his own college and mission board, and two years later drew many churches away from their conventions into the Union of Regular Baptist Churches. Baptist ranks in the prairie provinces and in British Columbia were also divided; some of the churches that aligned themselves with Shields's group fell under the influence of dispensational millenarianism and formed an independent fellowship. A Baptist layman of dispensational leanings, William Aberhart, had developed a large personal following as a Bible teacher in Calgary, Alberta, and in 1925 began to broadcast his lectures throughout the province. His stress upon an infallible Bible won many people, and his appeals for funds allowed him to found the Prophetic Bible Institute in 1927, and to build his own independent fundamentalist movement.

There was also some influence of fundamentalism in the larger Protestant denominations. The evangelical party of the Church of England gained strength under the leadership of Dyson Hague of Toronto, who had been one of the contributors to the pre-war series, *The Fundamentals*. Some of the continuing Presbyterians found the fundamentalist emphases congenial, a rather new note in Canadian Presbyterianism, although it had long been familiar in America.

Fundamentalism was not strong in the United Church of Canada, where the evangelical liberal heritage was so influential, but the challenge to liberal assumptions was felt. Unrest within Canada's largest Protestant body came more directly from the other side, from those who felt that the church should be more radical, especially as voiced in a somewhat critical, anti-bureaucratic spirit by members of the Canadian Student Christian Movement, founded in 1921. The social gospel, so important in the shaping of the United Church, was forced into crisis and decline as its basic concepts were challenged by theological currents from both right and left, and as encounter with stubborn social realities showed that the christianization of Canada was a lot farther off than had once been expected. The defeat of prohibition, a cause important to adherents of the social gospel, was a blow to the movement. Canada had been somewhat sheltered from the secularizing process that had long been an aspect of western civilization, but that process was speeded up by the war experiences. As John Webster Grant observed,

Those who campaigned energetically to complete the Christianization of Canada were the first to feel the effects of secularization, seeing their long-cherished goals begin to recede just when they seemed close to realization. The signs were already visible in the 1920s with the disarray of the liberal social gospel, the defeat of prohibition in one province after another, and the failure of the church union movement to retain its momentum after 1925.[13]

During the depression, the signs became even clearer.

Canada's economic situation made her especially vulnerable to the depression, which brought unemployment to a quarter of the labour force—at one point 100,000 were on relief in Montreal—while the impact of drought spelled disaster to vast wheat-growing areas of the west. In all the denominations there had to be serious cuts in budgets, salaries, programmes, foreign missions, and experimentation. Catholics and Protestants co-operated in providing relief to the particularly hard-hit prairie areas. An internationally known programme of economic co-operation was greatly expanded under the Catholic auspices of St. Francis Xavier University in Antigonish, Nova Scotia. The work that had been started long before the depression now became an important resource for farmers and fishermen. The encyclical *Quadragesimo Anno* provided theological justification for a significant undertaking.

In Quebec, the goal of much Catholic social thought was corporatism, the working-together of associations representing the various elements of society. Some interpreted corporatism in an authoritarian way that envisioned a clerically guided state, while others were more democratically inclined. The French Canadian national spirit became conspicuous again during the hard years of depression, this time with greater emphasis on economic issues. 'Depression, like war,' Mason Wade declared, 'has always set French and English Canadians at odds and strained the structure of Confederation.'[14] There were particular disagreements between the two cultures over attitudes toward the rise of Italian fascism, and toward the Spanish Civil War.

Early in the depression the radical social gospel movement came to life again. Church and lay leaders attracted to socialism founded in 1931 what was later named the Fellowship for a Christian Social Order. The bulk of its members were in the United Church; branches were formed in some of the conferences. The Fellowship's views, which called for the socialization of the organized agencies of production, were disseminated in Canada and the United States through a symposium edited by R. B. Y. Scott and Gregory Vlastos, *Towards the Christian Revolution* (1936). Taking a more political approach, a number of reformers of various denominational backgrounds participated with J. S. Woodsworth in the founding in 1933 of the Cooperative Commonwealth Federation (later

13 *The Church in the Canadian Era*, p. 217.
14 *The French Canadians, 1760–1945*, p. 865.

the New Democratic Party), which became a considerable force in Canadian politics. This development caused further tension between Protestants and Catholics, for the latter, faithful to the teachings of *Rerum novarum* and other encyclicals, found it difficult to make distinctions between European revolutionary and British evolutionary socialism. Archbishop Jean Marie Rodrique Villeneuve (1883–1947) of Quebec, who was made a cardinal early in 1933, strongly opposed the C.C.F.

A political development of a quite different type emerged in Alberta. As the depression tightened its grip on the prairies, political and economic references became especially pronounced in William Aberhart's lectures on prophecy. He was attracted to the ideas of Social Credit which proposed that every adult be credited with a regular monthly cash-dividend secured by the country's natural resources, and advocated this in his messages. Appealing to fundamentalists of many types, he soon developed a political base which brought him into power as premier in Alberta in 1935. It was, in H. H. Walsh's words, an illustration of 'that strange anomaly in Canadian religious development—a sectarian religion of a most other-worldly type creating a very this-worldly political party'.[15] In the United States, the quite different understanding of the separation of church and state, and consequently of religion and politics, inhibited such developments.

The depression was hard on Canada and its churches. Yet the time of testing did lead many Canadians to realize that the churches were important to them. The United Church moved towards consolidation, and a new concern for social justice was evident among Christians of widely divergent traditions.

Currents of Renewal in American Church Life

In the early years of the depression, many American Protestants looked for a revival of religion, assuming that in the crisis of the material order the people would turn again as of old to the things of the spirit. An editorial in the liberal weekly *Christian Century* called attention to the fact that 'this period of depression has brought forth no revival of religion. We are accustomed to expect revivals in such periods.'[16] But the Protestant era of American history, when Protestantism could assume it was the dominant faith and the custodian of national spiritual values, was ebbing. The repeal of prohibition in 1933 when Franklin Delano Roosevelt's 'New Deal' took over in Washington was one sign of a significant shift. The growing

---

15 *The Christian Church in Canada*, p. 320.
16 'Why No Revival?' *Christian Century*, lii (18 Sept. 1935), 1168–70.

influence of Roman Catholicism in the new Democratic administration was another. Demographic shifts meant that urban populations where the radical religious diversity of American life was most evident prevailed over the rural, where much Protestant strength was still concentrated, especially in the south. Yet at the time when the churches were quite weak in their influence, renewal currents were already flowing—but from an unexpected quarter, cutting across familiar expectations and party lines. Many did not for a long time recognize that renewal had indeed begun—and some never did. For theology had not enjoyed an important place in American church life, and it was in the theological realm that significant religious resurgence first appeared.

When World War I so disrupted European life, a many-sided religious and theological renaissance began; Karl Barth's biblical, churchly theology and Emil Brunner's dialectical theology were central strands in the new awakening. But all this was little known in the United States through the twenties; in Sydney Ahlstrom's vivid words, 'To most Americans of the 1920s, the notion of "crisis" and "despair" could arise only in the frightened and diseased minds of those who stalked the remote European ruins, the world of yesterday—or in the minds of expatriate individuals who preferred the ruins to the world of Cal Coolidge.'[17] But an awareness of certain limitations and superficialities in much of Protestant life and thought had been deepening in the minds of some of its leaders. The sense of crisis increased as the seriousness of the international situation because of the rise of totalitarianism was added to domestic anxieties.

Though many persons played a role in the emergence of a movement of theological reconstruction, the Niebuhr brothers were especially conspicuous and creative in the rise of neo-orthodoxy—a term used very broadly in North American usage to include a quite wide range of views. A member of the Evangelical Synod of the United States, a graduate of Eden Seminary and Yale Divinity School, Reinhold Niebuhr (1892–1971) served thirteen years in a Detroit pastorate and in 1928 became professor of social ethics at Union Theological Seminary in New York. In *Moral Man and Immoral Society* (1932), Niebuhr sharply criticized the idealism, optimism, and individualistic premisses of liberal Christianity and the social gospel. In *Reflections on the End of an Era* (1934) he drew insights from the Marxist analysis of industrial society. He expressed a deepening appreciation of classical Christian understandings of ultimate reality and the human predicament in *Beyond Tragedy* (1938) and *The Nature and Destiny of Man* (1941–3). He asserted that the

17 *A Religious History of the American People*, p. 937; cf. pp. 932–63.

'dramatic-historical' perspective of the Bible provides a truer view of human nobility and misery than the wisdom of scientists and philosophers. A tireless speaker, writer, editor, and polemicist, Niebuhr was a dramatic exponent of theological and ethical renewal. H. Richard Niebuhr (1894–1962), also a graduate of Eden and Yale who returned to the latter to teach theology and ethics, addressed himself more to philosophical, theological, and ethical problems, producing works that deeply influenced and shaped the movements of theological and church renewal—for example, *The Kingdom of God in America* (1937), *The Meaning of Revelation* (1941), and *Christ and Culture* (1951). In 1935 he co-authored an influential little book which called the churches to recover their own centres of authority and to cut themselves off from bondage to capitalism, nationalism, and anthropocentrism. 'The task of the present generation', he wrote, 'appears to be in the liberation of the church from its bondage to a corrupt civilization.'[18] There were many other important contributors to the rise and development of neo-orthodoxy, such as Walter Lowrie, Edwin Lewis, Walter M. Horton, and George W. Richards. A unique role was played by Paul Tillich (1886–1965), who left Hitler's Germany for New York to teach at Union in 1933. A philosophical theologian of great breadth and originality, he presented his distinctive position in many books, especially the three-volume *Systematic Theology* (1951–63). Even when neo-orthodoxy was given its broadest definition he did not really belong within it, but he played a central role in the general recovery of the theological dimensions of faith and life.

The American neo-orthodox movement was a complex development, varying in detail as it was articulated in various denominational and sectional settings. Though it reacted against liberalism at decisive points, there were also many continuing links—for example, neo-orthodoxy accepted the critical, historical approach to the Bible and tradition. An important reason for its power was that it cut across the fundamentalist/modernist stalemate, re-emphasizing religious and theological concerns important to the conservatives even as rigidities and dogmatisms were rejected. It accepted many of the social and intellectual achievements of liberalism, while not hesitating to criticize its idealistic premisses and optimistic illusions.

Neo-orthodox theologians stressed the transcendence and sovereignty of God and called attention to the reality and gravity of sin and self-centredness in human life. Though drawing on the results of modern

---

[18] H. Richard Niebuhr, Wilhelm Pauck, and Francis P. Miller, *The Church Against the World* (Chicago, 1935), p. 124.

biblical scholarship, they reasserted the importance of the divine self-revelation as recorded in the Bible, thus stimulating renewed interest in the study of the Scriptures and in biblical theology. The supreme self-disclosure of God was in Jesus Christ, neo-orthodox theologians affirmed, strongly emphasizing the importance of the doctrines of Christ and the Trinity. Though much aware of the historically conditioned and very human side of the life of the churches, they were deeply devoted to the church as the people of God and the body of Christ, and were seeking a fuller understanding of the nature and the wholeness of the church. This provided a stimulating context for a revival of interest in worship, and informed a resurgent interest in co-operative and unitive movements. With its realistic assessment of the precariousness of the human situation in modern civilization, neo-orthodoxy also focused fresh attention on ethical issues. The emphases of this seminal movement were felt in most theological parties and were reflected unevenly in patterns of worship, preaching, educational efforts, and religious publishing across a wide spectrum.

As neo-orthodoxy assessed the political and international situation in its realistic way, it tended to be critical of the pacifism with which liberalism had become entwined. Reinhold Niebuhr dramatically broke with pacifism early in the thirties and by the end of the decade was forcefully arguing for responsible American involvement in the tragic power struggles of the time. When the United States was plunged into World War II following the attack on Pearl Harbor late in 1941, pacifism remained a serious option for a relatively small minority. Most conscientious objectors entered non-combatant or civilian alternate service; a few went to prison for the sake of conscience.

The Christian churches generally supported the war effort as a necessity when it came. Believing that the survival of western civilization was at stake, most became convinced that there was no realistic alternative to meeting the military offensive of Hitler and his allies. The churches were generally much more restrained in interpreting the nation's role in the war than they had been in 1917–18; there was little glorification of the long and grim struggle. Much practical work in easing the shock of war on participants, their families, and refugees was undertaken by the churches and their agencies; some eight thousand chaplains served with the military at home and abroad. There was considerable concern that ways be found to bring about genuine peace with justice; Protestant, Catholic, and Jewish leaders were active in guiding their people to think and work for a lasting peace, and issued a joint statement of principles for an enduring and just settlement of issues.

In the decade and a half following the end of hostilities in 1945 a many-faceted revival of religion emerged. It came as a surprise to many, for it reversed the trends of the 1920s. Various reasons have been offered in explanation of this resurgence. The terrible experiences of war had turned the thoughts and aspirations of many persons toward spiritual concerns. There was a quest for a better, fuller life in touch with ultimate realities. Though the revival was widespread and very popular in many of its expressions, the apologetic work of neo-orthodoxy had helped to prepare the way, lending notes of a seriousness and intellectual respectability to theological and religious interests. There was also much deep-seated anxiety in American life, which derived from such things as the spectre of atomic destruction following the American atomic bombing of the Japanese cities of Hiroshima and Nagasaki in 1945, and the continuation of the arms race between the Soviet Union and the North Atlantic nations in the cold war. This armed stalemate repeatedly threatened to erupt into violence at one point or other on the globe, as it did in Korea in 1950. Less dramatic but very pervasive as a source of anxiety was the high mobility and increasing pace of change in American life just as the jet age began and the television was bringing the world into the home. As they addressed themselves to the questions of peace, life's meaning, and salvation, the churches met with a growing response. The percentage of church membership in the total population increased from an estimated 50 per cent in 1940 to almost 70 per cent in 1960; church attendance reached a peak in 1955 when it was estimated that just under half of the population was at religious services in a typical week. Both because of the vast increase in population—from about 130,000,000 in 1940 to just under 180,000,000 two decades later—and because of the great migration to the suburbs, there was a need for new church buildings; in 1960 the total amount spent passed a billion dollars. The general prestige of religion mounted, and the proliferation of religious books of all kinds broke previous records.

Virtually all forms of organized religion gained in this heady period of affluence and revival. Most of the denominations reported numerical gains, sponsored parish renewal movements, overhauled their religious education and youth programmes, and encouraged greater seriousness in worship. Seminary enrolments increased, and religious centres on university and college campuses flourished. At mid-century, Herbert Wallace Schneider reported that 'the large denominations which embrace over half our population have proved to be amazingly stable and have survived, despite many predictions to the contrary, a series of storms which have tested their intellectual and moral strength as severely as any "sifting time" in religious history'.[19]

Most of the newer religious movements also gained spectacularly in numbers in this post-war period. The remarkable growth of Jehovah's Witnesses had begun during the war itself, as the world-wide membership doubled to over 200,000 between 1942 and 1947, and was to grow even faster in the next five years. By 1960 the movement claimed about a million members throughout the world, a quarter of them in the United States.[20] The Pentecostal churches also flourished, and as a partial result of the success of the first World Pentecostal Conference at Zurich in 1947, a Pentecostal Fellowship of North America was founded the following year; this co-operative agency soon had a membership of fourteen denominations. Pentecostal teaching also permeated into most of the major churches, through such programmes as those sponsored by the Full Gospel Businessmen's Fellowship (founded in California in 1951), and through the radio and television work of preachers like Oral Roberts (b. 1918), then a Pentecostal preacher whose fame as an evangelist was surpassed only by Billy Graham.

Protestant theological parties adjusted in various ways during this period of religious revival. Liberalism, chastened by the tragedies of the times and by the strictures of neo-orthodoxy, continued to be an option as 'repentant' or neo-liberalism. Neo-orthodoxy, conspicuous in theological seminaries, was much less strident than before the war as it sought to work out the implications of its affirmations for the life of the churches and for ecumenical effort. Especially influential were the mature reflections of H. Richard Niebuhr in such books as *The Purpose of the Church and Its Ministry* (1956) and *Radical Monotheism and Western Culture* (1960). One of the most significant developments in this period was the resurgence of conservative evangelical Protestantism, as both a theological and a popular movement committed to mass revivalism. Fundamentalism had remained active during the depression in the evangelical parties of most denominations and in a number of the smaller bodies. Early in the 1940s it disavowed its anti-intellectual stance as it again sought to champion in a positive way the supernatural origin of Christianity and the authority of the inspired Bible, choosing to call itself conservative evangelicalism. In 1942 some of the smaller conservative and Pentecostal denominations combined with certain congregations and interested individuals from various traditions to form the National Association of Evangelicals. Its

[19] *Religion in 20th Century America* (Cambridge, Mass., 1952), p. 206.
[20] Marley Cole, *Jehovah's Witnesses: The New World Society* (New York, 1955), pp. 220–8.

statement of faith affirmed belief in the inspired and infallible Word of God. A year later the evangelicals founded Youth for Christ to gather in young people; it proved to be a potent instrument for refurbishing mass revivalism.

Combining familiar revival themes with a skilled use of communications techniques, William F. (Billy) Graham (b. 1918) emerged into public prominence at mid-century. He built up an impressive organization, conducted extensive revival campaigns in many of the world's major cities, and brought in thousands of 'decisions for Christ'. A Baptist preacher, Graham focused on traditional evangelical themes with overtones of millenarianism and patriotism. Care was taken to secure general denominational support before undertaking a crusade in a given place; the revivals fulfilled an important secondary function as rallying points for Protestant forces. Graham had a gift—enhanced by the organizational skill of his team—of sensing the religious moods and needs of various regions, and of addressing them. His critics found his theology old-fashioned and his social perceptions much too limited and conservative, much too attuned to the over-simplified anti-Communism so strong at the time. But Graham remained the best-known exponent of a renewed revivalism. Conservative evangelicalism had many other prominent leaders—pastors, scholars, teachers. A conspicuous force was a Baptist minister and professor, Carl F. H. Henry (b. 1912), author of a number of books, especially *The Uneasy Conscience of Modern Fundamentalism* (1947), who later became editor of an influential journal, *Christianity Today*.

Another facet of the religious reawakening was devoted to the search for inner peace and serenity, and drew on psychological insights in guiding people to have faith in themselves and in readily available resources of spiritual power. Immediately after the war a Reform rabbi, Joshua Loth Liebman, published his widely read *Peace of Mind* (1946) which brought reassurance to thousands of readers. Other works of varying quality addressed themselves to similar themes, but the most famous exponent of the inspirational message of inner peace was Norman Vincent Peale (b. 1898), minister of the Marble Collegiate Church in New York. Such books as *A Guide to Confident Living* (1948) and especially *The Power of Positive Thinking* (1952) became best sellers, brought long queues of people to the doors of his church, and made him a familiar television personality. Certain facets of New Thought teaching were reflected in his message. Religious leaders and writers of various religious heritages often employed themes from this broad current of the religious renewal in their daily work.

While it was still going strong in the 1950s, the revival came under penetrating criticism from certain participants in American religious life. According to Will Herberg, a Jew much influenced by the Niebuhrs, the religious upswing was to a great extent a search for identity and conformity in mass society, and many of its strands uncritically supported 'the American way of life' as its highest value. A college teacher of religion, A. Roy Eckardt, reported that many of the strands in the revival represented utilitarian folk-religion which addressed itself primarily to the security of individuals, and encouraged a folksy solidarity but neglected the deeper issues of both spiritual and social life. Martin E. Marty, a prominent church historian, found that the revival was not as much interested in historic faith as in religion in general, adapted to support America's 'real' religion of democracy. President Eisenhower spoke of deeply felt but generalized religious faith as important for sustaining free government.[21] That the multiform renewal of the post-war years had its limitations became especially clear when the tide quickly turned very early in the following decade. Yet the lives of many Americans were decisively influenced by the religious resurgence, and currents of authentic Christian spirituality flowed among the more ephemeral streams so deeply entangled with cultural realities.

Inasmuch as the Roman Catholic Church in the United States thought of itself as a distinctive minority with a special sense of mission, it was largely spared the debilitating effects of the spiritual depression of 1925-35 that so affected Protestantism. It gained greatly in national prestige during the presidency of Franklin Roosevelt; a number of Catholics were prominent during his long administration (1933-45). Some church leaders like John A. Ryan envisioned the possibility of a 'Catholic America' in the fullness of time. Many of the federal programmes on behalf of social justice, labour, the unions, and the underprivileged enacted by the 'New Deal' government were consistent in a general way with Catholic social emphases. Certain of the concerns long advocated by Ryan and other outspoken Catholic leaders found legislative expression. A biography of Ryan by F. L. Broderick was aptly entitled *Right Reverend New Dealer: John A. Ryan* (1963), for Ryan had a consistently high assessment of the New Deal. He once declared that

Never before in our history have the policies of the federal government embodied as much legislation that is of a highly ethical order. Never before in our

21 Herberg, *Protestant-Catholic-Jew: An Essay in American Religious Sociology* (Garden City, New York, 1955), esp. pp. 86-94; Eckardt, *The Surge of Piety in America: An Appraisal* (New York, 1958); Marty, *The New Shape of American Religion* (New York, 1959).

history have government policies been so deliberately, formally, and consciously based upon conceptions and convictions of moral right and social justice.[22]

Many Catholics did not share Ryan's enthusiasm, however, and some others who had been early supporters of the New Deal changed their minds. Prominent among them was Charles E. Coughlin, a priest of Royal Oak, Michigan, who had built up a considerable radio-following and become an advocate of Roosevelt's policies. But his advocacy of questionable monetary theories led to a break with the Democrats as he supported a third party in 1936. Two years later he advocated anti-Semitic views and inspired the forming of a 'Christian front'. His controversial national career came to an end early in the 1940s when he was forbidden by his superiors to continue his radio and political activities. More lasting contributions to American life were made by the Association of Catholic Trade Unionists (A.C.T.U., founded in 1937) which effectively supported unionism among Catholics, and by the lay editors of *Commonweal*, who interpreted Catholicism so as to support liberal democracy. By the 1940s, what had been in great measure a church of immigrants was now very much at home, and the sons and grandsons of the newcomers were rising in the socio-economic scale, some quite rapidly.

Before American entry into World War II the bishops had spoken clearly against Nazism and Communism, and they pledged their support to the nation after Pearl Harbor. In the armed services, Catholic personnel were thrown into close association with those of other faiths and of no faith, and chaplains learned to work together; all this helped to lessen mutual isolation and prejudices. During the days of the vast common national effort, the naturalization of the Catholic Church was largely completed. Emerging as the most powerful figure in the hierarchy was Francis J. Spellman (1889–1967), who had been educated at Fordham University and the North American College in Rome and had served for a time in the office of the papal secretariat of state in Rome. In 1939 he was made Archbishop of New York and Bishop of the Armed Forces of his country. As the chief link between Rome and the United States, he helped to arrange for a personal representative of President Roosevelt at the Vatican. Myron Taylor, an Episcopal layman, served in that capacity. Conspicuous for his patriotic activities during the war, Spellman was named a cardinal in 1946.

In the years following the war, Catholicism flourished in the genial atmosphere of the religious revival. Membership increased from some

[22] As quoted by David J. O'Brien, *American Catholics and Social Reform: The New Deal Years* (New York, 1968), p. 136.

twenty-one to forty-two million between 1940 and 1960; an increasing birth-rate, continuing immigration (especially of refugees), and the winning of converts were all factors in this impressive growth. The renewed vitality showed itself in many ways. New trends in biblical, theological, and liturgical thought were often stimulated from abroad, somewhat like neo-orthodoxy in Protestantism, with which it soon made contact. A new wave of attention to biblical scholarship and exegesis was encouraged in 1943 with the publication of an important encyclical of Pius XII, *Divino Afflante Spiritu*. Urged to take careful account of archaeological and philosophical insights in their interpretative work, Catholic biblical scholars were soon working in co-operation with others, and many priests began to put greater emphasis on the Bible in parish work. Theological reflection concerning the nature of the church took an important new turn in that same year as a result of another papal encyclical, *Mystici Corporis Christi*, with its emphasis on the church as the mystical body of Christ. The new emphases became known to many of the clergy and laity through the liturgical renaissance. The roots of that important development lay in nineteenth-century Europe; an influential interpreter of the movement in America was Virgil Michel (1890–1938) of the Benedictine abbey at Collegeville, Minnesota. Encouraged by another influential encyclical of Pius XII, *Mediator Dei* (1947), the advocates of liturgical renewal sought to increase lay participation in the mass, and to heighten awareness of the deeper spiritual meanings of worship.

Though nourished to some extent by these scholarly currents, much of the increase of Catholic fervour in the post-war period was of a more popular style. Fulton J. Sheen (b. 1895), a gifted teacher and magnetic speaker who won many converts while serving on the faculty of Catholic University, had developed a national radio-following. In the 1950s Bishop Sheen appeared on a regular television programme which was one of the central features of the high tide of the religious revival of those years. Sheen also wrote widely circulated books, especially *Peace of Soul* (1949). Another writer who stressed the Catholic aspects of deepened religious interest was Thomas Merton (1905–68), a convert whose autobiographical account of his journey to faith and to a vocation as a Trappist monk became famous as *The Seven Storey Mountain* (1948).

Both Catholicism and Protestantism profited from the religious resurgence; on the whole the historic animosities between the traditions were not intensified. Conspicuous leaders in both camps were well known across confessional lines, in part because of the spread of television in this period. Yet certain tensions persisted, and surfaced over several touchy issues. The naming by President Roosevelt of a personal representative at the Vatican disturbed many Americans, but when President Truman later proposed to name an ambassador to the Vatican, the resulting outcry forestalled the project. In 1947 an organization named Protestants and Other Americans United for the Separation of Church and State was founded; it expressed particular concern with the growing strength of Catholicism and interested itself in important contests in the courts on church–state issues. The question of the use of tax moneys for parochial schools was especially divisive. In a series of important Supreme Court decisions, beginning in 1947 with *Everson* v. *Board of Education*, the court insisted that direct aid to religious schools violated the Constitution. In later actions which declared that Bible reading and prayer in public schools were unconstitutional (*Abington School District* v. *Schempp* and *Murray* v. *Curlett*, 1963), the high court was sharply criticized. Much Protestant as well as Catholic resentment was stirred by some of these decisions, but in interpreting the First Amendment in a pluralistic religious situation, the court found that the separation of church and state extended to church-sponsored schools. The Catholic school system, however, the largest private educational operation in the world, continued to flourish without tax support through the period of revival, with more than 4,500,000 pupils in elementary schools, and a million more in high schools.

Social thought and action did not loom as large among either Protestants or Catholics in the post-war years as they had during the progressive era or during the depression. Discussions of Christian responsibility in the areas of economics and politics were generally grounded in theological and ethical considerations; social action programmes sought to be realistic in their aims, and were often focused on specific issues. The tension between conservative and liberal patterns of social reflection and programming continued; the approaches of the national and state councils of churches and of the N.C.W.C. usually had a liberal slant, while many congregations and some of the denominations remained strongly conservative. Such diverse figures as James W. Fifield, a Congregational minister and founder of Spiritual Mobilization, and Edward A. Keller, professor of economics at the University of Notre Dame, were articulate representatives of right-wing socio-economic viewpoints.

There was mounting concern in the churches over the unjust and unequal treatment of racial minorities. The delayed reaction to the detention in relocation camps of Americans of Japanese ancestry during World War II was one sign of a deepened sensitivity in racial matters;

another was a growing awareness in the churches of how unjustly Negroes were treated in American life and how deeply patterns of segregation had affected church life—it was often said that the most segregated hour in American life was at eleven on Sundays. The Federal Council of Churches had been active in the field of race relations since World War I, but immediately after the second war in 1946 it formally renounced patterns of segregation as a violation of the gospel of love, and pledged itself to work for a non-segregated society. In 1947 the Catholic Archbishop of St. Louis, Joseph Ritter (1892–1967) ended segregation in the parochial schools of his archdiocese, and 'when a group of Catholics organized to oppose the new policy by civil court action, the archbishop warned them, in a pastoral letter read from all the pulpits of the diocese on September 21, 1947, that they ran the risk of excommunication. Shortly thereafter, the group withdrew their action at court and disbanded.'[23]

The attention given to racial matters in the nation and in the churches was greatly increased by the historic Supreme Court decision of 1954, *Brown* v. *Board of Education*, calling for an end of segregation in the public schools. Black church leaders, long in the forefront of the struggle for racial justice, emerged into a new prominence, especially the talented young Baptist minister, Martin Luther King, Jr. (1929–68). Educated at Morehouse College, Crozer Theological Seminary, and Boston University, Dr. King led the black community of Montgomery, Alabama, in a long successful struggle against segregation in public buses. He founded the Southern Christian Leadership Conference to extend the drive for integration through non-violent means. He and other leaders drew much support from the churches, black and white, in this new effort of black people to gain their rights. King was not only an inspiring and prophetic leader, he was also a theological thinker whose writings presented an influential interpretation of Christian faith and ethics.

An important moral issue that troubled many Christians surfaced in the 1950s. Senator Joseph R. McCarthy, a Catholic, was an influential anti-communist whose activities helped to play down popular fears of Catholicism among many people. Yet he used his role as chairman of a Senate subcommittee on investigations to crusade against Communism in ways considered by growing numbers to be irresponsible. Those with only casual association with Communists were subject to cross-examination and often arbitrary dismissal. A mood of suspicion and fear spread. Several religious leaders protested, especially the Methodist Bishop G.

[23] William Osborne, *The Segregated Covenant: Race Relations and American Catholics*, pp. 112 ff.

Bromley Oxnam, and the moderator of the Presbyterian Church in the United States of America, John A. Mackay. The latter, president of Princeton Theological Seminary, was chiefly responsible for drafting 'A Letter to Presbyterians, Concerning the Present Situation in Our Country and in the World'. Declaring that 'treason and dissent are being confused', and that 'attacks are being made upon citizens of integrity and social passion which are utterly alien to our democratic habits', the letter asserted that 'the majesty of truth must be preserved at all times and at all costs'.[24] Adopted by the church, the document received much favourable attention at home and abroad, but was sharply attacked by others. It played some part in the rising tide of resistance against 'McCarthyism' and in the censure of the senator by his colleagues.

There were some significant developments in the field of co-operative, ecumenical, and unitive Christianity in this period. Several important mergers within denominational families took place. The trend toward consolidation within Lutheranism continued. Three synods of German background (Ohio, Iowa, Buffalo) merged in 1930 to form the American Lutheran Church. In 1961 this church entered a larger union with the Evangelical Lutheran Church and the United Evangelical Lutheran Church (of Norwegian and Danish backgrounds) to form The American Lutheran Church, which two years later the Lutheran Free Church also entered. Meanwhile, in 1962 the Lutheran Church in America was formed by the union of the United Lutheran Church of America (primarily German background), the Augustana Synod (Swedish), the American Evangelical Lutheran Church (Danish), and the Finnish Evangelical Lutheran Church. The various churches were well along the way to full use of English. Before 1900 all the pastors serving churches of Danish background, for example, were of Danish birth; by 1950 two-thirds of them were native-born. The mergers of the early 1960s brought the vast bulk of American Lutherans into three main bodies; the third was the conservative Lutheran Church—Missouri Synod. The Lutheran Church in America was the most ecumenically minded and the most in dialogue with other traditions; The American Lutheran Church occupied a middle position.

Another significant union was within Methodism in 1939, bringing together the small Methodist Protestant Church, which had withdrawn from the main body in 1828 seeking increased democracy in church government, and the northern and southern branches of the Methodist Episcopal Church, which had divided over the slavery question in 1844.

---

[24] Reprinted in Smith, Handy, Loetscher, *American Christianity*, ii, 551–2.

There were many issues to be faced before reunion could take place, and it took over three decades to do it. The status of Negro members in the new church was intensely debated; some white southerners thought it would be best to form an autonomous church for them as had been done after the Civil War. Finally, however, they were grouped in a separate 'jurisdiction' of a church in which all other jurisdictions were geographical. This compromise was later abandoned. The black denominations—African Methodist Episcopal, African Methodist Episcopal Zion, and Colored (later Christian) Methodist Episcopal—were not included. Two Methodist bodies of German background merged in the Evangelical United Brethren Church in 1946; twelve years later the small United Presbyterian Church joined with the northern Presbyterians to form the United Presbyterian Church in the United States of America. Later this communion produced a contemporary 'Confession of 1967' which reflected the impact of ecumenical and neo-orthodox theology.

These unions were within denominational families, but the formation of the United Church of Christ in 1957–61 brought churches together across confessional lines. There had been two preliminary unions; in 1931 the Congregational churches united with a small Christian church (General Convention) which had grown out of the movement for a primitive evangelical Christianity at the beginning of the nineteenth century; three years later the Reformed Church of the United States, of German and Swiss background, merged with the Evangelical Synod of the United States, which had brought together German immigrants of both Lutheran and Reformed background. In 1942, representatives of the Congregational Christian and Evangelical and Reformed churches began to discuss union; a Basis of Union went through many revisions before it appeared in 1949. Then court action by non-concurring Congregationalists stalled the formal action of union until 1957. The union became effective in 1961; only a few congregations did not enter the United Church. In some way analogous to the United Church of Canada, it represented of course a much smaller percentage of the total Protestant constituency of America.

In the field of co-operative Christianity, an important event occurred in 1950, when twelve agencies merged to form the National Council of the Churches of Christ in the United States of America. About thirty denominations had been co-operating through the Federal Council of Churches and other organizations devoted to missionary, educational, and other causes. Included in the merger was the United Council of Church Women, which had been founded in 1941, combining the resources of previous co-operative women's agencies devoted to missionary and other efforts. As the work of all the dozen agencies had grown and overlapped, it was recognized that the time had come to co-ordinate the co-ordinators. The churches in the new National Council had a combined membership of about 33,000,000 in 143,000 congregations. The council included a broad spectrum of Protestant church life, and sought to serve its member churches in missions, social action, and unity. Five black churches were in the membership—three Methodist and two Baptist —and they played a growing role in the Council's work. The black churches had often been considered as generally similar to those of the majority white population, but as co-operation increased, the distinctive style and mission of these churches became more obvious. This was illustrated by a careful survey of the Detroit area in the late 1950s by Gerhard Lenski. To the surprise of many, he found that 'the denominational groups within Detroit Protestantism no longer constitute self-contained socio-religious groups to any degree, while the racial groups do'. He found that among the black Protestants 'the communal bond is extremely strong, owing to the discriminatory practices of the whites', and that 'segregation tends to be the rule in the urban North almost as much as the rural South'.[25] The growing participation of blacks in co-operative Christianity helped to focus attention on the issues of racial justice.

Four charter members of the National Council of Churches were of Eastern Orthodox background—Russian Orthodox of North America, Syrian Antiochian Orthodox, Romanian Orthodox, and Ukrainian Orthodox, while the Greek Orthodox Archdiocese of North and South America soon joined, as did several other churches at a later date. As in the case of other churches so strongly affected by the influx of late nineteenth- and early twentieth-century immigration, the children and grandchildren of the newcomers were fully at home by the sixth decade, and many had become prosperous. Thus the council was no longer essentially a 'pan-Protestant' organization, for over-all Orthodox membership had passed the two million mark. The large Russian and Greek Orthodox churches had founded seminaries, and increasingly played a significant role in ecumenical life.

Many North American Christians participated in the series of conferences that led up to the formation of the World Council of Churches at Amsterdam in 1948. Its basis was the simple declaration that 'The World Council of Churches is a fellowship of Churches which accept our Lord Jesus Christ as God and Saviour'. Twenty-eight American and

---

[25] Gerhard Lenski, *The Religious Factor: A Sociological Study of Religion's Impact on Politics, Economics, and Family Life* (Garden City, N.Y., 1961), pp. 20, 36.

three Canadian churches were among the charter members. The World Council was an important channel for the theological renaissance of the post-war years, and deepened the acquaintance of many scholars and leaders of the American Churches with the biblical and revelational theologies so strong in Europe.

When the Second Assembly of the World Council met in Evanston, Illinois, in 1954, many Canadian and American Christians had their first direct observation of ecumenical encounter. Largely under the stimulus of this experience, the first North American Faith and Order Conference brought representatives from thirty-eight churches of the United States and Canada to Oberlin, Ohio, during the summer of 1957. The conference called attention to the local aspects of ecumenicity; as Paul S. Minear, a prominent New Testament scholar, expressed it

shepherds of the world-wide Church are coming to realize that concern for the Church's catholicity compels them to manifest this oneness in the church local. Shepherds of local congregations, on the other hand, are coming to realize that they cannot fulfill their vocation at home unless their congregation participates fully in the Church universal.[26]

Delegates of Eastern Orthodox communions participated actively, offering their conviction that the unity desired by the churches has been given in historical tradition and is embodied in the Orthodox Church. Several unofficial but accredited Roman Catholic observers were at the Oberlin conference—early signs of the coming thaw in the relations between Roman Catholics and other Christians.

As the 1950s drew to a close, there were high hopes for the continued vitality of the Christian churches—the religious, biblical, theological, liturgical, and ecumenical revivals had brought church membership and attendance to impressive heights, and the possibilities for genuine unitive advance seemed good. Yet there was much that passed for revival that lacked spiritual depth; churches identified too easily with the cults of achievement and success then so strong in a prosperous nation without subjecting them to intense scrutiny in the light of their own historic traditions. Some were aware of the superficialities of the renewal; others were to see them only after the tide turned.

Currents of Renewal in the Canadian Churches

Canada had entered World War II at its outbreak in September 1939, nearly two years before its southern neighbour. Though generally recognizing the necessity of the war, the churches determined not to fall into

[26] Paul S. Minear (ed.), *The Nature of the Unity We Seek* (St. Louis, 1958), p. 24.

the superpatriotic and uncritical justification of the war that had happened before, and for the most part succeeded. As in other lands, church support of the national effort was in providing chaplains, in comforting and helping distressed and bereaved families, and in entertaining and aiding those in military service. Much of the pacifism that had been so strong between the wars eroded, and despite some lapses when pacifist ministers lost pulpits, 'supporters of the war, remembering the aftermath of the previous one and in many cases their own earlier pacifism, sought to maintain an atmosphere of freedom'.[27] Yet some restrictions on freedom were seen as necessary, and there was little protest when Canadian-born citizens of Japanese descent on the coast of British Columbia were forced into detention camps in 1941, or when Jehovah's Witnesses were banned as a subversive movement.

In Quebec, where there was considerable difference of opinion concerning Canada's role in the war, the consensus was for moderate participation, with Canada's interests put before those of Britain. Conscription was unpopular, but the National Resources Mobilization Act of 1940 was accepted because it provided that those drafted would not be required to serve overseas without their consent. Cardinal Villeneuve of Quebec strongly supported national registration, and in 1941 called for the celebration of masses for victory in the parishes of his archdiocese—a gesture which put the Catholic Church's influence behind the war effort. He called for Canadian unity, and hailed those who enlisted in a righteous cause, both English and French Canadians. As the war dragged on and the cost of victory increased, the government passed a new law which could put conscripts in battle abroad; this was bitterly resented, especially by nationalist elements among the French Canadians, and there was a marked decline in enthusiasm for the war, and some criticism of the cardinal and other Catholic leaders. English-speaking Canadians, deeply aware of the military situation in Europe, had difficulty understanding French scruples in a time of national crisis. As Wade said,

A basic factor in the situation was the refusal of many English Canadians to recognize that Canada was a bi-ethnic, bi-cultural, and bilingual country. While there was improvement in mutual understanding among university people, intellectuals, and the younger generation less conditioned by old differences, there remained a fundamental misunderstanding.[28]

The French Canadians regarded conscription as a symbol of dominance by

---

[27] Grant, *The Churches in the Canadian Era*, p. 151.
[28] *The French Canadians, 1760–1945*, p. 953.

the majority. Though there were no riots as there had been during the previous war, long-standing tensions between English- and French-speaking peoples were inflamed again.

During the long years of war, the theological atmosphere in the Protestant communions changed. Karl Barth and Reinhold Niebuhr were widely read; neo-orthodox emphases on divine transcendence, human sinfulness, the atoning work of Christ, and the centrality of the Bible received increased attention in the life of the churches. Both liberals and conservatives were affected by the new trends. One of Barth's chief interpreters was Professor (later Principal) Walter Williamson Bryden of Knox College, a Presbyterian seminary. In the face of the issues of life and death that war brought home, many soldiers and civilians discovered that Christianity did have a relevant message for them. Realistic views of the economic and political order that were characteristic of the neo-orthodox trend countered the familiar concepts of both liberal and radical versions of the social gospel. Grant's summary is instructive: 'During these years the churches were moving from social perfection to social pragmatism, from conflict over absolute principles to the acceptance of a mixed economy, from concern for abstract justice to concern for practical welfare.'[29] In Roman Catholicism, new interest in Thomism enlivened theological work. The missionary work of both Catholics and Protestants expanded during the war years, and helped to fill the gaps caused by the inability of many European churches to carry on their work during the crisis.

In the fifteen years following the close of the war, Canada participated fully in a religious revival paralleling that of the United States, and the familiar indices of church membership, attendance at church schools and religious services, giving, the circulation of religious journals and books, and seminary enrolments all showed upward trends. Church building reached new peaks; for example, 'between 1945 and 1966, the United Church erected 1,500 new churches and church halls, and 600 new manses —many of them handsome rambling broadloomed ranch houses'.[30] Church growth was especially visible in the affluent suburbs, where the population explosion was centred. Churches of various denominational and theological backgrounds gained during the unprecedented and un-anticipated boom. Billy Graham's evangelistic crusades were well attended; the United Church conducted a series of national mission and evangelistic campaigns of its own. In both Catholic and Protestant

[29] *The Church in the Canadian Era*, p. 155.
[30] A. C. Forrest, in Kilbourn (ed.), *Religion in Canada*, p. 64.

churches, the role of the laity received greater prominence, and more responsible roles in ministry and mission were assumed by lay persons.

The co-operative and ecumenical spirit was also resurgent in these years of renewal. The Canadian Council of Churches was organized in 1944, with Anglican, Baptist, Disciple, Orthodox, Presbyterian, Quaker, Salvation Army, and United churches included in the membership. It was founded in anticipation of the formation of the World Council of Churches, and also as a result of the decision in the United States to merge the Federal Council of Churches into a National Council. The Federal Council had a North American purview, but its only Canadian member was the United Church; the logic of having a separate council for Canada was persuasive. As Grant declared,

The Canadian Council of Churches has become a useful and even indispensable organ of cooperation and consultation for the denominations that support it. It has never quite succeeded in stirring their enthusiasm or in commanding a loyalty comparable to that called forth by the Churches themselves.[31]

Interest in church union, long dormant after the controversies of the twenties, awoke again, as committees of the Anglican Church of Canada (the name was officially changed from the Church of England in Canada in 1955) and the United Church began to discuss that possibility. The unitive trend was also operative within denominational families. The Baptist Federation of Canada finally came into existence in 1944; eight years later most of the Lutheran bodies, which were growing rapidly, formed the Canadian Lutheran Council.

During the period of the religious revival, some of the smaller conservative bodies not related to ecumenical agencies were flourishing. In 1945 Jehovah's Witnesses emerged from underground to enjoy phenomenal growth—'their congregations doubled, to nearly 900 in twenty years, and the number of active ministers increased from 18,000 to 42,000'.[32] Membership in Pentecostal churches increased by 50 per cent during the 1950s. Their influence was especially strong in Newfoundland, which entered the Dominion in 1949. A relative newcomer, the Christian Reformed Church, spread rapidly, in part because of Dutch immigration after the war. Many strongly conservative Baptist congregations which had broken with the older associations became affiliated with the Fellowship of Evangelical Baptist Churches in Canada, founded in 1953. Conservative evangelicals, especially in the west, participated in the revival spirit even as they criticized the way some of its manifestations seemed

[31] *The Canadian Experience of Church Union*, pp. 82 ff.
[32] Forrest, in Kilbourn (ed.), *Religion in Canada*, p. 77.

bound by contemporary culture. Their various groups had enough in common in their biblical literalism that most could participate in such organizations and the Inter-Varsity Christian Fellowship and Youth for Christ.

The Doukhobors, cut off from other religious groups by their distinctive customs, did not share in the tides of revival. In part through poor leadership, their community organization came to an end in 1939; a new Union of Spiritual Communities of Christ took its place. The Sons of Freedom, a small minority of the Doukhobors, renewed their terrorist acts of arson and dynamiting after the war, bringing the whole group under a cloud. Terrorism came to a climactic conclusion in 1962. Then, following mass arrests and a long confusing trial which led to imprisonment for a number of the accused at the Mountain Prison near Agassiz, British Columbia, many of the remaining Sons of Freedom set out from their ruined villages on a long march west to camp near the prison. Their spirit of terrorism evaporated, and without the agitation of these Sons of Freedom the peaceful Doukhobors moved toward assimilation. In the words of scholarly investigators of this unusual group,

Where decades of police and bureaucratic action failed, a few years of exposure to the affluent society have succeeded. It now seems likely that the Doukhobors will maintain their separateness merely as one of the many small and picturesque religious groups of Canada; their dietary rules less complex than those of the Orthodox Jews; their theological concepts no more unorthodox than those of the Mormons; their economic organization far less radical than that of the still communitarian Hutterites; their pacifism no more vigorous than that of the Quakers. Only the strange chants of the Living Book, like an unsevered umbilical cord, will unite them with their increasingly remote past in the steppes and mountains of Russia.[33]

It would be hard to find a more powerful illustration of the way a prosperous modern society exercises a spell of conformity over its members.

Just as the Doukhobors were affected by the assimilative powers of North American life, more conventional Christians were even more moulded by the life of their time. The post-war revival of religion was genuine, but it was neither radical nor profound, and much it accomplished would soon be swept away.

The Confusion of Tongues

By the early 1960s, it was clear that the period of general revival in North American Christianity was over. Some of the many strands of a highly diversified church life continued to flourish; new enthusiasms and causes

[33] Woodcock and Avakumovic, *The Doukhobors*, p. 356.

gripped significant groups and attracted attention, often momentary. Caught in a time when long-familiar values and standards in society were challenged by counter-cultures, most of the churches were thrust into a time of troubles and confusion. Voices from both inside and outside the churches were suggesting that the patterns of western Christendom, so often adapted to suit the needs of the pluralistic populations of democratic industrial nations, were at last breaking down. As the decade wore on, it appeared that an era was coming to an end, yet the shape of the new had not yet emerged.

The 1960s began auspiciously enough for the churches. Though signs that the popular revival was over had been noticed, the churches were in a strong position, numerically and geographically. One sign of vitality in the Protestant world was the bold proposal of Eugene Carson Blake (b. 1906), the principal executive of the United Presbyterian Church in the United States of America, that his own denomination join with the Protestant Episcopal Church, the United Church of Christ, and the Methodist Church to form a plan of church union. Though reactions to Blake's call, extended in a sermon at the Episcopal Cathedral in San Francisco late in 1960, were mixed, the invitation was accepted, and early in 1962 the Consultation on Church Union (C.O.C.U.) gathered to begin its work amid rising interest. Six other denominations soon entered the consultation: the African Methodist Episcopal Church, the African Methodist Episcopal Zion Church, the Christian Churches (Disciples of Christ), the Christian Methodist Episcopal Church, the Evangelical United Brethren Church, and the Presbyterian Church in the United States. The consultation thus included three black denominations, and churches of episcopal, presbyterian, synodical, and congregational polity were involved. In addition, observers from many other communions, including Baptist, Orthodox, Moravian, Polish National Catholic, Roman Catholic, and three Canadian (Anglican, Presbyterian, United) churches, attended annual sessions. By mid-decade hopes for a union 'truly catholic, truly reformed and truly evangelical' were high. Informed extensively by the neo-orthodox, ecumenical theological syntheses shaped in the previous decade, a C.O.C.U. statement on the 'Principles of Church Union' expressed many agreements worked out by the official representatives of the negotiating churches. C.O.C.U. was only one of the signs of Protestant vitality—high seminary enrolments, church gatherings which combined missionary enthusiasm with social concern, and a continuing emphasis on the ministry of the laity were others.

For American Catholics, the decade began most auspiciously when the first Catholic president, John Fitzgerald Kennedy, was elected, overcoming the last barrier for Catholics in America. His sincere commitment to the separation of church and state was an important factor in his election. A youthful, popular, forceful leader, Kennedy as President opened what began as a decade of hope, of 'new frontiers' to conquer—poverty, injustice, inequality. He seemed to epitomize an important shift in Catholic mentality that was going on. For what was 'truly remarkable is the convergence of a John Kennedy and a John XXIII in the same moment of history'.[34] For the brief 'caretaker' pontificate of John XXIII (1958–63) seemed to be reversing the trend of centuries as dialogue with other Christians was seriously begun. Building on the work of his austere predecessor in the papacy, Pope John formed a Secretariat for Promoting Christian Unity, named official observers to attend the Third Assembly of the World Council of Churches at New Delhi in 1961, issued such progressive social encyclicals as *Mater et Magistra* (1961) and *Pacem in Terris* (1963), and summoned the Twenty-first Ecumenical Council, Vatican II, which met each autumn for four years from 1962 to 1965. He sought an updating (*aggiornamento*) of the church. In the early years of the pontificate of his successor, Paul VI, the liberal, ecumenical, and reformist elements at the council were conspicuous in the drafting of the sixteen officially promulgated texts, which dealt with such matters as the church, liturgy, revelation, ecumenism, bishops, priests, missions, the modern world, the laity, and non-Christians. A number of the North American hierarchy, especially Cardinals Joseph Ritter of St. Louis, Albert Meyer of Chicago, and Paul-Emile Léger of Montreal, were prominent for their leadership in reform at the council.

Of particular interest to Americans was the Declaration on Religious Freedom, of which John Courtney Murray, S.J. (1904–67), professor at Woodstock College, Maryland, was one of the principal authors. He became especially interested in the church–state issue when he joined some prominent Protestant leaders in protesting the 'secular' trend of Supreme Court decisions in 1948. Despite official restrictions, for decades he had been working toward an historical approach to an understanding of Catholicism and politics. Believing that democracy and religious freedom could be grounded in Catholic principles, he backed his views with impressive scholarship. The issue of the development of doctrine— long suspect among conservative Catholics—underlay many of the Council's debates, and emerged with particular force in the discussion of the controversial Declaration on Religious Freedom. Yet it passed

34 Eugene C. Bianchi, *John XXIII and American Protestants* (Washington, D.C., 1968), p. 126.

overwhelmingly, marking a milestone in church history with the statement that 'It is therefore completely in accord with the nature of faith that in matters religious every manner of coercion on the part of men should be excluded'.[35]

The Council had an immediate impact at all levels of church life. This was especially evident in the shift to the use of the vernacular in the liturgy after centuries of the Latin mass (except for Eastern rite Catholics), in the rise of collegiality of bishops and priests, in the adaptation to secular garb in which priests and nuns soon began to appear, and in the extensive participation of Catholics in ecumenical affairs. A number of 'bi-lateral conversations' between representatives of the Roman Catholic and of other traditions were begun; they helped to dispel mutual misunderstandings. Some American dioceses became members of state councils of churches, and the Catholic Church considered becoming a member of the National Council of Churches, and did join its Faith and Order Commission. The National Conference of Catholic Bishops was formed in 1966; it had more power than the old National Catholic Welfare Conference, which now became the United States Catholic Conference, a secretariat of the hierarchy. Canadian bishops had been meeting annually since 1943; after Vatican II their Canadian Catholic Conference took on a new importance.

A determination to do something about the way black people were so unequally and prejudicially treated was characteristic of the high hopes and morale of the churches in the early sixties. This matter has long remained as a serious blot on both religion and society. From the National Catholic Conference for Interracial Justice came the impetus for a national interfaith approach to the problem of racial justice, and Catholic, Jewish, Protestant, and Orthodox forces co-operated in calling a National Conference on Religion and Race in Chicago in January 1963. A continuing organization emerged, which played an important role in the passage of federal civil rights legislation in 1964, and encouraged the formation of local interfaith conferences on religion and race in a number of places. The dedication of many church persons from all traditions to the cause of equality was symbolized in mass participation in the March on Washington on 28 August 1963, when several hundred thousand people gathered in a great rally at which religious leaders were prominent, and which was climaxed by the eloquence of Martin Luther King, Jr. The

[35] Walter M. Abbott, S.J. (ed.), *The Documents of Vatican II* (New York, 1966), p. 690. The interventions of the bishops from the United States at the council are in Vincent A. Yzermans (ed.), *American Participation in the Second Vatican Council* (New York, 1967).

National Council of Churches' Commission on Religion and Race provided strong leadership for church participation in the civil rights movements of the 1960s. What had begun as a concern for integration broadened out to include the political and economic concerns of minority groups.

In Canada the gradual recognition that the religious boom of the 1950s had tapered off was not so much a cause for alarm as an occasion for consolidation and experimentation. Most of the larger churches made changes in their liturgical patterns, and new curricula of Christian education were put into use. For example, Grant has noted that 'the new curriculum of the United Church, which began to appear in 1962, was in many respects a classic example of Protestant modernization'.[36] Based on careful theological and pedagogical research, the new programme was generally well received; like C.O.C.U. and several new denominational curricula in the United States it reflected the neo-orthodox theological stamp of the fifties. Programmes for youth were recast along less paternalistic lines. In a number of denominations, women were questioning the familiar assumptions on which their organizations were based; in the United Church previously separated societies were brought together in official relationship to other church structures as United Church Women in 1962; a similar step was taken with the formation of Anglican Church Women in 1966. Missions to Indians and Eskimos were in transition as the process of cultural interchange was increasingly seen to be a two-way matter. Increasing emphasis was placed on the preparation of indigenous leaders by both Catholics and Protestants.

The dramatic changes in Catholic life which emerged out of Vatican II were felt in Canada with the appearance of vernacular liturgies, new trends in theological education, increased lay participation in parish work, and the swift extension of interreligious dialogue. One of the significant centres of ecumenical growth was in Montreal, where French Catholic and English Protestant clergy and laity entered into dialogue. In the discussions the small minority of French Canadian Protestants could often serve as mediators, gaining an acceptance and understanding long denied them. One illustration of the new ecumenical spirit was the co-operation of eight churches in proclaiming the gospel through use of audio-visual techniques at the Christian Pavilion of Expo '67, the celebration of the 100th anniversary of the Dominion of Canada at Montreal. In Claude de Mestral's words:

This was finally agreed upon by seven Churches: Roman Catholic, United, Anglican, Presbyterian, Lutheran, Baptist and Greek Orthodox—followed later

36 *The Church in the Canadian Era*, p. 186.

on by the Ukrainian Greek Orthodox Church. Never before had these Churches, representing over 90% of the Christian population, engaged in a joint missionary effort.[37]

In this period of ecumenical advance, the closest thing to C.O.C.U. with its concern for union across confessional lines was the renewed United Church-Anglican conversations, and a statement of principles for union was issued in 1965. The small Christian Church (Disciples of Christ) later entered the negotiations.

In both Canada and the United States dialogue between representatives of Christianity and Judaism increased. It grew in part out of the recognition that in religiously pluralistic societies deeper understanding and co-operation among the many institutions of faith are of mutual and common advantage. The Second Vatican Council's Declaration on the Relationship of the Church to Non-Christian Religions, while not fully satisfying from the point of view of many Jews and Christians, did insist that responsibility for Christ's crucifixion 'cannot be blamed upon all the Jews then living, without distinction, nor upon the Jews of today', and called for an increase in deepened understanding, respect, and dialogue.[38] Many of the councils of churches and denominations increased their contacts with Jewish agencies, and the writings of such Jewish authors as Martin Buber and Abraham Heschel became more familiar to many Christians. The Six Day War of 1967 strained some of these new relationships, for many Christians dismissed as a political question what is an important part of Jewish self-understanding—the survival and security of the new (1948) State of Israel. Christian attitudes to Jews, which had been shaped over the long centuries of Christendom, were slowly and unevenly changing; many responsible church leaders were seeking to minimize prejudicial and anti-Semitic references in Christian literature.

Though the churches in both countries entered the 1960s in a mood of confidence, a series of sweeping changes and reverses brought disappointment, confusion, and decline. Consciousness of the multiple problems of North American life—for example, racism, rural and urban poverty, pollution of the environment, inadequate medical care, inflation, crime rates—increased sharply. The evils seemed to multiply much faster than the remedial efforts of governmental, church, and other voluntary programmes which were designed to alleviate them. In the United States, the assassination of President Kennedy in November 1963 was especially

[37] Claude de Mestral, 'When Should the Church Speak', in Philip Le Blanc and Arnold Edinborough (eds.), *One Church, Two Nations?* (Don Mills, Ont., 1968), p. 163.
[38] Abbott (ed.), *The Documents of Vatican II*, pp. 665 ff.

disillusioning to young people who had pinned great hopes on his way of facing difficult modern problems. President Lyndon Johnson pledged himself to continue to march to the 'great society', but the escalation in 1965 of American involvement in the long, disastrous Vietnam War blunted the wars on poverty and racism and resulted in a growing resistance on the part of many young people not only to the war but to the broad pattern of American values and institutions that supported it. Many Christians joined in the opposition to the war, but the issue was long a divisive one in the churches.

Though it also was controversial, support in the struggle for racial justice and integration was also given by many Catholic, Protestant, and Orthodox Christians. Various minority groups were claiming a larger recognition of their rights, contributions, and needs in society and in the churches. American blacks, Indians, Hispanic Americans, and Chicanos were forming caucuses and pressing for greater attention and opportunities of leadership.

In the 1960s the concerns of the largest of these minorities were especially conspicuous. Distinct advances were made, but for most blacks the pace of change was much too slow. Their relative economic situation in relation to the whole population did not improve, and the prejudice of many whites toward blacks had not noticeably changed. Black anger was expressed in destructive urban riots, notably in the Watts section of Los Angeles in 1965. Discouraged by the caution and moderation of both black and white liberals, more militant black leadership appeared in the movement for black self-determination and black power in the later 1960s. The non-violent strategies of Martin Luther King came under criticism, and by the time of his tragic assassination at Memphis, Tennessee, in April 1968, which triggered another series of riots, concern for black liberation and power was challenging the earlier focus on reconciliation and integration. Within both black and white denominations and councils of churches there were many confrontations between moderates and militants. Black caucuses were active in denominations that had a minority of black members, and a National Conference of Black Churchmen was formed in 1966. The hopes of an earlier period that racial peace and justice might soon come were shattered by the realities of the turbulent sixties. At the end of the decade, a strident call for 'reparations' by the churches was made in the 'Black Manifesto'.

These tensions were not unknown among the small Canadian black communities. By the early part of the decade Canadian blacks had largely secured long-desired goals of provincial fair employment and accommodations acts and a federal bill of rights; Canadian-born blacks had teamed up with West Indians, whose primary goal was the liberalization of immigration restrictions, and with other ethnic minorities to win these victories. In Robin Winks's summary, 'Indians, Eskimaux, Ukrainians, and others no less eager to see legislation on civil rights, and Greeks, Italians, Hungarians, Chinese, and South Asians were not less vocal in their protests against the immigration policy.'[39] The emergence of black power, stimulated in part by visits by leaders from the United States, increased inner tension in the black churches, especially in Nova Scotia, as those who had long been in the vanguard of advance were challenged by new militant styles of leadership.

The major ethnic tension in Canadian society was heightened in this troubled decade. As Canadian Roman Catholic bishops stated the matter in 1967,

There is no concealing the fact that the chief malady of Canadian society consists in the deep discontent felt by a growing number of French-Canadians at the difficulties which their community must face in its attempts at growth; and in the uneasiness which the claims of the French-speaking arouse in other parts of the country.[40]

They called for deeper understanding and peace between the communities; the more militant were willing to talk about separation in some form. The ethnic tension had increased, but it was expressed less and less in religious terms; most churches officially strongly supported bi-culturalism and bilingualism.

Another movement for liberation was felt in the North American churches by the later 1960s. A number of church women who had participated in the civil rights crusade became seriously troubled as they reflected on the unequal treatment accorded them in both society and church, and as they analysed the patterns of male domination in leadership prerogatives, economic advantages, and double moral standards. Some denominations—for example, Baptist, Congregationalist (now in the United Church of Christ), Disciples, Friends, Methodists, and the United Church of Canada—had long ordained women, but few had been called to prominent pulpits or places of national leadership. Under the pressure of the times, United Presbyterians and the Lutheran Church in America opened the ordained ministry to women, but in the Episcopal/Anglican communion a drive to open the priesthood to women became very

39 *The Blacks in Canada*, p. 434, cf. p. 352.
40 As quoted by Philip LeBlanc, O.P., in LeBlanc and Edinborough (eds.), *One Church, Two Nations?*, p. xi.

controversial. Meanwhile, most of the older women's missionary societies had been merged into general denominational work; one observer of the scene reported that 'the majority of women who have kept their major concern for world mission believe that women have less and less a place of genuine influence and participation in administrative offices, board membership, and policy making'.[41] The emergence of women's liberation movements in church and society posed a clear challenge for many of the familiar patterns in church and theological life even as they opened fresh sources of energy and insight.

There were some developments in thought and feeling in the sixties which lessened the appeal of the traditional churches for many persons, especially the young. The familiar cry 'we are losing our youth', was heard again. The achievements of science and technology, exhibited in the attainment of instant world communication by television, in the techniques of transplanting human organs in medicine, in the wizardry of computers, and in the phenomenal advance of space travel, led some to find the conventional religious and theological patterns of the churches antiquated and irrelevant. They felt that the available human resources were quite sufficient to deal with the formidable problems of national and international life, and that religion as familiarly known had little of worth to say about how those resources could be organized and focused.

Both Canada and the United States had long been considered Christian countries, if not in law then in tradition and spirit. The logic of religious freedom combined with the facts of the vast diversity of religious groups forced growing numbers to admit that these countries could no longer be considered to be Christian nations in the old sense. In sections where one tradition was still largely dominant, as in parts of the south, this secular outcome was less visible, but over-all the trend was clear, however much it was disliked in many quarters. It was expressed in two crucial decisions of the Supreme Court, *Engel* v. *Vitale* (1962) and *Abington School District* v. *Schempp* (1963). In *Engel*, the use in public schools of a prayer drafted by the New York Board of Regents was declared to be a religious ceremony and hence prohibited under the 'no establishment' clause of the First Amendment; the other decision forbade the devotional reading of the Bible in tax-supported schools. The division of opinion over these important cases was sharp—some argued for the 'rights of majorities' in the schools they largely paid for, while others saw it as the logical outcome of genuine religious freedom in a pluralistic land. These decisions meant that the power of the voluntary Protestant establishment as shaped in the

---

[41] Beaver, *All Loves Excelling*, pp. 200-1.

nineteenth century was continuing to fade. Questions were being raised about the continued defensibility of maintaining military chaplains at public expense and about tax exemptions for churches and synagogues. In English-speaking Canada, Grant declared, 'the unofficial establishment of Christianity had virtually come to an end in 1960, although it would take time for many people to adjust mentally to a situation in which churches were no longer moral policemen but pressure groups or even interest groups'. In Quebec the forming of a ministry of education by the provincial government in 1964 was a sign of an important shift, for the Catholic Church had long been dominant in educational affairs. Two years later the Canadian hierarchy admitted 'that on such matters as birth control Christian legislators should make decisions in terms of their own understanding of the common good rather than of Catholic doctrine'.[42] Though some Christians welcomed this 'second disestablishment' of religion as liberating, and others accepted it as inevitable, probably the majority only dimly perceived it, and were deeply troubled when they did. Yet the fading of voluntary Christendom and its patterns contributed to the loss of direction and morale in the churches.

Indeed, the many swift-changing realities and moods of the 1960s evoked a variety of responses in the churches, many of them contradictory. The neo-orthodox synthesis that was so influential among religiously minded intellectuals in the previous period gave way to a wide variety of options. Though the previous positions still found defenders, there was a tendency among theological pioneers to prefer the immanental to the transcendental, the concrete to the abstract, the application to the principle. A number of influential leaders were inclined to be more concerned with the world than with the church, with practice rather than theory, and the style of theology shifted from monologue to dialogue. Liberal questions that had been largely by-passed during the neo-orthodox period were renewed—for example, the old quest for the historical Jesus was resumed. Various types of empirical, natural, and humanist theologies found new champions; for example, a second Humanist Manifesto appeared in 1973 on the 40th anniversary of the first. Indeed, a number of theological questions and attitudes that had marked the stormy 1920s were heard again in the 1960s.

New types of radical theology were propounded. Turning from the older pieties of the churches, a group of younger theologians stressed a theology of the secular, emphasizing that God is at work in the world, and the truly committed can best identify with the divine purpose there. A

[42] Grant, *The Church in the Canadian Era*, pp. 202-3.

young Harvard theologian, Harvey Cox, expressed a confident optimism in human abilities and social processes in *The Secular City* (1965) which was read widely in Catholic as well as Protestant circles. Great attention was briefly given in the latter part of the decade to the 'death of God' theology; some used the term to mean the death of Christendom, while for others it had more ontological meaning, but all who used the term were referring to the way inherited Christian tradition had lost its meaning for them. This approach was too abstract and negative to last long, but other styles of radical theology appeared, many growing out of particular causes. Black theology concerned with the liberation of the oppressed was expressed in various ways by such thinkers as Albert Cleage, James H. Cone, Major J. Jones, and J. Deotis Roberts. Theologies of liberation and revolution, influenced by forceful voices from the 'third world' beyond the European and North American centres of power, attracted considerable attention, especially among the young. An emphasis on the feminine in theology questioned the predominance of images of the male in reflections about God and in discussions of the ministry. The impact of such trends was felt in various ways and combinations across the Protestant spectrum, in Roman Catholicism, and probably least of all in Eastern Orthodoxy.

While the parade of theologies was moving through the churches, the resurgence of conservative evangelicalism with its bastion of biblical authority continued through the stormy sixties and into the seventies. Many of its leaders dealt with theological issues in a scholarly way, and showed increasing social concern as they faced the decline of the established culture, but the movement retained moral and religious patterns that had been central in its earlier history. Conservative evangelicals generally still worked for a Christian nation. For example, from his Canadian perspective Grant declared that they 'now seem to constitute the only important segment of the church that seriously believes in the continued existence of Christendom . . . not to the European version but to the rurally based Protestant piety of North American bible belts'.[43] Symbolically, they did not participate in the ecumenical Christian Pavilion at Expo '67 but presented their message in their own pavilion.

Another theological option that found increasing numbers of supporters in the major historic churches as well as in their own was Pentecostalist. By 1972 the Full Gospel Businessmen's Fellowship had grown to 300,000 members in 900 chapters; to its dinner meetings, often in hotel ballrooms, 'friends and acquaintances would be invited to hear the testimonies of

43 *Ibid.*, p. 221.

noted or unusual public figures who had experienced the joy and release from anxiety which had come to them through the "baptism of the Spirit" '.[44] Episcopal, Lutheran, Methodist, and, after the outbreak of a charismatic revival in Pittsburgh in 1966, Roman Catholic churches harboured Pentecostal reform movements.

By the end of the sixties millions of devoted church members, some of them much informed by one or another of the new currents of thought and life, continued their support of institutional religion. But the Christian churches generally were having a difficult time holding the loyalty of great numbers of their young people, many of whom were deeply influenced by the movements of resistance to the established patterns of culture and education, often in protest to American participation in the Vietnam War. Some were won to eastern religious movements of various kinds, but others to experience-oriented 'Jesus people' or 'Jesus freaks'— intense, simplistic, fluid, often communally based groups of diverse styles. Many were influenced by fundamentalist and Pentecostalist teaching. The conservative Inter-Varsity Christian Fellowship and Campus Crusade could often appeal to those who identified themselves with the Jesus people, but they were very critical of the familiar churches.

The combination of vast national problems and the great variety of voices calling Christians to this or that option—many advanced in such a way as sharply to challenge traditional patterns—brought considerable confusion and turmoil into the churches. A number of ministers left church work for other pursuits; many denominations were beginning to decline in membership and prestige. One study documented the decline in membership, church school enrolment, and overseas mission forces of Lutheran, Episcopal, Methodist, Presbyterian, and United churches in the United States; and reported that in 1957, according to a Gallup poll, 14 per cent of the people thought that religion was losing influence, but by 1968, 67 per cent thought so.[45] A sociologist of religion analysed the 'web of crises' of the Protestant churches, seeing these crises 'as emerging out of serious doubt about the most basic theological doctrines of Christianity and from a growing struggle over the meaning and purpose of the church'.[46] These doubts and struggles led to a crisis of authority. For many lay persons were not willing to go along with the activist, secular concerns of some conspicuous church leaders, thus widening a clergy–laity gap

[44] Hudson, *Religion in America*, p. 429.

[45] Dean M. Kelley, *Why Conservative Churches Are Growing: A Study in Sociology of Religion* (New York, 1972), pp. 1–11.

[46] Jeffrey K. Hadden, *The Gathering Storm in the Churches* (Garden City, N.Y., 1970), p. 239.

again. These tensions and reversals affected current projects; for example when the Consultation on Church Union in 1970 offered a 'Plan of Union for the Church of Christ Uniting', enthusiasm had markedly cooled, and it became apparent that there was much more preliminary work to do before the matter could be pressed.

The Roman Catholic Church was deeply affected by the reversals of the later sixties—the high hopes stimulated by Vatican II soon faded. Many who had been quite willing to reform the church were hardly prepared for the decline of authority and the radical suggestions and actions that emerged; many who had reluctantly gone along with moderate changes missed the Latin mass, the Marian piety, and the stricter rules of the old days. Thousands of priests, nuns, and brothers left their vocations; many of them married. The parochial school system, long the pride of Catholics, came under attack for its educational limitations just as it was caught by inflation on one side and the decrease in the number of sisters prepared to carry the educational burdens at minimal cost on the other. The real turning-point was the encyclical *Humanae Vitae* issued by Pope Paul VI in 1968, in which all artificial methods of birth control were condemned as the pope went against even the moderate practices suggested by a majority of the papal commission on the subject. At a time when over-population seemed to threaten human survival, the encyclical seemed to many Catholics to be morally insensitive. John Cogley wrote that 'the *Humanae Vitae* debacle marked a fundamental change in the character of American Catholicism. Reverential deference to the pronouncements of a reigning pontiff would probably never be the same again.'[47] A church that only a few years before had seemed so sure of its direction was caught between those who thought the changes were only half-hearted and incomplete and those who thought they had gone too far too quickly. The general confusion was reflected in habits of attendance at mass. A Gallup poll reported that while in 1955 in the United States 74 per cent of Catholics attended on an average Sunday, only 57 per cent did so by 1972.

In Canada the flood-gates of criticism of the churches were opened, somewhat ironically, at the request of Anglican officials who invited a journalist well known for his writings and television appearances to offer an outsider's opinion on what was going on in the churches. Pierre Berton's *The Comfortable Pew* (1965) skilfully probed the inconsistencies of modern church life: its wealth and property while it preached renunciation, its complacency and self-righteousness while it spoke of humility, its entanglement with cultural patterns of injustice of war while it lectured on

[47] *Catholic America*, p. 132.

peace and freedom, its inability to deal with sex while it harped on petty moralities. The book attracted wide attention—it sold some 200,000 copies in three years, and an American edition was published. It drew excited reviews and several replies: the United Church's *Why the Sea is Boiling Hot: A Symposium on The Church and the World* (1965) and *The Restless Church, A Response to the Comfortable Pew* (1966), a symposium sponsored by the Anglicans and edited by William Kilbourn. The issues raised were hotly debated in the Press and on the radio. Actually much of what was in the book had long been familiar to intellectual and theological communities, but now it became a matter of general debate, and took many people by surprise. Every aspect of the life of the church was opened to criticism—but recommendations as to what to do often conflicted sharply.

The Catholic Church in Canada was not spared in the new wave of criticism; much of it came from within. In 1960 a Catholic brother humorously criticized the way religious Orders sought to force school-children into their mould in *Les Insolences de Frère Untel* (translated two years later as *The Impertinences of Brother Anonymous*); on request thirty-four laymen expressed their opinions to the prelates bound for the third session of the Second Vatican Council (*Brief to the Bishops: Canadian Catholic Laymen Speak Their Minds*, ed. Paul T. Harris). Members of the clergy and the Orders were often active in encouraging reforming trends in the church. One observer of the Quebec scene noted that

in some instances, clerics and nuns are in the forefront of those who insist on the democratization of Church-State relations. These sentiments have been echoed and re-echoed by the various Catholic Action groups, many of whom are quite far to the left. Even within the confines of the parish and of the diocese, matters of financing, building, and even church calendars of spiritual activities are now determined by the laity.[48]

A spirit of experimentation accompanied the questioning of old ways; in liturgical, theological, educational, and ecumenical life, many new things, often in conflict with each other, were tried. In the swift tempo of change, yesterday's novelty often became today's bore. As elsewhere, some became sceptical of the church and drifted away, others were disillusioned as old securities and disciplines were eroded, while still others were disappointed because the changes were not sweeping enough.

In comparison with the religious and theological revivals of the 1950s among the North American churches, the reversals and rejections of the

[48] Laurier LaPierre, 'The Clergy and the Quiet Revolution', in LeBlanc and Edinborough, *One Church, Two Nations?*, p. 77.

succeeding decade seemed startling at the time, and many were reminded of the hard days of the twenties and thirties. Yet, somewhat chastened and less confident than before, in general the churches exhibited both a promising resiliency and a stubborn inertia in a difficult period. Congregational life went on, some parishes thriving and others merging or dying. Denominations reorganized—both because of financial pressure and in an effort to close the perpetual gap between theory and practice. Sometimes inner tensions boiled over in schisms—as in 1961 when a group broke away from the National Baptist Convention of the United States of America, Inc., over issues of denominational control and founded the Progressive National Baptist Convention which soon numbered half a million. Reunions occurred—chiefly the merging of the Evangelical United Brethren with the Methodists to form the United Methodist Church in 1968. In Canada most of the Brethren joined the United Church, while the western conference remained independent. In 1967 the Canada district of The American Lutheran Church became independent, and in the same year co-operated with the Canada section of the Lutheran Church in America to form the Lutheran Council in Canada. In that same year the Lutheran Council in the United States of America came into being, involving the three leading Lutheran bodies and involving 95 per cent of American Lutherans. Significant ecumenical and missionary achievements were recorded, and there were other signs of stability and continuity.

In all the churches there were evidences of deep and sincere piety; many felt that the time of testing was in part a time of cleansing. Some sections of the church, especially those influenced by conservative evangelicalism, continued to gain numerically at home and abroad, their very strictness in doctrine and practice offering security and predictability. If some priests and ministers left their vocations, a very much larger body did not; in American Roman Catholicism, for example, there were about 58,000 priests at work in 1970, of which 21,000 were members of Orders.

It is very difficult to secure reliable estimates of the exact size of the religious bodies in the two countries; the figures that follow are based on a useful annual year-book prepared under the auspices of the National Council of Churches. For Canada, the 1971 census indicated that 46·2 per cent of the population were counted as Roman Catholics, 17·5 per cent as of the United Church, 11·8 per cent as Anglicans, while the remainder were scattered among the smaller bodies, except for 4·3 per cent who said they belonged to 'no religion'. In round numbers, Catholics claimed nearly ten million, Anglicans just over and the United Church just under a million each, while about a quarter of a million were reported by the Canadian Jewish Congress, the several Lutheran bodies together counted 200,000, and the Presbyterian Church about 180,000.[49]

Comparable figures for the United States are even less exact. A Gallup poll in 1973 reported on the basis of a sampling of adults that 58 per cent claimed to be Protestants (a very inclusive category), 27 per cent Roman Catholics, 4 per cent Jews, 6 per cent 'others', and 5 per cent none. Rough estimates of inclusive membership of the leading denominational families in the early 1970s were as follows, in millions:

Roman Catholic	48½
Baptist	25+
Methodist	13 —
Lutheran	8¼
Jewish	6
Christian-Disciples-Church of Christ	4¾
Eastern Orthodox	4
Presbyterian	4—
Episcopal	3+
Latter-day Saints	2¼

That summary was only of the larger groupings; many other Christian bodies, some relatively small in size, maintained an active life and carried on mission work abroad.

Despite the ruptures with the past that occurred since the outbreak of World War I, the links of the churches with earlier centuries remained strong. Both church leaders and scholarly investigators of religion were observing that as the 1970s opened the average age of church members seemed to be high, and that young people were not being attracted in sufficient numbers to maintain the strength of the communions. The religious needs and hopes of this age seemed to be as great as ever, but were often expressed in terms other than those familiar to the western Christian traditions. The task facing the Christian churches at the beginning of the nineteenth century in both Canada and the United States was immense; they set about it with genuine sensitivity, spirituality, and energy. Serious mistakes were made, especially when cultural and social pressures dimmed the churches' vision of the gospel they existed to serve, and when wealth and power led to arrogance and triumphalism. The churches have faced

---

[49] Constant H. Jacquet, Jr. (ed.), *Yearbook of the American and Canadian Churches, 1974* (Nashville, 1974), *passim*. The Anglican membership figures included infants and children, while the United Church figures did not, so that the total 'constituency' of the latter church was larger.

many times of testing; those that lie ahead may be far more thorough than any recounted in this history.

The stamp of the centuries is heavy on the churches of the present. To understand how to treasure what was right and good in that complex past and how to abandon what was wrong or outdated will take all the wisdom and guidance which Christians seek in their worship of God as known in Jesus Christ.

BIBLIOGRAPHY

A vast amount of literature has been produced by and about Christian churches in North America. The suggestions that follow are selective, and are grouped under six headings:

1 General Works
2 The American Colonial Period
3 Canada: French and British Eras
4 The United States to 1860
5 Canada since Confederation
6 The United States since 1860

In most cases, books cited have bibliographical aids which will be of help in researching a particular topic.

I. GENERAL WORKS

The best compact history of religion in the United States is by Winthrop S. Hudson, *Religion in America*, 2nd edn. (Charles Scribner's Sons, New York, 1972). It focuses on institutional religion, is remarkably comprehensive for a book of 450 pages, and is fair and well-balanced in its judgements. Much more detailed, combining coverage of religious institutions and theological history with considerable analysis of the religious experience of immigrants, is Sydney E. Ahlstrom's massive and well-written *A Religious History of the American People* (Yale University Press, New Haven, 1972). These works largely replace previous one-volume histories of religion in America, but there is still great value in some of the older works. William Warren Sweet emphasized the importance of religion on the frontier in *The Story of Religion in America*, 2nd rev. edn. (Harper & Bros., New York, 1950); Clifton E. Olmstead summarized the contributions of many monographs and treatises in *History of Religion in the United States* (Prentice-Hall, Englewood Cliffs, N. J., 1960); William A. Clebsch interpreted religious history from a functional and secular point of view in *From Sacred to Profane America: The Role of Religion in American History* (Harper & Row, New York, 1968).

The pioneer documentary and bibliographical work was by Peter G. Mode, *Source Book and Bibliographical Guide for American Church History* (George Banta, Menasha, Wis., 1921). Though it still has value, it has been replaced by two other works. Indispensable for the serious student of American religion is Nelson R. Burr's *A Critical Bibliography of Religion in America* (Princeton University

Press, Princeton, N.J., 1961). It was done in collaboration with James Ward Smith and A. Leland Jamison, editors of a series of volumes on Religion in American Life. An extensive narrative bibliography in five parts, Burr's work is a mine of information on every aspect of the religious life of Americans. The period since its publication needs to be covered in as much detail; there is some help in a much briefer work by Dr. Burr in the series Goldentree Bibliographies in American History, *Religion in American Life* (Appleton-Century-Crofts, New York, 1971). A collection of edited sources has been prepared by H. Shelton Smith, Robert T. Handy, and Lefferts A. Loetscher, *American Christianity: An Historical Interpretation with Representative Documents*, 2 vols. (Charles Scribner's Sons, New York, 1960–3). The first volume of the Princeton series Religion in American Life contains a valuable collection of general essays: Smith and Jamison (eds.) *The Shaping of American Religion* (Princeton University Press, Princeton, N.J., 1961). An over-all theological interpretation of Christianity in America is by H. Richard Niebuhr, *The Kingdom of God in America* (Harper & Bros., New York, 1937); see also a source-book on theological writings edited by Sydney E. Ahlstrom, *Theology in America: The Major Protestant Voices from Puritanism to Neo-Orthodoxy* (Bobbs-Merrill, Indianapolis, 1967).

On historiographical trends in the study of American religion, consult the collection of essays edited by Jerald C. Brauer, *Reinterpretation in American Church History* (University of Chicago Press, Chicago, 1968); see also Henry Warner Bowden, *Church History in the Age of Science: Historiographical Patterns in the United States, 1876–1918* (University of North Carolina Press, Chapel Hill, 1971). A basic work which traces the rise, spread, and comparative size of the various churches in the country is by Edwin Scott Gaustad, *Historical Atlas of Religion in America* (Harper & Row, New York, 1962). Contemporary information, including statistical details, on most denominations of North America is provided by Constant H. Jacquet, Jr. (ed), *Yearbook of the American and Canadian Churches, 1974* (Abingdon Press, Nashville, 1974). Under various titles and editors the volume has been issued annually for many years, but Canada has been included only recently.

An early attempt to provide a general picture of Canadian church development was vol. xi (1914) of the series edited by Adam Shortt and Arthur G. Doughty, *Canada and Its Provinces*, 23 vols. (T. & A. Constable for the Publishers Association of Canada, Edinburgh, 1914–17). The essays in the volume were written by various authors largely from denominational viewpoints. An effort to provide a unifying principle for the study of Canadian religion using the 'frontier thesis' so popular at the time was E. H. Oliver, *The Winning of the Frontier* (Ryerson Press, Toronto, 1930). The first over-all one-volume Canadian church history was written by H. H. Walsh, *The Christian Church in Canada* (Ryerson Press, Toronto, 1956). This important contribution has now been largely replaced by a three-volume series under the general editorship of John Webster Grant,

A History of the Christian Church in Canada. Walsh penned the first volume, *The Church in the French Era: From Colonization to the British Conquest* (Ryerson Press, Toronto, 1966). The second, *The Church in the British Era: From the British Conquest to Confederation* (McGraw-Hill Ryerson, Toronto, 1972) was written by John S. Moir, while the general editor contributed the third volume, *The Church in the Canadian Era: The First Century of Confederation* (McGraw-Hill Ryerson, Toronto, 1972). There are several brief, popular accounts: Douglas J. Wilson's *The Church Grows in Canada* (Committee on Missionary Education, Canadian Council of Churches, Toronto, 1966); William Kilbourn, A. C. Forrest, and Patrick Watson collaborated in a richly illustrated sketch, *Religion in Canada: The Spiritual Development of a Nation* (McClelland & Stewart, Toronto, 1968). Documents on Canadian religious life have been edited by John S. Moir, *The Cross in Canada* (Ryerson Press, Toronto, 1966). A fine discussion of the development of the study of Canadian church history with useful bibliographical suggestions is by N. K. Clifford, 'Religion in the Development of Canadian Society: An Historiographical Analysis', *Church History*, 38 (1969), 506–23.

2. THE AMERICAN COLONIAL PERIOD

The English colonists in North America brought the culture and religion of the mother country with them, and such informative works as Wallace Notestein's *The English People on the Eve of Colonization, 1603–1630* (Harper & Bros. New York, 1954) and Carl Bridenbaugh's *Vexed and Troubled Englishmen, 1590–1642* (Oxford University Press, New York, 1968) make intelligible the pressures that brought the settlers to the New World. The role of Christianity in the movement of peoples across the Atlantic is studied in a readable work by Louis B. Wright, *Religion and Empire: The Alliance between Piety and Commerce in English Expansion, 1558–1625* (University of North Carolina Press, Chapel Hill, 1943). The history of the Puritan colonies of New England has long attracted much scholarly attention. The central figure in the renaissance of New England Puritan studies that began in the 1930s was Perry Miller, especially in the two-volume work, *The New England Mind*, published by the Harvard University Press, Cambridge, Mass. The first volume, sub-titled *The Seventeenth Century* (1939), is a detailed analysis of the ambitious intellectual synthesis of religious, philosophical, and scientific knowledge undertaken by Puritan leaders on both sides of the Atlantic; the second, *From Colony to Province* (1953), describes what happened to the expectations of the Puritan élite in the face of the realities of New England history. While there is no substitute for Miller's major volumes, a convenient introduction to his interpretation is a collection of some of his leading articles, *Errand into the Wilderness* (Belknap Press of Harvard University Press, Cambridge, 1956; reprinted as a Harper Torchbook, 1964). Other important contributions to the renaissance in Puritan studies include Samuel Eliot Morison, whose *Puritan Pronaos* (1936) has been revised as *The Intellectual Life of Colonial New England* (New York University Press, New York, 1956), and

Edmund S. Morgan, whose *Visible Saints: The History of a Puritan Idea* (New York University Press, New York, 1963) emphasizes the development in New England of the practice of the public relation of saving faith before the congregation.

With his focus on intellectual history, Miller overstated his case; considerable research since then has focused on a wider range of sources, including town, voting, economic, and tax records in revising his contributions. Some of the results are summarized by Darrett B. Rutman, *American Puritanism: Faith and Practice* (J. B. Lippincott, Philadelphia, 1970), and Larzer Ziff, *Puritanism in America: New Culture in a New World* (Viking Press, New York, 1973). Much attention has been concentrated on the Mather dynasty; a readable work is by Robert Middlekauff, *The Mathers: Three Generations of Puritan Intellectuals, 1596-1728* (Oxford University Press, New York, 1971). The early prominent dissenters from the Puritan system of Massachusetts Bay have also been carefully studied; on Anne Hutchinson see Emery Battis, *Saints and Sectaries: Anne Hutchinson and the Antinomian Controversy in the Massachusetts Bay Colony* (University of North Carolina Press, Chapel Hill, 1962) and David D. Hall (ed.), *The Antinomian Controversy, 1636-1638: A Documentary History* (Wesleyan University Press, Middletown, Conn., 1968); on the founder of Rhode Island consult Perry Miller, *Roger Williams: His Contribution to the American Tradition* (Bobbs-Merrill, Indianapolis, 1953), Ola E. Winslow, *Master Roger Williams: A Biography* (Macmillan, New York, 1957), Edmund S. Morgan, *Roger Williams: The Church and the State* (Harcourt, Brace & World, New York, 1967), and John Garrett, *Roger Williams: Witness Beyond Christendom, 1603-1683* (Macmillan, New York, 1970). Of the many books on the witchcraft executions at Salem Village in 1692, Chadwick Hansen's *Witchcraft at Salem* (George Braziller, New York, 1969) is especially recommended.

A good many volumes of edited sources on Puritan history have been published, few as thorough as Perry Miller and Thomas H. Johnson (eds.), *The Puritans* (American Book Company, New York, 1938), of which Miller (ed.), *The American Puritans: their Prose and Poetry* (Doubleday & Co., Garden City, New York, 1956) is a shorter version; also useful is Alden T. Vaughan (ed.), *The Puritan Tradition in America, 1620-1730* (Harper & Row, New York, 1972), and Michael McGiffert (ed.), *Puritanism and the American Experience* (Addison-Wesley, Reading, Mass., 1969). There has been increasing interest in Puritan attitudes to the Indians, for example Alden T. Vaughan, *New England Frontier: Puritans and Indians, 1620-1675* (Little, Brown & Co., Boston, 1965), and William Kellaway, *The New England Company, 1649-1776: Missionary Society to the American Indians* (Barnes and Noble, New York, 1961). The story of Puritanism's transformation in the later seventeenth and eighteenth centuries has been told in some illuminating volumes, such as Bernard Bailyn's *The New England Merchants in the Seventeenth Century* (Harvard University Press, Cambridge, Mass., 1955), Robert G. Pope's specialized study of *The Half-Way*

Covenant: Church Membership in Puritan New England (Princeton University Press, Princeton, N. J., 1969), and Richard L. Bushman's *From Puritan to Yankee: Character and the Social Order in Connecticut, 1690–1765* (Harvard University Press, Cambridge, Mass., 1967).

An important discussion of Puritanism outside New England has been provided by Babette M. Levy, *Early Puritanism in the Southern and Island Colonies* (American Antiquarian Society, Worcester, Mass., 1960). There was a strong Puritan influence in the early Church of England congregations in Virginia, later displaced by distinctively Anglican emphases, as is made clear in George Maclaren Brydon's *Virginia's Mother Church and the Political Conditions under which it Grew* (vol. i, 1607–1727, Virginia Historical Society, Richmond, 1947; vol. ii, 1727–1814, Church Historical Society, Philadelphia, 1952). The other strong Anglican establishment in the eighteenth century was in Maryland, discussed by Nelson Waite Rightmyer, *Maryland's Established Church* (Church Historical Society for the Diocese of Maryland, Baltimore, 1956). An informative, sprightly account of the Church of England in the colonies in the eighteenth century which over-emphasizes somewhat the power of that church is Carl Bridenbaugh's *Mitre and Sceptre: Transatlantic Faiths, Ideas, Personalities, and Politics, 1689–1775* (Oxford University Press, New York, 1962).

In colonial Presbyterianism, the tension between Puritan pietist and more confessionally oriented Scotch-Irish strands is analysed in a major interpretative work by Leonard J. Trinterud, *The Forming of an American Tradition: A Re-examination of Colonial Presbyterianism* (Westminster Press, Philadelphia, 1949); a glimpse of the vastness of the primary and secondary sources for the study of religion in colonial America is displayed in Trinterud (comp.), *A Bibliography of American Presbyterianism During the Colonial Period* (Presbyterian Historical Society, Philadelphia, 1968). A well-edited collection of sources for the study of Presbyterianism in all periods of American history was compiled by Maurice W. Armstrong, Lefferts A. Loetscher, and Charles A. Anderson, *The Presbyterian Enterprise: Sources of American Presbyterian History* (Westminster Press, Philadelphia, 1956).

The Religious Society of Friends (Quakers) was a major force in the colonial period. The standard work, by Rufus M. Jones (assisted by Isaac Sharpless and Amelia M. Gummere), is *The Quakers in the American Colonies* (Macmillan, London, 1923). Valuable studies which trace changes in Quaker life include two by Frederick B. Tolles, *Meeting House and Counting House: The Quaker Merchants of Colonial Philadelphia, 1682–1763* (University of North Carolina Press, Chapel Hill, 1948) and *Quakers and the Atlantic Culture* (Macmillan, New York, 1960), and also Sydney V. James, *A People Among Peoples: Quaker Benevolence in Eighteenth-Century America* (Harvard University Press, Cambridge, Mass., 1963). A definitive edition of the classic journal of the great Quaker humanitarian and anti-slavery leader of the eighteenth century has been edited by Phillips P. Moulton, *The Journal and Major Essays of John Woolman* (Oxford University

Press, New York, 1971). Roman Catholics were in a small minority in colonial America, but their story has been told in rich detail by John Tracy Ellis, *Catholicism in Colonial America* (Helicon Press, Baltimore, 1965). For a discussion of the early Catholic refuge in Maryland, consult Thomas O. Hanley, *Their Rights and Liberties: The Beginnings of Religious and Political Freedom in Maryland* (Newman Press, Westminster, Maryland, 1959). Still very useful for understanding the status of Catholics in the colonial period is Sr. Mary Augustine (Ray), *American Opinion of Roman Catholicism in the Eighteenth Century* (Columbia University Press, New York, 1936). On Catholics in Florida, which was in Spanish possession until the early nineteenth century, a fine account is by Michael V. Gannon, *The Cross in the Sand: The Early Catholic Church in Florida, 1513–1870* (University of Florida Press, Gainesville, 1965).

The Great Awakenings have long attracted scholarly attention; older studies are by Wesley M. Gewehr, *The Great Awakening in Virginia, 1740–1790* (Duke University Press, Durham, N.C., 1930), and Edwin S. Gaustad, *The Great Awakening in New England* (Harper & Bros., New York, 1957). Outstanding among a spate of source-books on the Awakenings is Alan Heimert and Perry Miller (eds.), *The Great Awakening: Documents Illustrating the Crisis and Its Consequences* (Bobbs-Merrill, Indianapolis, 1967). A penetrating brief treatment of the Awakenings in their social setting by a general historian is in the last book of the late Richard Hofstadter, *America at 1750: A Social Portrait* (Alfred A. Knopf, New York, 1971). The growth of the Baptists was directly related to the Great Awakenings; various aspects of the story are told by C. C. Goen, *Revivalism and Separatism in New England, 1740–1800: Strict Congregationalists and Separate Baptists in the Great Awakening* (Yale University Press, New Haven, 1962), William G. McLoughlin, *Isaac Backus and the American Pietist Tradition* (Little, Brown & Co., Boston, 1967), and William L. Lumpkin, *Baptist Foundations in the South: Tracing through the Separates the Influence of the Great Awakening, 1754–1787* (Broadman Press, Nashville, 1961). Several historians of education have studied the importance of the Awakening movements for their work, especially Lawrence A. Cremin, *American Education: The Colonial Experience, 1607–1783* (Harper & Row, New York, 1970), and Douglas Sloan (ed.), *The Great Awakening and American Education: A Documentary History* (Teachers College Press, New York, 1973).

New interest in the leading theological intellect of colonial America was aroused by Perry Miller's study *Jonathan Edwards* (William Sloane Associates, New York, 1949). Critical texts of Edwards's writings are in process of publication by Yale University Press; the first four volumes of The Works of Jonathan Edwards are as follows: Paul Ramsey (ed.), *The Freedom of the Will* (1957), John E. Smith (ed.), *Religious Affections* (1959), Clyde A. Holbrook (ed.), *Original Sin* (1970), and C. C. Goen (ed.), *The Great Awakening* (1972). A controversial volume which presses in oversimplified fashion but with much documentation the theme that it was the Edwardsean Calvinists rather than

their liberal opponents who prepared the way for the support of the American
Revolution by religious New England is by Alan Heimert, *Religion and the
American Mind: From the Great Awakening to the Revolution* (Harvard University
Press, Cambridge, Mass., 1966). The development of liberal theological thought
has been analysed carefully by Conrad Wright, *The Beginnings of Unitarianism
in America* (Starr King Press, Boston, 1955). The story of the tiny Jewish
minority has been told by Jacob R. Marcus, *The Colonial American Jews, 1492–
1776*, 3 vols. (Wayne State University Press, Detroit, 1970).

3. CANADA: FRENCH AND BRITISH ERAS

Two informative books that together give general coverage of Canadian Christian history to 1867 have already been mentioned, H. H. Walsh's *The Church in
the French Era* and John S. Moir's *The Church in the British Era*. Both are well
documented and have useful bibliographies. Moir has also edited a compact but
readable source-book on an important theme in Canadian church history:
Church and State in Canada, 1627–1867: Basic Documents (McClelland & Stewart,
Toronto, 1967). Documentary material on New France has been collected by
Cameron Nish (ed.), *The French Régime* (Prentice-Hall of Canada, Scarborough,
Ont., 1965). The nineteenth-century historian Francis Parkman wrote a number
of volumes on the struggle between France and Britain on the North American
continent; a number of his famous passages have been edited by John Tebbel,
The Battle for North America (Doubleday & Co., Garden City, N.Y., 1948).
Various recent books on Roman Catholicism in Quebec draw on the many
volumes in French written by Auguste Gosselin more than a half-century ago;
for example Lucien Lemieux, *L'Établissement de la première province ecclésiastique
au Canada, 1783–1844* (Fides, Montreal, 1968), and a handbook primarily for
laity, Nive Voisine (avec la collaboration de André Beaulieu et de Jean
Hamelin), *Histoire de L'Église catholique au Québec (1608–1970)* (Fides, Montreal,
1971). The exciting story of the Jesuit missionary enterprise among the Indians
has been told in a scholarly way by J. H. Kennedy, *Jesuit and Savage in New
France* (Yale University Press, New Haven, 1950). The voluminous sources of
the work of that Order were collected by R. G. Thwaites, *The Jesuit Relations
and Allied Documents*, 73 vols. (Burrows Bros., Cleveland, 1896–1901). An
important source of statistical and other information about the Catholic Church
in Canada in all periods is by Dominique de Saint-Denis, *L'Église catholique au
Canada: Précis historique et statistique*, sixième édition; *The Catholic Church in
Canada: Historical and Statistical Summary*, 6th edn. (Les Editions Thau, Montreal,
1956). The Catholic Church in colonial Louisiana fell under French-Canadian
ecclesiastical direction; the story has been carefully probed by Charles E. O'Neill,
Church and State in French Colonial Louisiana: Policy and Politics to 1732 (Yale
University Press, New Haven, 1966). A massive work that traces the story of
French Canadians since the conquest is by Mason Wade, *The French Canadians,
1760–1967*, rev. edn., 2 vols. (Macmillan, Toronto, 1968). There is also a French

edition. The references to Wade in this volume are from the first edition, *The French Canadians, 1760–1945* (Macmillan, London, 1954).

A number of Canadian denominational histories have been consulted in the preparation of this work; unless the title indicates otherwise, most of them deal also with the period after Confederation. Philip Carrington, *The Anglican Church in Canada: A History* (Collins, Toronto, 1963), is a more readable interpretation than Spencer Ervin, *The Political and Ecclesiastical History of the Anglican Church of Canada* (Trinity Press, Ambler, Pa., 1967), though there is much factual information in the latter. An important study of early Anglican history in Quebec is by Thomas R. Millman, *Jacob Mountain, First Lord Bishop of Quebec: A Study in Church and State, 1793–1825* (University of Toronto Press, Toronto, 1947). Useful for Presbyterian history are four books issued by Presbyterian Publications, Toronto: W. Stanford Reid, *The Church of Scotland in Lower Canada: Its Struggle for Establishment* (1936); Neil G. Smith, Allan L. Farris, and H. Keith Markell, *A Short History of the Presbyterian Church in Canada* (n.d.); *Enkindled by the Word: Essays on Presbyterianism in Canada* (1966), compiled by the Centennial Committee of the Presbyterian Church in Canada; and John S. Moir, *Enduring Witness: A History of the Presbyterian Church in Canada* (n.d. [1974]). The Baptist story is told by George E. Levy, *The Baptists of the Maritime Provinces, 1753–1946* (Barnes-Hopkins, Saint John, N.B., 1946), and Stuart Ivison and Fred Rosser, *The Baptists in Upper and Lower Canada before 1820* (University of Toronto Press, Toronto, 1956).

An informative collection of passages from the many volumes of a nineteenth-century writer on Methodist history has been edited by John Webster Grant, *Salvation! O the Joyful Sound: The Collected Writings of John Carroll* (Oxford University Press, Toronto, 1967). A fascinating study which deals with the interrelationship of religion and politics is by Goldwin French, *Parsons and Politics: The Role of the Wesleyan Methodists in Upper Canada and the Maritimes from 1780 to 1855* (Ryerson Press, Toronto, 1962); a central figure in the story is Egerton Ryerson, who had been studied in detail by C. B. Sissons, *Egerton Ryerson: His Life and Letters*, 2 vols. (Clarke, Irwin, Toronto, 1937–47).

An important topic in the history of Protestantism in the Maritime provinces has been analysed by Maurice W. Armstrong, *The Great Awakening in Nova Scotia, 1776–1809* (American Society of Church History, Hartford, Conn., 1948); see also J. M. Bumsted, *Henry Alline, 1748–1784* (University of Toronto Press, Toronto, 1971). The second part of a work by Gordon Stewart and George Rawlyk, *A People Highly Favoured of God: The Nova Scotia Yankees and the American Revolution* (Macmillan, Toronto, 1972) deals with Alline and the Awakening.

Books helpful for understanding some of Canada's smaller churches include the following: Reuben Butchart, *The Disciples of Christ in Canada Since 1830* (Canadian Headquarters' Publications, Churches of Christ [Disciples], Toronto, 1949); Carl R. Cronmiller, *A History of the Lutheran Church in Canada*, vol. i

(Evangelical Lutheran Synod of Canada, n.p., 1961); Arthur G. Dorland, *A History of the Society of Friends (Quakers) in Canada* (Macmillan, Toronto, 1927); and John R. Weinlick, *The Moravian Church in Canada* (Provincial Women's Board of the Southern Province, Winston-Salem, N.C., 1966).

Aspects of controversial questions of church and state have been probed in detail in various monographs. The Clergy Reserves, the university question, and the role of religion in elementary education are treated by John S. Moir, *Church and State in Canada West: Three Studies in the Relation of Denominationalism and Nationalism, 1841-1867* (University of Toronto Press, Toronto, 1959). The first of these issues is analysed further by Alan Wilson, *The Clergy Reserves of Upper Canada: A Canadian Mortmain* (University of Toronto Press, Toronto, 1968). A series of brilliant interpretative essays which focus largely on the 1840–67 period has been edited by W. L. Morton, *The Shield of Achilles: Aspects of Canada in the Victorian Age; Le Bouclier d'Achille: Regards sur le Canada de l'ère victorienne* (McClelland & Stewart, Toronto, 1968). E. R. Norman, *The Conscience of the State in North America* (University Press, Cambridge, 1968), compares the development of religious pluralism and the separation of church and state in Canada and the United States, and argues that the differences are not as great as might first appear, despite variations in chronology. An important work in historical sociology was written by S. D. Clark, *Church and Sect in Canada* (University of Toronto Press, Toronto, 1948). Both origins and later developments are traced in an informative study by D. C. Masters, *Protestant Church Colleges in Canada: A History* (University of Toronto Press, Toronto, 1966). A remarkable specialized work based on careful scrutiny of voluminous sources is by Robin W. Winks, *The Blacks in Canada: A History* (Yale University Press, New Haven, 1971).

4. THE UNITED STATES TO 1860

An older standard volume which deals with the attitudes of the American churches to the Revolution and to the development of nationalism was published originally in 1924 and reprinted over forty years later: Edward F. Humphrey, *Nationalism and Religion in America, 1774-1789* (Russell & Russell, New York, 1965). A convenient summary of 'Religion in the Revolutionary Generation' fills the first two chapters of William W. Sweet's *Religion in the Development of American Culture, 1765-1840* (Charles Scribner's Sons, New York, 1952). Seymour M. Lipset has drawn some suggestive comparisons, with attention to religious factors, in 'Counter-Revolution—The United States and Canada', in Thomas R. Ford (ed.), *The Revolutionary Theme in Contemporary America* (University of Kentucky Press, Lexington, 1967), pp. 21–64. The majority of the many books on the American Revolution discuss to some extent the role of religion; for a good example see Bernard Bailyn, *The Ideological Origins of the American Revolution* (Belknap Press of Harvard University Press, Cambridge, 1967). A valuable collection of essays on Christianity in the United States is by Sidney E. Mead, *The Lively Experiment: The Shaping of Christianity in America* (Harper & Row, New York, 1963); important sections discuss Protestantism during the revolutionary epoch, the rise of religious freedom, and the denominational church form as 'the shape of Protestantism in America'. An older book by Sanford H. Cobb, *The Rise of Religious Liberty in America* (Macmillan, New York, 1902) still has value; a massive later study on that theme by Anson Phelps Stokes, *Church and State in the United States*, 3 vols. (Harper & Bros., New York, 1950), was issued in 1964 by the same publisher in a revised, one-volume edition by Stokes and Leo Pfeffer. An analysis of the Separatist, Catholic, and Constitutional church–state traditions has been done by Elwyn A. Smith, *Religious Liberty in the United States: The Development of Church-State Thought Since the Revolutionary Era* (Fortress Press, Philadelphia, 1972). An excellent, highly detailed study of the Baptist contribution to religious freedom and the separation of church and state is by William G. McLoughlin, *New England Dissent, 1630–1833: The Baptists and the Separation of Church and State* (2 vols., Harvard University Press, Cambridge, Mass., 1971). In *The Critical Years: The Reconstitution of the Anglican Church in the United States of America, 1780–1789* (Seabury Press, New York, 1956), Clara O. Loveland traces the way the Church of England in the colonies was transformed into the Episcopal Church.

There are a number of general treatments of Protestantism in the United States, most of which put particular emphasis on the first two-thirds of the nineteenth century. Outstanding is Martin E. Marty's vivid interpretation, *Righteous Empire: The Protestant Experience in America* (Dial Press, New York, 1970); see also Jerald C. Brauer's *Protestantism in America: A Narrative History*, rev. edn. (Westminster Press, Philadelphia, 1965), and Winthrop S. Hudson's *American Protestantism* (University of Chicago Press, Chicago, 1961). Central to any understanding of Protestantism is an awareness of the importance of the revivalist tradition; good over-all treatments by general historians include Bernard A. Weisberger, *They Gathered at the River: The Story of the Great Revivalists and their Impact upon Religion in America* (Little, Brown & Co., Boston, 1958), William G. McLoughlin, *Modern Revivalism: Charles Grandison Finney to Billy Graham* (Ronald Press, New York, 1959), and the unfinished work by Perry Miller, *The Life of the Mind in America: From the Revolution of the Civil War* (Harcourt, Brace & World, New York, 1965). Important aspects of the larger history of revivalism are treated in such works as the following: John B. Boles, *The Great Revival, 1787–1805: The Origins of the Southern Evangelical Mind* (University Press of Kentucky, Lexington, 1972); Charles A. Johnson, *The Frontier Camp Meeting: Religion's Harvest Time* (Southern Methodist University Press, Dallas, 1955); Charles R. Keller, *The Second Great Awakening in Connecticut* (Yale University Press, New Haven, 1942); Whitney R. Cross, *The Burned-over District: The Social and Intellectual History of Enthusiastic Religion in Western New York, 1800–1850* (Cornell University Press, Ithaca, N.Y., 1950); and Timothy L. Smith, *Revivalism and Social Reform in Mid-Nineteenth-Century America*

(Abingdon Press, New York, 1957). The latter book is especially helpful in tracing links from the revivalism of the earlier nineteenth century to the religious developments of the latter part. If used with care, the autobiographies of such leading Awakeners as Lyman Beecher and Charles G. Finney make rewarding reading. Valuable source materials for the period from the Revolution to mid-century were collected in four volumes edited by William W. Sweet, *Religion on the American Frontier* (various publishers, 1931–46); the volumes dealt successively with the Baptists (1931), the Presbyterians (1936), the Congregationalists (1939), and the Methodists (1946).

A pioneering work in American church history was Robert Baird's *Religion in America*, originally published in Scotland in 1843 and in the United States a year later. Written with European audiences in mind, Baird stressed the importance of the spread of the voluntary societies as a feature of American religion. A modern critical abridgement by Henry Warner Bowden has been based on the large 1856 version of Baird's *Religion in America* (Harper & Row, New York, 1970); the substance of the author's revealing Book IV, 'The Voluntary Principle in America: Its Action and Influence' is included. The importance of the 'British example' in the development of the network of voluntary societies is documented by Charles I. Foster in *An Errand of Mercy: The Evangelical United Front, 1790–1837* (University of North Carolina Press, Chapel Hill, 1960). Foster over-emphasized the decline of the 'benevolent empire' in the panic of 1937; Clifford S. Griffin followed the story through the Civil War in *Their Brothers' Keepers: Moral Stewardship in the United States, 1800–1865* (Rutgers University Press, New Brunswick, N. J., 1960). The way the evangelical leadership hoped to make the United States a model Protestant nation by persuasive means under the conditions of freedom has been traced by John R. Bodo, *The Protestant Clergy and Public Issues, 1812–1848* (Princeton University Press, Princeton, 1954), and by James F. Maclear, ' "The True American Union" of Church and State: The Reconstruction of the Theocratic Tradition', *Church History*, 28 (1959), 41–62.

In *Salvation and the Savage: An Analysis of Protestant Missions and American Indian Response, 1787–1862* (University of Kentucky Press, Lexington, 1965), Robert F. Berkhofer, Jr. has analysed the Protestant attitude toward the Indians in this period; also useful is R. Pierce Beaver's *Church, State, and the American Indian* (Concordia Publishing House, St. Louis, 1966). The way the expectancy of the coming millennium gave a sense of direction and enthusiasm to the militant Protestantism of the time has been stressed by many authors; see especially Ernest L. Tuveson, *Redeemer Nation: The Idea of America's Millennial Role* (University of Chicago Press, Chicago, 1968). The anti-Catholic aspects of the evangelical campaigns have been treated by Ray A. Billington, *The Protestant Crusade, 1800–1860: A Study of the Origins of American Nativism* (Macmillan, New York, 1938, and various later editions, e.g. Quadrangle Books, Chicago, 1964). It was in this period that Methodism, founded as an autonomous church in 1784, grew to be the largest Protestant body in America; of the many Methodist histories note especially a collection of analytical essays edited by Emory S. Bucke, *The History of American Methodism*, 3 vols. (Abingdon Press, Nashville, 1964), and Frederick A. Norwood, *The Story of American Methodism* (Abingdon Press, Nashville, 1974), which pays considerable attention to the many varieties of Methodism. On the Disciples of Christ, an indigenous body born in the context of frontier revivalism, see David E. Harrell, Jr., *Quest for a Christian America: The Disciples of Christ and American Society to 1866* (Disciples of Christ Historical Society, Nashville, 1966), and George C. Beazley, Jr. (ed.), *The Christian Church (Disciples of Christ): An Interpretative Examination in the Cultural Context* (Bethany Press, St. Louis, 1973).

Various aspects of the theological history of the period are considered in many specialized studies, for example: G. Adolph Koch, *Religion of the American Enlightenment* (Thomas Y. Crowell, New York, 1968); Sidney E. Mead, *Nathaniel William Taylor, 1786–1858: A Connecticut Liberal* (University of Chicago Press, Chicago, 1942); H. Shelton Smith, *Changing Conceptions of Original Sin: A Study in American Theology Since 1750* (Charles Scribner's Sons, New York, 1955); George M. Marsden, *The Evangelical Mind and the New School Presbyterian Experience: A Case Study of Thought and Theology in Nineteenth-Century America* (Yale University Press, New Haven, Conn., 1970); James H. Nichols, *Romanticism in American Theology: Nevin and Schaff at Mercersburg* (University of Chicago Press, Chicago, 1961), and edited by the same author, *The Mercersburg Theology* (Oxford University Press, New York, 1966). A well-documented study by Yehoshua Arieli, *Individualism and Nationalism in American Ideology* (Harvard University Press, Cambridge, 1964) stresses the role of religion in fostering the intense individualism of nineteenth-century American life. Interrelationships between the intellectual and religious communities of the time are traced in good studies by Douglas Sloan, *The Scottish Enlightenment and the American College Ideal* (Teachers College Press, New York, 1971), and Wilson Smith, *Professors and Public Ethics: Studies of Northern Moral Philosophers Before the Civil War* (Cornell University Press, Ithaca, 1956). In *The Shaping of Protestant Education: An Interpretation of the Sunday School and the Development of Protestant Educational Strategy in the United States, 1789–1860* (Association Press, New York, 1966), William B. Kennedy has provided a compact survey of the educational effort of evangelicals. Two important articles show how dominant the Protestant perspective was in the development of public educational systems: David Tyack, 'The Kingdom of God and the Common School', *Harvard Educational Review*, 36 (1966), 447–69; and Timothy L. Smith, 'Protestant Schooling and American Nationality, 1800–1850', *Journal of American History*, 53 (1966–7), 679–95.

The anti-slavery movement which had arisen in the eighteenth century developed a new militancy in the nineteenth. The shaping of attitudes towards blacks in America has been traced in rich detail by Winthrop D. Jordan, *White*

Over Black: American Attitudes Toward the Negro, 1550–1812 (University of North Carolina Press, Chapel Hill, 1968), and *The White Man's Burden: Historical Origins of Racism in the United States* (Oxford University Press, New York, 1974), which covers much of the same ground as the earlier book but goes to 1863. A very important contribution to the comprehension of the anti-slavery movement was by Gilbert H. Barnes, *The Antislavery Impulse, 1830–1844* (Appleton-Century, New York, 1933; reprinted by Harcourt, Brace & World, 1964). Of the many books on abolitionism, most of which deal with the role of religion, see especially Dwight L. Dumond, *Antislavery: The Crusade for Freedom in America* (University of Michigan Press, Ann Arbor, 1961); Bertram Wyatt-Brown, *Lewis Tappan and the Evangelical War Against Slavery* (Press of Case Western Reserve University, Cleveland, 1969); Aileen S. Kraditor, *Means and Ends in American Abolitionism: Garrison and His Critics on Strategy and Tactics, 1834–1850* (Pantheon Books, New York, 1969), and Benjamin Quarles, *Black Abolitionists* (Oxford University Press, New York, 1969).

Recent research has been illuminating the nature of the slave communities and the place of religion among blacks, as in the studies by John W. Blassingame, *The Slave Community: Plantation Life in the Antebellum South* (Oxford University Press, New York, 1972), George P. Rawick, *From Sundown to Sunup: The Making of the Black Community* (Greenwood Publishing Co., Westport, Conn., 1972), and Eugene D. Genovese, *Roll, Jordan, Roll: The World the Slaves Made* (Pantheon Books, New York, 1974). There is a striking chapter on religion in Leon F. Litwack's *North of Slavery: The Negro in the Free States, 1790–1860* (University of Chicago Press, Chicago, 1961). In *The Negro Church in America* (Schocken Books, New York, 1964), sociologist E. Franklin Frazier was highly selective, but described how the 'invisible institution' of slave religion surfaced in the burgeoning black churches after the Civil War as 'a nation within a nation', Lawrence N. Jones has cast new perspectives on black church life in 'They Sought a City: The Black Church and Churchmen in the Nineteenth Century', *Union Seminary Quarterly Review*, 26 (1971), 253–72. A still useful older work is Carter G. Woodson's *The History of the Negro Church* (Associated Publishers, Washington D.C., 1921). On the efforts of white Christians to win slaves to Christianity, see Andrew E. Murray, *Prebyterians and the Negro: A History* (Presbyterian Historical Society, Philadelphia, 1960), and Donald G. Mathews, *Slavery and Methodism: A Chapter in American Morality, 1780–1845* (Princeton University Press, Princeton, 1965). H. Shelton Smith has given a richly documented review of white attitudes toward blacks in *In His Image, But . . . Racism in Southern Religion, 1780–1910* (Duke University Press, Durham, 1972).

On the history of Roman Catholicism in America, most of the books that will be mentioned deal also with the period after the Civil War to their dates of publication. A rather apologetic survey is by John Tracy Ellis, *American Catholicism*, 2nd edn. rev. (University of Chicago Press, 1969). Fr. Ellis also edited a fine source-book, *Documents of American Catholic History* (Bruce Publishing Co., Milwaukee, 1956). A readable survey by a layman is by John Cogley, *Catholic America* (Dial Press, New York, 1973). A rather detailed, analytical history which pays much attention to the conflicts arising among the major ethnic and cultural strands in the church is by Thomas T. McAvoy, *A History of the Catholic Church in the United States* (University of Notre Dame Press, Notre Dame, Ind., 1969). The fact-filled text is somewhat heavy, but with its useful bibliographies it is an indispensable book for the study of American Catholicism. More specialized topics are treated by Peter Guilday, *The Life and Times of John Carroll*, 2 vols. (Encyclopedia Press, New York, 1922); Charles H. Metzger, *Catholics and the American Revolution: A Study in Religious Climate* (Loyola University Press, Chicago, 1962); and Robert F. Trisco, *The Holy See and the Nascent Church in the Middle Western United States, 1826–1850* (Gregorian University Press, Rome, 1962).

On Jews in America, there is both content and bibliographical help in Abraham J. Karp (ed.), *The Jewish Experience in America: Selected Studies from the Publications of the American Jewish Historical Society*, 5 vols. (Ktav Publishing House, 1969), and Joseph L. Blau and Salo W. Baron (eds.), *The Jews in the United States, 1790–1840: A Documentary History*, 3 vols. (Columbia University Press, New York, 1966).

There is a vast literature on the development of religious communities, sects, and indigenous religious movements; the major bibliographical works should be consulted for particular groups. Though somewhat outdated (in part by its own success in stimulating research), Alice Felt Tyler's *Freedom's Ferment: Phases of American Social History to 1860* (University of Minnesota Press, Minneapolis, 1944) deals with such topics as Transcendentalism, Millennialism, Spiritualism, Mormonism, Shakerism, and other communitarian movements as well as with temperance, peace, anti-slavery, and women's rights crusades. On Transcendentalism, a good starting-point is the impressive source-collection edited by Perry Miller, *The Transcendentalists: An Anthology* (Harvard University Press, Cambridge, Mass., 1950). The impact of the movement on Unitarianism is examined by William R. Hutchison, *The Transcendentalist Ministers: Church Reform in the New England Renaissance* (Yale University Press, New Haven, 1959). On the Latter-day Saints (Mormons), the best single work is by Thomas F. O'Dea, *The Mormons* (University of Chicago Press, Chicago, 1957); see also Marvin S. Hill and James B. Allen (eds.), *Mormonism and American Culture* (Harper & Row, New York, 1972), and a compilation by William Mulder and A. Russell Mortensen (eds.), *Among the Mormons: Historic Accounts by Contemporary Observers* (Alfred A. Knopf, New York, 1958). A book which defines the 'communitarian point of view' and then focuses on the Owenite communities is by Arthur E. Bestor, *Backwoods Utopias: The Sectarian and Owenite Phases of Communitarian Socialism in America, 1663–1829* (University of Pennsylvania Press, Philadelphia, 1950). Edward Deming Andrews wrote many books on the

Shakers; a good summary is his *The People Called Shakers: A Search for the Perfect Society*, new enl. edn. (Dover Publications, New York, 1963); see also Henri Desroches, trans. by John K. Savacool, *The American Shakers: From Neo-Christianity to Pre-Socialism* (University of Massachusetts Press, Amherst, 1971). On the significant community that gathered around John Humphrey Noyes, consult Maren Lockwood Carden, *Oneida: Utopian Community to Modern Corporation* (Johns Hopkins Press, Baltimore, 1969), and Constance Noyes Robertson, *Oneida Community* (Syracuse University Press, Syracuse, N.Y., 1970).

5. CANADA SINCE CONFEDERATION

The basic book has already been mentioned in the first section: Grant's *The Church in the Canadian Era*. The references at the end of each of the ten well-written chapters and in the concluding bibliographical note point the way to further research. A general history which has considerable emphasis on religious movements is by A. R. M. Lower, *Colony to Nation: A History of Canada*, 4th rev. edn. (Longmans, Don Mills, Ont., 1969). A Protestant interpretation of 'Christian Canada' somewhat analogous to the 'Christian America' emphasis was written during World War I by William T. Gunn, *His Dominion* (Canadian Council of the Missionary Education Movement, Toronto, 1917); an analysis of the erosion of that vision is given by N. K. Clifford, 'His Dominion: A Vision in Crisis', *Studies in Religion/Sciences religieuses*, 2 (1973), 315–26.

On Canadian social Christianity, basic works are by Stewart Crysdale, *The Industrial Struggle and Protestant Ethics in Canada* (Ryerson Press, Toronto, 1961); Jean Hulliger, *L'Enseignement social des evêques Canadiens de 1891 à 1950* (Fides, Montreal, 1958); and the detailed study by Richard Allen, *The Social Passion: Religion and Social Reform in Canada, 1914–1928* (University of Toronto Press, Toronto, 1971). Most Protestant (and some Catholic) advocates of social Christianity were believers in the temperance movement; the story has been told by Ruth E. Spence, *Prohibition in Canada: A Memorial to Francis Stephens Spence* (Ontario Branch of the Dominion Alliance, Toronto, 1919).

The drive for a Protestant union, leading to complex negotiations and bitter controversies and resulting in the formation of the United Church of Canada at the cost of the division of Presbyterianism, produced a voluminous literature. The basic historical work is still Claris E. Silcox's *Church Union in Canada: Its Causes and Consequences* (Institute of Social and Religious Research, New York, 1933). Among books prepared while the negotiations were in progress were those by Robert Campbell, *The Relations of the Christian Churches: To One Another, and Problems Growing Out of Them, Especially in Canada* (William Briggs, Toronto, 1913), and E. Lloyd Morrow, *Church Union in Canada: Its History, Motives, Doctrine and Government* (Thomas Allen, Toronto, 1923). After union, Ephraim Scott wrote *'Church Union' and the Presbyterian Church in Canada*

(John Lovell & Son, Montreal, 1928) criticizing the union, while Thomas B. Kirkpatrick wrote *Our Common Faith* (Ryerson Press, Toronto, 1928), a positive exposition of the United Church's Twenty Articles, with a brief history of the church union movement by Kenneth B. Cousland. Later studies of United Church teachings were made by Randolph C. Chalmers, *See the Christ Stand: A Study in Doctrine in the United Church of Canada* (Ryerson Press, Toronto, 1945), and Stewart Crysdale, *The Changing Church in Canada: Beliefs and Social Attitudes of United Church People* (United Church of Canada, Toronto, 1965). A compact reinterpretation of the story of the union has been provided by John Webster Grant, *The Canadian Experience of Church Union* (Lutterworth Press, London, 1967). On continuing ecumenical developments, see the work edited by the same author, *The Churches and the Canadian Experience: A Faith and Order Study of the Christian Tradition* (Ryerson Press, Toronto, 1963). An important symposium edited by Philip Le Blanc and Arnold Edinborough, *One Church, Two Nations?* (Longmans, Don Mills, Ont., 1968) traces the decline of the ecumenical spirit in the late 1960s.

A number of denominational histories that deal with periods both before and after Confederation were mentioned in section 3; note also John T. McNeill's *The Presbyterian Church in Canada, 1875–1925* (General Board, Presbyterian Church in Canada, Toronto, 1925); J. H. Riddell, *Methodism in the Middle West* (Ryerson Press, Toronto, 1946), the bulk of which covers the period from Confederation to 1925; and Leslie K. Tarr, *This Dominion His Dominion* (Fellowship of Evangelical Baptist Churches in Canada, Willowdale, Ontario, 1968). Both large and small religious bodies are discussed in S. D. Clark's *Church and Sect in Canada*, while W. E. Mann followed Clark's lead in a detailed study of *Sect, Cult, and Church in Alberta* (University of Toronto Press, Toronto, 1955). Important treatments of smaller groups are by George Woodcock and Ivan Avakumovic, *The Doukhobors* (Oxford University Press, Toronto, 1968); Frank H. Epp, *Mennonites in Canada, 1786–1920: The History of a Separate People* (Macmillan, Toronto, 1974); Orland Gingerich, *The Amish of Canada* (Conrad Press, Waterloo, Ont., 1972); and Victor Peters, *All Things Common: The Hutterian Way of Life* (University of Minnesota Press, Minneapolis, 1965).

The stories of the lay-led 'Y's' have been told by Murray G. Ross, *The Y.M.C.A. in Canada: The Chronicle of a Century* (Ryerson Press, Toronto, 1951), and Josephine P. Harshaw, *When Women Work Together: A History of the Young Women's Christian Association in Canada* (Y.W.C.A. of Canada, Toronto, 1966). C. B. Sissons, *Church and State in Canadian Education* (Ryerson Press, Toronto, 1959) and Franklin A. Walker, *Catholic Education and Politics in Ontario* (Nelson, Toronto, 1964) offer interpretations of educational history from Protestant and Catholic viewpoints respectively. A critique of Canadian Christianity in the mid-sixties was penned by Pierre Berton, *The Comfortable Pew* (J. B. Lippincott, Philadelphia, 1965); William Kilbourn edited a reply, *The Restless Church: A Response to the Comfortable Pew* (J. B. Lippincott, Philadelphia, 1966).

6. THE UNITED STATES SINCE 1860

There is a very good chapter on the churches and the Civil War in Ahlstrom, *A Religious History of the American People*; certain aspects of the topic have been treated in detail, for example: Benjamin J. Blied, *Catholics and the Civil War* (privately printed, Milwaukee, 1945); Chester F. Dunham, *The Attitudes of the Northern Clergy toward the South, 1860–1865* (Gray Company, Toledo, 1942); Bertram W. Korn, *American Jewry and the Civil War* (Meridien Books, Cleveland, 1961); and James W. Silver, *Confederate Morale and Church Propaganda* (Peter Smith, Gloucester, Mass., 1964). On the churches in the south since the war, an informative book by Samuel S. Hill and others is especially recommended, *Religion and the Solid South* (Abingdon Press, Nashville, 1972); see also Paul M. Gaston, *The New South Creed: A Study in Southern Mythology* (Alfred A. Knopf, New York, 1970), and Kenneth K. Bailey, *Southern White Protestantism in the Twentieth Century* (Harper & Row, New York, 1964). There are good studies of the two largest denominations in the last thirty-five years of the nineteenth century: Hunter D. Farish, *The Circuit Rider Dismounts: A Social History of Southern Methodism, 1865–1900* (Dietz Press, Richmond, Va., 1938), and Rufus B. Spain, *At Ease in Zion: Social History of Southern Baptists, 1865–1900* (Vanderbilt University Press, Nashville, 1967). An over-all history of the latter denomination is by Robert A. Baker, *The Southern Baptist Convention and Its People, 1607–1972* (Broadman Press, Nashville, 1974). The Southern Presbyterian experience has also been given a thorough interpretation in an impressive series by Ernest Trice Thompson, *Presbyterianism in the South*, vol. i, *1607–1861*, vol. ii, *1861–1890*, vol. iii, *1890–1972* (John Knox Press, Richmond, 1963–73).

For the study of Christianity primarily in its northern context, an interpretation of the evangelical effort to make America a fully Christian nation is suggested by Robert T. Handy, *A Christian America: Protestant Hopes and Historical Realities* (Oxford University Press, New York, 1971). A particularly valuable collection of sources focused on the urban north has been edited by Robert D. Cross, *The Church and the City, 1865–1910* (Bobbs-Merrill, Indianapolis, 1967); previously Aaron I. Abell had discussed *The Urban Impact on American Protestantism, 1865–1900* (Harvard University Press, Cambridge, 1943). On the impact of immigration on American life, John Higham's *Strangers in the Land: Patterns of American Nativism, 1860–1925* (Rutgers University Press, New Brunswick, 1955) is especially recommended; see also Donald L. Kinzer's *An Episode in Anti-Catholicism: The American Protective Association* (University of Washington Press, Seattle, 1964). A remarkably perceptive study of religion in the post-Civil War period is by Paul A. Carter, *The Spiritual Crisis of the Gilded Age* (Northern Illinois University Press, DeKalb, 1971). Protestant missions reached their highest levels of enthusiasm between the Civil War and World War I; an important survey with rich bibliographical references is by R. Pierce Beaver, 'Missionary Motivation through Three Centuries' in Brauer (ed.), *Reinterpretation in American*

Church History, pp. 113–51. A massive study of missions at the turn of the century was made by James A. Dennis, *Christian Missions and Social Progress: A Sociological Study of Foreign Missions*, 3 vols. (F. H. Revell Co., New York, 1897–1906). For a critical view of mission activities in a field of particular interest to Americans, consult Paul A. Varg, *Missionaries, Chinese and Diplomats: The American Protestant Missionary Movement in China, 1890–1952* (Princeton University Press, Princeton, 1958). R. Pierce Beaver has given important clues to the historical role of women in American Protestant life in *All Loves Excelling: American Women in World Mission* (William B. Eerdmans, Grand Rapids, Mich., 1968); see also Alan P. Grimes, *The Puritan Ethic and Woman Suffrage* (Oxford University Press, New York, 1967), and the important collection of documents edited by Aileen Kraditor, *Up from the Pedestal: Selected Writings in the History of American Feminism* (Quadrangle Books, Chicago, 1968).

A suggestive interpretation of the creation of an extensive network of Sunday schools is by Robert W. Lynn and Elliott Wright, *The Big Little School: Sunday Child of American Protestantism* (Harper & Row, New York, 1971). A thoughtful discussion of the problems of religion in public education is by Robert Michaelsen, *Piety in the Public Schools: Trends and Issues in the Relationship between Religion and the Public School in the United States* (Macmillan, New York, 1970). On the relationships between the temperance movement and the churches, the following provide good introductions and bibliographical aids: Paul C. Conley and Andrew A. Sorenson, *The Staggering Steeple: The Story of Alcoholism and the Churches* (United Church Press, Philadelphia, 1971); Joseph A. Gusfield, *Symbolic Crusade: Status Politics and the American Temperance Movement* (University of Illinois Press, Urbana, 1963), and James H. Timberlake, *Prohibition and the Progressive Movement, 1900–1920* (Harvard University Press, Cambridge, Mass., 1963).

The emergence of Protestant theological liberalism in the later nineteenth century is traced by Daniel D. Williams, *The Andover Liberals: A Study of American Theology* (King's Crown Press, New York, 1941), and Kenneth Cauthen, *The Impact of American Religious Liberalism* (Harper & Row, New York, 1962), while well-chosen illustrative documents have been edited by William R. Hutchison, *American Protestant Thought: The Liberal Era* (Harper & Row, New York, 1968). A good study of a major forerunner of liberalism with representative selections is edited by H. Shelton Smith, *Horace Bushnell* (Oxford University Press, New York, 1965), and the most prominent pulpit exponent of nineteenth-century evangelical liberalism has been analysed by William G. McLoughlin, *The Meaning of Henry Ward Beecher: An Essay on the Shifting Values of Mid-Victorian America, 1840–1870* (Alfred A. Knopf, New York, 1970).

The standard work on Protestant social Christianity is by C. Howard Hopkins, *The Rise of the Social Gospel in American Protestantism, 1865–1915* (Yale University Press, New Haven, 1940); the nineteenth-century background has been skillfully probed by Henry F. May, *Protestant Churches and Industrial America* (Harper & Row, New York, 1949); a selection of the writings of three social gospel leaders, edited by Robert T. Handy, is *The Social Gospel in America, 1870–1920: Gladden, Ely, Rauschenbusch* (Oxford University Press, New York, 1966). On the impact of World War I on the churches, there is a critique by Ray H. Abrams, *Preachers Present Arms* (Round Table Press, New York, 1933); a corrective to Abrams's selectivity can be found in the dissertation by John F. Piper, Jr. 'The Social Policy of the Federal Council of the Churches of Christ in America During World War I' (Ph.D. thesis, Duke University, Durham, 1964). The story of the collapse of the Interchurch World Movement as an early casualty of post-war disillusionment has been analysed by Eldon Ernst, *Moment of Truth for Protestant America: Interchurch Campaigns Following World War One* (American Academy of Religion and Scholars' Press, Missoula, Montana, 1974). The social gospel revived following the war; the basic materials were surveyed by Robert M. Miller, *American Protestantism and Social Issues, 1919–1939* (University of North Carolina Press, Chapel Hill, 1958); a lively interpretation appears in Paul A. Carter's *The Decline and Revival of the Social Gospel: Social and Political Liberalism in American Protestant Churches, 1920–1940*, rev. edn. (Archon Books, Hamden, Conn., 1971), while Donald B. Meyer focused on the political aspects of social Christianity with particular emphasis on Reinhold Niebuhr in *The Protestant Search for Political Realism, 1919–1941* (University of California Press, Berkeley, 1960).

The 1920s were marked by the fundamentalist/modernist controversy; some of the movements which prepared the way for fundamentalism have been carefully probed by Ernest Sandeen, *The Roots of Fundamentalism: British and American Millenarianism, 1800–1930* (University of Chicago Press, Chicago, 1970); see also C. Norman Kraus, *Dispensationalism in America: Its Rise and Development* (John Knox Press, Richmond, 1958). A useful source-book on the Fundamentalist controversy, edited by Willard B. Gatewood, Jr. is *Controversy in the Twenties: Fundamentalism, Modernism, Evolution* (Vanderbilt University Press, Nashville, 1969). For the general twentieth-century theological scene, consult Arnold S. Nash (ed.) *Protestant Thought in the Twentieth Century: Whence and Whither?* (Macmillan, New York, 1951) and William R. Miller (ed.) *Contemporary American Protestant Thought: 1900–1970* (Bobbs-Merrill, Indianapolis, 1973)—the first is a symposium, the second an anthology.

Most of the denominational histories which have been mentioned in previous sections also deal with the period since the Civil War, but books which focus primarily on the latter period include Lefferts A. Loetscher's *The Broadening Church: A Study of Theological Issues in the Presbyterian Church Since 1869* (University of Pennsylvania Press, Philadelphia, 1954), E. Clifford Nelson, *Lutheranism in North America, 1914–1970* (Augsburg Publishing House, Minneapolis, 1972), and David E. Harrell, Jr., *The Social Sources of Division in the Disciples of Christ, 1865–1900* (Publishing Systems, Atlanta, 1973).

The state of the black churches was surveyed early in the 1930s by Benjamin E. Mays and Joseph W. Nicholson, *The Negro's Church* (Institute of Social and

Religious Research, New York, 1933). Increasing attention has been given to the evil effects of racism in America, as by C. Vann Woodward, *The Strange Career of Jim Crow*, rev. edn. (Oxford University Press, New York, 1957), Thomas F. Gossett, *Race: The History of An Idea in America* (Southern Methodist University Press, Dallas, 1963), and August Meier, *Negro Thought in America 1880–1915: Racial Ideologies in the Age of Booker T. Washington* (University of Michigan Press, Ann Arbor, 1963). Analyses of Protestant and Catholic entanglements with colour problems have been presented by David M. Reimers, *White Protestantism and the Negro* (Oxford University Press, New York, 1965), and William A. Osborne, *The Segregated Covenant: Race Relations and American Catholics* (Herder & Herder, New York, 1967). The histories of some of the younger black religious movements have been discussed by Arthur H. Fauset, *Black Gods of the Metropolis: Negro Religious Cults of the Urban North* (University of Pennsylvania Press, Philadelphia, 1944), and Joseph R. Washington, Jr., *Black Sects and Cults* (Doubleday & Co., Garden City, New York, 1972). The impact on religion of the rise of black power has been interpreted by James H. Cone, *Black Theology and Black Power* (Seabury Press, New York, 1971), and *A Black Theology of Liberation* (J. B. Lippincott, Philadelphia, 1971). Other interpretations of black theology which include considerable historical reflections are by Major J. Jones, *Black Awareness: A Theology of Hope* (Abingdon Press, Nashville, 1971), and J. Deotis Roberts, *Liberation and Reconciliation: A Black Theology* (Westminster Press, Philadelphia, 1971).

A highly informative book on Pentecostalism in North America and elsewhere is by Walter J. Hollenweger, *The Pentecostals* (S. C. M. Press, London, 1972), translated by R. A. Wilson from the German. Useful also are studies by Vinson Synan, *The Holiness-Pentecostal Movement in the United States* (William B. Eerdmans, Grand Rapids, 1971), and a handbook of American Pentecostal bodies by John T. Nichol, *Pentecostalism* (Harper & Row, 1966; rev. edn., Logos International, Plainfield, N. J., 1971).

General works which deal with Roman Catholicism in the United States have already been mentioned, but a few which deal with topics that relate primarily to the period since the Civil War can be emphasized. American involvement in the two Vatican Councils is discussed in James Hennesey, *The First Council of the Vatican: The American Experience* (Herder & Herder, New York, 1963), and in Vincent Yzermans (ed.), *American Participation in the Second Vatican Council* (Sheed & Ward, New York, 1967). A massive study that gives the reader a good insight into late nineteenth-century Catholic history as well as illuminating its major subject is John Tracy Ellis's *The Life of James Cardinal Gibbons, Archbishop of Baltimore, 1834–1921*, 2 vols. (Bruce Publishing Co., Milwaukee, 1952). The role of Catholics of German background to World War I is treated perceptively by Colman J. Barry, *The Catholic Church and German Americans* (Bruce Publishing Co., Milwaukee, 1953). The story of the Americanist crisis has been probed by Robert D. Cross, *The Emergence of Liberal Catholicism in America*

(Harvard University Press, Cambridge, Mass., 1958), Thomas T. McAvoy, *The Great Crisis in American Catholic History, 1895–1900* (Henry Regnery Co., Chicago, 1957), and Gerald P. Fogarty, *The Vatican and the Americanist Crisis: Denis J. O'Connell, American Agent in Rome, 1885–1903* (Università Gregoriana Editrice, Rome, 1974). An important early chapter in the story of Catholic social Christianity has been recounted by Henry J. Browne, *The Catholic Church and the Knights of Labor* (Catholic University Press, Washington, 1949), while a readable general treatment of the larger movement has been contributed by Aaron I. Abell, *American Catholicism and Social Action: A Search for Social Justice, 1865–1950* (Hanover House, Garden City, N.Y., 1960). Philip Gleason, *The Conservative Reformers: German-American Catholics and the Social Order* (Notre Dame University Press, Notre Dame, Ind., 1968) deals primarily with the social thought and action of Catholics of German background in the twentieth century. The 1930s are especially emphasized in David J. O'Brien's *American Catholics and Social Reform: The New Deal Years* (Oxford University Press, New York, 1968), and George Q. Flynn, *American Catholics and the Roosevelt Presidency* (University of Kentucky Press, Lexington, 1968).

Books on Eastern Orthodox history published in North America often deal primarily with the ancient and Byzantine backgrounds; for example, John Meyendorff's illuminating *The Orthodox Church: Its Past and Its Role in the World Today* (Pantheon Books, New York, 1962), translated from the French by John Chapin, has only a few pages on the United States; there is a short chapter on 'The Church in America' in Demetrios J. Constantelos, *The Greek Orthodox Church: Faith, History, and Practice* (Seabury Press, New York, 1967). Alexander A. Bogolepov threw much light on Eastern church history in a plea for Orthodox unity in North America: *Toward an American Orthodox Church: The Establishment of an Autocephalous Orthodox Church* (Morehouse-Barlow, New York, 1963). C. Samuel Calian wrote in rather general ecumenical terms but included a good bibliography in discussing *Icon and Pulpit: The Protestant-Orthodox Encounter* (Westminster Press, Philadelphia, 1968).

Comprehensive coverage of the ecumenical movement in twentieth-century America with excellent bibliographical aids can be found in two volumes by Samuel McCrea Cavert, *The American Churches in the Ecumenical Movement, 1900–1968* (Association Press, New York, 1968), and *Church Cooperation and Unity in America, A Historical Review: 1900–1970* (Association Press, New York, 1970). On Catholic-Protestant ecumenical developments, see Eugene C. Bianchi, *John XXIII and American Protestants* (Corpus Books, Washington, D.C., 1968), and Lerond Curry, *Protestant-Catholic Relations in America: World War I through Vatican II* (University of Kentucky Press, Lexington, 1972). On Jewish-Christian relationships, illuminating books have been written by Arthur Gilbert, *A Jew in Christian America* (Sheed & Ward, New York, 1966) and A. Roy Eckardt, *Elder and Younger Brothers: The Encounter of Jews and Christians* (Charles Scribner's Sons, New York, 1967).

The literature related to the emergence of new religious movements since the Civil War, especially those related to New Thought, is extensive and much of it controversial. General books which provide helpful overviews and guides for further study include the following: three by Charles S. Braden, *These Also Believe: A Study of Modern American Cults and Minority Religious Movements* (Macmillan, New York, 1949), *Christian Science Today: Power, Policy, Practice* (Southern Methodist University Press, Dallas, 1958), and *Spirits in Rebellion: The Rise and Development of New Thought* (Southern Methodist University Press, Dallas, 1968); J. Stillson Judah, *The History and Philosophy of the Metaphysical Movements in America* (Westminster Press, Philadelphia, 1967); and Donald B. Meyer, *The Positive Thinkers: A Study of the American Quest for Health, Wealth and Personal Power from Mary Baker Eddy to Norman Vincent Peale* (Doubleday & Co., Garden City, N.Y., 1956).

On the religious situation since 1950, several sociological studies provide helpful perspectives, especially Will Herberg, *Protestant-Catholic-Jew: An Essay in American Religious Sociology* (Doubleday & Co., Garden City, N.Y., 1955), Gerhard Lenski, *The Religious Factor: A Sociological Study of Religion's Impact on Politics, Economics, and Family Life* (Doubleday & Co., Garden City, N.Y., 1961), and Milton Gordon, *Assimilation in American Life: The Role of Race, Religion, and National Origins* (Oxford University Press, New York, 1964). One of the surprising developments of the late 1960s is described in books by Ronald M. Enroth, Edward E. Ericson, Jr., and C. Breckinridge Peters, *The Jesus People: Old-Time Religion in the Age of Aquarius* (William B. Eerdmans, Grand Rapids, 1972) and Erling T. Jorstad, *That New-Time Religion: The Jesus Revival in America* (Augsburg Publishing House, Minneapolis, 1972); a general symposium on the state of religion in that period is edited by Robert N. Bellah and William G. McLoughlin, *Religion in America* (Houghton Mifflin, Boston, 1968).

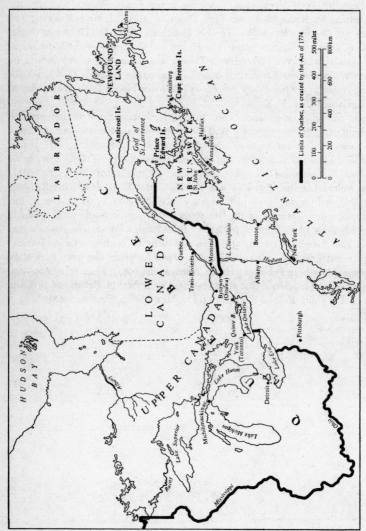

MAP I. CANADA BEFORE CONFEDERATION

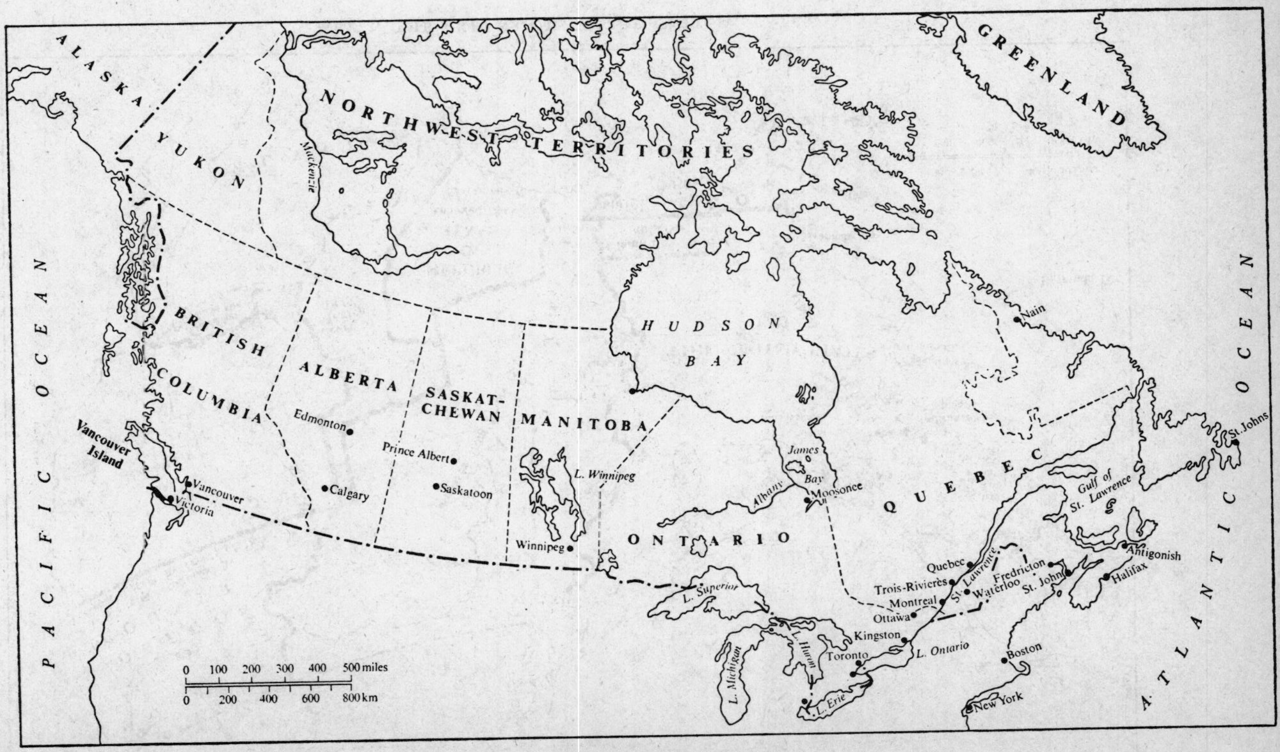

MAP 2. DOMINION OF CANADA

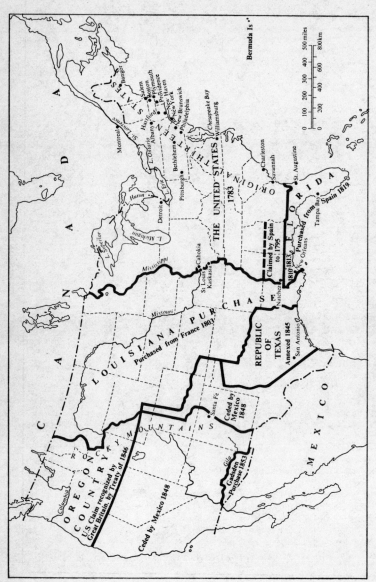

MAP 3. THE EXPANSION OF THE UNITED STATES

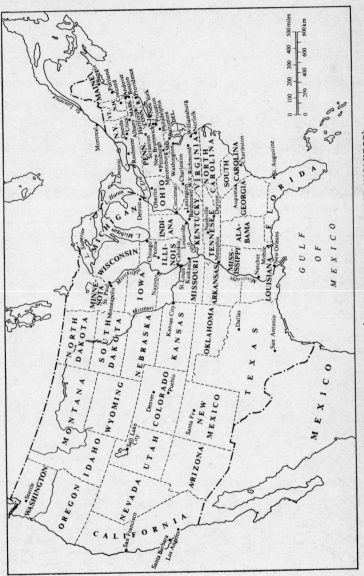

MAP 4. UNITED STATES (ALASKA AND HAWAII NOT INCLUDED)

INDEX